D1210133

Thrift and Thriving in America

Thrift and Thriving in America: Capitalism and Moral Order from the Puritans to the Present

Edited by
Joshua J. Yates
and
James Davison Hunter

OXFORD
UNIVERSITY PRESS

Oxford University Press, Inc., publishes works that further
Oxford University's objective of excellence
in research, scholarship, and education.

Oxford New York
Auckland Cape Town Dar es Salaam Hong Kong Karachi
Kuala Lumpur Madrid Melbourne Mexico City Nairobi
New Delhi Shanghai Taipei Toronto

With offices in
Argentina Austria Brazil Chile Czech Republic France Greece
Guatemala Hungary Italy Japan Poland Portugal Singapore
South Korea Switzerland Thailand Turkey Ukraine Vietnam

Published by Oxford University Press, Inc.
198 Madison Avenue, New York, New York 10016

www.oup.com

Library of Congress Cataloging-in-Publication Data
Thrift in America : capitalism and moral order from the Puritans to the present /
edited by Joshua J. Yates, James Davison Hunter.
p. cm.
Includes index.
ISBN 978-0-19-976906-3 (cloth : alk. paper) 1. Saving and
investment—Moral and ethical aspects—United States—History.
2. Thriftiness—United States—History. 3. Capitalism—United States—History.
I. Yates, Joshua J. II. Hunter, James Davison, 1955–
HC110.S3T46 2010
339.4'30973—dc22 2010027023

1 3 5 7 9 8 6 4 2
Printed in the United States of America
on acid-free paper

CONTENTS

ACKNOWLEDGMENTS

Large and ambitious scholarly projects such as this one are always the work of many minds and hands. We would like to acknowledge a number of people who made essential contributions at one critical juncture or another for which we will remain deeply grateful.

For their vital administrative efforts on behalf of the project and volume, we would like to single out Josephine Tramantano, Charity Naveret, and Susan Witzel. We would like to thank them for helping us keep all the separate parts moving in all the right directions.

For carrying out a yeoman's share of the early background research for the project, and providing essential administrative and intellectual support along the way, we would like to thank David Franz. We are likewise grateful to Wilson Brissett for taking over many of these important duties in the latter stages of writing.

For early editorial support we would like to recognize Jennifer Seidel, while for their outstanding final copyediting, we would like to thank Michael O'Connor and the editorial staff at Oxford University Press. The lion share of the editorial credit, however, must go to Emily Gum whose careful eye and sensitive ear proved crucial time and again. She made everyone involved look better than we deserve.

Substantively, we were the beneficiaries of an outstanding group of scholarly advisors, including T. J. Jackson Lears, Kiku Adato, Barbara Defoe Whitehead, David Blankenhorn, and David Bosworth. In addition, we would like to thank Patrick Deneen and George Thomas, two early readers, for providing us invaluable critical feedback on initial drafts of the book. Taken together, each of these scholars helped us bring conceptual and narrative coherence to a large edited volume featuring scholars from across the humanities and the social sciences, without, we hope, sacrificing the many stubborn incongruenities and counter-narratives that make the topic so historically and analytically rich. To the extent that we have been successful, we owe a significant debt of gratitude to their wise and critical counsel.

The idea for this volume itself grew out of a multi-year initiative to study the historical and contemporary significance of thrift in American thought and life. The initiative began as a collaboration between the Institute for Advanced Studies in Culture and the Institute for American Values and was made possible by generous financial support from the John Templeton Foundation.

An occasion of great sorrow was the death of Steven Innes during the early stages of this project. He was an esteemed colleague who will be missed by many. Upon his death, James Calvin Davis kindly helped to conduct the final editing of Steven's chapter, which is here produced posthumously.

The passing of Steven put us in mind that producing this volume has had its fair share of challenges. Indeed, there were moments when we wondered whether it would ever see the light of day. That we were able to persevere and see the project through to a successful conclusion is, once again, due to the efforts and encouragement of many people.

First, we would like to acknowledge the ever-patient guidance and encouragement we received from Kimon Sargent, the project's program officer at the Templeton Foundation. Similarly, we would like to offer our word of thanks to Jean Bethke Elshtain for her generous counsel at a crucial point in the process.

In everything, we would like to communicate our great appreciation and admiration to all of our contributing authors (even those whose essays did not make it into the final version of the volume). Although the way was long, and although filled with many toils and snares, we achieved our goal, all thanks to their steadfast commitment to the project and, of course, to the enormous effort they each invested in it.

At a more personal level, we would like to thank a number of colleagues, friends, and family whose unflagging support and interest in the project was a gift beyond measure. In this respect, we would like to thank Joseph and Cynthia Yates, Chuck Mathewes, Jennifer Geddes, Slava Jakelic, Tim Peck, Ed and Carmen Gitre, Katie Pennock, Julie McDermott, and Patrick Larochelle. We would especially like to acknowledge Jeff and Heather Dill for their unwavering moral support and for many hours of listening.

Of course, there would be no successful conclusion at all without the keen interest shown by Oxford University Press in the project. For that we are indebted to our editor, James Cook, who took up the book and worked with us to ready it for publication.

Finally, I (Josh) would like to thank my wife, Molly, and my children, Ellen, Benjamin, John, and Meredith, for their unfailing and selfless support over the past five years, and for the inevitable sacrifices that such support often demanded of them. This accomplishment is as much yours as mine. I (James) am, as ever, grateful for the partnership of my wife, Honey.

LIST OF CONTRIBUTORS

Kiku Adatto is a Lecturer on Social Studies at Harvard University.

Joyce Appleby is Professor Emerita in History at the University of California at Los Angeles.

Steven Brint is Professor of Sociology at the University of California, Riverside, and Director of the Colleges and Universities 2000 Project.

Wilson Brissett is Assistant Professor of English at the U.S. Air Force Academy.

Lendol Calder is Professor of History and Chair of the History Department at Augustana College.

James Calvin Davis is Associate Professor of Religion at Middlebury College.

Robert H. Frank is the Henrietta Johnson Louis Professor of Management and Professor of Economics at Cornell University's Johnson Graduate School of Management.

Steven Fraser is the author of *Labor Will Rule: Sidney Hillman and the Rise of American Labor*, which won the Phillip Taft Prize for the best book in Labor History.

Lawrence B. Glickman is Carolina Trustee Professor of History at the University of South Carolina and the author of *A Living Wage: American Workers and the Making of Consumer Society* and the Editor of *Consumer Society in American History: A Reader.*

Daniel Walker Howe is Rhodes Professor of American History Emeritus at Oxford University and Professor Emeritus of History at the University of California at Los Angeles.

James Davison Hunter is LaBrosse-Levinson Distinguished Professor in Religion, Culture and Social Theory at the University of Virginia and Executive Director of the Institute for Advanced Studies in Culture.

Stephen Innes was James Madison Professor of American History at the University of Virginia.

T. J. Jackson Lears is Board of Governors Professor of History at Rutgers University and the Editor-in-Chief of *Raritan Quarterly Review*.

Charles Mathewes is Professor of Religious Studies, and Faculty Fellow at the Institute for Advanced Studies in Culture at the University of Virginia.

Kathleen D. McCarthy is Professor of History at the Graduate Center of the City University of New York and Founding Director of the Center on Philanthropy and Civil Society.

Deidre McCloskey is Distinguished Professor of Economics, History, English, and Communication at the University of Illinois at Chicago.

J. R. McNeill is Cinco Hermanos Chair in Environmental and International Affairs at Georgetown University.

Kristopher Proctor is a PhD Candidate in Sociology at the University of California Riverside.

Patrick Rael is Associate Professor of History at Bowdoin College.

David M. Reimers is Emeritus Professor of History at New York University.

Jennifer Scanlon is Professor and Director of the Gender and Women's Studies Program at Bowdoin College.

George Vrtis is Assistant Professor of Environmental Studies and History at Carleton College.

Joshua J. Yates is Research Assistant Professor at the University of Virginia and Director of the Program for Cultural, Capitalism, and Global Change at the Institute for Advanced Studies in Culture.

Olivier Zunz is Commonwealth Professor of History at the University of Virginia.

Thrift and Thriving in America

1 }

Introduction

THE QUESTION OF THRIFT

James Davison Hunter and Joshua J. Yates

Until quite recently, thrift was a concept with which most Americans were only dimly familiar. For many under the age of seventy, a chance encounter with the word *thrift* could easily bring them up short for a lack of anything meaningful to say. From some, thrift was a relic from an earlier time, perhaps conjuring images of the tightwad or the miser, while for others, secondhand clothing stores might very well have been the first and only things that came to mind. Of course, for those seventy or older, thrift still resonated as a deeply ingrained habit. This was largely due to the searing experience of the Great Depression and World War II, and the forced scrimping, saving, and rationing of their childhood years. They could remember back to a time when thrift, or at least the ideal of thrift, was once part of a constellation of celebrated economic virtues such as prudence, industry, and punctuality, and thus a hallmark of middle-class respectability; they could recall an era when thrift was taught in schools, exhorted from the pulpits, and encouraged by the government in the form of federally supported "thrift institutions" like the building and loan associations memorably romanticized in Frank Capra's *It's a Wonderful Life.* This septuagenarian-and-over set was also likely to remember when, sometime in the mid-twentieth century, thrift appeared to lose its place of prominence and gradually to fade as a meaningful ideal amid the postwar abundance that so dramatically altered the everyday lives of most Americans. For the next half century, thrift seemed to go the way of chastity, teetotalism, and other quirky artifacts from a more morally uptight past. So severe was its fifty-year slide into irrelevance, that by the first decade of the twenty-first century, the average American family was only two paychecks away from poverty and carried around $9,000 in revolving debt (mostly from credit cards). At the same time, personal savings rates hit zero for the first time since the Great Depression—only times were economically good. For a handful of moralists, few images more dramatically, or forebodingly, symbolized the consequences of America's collective self-transformation into a postthrift society than when, in 2008, the national debt passed the $10 trillion mark and the National Debt Clock in Times Square ran out of digits.

In the wake of the 2008 financial crisis, thrift has rather suddenly thrust its way back into the public eye, and there are signs that its prospects may be turning around, though how permanently we do not know. Economists are again extolling its virtues, think tanks are studying the effects of the precrisis "debt culture," foundations are investing in ways to encourage frugality and financial literacy, journalists are rediscovering and debating the virtues of thrift and its paradoxes, and average citizens are once again saving more.[1] After four years of hovering around zero, personal savings rates have come back up, while levels of individual indebtedness have declined as people pay off their credit cards and spend less.[2]

Still, whether its fortunes are waxing or waning, thrift nevertheless remains largely a virtue of necessity for most people, and it can be difficult to credit this fact with anything especially noteworthy. People have, after all, always engaged in thrifty behavior when times turned hard. Even in the face of economic hardship, the effort to make ends meet lacks any extraordinary pathos. It is understandably tough for most people to feel the emotional pull of "buying used," paying in cash, cutting coupons, reusing tea bags, stitching up threadbare socks, and saving for a rainy day. These are the utterly banal but necessary practices of getting by when you don't have enough and when there is real concern about what tomorrow will bring. Conventionally conceived, thrift is thus the thoroughly unremarkable social ethic of material scarcity, which under the conditions of modern capitalism translates to that most prosaic but obligatory issue: saving money.

But is this all there is to say about thrift, either today or in the past? The argument of this book is that there is a great deal more to be said, and given present efforts to dig the old parsimonious virtue out of mothballs, it is an auspicious time to reconsider what in fact turns out to be a far more complex and interesting—even surprising—story.

To begin with, even as a monetary virtue, thrift has not just been a form of individual frugality—that is, about the accumulation of personal wealth—but a means to social goods for groups and society. For example, Negro Savings Clubs, various mutual aid societies, municipal savings banks, and labor and credit unions functioned not only as generators of individual wealth but as the earliest examples of mass philanthropy and collective thrift. Not just a story of enrichment but a narrative of liberation and participation in the public weal: saving (or spending wisely) was a path to empowerment, independence, and full citizenship. In a similar way, the National Thrift Movement of the 1920s was regarded as essential to the war effort in America. Every American could participate in the defeat of Germany by purchasing savings bonds and carefully using the resources available to them. In each case, savings was a collective project whose purpose was the greater good.

More interesting still is thrift as an idea historically nested within an evolving set of values central to the changing culture of capitalism in the West and, in this context, the changing moral economy of the self. Thus, at the level of social institution and moral psychology, thrift has been a part of a cluster of normative characteristics that signal limitation, self-restraint, reticence, temperance, conservation, and stewardship. These have been configured in different ways at different times, and more often than not, they have clustered in contradictory ways. At times, these attributes have functioned as enablers of capitalist production; in others, a limit, a restraint, and even a form of resistance and antagonism to the market's reach.

Thrift and the thrift ethos, we learn, has been a particular and powerful moral idea, disposition, and practice that has indelibly marked the character of American life. In a multitude of ways that transcend the inevitable need for individual frugality, thrift remains intensely relevant to the complex problems we face today.

But here we get ahead of ourselves.

A "Virtue" without a History

One reason to take a serious look at thrift has to do with its interesting place in moral philosophy and moral theology: it is absent. One searches in vain in encyclopedias of philosophy, ethics, or theology for an article on thrift, or even on frugality. When we turn to those two classic monuments to high Victorian erudition, the *Encyclopedia of Religion and Ethics* and the eleventh edition of the *Encyclopaedia Britannica*, we find "thrift" conspicuous by its absence. Neither contains articles on thrift. If one chooses a slightly more eccentric reference source, Mortimer Adler's fascinating *Syntopicon* to "The Great Books," one finds "thrift" only in a small subsection of the chapter on wealth, with references to a few passages from some of the classic texts in economics by Smith, Marx, Veblen, Tawney, and Keynes.[3] Even the most up-to-date reference works on ethics—not least those devoted to business ethics—contain little or no discussion of thrift or its twin, frugality.

As to the practice of thrift, there are some scattered reflections in economic history, in such works as Joseph Schumpeter's monumental *History of Economic Analysis* and in Tawney's *Religion and the Rise of Capitalism*. Some recent spadework has been done on popular attitudes toward money, commerce, and thrift in the late Middle Ages, but here again, the work is more indicative than systematic.[4] In sociology, of course, there is a massive literature on *The Protestant Ethic and the Spirit of Capitalism*, but so much of this work deals with the argument itself in the attempt to modify Max Weber's thesis or to debunk it altogether. The historical sociology on the meaning and practice of thrift during the rise of capitalism is sadly thin.

Consider, too, the genre of social criticism addressing American greed and extravagance. At what seemed to be the zenith of American prosperity, the 1950s, conservatives such as Russell Kirk exhorted Americans to go beyond the dreams of avarice, while liberals such as John Kenneth Galbraith criticized the affluent society. However, neither of these criticisms contained any real analysis of thrift or offered any exhortation on the subject.

Our effort here, of course, is not to provide an exhaustive review of economic history and philosophy but rather to suggest from a cursory sweep that, for all practical purposes, *thrift is an idea, a virtue, and a practice without a history*. In the main, scholars in the social sciences and humanities have ignored it.

Why is thrift of such little interest? The answer is not clear. Perhaps it is because thrift is so "common," so "petite bourgeois." Smith himself referred to ideals such as thrift, discipline, and self-restraint as the "awful virtues" for just this reason. One can have serious and lengthy philosophical or theological arguments about other virtues, such as courage, justice, prudence, and even temperance, but thrift? It hardly seems worth the time and effort, and so it fails to attract anyone's attention. At the very least, this absence of curiosity from the scholarly community is striking. Given the lacunae in our knowledge of thrift, we are compelled to take a closer look.

Historicizing Thrift

A second reason for sustained inquiry on the topic of thrift has to do with its rather sudden and seemingly arbitrary appearance in history. Under what conditions does thrift emerge as a common practice deserving the name? Under what circumstances does it become exemplary? As it turns out, those conditions are rather exceptional.

One might expect thrift to surface in classical discussions of the merchant, but its absence is again remarkable. To be sure, it is next to impossible, for example, to find in either Greek or Roman literature a merchant who is construed as a hero. When merchants appear in the literature of classical antiquity, they seem to appear in comedies, not tragedies. We see a similar attitude toward merchants when turning from literature to history and philosophy. None of the Greek or Roman heroes described by Plutarch, for instance, is a merchant, or even an entrepreneur.

Plato, Aristotle, and their Greek and Roman successors paid little attention to merchants or to economic problems more generally. Plato does allude to merchants and the merchant class in both *The Republic* and *The Laws*, and one of the minor Platonic dialogues is about "lovers of gain." At one point in *The Republic*, Plato describes in unsympathetic language both the "feverish city," the city of unchecked getting and spending, and the city of "utmost necessity," the frugal, almost ascetic city. Yet Plato's political philosophy contains little on the subject of political economy. One might think that Aristotle, being more "empirical" and pragmatic than Plato, would be more concerned with economics. However, for Aristotle—as it was for all the great thinkers of classical antiquity—economics was, essentially, *home* economics, the economy of the household. There were undoubtedly men and women who practiced thrift, but no one ever thought about it as such. The concept of "thrift," then, would have meant little to a Greek or Roman.

In terms of the economic teaching of the biblical tradition, we find a different understanding altogether. In the wisdom literature, one can find a commonsense morality that extols frugality, sobriety, and prudence. The lazy, the vagabond, and the spendthrift are all criticized and denounced. The more dominant economic teaching of the Hebrew scriptures is found in the prophetic literature, but here the theme is on justice and on the necessity of socioeconomic transformation—not for its own sake but rather because this was what was required of a just, merciful, and holy God. In the New Testament and in early Christianity, we see both a continuation and a deepening of this Hebraic tradition. Jesus himself says little about thrift. Frugal stewards and maidservants appear in his parables, but their frugality is not the reason they are exemplary. The prodigal son in Jesus's parable wastes his inheritance, but his father forgives him, even to the extent of staging a not very thrifty banquet. Moreover, Jesus tells a rich young ruler to take what he has and give it all to the poor. The frugal steward is chastised while the entrepreneurial servants are commended for investing their talents. And one of the pictures of heaven that Jesus gives is of an extravagant feast. These and other parables and sayings indicate that Jesus cared far more about charity and grace than about thrift.

These teachings extend into patristic and medieval theology and philosophy. Here, too, thrift has no pride of place. None extolled thrift or frugality. In the writings of Thomas Aquinas, for example, frugality is at best mentioned in passing as a type of prudence. But he took prudence, one of the seven cardinal virtues, to mean "good sense." Nor was prudence viewed as the foremost economic virtue. Justice, in the sense of fairness, had that distinction.

Neither the ancient nor the medieval sources of the Western tradition, then, have much to say about the idea or virtue or practice of thrift—indeed, perhaps more to the contrary. For the aristocratic warrior, courage was the supreme virtue. For the philosopher or sage, it was usually wisdom. For the Christian saint, it was the theological virtues of faith, hope, and charity—the greatest of which was charity. Though classical and biblical traditions are so fundamentally different, one possible point of commonality between them in their understanding of wealth was the view that wealth should serve some notion of a common good. In classical philosophy, economic questions were inescapably moral questions. Thus, a proper economic virtue would have been liberality or a public-spirited generosity. The good citizen of Athens used his money to benefit the polis; the prosperous Roman was expected to use his wealth for the good of the Republic, and later the Empire. For the Jews, there was the tradition of jubilee, a year when the community was renewed in part by the forgiveness of old debts. And in the early church, wealthy believers were expected to relinquish their wealth or to be charitable toward the poor. In all, thrift does not exist as a category of moral reflection or practical ethics.

But then something changed.

It has become commonplace to say that a transformation began to take form in the economies of Europe somewhere between the fourteenth and sixteenth centuries. Needless to say, it was a gradual shift, but its nature and scope were profound. The nature of the transformation was from an economy that was primarily agrarian and founded on barter to one that was increasingly commercial and founded on money. The transformation was also global in character. A world in which a merchant in Amsterdam, London, Genoa, or Lisbon could send his ships to Mexico, China, India, and Brazil was a world far different from one in which his most distant trading partners were in Byzantium or Alexandria. The age of exploration, then, opened new markets for European merchants and made new resources available for both the emerging merchant class and the emerging nation-state. As the merchant class grew richer and stronger and central governments grew in power, the old landed aristocracy grew poorer and weaker. One image encapsulates this transformation well. In medieval Europe, even the most bustling commercial town was centered on the cathedral. By the seventeenth century, however, even the most pious communities were oriented toward the market. The story of this transformation is endlessly complex, but overall we see the market displacing the church as a focal point of public life just as it redirected the aspirations of citizenship away from concern with the common good to a preoccupation with aggregating private goods. Commerce, then, increasingly displaced religious and civic piety as the exemplary activities of social life. The sum and substance of this transformation was, of course, the birth of capitalism.

This new world generated new institutions and habits of life and thus required a new self-understanding and a new morality to make sense of it. It is a caricature, but one with some historic grounding: gradually but ineluctably, Western cultures were moving from an ethics of virtue to an ethics of interest. The problem with this shorthand is that it glosses over an incredibly intricate, complex, and uneven change, each part of which defies simple summary.

That said, few would disagree about the significance of the Protestant reformer John Calvin in articulating the new moral sensibilities of the age. While Calvin never wrote an extended treatise on ethics, he nevertheless fashioned an ethics tailored specifically for the middle class. For the first time in Western thought, we witness a moral theory in which the paramount virtues are not courage or justice but prudence, temperance, and thrift. Calvin's exemplary human being is not a warrior like Achilles, a statesman like Pericles, or a philosopher like Socrates. He is not even a medieval saint or monk. Instead he or she is a churchgoing, law-abiding, hardworking member of the middle class. In a sense, Calvin (who translated Seneca in his youth) offered a kind of Christianized Stoicism, a Stoicism for the Protestant bourgeois. Like Stoic ethics, Calvin's morality stressed self-control, discipline, restraint, and, not least, perseverance. The Catholic element is also undeniable: Calvin's table of virtues are also the virtues of the monastic. Calvin's greatest innovation was to claim that common laypeople could practice the virtues of a monk or nun, not toward the ends of mystical, otherworldly experience but rather in ways that sanctified the activities of their ordinary, day-to-day lives.

For Calvin, of course, frugality was about more than saving money. The Protestant men and women of sixteenth-century Geneva wore plain clothes (finery was forbidden), ate plain food (fine food was forbidden), and sang plain songs in church (musical instruments were forbidden) and even in the tavern (boisterous rhymes were also forbidden). In short, life in Geneva was plain, simple, and, to tell the truth, a little boring. That said, the "respectable morality" of the emerging Protestant middle class did make for a relatively prosperous, orderly, and stable society. Calvin's affirmation of the ordinary was, unintentionally, in service to what became historically extraordinary.

It would be pointless here to enter the great debate over Weber's thesis about Protestantism and capitalism.[5] Whatever the causal relationship, it can be argued fairly and uncontroversially that the Protestant Reformation coincided with one of the greatest shifts in economic history. Whatever else might be said, Calvinism both justified the commercial activities of the emerging merchant class and provided restraining boundaries for their actions. Commerce and industry had become callings for ordinary people, frugality was explicitly promoted, and avarice and extravagance were discouraged.

At this stage it is not necessary to pursue the role and significance of Thomas Hobbes, Adam Smith, John Locke, or a host of others to make our point. At the end of our potted history, we see the sheer historical and sociological contingency of the idea, virtue, and practice of thrift. "Thrift," in all of these expressions, was an invention of early modernity, as a critical component in the emergence of a market economy. The newfound wealth of the middle classes, and the monetary problems of the early modern state, led philosophers, theologians, and popular moralists to think about money, and responsible attitudes toward it, in a different way. Put differently, thrift as we have come to know it is essentially unintelligible outside of the way of life represented by early modern and modern capitalism.

The Story of Thrift in America

Why, then, study thrift? Beyond filling the gaps in our understanding of this idea, virtue, and practice, a social history and moral philosophical reflection on thrift is a window into the changing culture of capitalism, and this claim begins to gesture at the ambition of this volume.

Assembling a distinguished group of scholars from across the social sciences and humanities, *Thrift in America* offers a conceptually fresh, empirically vibrant, and largely unprecedented account of thrift in American history. Underpinning the rich diversity of disciplinary perspectives are two overarching claims: (1) what is striking from even a cursory glance at the history of thrift is its astonishing capaciousness and dynamism, challenging the narrow and attenuated rendering of thrift as mere frugality; and (2) the idiom of thrift has served as the primary language Americans have used for articulating the normative dimensions of economic life throughout their history.

Thrift in America makes these claims by telling two stories about thrift in America—or, rather, by telling a story within a story. The first, bounded, story examines "classic thrift"—conventionally understood as frugality. It tells of its cultural origins and ascendancy, but also how it gradually lost its normative appeal in the mainstream of American life and became marginalized (although not completely expelled). Here we are challenging a familiar rise-and-fall narrative about the history of thrift that goes something like this: the idea of thrift has its origins among the Puritans and achieves its greatest currency in the eighteenth and nineteenth centuries, but by the late twentieth century, it has foundered and is all but forgotten.

This narrative at first sounds plausible. Yet as one begins to dig into the subject, one realizes how much more there is to this story. In the place of a simple history of ascent and decline is a complex account of institutional and cultural realignment leading, in turn, to significant alterations in thrift. In this more complicated account of the ebb and flow of the thrift ethos across profound historical transformations, the tensions of realignment play out in manifold, often crosscutting ways yet always bearing as much on the ordering of our individual daily lives as on our attempts to define public virtue and the good society.

The second, more expansive story reveals, in one historical case after another, how remarkably rich, dynamic, and versatile thrift has been in practice, concerned as much with our uses of time, natural resources, manpower, and the passions as it is with saving money. Its shows how its purposes are as varied as its objects: thrift for human survival, religious calling, political independence and self-rule, environmental conservation, racial hegemony, philanthropy, manhood and womanhood, collective security, and social protest. Thrift is an idea that has been reconfigured in different times and under different circumstances, showing itself to be remarkably malleable in application and purpose.

Thrift "Well Understood"

Among the original contributions of this collection is putting thrift in this more expansive light, where it reveals how, when Americans have considered the normative dimensions of economic life, they have historically done so through the cultural idiom of thrift. Extending well beyond commonsense notions, thrift in this deeper sense has been more concerned with ends than with means. The etymology of the word *thrift* is revealing in this regard. In the *Oxford English Dictionary* (*OED*), the first definition of thrift refers to an older sense of the word, when it was less a virtue than a condition. It reads as follows: "The fact or condition of thriving or prospering; prosperity, success, good luck, in early use sometimes fortune, good or bad, etc."[6]

The *OED* illustrates this particular definition with several quotations, most of them drawn from medieval literature and written in medieval English. However, the last citation comes from 1679. It is from a devotional text by the author of *Pilgrim's Progress*, John Bunyan, called *Fear of God*. In Bunyan's words, "Every grace is nourished by the Word, and without it there is no thrift in the soul."[7] For Bunyan, and his contemporaries, "thrift" was a condition, a state of being, and even of blessedness. Even for this mid-seventeenth-century Puritan, thrift was still understood to mean a condition of thriving. It was not until later that the word came to be understood as a virtue, and a specifically monetary virtue. Two hundred years after Bunyan, we have the meaning with which we are most familiar: thrift as "economical management, economy, sparing use or expenditures of means, frugality, saving, etc."[8]

Nevertheless, the early meaning of thrift—that is, the condition of thriving—has always been the subtext of the late one, and at times has even been used to critique the more narrowly conceived applications of thrift as frugality. Thrift in this deeper sense moves beyond the instrumentalities of "more or less" and begs the question: *What does it mean to thrive?* In short, thrift for what? More or less of what, and for what end? Such questions locate thrift's distinctive moral gravity. As we contend in the volume's concluding chapter, sustained consideration of thrift in this second sense supplies a badly needed normative vocabulary for thinking and talking about present economic, environmental, and social challenges. If there is a moral to the story of thrift, it is that our ability to sustain and extend the conditions for genuine human thriving depend, first and foremost, upon our ability to sustain and extend a conversation about the inescapably normative dimensions of economic life. We suggest that this is the promise of thrift, "well understood."

Thrift and Moral Order

As already noted, thrift shares a family resemblance with other practices and other moral goods such as self-restraint, reticence, temperance, conservation, and stewardship; in turn, these ideas are often defined in relation to notions of justice, charity, and the public good. In this way, thrift and its analogues never exist apart from a larger cultural framework, or moral order. At its simplest, moral orders provide the normative terms by which a people's way of life is defined and organized. Such normative terms supply the many permissions and interdictions—society's "yeses" and "nos"—that not only are embedded in its laws and governing institutions but are more or less internalized so that they become "second nature" to most of the people who constitute the society. Such systems of controls and permissions uphold and police the boundaries of a particular formulation of what a society holds as its highest ideals and authoritative goods—that is, its definitions of the good life and the good society (the "sacred" in anthropological terms). On the positive side, moral orders are empowering in that they fund the legitimating stories, rationales, and role identities by which people can act intelligibly as members of the same society. But moral orders also constrain. When individuals deviate from the norms of a given moral order, as they do on a regular basis, they expose themselves to communal censure or even official punishment, in addition to suffering the internal weight of guilt and shame that can come with even the smallest transgression. That said, moral orders are never static, monolithic, or all-encompassing but are almost always ideologically loaded and contested, rife with contradiction, and constantly evolving.

Moral order is a difficult subject to elucidate, not least when it comes to the sphere of life we call the "economy." The very idea that the financial structures and transactions that constitute so much of modern life presuppose a moral order would strike many people as incomprehensible, if not wrong. We tend to think of the moral dimensions of the market in terms similar to how we think of any complex machine or technology; that is, we do not think about them in moral terms at all, or if we do, we think of them as morally neutral. Personal decisions about consumption or structural injustices have moral weight, but not the laws of supply and demand. Of course, in moments of financial crisis there is no shortage of moralizing about the market, but again, it is typically directed at greedy, colluding executives or spendthrift consumers, rather than the economy itself.

That said, we believe that one can in fact discern a broad-gauged typology of thrift ethics that correspond to distinct moral orders across the wide sweep of American history. Here we can anticipate the general lines of the story we see in the pages that follow: "Puritan thrift," "classic thrift," "consumer thrift," "collective thrift," "reactionary thrift," and "green thrift"—each rises to prominence within a given historical period and offers paradigmatic expression of a dominant moral order. From its rather nondescript and enigmatic origins to its first explicitly public affirmations, the rise of the thrift ethos in the history of American life and thought occurred centrally within the religious, social, and economic orbit of the English and North American Puritans. Such affirmations were pursued within a culturally and historically distinct moral order—what we call the "Holy Common-Wealth." Puritan thrift engendered a powerful combination of individual moral striving with a collective project of mutual aid and social reform. It did so, moreover, within a robust religious and civil institutional context. This admixture of the personal and the public, however, marked a cultural tension within the Holy Common-Wealth—one whose relative fragility would be revealed in the early years of the Republic.

The post-Revolutionary era in the newly formed United States brought rising levels of consumption and economic growth, the further establishment of a strong middle class, and, not surprisingly, heightened anxiety over the influence of luxury on moral and civic values. Thrift is hotly contested during these years, and its availability as a mode of social critique from a variety of perspectives signals the continuing centrality of thrift within national debates over citizenship, middle-class respectability, and regional difference. This is the dawning era of "classic thrift," and the distinctive moral order to which it gave expression—what, following historian T. J. Jackson Lears, we call the "Victorian-Individualist Synthesis." Like its Puritan forerunner, the ethic of thrift in its bourgeois formulation emphasized self-discipline, hard work, sobriety, honesty, diligence, and industry. It was animated by a morally inflected striving for respectability, independence, and manliness, which at least formally found its writ in a pan-Protestant ethical sensibility. The crucial differences came as thrift and this ethical sensibility gradually detached themselves from the Puritan providentialist cosmology that originally underwrote them. Thrift in this dispensation found new sanction in a rich and dynamic amalgamation of civic republican, Protestant, Stoic, and democratic sensibilities, but it did so primarily as a private affair.

The massive cultural shifts marked by urbanization and industrialization at the turn of the twentieth century began to challenge the classic notion of thrift developed under the Victorian-Individualist Synthesis. New economic realities, including the expansion of a credit economy, gave rise to a version of "consumer" thrift that required new forms of financial discipline even as the importance of "classic" thrift was downplayed to accommodate innovations like the installment plan. This brave new economic era, however, brought unprecedented risks as well. In the face of world wars, economic depression, and other disruptions caused by industrial capitalism, a renewed call for "collective" thrift (in a variety of forms) achieved prominence as a necessary means of guaranteeing citizens some basic minimum standard of material well-being. By the First World War, these changes had sufficiently decoupled thrift from earlier moral registers and began refashioning it within a new formulation of moral order, what we call, again following Lears, the "Managerial-Civic Compromise." Here, the bureaucratic search for efficiency, the institutionalization of an industrial division of labor, and the interdependence of both with an increasingly powerful federal government formed the basis of a new way moral order would relate to capitalism.

Though compelling for a time, the historic compromise between labor, capital, and the state would eventually prove tenuous. It was not long before the unprecedented explosion of economic growth that followed the Second World War caused the central meanings of thrift to transform yet again. As the Great Depression faded to the back of the collective memory and the postwar boom took off, a new sense of established (perhaps even permanent) abundance, seen in the expansion of home ownership and the market for consumer goods, replaced the long-standing notion that scarcity was the fundamental grounding for economic thinking. Many distinguished economists agreed with this thinking, and while the most radical predictions (like the near extinction of work) have long been abandoned, the condition of abundance has continued to dominate the last sixty years of American economic thought.

One of the central concerns of Thrift in America is thus to lay the groundwork for asking a pressing question: What happens to thrift in an age of late capitalist abundance? The consumerist era of endless growth and "easy" credit seems to have left behind the seemingly old-fashioned practice of financial frugality. But, again, these volumes develop a thicker methodology for approaching thrift—as an indicator of an underlying moral order—that seeks to look beyond this quick dismissal. Understanding the contextual transformations surrounding the history of thrift in earlier eras prepares us to compose a more complex portrait of its meaning in the present.

There are many signs that thrift has *not* disappeared as completely as indicated by a first glance. Just as new forms of thrift emerged in response to economic shifts in the late nineteenth and early twentieth centuries, yet newer forms are evolving to answer our particular situation now. In many instances, these new forms are radically individualist and expressivist, and they mirror the broader fragmentation of American society. We call these new forms, for heuristic purposes, "free-agent" thrift. It is most clearly represented by the often demanding practices and lifestyles of the highly flexible, mobile, and consumerist professional-managerial elite. At the level of moral order, what we have is more like an experiment—what we call the "Free-Agent-Expressivist Experiment"—that wagers we can do without a conception of the commonweal, or even without a common language by which to discuss the normative dimensions of economic life. But, again, this is not the whole story. Thrift also has "reactionary" formulations in the discourse of environmentalist and antiglobalization movements, which often draw upon the language of restraint to ground their critiques of American-style global capitalism. It may even be argued, we think credibly, that the rise of the environmental movement, with its concern for ecological sustainability, the conservation of natural resources, and the preservation of the planet's biodiversity, represents one of the most important transformations in the history of thrift—to wit, the rise of "green thrift."

As an inquiry into the changing moral culture of capitalism, the story that unfolds in these chapters reveals a number of tensions, contradictions, and paradoxes in the evolution and changing meanings and purposes of thrift. As we mentioned earlier, thrift is an idea that has been reconfigured in different times and under different circumstances, revealing its remarkably malleable application and purpose. All of these themes appear and reappear over the course of this investigation, and all provide insight into the moral culture of capitalism in various moments of its history. Yet, despite thrift's surprisingly dynamic and variable character, we believe a meaningfully coherent story can be told. The chronological progress of this volume charts the transformations of thrift in relation to the shifting background of American cultural and economic life and offers an account of the social and moral history of thrift in America as a way of addressing more adequately the complicated economic era in which we now live.

A Controversial Virtue

In his contribution to this volume, the Pulitzer Prize–winning American historian Daniel Walker Howe writes: "Thrift has been a perennially contested virtue, even among those who claim to honor it." This is an important reminder and one that moves us to make two critical qualifications about the story of thrift we have just offered.

First, the reader will discover certain points of discord between certain chapters and, in one or two instances, between some of the contributors and the editors regarding this story. The substance and structure of the typological narrative we develop are thus fully our own. They draw faithfully but selectively from individual chapters, and not equally from every chapter. This means that there are unresolved points of tension and even apparent contradictions to be found in the volume. For instance, the tension between accounts placing explanatory weight on changes in the structures of capitalism versus those that favor changes in moral order pervade this entire collection. This is of course a very old dispute in the social sciences and one that we make no attempt to resolve. Rather, we merely suggest that material and ideal interests generally stand in dynamic tension, and it is left to individual scholars to determine which, in a given historical instance, should be given the greater explanatory emphasis (a decision that will doubtless reflect certain disciplinary biases). Whatever the case may be in specific instances, both sides of the dialectic clearly play pivotal roles throughout the multifaceted history of thrift in America.

Some contributions, however, raise significant questions about the overall importance of thrift in American history, however conceived, and could be construed as offering a counternarrative to the one we have put forward in this introduction—namely, our claim that the cultural idiom of thrift has served as *the* primary language for thinking and talking about the normative dimensions of economic life throughout American history. The environmental historians J. R. McNeill and George Vrtis, for instance, make a compelling case that Americans have been quite possibly the most profligate people in human history, at least when it comes to their ecological footprint. All the lofty rhetoric of thrift aside, when judged against long-standing habits of environmental heedlessness and the improvident handling of natural resources, the actual record of thrift in American history (from the very earliest colonial days) seems a paltry affair. Americans, they point out, are famous not for thrift but for pioneering the world's first "high-energy society," which has generated unprecedented material abundance at the cost of unprecedented levels of waste and pollution.

For slightly different reasons, the economic historian Deirdre McCloskey also challenges the significance of thrift in American history. In her case, McCloskey questions the received historiography, which portrays thrift as that essential bourgeois discipline that made capitalist accumulation—and thus capitalism itself—possible. According to McCloskey, the historical evidence shows that irrespective of how thrifty Americans may or may not have actually been, thrift had little or nothing to do with the rise of capitalism, or the historically unprecedented explosion of economic growth that came with it. Putting it tersely, McCloskey maintains that people everywhere and at all times have always only been as thrifty as they had to be, and as prodigal as they possibly could be. In the case of the United States, the combination of political freedom (so conducive to technological innovation) and the sheer abundance of land and natural resources proved decisive in setting up a particular cultural format that from the very beginning encouraged Americans toward extraordinary wealth construction and extreme prodigality. Taken together, the contributions by McCloskey and by McNeill and Vrtis do indeed seem to offer a potentially powerful counterstory, one that must be taken seriously.

While wanting neither to gloss over genuine points of divergence nor to force any false coherence, we nevertheless believe that our historical typology aligns quite well with the arguments advanced by both McCloskey and McNeill and Vrtis. When we claim that thrift has been the primary normative language of economic life, we are not claiming that thrift was responsible for the rise of capitalism, nor are we arguing that Americans were once especially thrifty in regard to the natural environment. We quite agree with McCloskey that once a certain level of prosperity is reached, thrift does in fact become a functional part of the moral order—part of the cultural system of permission and controls mentioned earlier—that helps regulate the moral ambiguities of newly accumulated wealth for a newly emerging social class, itself adjusting to the changing demands of the modern division of labor. Thrift thus doubled nicely both as a justificatory rationale for those enjoying this new wealth and as a form of social control over subordinate groups (e.g., African Americans and the poor). The essential point for us is that thrift was not incidental to the development of capitalism. Similarly, we readily concur with McNeill and Vrtis that while American culture has historically combined competing impulses toward thrift and profligacy, the unusual material abundance of American society has inclined Americans to be profoundly spendthrift in their relationship to their natural and physical surroundings. And yet, as they also admit, there have been important, if sporadic, but ultimately mounting movements of resistance to environmental degradation over the decades, typically pursued in the name of conservation, greater efficiency, and environmental responsibility. Only where they seem to be skeptical of the role thrift has played in motivating such resistance, we see thrift (albeit broadly conceived) at the heart of such movements. Indeed, one might credibly argue that the story of thrift in the late twentieth and early twenty-first centuries is nothing less than the story of thrift's reformulation into an ethic of environmental stewardship and sustainability. To be sure, these are only some preliminary considerations, and any resolution must await further research.

This leads us to the second qualification, which can be stated more succinctly. Our historical typology is not intended to provide an exhaustive account of thrift or of the changing relationship between capitalism and moral order over the course of hundreds of years of American history. Trying to provide anything like a definitive theoretical synthesis or philosophical statement would be premature at this stage. Rather, we envision this work as a first installment in what we hope will become a series of future studies on this and related topics in economic culture. The reader should therefore consider this volume to be an initial foray into an as yet uncharted territory and as a catalyst for ongoing study and debate.

With such crucial qualifications in mind, we believe that the sustained, interdisciplinary investigation of thrift accomplished in this volume provides a unique and heretofore inaccessible window into the cultural dimensions of economic life from the Puritans to the present. Of all the things we are able to see through it, perhaps the most important (and surprising) are the shifting notions of what Americans think it means and takes to "thrive" under the evolving conditions of modern capitalism.

Overview of Volume

PART I: THE EMERGENCE OF THRIFT IN EARLY AMERICA, 1630–1880

Rather than the narrow, attenuated, and rather banal topic many take it to be, the American historian Daniel Walker Howe shows thrift to be a subject of long-standing and often bitter disputes over which vision of human thriving would define the character of American society. As he contends in "The Controversial Virtue of Thrift in the Early American Republic," the very notion of thrift has thus been from the earliest days a robustly contested idea, practice, and public ideal. The competition to define thrift has played out between Calvinist theology, classical republican thought, and Scottish moral philosophy, and against the transition from early America's largely agriculture-based economy to the industrialized, urbanized America of the late nineteenth century. The results were multifarious. On the one hand, city living multiplied temptations to spend and indulge. On the other hand, it helped bring into being a prosperous middle class that embraced thrift as a guiding virtue. Thrift thus underwent various recalibrations as the young nation vacillated between rural and urban development, between consumptive refinement and productive sobriety, and between private and public interests. In each case, thrift has been subject to competing definitions and demands.

However, as the economic historian Deirdre McCloskey demonstrates in "The Prehistory of American Thrift," for the opening chapter in the story of thrift in the United States we have to go back to developments in England and, before that, in Holland. The basic story is of course well known: With the relative leveling of society in the wake of the Renaissance, and especially the Reformation, aristocratic virtues gradually lost their long-held social dominance. In their place arose new commercial and civic virtues that legitimated the rising capitalist order. But McCloskey is quick to show that the lesson of this early history is not what many have assumed. With apologies to Marx and Weber, her analysis questions the oft-repeated assumption that it was an increase in savings due to thrift that drove the rise of capitalism as the dominant economic order in the Anglo-American world. Rather, McCloskey shows that all of the historical evidence points instead to a combination of relative political freedom and technological innovation that led to the most dramatic economic growth—by a factor of eighteen—in world history. That said, she concedes that thrift's social status did change in the period leading up to the Industrial Revolution from an utterly unremarkable feature of human existence to a marker of middle-class respectability and comportment. Along with all the economic virtues, thrift became an important regulating ideal.

At the radical end of the socioeconomic (and theological) changes wrought by both the spread of commerce and the Reformation were the English Puritans. Borrowing much in the way of religious and economic advice from the Dutch, Puritans built a commercial system around a deep sense of thrift. In "Saving Grace and Moral Striving: Thrift in Puritan Theology," religious historians James Calvin Davis and Charles Mathewes develop the rich theological framework within which the Puritan ideal of thrift first developed. The Puritans believed quite explicitly that thrift was a necessary condition for human thriving because it was the proper response to divine grace. As such, Puritan thrift expressed an ethic of responsible, profitable, and pious management of time, talents, and treasure. As important as such "inner-worldly asceticism" may have been as a mark of salvation to the individual believer, thrift was not reducible to a private, individual practice for the Puritans. Rather, it was as much a spiritual calling for whole communities as it was for the individuals who constituted them.

The paradoxical result of Puritan thrift, to which observers since Weber have repeatedly pointed, and of which the Puritans themselves were acutely aware, was how what started out as a deeply pious attitude toward the methodological practice of godly accumulation eventually seemed to lead to a highly effective, but ultimately worldly, technique for material acquisitiveness. How, in other words, did the Puritans ever come to produce Benjamin Franklin? The late historian Stephen Innes takes up this long-standing question in "Thrift and Prosperity." Innes locates part of the answer in the unique social and cultural circumstances of Puritan New England that allowed for the fullest implementation of the Puritan politics of virtue, and of the creation of key institutions that reinforced compliance to this politics within the Puritan community. On Innes's reading, thrift and thriving were thus as much public as private matters. Innes thus also underscores the centrality of social criticism among the Puritans as a form of social control, paying special attention to the ways they treated economic success with suspicion, if not equating it with spiritual and moral failure. Beginning with the Puritan jeremiad, this tradition of critique continues in both religious and secular formulations down to the present.

Anxiety over the status of luxury only grew more acute in the transition from colonial hardship to national prosperity in the era of the early Republic, as American historian Joyce Appleby shows in "Moderation in the First Era of Popular Consumption." Fear of famine was largely eliminated, concentration on bare survival made way for concern with economic growth, and ordinary people began to produce, and enjoy on a large scale, "goods to comfort and adorn body and home." Moderation, restraint, and self-discipline—variations on the theme of thrift—were not abandoned, argues Appleby, but their religious and moral justifications were gradually supplemented and in some cases replaced by instrumental and economic ones.

Moving further away from the Puritan vision of the Holy Common-Wealth, both secular and sectarian associations took on a larger role in shaping the broader moral culture of the United States. In "Spreading the Gospel of Self-Denial: Thrift and Association in Antebellum America," historian Kathleen McCarthy charts the democratization and diversification of thrift in the nineteenth century and explores how American voluntary associations preached the gospel of thrift to men, women, and children of every station and, in the process, helped fortify the foundations for commercial society. In this period, Americans created a variety of charitable organizations, which, in the effort to combat poverty, emphasized the importance of abstemious behavior. Religious groups continued to inculcate moral restraint as well, and the Second Great Awakening gave birth to the "benevolent empire," through which the new Sunday school movement inculcated thrift as well as the related virtue of temperance. At the same time, Americans were busy creating mutual aid societies and lodges, largely secular, whose purpose was to preach the thrift ethic to the working class.

Historian Patrick Rael traces the role that notions of thrift played in the history of race in pre–Civil War America in "African Americans, Slavery, and Thrift from the Revolution to the Civil War." In particular, he highlights how white Americans reserved "the virtues of thrift—industriousness, discipline, and self-control" for themselves, while ascribing to blacks "thrift's antitheses—laziness, improvidence, and profligacy." In this way, the moral economy of thrift was used to justify the institution of slavery. At the same time, the national discourse of thrift was fragmenting, as the North and South developed competing conceptions of thrift, which reflected the contrasting needs of their economies. The northern states emphasized the bourgeois work ethic, industrialization, and urban life. The southern states stressed a conception rooted in an agricultural and slave-based economy. Northern thrift, according to Rael, contributed to the creation of an economy much more diversified and powerful than that of the South, an advantage that proved decisive in the Civil War.

The story developed in part I challenges the easy narrative of decline from a once-virtuous past to a prodigal American modernity. That the discourse and practice of thrift have changed over the course of early American history is undeniable. The Puritan Holy Common-Wealth fades, but key aspects of its moral economy persist into the early national period. In addition, there are innovations that bear on the history of thrift—the rise of mutual aid societies and collective forms of thrift that sought to respond to new social and cultural realities. Clearly, the early career of thrift is complicated and contested. The dominant movement in this era, though, seems to be toward the formation of a post-Puritan notion of thrift. The exhortations and jeremiads once aimed at entire congregations and communities by the Puritan divines were, in time, transposed into the secular dogma of individual responsibility famously epitomized by the best-selling advice of Benjamin Franklin's "Poor Richard": "Trouble springs from idleness; toil from ease"; "Early to bed and early to rise, makes a man healthy, wealthy, and wise"; "Diligence is the mother of good luck."[9] More narrowly economic and private in focus than the Puritan vision, this new form of thrift came with a clear duty toward charity and benevolence, but one that was more and more concerned with personal propriety and individual material well-being.

Yet, part I not only concentrates on the moral, philosophical, and religious sources of classic thrift and the Victorian-Individualist Synthesis to which it gave expression; it also highlights its significant cultural counterpoints—historic patterns and rituals of excess, indulgence, consumption, and waste. This period had its fair share of gambling and financial risk-taking. It also witnessed countercultural deployments of thrift, especially around race and gender issues. It saw the initial stages of a further transposition of thrift in terms consistent with rising consumption and a growing emphasis on personal refinement and polite culture.

Taken as a whole, the rise of thrift in both its Puritan and later bourgeois formulations represents the remarkable transvaluation of ideals that accompanied the shift to capitalism in the late eighteenth and early nineteenth centuries throughout the West. Throughout this period, attitudes toward commerce, banking, financial speculation, and other practices of wealth accumulation changed dramatically. In the words of the economic historian A. O. Hirschman, values that had stood condemned for millennia as the vices of "greed, love of lucre, and avarice" in the moral registers of both classical and Christian thought had become "virtuous."[10]

PART II: THE MODERNIZATION OF THRIFT: YEARS OF TRANSITION AND TRANSFORMATION, 1880–1950

Between 1880 and 1950, classic thrift found itself gradually being displaced from the mainstream of American culture by two new forms thrift, each representing what T. J. Jackson Lears describes in his opening chapter as the reconfiguration of thrift for a managerial age. The first is what might be called "consumer thrift." Counterintuitive (even contradictory) from the perspective of both Puritan and classic thrift, with their complementary preoccupation with a saving and work-centered ethic, consumer thrift captures the highly trained forms of discipline that were then emerging under a new, consuming-oriented phase of capitalism. In this light, the advent of the installment plan and the widespread introduction of buying consumer goods "on time" are emblematic not of the end of thrift, but rather of a further transformation. As Lendol Calder puts it: "In this new order of perception, credit emerges as thrift applied to a new commodity: time."

Simultaneously with consumer thrift, however, arises a new, secularized (and increasingly nationalized) version of "collective thrift." It had become clear that the private, individualistic features of classic thrift, however responsible and benevolent, were simply insufficient in the face of extreme cycles of boom and bust or amid the turbulence of world war. Only collective thrift in a combination of forms—corporate- and state-based, mass philanthropic, even civic-patriotic—had the potential to guarantee citizens in industrializing nations some basic minimum standard of individual well-being and geopolitical security.

By no means did classic thrift disappear in this period. During the early decades of the twentieth century it arguably achieved its greatest institutional prominence. It was strenuously advocated for by a host of national associations, most prominently the YMCA, the American Bankers' Association, the U.S. Chambers of Commerce, the American Home Economics Association, the Federated Council of Churches, and the National Association of Education. On an annual basis beginning in 1917, these and many other groups celebrated classic thrift during National Thrift Week (held the week of January 17 to commemorate Benjamin Franklin's birthday). By the middle of the 1920s, a full-fledged National Thrift Movement had arisen whose explicit goal was to school Americans in the "Ten Commandments of Thrift." Among their most successful accomplishments was the establishment of a program of "thrift accounts" in elementary and secondary schools across the country. Yet, despite such popular initiatives, it had become clear that classic thrift was no longer the undisputed route to middle-class respectability; it had lost its hegemonic status as competing pictures of thrift were becoming attractive to Americans of all ages. It is arguably because of this fact that something like the National Thrift Movement became necessary in the first place. When seen in the light of subsequent history, therefore, what at the time might have seemed like a dynamic and vibrant social movement might now be judged as classic thrift's grand finale.

In "The Modernization of Thrift," Lears chronicles the rise of this managerial ethos. No longer worried, as were the moralists, about the drift toward hedonism, the new managerial thrift emphasized "efficiency" as a means to higher productivity. This shift reemphasizes the movement toward a new psychology of "abundance" that characterizes this whole era of American history. The apotheosis of the managerial ethic was found in Progressives like economist Richard Ely, who championed the practice of thrift in relation to resources in industrial productivity and thought this moral watchfulness in one area was certain to produce increased wages for workers in another. The optimism of this sort of approach fell apart in the stock market crash of 1929, and the response over the course of the Great Depression was the need for collective, not merely individual, methods of saving. Another key aspect of the new managerial age was the growth of consumer culture based on planned obsolescence and ever-changing styles. The result was a compromise between labor, management, and government that tied increasing consumption and productivity together as the major engines of American economic growth for the better part of the twentieth century.

James Davison Hunter, in "Thrift and Moral Formation," charts the displacement of the classic discourse of thrift in the moral education of children. Shifting away from older lessons about magnanimity and the importance of avoiding miserliness, American education in this age became acutely focused on the potential instability of economic life in the new urban centers. As a result, national movements supporting thrift were spawned, creating savings plans at banks, post offices, and even public schools—it was, in the sense of moral exhortation, the golden age of thrift. This moment of triumph would not last long, however. The revolution in productive efficiency in the 1920s quickly began to shift opinion away from the psychology of scarcity that created the thrift ethos and toward a new sense of American prosperity and abundance. Soon, the new economic philosophy of "consumptionism" was dominant, and the individual thrift that proved powerless in response to the Great Depression was on the out. New curricula encouraged parents to take their children on shopping trips and train them to be wise and efficient consumers.

This new sense of "consumptionism," however, is thicker than we are accustomed to thinking. Lawrence B. Glickman, in "The Virtue of Consumption: Challenging Thrift in an Age of Transition," builds the case for the growth of "moral consumption" in this same era. Thrift, he asserts, was not only a moral virtue; it was understood as one of the central building blocks of civilization, a republican way of life that supported the larger identity and goals of the nation. The challenges to thrift that began to arise in the era after the Civil War, then, took the shape of alternate views of the composition of civilization itself. One early example was the consumer activism of the abolitionist era that cast spending in a new, morally positive light. Soon even workers' groups were touting consumption as the path to a more civilized life. In the new industrial manufacturing culture, advocating for steady and increasing consumption often became equated with support of the industry itself. This idea easily spun over into the New Deal logic that spending and increased production was the way to heal the economy in the new age of abundance.

Jennifer Scanlon, in "Thrift and Advertising," details the role of advertising in developing the new ethic of consumer thrift in the twentieth century. She explains how advertising professionals targeted housewives as the controllers of domestic spaces and pitched to them a new sense of efficiency and self-control as the values necessary for a way of life characteristic of the modern age. Scanlon elaborates the connections between this modern ethic of discipline and the older classic notion of thrift to show how the cultural forms of restraint were transformed across this particular set of economic relations in the middle of the twentieth century.

Paralleling this surprising story of consumerist discipline, Lendol Calder, in "Hard Payments: Consumer Credit and Thrift," works against several deeply entrenched assumptions by dealing with the transformation of credit across the late nineteenth and early twentieth centuries. First, he tackles the notion that credit is an essentially modern invention by detailing the history of informal modes of credit (like the tab at the country store) that existed long before the twentieth century. Next, he shows how the twentieth century saw a proliferation of novel forms of consumer credit, not least the diffusion of the installment plan. But, finally, he refuses to identify this movement with straightforward thriftlessness. He argues instead that the new forms of credit fostered a new form of penny-pinching, or thrift. To be sure, the discipline of allotting money carefully so that one can afford to make all the monthly payments that accrue in the modern credit era not only reinstitutes thrift but recalibrates it to the patterns of mass consumption in the process. But, again, such transformation of thrift comes with a price: the credit may be easy, but the discipline of monthly interest payments is "hard."

Olivier Zunz, in "Mass Philanthropy as Public Thrift for an Age of Consumption," tells the story of the development of modern mass philanthropy, which used investigative problem solving in conjunction with government initiatives to make use of the enormous corporate wealth created by the revolution in industrial production. But individual Americans also participated in the new philanthropic spirit, putting to use the savings they had accumulated through practices of frugality and new prosperity. Fund-raising techniques came to rely largely on "nickel-and-dime" strategies to raise large amounts of money from a wide swath of the population. This charitable ethic was supported by the fund-raising effort around World War I, which raised the activity of giving to the level of patriotic duty.

David Reimers, in "Immigrants and Thrift," describes the economic and cultural struggles of immigrants from Europe, Asia, and Mexico in the age of industrialization. In order to deal with the trauma of relocation and economic hardship, many immigrants formed associations that held collective savings, provided insurance, and performed charitable functions among the immigrant communities. In this way, he reveals how immigrants participated in the long-standing American tradition of voluntary association but also how immigrant populations injected into American economic culture the practices of mutual aid and collective security that redefined thrift for a new century and a new citizenry.

Kiku Adatto, in "Saving for Democracy: Thrift, Sacrifice, and the World War II Bond Campaigns," details the further growth of a collective notion of thrift as she recounts the war bond campaign of the Second World War. Here we see a notion of thrift fully embedded in a social attempt to serve the greater good. Saving money was equated directly with service to the nation and was pitched as a duty of sacrifice to support the war effort. One of the central characteristics of this campaign was that it enabled everyone down to newspaper boys to participate in a society-wide thrift movement. As such, the World War II war bond effort put thrift in the service of democracy, both in the sense that it directly supported the war being fought for democratic ideals and in the sense that it allowed the participation of all sectors in the American war effort. This national ethic of collective thrift for the greater good, Adatto argues, largely died in the prosperity that followed World War II, and it has not been restored even during subsequent wars in the latter part of the twentieth century.

Though compelling for a time, what we are calling the Managerial-Civic Compromise between labor, capital, and the state would eventually prove unsustainable. The unprecedented explosion of economic growth that followed the Second World War would cause the central meanings of thrift to transform yet again. Amid the ebullience of postwar prosperity, the memory of the Depression receded and a new psychology of abundance began rapidly replacing the old psychology of scarcity. A number of factors facilitated this shift, including the powerful combination of extraordinary increases in industrial productivity and the rise of modern advertising and popular entertainment. Together, these allowed (and encouraged) unprecedented numbers of Americans to own their own homes, put automobiles in their driveways, and bring a seemingly endless array of consumer goods, appliances, and labor-saving devices into their households. This is a familiar story.

Perhaps less well known is how economic theory also changed its mind during this era. A new generation of economists, from Simon Patten to John Maynard Keynes to Walter Rostow, heralded the dawn of a new social and economic epoch of affluence. In this new age, classic thrift became a virtue-relic of a more primitive past, at least for elite academic sensibilities. The economist Paul Samuelson, who would later go on to win the Nobel Prize in Economics, expounded what was then thought to be the definitive revision of the old economic view—the so-called paradox of thrift—arguing that classic thrift may still be useful to the individual in a pinch, but it is absolutely inimical to the economic growth of the nation as a whole. If Americans saved rather than spent their incomes, an economy predicated as much on consumption as production would only falter.

Underlying this perspective was a confidence that, according to Keynes, mankind was solving his economic problem.[11] In this new epoch of abundance, humans had finally been liberated from the miserable and degrading mind-set that sanctioned a calculating self-centeredness, inhuman forms of material asceticism, and an overall inability (having neither the time nor the inclination) to appreciate the finer things in life. Thus emancipated, humans could now pursue their authentic, self-actualizing, and "other-directed" (today we might say "postmaterial") interests to the benefit of society and themselves. However it may have made sense in a time of material scarcity, classic thrift had become a hindrance to the fundamental human need to express "higher wants" in an age of abundance. "There will be great changes in the code of morals," Keynes promised. "We shall be able to rid ourselves," he added, not mincing words, "of many of the pseudo-moral principles which have hag-ridden us for two hundred years, by which we have exalted some of the most distasteful of human qualities into the position of the highest virtues."[12]

In a variety of ways, thrift was therefore forced to change its complexion as notions of social and moral progress—that is, what it meant to thrive (now encapsulated by the phrase "living standard")—were forced to keep up with the wider changes wrought on society by the evolution of capitalism. Instead of "coaxing wealth from scarcity," now the ends of thrift had to be adjusted to the demands of living well in abundance, whether this was expressed in terms of consumer discipline or in terms of state and corporate welfare. The midcentury dreams of a number of prominent public intellectuals from Keynes to John Kenneth Galbraith to David Reisman seemed close at hand: America, and the world soon behind it, had entered an epoch "after thrift." Such dreams, however, would not last long.

PART III: THRIVING AFTER THRIFT? PROSPERITY AND CRISIS SINCE 1950

Moving from the middle of the twentieth century to the present, this final part focuses on the implications of thrift's changing career for contemporary American society. It highlights important ways in which thrift persists today—how it continues to evolve toward new, even radically new, ends, how older versions of the thrift ethos have resurfaced in unexpected places. Nevertheless, the story is far from one of straightforward continuity. Indeed, by the closing decades of the twentieth century, the idiom of thrift, whether individual or collective, classic or consumerist, had grown increasingly incoherent. By any measure of its vital statistics, thrift's prospects looked bleak. This incoherence, and our resulting inarticulacy about it, demonstrate the degree to which thrift had lost its cultural force—how its abstemious energies had dissipated, how its rhetorical appeal had lost its former vividness, resonance, and depth. A once-defining idiom of middle-class respectability, thrift had become conspicuously absent in public discourse. Where the ethos of thrift still found expression, largely at the margins of contemporary culture, it was a rather antiquated affair. As a result, thrift had effectively lost its capacity to organize and give meaning to both private and public life.

In this way, the most striking thing this volume reveals about the character of thrift today may be that its persistence is as difficult to depict as its evolving forms are to decipher. Whereas it is clear in retrospect how thrift has embodied formerly dominant formulations of moral order in the history of American economic life since the Puritans, we can only be provisional about what the continued evolution of thrift tells us about capitalism and moral order in the present. We live during a time when the very concept of a single unifying moral order is hard to fathom, and, complicating matters further, our analyses are clearly limited to the ambiguities and exigencies of the present. We may very well live at the end of thrift. However, we may also be living between dominant forms of thrift—such was the case for those Americans living between the decline of Puritan thrift and the rise of classic thrift or, similarly, between the denouement of classic thrift and the ascendance of consumer and collective thrift. In the same way, we too may be on the verge of a new hegemonic form of the thrift ethos. As we shall see, there is compelling evidence to suggest that a new normative ethic (sharing affinities with the "new economy") has already been shaping our lives while a reactionary thrift ethos mobilizes in resistance.

As the opening chapters of part III demonstrate, the commonsense assessments of thrift's dissipation are empirically sound. On a variety of measures, thrift really has fallen on hard times. In "Why Do Americans Save So Little and Does It Matter?" economist Robert Frank shows that the aggregate personal savings rate is for the first time since the Great Depression below zero and that the average American family currently carries almost $9,000 in unpaid credit card balances. "It is difficult," he concludes, "to second-guess the claim that Americans save too little." But Frank sees the problem as only partially one of individual self-control. The more difficult issue comes as a collective action problem. He argues that for many middle-class Americans saving and spending decisions are greatly influenced by a larger social context where competing moral goods clash. Should a middle-income family, for example, move to a neighborhood that is in a good school district but that costs more than they can responsibly afford, or should they stay in a neighborhood that they can afford, but with much poorer schools? The choice between financial responsibility and security, on the one hand, and the well-being of one's children, on the other, represents a genuine dilemma for many Americans, a dilemma that can only be resolved collectively.

In "The Rise and Fall of 'Collective Thrift': Social Insurance, Economic Planning, and the Decline of Modern American Liberalism," social historian Steven Fraser shows why collective thrift may not be as readily forthcoming a remedy for addressing the collective action problems that stymie individual thrift. Detailing the rise of mid-twentieth-century experiments in collective thrift—from government-sponsored Social Security, unemployment insurance, and subsidized medical care, to corporate-sponsored pension plans—Fraser also shows how short-lived many of these initiatives proved to be. In an era of global capital, increased foreign competition, and a renewed confidence in market solutions, political attitudes turned decidedly against collective thrift in all but a few forms by century's end. Fraser documents how, over the past twenty years, Americans have seen the systematic dismantling of public welfare programs and the privatization of collective thrift. A central consequence of this reversal has been a dramatic shifting of the burden of risk onto the shoulders of individuals. For working- and middle-class Americans this means, for instance, increasing reliance on "defined contribution plans," like 401(k)s, rather than "defined benefit plans" provided by employers. For poor Americans, this means less time on the dole and less public assistance overall. The general trend is what he calls the "financialization" of the economy, which rewards short-term speculation over long-term investment and promotes the public inclination "to seek individual or private solutions to all economic dilemmas."

Sociologists Steven Brint and Kristopher Proctor and American studies scholar Wilson Brissett narrow the field of vision to the state of thrift among elite and nonelite Americans. While the former examine the demographic segment of the American public historically most marked by the thrift ethos, the "professional-managerial" class, the latter investigates the ramifications of the ongoing struggle between "pro-thrift" and "anti-thrift" institutions upon working-class and underclass Americans. As the earlier sections of the volume have repeatedly demonstrated, the practice of thrift is esteemed as a virtue mainly by those who can afford to practice it. For the rest, thrift has been at best a virtue of necessity and, at worst, a form of moralizing condescension. This pattern largely continues in the present, though, as these chapters suggest, in some new, and newly perverse, ways. Today, the ideal and practice of thrift have increasingly had to compete with "payday" lending's deceptive promise of easy money and the state-run lottery's fraudulent offer of a lucky break.

In "Middle-Class Respectability in Twenty-First-Century America: Work and Lifestyle in the Professional-Managerial Stratum," Brint and Proctor survey the economic, work, and lifestyle habits of the "professional-managerial" class, again, those strata of citizens who have traditionally been thrift's most consistent and enthusiastic boosters. Their research resists the popular impression (and caricature by social critics) that this group is today among the most consumerist of Americans. They admit that members of this class are relatively more likely to think of their consumption as an opportunity for self-expression, but argue that this is neither crass materialism nor does it lack in strenuous forms of self-restraint. "If today's upper middle class does not save more proportionally than its predecessors," they write, "it nevertheless practices many forms of cultural and, indeed, moral restraint to maintain conditions favorable to thriving." For example, Brint and Proctor find that these Americans go to school longer, work longer hours, spend more time engaged in physical exercise, and go to greater pains to make their consumption ethically and spiritually meaningful. Not surprisingly, they also find that rather than material scarcity, the most precious, and by far the rarest, resource in their lives is time. Thus, far from a riot of hedonism and permissiveness, these Americans are, on the whole, a highly disciplined group. Due to the increasing pressures of global capitalism, which has seen the professional-managerial stratum become a truly worldwide phenomenon, it appears they have to be disciplined if they want to stay competitive.

But if the pressures of global capitalism are shaping a new kind of thrift among the upper-middle classes, what is going on among poorer Americans? In "Thrift in the Other America," Wilson Brissett takes a look at thrift among low-income populations today. Poverty is one area of the economy that is already loaded with moral meaning, but Brissett steers clear of the easy moral pronouncements that characterize political debates over the issue and instead offers analysis of institutions that support and discourage thrift among the poor. Personal savings itself is institutionally arranged to be easily available to the prosperous and relatively inaccessible to the low-income worker. The sale of lottery tickets and the high-interest lending of payday loan centers, on the other hand, are available at every corner store and strip mall. In this way, government and mainstream market forces are discouraging the practice of thrift among low-income populations (often, as in the case of credit card companies, in the name of "democratization") more forcefully than ever before. The rising tide of this "debt culture" has been countered by the growing influence of Community Development Financial Institutions (CDFIs), which offer a range of services from savings accounts to mortgage lending to venture capital investing in low-income areas and usually enjoy support from government funding and partnership with commercial financial organizations. They have popularized the notion of a "double bottom line" that measures investment success by both financial return *and* social impact. The overall impact of CDFIs, however, has been too small to counteract substantially the anti-thrift forces among the American poor.

Taken together, these initial chapters in part III offer evidence suggestive of the newest normative ethic to emerge on the American scene, what we will for heuristic purposes call "free-agent" thrift. Like all forms of thrift before it, free-agent thrift similarly enacts the evolving affinities between capitalism and moral order—the reconfiguration of thrift for a "postmaterial" age; in this case, thrift comes to enact the terms of neoliberal capitalism. Accordingly, it also represents an emerging character type: the proper subjects of "free markets" are "free agents," individuals oriented not only to material security but also to authentic expressions of work, leisure, and social concern.

On the positive side, free-agent thrift prescribes a distinctive normative orientation conducive for individual thriving, at least for those able to benefit from their position in the global economy. It combines a vision of virtuous consumption with a work ethic that privileges authenticity and autonomy as much as industrious time management, sober self-control, and diligent delayed gratification. The transcendental echo of Puritan thrift is clear—"improve every moment" with pious industry in the service not just of material gain but of "spiritual" uplift. It also connects long-standing concerns with gentility, refinement, and self-cultivation with a cosmopolitan concern for tolerance, social justice, and equality.

On the negative side, free-agent thrift is akin to consumer thrift without the safety net of collective thrift to fall back on. It represents a massive shift in the burden of risk from the corporation and the nation to the individual citizen, a burden that many Americans are neither financially equipped to carry nor psychologically prepared to bear in the face of global economic turbulence. It is empowering, even exhilarating, if you are one of the educated professionals who can move easily from one job to another, competent in literacy and numeracy, administrative efficiency, and economic competitiveness, but distressing if you are not. As Richard Sennett has recently put it, "Only a certain kind of person can prosper in an unstable, fragmentary social condition."[13]

In the end, we are left wondering whether the free-agent ethic is simply a further evolution of thrift or whether it bends it out of all recognition.

But how are we to evaluate such a question? The inarticulacy, fragmentation, and dissipation of thrift surely render problematic any attempt to answer this question definitively. Confounding such attempts further are questions about what has changed in the status of moral order itself. Indeed, there does not seem to be any coherent moral order today—no Victorian-Individualist Synthesis or Managerial-Civic Compromise—by which to orient our ideals and practices in the interests of individual or collective well-being. As said earlier, what we have, rather, is more like an experiment—the Free-Agent-Expressivist Experiment—that wagers we can do without this public ideal, without some common language by which to talk about the normative dimensions of economic life, about the character of moral economy and the conditions for human flourishing. The trouble with this experiment, some would say, is that it leaves out plenty of people and it is not altogether clear that those who stand to benefit from it are themselves thriving.

In response to the conditions of inarticulacy, fragmentation, and dissipation, and in direct opposition to what is perceived to be the negative consequences of the Free-Agent-Expressivist Experiment, it is not surprising to find some Americans calling for a radical reconfiguration of thrift as a form of resistance. In this last section of part III, environmental historians J. R. McNeill and George Vrtis and sociologist Joshua J. Yates report on the origins and institutionalization of the other significant reformulation of thrift in the contemporary period: the greening and radicalizing of thrift to combat the creative destruction of market forces.

In "Thrift and Waste in American History: An Ecological View," McNeill and Vrtis tell the history of how Americans have wrestled with the competing social visions of economic growth and ecological thrift. On the one hand, the story of waste is a story of American exceptionalism: endowed with unusual material abundance, technical know-how, and political freedom, Americans created "a cultural format in which endless consumption rivaled spiritual grace as the path to worthiness and fulfillment." Yet, in contrast to what they call the "cornucopian vision," there arose a concern for ecological conservation and protection that would eventually give birth to the modern environmental movement. Nature and culture form, in McNeill and Vrtis's telling, a double helix in American history, causing the perennial struggle between thrift and profligacy to swing decidedly in favor of the latter. Still, the American propensity for excessive wastefulness provoked periodic backswings in the direction of careful husbandry, the repercussions of which are still at work today in the greening of thrift.

In "Disputing Abundance: The Antiglobalization Protest Movement and Our Changing Natural Imaginary," Yates shows how the rhetoric of thrift in the antiglobalization protest movement serves as an illuminating backdrop against which to trace another surprising reformulation of thrift in the present. Where traditionally thrift has been thought necessary to free, prosperous, market-based societies, today it is commonly dismissed as either outmoded or inimical to free markets, to societies premised on a virtual, corporate-dominated, technologically produced abundance. In the movement's rendering, the spirit of thrift is enlisted in the resistance to the very society it was deemed instrumental in building. Yates investigates how thrift is used in the effort to counter and subvert what movement activists believe to be the ideological premise of managerial and now global capitalism: the assertion that we live in an era of unlimited and inexhaustible material abundance. Yates also discusses what movement leaders advance as the constructive face of reactionary thrift—an affirmation of social and environmental justice. Over against their litany of grievances—the destruction of local communities and cultures, the propagation of social and economic inequality within and across societies, and the devastation of the environment—activists advocate an assortment of thrifts, both old and new. They promote versions of classic thrift such as frugality and "simple living"; collective thrift, in terms of public regulation of natural resources, fair wages, and social safety nets; and, perhaps most notably, green thrift in the form of ecological conservation, the protection of "the commons," and "sustainable growth."

Of course, environmentalists and antiglobalization protesters are not the only ones unhappy with the state of the market and the status of thrift in American life. More mainstream critiques come from a number of directions. Over the past half century, popular figures from Vance Packard to the authors of the financial self-help best seller *The Millionaire Next Door* have extolled the virtues of old-time thrift. Others, like the recent Tea Party protesters, mobilize on behalf of libertarian ideals of economic freedom and against spiraling federal budgets and overreliance on foreign credit. Still others, from John Kenneth Galbraith to more recent elite critics like Juliet Shore, Thomas Frank, and Barbara Ehrenreich, have made their living condemning consumerism and economic inequality. As this volume has repeatedly shown, however, none of the existing critiques is entirely new; they not only stand in long traditions of moral evaluation, but they are also constitutive of the thrift ethos in all its forms. However inarticulate, fragmentary, and dissipated it may have become, the common, underlying meaning of thrift—the question about what it means to thrive—is clearly still an animating concern for many Americans regarding the normative dimensions of economic life.

This is the essential question to which we turn in the concluding chapter of the volume, "Thrift and Thriving: Toward a Moral Framework for Economic Life." It is our contention that the reappraisal of the history of thrift offered in this volume not only leads us to ask this question but provides resources for answering it. We believe the original contribution of this volume is to show

how the enduring question of thriving has always been the subtext of thrift more narrowly understood and, in turn, has repeatedly inspired both powerful forms of social critique and movements of social reform that continue to inform our culture down to the present day. We contend that sustained consideration of thrift in this deeper sense supplies a badly needed normative vocabulary for thinking and talking about present economic, environmental, and social challenges. As stated previously, if there is a moral to the story of thrift, it is that our ability to sustain and extend the conditions for genuine human thriving depend, first and foremost, upon our ability to sustain and extend a conversation about the inescapably normative dimensions of economic life. We suggest that this is the promise of thrift, "well understood."

Notes

1. For a sample of thrift's new public visibility, see the following: Nancy Gibbs, "The Great Recession: America Becomes Thrift Nation," *Time*, April 15, 2009; "Thrift: The Double-Edged Virtue," cover story in the Summer 2009 issue of the *Wilson Quarterly* (vol. 33, no. 3); Casey Mulligan, "The Recession and the 'Paradox of Thrift,'" Economix, blog of the *New York Times*, November 4, 2009, http://economix.blogs.nytimes.com/; Theodore Malloch, *Thrift: Rebirth of a Forgotten Virtue* (New York: Encounter Books, 2009); Yasser Abdih and Evan Tanner, "Frugality: Are We Fretting Too Much? Household Saving and Assets in the United States," *IMF Working Paper* (September 2009); "For a New Thrift: Confronting the Debt Culture," A Report to the Nation from the Commission on Thrift, sponsored by the Institute for American Values, the New America Foundation, Public Agenda, Demos, the Consumer Federation of America, and the National Federation of Community Development Credit Unions and funded by the Sir John Templeton Foundation.

2. Personal savings rates have surged to their highest levels in more than fifteen years, up to 6 percent by May 2009 (http://research.stlouisfed.org/fred2/data/PSAVERT.txt, accessed February 1, 2010). Moreover, according to the Federal Reserve, household debt fell for the first time since we started keeping track of such data in 1952 (http://money.cnn.com/2008/12/11/news/economy/flow_of_funds/index.htm, accessed February 1, 2010). That said, when factoring in both corporate and government debt levels, the total U.S. savings rate continues to crater at all-time lows (http://2.bp.blogspot.com/_pCDyiFU-v9XU/SoTnRhbNIVI/AAAAAAAAH_s/taQ3BCxwZok/s1600-h/Savings+Rate.jpg, accessed February 1, 2010).

3. Mortimer Adler, ed., *The Syntopicon: An Index to the Great Ideas*, 2nd ed., 2 vols. (Chicago: Encyclopaedia Britannica, 1990).

4. See, e.g., Edwin Brezette de Windt, ed., *The Salt of Common Life: Individuality and Choice in the Medieval Town, Countryside, and Church* (Kalamazoo, MI: Medieval Institute, 1995); and Ann Wroe, *A Fool and His Money* (New York: Hill and Wang, 1996), a study of a late-medieval merchant's legal problems.

5. Our view is best articulated by Georgia Harkness in *Calvin: The Man and His Ethics* (New York: Henry Holt, 1931), 201: "Calvin no more created the commercial enterprise of his day than the Pope created the empire of Charlemagne, but like the Pope, he greatly favored what was already in the process of development by conferring on it a divine sanction."

6. *Oxford English Dictionary*, 2nd ed., s.v. "thrift," n. 1.

7. John Bunyan, *The Fear of God* (London: Religious Tract Society, 1839).

8. *Oxford English Dictionary*, 2nd ed., s.v. "thrift," n. 3a.

9. Benjamin Franklin, *Writings* (New York: Library of America, 1987): "Poor Richard Improved, 1756," p. 1286; "Poor Richard, 1735," p. 1198; "Poor Richard, 1736," p. 1200.

10. Albert O. Hirschman, *The Passions and the Interests: Political Arguments for Capitalism before Its Triumph* (Princeton, NJ: Princeton University Press, 1977), 9.

11. John Maynard Keynes, *Essays in Persuasion* (New York: Norton, 1963), 360.

12. Ibid., 363.

13. Richard Sennett, *The Culture of the New Capitalism* (New Haven, CT: Yale University Press, 2006), 3.

PART } I

The Emergence of Thrift in Early America, 1630–1880

2 }

The Controversial Virtue of Thrift in the Early American Republic

Daniel Walker Howe

"Thrift, thrift Horatio!" William Shakespeare's Hamlet uses the word *thrift* in bitter satire to describe the unseemly haste with which his mother remarried after his father's death. "The funeral-bak'd meats did coldly furnish forth the marriage tables." Hamlet's sarcasm is directed not at the cooled leftovers themselves but at the emotional coldness displayed by his mother and new stepfather. Their thrift revealed lack of proper human feeling. Not everyone in Shakespeare's time considered thrift a virtue or tried to live by its code, nor does everyone today. Thrift has been a perennially contested virtue, even among those who claim to honor it.

Thrift as treated in this chapter is not equated with the meager rations of the poor; indeed, many poor people are not thrifty. The thrift discussed here is a voluntarily chosen attitude toward life, a determination to keep expended resources proportionate to requirements. A thrifty person practices restraint and distinguishes between mere wants and real needs. Such a person is often strongly oriented toward the future, since thrift as here defined includes saving for future goals and reflects a will to control the future and one's own place in it. Thrift thus implies a willingness to defer gratification. It is correlated with a value on self-fulfillment but not self-indulgence. Yet thrift is by no means necessarily self-seeking; one can be thrifty, for example, out of respect for God's creation or to conserve resources for one's children or for future generations of humanity. How best to practice the virtue of thrift is by no means always clear, and in the early American republic bitter debates arose over what constituted true thrift, in both private and public life.

Thrift as an American Virtue

At the heart of America's culture of thrift was religion, specifically the Reformation. Seventeenth-century Calvinist preachers exhorted their people to practice a stern work ethnic, to rise early and go to bed late, and to serve God in their various callings. As John Cotton told his Boston congregation in 1651, a good Christian should "lose no opportunity to bestir himself for profit," yet should do so only for the glory of God, keeping himself "deadhearted to the world."[1] Puritan social morality demanded not only hard work but also thrift. "Tis ordinarily a Sin," Cotton's clerical grandson warned a later generation of New Englanders, "for a man to Spend more than he Gets, or to make his Layings out more than his Comings in."[2] The Pennsylvania Quakers, an offshoot of English Puritanism, practiced an even stricter ethic of self-denial and thrift. Shakespeare disliked Puritans (after all, they closed down theaters when they could) and satirized them in the character Malvolio in *Twelfth Night*. But in America, the attitude toward thrift characteristic of the Puritans and their evangelical successors became widely prevalent.

During the eighteenth and nineteenth centuries, itinerant evangelists carried the message of provident care to the remotest corners of the English-speaking world. Exhortations to thrift as a religious virtue were typical social admonitions of the international, interdenominational Evangelical movement. Despite sectarian and theological divisions over issues like free will, infant baptism, and ecclesiology, Evangelicals could agree on the gospel of hard work and an austere lifestyle. Baptists and Methodists, German Lutherans and Anabaptists joined with Congregationalists and Presbyterians, Calvinists and Arminians to endorse the practice of thrift. And the young United States was, of all countries, one of those most influenced by the Evangelical movement. The many voluntary organizations founded to address particular charitable and reform causes supported by the Evangelical movement further promoted thrift by encouraging people to set aside some of their income for contribution and also by pooling their contributions for investment.[3]

Social commentators in the independent United States reinforced the Puritan-Evangelical religious heritage with secular imperatives to self-restraint. In the absence of a ruling class, a national established church, or even strong institutional controls, republican citizens would have to learn to practice self-government. Sometimes commentators invoked the virtuous ancients of classical republicanism, who urged citizens to self-sacrifice for the welfare of the commonwealth. Closer in time and even more directly relevant were the writings of the eighteenth-century Scottish moral philosophers, who secularized Scotland's Reformation intellectual heritage. Led by Thomas Reid and Dugald Stewart, these philosophers analyzed human nature in terms of a hierarchy of faculties. They emphasized the importance of nurturing the higher, the rational, faculties—conscience and prudence—so as to enable them to control the more powerful but less reliable passions in human nature. Benjamin Franklin's autobiography and his Poor Richard maxims exemplified and translated into popular idiom the eighteenth-century moral philosophy of impulse control and the virtue of thrift.[4]

Following the example of the Scottish Presbyterian John Witherspoon, who came to Princeton in 1768, American educators made the Scottish philosophy their capstone for higher education in the early Republic. As taught in American colleges, this school of moral philosophy included a comprehensive study of all aspects of human nature, normative as well as descriptive. From this Scottish American moral philosophy all of the present social sciences descend: psychology, sociology, anthropology, and—most famously—economics, pioneered by a Scottish moral philosopher named Adam Smith.[5] A leading exemplar of nineteenth-century American moral philosophy was Francis Wayland, Baptist minister, president of Brown University, and author of the most widely used antebellum textbook on economics. An important component of the approved republican ethos was the virtue of thrift, which involved rational foresight and the subordination of impulse to long-range objectives. Like other moral philosophers of his school, Wayland applied the virtue of thrift to both private life and public policy. His *Elements of Political Economy* (1837) parallels his *Elements of Moral Science* (1835) in substance and presentation. Both books treat their subjects practically as well as theoretically, including substantive advice on matters public and private. Both incorporate Christianity into their moral code. They favor keeping government taxes and coercion minimal but encourage investment in education as a form of enlightened thrift. Both books argue that aid to the poor is best handled by private charities, but they acknowledge that public action is necessary is some cases. Whenever possible, some work should be required of aid recipients, so as not to undermine their self-respect and their habits of thrift.[6]

Besides religious and academic endorsement, a third encouragement to thrift was political. As the eighteenth century went by, the volume of trade within the Atlantic world increased. Colonial Americans, whether large planters, small farmers, fishermen, or merchants, consumed many commodities they did not make themselves, including coffee, tea, manufactured tools and weapons, textiles, and clothing. They also imported slaves through the Royal African Company, a chartered monopoly based in Liverpool. In return, the mainland colonies sold their tobacco, indigo, timber, and codfish in Europe, their meat and grain to the West Indies, their rum to Africa. Americans discovered that the existence of this trade gave them leverage with British policy makers when they wanted to express grievances. By boycotting British goods, they could pressure British merchants to appeal to Parliament to conciliate the colonists. Thus, although the Americans enjoyed no direct representation in Parliament, they could still make their wishes known and felt. The American Revolution involved many colonists in cooperative nonconsumption—in other words, in politically motivated thrift. "Save your money and you will save your country," exhorted a Philadelphia newspaper in 1767.[7] "Can he be a true lover of his country," demanded a Connecticut writer, "who would be seen strutting about the streets, clad in foreign fripperies," when he could "be nobly independent in the russet grey" of homespun cloth?[8] Wearing homemade clothing became a badge of patriotism. But this kind of political frugality became controversial and coercive when forced on reluctant fellow subjects, some of whom became Loyalists in reaction against it.

The patriots won their struggle in the end, but history did not come down unambiguously on the side of thrift. The expansion of trade and communication in the eighteenth-century Atlantic world fostered the emergence of polite culture. This, the precursor of today's consumer culture, encouraged men and women to value beauty in their lives and good manners in their social intercourse. Polite culture, like the Puritan work ethic, constituted a form of self-discipline and restraint on violence and passion. It helped civilize the environment and established acceptable rules for dealings among strangers. It thus encouraged the development not only of commerce but also of a "public sphere" of rational and responsible discussion of public issues. Simultaneously, however, polite culture created certain problems. It could easily come into conflict with the virtue of thrift. Politeness privileged leisure over work and tasteful consumption over sheer self-denial. Some warned that Americans were being "insensibly drawn into too great a degree of *luxury* and *dissipation*."[9]

Even Americans whose patriotism was above reproach found polite culture agreeable. Thomas Jefferson unambiguously embraced polite culture rather than thrift in his personal life. He built an architectural masterpiece for a home, lived well, and died broke. As transportation and communication improved throughout the nineteenth century, the values of both polite culture and the Evangelical movement penetrated to almost all classes and regions of the United States. Most Americans tried to have it both ways, juggling the values of refinement and thrift to the extent their resources permitted. Even modest homes in the hinterland welcomed the traveling peddler with his little luxuries. Inevitably, some Jeremiahs would lament the corruption of ancestral austere virtue, as the Wesleyan Methodists did within the Methodist tradition, or as Elias Hicks did among the Quakers. But to the majority, their amenities seemed a modest, deserved reward for diligent labor and thrift.

Throughout the antebellum period, contemporary observers, notably Frederick L. Olmsted in the 1850s, found the South on the whole less thrifty than the North. A number of factors conspired to make the Puritan ethic less pervasive in the South. The institution of slavery inevitably undercut the dignity of manual labor. The master class fell under the spell of certain European ideas of aristocratic honor, including, for example, the practice of dueling (acquired from French officers during the Revolution) in defiance of Evangelical Christian norms. The South became a cultural battleground, where Evangelical values, such as diligent work and thrift, had to compete not only with polite culture but also with older codes of conduct like Celtic tribalism, which was more tolerant of indolence, violence, blood sports, and hedonism.[10] Many in the southern plantation aristocracy followed Jefferson's practice and went into debt. Modern economists, however, declare antebellum slave agriculture quite economically efficient—if deplorably immoral. Certainly the conversion of southern political leaders like George McDuffy and John C. Calhoun from tariff protection to free trade reflected a perfectly rational sense of the economic interests of cotton producers. Slaves represented a substantial investment, and most slaveholders had more money tied up in their human property than they did in land or any other form of investment. Slave management was therefore, among other things, a form of master-class thrift, though one that went largely unrecognized as such. A large interstate slave trade demonstrated the willingness of masters to treat enslaved persons as commercial commodities.[11] While it seems highly unlikely that southerners paid less attention than northerners to profit in their behavior, there does seem to have been a difference in their attitude. Northerners were more likely to regard thrift as a *virtue*. Southern literary writers tended to depict their section's own merchants as "outsiders," for example, as Yankees or Jews, thereby implying that commercial thrift was not a truly southern virtue.[12]

The Domestic Virtue of Thrift

When Jefferson delivered his inaugural address in 1801, and for many years thereafter, most Americans earned their living through agriculture. They practiced what historians have come to term *composite farming*, meaning that they produced partly for the consumption of their own family and partly for the market. The virtue of thrift constituted an integral part of this way of life, followed by both men and women. Virtually no farm families expected to satisfy all their wants by purchase. When a husband hammered together a stool and his wife made the children's clothes, they were not being thrifty in the same way that someone shopping for groceries today is being thrifty by remembering to use a coupon. They were performing their occupations, earning their living, just as much as when the man plowed the field or the woman churned the butter to sell in the village. Their thrift was central, not peripheral, to their lives; it was a necessity, not an option. Thrift demanded that the family set aside enough corn or potatoes to be able to seed next year's crop and go on farming. Significantly, the very word for their occupation, *husbandry*, also meant thrift, as in the expression "to husband resources."[13]

So many and varied were the aspects of farm labor that individual, unmarried farmers were exceedingly rare; to operate a farm household took both a man and a woman. And so the word *husband*, originally meaning "farmer," came to mean "married man." With hired labor scarce and expensive, the preferred sources of agricultural labor were family members, neighbors offering reciprocal favors, or (for those who could afford the investment) bound workers, indentured or enslaved. Thrifty foresight, not irresponsibility, prompted farm couples to have many children. In 1800 the white birthrate stood at an average of seven children per woman; by 1860, when it had declined to five, the rural percentage of the population had fallen from 95 to 80.[14]

Following the principle of "safety first," newly settled agricultural families generally began by growing food for their own consumption but turned as quickly as possible to supplementing this with something they could market. In the long run, those who achieved the greatest degree of self-sufficiency were large landowners commanding a large labor force (perhaps enslaved), who could afford to grind their own grain and employ their own artisans, like blacksmiths, carpenters, and saddlers. When an ordinary farming family needed something they could not produce for themselves, they might trade goods or services with a neighbor or visit the local storekeeper. With currency chronically scarce, people seldom paid for their purchases with actual coins or banknotes. Instead, the storekeeper kept an account book, which recorded who owed what. When the husband bought a tool he was debited; when the wife brought in a surplus cured ham she was credited. In many little towns, the storekeepers still kept their accounts in shillings and pence fifty years after the Revolution. If customers had been paying cash, it would have made sense to convert to dollars and cents, but since nobody expected this, why not go on using the old-time familiar units of exchange?[15]

We might suppose that on the frontier people would perforce be more thrifty, since they were farther removed from the transportation that brought commercial goods and would find it more difficult to market their produce for cash. However, there is evidence to the contrary. Those on the western edge of white settlement would often resort to hunting and gathering, on the whole a less-efficient means of sustenance than agriculture. If they were squatters on the public domain, they had no economic interest in improving their land unless and until they could acquire title to it. In the meantime their use of the land and its natural resources would be exploitative and wasteful. When frontiersmen did own their land, they often held it for resale to others; that is, they were primarily small-scale speculators and only secondarily farmers. On the frontier there was always a surplus of single males. They might be adventurous souls, missionaries, or honest traders. Often, however, they were rootless men who had moved before and who would move again, perhaps in a succession of economic failures, restless and perennially looking for their luck to change. These were the aggressive whites whom the Native Americans learned to dread.[16] The stable, thrifty family farmers usually characterized the second wave of white settlement, not the first. The loss of such people to the West became the subject of recurrent lamentation in Atlantic coast regions like New England, Virginia, and South Carolina. One of the principal incentives for their departure was the exhaustion of the soil in older areas. To discourage out-migration and depopulation, responsible farmers in the East began as early as the eighteenth century to advocate and practice soil conservation, fertilization, crop rotation, and other measures of land thrift. But in America as a whole, these practices remained the exception rather than the rule.[17]

The early stages of the Industrial Revolution did not in fact "revolutionize" composite agriculture; this way of life had endured for a long time and weathered many historical changes. Indeed, improvements in industry *facilitated* the household economies. When women could buy a better spinning wheel, made in the factory instead of at home, they bought it and went on spinning. When mill-made textiles became so cheap that it no longer made sense to weave at home, housewives bought textiles to sew together and were able to make their family more clothes. Finally, the sewing machine arrived. After the Civil War, farm women brought it into the home, too, and sewed more and nicer clothes than ever. (Sometimes women would design a dress at home by picking apart an old garment and using it as a pattern.) By this time, the housewife had long been able to subscribe to magazines like *Godey's Ladies' Book*, which democratized polite culture for a mass audience and offered her fashion guidance. She wanted to combine the virtue of thrift with good taste. And if she now needed to spend less time making clothes, she spent more time cleaning.[18]

The thrifty values that underlay composite farming as a way of life actually fostered industrialization. The Puritan ethic, by affirming the dignity of the worker, encouraged the adoption of laborsaving technology to make work more efficient, in agriculture as well as in manufacturing. Prosperous farmers could afford to buy manufactured products like steel plows instead of wooden ones.[19] The "putting out" system had long brought industrial production of woven cloth and shoes into countless farm homes. And when the textile mills first opened, farm families welcomed the chance to send their unmarried daughters off to work in them, hoping to receive some of their earnings back home. People were accustomed to deriving income from a variety of sources and pooling the contributions of family members. In July 1821, Anne Clarke wrote home to her father Joseph that she had to "deny myself many comforts and submit to many privations" so as to be able to send money home to help her father pay off the mortgage.[20]

From Mandatory Thrift to Optional Thrift

In the 1790s only one American in twenty lived in a town with a population exceeding 2,500 (quite a low threshold for "urban" life). Starting in the 1820s, more people began to move from the countryside to the city. By 1840, 11 percent of Americans lived in an urban place, and by 1860, it was 20 percent. Town families had a different way of life, which affected the practice of thrift. In the city, there was far more division of labor and task specialization. Urban thrift became more compartmentalized, rather than intrinsic to everyday life and work as it had been on the farm. With the husband away from home more of the time, working for a wage, the wife managed the household, and most aspects of thrift now fell within what was considered her sphere. New patterns of thrift emerged. With children no longer an economic asset, urban couples chose to have fewer of them.[21] In the city, people were less likely to trade services with neighbors and more likely to seek institutional aids to thrift: savings banks, mutual assistance associations, and insurance companies. Firewood now could not be found on one's own land; it had to be bought. To save fuel, urban families purchased stoves, which burned wood more efficiently, to replace fireplaces for cooking and heating. Deliveries of ice were practical in cities, so it became feasible to have an icebox and keep food fresh longer, opening up a new range of possible economies. Urban merchants could afford to insist on cash payment at the time of purchase and did not have to cater to a tiny clientele with elaborate arrangements for credit; as a result of this and other economies of scale, they could undersell the country storekeeper and stock a wider variety of goods.[22]

In the cities, particularly in the new occupations in manufacturing, people practiced "time-thrift." Workers needed to be punctual in reporting to the job and in making proper use of the time for which they were being paid. The rigid work discipline enforced in factories seemed onerous to people accustomed to the more elastic hours of preindustrial production; punctuality, for example, was more critical in a factory than it had been in an artisan shop. We should not forget, however, that nature imposes strict temporal imperatives on farmers: a crop must be planted and harvested on time; the cows must be milked on schedule. Plantations operated with slave labor were even more "mastered by the clock" than farms using free labor.[23] The success of the clockmaker Eli Terry in mass-producing clocks in antebellum America—common in urban and even in rural areas by the 1840s—demonstrated not only an achievement of manufacturing and distribution but also the time consciousness of the consumers.[24] An amazed traveler along the western frontier commented during 1844 that "in every cabin where there was not a chair to sit on, there was sure to be a Connecticut clock."[25]

The migrants to the cities—most of whom, after all, came from rural backgrounds in the Old World or the New—continued to practice thrift, sometimes to better effect than they had managed in their previous homes. Urban employers had to keep wages high enough to compete with opportunities for hired labor in agriculture. To be sure, some men, in both urban and rural settings, squandered their wages on drink. But working-class people found ways to save money in the city. It is an error to imagine that thrift was the exclusive cultural property of rural people or white Anglo-Saxon Protestants. No social group had a monopoly on thrift. Charles Ball escaped from slavery and worked as a free man in Baltimore, Annapolis, and Washington until he had accumulated $350, enough to start a twelve-acre farm in 1820. (Several years later, sadly, he was apprehended and sent back to bondage in Georgia.)[26] A scant thirty months after arrival at New York in 1851 from famine-racked Kenmare, Ireland, Ellen Holland deposited in the Emigrant Savings Bank $110—equivalent to about $2,350 today. (That the account was in her name proved convenient when her husband died soon after in the disease-ridden slum of Five Points.)[27] Catholic clergy such as John Hughes, first archbishop of New York, like Protestant ministers, exhorted their flocks to thrift and honest work.[28]

But the cities also held out temptations for people in pursuit of middle-class standing to overextend their financial resources. City life provided opportunities for them to socialize, to see and be seen, and therefore encouraged more emphasis on tasteful consumption and competitive display. Improved access to magazines and newspapers exposed them to tempting advertisements. The textile industry that transformed production also affected consumers, especially in urban areas. There, people were more likely to buy clothes rather than make them at home. An army of young men arrived from the country to perform new urban clerical jobs. They aspired to be middle-class rather than working-class men, and they could now look the part by wearing inexpensive ready-made suits and detachable white collars.[29] An army of young women arrived in the cities seeking employment in the textile industry but willing to take jobs in domestic service. Some of them found that prostitution paid better than either of those occupations, and it enabled them to indulge what had been only fantasies of consumption.[30]

Amid the ethnic pluralism of the most cosmopolitan cities, newcomers from the farms witnessed festivals one never saw in the dour Calvinist countryside. In New Orleans they celebrated Mardi Gras. In New York, the Episcopalians and the Dutch dared to celebrate Christmas—cautiously at first, but with growing enthusiasm after the publication of Clement C. Moore's poem "A Visit from Saint Nicholas" in 1823. Christmas in the city evolved into a consumer's holiday, a moment of release and merrymaking.[31] By 1843 Charles Dickens's *Christmas Carol* would deplore the miserly asceticism of Ebenezer Scrooge in the most famous literary satire on the Puritan ethic since Shakespeare. All this made it harder for the sons and daughters of the farms to observe the restraints they had practiced in the privacy of rural isolation and cultural provincialism. In the city, thrift—a necessity on the farm that practiced composite agriculture—became a choice.

At this pivotal moment in the history of thrift came Lydia Maria Child's book *The Frugal Housewife*, first published in 1829 with reprintings until 1870. (By 1835 it was in its twentieth edition.) When an Englishwoman published a book with the same title, Child changed the title of later editions of her book to *The American Frugal Housewife*.[32] Born Lydia Maria Francis, she grew up in an intellectual and religious family, the sister of Convers Francis, who became dean of Harvard Divinity School. She married a Whig lawyer named David Child. The couple involved themselves deeply in a long series of reform causes involving the rights of Native Americans, African Americans, and women. David's law practice consequently suffered, and to shore up their finances, Maria (as she preferred to be called) wrote a series of commercially successful novels, children's books, and advice manuals.[33] *The American Frugal Housewife* addressed women living in the midst of the dramatic transportation improvements that enabled farm families to produce more wholeheartedly for the market and, as a consequence, obtain more cash to spend on consumer goods. These economic and social changes transformed the domestic life of ordinary women, creating an audience in search of advice on how to deal with them. (Earlier manuals had been aimed at wealthy women, providing advice on how to manage servants, entertainments, and decorations.) For generations women and men alike had learned their respective aspects of husbandry, as they grew up, from their parents' examples. That an advice book met a felt need for guidance shows how rapidly the familiar patterns were now changing.

Child's book treats problems common to housewives in cities, small towns, and the countryside—especially the latter. It is aimed at women from the modest lower middle class. They may employ a "hired girl" to help with the chores, but the author assumes her reader is one who involves herself closely with housework, cooking, child rearing, and caring for sick family members, one who is "not ashamed of economy." Her work never mentions enslaved domestics and was sold principally in the North. Her advice provides fascinating detail about everyday life. It tells how to brew homemade beer, which was intended for all members of the family, including children. Buying vinegar by the gallon is uneconomical, the author declares; you should buy vinegar by the barrel; if you then add occasional slops to this barrel, they will turn to vinegar too and you will have a perpetual supply. Teach your children to assume responsibility for keeping their own clothes mended, and they will learn both how to sew and habits of responsible thrift. The book assumes a clear division of labor between husband and wife and that most aspects of thrift in consumption by now fall within the woman's domestic sphere. It warns against many varieties of conspicuous consumption, against trying to keep up with the Joneses, and (perhaps most emphatically) against bringing up daughters to be concerned about social life, flirtations with boys, and making an impression on their peers.

The next stage in the mass-marketing of the virtue of thrift came with Catharine Beecher's *Treatise on Domestic Economy* of 1841.[34] This work (as its title indicated) was longer and more analytical than Child's, and it treated its subject matter with academic high seriousness. Child had also written children's poems ("Over the river and through the wood, To Grandmother's house we go"), whereas Beecher had written *Elements of Mental and Moral Philosophy*. (Her philosophy shared the general outlook of the Scottish American moralists.) Where Child began her book with a miscellany of practical maxims, Beecher led off with a discussion of the role of women in republican society as guardians of virtue, quoting extensively from Alexis de Tocqueville. For Beecher, a woman's learning to be thrifty was part of her larger project of self-improvement. Thrift constituted one aspect of the homemaking career; this career required conscious professional preparation, just as any skilled male occupation did.[35]

During the decade since Child first published *The Frugal Housewife*, America's cities and towns had developed a middle class for Beecher to address. Both authors agreed in emphasizing time-thrift as well as thrift in expenses. But Beecher implicitly addresses women of not only a higher educational level but also a higher income level; her book cost fifty cents; Child's, twenty-five. Beecher advises the housewife to put out simple sewing to poor women and spend the time saved on more ambitious needle projects of her own, whereas Child had cautioned that putting out sewing was unnecessarily extravagant. Beecher combines her teaching of thrift with the teaching of good taste, for example, by explaining that it is more tasteful to maintain a consistency of good quality in household furnishings than to display a single ostentatiously expensive piece surrounded by cheap ones. She assures her affluent readers that "the unequal distribution of property is no evil" and, while advising them to keep careful accounts, discourages sharp bargaining with household employees or shopkeepers.[36]

Together, the advice manuals that Child and Beecher wrote for housewives illustrate significant changes in American life. No longer is household management governed by immemorial tradition. People move to new locations and have to learn how to re-create their lives in novel circumstances. They now look to secular authorities as well as religious ones for guidance. Women have attained enough respect, at least within the domestic "sphere," to constitute themselves such authorities. Innovations in printing, papermaking, transportation, and the business of publishing—what historians call the "communications revolution"—have made books cheaper and facilitated their distribution. Protestant churches and public schools, working together, have increased literacy, even among females, to create a mass women's audience for the printed media.

Yet the thrift that Child and Beecher celebrated was only an option, not a necessity. The evangelists of thrift by no means had all their own way in the young republic. In fact, antebellum Americans could be shockingly unthrifty in many ways. They squandered those resources that they had in abundance, even while practicing the strictest economy on others that were hard for them to make or buy. Maize as a crop was labor-thrifty but land-intensive. The same farmers who used their coffee and salt with care heedlessly mined their soil of its nutrients and then moved on to new fields, leaving eroded gullies behind them, because land was plentiful.[37] They slaughtered by the million the passenger pigeons that once darkened the sky—until, suddenly, there were none left. Beaver were hunted nearly to extinction. The early trains and steamboats burned wood for fuel, denuding the country of forests because Americans did not care to go to the trouble to mine coal as Europeans did. Forty-niners en route to California littered their trail across the plains with abandoned utensils once they realized that they could get along without much of the gear that unscrupulous salesmen had pressed on them in St. Louis. America seemed so vast, so rich, so full of resources that the temptation to waste them was almost irresistible. Even the American Indians would set forest fires to drive out game for killing. The number of buffalo had already been significantly diminished by the American Indians after they domesticated the horse in the eighteenth century, even before the whites decided in the nineteenth to wipe out the great herds in order to turn the Plains over to cattle and wheat and confine the tribes to reservations.[38]

The Public Virtue of Thrift

As the practice of thrift demonstrated an individual's power of self-government, the political practice of thrift was believed to vindicate the self-government of the American commonwealth. Thrift had always been an important issue in both the public sector and the private sector of the American economy. Voters and policy makers alike applied attitudes derived from the private sector toward thrift in the public sector. Even political economists did not then distinguish microeconomics from macroeconomics. Jefferson's personal experience with indebtedness helps explain his fear of the national debt and pursuit of the strictest public economy. Although willing to spend money to purchase Louisiana and acquire an "empire for liberty," he generally practiced an austere thrift in public policy, preferring, for example, to construct coastal gunboats rather than a seagoing navy because they were cheaper.[39]

Such public economy conformed to common views of domestic economy. American farmers and employers found labor dear and land cheap, in contrast with Europe's high-cost land and cheap labor. Family farmers seldom owed rent to a landlord and never owed tithes to an abbot or bishop; they did, however, commonly owe mortgage payments to a banker. Popular resentment of bankers flourished accordingly and could be exploited politically. Politicians in the Jeffersonian-Jacksonian tradition treated the federal Treasury like the assets of a yeoman farmer. They wanted land cheap and plentiful. This implied dispossessing the American Indians, opening up new lands to white settlement quickly and inexpensively, granting preemption rights to squatters on public property, and perhaps "graduating" the price (i.e., periodically dropping the cost of each parcel until it sold). It also implied westward expansion of U.S. territory at the expense of previous occupants, both American Indians and Mexicans, in the pursuit of what Democrats called America's "manifest destiny." But while encouraging profligacy with the government's land, the Jeffersonian-Jacksonian policy makers practiced extreme thrift with the government's financial revenues. They focused on repaying the national debt as promptly as possible, like a prudent farmer paying off his mortgage.[40]

John Quincy Adams challenged this mind-set with a rival vision of national economy in his first annual message to Congress in 1825. Adams declared that it would be more cost-effective in the long run to practice thrift with land and spend somewhat more of the government's cash. He favored selling federal lands for what they would bring on the market and investing the proceeds in infrastructure—such as transportation and education. If the lands were given away, only the recipient gained; if they were sold for public benefit, all taxpayers in the society gained. With good transportation and public schools, land values would rise, benefiting both the purchasers (and settlers) and the federal government, as owner of the unsold parcels. Thus, while his Jacksonian rivals envisioned an America expanding quantitatively across space, Adams and those in his Whig tradition envisioned America expanding qualitatively through economic development over time. The cultivation of thrift and other virtues was part of the duty of "improvement" placed on each individual by Christianity and moral philosophy. Adams declared that "moral, political, [and] intellectual improvement" were "duties assigned by the Author of Our Existence to social no less than to individual man." While willing to spend federal money on what they called "internal improvements," Adams and the Whigs wanted to treat the continent with thrift and husband its resources, developing them gradually and turning them to public benefit.[41] The Whigs staked their hopes on the future and intended to control it. They were willing to pay taxes as an investment in the future. By contrast, Jacksonian Democrats liked American society the way they found it and wanted it to expand. Their attitude toward the continent and its resources was oriented toward the present rather than the future.

The Democratic attitude toward public thrift found classic expression in Andrew Jackson's veto of the Maysville Road bill in 1830 and his veto of the recharter of the National Bank in 1832. In the first of these, Jackson argued that the Maysville Road bill was a merely local measure unworthy of national support (ignoring that it constituted a segment of a projected road from Buffalo to New Orleans). The government's top priority, he insisted, must be debt retirement. The practice Jackson most feared was the one his generation named "logrolling": the exchange of favors by politicians analogous to the exchange of favors by rural neighbors needing to remove felled trees from their fields before plowing. The people must not be taxed to pay for "irregular, improvident, and unequal appropriations of the public funds."[42]

In his bank veto, Jackson's leading argument against recharter was that the government did not get its money's worth: a banking monopoly worth (he claimed) $17 million was being sold for only $3 million. Furthermore, the terms of the charter gave financial benefits to foreign investors and American bankers not provided to ordinary people. "The rich and powerful too often bend the acts of government to their selfish purposes," Jackson famously declared. "In the full enjoyment of the gifts of Heaven and the fruits of superior industry, economy, and virtue, every man is equally entitled to protection by law." The National Bank bill bestowed special privileges on a favored few, he argued. The true strength of American government, President Jackson insisted, "consists in leaving individuals and States as much as possible to themselves." Jackson had powerfully invoked both popular antibank feeling and the faith of many ordinary Americans, mostly engaged in agriculture, that they could get along best if left to practice the virtue of thrift on their own.[43]

On the other hand, the Whigs considered banks, and the National Bank in particular, the friend of thrifty savers and prudent borrowers needing credit. Whigs wanted to encourage the issue of paper money by banks in order to overcome the chronic shortage of currency. (Neither state nor federal governments then issued paper currency.) However, banknotes created problems of their own: those of irresponsible wildcat banks might prove worthless, and the many different banks issuing them, each with its own design, facilitated counterfeiting. Of all banknotes those of the National Bank were the most trustworthy and stable in value across the country, so Whigs liked the National Bank. Democrats, however, mindful of the possibilities for fraud, tried to eliminate paper money (at least in small denominations) and rely entirely on gold and silver coins—"hard money," in the terminology of the time. During the 1830s the most salient political issues dividing the major parties concerned banking and currency. The Whig policy of "soft money" facilitated economic expansion and actually made it easier for borrowers to pay back loans, even though the Democrats claimed to support the interest of the farmer against the banker. Actually, the Democrats did not wish to encourage borrowing, either public or private. Bankers' eagerness to lend money for a profit tempted many people to overreach and got them into trouble. When Congress passed the first nationwide bankruptcy law in 1840, the Whig majority supported it, but the Democrats, not wishing to encourage feckless extravagance by forgiving debts, voted against it.[44]

While the Democrats endorsed laissez-faire, the Whigs supported a tariff on imports to encourage domestic production of commodities, mostly manufactured goods, that needed protection against foreign competition. This policy furthered the Whigs' goal of economic diversification. Although different from the strict economic individualism of the Democrats, the Whig attitude toward personal and national thrift had a historical legitimacy of its own. Back at the time of the Revolution, those who advocated resisting parliamentary taxation of the colonies had linked the practice of austerity with the development of domestic manufactures. Even after "manufacturing" ceased to mean "handcrafting," and textile mills replaced spinning wheels, this political association persisted. The Whig party of John Quincy Adams and Henry Clay endorsed both the Evangelical movement, with its frugal work ethic and moral reforms, and the encouragement of industrialization by protective tariffs. Whigs and Democrats both endorsed thrift, but the two parties meant different things by it.[45]

When financial panics in 1837 and 1839 plunged the United States into its worst depression prior to 1929, the two parties reacted very differently. Democratic president Martin Van Buren, Jackson's designated heir, offered his suffering country nothing by way of relief. "Those who look to the action of this Government for specific aid to the citizen to relieve embarrassments arising from losses by revulsions in commerce and credit lose sight of the ends for which it was created and the powers with which it is clothed," he told Congress. All the public could expect from the government was "strict economy and frugality" and a warning not "to substitute for republican simplicity and economical habits a sickly appetite for effeminate indulgence."[46] Clay, leader of the Whig congressional opposition, saw things very differently. He deplored Van Buren's "cold and heartless insensibility" and invoked his own American System of integrated development as a pathway to economic recovery. "We are all—people, States, Union, banks—bound up and interwoven together, united in fortune and destiny, and all, all entitled to the protecting care of a paternal government."[47] The depression gave the Whigs their one clear victory, in the election of 1840, but the tragic death of their president, William Henry Harrison, after a single month in office eliminated their chance to shape national economic policy.

Thrift and Social Criticism

As the nineteenth century went by, thrift became an object of social reformers. Efforts appeared to encourage popular thrift by means of legislation. Reformers worried that the poor were not practicing the virtue of thrift and needed to be encouraged or coerced into it. Gambling had long been a favorite pastime among the nonthrifty of all social classes. Traditionally, governments at all levels had indulged this fondness by licensing lotteries in return for a share of the proceeds. As the nineteenth century went on, and the Evangelical movement spread, public opinion changed. First governments stopped licensing lotteries. Then they declared all gambling a vice and a crime that robbed the family of the workingman of their bread to feed his addiction to gambling.[48] The criminal law likewise took up the enforcement of the virtue of thrift in the case of alcohol. Early evangelists preached temperance, that is, moderation in the consumption of alcohol. Later evangelists encouraged total abstinence from alcohol. Eventually they turned to the power of government for assistance. Local governments had long possessed the power to grant or withhold licenses to sell liquor. The movement for outright legal prohibition of alcohol won its first victory at the state level in Maine in 1851. The principal arguments against alcohol were the protection of women against domestic violence by drunken husbands and the need for thrift among the poor.[49] Finally, one of the most important legislative measures of thrift was undertaken by the federal government after the Civil War. Even while the bison were being destroyed, the creation of Yellowstone National Park by the Grant administration showed that the conservation of natural wilderness had come to seem important enough for the government to ensure it.

Ideas about the practice of thrift proved important to many other programs for reforming or restructuring American society. Thrift preoccupied not only mainstream America but also the utopian dissenters from its way of life. New Harmony, Indiana, founded by the secularist Robert Owen; the "phalanxes" founded by the disciples of Charles Fourier and Albert Brisbane; the Shaker communities scattered from Maine to Kentucky; the "perfectionists" of Oneida, New York; and the Utah Mormons—each of these communities modeled its own thrift along with its own distinctive redefinition of gender relations. On the whole, religious utopian communities chalked up more successful records than secular ones. Through pious hard work and simple living, aided by technological innovation, Shakers, Mormons, and members of the Oneida community achieved economic prosperity, much as medieval monastic communities did.[50] Indeed, as early as 1830 there were eleven Roman Catholic religious orders in the United States practicing the original form of Christian austerity and asceticism. Taken together, these various communities illustrate the point that socialists as well as capitalists can honor the virtue of thrift. Even in much more recent times, socialist nations in pursuit of economic development have sought, like industrializing capitalist countries, to encourage or coerce an ethic of hard work and thrift.

Henry David Thoreau's one-man utopian retreat at Walden Pond used the practice of extreme thrift as a spiritual exercise and a metaphor for seeking the meaning of life. His account in *Walden* opens with a section called "Economy," the longest one in the book. The section can be read on several levels. In the first place, it is his acknowledgment of economic activity as fundamental to all human life, including his own experiment. Faithful to his Puritan-Yankee cultural heritage, he affirms that simplicity and thrift are virtues. He wishes to disarm potential critics who would dismiss him as impractical by demonstrating at the outset his concern for the practical. Thoreau's enterprise was speculative in both senses of that word. It was meditative; it was also a risky venture, and he who undertakes it must calculate his assets as carefully as a merchant undertaking a voyage. Thoreau's individual undertaking is also analogous to that of a society on a utopian mission; he must be concerned with the realities of getting a living just as its members would be.

Yet Thoreau's section on economy is also a satire on conventional bourgeois thrift. When Thoreau says, "I have always endeavored to acquire strict business habits," he is being ironic.[51] He deplores the kind of unreflective, conformist thrift that he believes has trapped his neighbors in prisons of their own making. He escapes to Walden Pond in search of self-renewal in an atmosphere uncluttered by the paraphernalia of commercial civilization. He believes these cost far too much in time and effort to be a good bargain. Accordingly, his thrift constitutes an effort to reduce life to its bare essentials—to dispense with material distractions, useless hoarding, and what Thorstein Veblen would later call conspicuous consumption. His solution (like that of the Shakers and early Quakers) is the simple life. "Most of the luxuries, and many of the so called comforts of life, are not only not indispensable, but positive hindrances to the elevation of mankind," Thoreau declared. "None can be an impartial or wise observer of human life but from the vantage ground of what *we* should call voluntary poverty."[52]

Walden stands in a long tradition of literary treatments of thrift, Daniel Defoe's *Robinson Crusoe* being the archetype. Thoreau's sojourn at Walden Pond is a symbolic, nearby, and voluntary exile; Crusoe is forced by shipwreck to deal with years of isolation on a remote island. But Defoe's character is utterly utilitarian and humorless; his narrative exists on an entirely literal level. The social implication of Defoe's novel is a straightforward endorsement of the Puritan ethic of its Dissenting author. A more illuminating eighteenth-century precursor of Walden is *The Autobiography of Benjamin Franklin* (not actually published in full until 1868, that is, after *Walden*). To compare Thoreau's thrift with that of Franklin casts light on both. The two writers present themselves as models for others to imitate; as a result, both can appear irritatingly conceited. Both of course are penny-pinchers who tell the reader they practice asceticism not only out of frugality but also as an aid to insight. (In the *Autobiography*, Franklin claims that a spartan diet in youth helped him think clearly, though by the time of its writing he had been thoroughly won over by French cuisine and wines.) Franklin was extremely interested in material success, political power, and the esteem of others—all of them empty baubles, according to Thoreau. From Franklin's point of view, much of the benefit of practicing the Puritan ethic stems from the approval other people bestow on it. (His youthful industry, "visible to others," won him "character and credit" in their eyes, he recalls.) Hardly anyone in the world was more famous and widely admired than the elderly Franklin. Thoreau, by contrast, was criticized after his death by even his close friend and fellow transcendentalist Ralph Waldo Emerson for having "no ambition."[53] In sharp contrast to the pragmatic Philadelphian, Thoreau exemplified the artist alienated from society and its conventions. "The life which men praise and regard as successful is but one kind," he wrote in *Walden*. "Why should we exaggerate any one kind at the expense of the others?"[54] In the twentieth century, other alienated intellectuals would follow Thoreau's example, using advice on thrift as an instrument of social criticism.

Varying attitudes toward thrift had different implications for social criticism, as household reformers Child and Beecher demonstrated. Child became an ardent supporter of both the abolition of slavery and equal rights for women. That women and blacks practiced the virtue of thrift demonstrated to her that they had rational foresight, self-control, and ambition—in other words, they possessed the human qualities that justified their independence and full participation as citizens. But when Child published her *Appeal in Favor of That Class of Americans Called Africans* (1833), endorsing abolition of slavery and black equality, sales of her magazine and books plummeted. Abolitionism was not popular with the yeoman farmers' wives who constituted the bulk of her audience. Child stuck to her guns and went so far as to help the self-emancipated Harriet Jacobs publish her famous narrative, *Incidents in the Life of a Slave Girl* (1861).[55]

Beecher took a different approach. She treated thrift as an appropriately feminine virtue because it exemplified the self-effacing self-sacrifice that demonstrated women's moral superiority to men. She too deplored slavery; Beecher, however, insisted that women should seek to influence public opinion indirectly, more subtly—not through explicit political agitation, public speaking, or trying to get the vote. By setting a proper moral tone, encouraging religion and refined sentiment, women, she believed, could indirectly exert a calming influence on politics. She supported not abolitionism but the colonization movement, perceived at the time as a moderate means of emancipating slaves, one less threatening to whites. Beecher approved of the famous novel written by her sister Harriet Beecher Stowe, *Uncle Tom's Cabin*, as encouraging sympathy for the slaves in a nonpolitical way appropriate for a woman.

Eventually the thrift advocated by Child and Beecher found a common political analogue in the free labor ideology exemplified by Abraham Lincoln. Slavery contradicted the whole ethic of thrift, free labor advocates insisted. It encouraged slaves to careless indifference rather than the practice of an economy from which they could not benefit. It also encouraged masters to thriftless self-indulgence and competitive display. Free labor's northern supporters demanded that slavery be banned in the western territories so these lands could provide opportunities for thrifty yeomen and room to expand a diversified economy.[56] Southern propagandists, meanwhile, were becoming ever less enthusiastic about thrift as a virtue and more likely to stigmatize it. In the sectional recriminations leading up to the Civil War, southerners frequently accused their northern countrymen—especially those in the antislavery movement—of being money-grubbers governed by avarice.[57]

Lincoln's support for the free labor program reflected his personal values and experience writ large. He himself had risen from humble origins by hard work and thrift. He had worked for wages, had run a country store, and had industriously studied law. He saw himself as the embodiment of free labor. Opportunity for advancement and self-fulfillment lay at the heart of his vision of American society.[58] Only through developing the rational power of prudential self-interest—that is, the virtue of thrift—could a person achieve such advancement. Like the moral philosophers of the colleges he never attended, Lincoln strongly believed in subordinating the "passions" to what he termed "cold, calculating, unimpassioned reason."[59] Lincoln abstained from alcohol and endorsed the temperance movement as an example of self-government at both the individual and the collective level.[60]

This idea of improvement was essential to both Lincoln's personal self-image and his political philosophy. Lincoln endorsed not only thrift but hard work, ambition, and honesty—all the economic virtues. He envisioned wage labor as a transitional phase for ambitious individuals; they could save their money and become independent businessmen or farmers if they wished. As he told an audience of urban workingmen, "I want every man to have the chance—and I believe a black man is entitled to it—in which he *can* better his condition—when he may look forward and hope to be a hired laborer this year and the next, work for himself afterward, and finally to hire men to work for him!"[61] Nor were Lincoln's goals narrowly mercenary. Like many thrifty people, he was strongly oriented toward the future, in both his personal life and his public policies. He was deeply committed to the goal of self-realization. Despite having no formal education, he became a respected appellate counsel at law. He not only read but internalized Shakespeare and the Bible. He sent his son to Harvard.[62]

In public policy, Lincoln sought to create opportunities for people to improve themselves. As president, he fulfilled at last Adams's dream of federal support for education by signing the act creating the land-grant colleges. In a society such as Lincoln envisioned—of thrifty, industrious people marketing their own labor, able to pursue education at all levels, choosing from a wide variety of occupations, and secure in the possession of their own savings—there was no legitimate place for human slavery. Like the white man, the black man enjoyed a natural right to the fruits of his own labor. Lincoln put it forcefully in his first debate with Stephen Douglas: "In the right to eat the bread, without leave of anybody else, which his own hand earns, *he is my equal and the equal of Judge Douglas, and the equal of every living man*."[63]

At the level of state policy, Lincoln strongly supported "internal improvements." Only by improving the transportation facilities of frontier Illinois (dredging rivers, digging canals, and encouraging the building of railroads) could farmers get their crops to market, he believed; and only by encouraging the growth of commerce and towns could boys like young Lincoln have vocational opportunities other than farming like their fathers. At the national level Lincoln supported the protective tariff because he feared that without protection for America's infant industries, the country would be doomed to permanent status as an exporter of agricultural staples and raw materials and an importer of manufactured goods. Because Britain enjoyed such a head start in the Industrial Revolution, a measure of protection would level the playing field for American competitors. Industrialization was important for the United States because it would create a diversified economy with new economic opportunities. Lincoln's social vision required that individuals be free to choose fulfilling occupations, but in order for careers to be open to talent the careers had to first exist. Lincoln's support for the tariff reflected his willingness to use the power of government to shape an economic order to conform to his moral objectives. His determination to ban slavery in the territories reflected the same willingness.[64] A year and a half after it began, Lincoln converted the war to save the Union into a war to save the Union and free the slaves. He died just as the war was ending, a victim of southern white terrorism, which would claim many more victims during the era of Reconstruction.

Conclusion

Citizens of the overwhelmingly agricultural young American republic practiced thrift as an integral part of their daily lives. Their thrift was both an economic necessity and a cultural ideal, mandated by their predominantly Protestant heritage. When forging public policies, Americans tried to apply their familiar principles of thrift. But a seemingly common commitment to thrift could not reconcile disagreements over what kind of society America ought to become. Should thrift be practiced in ways that would preserve America as a land of independent family farms, with equal opportunity (at least for white males) to acquire land? Or should thrift be practiced so as to help transform America into a developed economy that would provide diverse opportunities for diverse talents? Rival conceptions of thrift, public and private, lay at the heart of the Second Party System of antebellum politics and even at the heart of the most radical versions of social criticism then on offer. The climactic paroxysm of the early Republic, the Civil War, expunged slavery from the nation as incompatible with a democracy of thrift.

Economic, social, and cultural changes during America's twentieth century steadily undermined the practice of republican thrift and the value system that went with it. An ever-shrinking percentage of the population worked on family farms, and composite agriculture became a historical memory. Abundance replaced scarcity. Advertising and consumer credit encouraged people to seek immediate gratification. Personality replaced character. Educators and philosophers seemed to lose faith in self-improvement as the rigorous development of certain faculties. Indulgence replaced discipline. Women left the home to work and chose to buy many of the goods and services they had previously, thriftily, provided within the household: food, clothing, and child care. Government interventions in the economy have had ambiguous consequences for thrift. If Social Security, Medicare, and the capital gains tax diminished incentive to save, insurance of bank deposits and the regulation of Wall Street encouraged savings by protecting them. Tax deductions for mortgage payments encouraged home ownership. Through all these changes, thrift has retained at least some advocates and practitioners. Its continued relevance as a controversial value is demonstrated by arguments over the environment. Perhaps most surprisingly, the reform of the welfare system a few years ago returned the practice of personal thrift to the arena of political debate.[65]

Notes

1. John Cotton, *Christ the Fountaine of Life* (1651), quoted in Daniel W. Howe, "The Impact of Puritanism on American Culture," in *Encyclopedia of American Religious Experience*, ed. Charles Lippy and Peter W. Williams (New York: Scribner's, 1988), 2:1066.

2. Cotton Mather, *A Christian at His Calling* (1719), quoted in Stephen Foster, *Their Solitary Way: The Puritan Social Ethic in the First Century of Settlement in New England* (New Haven, CT: Yale University Press, 1971), 107.

3. Kathleen McCarthy, *American Creed: Philanthropy and the Rise of Civil Society* (Chicago: University of Chicago Press, 2003). See also Robert Wuthnow and Tracy Scott, "Protestants and Economic Behavior," in *New Directions in American Religious History*, ed. Harry Stout and D. G. Hart (New York: Oxford University Press, 1997), 260–95.

4. Daniel W. Howe, *Making the American Self: Jonathan Edwards to Abraham Lincoln* (Cambridge, MA: Harvard University Press, 1997), 21–33.

5. On Scottish American moral philosophy, see Donald H. Meyer, *The Instructed Conscience: The Shaping of the American National Ethic* (Philadelphia: University of Pennsylvania Press, 1972).

6. Francis Wayland, *Elements of Political Economy*, 3rd ed. (Boston: Gould, Kendall, and Lincoln, 1840), 393–432; Wayland, *Elements of Moral Science*, ed. Joseph Blau (1835; Cambridge, MA: Harvard University Press, 1963), 345–50.

7. *Pennsylvania Journal*, December 10, 1767, quoted in Edmund Morgan, "The Puritan Ethic and the American Revolution," *William and Mary Quarterly*, 3rd ser., 24 (January 1967): 10.

8. *New London Gazette*, November 27, 1767, quoted in Timothy H. Breen, *The Marketplace of Revolution: How Consumer Politics Shaped American Independence* (New York: Oxford University Press, 2004), xvi.

9. Morgan, "Puritan Ethic," 9. See also Richard Bushman, *The Refinement of America* (New York: Knopf, 1992).

10. Bertram Wyatt-Brown, *Southern Honor* (New York: Oxford University Press, 1982); Grady McWhiney, *Cracker Culture: Celtic Ways in the Old South* (Tuscaloosa: University of Alabama Press, 1988).

11. Robert Fogel and Stanley Engerman, *Time on the Cross: The Economics of American Negro Slavery* (Boston: Little, Brown, 1974). Despite many critiques of it, the basic argument of this work—the economic efficiency of slavery—has stood the test of time. See, e.g., Peter Coclanis, *The Shadow of a Dream: Economic Life and Death in the South Carolina Low Country* (New York: Oxford University Press, 1989); Steven Deyle, *Carry Me Back: The Domestic Slave Trade in American Life* (New York: Oxford University Press,

2005); and James L. Huston, *Calculating the Value of the Union: Slavery, Property Rights, and the Economic Origins of the Civil War* (Chapel Hill: University of North Carolina Press, 2003).

12. Frank Byrne, "The Merchant in Antebellum Southern Literature and Society," *American Nineteenth Century History* 6 (March 2005): 33–56.

13. Richard Bushman, "Markets and Composite Farms in Early America," *William and Mary Quarterly*, 3rd ser., 55 (July 1998): 351–74; Allan Kulikoff, *From British Peasants to Colonial American Farmers* (Chapel Hill: University of North Carolina Press, 2000); Brian Donahue, "Environmental Stewardship and Decline in Old New England," *Journal of the Early Republic* 24 (Summer 2004): 234–41.

14. Herbert S. Klein, *A Population History of the United States* (Cambridge: Cambridge University Press, 2004), 78; Mark Caines and John Garraty, *Mapping America's Past* (New York: Holt, 1996), 94–95.

15. Jack Larkin, *The Reshaping of Everyday Life, 1790–1840* (New York: Harper and Row, 1988), 38, 53.

16. See Alan Taylor, "Land and Liberty on the Post-Revolutionary Frontier," in *Devising Liberty*, ed. David Thomas Konig (Stanford, CA: Stanford University Press, 1995), 81–108.

17. Brian Donahue, *The Great Meadow: Farmers and the Land in Colonial Concord* (New Haven, CT: Yale University Press, 2004); Steven Stoll, *Larding the Lean Earth: Soil and Society in Nineteenth-Century America* (New York: Hill and Wang, 2002).

18. Laurel Thatcher Ulrich, *The Age of Homespun* (New York: Knopf, 2001); Wendy Gamber, *Female Economy* (Urbana: University of Illinois Press, 1997), 135; Ruth Schwartz Cowan, *More Work for Mother: The Ironies of Household Technology* (New York: Basic Books, 1983), 131.

19. Peter McCelland, *Sowing Modernity: America's First Agricultural Revolution* (Ithaca, NY: Cornell University Press, 1997).

20. Anne Clarke to Joseph Clarke, July 8, 1821, quoted in Catherine Kelly, *In the New England Fashion: Reshaping Women's Lives in the Nineteenth Century* (Ithaca, NY: Cornell University Press, 1999), 43.

21. See Carnes and Garraty, *Mapping America's Past*, 94–95.

22. On the transition in retailing from rural peddling to urban shopkeeping, see Joyce Appleby, *Inheriting the Revolution: The First Generation of Americans* (Cambridge, MA: Harvard University Press, 2000), 82–84.

23. Mark M. Smith, *Mastered by the Clock: Time, Slavery, and Freedom in the American South* (Chapel Hill: University of North Carolina Press, 1997).

24. On Eli Terry, see Donald Hoke, *Ingenious Yankees* (New York: Columbia University Press, 1990), 52–99.

25. Quoted in David Jaffee, "Peddlers of Progress and the Transformation of the Rural North," *Journal of American History* 78 (September 1991): 517.

26. Charles Ball, *Slavery in the United States* (1836), in *Recollections of the Early Republic*, ed. Joyce Appleby (Boston: Northeastern University Press, 1997), 103–29.

27. Tyler Anbinder, "From Famine to Five Points," *American Historical Review* 107 (April 2002): 351–87.

28. Martin Meenagh, "John J. Hughes, First Archbishop of New York" (D.Phil. thesis, Oxford University, 2003).

29. Michael Zakim, *Ready-Made Democracy: A History of Men's Dress in the American Republic, 1760–1860* (Chicago: University of Chicago Press, 2003).

30. Christine Stansell, *City of Women: Sex and Class in New York, 1789–1860* (New York: Knopf, 1986).

31. Penne L. Restad, *Christmas in America* (New York: Oxford University Press, 1995); Stephen Nissenbaum, *The Battle for Christmas* (New York: Vintage Books, 1996).

32. Lydia Maria Francis Child, *The American Frugal Housewife, Dedicated to Those Who Are Not Ashamed of Economy, by Mrs. Child*, 22nd ed. (New York: Samuel S. and William Weed, 1838).

33. Carolyn Karcher, *The First Woman of the Republic: A Cultural Biography of Lydia Maria Child* (Durham, NC: Duke University Press, 1994).

34. Catharine Beecher, *A Treatise on Domestic Economy*, ed. Kathryn Kish Sklar (1841; A Treatise on Domestic Economy: Schocken Books, 1977).

35. See Kathryn Kish Sklar, *Catharine Beecher: A Study in American Domesticity* (New Haven, CT: Yale University Press, 1973).

36. Beecher, *Treatise on Domestic Economy*, 184.

37. H. J. Habakkuk, "Britain and America: The Economic Effects of Labour Scarcity," in *Britain and America: Studies in Comparative History*, ed. David Englander (New Haven, CT: Yale University Press, 1997), 51–81.

38. Andrew Isenberg, *The Destruction of the Bison* (Cambridge: Cambridge University Press, 2000).

39. Herbert Sloan, *Principle and Interest: Thomas Jefferson and the Problem of Debt* (New York: Oxford University Press, 1995).

40. See also Harry Watson, *Liberty and Power: The Politics of Jacksonian America* (New York: Hill and Wang, 1990); and Daniel Feller, *Jacksonian Promise: America, 1815–1840* (Baltimore: Johns Hopkins University Press, 1995).

41. John Quincy Adams, "First Annual Message" (December 6, 1825), in *Messages and Papers of the Presidents*, ed. James D. Richardson (Washington, DC: Government Printing Office, 1900), 2:311.

42. Andrew Jackson, "Veto Message" (May 27, 1830), in *Messages and Papers of the Presidents*, ed. James D. Richardson (Washington, DC: Government Printing Office, 1900), 2:489.

43. Andrew Jackson, "Veto Message" (July 10, 1832), in *Messages and Papers of the Presidents*, ed. James D. Richardson (Washington, DC: Government Printing Office, 1900), 2:590.

44. Charles Sellers, *The Market Revolution: Jacksonian America, 1815–1846* (New York: Oxford University Press, 1991); William Shade, *Banks or No Banks: The Money Issue in Western Politics* (Detroit, MI: Wayne State University Press, 1972).

45. See also Lawrence F. Kohl, *The Politics of Individualism: Parties and the American Character in the Jacksonian Era* (New York: Oxford University Press, 1989).

46. Martin Van Buren, "Third Annual Message" (December 4, 1839), in *Messages and Papers of the Presidents*, ed. James D. Richardson (Washington, DC: Government Printing Office, 1900), 3:554.

47. Henry Clay, "Speech on the Sub-Treasury" (September 25, 1837), in *Life, Correspondence, and Speeches*, ed. Calvin Colton (New York: A. S. Barnes, 1857), 6:74.

48. Gaillard Hunt, *Life in America One Hundred Years Ago* (New York: Harper, 1914), 175–81.

49. W. J. Rorabaugh, *The Alcoholic Republic* (New York: Oxford University Press, 1979).

50. For a comparative study of the three groups, see Lawrence Foster, *Religion and Sexuality: Three American Communal Experiments of the Nineteenth Century* (New York: Oxford University Press, 1981).

51. Henry David Thoreau, *Walden: A Fully Annotated Edition*, ed. Jeffrey S. Cramer (New Haven, CT: Yale University Press, 2004), 19. It is also a reference to Thoreau's experience in his father's pencil factory.

52. Ibid., 14.

53. Ralph Waldo Emerson, "Thoreau," in *Selected Essays*, ed. Larzer Ziff (Harmondsworth, UK: Penguin Books, 1982), 412.

54. Thoreau, *Walden*, 18.

55. See Jean Yellin, *Women and Sisters: The Antislavery Feminists in American Culture* (New Haven, CT: Yale University Press, 1989).

56. Eric Foner, *Free Soil, Free Labor, Free Men* (New York: Oxford University Press, 1970).

57. Kenneth Startup, "'A Mere Calculation of Profits and Loss': The Southern Clergy and the Economic Culture of the Antebellum North," in *God and Mammon: Protestants, Money, and the Market, 1790–1860*, ed. Mark Noll (New York: Oxford University Press, 2002), 217–35.

58. Gabor Boritt, *Lincoln and the Economics of the American Dream* (Urbana: University of Illinois Press, 1994).

59. Abraham Lincoln, "Address before the Young Men's Lyceum" (1838), in *The Collected Works of Abraham Lincoln*, ed. Roy P. Basler (New Brunswick, NJ: Rutgers University Press, 1953), 1:115.

60. Abraham Lincoln, "Temperance Address" (1842), in *The Collected Works of Abraham Lincoln*, ed. Roy P. Basler (New Brunswick, NJ: Rutgers University Press, 1953), 1:276–79.

61. Abraham Lincoln, "Speech at New Haven, Connecticut" (1860), in *The Collected Works of Abraham Lincoln*, ed. Roy P. Basler (New Brunswick, NJ: Rutgers University Press, 1953), 4:24–25.

62. Two judicious assessments of Lincoln's outlook are Richard Carwardine, *Lincoln* (London: Longman, 2003); and Allen Guelzo, *Abraham Lincoln, Redeemer President* (Grand Rapids, MI: Eerdmans, 1999).

63. Abraham Lincoln, "First Debate with Stephen A. Douglas" (1858), in *The Collected Works of Abraham Lincoln*, ed. Roy P. Basler (New Brunswick, NJ: Rutgers University Press, 1953), 3:16 (emphasis in original).

64. See also Howe, *Making the American Self*, 136–49.

65. Topics in this chapter are explored more fully in Daniel Walker Howe, *What Hath God Wrought: The Transformation of America, 1815–1848* (Oxford: Oxford University Press, 2007). All material adapted from that book is used with the permission of Oxford University Press.

3 }

The Prehistory of American Thrift

Deirdre McCloskey

The prehistory of North American thrift is English. A plantation owner in seventeenth-century Virginia thought of himself as a British subject. In Massachusetts John Winthrop and Anne Bradstreet were born English and anyway viewed their city of God in the New World as an extension of English Puritanism. The "long, rather listless pieces" of poetry by Bradstreet before she found her American voice, Adrienne Rich writes, "seem to have been composed in a last compulsive effort to stay in contact with the history, traditions, and values of her former world."[1] At the other end of the century and a half of colonial North America one finds Benjamin Franklin, that apostle of bourgeois virtues, worrying and worrying about his Englishness. He spent a year as a printer and then two long trips as a diplomat in London, two decades in total, and right up to 1776 thought of himself as a citizen of the British Empire. He split from his beloved illegitimate son, William, a colonial governor and later a banished Tory, on the issue of Englishness.

The word *thrift* in English is still used as late as John Bunyan to mean simply "wealth" or "profit," deriving from the verb *thrive*—as *gift* derives from *give* and *drift* from *drive*. Its third sense in the *Oxford English Dictionary* is our modern one, dating significantly from the sixteenth century: "food is never found to be so pleasant . . . as when . . . thrift has pinched afore" (1553); "so I will if none of my sons be thrifty" (1526).

This sense of thrift, anywhere, can be viewed as a mix of the cardinal virtues of temperance and of prudence in things economic. Temperance is the cardinal virtue of self-command facing temptation. Lead me not into temptation. Prudence, by contrast, is the cardinal virtue of practical wisdom. It is reason, know-how, savoir faire, rationality. Prudence without temperance does not in fact do what it knows it should thriftily do. Temperance without prudence does not know what to do. Prudent housewives in the "Ladder to Thrift," as the English agricultural rhymester Thomas Tusser put it in 1574, "make provision skillfully."[2] Without being full of skill—that is, prudent—they do not know how to be thrifty in saving tallow for candles or laying up salt mutton for Christmas.

Prudent temperance in a sense has no history, in that it is ever present in human society. The Hebrew Bible, for example, speaks of thrift, usually associated with diligence: "The sluggard will not plough by reason of the cold; therefore shall he beg in harvest, and have nothing" (Prov. 20:4 KJV); "Seest thou a man diligent in his business? he shall stand before kings" (Prov. 22:29 KJV). Jesus of Nazareth and his tradition used parables of thrift to point to another world. "Eat and drink," advises the Koran, "but be you not prodigal; [God] loves not the prodigal" (7:31).[3]

Of course faiths other than the Abrahamic ones admire on occasion a godly thrift. The Four Noble Truths of Buddhism, to be sure, recommend that life's sorrow can be dissolved by the ending of desire, in which case advice to be thrifty would have no point. Buddhism is similar in this respect to Greek and Roman Stoicism, which advocated devaluing this world's lot, an inspiration to Christian saints of thriftiness early and late. But consider the "Admonition to Singāla," consisting of a few hundred lines in the Buddhist canon, described as "the longest single passage . . . devoted to lay morality." In the midst of it Buddha is represented as bursting into poetry in praise of friendship. The reward?

> The wise and moral man
> Shines like a fire on the hilltop,
> Making money like a bee,
> Who does not hurt the flower.
> Such a man makes his pile
> As an anthill, gradually.
> The man grown wealthy thus
> Can help his family
> And firmly binds his friends
> To himself. He should divide
> His money in four parts;
> On one part he should live,
> With two expand his trade,
> And the fourth he should save
> Against a rainy day.[4]

As the editor remarks, the verses "effectively give the lie to the picture, still popular in some circles, of ancient India as a land of 'plain living and high thinking.' The last three verses are evidently a product of a society quite as acquisitive as that of present-day Europe or America."[5] More so, actually, if one is to take literally the recommended savings rate of fully 75 percent—with no allowance for charity, something that bothered the Buddhist commentators.

From the huts of the Aborigines to the lofts of Chicago, humans need to live within their incomes, being by their own lights "thrifty."

In England the thirteenth-century writers of advice books to Norman-English landowners start with thrift and go on to the details of husbandry. The third paragraph of *The Husbandry* by Walter of Henley, after a bow in the second paragraph to the passion of Jesus, prays "that according to what your lands be worth yearly . . . you order your life, and no higher at all."[6] It continues then in the same vein for five more paragraphs. The anonymous *Seneschaucy*, also written in medieval French in the late thirteenth century, instructs the lord's chief steward "to see that there is no extravagance . . . on any manor . . . and to reduce all unnecessary expenditure . . . which shows no profit. . . . About this it is said: foolish spending brings no gain."[7] The passage deprecates "the practices without prudence or reason" (*lez maners saunz pru e reyson*). So much for a rise of prudence, reason, rationality, and thrift in, say, the sixteenth century. Prudent temperance rose with Adam and Eve.

The prehistory of thrift, in other words, extends back to the Garden of Eden. It is laid down in our genes. A protoman who could not gain weight readily in feast times would suffer in famine. Therefore, his descendent in a prosperous modern society has a weight problem. Prudent temperance does not require a stoic or monkish abstemiousness. A plowman burning 3,000 calories a day had better get them somehow. One should be thrifty in eating, says Tusser, but not to the point of denying our prudent human solidarity:

> Each day to be feasted, what husbandry worse,
> Each day for to feast, is as ill for the purse;
> Yet measurely feasting, with neighbors among,
> Shall make thee beloved, and live the more long.[8]

From the sixteenth through the eighteenth century, then, the average English and American-English person surely practiced thrift. But this did not distinguish her from the average English person before or after, or for that matter from the average person anywhere since Eden.

> "My other piece of advice, Copperfield," said Mr. Micawber, "you know. Annual income twenty pounds, annual expenditure nineteen nineteen six, result happiness. Annual income twenty pounds, annual expenditure twenty pounds ought and six, result misery."
>
> To make his example the more impressive, Mr. Micawber drank a glass of punch with an air of great enjoyment and satisfaction, and whistled the College Hornpipe.
>
> I did not fail to assure him that I would store these precepts in my mind.[9]

Thrift in the sense of spending exactly what one earns is forced by accounting. Not having manna from heaven or a Santa Claus, the world must get along on what it gets. The world's income must equal to the last sixpence the world's expenditure—*expenditure* understood to include investment goods. So too Mr. Micawber. If he spends more than he earns, he must depend on something turning up, that is, a loan or gift or inheritance. He draws down his credit. In the meantime, his diminishing balance sheet—what he owns and owes—pays to the last sixpence for his punch and his house rent.

Thrift in the sense of earning *much* more than one spends, and thereby accumulating assets in that balance sheet, is again a matter of accounting. You must expend everything you earn somehow, on bread or bonds or building houses or whatever. But of course you can expend foolishly or well—on bombs or on college educations. If you refrain from silly consumption of Fritos and other immediate-consumption goods—"abstaining from consumption," in the economist's useful way of putting it—you necessarily save; that is, you add to your hoard buried in the back garden or to a bank account or to your investments in educations or roadways or battleships.

There is nothing modern, I repeat, about such accounting. It comes with life and the first law of thermodynamics, in the Kalahari or in Kansas City. In particular, the preindustrial European world I am here contrasting with modern times needed urgently to abstain from consumption—*consumption* understood as immediate eating and other immediate expenditures that are not investments in a future. Yields of rye or barley or wheat per unit of seed planted in medieval and early modern agriculture were only 3 or 4; they are over 100 now. The low yields forced Europeans to refrain from a great deal of consumption if they did not want to starve in the next year. One-quarter to one-third of the grain crop went back into the ground as seed in the fall or the spring, to be harvested the next September. In an economy in which the grain crop was perhaps three-fourths of total income, that portion alone of medieval saving implied an aggregate, social saving rate of upward of 25 percent. The usual rate of saving in modern industrial economies is seldom above 10 percent.

Furthermore, trade in grain was restricted in climatic extent, so grain storage even for consumption in people's mouths, and not just for investment in next year's seed, was also high by modern standards. Grain storage amounted to another desperate form of saving, crowding out more modern forms.[10] In recent times, if the grain crop does poorly in America, the world market easily supplies the difference from a different clime. In the late Middle Ages grain did flow from the Midlands to London or from Burgundy to Paris. But it began to flow to Western Europe in large amounts from as far away as Poland only gradually in the sixteenth and seventeenth centuries, through the efforts of thrifty Dutch merchants and shipbuilders, and only in the nineteenth century from as different a climate as Ukraine or, finally, from North and South America or even Australia. Until the eighteenth century, therefore, the grain crops here and there in the relevant and narrow market area tended to fail together. The potato famine of the 1840s was the last replay of a sort of undiversified catastrophe that was commonplace in the 1540s and more so in the 1340s. In such circumstances you stored and saved, in gigantic percentages of current income, or you starved.

Such scarcities were broken in the New World of British Americans. They ate better than their Old World cousins within a generation of the first settlements.[11] The feat was not hard, for their English cousins were passing then through the worst times for the working man and woman since the early fourteenth century.[12] Plentiful land, at any rate out on the literal frontier, made it unnecessary to save so much in grain, and freed the sum for other investments. Yet although the North American English became, even as a colony, well off by British standards, British North America was by no means the home of the Industrial Revolution. It was too small, too tempted by agriculture, too far away. The Northeast of the soon-to-be United States, like southern Belgium and northern France, was to be sure a close follower, in the 1790s and 1800s. But the leaders, from the 1760s, were northwest England and lowland Scotland, lands of grindingly necessary thrift.

The point is that there is no aggregate increase in thrifty savings to "explain" the modern world. Thrifty saving is not peculiar to capitalism and has nothing to do with an alleged rise of prudence or greed or anything else in the childhood of the modern world. Actual saving was high before modern times and did not change much with modern capitalism.

So too actual greed. In 1904 Max Weber, writing when the German Romantic notion that medieval society was more sweet and egalitarian than modern capitalism was beginning to crumble in the face of historical research, thundered against the idea that greed is "in the least identical with capitalism, and still less with its spirit." He writes, "It should be taught in the kindergarten of cultural history that this naïve idea of capitalism must be given up once and for all."[13] *Auri sacra fames*—"infamous lust for gold"—is from the *Aeneid*, not from Benjamin Franklin or *Advertising Age*.[14] The lust for gold "has been common to all sorts and conditions of men at all times and in all countries of the earth."[15]

The case is the same with actual luxury, the opposite of thrift. "Depend on it, sir," said Samuel Johnson in 1778, "every state of society is as luxurious as it can be. Men always take the best they can get," in lace or food or educations.[16] Karl Marx noted cannily that "when a certain stage of development has been reached, a conventional degree of prodigality, which is also an exhibition of wealth, and consequently a source of credit, becomes a business necessity. . . . Luxury enters into capital's expenses of representation."[17] True. Otherwise it would be hard to explain the high quality of lace on the collars of black-clad Protestant Dutch merchants in paintings of the seventeenth century or, indeed, the market for the expensive oil paintings in the hundreds of thousands representing the merchants and their world.

Readers of the magnificent historical chapters 25–31 of Marx's *Capital* find all this hard to believe. Marx's eloquence persuades them that someone writing in 1867, very early in the professionalization of history, nonetheless got the essence of the history right. The history Marx thought he perceived went with his logic that capitalism just *is* the same thing as greed—"the restless never-ending process of profit-making alone . . . this boundless greed after riches," as he put it, drawing on an anticommercial theme originating in Aristotle.[18] Greed is the engine that powers his "equation" (as he imagined it to be) of M → K → M': that is, money starting as an amount M gets invested, through thriftiness, in Kapital, which is intrinsically exploitative, generating surplus value appropriated by the capitalist to arrive at a new, higher amount of money, M'. And then again and again and again, "endlessly."[19] The root of the word Marx uses here, which was echoed during the Dark Ages in rural monkish economic theory and still resonates in Marx-influenced notions of capitalism, originated twenty-four centuries before Marx in the Greek aristocratic disdain for commerce: people of business, declared aristocratic Plato and aristocrat-loving Aristotle, are motivated by *apeiron*—unlimited—greed.

For all Marx's brilliance—anyone who does not think he was the greatest social scientist of the nineteenth century has not read enough Marx—he got the history almost entirely wrong. Whatever the value of his theories as a way of asking historical questions, almost no important fact you read in Marx is historically correct. This is not some special Marxian fault. The same is true of the other practitioners of merely philosophical history before the facts started arriving at last, during the twentieth century: David Hume, Jean-Jacques Rousseau, Adam Smith, Georg Hegel, Ferdinand Tönnies, Émile Durkheim, and even, a very late instance, on many points Weber, and still later Karl Polanyi.[20] The theory of capitalism that educated people still carry around in their heads springs from Marx, Saint Benedict, and Aristotle, filtered through these eloquent modern men. It is economically mistaken. And the point here is that it is historically mistaken as well.

The myth of *Kapitalismus* is that thrift among the bourgeoisie consists precisely in the absence of a purpose other than accumulation "for its own sake." The late Robert Heilbroner wrote, "Capitalism has been an expansive system from its earliest days, a system whose driving force has been the effort to accumulate ever larger amounts of capital itself."[21] Weber wrote, too, in 1904, that "the *summum bonum* of this ethic [is] the earning of more and more money. . . . Acquisition . . . [is] the ultimate purpose of life."[22] Weber here, contrary to the thundering just quoted, agreed with Marx, money-to-capital-to-money: "Accumulate, accumulate!" declared the man himself in 1867. "This is Moses and the prophets!"[23]

At the level of individuals there has never been any evidence for the historical change that is supposed to characterize modern forms of greedy thrift. The chief evidence that Weber gives in *The Protestant Ethic and the Spirit of*

Capitalism is a humorless reading of Franklin's autobiography. Like many other readers of Franklin, especially non-American readers, Weber took the checklist of virtues a young man used to discipline himself as the man's essence. He failed to note Franklin's actual behavior as a loving and passionate friend and patriot or his amused ironies about his young self.[24] Weber modified the pointlessness of the Marxian impulse to "accumulate, accumulate" by claiming that "this philosophy of avarice" depends on a transcendent "*duty* of the individual toward the increase of his capital," becoming a "worldly asceticism."[25] But his Franklin, who after all had lost most other traces of his ancestors' Calvinism, whether spiritual or worldly, abandoned at age forty-two "endless" accumulation and devoted the rest of his long life to science and public purposes. So much for "ever larger amounts of capital itself" or a "duty toward the increase of capital" or the drive to "accumulate, accumulate."

Many fine scholars have taken in with their mother's milk a belief that modern life is unusually devoted to gain and that thrift is therefore something recent, dirty, and bourgeois, though lamentably profitable. "The unlimited hope for gain in the market," writes the otherwise admirable political theorist Joan Tronto, "would teach people an unworkable premise for moral conduct, since the very nature of morality seems to dictate that desires must be limited by the need to coexist with others."[26] But running a business, unlike professing at a university, would teach anyone that gain is limited. Dealing in a market, unlike sitting in the Reading Room of the British Museum writing burning phrases against the market, would teach that desires must be limited by the need to coexist with others. The tuition of a market society in scarcity, other-regarding, and liberal values works as an ethical school. As the historian Thomas Haskell put it in 1985, "Contrary to romantic folklore, the marketplace is not a Hobbesian war of all against all. Many holds are barred. Success ordinarily requires not only pugnacity and shrewdness but also restraint," temperance.[27]

Even so fine a historian as Alan Macfarlane believes the Aristotelian/Marxist/Weberian lore. "The ethic of endless accumulation," he writes, "as an end and not a means, is the central peculiarity of capitalism."[28] If it were, the miser would be a strictly modern figure and not proverbial in every literature in the world. "In this consists the difference between the character of a miser," wrote Smith in 1759, "and that of a [thrifty] person of exact economy and assiduity. The one is anxious about small matters for their own sake; the other attends to them only in consequence of the scheme of life which he has laid down for himself."[29] "Accumulate, accumulate" is not a "scheme of life" in the ethical sense that Smith had in mind.

At the level of the society as a whole there *is* "unlimited" accumulation, at any rate if war and rapine and rats do not intervene. Corporations, having legally infinite lives—though in truth 10 percent die every year—are to be sure sites of accumulation. The individual economic molecules who make up the river of capitalism may not always want to accumulate beyond age forty-two, but the river as a whole, it is said, keeps rolling along. True, and to our good. The machines and improved acreage and splendid buildings and so forth inherited from an accumulating past are good for us now.

But there is no historical case for "accumulate, accumulate" being peculiar to capitalism. Infinitely lived institutions like families or churches or royal lineages existed before modern capitalism and were themselves, too, sites of accumulation. Thus improved acreage spread up the hillsides under the pressure of population before the Black Death. Thus the medieval cathedrals were raised over centuries. Thus Oxford colleges were built, and endowed in real estate.

The prehistory of thrift was itself revolutionized during the 1960s when economic historians realized with a jolt that thriftiness and savings could not explain the Industrial Revolution. The rise in savings was too small.[30] "The bourgeoisie," wrote Marx in 1848, "during its rule of scarce one hundred years has created more massive and colossal productive forces than have all the preceding generations together."[31] It was a prescient remark. But the classical economists from Smith to Marx were writing before the upsurge in real wages of British and Belgian and American working people in the last third of the nineteenth century, and long, long before the explosion of world income in the twentieth century. They imagined a moderate rise of income per person, perhaps at the most by a factor of two or three, such as might conceivably be achieved by Scotland's highlands becoming similar to capital-rich Holland (Smith's view) or by manufacturers in Manchester stealing savings from their workers (Marx's view) or by the savings generated from globalization being invested in European factories (John Stuart Mill's view).

The classical and mistaken view overturned by the economic historians of the 1950s and 1960s is that thrift implies saving, which implies capital accumulation, which implies modern economic growth. It lingered in a few works such as Walt Rostow's *Stages of Economic Growth* (1960) and most unhappily in what William Easterly (2001) has called the "capital fundamentalism" of foreign aid, 1950 to the present. The belief was that if we give Ghana large amounts of savings over several decades, leading to massive capital investments in artificial lakes and Swiss bank accounts, and give Communist China not a penny, Ghana will prosper and Communist China will languish.[32]

What actually happened from 1800 to 2000—and, once it was fully recognized, what killed the notion among most economists and economic historians that thrifty saving was the way to massive and colossal productive forces—was a rise of income per person by a factor of not two or three but *eighteen*.[33] That is how much income per head in places like the United States and Japan have risen since such countries invented or adopted modern techniques of making steel or lighting houses. It is not 18 percent, understand, such as classical notions of thrifty capital accumulation could explain with ease, or even a near tripling of 180 percent, which they could perhaps explain, with a good deal more trouble. It is a factor of 18, fully 1,700 percent—which they cannot explain at all.

What, then, explains it? New thoughts, what the economic historian Joel Mokyr calls the "industrial enlightenment." The ideas of steam engines and lightbulbs and computers, not new accumulations from saving, made northwestern Europe and then much of the rest of the world rich.[34] Accumulation of physical capital is not the heart of modern capitalism, as economic historians have understood since their researches of the 1950s and 1960s and as economists have understood since the calculations by Moses Abramowitz and Robert Solow in the 1950s—and before them the calculations by G. T. Jones in 1933.[35] Its heart is innovation.

Of course, if you think up a waterpower-driven spinning machine, you need some savings to bring the thought to fruition. But another of the discoveries of the 1960s by economic historians was that the savings required in England's heroic age of mechanization were modest indeed, nothing like the massive "original accumulation of capital" that Marxist theory posits. Early cotton factories were not capital-intensive. The source of the industrial investment required was short-term loans on inventories and loans from relatives, not savings ripped in great chunks from other parts of the economy.

The classical and Marxist idea that capital begets capital, "endlessly," is hard to shake. It has recently revived a little even among economists, in the form of the so-called new growth theory, an attempt to give M → K → M' a mathematically spiffed-up form. The trouble is that, as I have noted, savings and urbanization and state power to expropriate and the other physical-capital accumulations that are supposed to explain modern economic growth have existed on a large scale since the Sumerians. Yet modern economic growth, that wholly unprecedented factor of 18, is a phenomenon of the past two centuries alone. Something happened in the eighteenth century that prepared for a temporary but shocking "great divergence" of the European economies from those of the rest of the world.[36]

The *marxisant* analysis is that what happened is the "original accumulation of capital." The original or primitive accumulation was according to Marx the seed corn, so to speak, or better the starter in the sourdough, in the growth of capital. We are back to thrift or savings not by historical fact but by blackboard logic. "The whole movement," Marx reasons, "seems to turn on a vicious circle, out of which we can only get by supposing a primitive accumulation, . . . an accumulation not the result of the capitalist mode of production, but its starting point."[37] As the economic historian Alexander Gerschenkron put it in 1957, with a certain sarcasm, it is "an accumulation of capital continuing over long historical periods—perhaps over several centuries—until one day the tocsin of the industrial revolution was to summon it to the battlefields of factory construction."[38]

Looking at the thrift necessary for such an accumulation in a cheerful way, the starting point was a supposed rise of thriftiness among Dutch or especially

English Puritans. Marx characterized such tales as praise for "that queer saint, that knight of the woeful countenance, the capitalist 'abstainer.'"[39] We can join him for a moment in disbelieving the optimistic tale, noting further, and contrary to his own pessimistic tale, that abstention is universal, as I have said, and that saving rates in Catholic Italy or for that matter Confucian China were not much lower, if lower at all, than in Calvinist Massachusetts or Lutheran Germany.

Marx's notion in *Capital*, on the contrary, is that an original accumulation was a sine qua non and that there was no saintliness about it. The original accumulation was necessary because masses of savings were necessary and because "conquest, enslavement, robbery, murder, briefly, force, play the greater part."[40] He instances enclosure in England during the sixteenth century (which has been overturned by historical findings that such enclosure was minor) and in the eighteenth (which has been overturned by findings that the labor driven off the land was a tiny source of the industrial proletariat and occurred mainly in the south and east where little industry was going on). He gives a large part, then, to regulation of wages in making a proletariat in the sixteenth century (which has been overturned by findings that half of the labor force in England as early as the thirteenth century already worked for wages). And then he turns to the slave trade: "Liverpool waxed fat on the slave-trade. This was its method of primitive accumulation" (which has been overturned by findings that the alleged profits were no massive fund).[41] Later writers have proposed as the source of the original accumulation the exploitation by the core of the periphery (Poland, the New World);[42] the influx of gold and silver from the New World (strange as it is then that imperial Spain did not industrialize); the exploitation of workers themselves during the Industrial Revolution, out of sequence; other loot from imperialisms old and new; or, following on Marx's assertion in *The Communist Manifesto*, even seventeenth-century piracy.

None of these, it has been found, make very much historical sense, and the findings are not very surprising. After all, conquest, enslavement, robbery, murder, and, briefly, force have characterized the sad annals of humankind since Cain and Abel. Why didn't earlier and even more thorough expropriations result in an industrial revolution and a factor of 18, that 1,700 percent increase in the welfare of the average Briton or American or Taiwanese? Something besides thrifty self-discipline or violent expropriation must have been at work in northwestern Europe and its offshoots in the eighteenth century. Thrifty self-discipline and violent expropriation have been too common in human history to explain a revolution unique to Europe around 1800.

And as a practical matter a pile of physical capital financed from, say, Piet Heyn's seizure of the Spanish treasure fleet in 1628 would by the year 1800 melt away to nothing. It does not accumulate. It depreciates. The confusion is between financial wealth in a bank account, which is merely a claim by this person against that person to the society's real wealth in a house or ship or education. Real wealth is what needs to be available for real investment. You cannot build a factory with pound notes or dig a canal with gold coins. You need bricks and wheelbarrows and skilled people to wield them. Mere financing can hardly be the crux, or else the Roman church in its command of tokens of wealth would have created an industrial society in 1300. Or Philip II—who after all was the beneficiary of those treasure fleets that the English and Dutch privateers preyed on—would have financed an industrial revolution in Spain. So any original accumulation supposed to be useful for any real industrialization must be available in real things. But "what is with you [in real, physical things] comes to an end, but what is with God abides" (Koran 16:96); "These lovely [earthly] things," writes Saint Augustine, "go their way and are no more.... In them is no repose, because they do not abide."[43] A real house built in 1628 out of Piet's profit would be tumbled down by 1800, unless in the meantime its occupants had continued to invest in it. A real educated person of 1628 would be long dead, a real machine would be obsolete, a real book would be eaten by worms. The force of depreciation makes an original accumulation spontaneously disappear.

This is not to say, note well, that conquest, enslavement, robbery, and murder play no part in European history. A Panglossian assumption that contract, not force, explains, say, the relation between lord and peasant defaces the recent work on "new" institutionalism, such as that of Douglass North.[44] But, pace Marx, modern economic growth did not and does not and cannot depend on what can be gained by stealing from poor people. Stealing from poor people, when you think about it, could hardly explain enrichment by a factor of 18. Would you do so well by robbing the homeless people in your neighborhood or by breaking into the residence of the average factory worker? Does it strike you as plausible that British national income depended much on stealing from an impoverished India? If it did, why did real income per head in Britain go up sharply in the decade after Britain "lost" India?

Modern economic growth has not depended on saving or on stealing to get the saving. It has depended instead on the invention of entirely new ways of propelling ships or making shoes. And nowadays it depends—if your country is, as Gerschenkron put it, "relatively backward"—on leaping over the slow, early stages of invention and investment by adopting what has already been invented, getting cell phones now instead of laboriously investing in landlines and then inventing substitutes. It is why China and India can now grow at rates inconceivable in the eighteenth and early nineteenth centuries, before the inventions were well launched. It is why in the late nineteenth century Sweden and then in the late twentieth century Japan and South Korea caught up so very quickly. "Capitalist production," Marx declares, "presupposes the pre-existence of considerable masses of capital."[45] No, it does not. A modest stream of withheld profits will pay for repairing the machines and acquiring new ones, especially the uncomplicated machines of 1760. (In 1760 the most complicated "machine" in existence was a first-rate ship of the line, continuously under repair.) And so far as the starter is concerned, as in sourdough it is small and could come from anywhere, not only from some great original sin of primitive accumulation.

What did happen in the seventeenth and eighteenth centuries, it would appear, is so to speak an original accumulation of inventive people, such as James Watt and Franklin. Such people sought bourgeois and thrifty ways of making and doing things, turning away from the projects of honorable display characteristic of an aristocratic society. By the eighteenth century they were launched on careers of producing a wave of gadgets that has not yet ceased rolling over us. An original accumulation of habits of free publication and vigorous discussion, as Mokyr argues in *The Gifts of Athena*, created "a world in which 'useful' knowledge was indeed *used* with an aggressiveness and a single-mindedness that no other society had experienced before was the unique Western way."[46] We do not yet know for sure why this happened in northwestern Europe and did not happen until later elsewhere, though many economic historians suspect that Europe's political fragmentation leading to comparative freedom for enterprise was important.[47] What did *not* happen, we do know, was a big rise in European thrift.

So nothing much changed from 1348 to 1600 or from 1600 to 1800 in the actual circumstances of thriftiness. And the modest changes did not matter much. The Dutch- and English-speaking people who initiated the modern world exercised personal thrift, or did not, as they still do, or do not. But changes in aggregate rates of saving drove nothing of consequence. No unusual Weberian ethic of high thriftiness or forceful expropriation started economic growth. East Anglian Puritans learned from their Dutch neighbors and coreligionists how to be thrifty in order to be godly and to work hard, as John Winthrop puts it, "to entertain each other in brotherly affection."[48] That is nice, but it is not what caused industrialization—as indeed one can see from the failure of industrialization even in the Protestant and prosperous parts of the Netherlands, or for that matter in East Anglia itself. The habits of thriftiness and luxury and profit, and the routines of exploitation, are humanly ordinary and largely unchanging. Modern economic growth depends on ingenuity in crafting gadgets, and this in turn appears to depend on free societies. It does not depend on massive investment or an original accumulation of capital.

What did change from 1600 to 1800, however, and did so dramatically, was the high-cultural *attitude* toward thrift. Thriftiness and other specifically economic virtues—such as prudent calculation of costs and benefits, an admiring attitude toward industrial novelties, or an acceptance of ethically acquired profits—became fully respectable, honorable, admired, permitted, and encouraged, not obstructed and disdained, first in Holland and then at last in England, and even a bit earlier in England's remote American colonies and in England's impoverished neighbor, Scotland. This *was* unique in world history, and the change had stupendous economic consequences. A change in the superstructure determined a change in the base.

Away from northwestern Europe and its offshoots around 1800 the economic virtues were still not respectable—in the opinion of the dominant classes, at any rate. Right up to the Meiji Restoration of 1867, after which things in Japan changed with lightning speed, leading opinion scorned the merchant. In Confucian cultures more widely the merchant was ranked as the lowest of the classes: in Japan, the order was the daimyo, the samurai, the peasant, and then the merchant. A merchant in Japan and China and Korea was not a "gentleman," to use the European word, and had no honor.

Likewise circa 1600 in William Shakespeare's England the economic virtues were not at all respectable. They were sneered at. The only one of Shakespeare's plays that speaks largely of merchants offers no commendation of thrift. Shylock's "well-worn thrift" is nothing like an admired model for behavior. It is the lack of thrift in aristocratic Bessanio, the "disabling of his estate," itself viewed as amusing and blameless—since had he but the means he could hold a rival place with Portia's wealthy and aristocratic suitors—that motivates the blood bargain in the first place.

This does not mean that Shakespeare's contemporaries were not greedy. But their greed expressed itself in an aristocratic notion that Lord Bessanio simply *deserved* the income from his lands or borrowings or gifts from friends or marrying well or any other unearned income he could assemble—and then gloriously spend. The gentry and especially the aristocracy in Shakespeare's England discounted bourgeois thrift and scorned the bourgeois work that earned the income to be thrifty about. Gentlemen, and especially dukes, did not trouble to pay their tailoring bills. As late as 1695 the English economic writer Charles Davenant complained that "if these high [land] taxes long continue, in a country so little given to thrift as ours, the landed men must inevitably be driven into the hands of . . . usurers."[49] The unthrifty were the landed English gentlemen puttin' on the style. Francis Bacon had been in Shakespeare's time the very type of such a man, given to "ostentatious entrances, arrayed in all his finery, and surrounded by a glittering retinue"; he was chronically unthrifty, always in debt, and tempted therefore to misuse the lord chancellor's mace, when finally his ambition achieved it, by soliciting bribes from both parties in legal disputes.[50] About the same time as Bacon's disgrace, a prudent temperance had made Plymouth Colony and Massachusetts Bay succeed where Jamestown had failed, because the adventurers of Jamestown were gentlemen, not thrifty Puritans.

All of Shakespeare's works record an aristocratic refusal to calculate. Think of Hamlet's indecision, Lear's proud impulsiveness, King Leontes's irrationalities in *A Winter's Tale*. Such behavior is quite unlike the prudent examining of ethical account books even among late and worldly Puritans like Daniel Defoe or among their even later and even more worldly descendants like Franklin. What is correct in Weber's emphasis on worldly asceticism is that the Puritans wrote a good many fictions such as autobiographies stressing it.

Because it elevates an ignoble prudence, aristocrats are scornful of such calculation. That does not mean that they in fact did not calculate. They'd better. As the king prays to the god of battles in *Henry V*:

> steel my soldiers' hearts.
> Possess them not with fear. Take from them now
> The sense of reck'ning, [if] th'opposèd numbers
> Pluck their hearts from them. (4.1.272–74)[51]

And indeed his "ruined band" before Agincourt, as he had noted to the French messenger, was

> with sickness much enfeebled,
> My numbers lessened, and those few I have
> Almost no better than so many French. (3.6.131–33)

Imagine that. At the battle that followed, on the Feast Day of Crispian in 1415, his numbers of 5,000 or 6,000 (to take the conventional estimate, recently disputed) did not prudently flee from an enemy of 25,000.

One reason, Shakespeare avers, was the king's religious faith. As Henry says to Gloucester, "We are in God's hand, brother, not in theirs" (3.6.155), though the expression of religious faith here, as usually in Shakespeare, is formulaic and questionably sincere. In a highly religious age few characters in Shakespeare make religious faith their guiding theme, and some of these are scheming clerics with unfaithful purposes, like the bishops in the early scenes of *Henry V*. Contrast John Milton, writing a half century later, in whom the Puritans find their noblest voice. (The word *thrift*, by the way, appears nowhere in Milton's justifying of the ways of God to man.)

The alternative and central virtue in *Henry V* is not Christian faith but aristocratic courage:

> 'tis true that we are in great danger;
> The greater therefore should our courage be. (4.1.1–2)

Shakespeare emphasizes in 1599 such aristocratic virtues and not, for example, the prudence of the warhorse-impaling stakes that on Henry's orders the archers had in fact been lugging through the muddy French countryside for the week preceding October 25.[52] The stakes are mentioned in Shakespeare's sources but not in the play. Such prudence is a calculative virtue, as are justice and temperance, among the seven principal virtues. They are cool. The two warm and earthly virtues, love and courage, with at least secular versions of the warm virtues faith and hope, which together make the four praised most often by Shakespeare, are specifically and essentially *non*-calculative.

Writing in 1900, Georg Simmel claims in *The Philosophy of Money* to detect a "psychological feature of our times which stands in such a decisive contrast to the more impulsive, emotionally determined character of earlier epochs. . . .

Gauging values in terms of money has taught us to determine and specify values down to the last farthing."[53] In a word, thriftiness reigns now, as against the warm noncalculativeness of earlier folk. This is false, of a piece with Weber's claim that a rise of rationality characterizes the modern world. The Great War was soon to make such optimistic Eurocentrism look strange indeed. Ernest Renan, professor of Hebrew at the Collège de France from 1862—most famous for his claim that Jesus was a good chap if a trifle primitive and oriental—declared that "we must make a marked distinction between societies like our own, where everything takes place in the full light of reflection, and simple and credulous communities," such as those that Jesus preached in.[54] After the events of the twentieth century in Europe, which exhibited irrationality, impulse, credulousness, and rather little of the full light of reflection, one stands amazed that anyone can still believe in the unusual rationality or prudence or thriftiness of the modern European world.

In fact people always and everywhere have been both more or less rational and more or less impulsive. They exhibit the seven virtues, and the numerous corresponding vices, all. In medieval Europe one can see in Walter of Henley's book *The Husbandry* and the *Seneschaucy* the pervasiveness of a money economy. In 1900 Simmel had little way of knowing how wrong his notions of the "rise of the money economy" were to prove in actual as against philosophical historical research. At that time only a few lone geniuses like Frederick Maitland had it right. It has subsequently been discovered that everything was for sale for money in olden times—for instance, husbands and eternal salvation. People in 1300 thought of values down to the last farthing.

Where Simmel is correct, however, is again that attitudes and commonplace rhetoric about prudence and temperance did change from 1600 to 1800. Shakespeare's *Henry V* does not of course tell what the real, historical king was doing or thinking or saying in the weeks leading up to the battle (though some of the speeches were inspired by passages in *Holinshed's Chronicles*). *Henry V* tells about sixteenth-century attitudes, rhetorics, ideologies—what was expected to be mouthed by stage noblemen in the last years of Elizabeth's England. It was a place in which only rank ennobled and honor to the lowborn came only through loyalty to the nobles. Before the taking of Harfleur ("Once more unto the breach, dear friends" [3.1.1]), Henry declares,

> there's none of you so mean and base
> That hath not noble lustre in your eyes. (3.1.29–30)

And before Agincourt, he says:

> For he today that sheds his blood with me
> Shall be my brother; be he ne'er so vile,
> This day shall gentle his condition. (4.3.61–63)

On the eve of the battle, out of earshot of Henry, the king's uncle grimly notes the disadvantage in numbers: "There's five to one. Besides, they all are fresh," at which the Earl of Salisbury exclaims in agreement, "God's arm strike with us! 'Tis a fearful odds" (4.3.5). The king comes onto the scene, and the Earl of Westmoreland continues the calculative talk:

> O that we now had here
> But one ten thousand of those men in England
> That do no work today! (4.3.16–18)

To which Henry, now fully on the scene, replies, scorning such bourgeois considerations:

> If we are marked to die, we are enough
> To do our country loss; and if to live,
> The fewer men, the greater the share of honor. (4.3.20–22)

And he ends most gloriously. One can imagine how British audiences reacted to Laurence Olivier's version in the heroic days of 1944:

> And gentlemen in England now abed
> Shall think themselves accursed they were not here,
> And hold their manhoods cheap whiles any speaks
> That fought with us upon Saint Crispin's Day. (4.3.34–37)

This is not bourgeois, prudential rhetoric, and counts not the cost.

The English were notorious in the Elizabethan Age for such proud, impulsive, decidedly unbourgeois behavior, supported by the corresponding elevation in their talk of aristocratic values. A Dutch businessman in the early seventeenth century declared that the English "are bold, courageous, ardent and cruel in war, but very inconstant, rash, vainglorious, light and deceiving, and very suspicious, especially of foreigners, whom they despise."[55] The Low Countries were at the time the point of contrast. Well into the eighteenth century Holland served as a model for the English and Scots of how to be thrifty and bourgeois—and certainly how to talk it.

The rising class in the English sixteenth and seventeenth centuries was not the bourgeoisie but the gentry, viewed as one of two classes of "gentlemen" below England's exceptionally tiny aristocracy. Yet a mere hundred years after Shakespeare the English, surprisingly, were very busy transforming themselves from admirers of the aristocracy into admirers of the bourgeoisie. Even the gentry and aristocracy gradually became businesslike about their landholdings. In the 1690s, with a Dutch king, the William of William and Mary, the British proceeded to adopt Dutch institutions—such as a central bank and a national debt and a stock market—and undertook to cease being inconstant, rash, vainglorious, light, and deceiving (though remaining "suspicious and despising of foreigners"), or at least to cease talking about it. Evidently something changed during the late seventeenth century in the evaluation of prudent temperance as against courageous hope, and so too in the evaluation of thrift.

The admiration had long-term consequences. The elite's behavior changed some, but its theory of behavior, once hostile to bourgeois values, changed more. The king did not believe any longer that he could by right seize money from the city of London. The effective rulers of Britain became more and more mercantilist (c. 1700) and then free trading (c. 1840)—anyway more and more concerned with national profit and loss. As Charles Louis de Secondat, Baron de Montesquieu, put it in 1748, "Other nations have made the interests of commerce yield to those of politics; the English, on the contrary, have ever made their political interests give way to those of commerce."[56] Well, not ever, but by 1748, often. Such an ordering of ideas was second nature to the Dutch in 1600. It had to be learned by the British. The British became known as unusually calculating instead of, as before, unusually careless in calculating. The actual change in individual behavior was not great. Right up to the nineteenth century the rest of the world was astonished by the aristocratic/peasant brutality of British soldiers. But the change in ideology was great and permanent and finally softening.

In his survey of its history 1727 to 1783 Paul Langford characterizes England as by then thoroughly bourgeois, "a polite and commercial people" (in the phrase from William Blackstone that Langford uses as his title). As early as 1733, Langford claims, a century before the Reform Bill that gave some few of them a direct political voice, "the shopkeepers and tradesmen of England were immensely powerful as a class." He speaks of buying power. "The seeming passion for aristocratic values" evinced, for example, in the vogue for spas such as Bath and a little later seaside resorts such as Brighton, depended on a middle-class clientele—the upper-middling sorts described in Jane Austen's novels, not the lesser merchants in the cities but a gentry increasingly accepting merchant values. "Bath owed its name to the great but its fortune to the mass of middling."[57] Langford quarrels repeatedly with the more usual notion that aristocratic values ruled in the age of the Whig grandees.[58] Britain in the eighteenth century, Langford claims, was if anything a plutocracy, not an aristocracy, a place where wealth, even wealth gained in bourgeois ways, gave power.

It was the base. In the superstructure still more was happening. The first voice of bourgeois theorizing in English is Joseph Addison. "With *The Spectator* [1711–12 and 1714] the voice of the *bourgeois*," Basil Willey declares, "is first heard in polite letters, and makes his first decisive contribution to the English moral tradition." Addison was "the first lay preacher to reach the ear of the middle-classes," though it would seem that for the less highbrow, middling sort Defoe scoops him by a decade or so, and Addison's colleague Richard Steele lasted longer in the pulpit. "The hour was ripe for a rehabilitation of the virtues" [against aristocratic Restoration cynicism]. Addison and Steele "were the very men for the task."[59] Decades later the Dutch returned the favor of the Addisonian project of translating the bourgeois virtues of Holland. They published "Spectatorial Papers" in explicit imitation, against a perceived corruption even in Holland of the bourgeois virtues by French manners, effeminacy, nepotism, and sleeping late.[60]

A long-evolving orthodoxy in English history claims that, on the contrary, England long espoused a "gentlemanly capitalism" hostile to bourgeois values.[61] Right through late Victorian times and beyond, it is said, capitalism was trammeled by estate-yearning and cricket-loving people. It seems a dubious claim. To lament the economic "failure" of the first industrial nation, which has remained from 1700 to the present one of the richest countries in the world, has always seemed a trifle strange. From the time of atmospheric steam engines to the present, England and Scotland together have been world centers for invention: modern steel, radar, penicillin, and magnetic resonance imaging, to name a few.[62] A surprisingly high percentage of world inventions still come out of little Britain. And as E. P. Thompson pointed out early in the debate about gentlemanly capitalism, the landed aristocrats themselves, and their protective belt of gentry, came to be bourgeois in values. They labored at high farming the way their financiers in London labored at deal making and their manufacturing countrymen in Lancashire labored at spinning cotton. And they honored such labor.

As Stephen Greenblatt notes, in Shakespearean England "there was virtually no respect for labor; on the contrary, it was idleness that was prized and honored."[63] Real aristocrats fight; priests worship; the rest work. Prey, pray, and pay. "As for gentlemen," writes one of their number in Shakespeare's time, "whosoever . . . can live idly and without manual labor . . . he shall be called master."[64] Into the twentieth century in England the word *gentleman* meant, "often, a man whose means enable him to live in easy circumstances without engaging in trade"—a man who did not need to work at anything.[65] The shift in the meaning of the word—its present meaning of course is "any adult male in sight," as in "ladies and gentlemen of the jury"—follows the spread of work-admiring middle-class values.

Bourgeois labor is dealing, managing, advising. It is verbal work, the issuing of orders, the speaking of ideas, the calculating of amounts—what you and I are doing now, for instance. Unsurprisingly, the word *gentleman* in English shifts away from the honoring of idleness and toward the admiring of the economic virtues of thrift and diligence first in bourgeois America. Everyone in the American middle class, from the small-town plumbing contractor to the captain of industry, admires purposeful, energetic work with words and in a democratic spirit does not disdain helping out occasionally with the manual labor, either. Get busy! Even professors in America are businesspeople, as, for instance, Morris Zapp in David Lodge's early academic novels or Stanley Fish in real life. Busy, busy, busy. An American professor does the job, he says to himself proudly, whether the work is of brain or of hand. Get the job done. Henry Ford inspected the line. Sam Walton stocked the shelves.

In *On Duties* (c. 44 B.C.) Cicero declares that the four pagan virtues constitute a man's *honestas*, there meaning simply "rectitude, moral worthiness."[66] But in Latin *honestas* also means "honor" in the aristocratic sense—that is, reputation—as does exclusively its reconstructed root *honos* without suffix and the usual *honōs* (genitive *honōris*) or simply *honor*. The Romans used rather the original of our *sincere*, originally meaning "pure," for what we now call *honest*. *Sinceritas* was not highly esteemed in a shame culture of aristocrats, and in fact this particular form is not attested before Augustus. At Rome and in its offshoots ethical goodness was what was worthy of esteem in a man of honor. "To live honorably" is the modern English translation of the advice in Justinian's treatise on Roman law in A.D. 533, *honeste vivere*, not our modern "live honestly."[67] Truth telling was distinctly secondary to this notion of *honestas*. Think of the haughty virtues, the *dignitas*, the willingness to say what is appropriate, not what is true, of Henry V or of a Mafia don.

Othello's repeatedly addressing his friend as "honest Iago" (*Othello* 1.3.293, 2.3.160) and, just before he discovers Iago's lies, as "My friend, your husband, honest, honest Iago" (5.2.162) is therefore not quite so crude a case of dramatic irony as appears to us now. In *Othello* as most usually in Shakespeare the word *honest* means chiefly "honorable," as men still speak in jest of the purity of an "honest" woman. This sense with reference to women is also very common in Shakespeare. For example, it is used eight times in *Othello* about Desdemona: "I do not think but Desdemona's honest" (3.3.230).

Consider these lines:

> O brave Iago, honest and just,
> That hast such noble sense of thy friend's wrong. (5.1.32–33)

Iago is here characterized as a warrior—*brave* and *noble* as an honorable warrior should be—though as it will turn out he has neither integrity nor a sense of justice. In *Othello* the word is used twenty-five times about dishonorable Iago: of these references, nine are made by Iago himself and fourteen by the tragically misled Othello. The play cites *honest* and *honesty* fully fifty-three times—as against only five times in *Macbeth*, ten in *King Lear*, sixteen in *Hamlet*, or twenty-nine even in *The Winter's Tale*—all of which, like most of Shakespeare, are centrally concerned with honor and falsity.[68] In 1713 Anthony Ashley Cooper, Third Earl of Shaftesbury, was still using *honest* to mean "honorable, virtuous." He inquired, "What honesty or virtue is, considered by itself," and concluded piously that "it is impossible for an atheist to be virtuous, or share any real degree of honesty, or merit."[69]

The same happens in French: *honnête* has an obsolete sense of "civil, courteous"; and *honnêteté* an obsolete sense of "virtue, decency." By now *honnête* means only telling the truth. The same shift occurs, too, in Germanic languages, with an entirely different root word. The usual Dutch or German words for *honesty* now mean telling the truth, but in olden days—as in Latin-derived languages before the rise of the bourgeoisie to social prestige—they meant noble honor. In modern Dutch, *eerlijkheid* means simply "honesty," as in *eerlijkheid duurt 't langst*, "honesty lasts the longest" (i.e., "honesty is the best policy"). But it arises, as in French and English, from honor words in a very different society. The Dutch element *eer* itself still today means "honor": *eerbaarheid*, "chastity"; *eergevoel*, "sense of honor" (lit. "honor feeling"); *eren*, "to honor or revere" (as in Dutch hymns to *de Heer*); *erezaak*, "a point of honor"; and even old *eerverlies*, "corruption of blood lines."

The *Oxford English Dictionary* notes that *honest* meaning "held in honor" or "respectable" (sense 1a), from *honestas* by way of French, was obsolete after 1692. It is just about the time, as I said, that England became as bourgeois and thrifty as the Dutch Republic. The last citation in the *OED* of the meaning "commendable" (sense 2a) cites Alexander Pope's *Iliad* of 1715–20. It is just about the time England and Europe generally had their first fully capitalist financial crash. Financial crashes characterize capitalism precisely because a market society depends on the *honesty* of strangers, in the modern sense. The Dutch tulip boom and bust in the 1630s had depended on it. The meaning of *honesty* as "sincere," says the *OED*, is "the prevailing modern sense" (sense 3c), though used occasionally this way from Middle English. In *Othello* the two senses of it, honorable and sincere, mingle, to ominous effect.[70]

It is no surprise that in a commercial democracy such as ours the word *honesty* has come to signify instead *our* master virtue, the egalitarian and bourgeois equivalent of an aristocratic and anticommercial "honor." John Casey is astonished that honor "today . . . finds almost no place in the thought of moral philosophers," though it was central in the Renaissance and before.[71] But that is because honor has been replaced by honesty, which in a bourgeois society plays an identical social role. In *The Stones of Venice* John Ruskin remarks, after a long disquisition on the origin of virtue lists, "It is curious that in none of these [Italian] lists do we find either *Honesty* or *Industry* ranked as a virtue, except in the Venetian one."[72] Surely it is not so curious, considering the frankly bourgeois and busy character of the Venetian Republic at its height, in contrast with the honor-obsessed cultures of contemporary feudal societies like France or England. As Ruskin notes, later the virtue of "industry, in Northern [that is, protobourgeois French, German, Dutch, and English] art and Northern morality, assumes a principal place."[73]

What, then, of the society the English were imitating, the Dutch? By 1600 the Dutch were already thoroughly bourgeois and devoted to bourgeois notions of the value of thrift. As the Dutch Liberal historian Johan Huizinga wrote in 1935, "We [Dutch] are essentially unheroic. Our character lacks the wildness and fierceness that we usually associate with Spain from Cervantes to Calderòn, with the France of the *Three Musketeers* and the England of Cavaliers and Roundheads. . . . A state formed by prosperous burghers living in fairly large cities and by fairly satisfied farmers and peasants is not the soil in which flourishes what goes by the name of heroism. . . . Whether we fly high or low, we Dutchmen are all bourgeois—lawyer and poet, baron and laborer alike."[74]

Simon Schama detests this notion that the Dutch were "bourgeois," because he associates the word with vulgar Marxism, in which *bourgeois* means "bad person." ("Oh, Daddy, you're so *bourgeois*!" exclaims the teenage girl.) Schama prefers *burgher*, which he understands as public-spirited "citizen" as against the Mr. Moneybags of Marxist fable. "To be a Dutch burgher," Schama declares, "meant avoiding being either godless or helpless."[75] Quite. "Money-making, which the Calvinist Church so detested," writes Schama (who, we should note, is right again—people who in thinking the opposite believe they are following Weber are wrong), "was tolerated by distinguishing between proper and improper ways of making fortunes, and the concept of wealth as stewardship."[76] The Left could here note sarcastically, and accurately, that in the seventeenth century the proper "stewardship" included piracy, slave trading, and shocking colonial exploitation. "To be Dutch," he concludes, "still means coming to terms with the moral ambiguities of materialism," now as in the Golden Age.[77]

But coming to terms with the moral ambiguities of materialism is the life of *any* bourgeois person, Dutch or Florentine, American or English, Japanese or South Asian. The question always is, What is your admirable thrift *for*? The early Medici bankers, two centuries before Schama's Dutch, writes Tim Parks, faced the same problem in ethical mechanics. "Precisely because [Cosimo il Vecchio] cares about his eternal soul he is aware of a fierce tension between the competing demands of the sacred and the secular. A rich and powerful man who is also a devout Christian must needs be anxious."[78] Such a bourgeois anxiety, Parks notes, would not characterize the late Medici, who were by that time aristocratic dukes rather than high-bourgeois bankers.

The anxiety-producing tension between the sacred and the profane has been an obsession in Christianity since the Sermon on the Mount. A hungry peasant or a well-heeled aristocrat has, as we say, no issues with money and consumption. It's "eat black bread every chance you get" or "endow St. Paul's with stained glass." No issues there. But the *middenstand* live with the moral ambiguities of materialism. It is why thrift is a bourgeois issue. The bourgeoisie have after all so very much of that matter to be thrifty or profligate about, and they know how it was earned, because they just earned it. Should a tithe for my church be reckoned before or after taxes? Is it hubris for Silas Lapham to build a vulgar house in the Back Bay? Should Emma Woodhouse persuade Harriet Smith not to marry a mere farmer?

As Schama himself concedes, "The tensions of a capitalism that endeavored to make itself moral were the same whether in sixteenth-century Venice, seventeenth-century Amsterdam or eighteenth-century London."[79] *That* is the right tactic for discussions about the rise of the bourgeoisie and the gospel of thrift: namely, to note and analyze its ethical tensions. The mistake is to flee from the very word *bourgeois* because some people use it to mean "bad bosses," or indeed from the word *ethics* because some people use it to mean "inessential rules of business just short of indictable crimes," or *morality* because some people use it to mean "puritanical, sex-obsessed hypocrisy."

"The effort to moralize materialism" is told in the Netherlands, of course, in characteristically Dutch ways, which Schama persuasively illustrates. But is the moral effort especially Dutch? *Ik denk het niet.* I don't think the Dutch moralized their riches and other bourgeois do not. The American bourgeoisie moralizes its riches as just rewards for cowboy courage, or as a gospel of philanthropy of the Carnegie-Mellon type, or as a democratic creed of opportunity seized. The Hindu bourgeoisie moralizes its riches as the favor of Ganesh or the expression of spiritual worth from a previous reincarnation or as provisioning for those pesky cousins. As behavior, of course, a sheer materialism without sincere reference to the transcendent is common enough in all societies, bourgeois or not. But it is the official theory of none. Official theories are about the transcendent, a beyond. Every human, whether bourgeois and thrifty or aristocratic and spendthrift, seeks it.

The Dutch were not exceptional in their positive evaluation of thrift; they were merely a century early compared with the English or the Americans and a century later compared with the Florentines and Venetians. *Bourgeois* can mean, if we wish to use words this way—and can get over being spooked by Marx—"city dweller practicing an honored profession or owning a business or functioning at a managerial level in someone else's enterprise, including governmental and nonprofit enterprises." Such a person faces a particular set of ethical problems. She has the anxious ethical task of learning how to be a counselor yet be self-prudent, to be a saleswoman yet be other-loving, to be a boss yet be just, to be a bureaucrat yet be courageous, to be a scientist yet be faithful. Above all she needs to be thrifty but virtuous. Schama is right to emphasize the ethical tensions of capitalism. But the Dutch are merely an early instance, as the Venetians and Florentines and Genoese were still earlier, with the Hanseatic League in attendance, and Osakans and Singaporeans later, of a by now worldwide social class and a by now worldwide ethical problem, namely, the tensions of bourgeoisness ascendant.

There are many tales told about the prehistory of thrift. The central tales are Marxist or Weberian. Both are mistaken. Accumulation has not been the heart of modern economic growth, nor has it been the heart of the change from the medieval to the early modern economy or from the early modern to the fully modern economy. If you personally wish to grow a little rich, by all means be thrifty and thereby accumulate. But if you wish your society to be remarkably rich, you should rather work for it to be open to new ideas and thereby educate. *Thrift* has been much honored in American civic theology. But like many other of the sacred words, such as *democracy* or *equality* or *opportunity* or *progress*, its rhetorical force turns out to be more important historically than its material force. It's time for the old tales of thriftiness to be retired.

Notes

Portions of this essay are taken from my recent book, *The Bourgeois Virtues: Ethics for an Age of Commerce* (Chicago: University of Chicago Press, 2006), which I heartily recommend, and from a sequel to that book, *Bourgeois Dignity: Why Economics Can't Explain the Modern World* (2010), and, in progress, *The Bourgeois Revaluation: How Innovation Became Ethical, 1600–1848.*

1. Adrienne Rich, "Anne Bradstreet and Her Poetry," in *The Works of Anne Bradstreet*, ed. J. Hensley (Cambridge, MA: Harvard University Press, 1967), xiv–xv.

2. Thomas Tusser, *Five Hundred Points of Good Husbandry* (1574; London: Lackington, Allen, 1812), 19.

3. *The Koran Interpreted*, trans. A. J. Arberry (Oxford: Oxford University Press, 1998). All quotations from the Koran come from this translation.

4. Digha Nikayu, in *Sources of Indian Tradition*, ed. William Theodore de Bary (New York: Columbia University Press, 1963), 1:122.

5. A. L. Basham, in *From the Beginning to 1800*, vol. 1 of *Sources of Indian Tradition*, 2nd ed., ed. Ainslee Embree (New York: Columbia University Press, 1988), 151.

6. Walter of Henley, *The Husbandry*, in *Walter of Henley and Other Treatises on Estate Management and Accounting*, ed. Dorothea Oschinky (Oxford: Clarendon, 1971), 309.

7. *Seneschaucy*, in *Walter of Henley and Other Treatises on Estate Management and Accounting*, ed. Dorothea Oschinky (Oxford: Clarendon, 1971), 269.

8. Tusser, "Good Husbandly Lessons," in *Five Hundred Points*, 26.

9. Charles Dickens, *David Copperfield* (New York: Modern Library, 2000), 116.

10. Deirdre N. McCloskey and John Nash, "Corn at Interest: The Extent and Cost of Grain Storage in Medieval England," *American Economic Review* 74 (March 1984): 174–87.

11. Robert W. Fogel, *The Escape from Hunger and Premature Death, 1700–2100: Europe, America, and the Third World* (Cambridge: Cambridge University Press, 2004).

12. Stephen Innes, "Introduction: Fulfilling John Smith's Vision," in *Work and Labor in Early America*, ed. Stephen Innes (Chapel Hill: University of North Carolina Press, 1988), 5.

13. Max Weber, *The Protestant Ethic and the Spirit of Capitalism*, trans. Talcott Parsons (1904–5; New York: Scribner's, 1958), 17. Weber also writes, "The notion that our rationalistic and capitalistic age is characterized by a stronger economic interest than other periods is childish." Max Weber, *General Economic History*, trans. Frank Knight (1923; London: Allen and Unwin, 1927), 355.

14. The *Aeneid of Virgil* 3.73, author's translation.

15. Weber, *Protestant Ethic*, 17.

16. *Boswell's Life of Johnson*, April 14, 1778, quoted in Peter Mathias, "Dr. Johnson and the Business World," in *The Transformation of England: Essays in the Economic and Social History of England in the Eighteenth Century* (New York: Columbia University Press, 1979), 302.

17. Karl Marx, *Capital: A Critique of Political Economy*, ed. F. Engels, trans. S. Moore and E. Aveling (1867; New York: Modern Library, n.d.), 1:651 (24.3).

18. Ibid., 1:170–71 (4).

19. See, e.g., ibid., 1:641 (24.1) and 1:784 (26): "We have seen how money is changed into capital; how through capital surplus-value is made, and from surplus value more capital."

20. Santhi Hejeebu and I have laid out the case against Karl Polanyi's economic history in "The Reproving of Karl Polanyi," *Critical Review* 13 (Summer/Fall 1999): 285-314.

21. Robert Heilbroner, *The Worldly Philosophers: The Lives, Times, and Ideas of the Great Economic Thinkers*, 7th ed. (1953; New York: Simon and Schuster, 1996), 201. Cf. 156, "an owner-entrepreneur engaged in an endless race," and so forth.

22. Weber, *Protestant Ethic*, 51 (emphasis added).

23. Marx, *Capital*, 652 (24). And "accumulation for accumulation's sake, production for production's sake."

24. See D. H. Lawrence, "Benjamin Franklin," chap. 2 of *Studies in Classic American Literature* (1923; Harmondsworth, UK: Penguin Books, 1971). The most well known of the amused ironies is Franklin's comment on a late addition to his list of virtues, humility: "I cannot boast of much success in acquiring the *reality* of this virtue; but I had a good deal with regard to the *appearance* of it." (Claude-Anne Lopez remarked once that Franklin will lack a full biography until someone with a sense of humor attempts it.)

25. Weber, *Protestant Ethic*, 51 (emphasis added).

26. Joan C. Tronto, *Moral Boundaries: A Political Argument for an Ethics of Care* (New York: Routledge, 1993), 29.

27. Thomas Haskell, quoted in Innes, "Introduction," 39n61.

28. Alan Macfarlane, *The Culture of Capitalism* (Oxford: Blackwell, 1987), 226.

29. Adam Smith, *The Theory of Moral Sentiments*, Glasgow ed., ed. D. D. Raphael and A. L. Macfie (1759; Indianapolis: Liberty Classics, 1982), 173 (3.6.6).

30. Simon Kuznets and later Charles Feinstein provided the rigorous accounting of the fact. It was anticipated in the 1950s and 1960s by virtually the entire profession of British economic historians, in detailed studies of banking and manufacturing. Peter Mathias gives a good summary and remarks that "considerable revaluation has recently occurred in assessing the role of capital." Peter Mathias, "Credit, Capital and Enterprise in the Industrial Revolution," in *The Transformation of England: Essays in the Economic and Social History of England in the Eighteenth Century* (New York: Columbia University Press, 1979), 88–115.

31. Karl Marx, *The Communist Manifesto*, Norton Critical Edition (New York: Norton, 1988), 59.

32. Walt W. Rostow, *The Stages of Economic Growth: A Non-Communist Manifesto* (Cambridge: Cambridge University Press, 1960); William Easterly, *The Elusive Quest for Growth: Economists' Adventures and Misadventures in the Tropics* (Cambridge, MA: MIT Press, 2001).

33. Angus Maddison, *The World Economy: A Millennial Perspective* (Paris: Organization for Economic Cooperation and Development, 2001).

34. Deirdre N. McCloskey, "The Industrial Revolution, 1780–1860: A Survey," chap. 6 of *The Economic History of Britain, 1700–Present*, ed. Roderick Floud and Deirdre McCloskey (Cambridge: Cambridge University Press, 1981), 1:103–27.

35. G. T. Jones should be better known among economists. A student of Alfred Marshall, he anticipated the mathematics of the "residual." He died young, and his work was forgotten except by economic historians. G. T. Jones, *Increasing Returns* (Cambridge: Cambridge University Press, 1933).

36. Kenneth Pomeranz, *The Great Divergence: China, Europe, and the Making of the Modern World* (Princeton, NJ: Princeton University Press, 2001).

37. Marx, *Capital*, 784.

38. Alexander Gerschenkron, "Reflections on the Concept of 'Prerequisites' of Modern Industrialization," in *Economic Backwardness in Historical Perspective: A Book of Essays* (Cambridge, MA: Harvard University Press, 1962), 33.

39. Marx, *Capital*, 656 (24.3).

40. Ibid., 785.

41. Ibid., 833.

42. Immanuel Wallerstein, *Capitalist Agriculture and the Origins of the European World-Economy in the Sixteenth Century*, vol. 1 of *The Modern World-System* (New York: Academic Press, 1974).

43. Arberry, trans., *Koran Interpreted*, 269; Augustine, *Confessions*, trans. F. J. Sheed (New York: Sheed and Ward, 1943), 4.10.

44. See Douglass North's *Understanding the Process of Economic Change* and Sheilagh Ogilvie's devastating empirical inquiry into the Panglossian hypothesis. Douglass C. North, *Understanding the Process of Economic Change*, Princeton Economic History of the Western World (Princeton, NJ: Princeton University Press, 2005); Sheilagh Ogilvie, "Guilds, Efficiency, and Social Capital: Evidence from German Proto-industry," *Economic History Review* 57 (May 2004): 286–333.

45. Marx, *Capital*, 794.

46. Joel Mokyr, *The Gifts of Athena: Historical Origins of the Knowledge Economy* (Princeton, NJ: Princeton University Press, 2002), 297.

47. See. e.g., Jean Baechler, *The Origins of Capitalism*, trans. Barry Cooper (Oxford: Blackwell, 1975); William H. McNeill, *The Pursuit of Power: Technology, Armed Force, and Society since a.d. 1000* (Chicago: University of Chicago Press, 1982); E. L. Jones, *Growth Recurring* (Oxford: Oxford University Press, 1988); Charles Tilly, *Coercion, Capital, and European States, a.d. 990–1900* (Oxford: Blackwell, 1990); Alan Macfarlane, *The Riddle of the Modern World: Of Liberty, Wealth, and Equality* (Basingstoke, UK: Palgrave, 2000).

48. John Winthrop, quoted in Stephen Innes, "Puritanism and Capitalism in Early Massachusetts," in *Capitalism in Context: Essays on Economic Development and Cultural Change in Honor of R. M. Hartwell*, ed. J. A. James and M. Thomas (Chicago: University of Chicago Press, 1994), 106.

49. Charles Davenant, quoted in Charles Wilson, *England's Apprenticeship: 1603–1763*, (New York: St. Martin's Press, 1965), 155–56.

50. Lisa Jardine and Alan Stewart, *Hostage of Fortune: The Troubled Life of Francis Bacon, 1561–1626* (London: Victor Gollanzm, 1998), 433.

51. William Shakespeare, *The Norton Shakespeare*, ed. Stephen Greenblatt (New York: Norton, 1997). All Shakespeare quotations come from this translation; references are to act, scene, and line.

52. John Keegan, *The Face of Battle: A Study of Agincourt, Waterloo, and the Somme* (New York: Penguin Books, 1978), 90.

53. Georg Simmel, *The Philosophy of Money*, 2nd ed., ed. D. Frisby, trans. T. Bottomore, D. Frisby, and K. Mengelberg (London: Routledge, 1990), 444.

54. Ernest Renan, quoted in James Wood, *The Broken Estate: Essays on Literature and Belief* (New York: Random House, 1999), 262.

55. Quoted in Jeremy Paxman, *The English: A Portrait of a People* (London: Penguin Books, 1999), 35.

56. Charles Louis de Secondat, Baron de Montesquieu, *The Spirit of the Laws* (1748), 2.7, quoted in Innes, "Puritanism and Capitalism," 96.

57. Paul Langford, *A Polite and Commercial People: England 1727–1783* (Oxford: Oxford University Press, 1992), 5, 30, 107.

58. Ibid., 5, 61, 105.

59. Basil Willey, *English Moralists* (London: Chatto and Windus, 1964), 221, 223, 228.

60. Dorothee Sturkenboom, *De elektrieke kus. Over vrouwen, fysica en vriendschap in de 18de en 19de eeuw. Het verhaal van het Natuurkundig Genootschap der Dames in Middelburg* (Amsterdam: Augustus, 2004).

61. Pat Hudson gives a brief but penetrating introduction to the issue in her lucid classic, *The Industrial Revolution* (Sevenoaks, Kent, UK: Edward Arnold, 1992), 218–25.

62. This has been argued in detail by David Edgerton, *Science, Technology, and the British Industrial "Decline," 1870–1970* (Cambridge: Cambridge University Press, 1996), and *Warfare State Britain, 1920–1970* (Cambridge: Cambridge University Press, 2005).

63. Stephen J. Greenblatt, *Will in the World: How Shakespeare Became Shakespeare* (New York: Norton, 2004), 76.

64. Quoted in ibid., 77.

65. As elsewhere, unattributed word-lore is from *The Oxford English Dictionary*.

66. Marcus Tullius Cicero, *De officiis* [Concerning Duties], trans. W. Miller, Loeb Classical Library (Cambridge, MA: Harvard University Press, 1913), 1.61.

67. Justinian, *Institutes*, trans. P. Birks and G. McLeod (Ithaca, NY: Cornell University Press, 1987), 1 (1.1).

68. These data were collected using the complete, searchable texts available at http://shakespeare.mit.edu.

69. Anthony Ashley Cooper, 3rd Earl of Shaftesbury, *Characteristics of Men, Manners, Opinions, Times*, 6th (1732) ed. (Indianapolis: Liberty Fund, 2001), 2:4. Cf. 2:8: "honest or moral character."

70. See, e.g., *Othello* 1.3.283, 293, 382; 2.1.198; 2.3.6, 125, 160, 230, 249, 309–15; 3.1.20–21, 38; 3.2.5; 3.3.105–7, 123, 130, 134, 158, 229, 247, 262, 380–89, 417, 438; 5.1.32; 5.79, 155, 161.

71. John Casey, *Pagan Virtue: An Essay in Ethics* (Cambridge: Cambridge University Press, 1990), 83.

72. John Ruskin, *The Stones of Venice* (1851–53; New York: Wiley, 1880), 329 (2.8.64).

73. Ibid., 328 (2.8.64).

74. Johan H. Huizinga, "The Spirit of the Netherlands," in *Dutch Civilization in the Seventeenth Century and Other Essays*, trans. A. J. Pomerans, ed. Pieter Geyl and F. W. N. Hugenholtz (1935; London: Collins, 1968), 110–12.

75. Simon Schama, *The Embarrassment of Riches: An Interpretation of Dutch Culture in the Golden Age* (New York: Knopf, 1987), 420.

76. Ibid.

77. Ibid., 609.

78. Tim Parks, "The Cosimos," review of *Cosimo de' Medici and the Florentine Renaissance*, by Dale Kent, and *The Medici, Michelangelo, and the Art of Late Renaissance Florence*, by Cristina Acidini Luchinat et al., *New York Review of Books*, December 19, 2002, 76.

79. Schama, *Embarrassment of Riches*, 49.

4 }

Saving Grace and Moral Striving

THRIFT IN PURITAN THEOLOGY

James Calvin Davis and Charles Mathewes

Any examination of thrift in American culture must begin by understanding the significance of thrift in the Puritan moral worldview. Thrift was an important moral discipline to the Puritans; they understood it to respect God's sovereignty, cohere with the ultimate ends of human existence (i.e., stewardship and worship), and serve the evangelistic cause. The moral imperative to exercise thrift was rooted in the experience of grace and embedded within the broader theological themes of providence, sanctification, and calling. At the same time, thrift was not treated as an unqualified good, as some readers of Max Weber seem to think; it was always governed by the theological conviction that all must serve the common good. Nonetheless, the Puritans believed that the experience of God's grace invited and compelled a person to live a life normally characterized by, among other virtues, thrift. How this tradition got from grace to thrift—that is, from the reception of excessive and unmerited beneficence to a response characterized by restraint and restriction—is the question that governs this essay.

We define *thrift* as a practical habit expressive of a whole habitus, one with deep theological implications, a way of being in the world that treats the world with a conserving care. This quite broad definition sets us on a different and more fruitful track than that taken by those who would define thrift more narrowly, as the fact of the saving of wealth by humans. Certainly such definitions have a great deal of analytic clarity. But they are typically offered as part of an argument that thrift has no history, that it has been a fact of human existence since the beginning—and that there is therefore nothing interesting to say about thrift's career in modernity. As Deirdre McCloskey puts it, in her important (and factually rich) contribution to this volume, because "actual saving was high before modern times, and did not change much with modern capitalism,"[1] therefore there is no "there" there—there is no discrete issue of the peculiar career of "thrift" in the modern world. But this is mistaken on two counts. First of all, it relies on a contestable perennialism that, however axiomatic it is to a particular brand of social science, makes it difficult for its adherents to recognize important historical changes when they occur. (So, for example, the fact that the United States' individual savings rates have dropped to a *negative* rate—so that we are collectively borrowing more money than we make—is likely to be dismissed by such an axiomatic approach as a short-term trend that will inevitably be corrected, rather than investigated as an interesting cultural phenomenon.) One's scholarly tools ought to make one more sensitive to potential sites of fruitful investigation, not less. Second, and more important for our purposes, it misunderstands the object under investigation. We are not asking simply about the fact of economic savings, the act of saving wages or products earned or created "now" for some time "later"; rather, we are concerned with the meaning that people have attached to this act. And whatever you say about average saving rates across time, it is pretty clear to us that the idea of thrift, its inner meaning, and its place in a larger way of life have changed dramatically over time.

None of this is to say that there were no antecedents to the modern idea of thrift. That idea did not spring ex nihilo out of some sort of fundamentally killjoy mentality that crabbed the Puritan mind; the recourse to the Puritans' understanding of economic conservation was prompted by their own historical experiences, and especially by their abhorrence of what they saw as a moral and theological crisis in early modern England. This puts the lie to nostalgic medievalists' assaults on thrift as fundamentally hostile to happiness. For the Puritans, thrift is contrasted not to the gratuitous joyous giving of feast days but rather to the dissoluteness and the "crisis of drunkenness" that Puritans were not alone in perceiving in the England of the early seventeenth century. In this context, thrift was offered neither as a strategy for economic success, nor as a technology of moral perfection (i.e., a deeply impious kind of power); rather, it was offered as the core of a profound "reform of manners" that would counter this sort of moral dissipation and the pathetically self-aggrandizing and dangerously self-destructive "worldliness" that such dissipation reveals. Thrift was an integral component of the Puritans' understanding of their position *coram Deo*, "before God." It is misunderstood if it is caricatured as miserliness. Thrift was the way to joy; it was the response to grace; it was part of a larger vision of how to inhabit the gift of time itself from God.

The elements of this picture, and much of its organization, predated the Puritans' particular development of it. Hence, to understand the Puritans we explore, in the first section, the deep theological roots of this picture, particularly as found in the Puritans' Augustinian legacy. After doing that, we turn, in the second section, to a direct discussion of the Puritans' depiction of thrift, paying special attention to the theological roots of their thrift proposals.

The Augustinian Legacy

Puritanism is unintelligible without recourse to the theological traditions from which it took its language and cosmology, and preeminent among those is the Augustinian tradition: that tradition of Western Christian thought stemming from Augustine, running through medieval monasticism, and reasserted in the theological vision of Protestant Reformers, particularly John Calvin. Indeed, it would not be wholly inaccurate to say that Puritanism *just is* one appropriation of Augustinianism. In this section we identify the deep structures of Puritanism's theological and sociopolitical imagination in Augustine's thought and explain how the tensions latent in that inheritance led to the dynamics and conflicts that occupied the Puritans and their descendants, up to the present day.

AUGUSTINE: MENDICANTS AND MARTYRS

To understand Augustinianism we must understand Augustine; but our usual pictures of Augustine misunderstand him quite dramatically, precisely because they depict him as a great thinker. This is terribly misleading. Augustine was not an intellectual working in luxurious *otium*, that leisure for which Augustine in his letters repeatedly longed. He was, first and foremost, a bishop, and a bishop at a time when the episcopacy began to assume a central civic role in the life of late antique city. Augustine was pastor to the catholic Christians in his see of Hippo Regius and leader of the monastic community associated with the basilica there, and all of his writing was shaped by the pressing needs of his daily life.

These implications were manifest differently in the "religious" life of the monastery and the secular life of the laity, but they essentially pointed to the same lessons. Speaking monastically, Augustine emphasized the need for visibility and presence, for the monks not to be hidden but to be a public exemplum of the Heavenly Jerusalem that was the destiny of all Christians. As part of their exemplarity, not only did they have to hold all in common (i.e., not have private possessions), but also they in themselves were not to be secreted away somewhere; they were to be visible even in their foibles, violating the frontiers of decorum that separated domestic privacy from public presence in the ancient world. The monks were called to be open in their confessions of weakness and their acknowledgment of difficulty and struggle. Augustine not only urged that this be embodied but also embodied it himself. In his *Confessions*, he discussed matters so private as to make readers even today squirm with displaced embarrassment for him. Speaking communally, he never tried to hide problems or conflicts in the monastery from the world at large; rather, he preached about them publicly and wrote letters about them, letters he knew would spread beyond their intended recipients.[2]

Speaking civically and ecclesially, Augustine always saw his flock as struggling and never flinched from acknowledging that, either to them or to himself. He was, in R. A. Markus's felicitous phrase, a defender of "Christian mediocrity"—of the idea that humans could not make themselves perfect, no matter how hard they tried, and that to think one had to *deserve* God's approval was fundamentally confused.[3] With the audacity of an enthusiastic preacher, Augustine dared to link the quotidian difficulties of his flock with the most holy body of Christian witnesses, the martyrs. In one sermon, he urged:

> We need not hope for that kind of persecution which our ancestors endured at the hands of the earthly powers that be, in order to become martyrs. The world doesn't stop, there is no end to the multitude of trials and temptations. Sometimes you're suffering from a fever, and you are fighting in the arena. . . . You're weak, and you're battling away, and you're winning. . . . Don't count yourself as not being a martyr. Your feast day is not indeed in the calendar, but your crown is ready waiting for you. . . . How many martyrs have left this world from their beds, and as conquerors over that infirmity have passed to the realms above![4]

"The world itself," he says in another sermon, "can be our desert."[5] To identify everyday life with martyrdom, and the ordinary *saeculum* with the holy *eremus*—to place them on a continuum at all, really—was a shocking thing in a time when the magical powers of the holy were granted enormous ontological weight.[6] In his depiction of both consecrated religious life and the life of ordinary Christian laity, Augustine emphasized the sacramentality of everyday human life. The encounter with God takes place not in exceptional moments but in the quotidian minutiae of everyday living; it is there, in the everyday, that we should come to feel the soul-encompassing grip of God's love for us, God's obligations on us, and the primacy of God's grace for us.

This apprehension of the sacramentality of everyday life—albeit at best, because of sin, only ambiguously apprehended—is the keynote of Augustine's vision of human existence before God. Our existence is fraught with moral and spiritual ambiguity, both as regards our own character and in the world as we experience it. Ambiguity is not the same as pessimism, and Augustine is not, as many suggest, a gloomy or grim realist; for beneath this ambiguity lurked a powerfully joyful sense of the eschatological destiny of Creation. But while the world will finally be revealed (or perhaps determined) by God to be a site of joyous glorification of God, at present our world is systematically ambiguous.

This emphasis on ambiguous sacramentality shapes Augustine's vision of how we should inhabit the world. The world's sacramentality is real, though to us in our fallen state obscure; the world speaks of God, but only for those who have ears to hear. God is working to sanctify all aspects of our life, and the world itself is significant of God, fundamentally God's language, which we are called to understand. Therefore our actions in this world are also, and perhaps more basically, a mode of inquiry—attempts to learn to speak that language properly, and thereby come to participate in God's ecstatic joy. In this process what is crucial is how we use the situations in which we find ourselves. Graceful behavior flows naturally from sanctified discernment, which sees God's hand operating in all things and responds appropriately.

It is from this intuition that the "thrift" disposition will later emerge, for it implies that all aspects of existence ought to be sanctifying for us. Our religious obligations are not one segment of our lives but in fact saturate our whole existence. Being thrifty is a way of properly stewarding God's gifts, the better to appreciate each one's distinct preciousness. Just as the root of *thrift* is *thrive*, so for Augustine right use is not life-denying but life-affirming, showing the way to what Saint Paul called "life abundant."

In many ways, misunderstandings of this position misshape contemporary assessments of its plausibility. Perhaps most centrally what we often miss about this vision is its implication that humans are fundamentally responsive, not spontaneous and unconstrained in their being and doing. We are created in love with God, and after the Fall we "have a past," as was once said of people with dubious moral histories, and are bent in self-love. God's gift of grace reorients our vision and our affections, making us see the real structure of things and enabling us, albeit always with a divided heart, to desire to do the right thing as well. In all situations the human is fundamentally responsive—a subject, a patient, a sufferer. Augustine's choice of metaphors for grace are noteworthy. The world is a hospital of grace, a site of healing, not achievement; grace is a medicine, not a steroid.

This picture may be fundamentally foreign to modern thought, but it was pretty common before modernity. Augustine was unusual only in the extent to which he worked out its implications.[7] He used it to transform the traditional moral language of virtue from a heroic, agonal, and warlike language into one of suffering. Here the virtues are ways we resist, through grace, our stubborn and prideful willfulness, our attempt to be our own gods. The virtues are disciplines, granted to us by grace, that allow us to recognize our necessary vulnerability, our need of others and especially the divine Other, to achieve our blessed end. The theological virtues in particular provide a grammar in which to understand our action. They structure our experience of time in a way that makes time itself sanctified and sanctifying, so they provide a fundamental way to understand ourselves as responding to grace—the way we inhabit time, the way we *receive* time. This is not an expression of or longing for power, a technology for spiritual or moral achievement. Moral excellence is found not in an illusion of radical independence but in recognizing our dependencies and filiations; we should aim most fundamentally to be mendicants, begging constantly for forgiveness, entreating God to "grant what you command and command what you will," as Augustine famously put it in book 10 of the *Confessions*. Hence, Augustine presented the Christian life as a life of suffering, of training in longing, of acknowledging and deepening our vulnerability to God, of seeking God's voice in all things and responding to all things as if God were acting on us through those things.

This combination—emphatic public acknowledgment of suffering and weakness with the idea that all aspects of life may be sacramental—played a large role in provoking the so-called Pelagian controversy.[8] The nature and meaning of this controversy are controversial as well. Often this controversy is presented as if it were an academic spat between rival philosophical views over free will and divine providence, or as a political battle by enlightened liberals for human dignity over against Augustine's conservative pessimism. But in fact the controversy was actually a battle between different social imaginations, a battle over the nature of the spiritual hierarchy of the cosmos and, ultimately, a battle about the nature of God; the political and academic languages of our own day are simply anachronistic.[9] Pelagius was an elite ascetic of a sort familiar in the Mediterranean world for almost a millennium, and he thrived in the traditional elite spiritual economy of the perfect and their (largely upper-class) disciples. Such figures had much invested in a particular understanding of religious authority. He and his followers depicted God as a noble Roman landlord, starchy with *dignitas*, magnanimously yet unsmilingly dispensing favors to those who merited it—a role that was well established socially and that was readily understood and accommodated in shaping a life. The language of merit for such figures was not finally something derived from a presumption of human perfectibility; rather, the Pelagians simply could not imagine that God could be radically unlike the social elites of their day. Ironically, the Pelagians, self-proclaimed defenders of the human capacity to change, could not imagine things being radically different. For them, the spiritual economy of the age, as well as the social-economic systems thereof, would continue as it always had. In contrast, Augustine represented the church's new and decidedly un-elite future; as a bishop with a flock, he became increasingly antielitist over his career, insisting that ascetical self-understandings are available to all.[10] He took his images of God from a different source—from the image of the father of the prodigal son, who ran across his fields toward the son who had scorned and shamed him, eschewing decorum and dignity out of joy and love, scandalizing the standards of the time. For Augustine, human life even after redemption is messy and murky, not at all clean and clear, revealing one's own weaknesses and frailties. The house of the Lord is not the ancient gymnasium of the spiritual elect; it is, as we saw, a hospital, in which the sick—all of us called to the kingdom of God—are gradually nursed back to health. Augustine, defender of Christian mediocrity, was a revolutionary, demanding a far greater transformation of life and society than did Pelagius.

The Pelagian controversy rages on to this day as a struggle between defenders of grace and defenders of free will. Augustine was interested not in settling this philosophical question but in keeping alive the tension between divine grace and human agency, thereby setting the terms (quite literally) for later Western theology. Augustine was self-conscious of the tension he was bequeathing and did not want to resolve it. Augustine's late writings contain two remarkable small essays, *On the Gift of Perseverance* and *On the Predestination of the Saints*, which counsel preachers on how to properly explain to congregations the relationship among grace, predestination, and their own agency.[11] His thought framed for its inheritors this question: How can a doctrine of powerful prevenient grace, such as Augustine affirms, coexist with (and ultimately find a functional place within) a moral life plan that can be intentionally undertaken by believers as a way of life? The puzzle was pointedly taken up by Calvin, the sixteenth-century Protestant Reformer who made sense of the tension between the absolute priority of divine grace and the importance of moral agency by accentuating the sacramentality of our worldly existence and giving human agency an explicit theological motive: gratitude.

JOHN CALVIN: THE DISCIPLINE OF GRATITUDE

Everyone knows that Calvin was an Augustinian, especially in his doctrines of sin and predestination. Calvin's context, his background, and his own irreducible quiddity notwithstanding, he stands firmly in the line of his Augustinian antecedents. Calvin's work can be understood as an inquiry into shaping individual and communal life in light of God's electing action: it is in the ordinary living out of one's vocation that we meet the holy and welcome it into our lives and societies. Calvin begins his most famous work, the *Institutes of the Christian Religion*, by tying together the knowledge of God and ourselves, and the theme played there repeats throughout that work: ordinary time and the activities and responsibilities it contains become holy through involvement in the redemptive scheme of a sovereign and gracious God. As a result, both the disciplined inner life and the organized outer life become the means of experiencing grace and inclusion in the kingdom—that is, sanctification leads to a renewed embrace of virtue, law, and one's vocational responsibilities. What Calvin gives special priority are both the high aspirations and the essential motivations for this sanctified, virtuous, grace-responsive life.

The influence of the Augustinian tradition on Calvin was crucially complicated by his training in the culture of Renaissance humanism and especially by his own engagement with Stoicism. (His first book was a commentary on Seneca.) What Calvin took from the Renaissance was what the humanists found in ancient non-Christian philosophy: a way to talk and deliberate about the nature and proper ordering of human life, a style of thought that was fundamentally different from and opposed to (what they saw as) the desiccated and overtechnical jargon of late medieval scholasticism. The cost of the humanist liberation from scholasticism could be (overtly or covertly) a non-Christian picture of the nature and destiny of humanity, whether that was

Neoplatonic or Stoic. While many of the humanists were prepared to pay that price,[12] Calvin was not. To understand why he was not, we must understand the profound differences separating the Stoic worldview from an Augustinian Christian one.

The Stoics based their moral pedagogy on a pantheistic cosmology of sheer immanence. They held that God and the world are only conceptually distinct, with the cosmos being the substance of God and with God the *logos*—the ordering rational principle—being internal to nature.[13] Nature, as ordered by reason, is all there is; and all that is, is fully present in itself. Properly speaking, nothing signifies anything else; each thing is what it is and is not another thing. The Stoic thinks that all is ultimately *insignificant* because all is immanent and so more of the same (what G. W. F. Hegel would call "bad infinity"). The pragmatic upshot of this picture for moral pedagogy is something like fatalism. The goal of the Stoic is to govern one's responses to reality by having a proper valuation of the things affected by reality and, thereby, to submit to necessity in insensible *apatheia*, buffeted by nature, whether for good or ill.

Calvin's understanding of God and of the human differs radically from this Stoicism. Certainly God is no watchtower God, an Aristotelian observer indifferent to the world. Rather, God is radically involved in creating, sustaining, and redeeming the world. This is why Calvin rather notoriously will allow, in a statement that many misread as Stoic, that those who are pious and wise can say that "nature is God," because when we are properly trained, we can discern God's purposes for us shining through nature.[14] But nature is only rightly understood for Calvin when it is understood as *Creation*. God, finally, is not simply and exhaustively present in the immanent and immediate flux of Creation as we find it. God is fundamentally distinct from Creation; Creation is not necessary to God. Yet Creation is, by God's grace, *significant* of God, though that significance is discerned only if it is read aright. (Calvin talks about the graceful person using the "spectacles" of Scripture to read the book of the world aright.)[15] Stoic Fortuna and Christian Providence, as well as Stoic nature and Christian Creation, are fundamentally different ideas, reflecting radically different understandings of the universe (1.16.8).

Furthermore, Calvin thinks the "iron philosophy" of Stoicism built on their metaphysics is psychologically monstrous (e.g., 3.8.9–11). The insensibility the Stoics promote contradicts the "disposition to godliness" they profess to admire (3.8.10). Submission to God's will is not submission to the blind, random necessities of nature: "To bear the cross is not to be utterly stupefied and to be deprived of all feeling of pain" (3.8.9). On the contrary, what such submission promotes is a heightened sensitivity to suffering, albeit suffering of the proper sort—that is, suffering in trust that God will bring good out of the evil we presently endure: "We do not hear that barren incantation, 'We must yield because it is necessary,' but a living and fully effective precept, 'We must obey because it is unlawful to resist; we must bear patiently, since impatience would be insolence against God's righteousness'" (3.8.11). Again, God's will is mediated through the manifold realities of Creation, but it is not identified with Creation. Scripture helps us to read Creation aright, to discern more definitively God's will for us. Reading it makes us sensible not only of the ambiguous status of a Creation caught between sin and grace but also of God's merciful loving-kindness. This then enables the elect's inner apprehension (affective and cognitive) of his or her *election*, which in turn instigates and cultivates affective gratitude in the heart of the faithful. To be a human, then, is to be a creature whose affective response is never finally focused on harmonizing with the melodies of immanent nature, simply because our affective responses are not ultimately responses to nature itself. To attempt to tie the emotions down to the world is a futile and mutilating activity.

Instead Calvin teaches what we may call a discipline of gratitude. In seeing the world as significant of God's providence, we should come to experience God's election of us, so that the central emotion we will feel, and that we ought to cultivate, is ecstatic gratitude and joy. Of course, election in this life has a cruciform character, and so the deeper we enter into this election, the more profound and more profoundly felt our suffering will be. But the elect understand that their suffering bears and shows forth the course of God's providence, and they embrace it with the grateful enthusiasm of redeemed participants in the providential transformation of the world.

It is here that Calvin's perhaps most distinctive contribution to the Augustinian tradition, and certainly most decisive development for the Puritans, is best seen in his explication of the process of sanctification, especially in his well-known development of the "third use of the Law." For previous Protestants, "the Law"—understood as God's commands to us to act in certain ways—had two uses. First, it was a deterrent, restraining evil by encouraging some behaviors and proscribing others; second, it was a "converting ordinance," convicting us of our sinfulness by convincing us that we can never fulfill God's moral requirements, provoking us to despair of our own capacities, and hence driving us to fall at the mercy of God's grace alone. Calvin added a third, "pedagogical" use, whereby the law continued to serve an important function for "believers in whose hearts the Spirit of God already lives and reigns." For the regenerate, the law continued to serve as a guide to the right living that is expected of God's people. Grace empowers the sanctified life, but the law teaches the Christian about what properly constitutes grateful obedience: "Here [the law] is the best instrument for them [believers] to learn more thoroughly each day the nature of the Lord's will to which they aspire, and to confirm them in the understanding of it." In this way, the law remained an important source of moral guidance for the Christian life. Yet the guidance it provided served a more ultimate end than simple adherence to the law itself. The law, one might say, described the kind of character rightly associated with a grateful, and grace-filled, heart: "The law points out the goal toward which throughout life we are to strive." In other words, adherence to the law was the means to a greater end: the cultivation of Christian character, or virtue, and the preeminent mark of that virtue was gratitude for what God has done (2.7.12–13).

Given this, it is no surprise that cultivation of true virtue goes far beyond behavior; it encompasses one's feelings and vision as well. And here we see one place where Calvin's training as a humanist comes together with his Augustinian heritage to profoundly shape his theology. For the humanists were worried about the problems of abundance—not only the abundance of goods but also the abundance of human passion and emotion. Much Renaissance thought was a reflection on the dangers of abundance, what Simon Schama has called the "embarrassment of riches"—materially the rise of trade, wealth, and adornment, especially because of the discovery (and speedy exploitation) of the New World. This partially explains the Renaissance's enthusiasm about the recovery of ancient pagan philosophy, especially Stoic and other critiques of luxury and improper worldliness. Many of Calvin's humanist contemporaries—such as Desiderius Erasmus, Ignatius of Loyola, Niccolò Machiavelli, Baldassare Castiglione—wrote works that were not simply philosophical speculation but that promoted a way of being in the world; they sought to shape the behavior, disposition, etiquette, and manners of their audience. Calvin's concern for the proper use of time and opportunity stemmed from the combination of humanist philosophy of life and a Christian theology of stewardship. In an era of manuals addressing self-presentation and self-fashioning, his work sculpted readers to present themselves as courtiers in the heavenly court. He meant the *Institutes* to be not primarily a *summa theologiae* but a *summa pietatis*: that is, the *Institutes* were not primarily a systematic body of theological propositions but a rhetorical work meant to shape readers' affections and behavior, to induce in them a proper piety, and to teach them how (and toward whom) that piety should be oriented. In other words, gratitude to God for his benevolence spurs the Christian to answer with responsible—thrifty, perhaps—application of God's gifts to the transformation of the world. The experience of excess in justification leads to the practice of discipline and restraint in the sanctified life.[16]

Calvin left to those who came after him some profound challenges. How, after all, does sanctification manifest itself outwardly? This is both a theological and a sociomoral problem, and Calvin felt it deeply; his analysis of the shape of both the sanctified individual Christian life and the "holy commonwealth" was among the most deeply and frequently revised topics in successive editions of the *Institutes*. But he never settled these issues satisfactorily, to himself or anyone else. He left his intellectual descendants to struggle with the problem of how to understand social communities and institutions when they are caught in the tension between the first and third uses of the law—how, that is, to undertake the long-term project of incrementally transforming society from one that served God's kingdom in spite of itself to one whose citizens and institutions served the kingdom willingly and gratefully. The Puritans in particular were much taken with this question. They assumed that one's response to grace was both personal and social, individual and corporate; hence a "sanctified virtue" like thrift had implications for both individual discipline and one's responsibility to the common good. But how can we ensure that true virtues, and not their secular *simulacra*, would be cultivated? Only through understanding the grip of this question—Calvin's formulation of the Augustinian tradition's existential question—can we understand the centrality of the idea of thrift for the Puritans.

Thrift and Puritan Moral Theology

In different settings, with different concerns, each developing themes worked on by those that came before, Augustine and Calvin can be seen as articulating a single view of how to live in the "after-word," of how to live in response to grace. This view has three fundamental pieces. First of all, they affirm that the world is significant. It is not just some aspect of human life but the whole scope of human life—from its most mundane aspect to its most elevated—that bears the sacramental glory of God. Because of this, life in the world must be subject to the proper discipline in order to sculpt a whole life appropriately shaped to serve and praise God. Second, they affirm that the shaping of life must begin with the conversion of affection and perception—an affective and visual metanoia. It is only through this radical conversion of the heart that the actions they recommend find their place. Third and finally, they affirm that from this transfigured perception flows a new disciplined way of being: a faith without works is dead. The Puritans took up these themes in their own setting and developed from them the core of the thrift ethos that is our present concern.

SAVING GRACE AND MORAL STRIVING

Seventeenth-century Puritan moralists identified thrift as an important component of their conception of the moral life.[17] Thrift represented a set of moral values centered around "saving, not willing that any thing be lost"; this spirit of restraint and conservation stands in opposition to excessive or wasteful dispensing of goods.[18] Sometimes Puritan thinkers talked about thrift with the language of *parsimony*, which William Ames defined as the "virtue of spending only what is worthy and necessary," a minimalist conception of the moderate use of goods. Other times they used the term *frugality*, which Ames identified as the "virtue of conducting our affairs with profit and benefit" and which Richard Baxter called "an act of fidelity, obedience, and gratitude, by which we use all our estates so faithfully for the chief Owner, so obediently to our chief

Ruler, and so gratefully to our chief Benefactor, as that we waste it not any other way."[19] Already these basic definitions suggest that the Puritans understood this moral value, like the moral life as a whole, to be firmly rooted in the larger theological themes of the Augustinian tradition: providence, grace, and gratitude. For the Puritans, thrift was an essential component of a moral life that was itself the proper grateful response to the experience of grace.

Puritan moralists could commend thrift to an audience that included the unregenerate as a moral virtue consistent with what is fundamentally good for "worldly" human beings qua "worldly" human beings.[20] More often than not, however, they based their explications of thrift on explicit theological claims, pushing the virtue as a proper part of the moral life of the elect. The Puritans' commitment to the theological doctrine of predestination, like Calvin's, did not make them less interested in moral accomplishment; if anything, it intensified their preoccupation with the moral life. The Puritans famously believed that while all human beings were mired in sin and rightly deserving of eternal damnation, some were elected by God's free grace to redemption. Such gratuitous salvation does not induce in the saved spiritual somnolescence, however, but instead radically reorients their wills and moves them toward lives of manifest active gratitude. Having been justified by grace, believers are sanctified by it, too. They are bestowed with the divine power to turn from their sinful ways to lives of piety and holiness. The elect are thus spurred by the assurance of God's grace to respond with lives of moral accomplishment. Furthermore, for the elect, moral striving serves not as an attempt to barter with God over eternal life (a haggle that Calvin thought would lead only to despair and failure) but as an effort to demonstrate one's thankfulness for a salvation already accomplished. How better to demonstrate one's appreciation for new life than to dedicate that life to the will and wishes of the divine benefactor? In other words, gratitude for justification (God's act of making the elect right with God through Jesus Christ) leads to sanctification (the conversion of a life lived in sin and selfishness to one lived for God and others). Grace and gratitude stand as both the empowering agents and the motivating factors for moral performance among the regenerate.[21]

At the same time, the Puritans believed (as did Calvin) that there was some value in moral striving for those who were not sure of their eternal status, for the cultivation of moral virtues and adherence to the law could also serve as a means by which persons prepared themselves for the reception of divine grace. To be clear, the Puritans were teaching not that we make ourselves worthy of grace by moral striving but instead that we simply put ourselves in a position to recognize the intervention of God and to be receptive to God's calling. Again, one's action was better seen as making oneself more fully available to God than as somehow competing with God. Thus Puritans like Baxter could recommend character development in their casebooks both as an exercise in "finding God" and as instruction to the converted.

Finally, moral striving was useful to the converted as a way of testing, so to speak, one's sense of Christian calling. If one's sense of call was genuine, then a believer should be able to discern the signs of special grace in the pattern of living. In other words, moral accomplishments would betray the presence of divine grace. This uncertainty around the calling and the need for evidence produced a rich Puritan literary tradition,[22] but more important for our purposes, it also provided an additional motivation for Christians to develop godly character.[23] Thus, Christian morality enjoyed at least three theological motivations: preparation for the experience of conversion, gratitude for the reception of grace, and confirmation of the genuineness of one's calling. Without reducing it to "works righteousness," the Puritans were able to commend moral discipline to the converted and to those seeking conversion alike, as both an evangelistic exercise and a living out of one's calling.

It is in this context of a sanctified life that Puritan moralists most often commended the virtue of thrift. And "virtue" it was for the Puritans: no less a Puritan mind than Ames explicitly used the term in his discussion of thrift-related values. Indeed, for a theological tradition allegedly betrothed to intense legalism, the language of virtue is quite prevalent in discussions of moral norms like thrift. The Puritans saw little contradiction between their commendation of virtue and the priority they placed on adherence to moral principle and law. To the contrary, they thought law and virtue worked in tandem in the Christian moral life. Working from Calvin's "three uses of the law," the Puritans argued that rules and laws provide a framework for the deeper task of developing "habits of the heart," true morality that stems from proper motivation and orientation. With the guidance and structure of the law, Christians discipline themselves in their moral performance until morality becomes internalized, until it is a matter of character more than an adherence to external legislation. The Puritans thought that the wisdom and authority of law never became irrelevant, but the objective of moral teachings was to internalize and habituate a Christian sense of the good and the right. As a result of this, they recommended norms like thrift both on the authority of biblical command and as part of the ideal Christian character. So while the practice of thrift might begin as a response to specific obligations in particular economic circumstances, ultimately it became a habit of the heart, a generalized attitude that subsequently informed the Christian's action in those and other circumstances: "The intending of God's glory or our spiritual good, cannot be distinctly and sensibly re-enacted in every particular pleasure we take, or bit we eat, or thing we use; but a sincere, habitual intention well laid at first in the heart, will serve the right use of many particular means."[24] For the Puritans, then, thrift was both command and character; it was a biblical obligation that, through the adherence to rule, was ideally habituated by the Christian. We will look first at the most obvious manifestation of this thrift ethos—in the Puritans' treatment of material possessions—and then we will turn to assessing the ways in which this thriftiness was rooted in a deeper habit, one that shaped the Puritans' way of inhabiting time.

MATERIAL THRIFT

Thrift in the use of possessions, what we might call material thrift, is perhaps the expected use of the term. In this sense, thrift required the careful accumulation, management, and distribution of material wealth in such a way as to maximize responsible usage and avoid unjustifiable excess.[25] Thrift requires the responsible, profitable, and pious use of the material resources we have at our disposal—goods and money—and the avoidance of "vaine and unprofitable" uses.[26] This obligation descended to the smallest units of material possession: "We must see that nothing of any use be lost through satiety, negligence, or contempt; for the smallest part is of God's gifts and talents, given us, not to cast away, but to use as he would have us; and there is nothing that is good so small, but some one hath need of it, or some good use or other may be made of it."[27] At work in the Puritan commitment to thrift was the understanding that "God gave us those things which we have not as to absolute Lords, but as to Possessors at will, that we should dispense the things committed to our trust to his honor, and according to his will."[28] In other words, a profound sense of gratitude and obligation to stewardship underwrote the Puritan commitment to thrift.

This moderate use of wealth required that its possessors avoid "prodigality," or the waste of material wealth on excessive expenditures. Baxter defines this as "that sin of unfaithfulness, disobedience, and ingratitude, by which either by act or omission we misspend or waste some part of our estates to the injury of God . . .that is, besides and against his interest, his command, and his pleasure and glory, and our ultimate end."[29] Where the line between proper enjoyment and excess lay was difficult to identify and was seldom delineated clearly. Baxter defined excess as "when it is above the proportion of your own estate, or the ordinary use of those in your own rank, or when it plainly tendeth to cherish gluttony or excess in others: but these answers are no exact solution. I add therefore, that it is excess when any thing is that way expended, which you are called to expend another way."[30] In other words, excess is "when in rational probability a greater good may be done by another way of expense, *consideratis considerandis*, and a greater good is by this way neglected, then you had a call to spend it otherwise."[31] Most problematic in this measure of prodigality is the connection between proper use of wealth and social rank. Here Baxter echoes a common Puritan theme when he fears the use of material wealth will be used to climb beyond one's place in the social order.[32] If rooting the definition of prodigality in social status is a familiar though troubling theme among Puritan moralists, even more characteristic is Baxter's insistence that prodigality is any use of possessions that runs counter to God's honor or the common good. For

Baxter and his colleagues, it was unjustifiable excess when material wealth was not put to the use most profitable for the common good and service to God. Again, this is not to say that Baxter and the other Puritans could imagine no justifiable use of wealth for the owner's own pleasure. They understood moderate enjoyment of one's wealth as consistent with service to God, insofar as God bestows wealth in part to serve our human needs for leisure, recreation, and the experience of beauty. When such enjoyment came at the expense of attention to needs in the commonwealth or orientation to God's service, however, it constituted an excessive expenditure, or prodigality. Such prodigality amounted to "flesh-pleasing," which Baxter described as "the grand idolatry" that betrayed a fundamental preference for carnal enjoyment over serving God and a preoccupation with one's own desires over the needs of others.[33]

Indeed, these dual themes of gratitude and sensitivity toward the common good go a long way in explaining why the Puritans considered prodigality such a grievous sin. Specifically, prodigality threatened the good of the commonwealth in several ways. First and most basically, prodigality wastes goods that otherwise could be invested in the good of the civil community. In particular, it robs the poor of resources that might come to their aid, an act so treacherous that Baxter called prodigality an "inhuman vice" because of the burden it places on the poor.[34] Second, the Puritans expected that prodigality led to other vices that compromised a person's social contribution, such as gluttony, intemperance, dishonesty, and association with immoral company. They assumed that lavish living would lead to this further breakdown in character because the need to feed an increasingly uncontrollable lifestyle would require a person to put himself in unsavory circumstances. More generally, however, the Puritans assumed prodigality would lead to further vice because of their subscription to an understanding of moral character in which the virtues were part of an integrated whole, rather than discrete and unrelated practices or habits. The virtues were both products and essential components of godly character, and a deficiency in one component of that character put at risk the practice of other virtues. Especially because prodigality betrayed an allegiance to the "belly-god," the Puritans expected that those who suffered from this vice would be prone to other sins as well and, as such, would be unprofitable members of the community at best, threats to it at worst.

Not only is prodigality morally problematic, however; more deeply still, it is theologically dubious. As was the case with Calvin, the Puritans believed that the entire life of faith was predicated on gratitude—for saving grace, to be sure, but also for the other gifts God has given to sustain human living and provided for our enjoyment and flourishing. Gratitude is the motivation that underwrites the sanctified life, and a grateful response to divine generosity would be to take the gifts given—including life itself and our material wealth—and use them in such a way that brings God honor and fulfills God's purposes for them. By contrast, prodigality was a fundamental betrayal of both God's priority of ownership and God's graciousness to human beings. All of creation was created by God, belongs to God, and is intended to serve God's own purposes—namely, "the manifestation of the glory of his eternal power, wisdom, and goodness."[35] Prodigality, however, ignores those divine purposes and wastes God's gifts on carnal ends. While an appreciation for God's providence and generosity should render in us a grateful disposition that manifests itself in the practice of thrift, prodigality stems from an ungrateful heart.

At its core, argued the Puritans, prodigality was much more than a sinful act; it was a sign of that fundamentally errant disposition that they called *worldliness*. According to Baxter, prodigality was a product of worldliness, "a perverting of the very drift of a man's life, as employed in seeking a wrong end, and not only of some one faculty or act; it is an habitual sin of the state and course of mind and life."[36] Worldliness was a matter of misdirected love, so insidious because rather than being a product of momentary passion, it was a disposition cultivated by deliberation and habit: "It is a sin of interest, love, and choice, set up against our chiefest interest."[37] Worldliness represented the considered rejection of God as one's chief end in preference for the satisfaction of one's own immediate, carnal desires. It is a sin fundamentally of immanence and immediacy, of imagining that one could be satisfied in the moment as one experiences it as a fallen creature in a temporary world. As such, worldliness amounted to idolatry, the denial of God as our true end—of God's honor as the end for which human beings were created—in favor of ourselves and our temporal concerns. Baxter suggested that in giving in to worldliness we have, in effect, dehumanized ourselves, relegating ourselves to the level of the "brutes."[38]

By contrast, the Puritan dedication to thrift was rooted in a recognition of God as human beings' chief end, in an expression of gratitude for God's benevolence and in a commitment to the realization of God's priorities in the commonwealth. In other words, thrift, like its opposite, was a habitual practice grounded in a deeper religious and moral disposition of character. Material thrift required, for the Puritans, a fundamental shift in attitude, ultimate values, and focus; it was a practice rooted in a disposition characterized by "fidelity, obedience, and gratitude": fidelity to one's fellow citizens but also to God, obedience to God's expectation of good stewardship, and gratitude for the generosity of all God's graces.[39] While worldliness focuses on the self in the here and now, thrift cautions moderation in the use of material possessions in ways consistent with God's intentions and the good of the commonwealth. While worldliness is motivated by greed, godly thrift is motivated by gratitude.

This Puritan protection of thrift did not represent a veiled rejection of private property, the renunciation of which certain Anabaptist groups in post-Reformation Europe and America still advocated. From the Puritans' Calvinist perspective, such a rejection of property implied a lack of gratitude for material possessions as gifts from God as well as a lack of awareness of how those possessions might be used by individuals to honor God and serve the commonwealth. The Puritans generally understood private property to be an institution properly derived from postlapsarian natural law. Ames taught that private property was not an originally intended component of the human condition, but after the Fall it was a division deemed necessary "by reason of the multiplication of mankind and the prevailing of iniquity."[40] Under these conditions, private property was a good in that it ensured the "more peaceful and quiet settling of things" minimizing (theoretically, at least) contentious disputes over the possession and use of goods and land. Besides its negative aspect, however, the institution of private property maximized the usefulness of the goods of creation, the Puritans believed, by providing an order and motivation to their use. Private property, then, was justified by natural law (or the law of nature after the Fall, anyway) and by its practical usefulness, and none of the Puritans' railings against lavish use of property was meant as a challenge to the possession of it in itself.

Neither was the Puritan commendation of thrift meant to endorse savings motivated by an artificial scruple against spending or a selfish desire for acquisition. Saving just to save might be driven by an irrational fetish or ungrounded legalism, but Christian thrift draws its motivation from thanksgiving and its vector from the telos of human existence: namely, to honor God through discipline and doing good for others. Similarly, both thrift and miserliness can motivate savings, but while the former is provoked by gratitude and the desire to honor God, the latter is driven by greed. As such, thrift was compatible with charity in a way miserliness could not be: "It is required that this care [i.e., parsimony] does not proceed from the love of riches, but out of conscience towards God, whose benefits we ought not to abuse, and out of a foresight of providing for our necessities, and doing good to others. For honest thrift doth not hinder, but rather promote [sic] liberality and other virtues."[41] The distinction between godly thrift and miserliness is an important one to make because many subsequent interpreters of the so-called Weberian thesis have concluded that an imperative to save is the contact point between the Puritan ethic and a capitalistic ethos, which encourages private investment. There is something to this connection, for it is hard to deny that a theological ethos that encourages hard work and blesses material acquisition while simultaneously restricting both the enjoyment of that wealth and the dispersal of it to others would leave only one legitimate economic option: the reinvestment of that wealth into both private industry and community infrastructure. But there is one key difference between Puritan moral economy and the capitalistic worldview for which it is given so much credit, a difference Weber himself explicitly noted: for the Puritans the imperative to save was always defined *and restricted by* a particular understanding of God's intentions for human beings and a commitment to the common good. These parameters set limits on the Puritan conception of thrift that distinguished it from the modern capitalist's self-oriented motivation to save.[42]

Savings and the wealth it produced were for the Puritans a deep moral issue, and one on which they increasingly reflected over the years, as their communities grew in wealth. Great wealth was itself a morally neutral good: "Riches as they are considered absolutely and in themselves are morally neither good nor bad, but things indifferent which men may use either well or ill."[43] What made "riches" good or bad was, of course, how they were used. The Puritans did not understate the obstacles that wealth and the temptation to love wealth could become for the life of faith; when love of riches eclipsed love of God and concern for fellow citizens, the Christian risked idolatry.[44] But wealth and the comforts it could provide were not to be despised either. Wealth could be an indication of God's favor—it certainly was a sign of God's benevolence—and so the Puritans encouraged one another to be thankful for wealth and the comforts it purchased, such as food, security, leisure, and aesthetic enjoyment. Wealth also could be an "instrument of piety," a means by which to discharge the duty to bring honor to God and serve the common good.[45] Wealth could serve important social functions by situating a person to aid others in the commonwealth, but it also could benefit the commonwealth by providing a symbolic reminder of social ordering, by which civil society maintains its stability. In other words, most Puritan moralists believed that a certain amount of wealth was appropriate for civil magistrates and other leaders of the community, not only because of the practical benefit possible by having such resources at their disposal but also because of the symbolic gesture it provided toward the importance of authority in the commonwealth.[46] Thus, the virtue of thrift did not constitute the rejection of wealth, the use of wealth, or even the enjoyment of wealth. Few Puritan moralists instructed their rich parishioners to abandon their wealth; instead, they advised them to use what God had given them wisely, moderately, and compassionately.[47] Clearly, it was a delicate balancing act for the Puritans between showing adequate gratitude for God's good gifts and loving them too much, but the Puritans never denied that material possessions in themselves (or their enjoyment) could be good.

One such moral restriction on the appropriateness of thrift was the presence of the poor in the commonwealth. As a prima facie obligation, providing for the poor trumped many private uses of wealth beyond the level of physical and social necessity. This is not to say that the obligation to the poor was open-ended or absolute. Excessive spending occasionally could be justified in particular cases, even if that money alternatively could be applied directly to the needs of the poor.[48] More broadly, the Puritans did not think charity to the poor was in all cases an unambiguous good. Charity could itself be an exercise of prodigality, when given indiscriminately or with wrong intention (e.g., to augment one's public reputation).[49] Charity could also be socially counterproductive. The Puritans distinguished between those who were poor because of tragic misfortune and those who were poor because of their own character flaws. The so-called idle poor were a frequent target of the Puritans' moral indignation, and Puritan teachers counseled their charges not to contribute to the laziness of the idle poor by providing handouts. At the very least Christians were obligated to discriminate between those who sought their help because of misfortune and those who opened their hands because they refused to work.

Even beyond this distinction of desert among the recipients of charity, Puritan morality did not obligate Christians to give everything away to the poor. Their reluctance to instruct their parishioners to give away all unnecessary wealth to charity was rooted partially in an appreciation for the institution of private property and partially in the belief that enjoyment of that property was, to a degree, a proper expression of thanksgiving to the God who provided it. But the justification of thrift instead of charitable giving was also rooted in a sophisticated appreciation for the social power of wealth. Wealth provided certain leaders not only with economic resources but also with political power to serve the needs of the community, so that ultimately the private accumulation of wealth might better serve the needs of the poor than the yield of that wealth to charitable giving. In other words, wealth, especially in the hands of important members of the civil community, helped Christians discharge their particular callings in the transformation of the commonwealth into a godly community. In this way, the commendation of thrift was compatible with the imperative to charity. Thrift represented a wise and moderate accumulation, use, and enjoyment of material wealth in ways that furthered the good of the commonwealth, that fulfilled the individual Christian's sense of calling in the world, and that consequently served as an expression of Christian gratitude.

TEMPORAL THRIFT

To understand thrift merely as a way of managing the material goods with which one is graced, however, is not to have grasped the full extent of its meaning. For material thrift was only one side of the coin; the other, less appreciated but no less valuable aspect of it was what it meant to live a thrifty life in time. Although they did not use precisely this term in talking about time, the Puritans clearly believed that what we might call temporal thrift was at least as important a virtue as the exercise of frugality in material wealth. This is seen in the Puritans' insistence that time be used efficiently and responsibly for the work that they believed every Christian had been given in his or her calling: "Remember then that God never gave thee one minute to spend in vain; but thy very ease, and rest, and recreations must be but such and so much as fit thee for thy work; and as help it on, and do not hinder it."[50] Because time is a scarce commodity, it should not be wasted away on pursuits that do not serve those ends for which human beings were created, to honor God and to benefit the common good. All of our time should be "saved" and wisely spent for endeavors that contribute to those ends; and everything we spend time pursuing should be in service to those ends.

The best way to grasp the Puritans' urging of temporal thrift is to appreciate their abhorrence of what they took to be its opposite: wasting time, and the vices of sloth and idleness from which such waste derived. As Baxter describes it, sloth is the malevolent disposition in the pair, the habit of being slow and lazy. Idleness, for its part, was the actual practice of doing nothing, the manifestation of a slothful character in action, "the actual neglect or omission of our duties."[51] Baxter calls this pair "one of the greatest time-wasting sins" and an enemy of thrift, because the slothful refuse to take advantage of the opportunities they are given to serve God and the common good. They squander their time as a big spender wastes his money, doing nothing instead of laboring in the particular calling God has given them.

As a result, the slothful offend God and harm the commonwealth. Sloth and idleness offend God because they betray a lack of gratitude for God's benevolence, for the divine gift of time, for saving grace, and for the opportunities to put the blessings of this life to work for God's glory. Idleness amounts to robbing God in that it deprives God of the use of our lives, a use to which God—as provider of that resource—is entitled. In addition to denying God's benevolence, sloth and idleness wound both the commonwealth and ourselves, because we and our fellow citizens are deprived of the contribution we could make to the common good by applying ourselves and using our time more responsibly. Idleness often led to poverty, and the idle poor were a significant drain on the health of any commonwealth. "Idleness and sloth are consumers of all the mercies of God," wrote Baxter, and because the idle poor spend time on purposeless inactivity, they frustrate the two ends to which we are directed to orient our lives: God's glory and service to the common good.[52]

As time wasters, sloth and idleness are dangerous in themselves, but the Puritans also worried about these vices giving rise to other sins. As we have seen, the virtues formed an integrated whole in the Puritan understanding of Christian character, so that a deficiency in one area likely would lead to deficiencies in others. Furthermore, virtue needed to be dynamic, and a slothful person inactive in godly service was at risk for having the rest of his Christian character "rust," or atrophy.[53] In addition, Puritan moralists believed that good, hard work served as a distraction from the temptations of the world, like lust, drunkenness, and gluttony. Those who did not use their time to engage in holy work were at risk of falling into those temptations. Finally, the Puritans feared idleness because it seemed to them so unnatural. Human beings, like many other creatures, were made to labor. The goodness of hard work is reflected in the natural law, so that idleness amounted to a rejection of that natural law. The result was that "idleness maketh thee the shame of creation."[54]

The list of things to worry about may seem long to us; it includes "excessive sleep," "inordinate sport and games," and "unnecessary pomp and curiosity in retinue, attendance, house furniture," and bodily adornments.[55] Why excessive sleep should be described as idleness is probably clear; too much time at play, beyond the needs of recreation aimed at refreshment, also represented a waste of time that could be spent discharging one's Christian duties in the world. In his rejection of excessive leisure, Baxter surely had in mind the feast-day revelry popular in seventeenth-century English culture and so taxing to the Puritan conscience, but he also took aim at the "reading of vain books, romances, and feigned histories." In fact, Baxter was not only bothered by his day's version of dime-store romance novels; he also cautioned against wasting time on "unprofitable studies, undertaken but for vain-glory, or the pleasing of a carnal or curious mind."[56] From sporting games to study with no practical purpose—all of these pastimes violated the Puritan respect for thrift because they wasted time better spent on doing the work of one's calling.

One popular way of discussing temporal thrift among Puritan moralists was by reference to the biblical notion of "redeeming the time": "See then that ye walk circumspectly, not as fools but as wise, redeeming the time, because the days are evil."[57] While the Calvinist tradition did not generally subscribe to an imminent eschatology (i.e., a belief that the end of the world was coming very soon), seventeenth-century Calvinists did believe that history was progressing toward its culmination in the reemergence of the kingdom of God. Puritan theologians acknowledged openly, of course, that they could not say for certain when the end of the world would occur, and they were just as honest in recognizing the obvious fact that we can seldom pinpoint what moment will mark the end of individual lives. But precisely because of the uncertainty surrounding the span of our lives or of this age itself, Puritan moralists echoed the biblical warning that Christians should live as if their time in this world would be short, using each day wisely in ways that honored God and served God's reign. Using the days wisely meant applying them to the discharge of one's calling in the world, rescuing time from the sinful habits of human petulance for the work of God's kingdom. This is what Calvinists referred to as "redeeming the time," the seizure of every temporal opportunity to work toward the fulfillment of the church's (and the individual Christian's) mission. The Puritans encouraged the engagement of duty with zeal, a virtuous "fervor or earnestness" that motivates the Christian to do his duty "willingly, and heartily, and entirely."[58] To ward off idleness, the Puritans advocated the practice of diligence—seizing every opportunity to discharge one's duties in the world. And not only in one's religious life, but even in the apparently mundane work for which one was responsible was one to be zealous and diligent, for even in that work there were opportunities to honor God and contribute to the common good.[59] Practicing material thrift presumably required economic opportunities, but time was a universal commodity. Thus temporal thrift was all the more important, and the supporting virtues of zeal and diligence the "best improvers of time and mercy."[60] Redeeming the time required that time be regarded with a spirit of stewardship, just as are material possessions, and that it be used efficiently, responsibly, and moderately. In a word, redeeming the time required that Christians practice temporal thrift.

In an approach similar to their treatment of material thrift, the Puritans considered temporal thrift to be not only a proper response to biblical law but also a reflection of true Christian character. Temporal thrift was a virtue, a habituation, a disposition that reflected a genuine gratitude for time as a gift of God's benevolence and a respect for the uses for which God bestows this gift. Indeed, the reason for this gift of time, according to the Puritans, was to do the work of our callings, our particular roles in life that contribute to the public benefit and bring honor to God. As a result, Christians should labor to internalize this habit of taking advantage of every moment to serve that calling: "Time being man's opportunity for all those works for which he liveth, and which his Creator doth expect from him, and on which his endless life dependeth, the redeeming or well improving of it must needs be of most high importance to him."[61]

Complaints about temporal dissoluteness are surprising for the sorts of things that fell within their scope, not only for their character. Gluttony and "unnecessary pomp" in dress and bodily adornment were also violations of the obligations of temporal thrift, according to Baxter. What is interesting about his observations here is that he sees this kind of excessive behavior as a violation of *temporal* thrift, not just of material thrift. To be sure, Baxter considered gluttony and pomp a waste of money, too, but what concerned him perhaps more was the loss of the time spent preening oneself or wasted away in drunkenness or fullness. Baxter's treatment of excessive adornments as violations of temporal thrift is revealing on at least two counts. On the one hand, we see reflected in it Baxter's stated priority for temporal thrift over material thrift. Despite the fact that the term *thrift* is more commonly used in economic spheres, Baxter and Puritans like him indicated that the wasting of time was a greater sin than the wasting of money. Correspondingly, temporal thrift seems to have been the higher of these two important virtues.

But on the other hand, Baxter's discussion of the wrongness of excessive adornment speaks of the fundamental connection between material and temporal thrift. At the heart of all the vices to which thrift responds is the waste of God's gifts, whether material goods or temporal opportunities. Therefore, of paramount importance to both material and temporal thrift is the conservation of God's benevolence in all its forms. To waste time, money, material goods, or any other gift of God's benevolence was to live contrary to the end for which human beings were created, to bring glory to God and "enjoy him forever." Wastefulness betrays a lack of gratitude for divine blessings, a preference for selfish desires over holy priorities and the common good, and an inordinate love of the things of this world. Fundamentally, wastefulness betrays bad character:

> But the master-thief that robs men of their time is an unsanctified, ungodly heart; for this loseth time whatever men are doing: because they

> never truly intend the glory of God; and having not a right principle or a right end, their whole course is hell-wards; and whatever they do, they are not working out their salvation: and therefore they are still losing their time, as to themselves, however God may use the time and gifts of some of them, as a mercy to others. Therefore a new and holy heart, with a heavenly intention and design of life, is the great thing necessary to all that will savingly redeem their time.[62]

According to the Puritans, the practice of thrift with time and possessions signaled the presence of such a "holy heart," a virtuous character touched by grace.

And in the end it is this wastefulness that the Puritans find most abhorrent. Many critics today seem not to be able to imagine that the Puritans could have had any reason for this abhorrence that does not reduce finally to an anal-retentive attitude toward everything. In this way the Puritans get reduced to nothing more than a bunch of severe neat freaks with quaint English accents, black clothes, and the occasional blunderbuss. But the failure of imagination here is ours, not theirs. In fact, part of their anxiety about wastefulness came from their awareness of how close this vice is to how humans are supposed to behave; it seemed a perverse parody of the active gratitude that humanity was meant to enact.

And of course it seemed a perverse parody of gratitude to the Puritans because that is what it was to them. From Augustine through Calvin to the Puritans and beyond, the theological ethics of thrift is based on a theological anthropology that depicts the human as always excessive—excessive in good and evil, in gratitude and resentment, in sin and grace: ours is a gratuitous self, in all its actions. This anthropology reflects similarly organized cosmology, and this anthropology and cosmology are both rooted in what is properly theology—a picture of a God who did not need a Creation, and who so loves Creation as to desire to bless it with the divine Presence and to bring it, in turn, into that Presence, in an endless litany of glory and praise. To try to understand the Puritans without keeping this picture of the human, the cosmos, and God in mind is not to give them credit for actually having the theological beliefs that they did.

Conclusion: Thrift, Restraint, and Excess in the Puritan Tradition

How does a theological scheme such as this one, which is predicated on excess—namely, the excess of God's benevolence and grace—lead to a moral program that emphasizes restraint as much as it does? After all, in their commendation of thrift, the Puritans allegedly rejected excess in many facets of the religious and moral life, even as they justified this restraint out of gratitude for the excess of God's benevolent grace. Eating, drinking, leisure activities, parties, and music were all significantly restricted out of an emphasis on thrift and moderation, an emphasis that itself was explained as the proper response to God's unwillingness to restrain himself in doling out forgiveness. Perhaps most indicative of this apparent theological contradiction was the Puritans' attitude toward feast days in the church. While the cycle of fasting and feasting was a central part of the liturgical life of the medieval church, symbolizing the tension between sin and grace in the Christian experience, the Puritans rejected such a calendar, and they were especially damning of the many feast days celebrated in the English church. To reject this liturgical response to God's excess with periodic excesses of our own would seem to suggest either a contradiction in this picture's theological values or a misunderstanding of the ritualistic basis of the Christian calendar.

In reality, however, the Puritans were not inconsistent in their celebration of theological excess, and their rejection of English feast days was based on the conviction that the established church itself, and not they, had lost the real intention of the liturgical cycles. Puritans like Ames feared that the liturgical fasts were artificially inspired, thus lacking real meaning for the majority of practitioners, and that the frequent feasting which the engorged church calendar now excused had dissolved the paradox between bad news and good, sin and grace, restraint and excess.[63] In response, they rejected the "papist" celebration of set fast and feast days and deplored the cultural excesses that had developed on those days, but they did not eliminate the observance of the theological tension between excess and restraint. The Puritans famously called periodically for seasons of fasting, but they also (again, rather famously) retained days of thanksgiving, tying both experiences back to the life of particular Puritan communities and congregations. Thus, instead of having feasting and fasting dictated by the simple turn of the liturgical calendar, those seasons were initiated ad hoc in response to particular experiences of grace and trial in the community itself. By replacing liturgical feasting and fasting with more occasional practices, the Puritans were able to root the ritual again in the dual themes that inspired and motivated their entire understanding of the Christian life—gratitude for grace and attention to the common good. Furthermore, their resistance to a regular cyclical pattern of a liturgical calendar, while perhaps pursued too zealously (for some tastes, anyway), nonetheless reflected their conviction that God was perpetually doing a *new thing* and that the danger for humans was to fall into stale patterns of obedience without inward vivification. Not knowing when the next feast day was coming was itself an ascetical practice, for it kept the Puritans on their toes, as it were, when seeking God.

Seen this way, the virtue of thrift undoubtedly appears to be one of those impulses of restraint so prevalent in Puritan moral theology, but this restraint was defined, motivated, and restricted by the experience of "excess"—the excess of God's grace. The virtue of thrift counseled moderation in the use of material resources and efficiency in the use of time not to deny Christians the experience of excess but in the hopes of creating excess. But the hoped-for excess that resulted from a community of believers developing Christian character was a communal excess, not an individual experience, and it was aimed at spiritual excess, not material. In other words, in their commendation of thrift and virtues like it, the Puritans were not rejecting the unrestrained experience of abundant pleasure and beauty. They were instead counseling restrained experience of the aesthetics and pleasures of this world out of a preference for, as Calvin characterized it, "spiritual inebriation," intoxication from spiritual fellowship with God with an eye toward the abundant celebration hoped for in the world to come. The Puritans did not reject the experience of excess; they simply had another target for their excess—the experience of union with God and the good of the commonwealth.

Thus while superficially it might seem a contradiction that a theology that begins with the confession of divine excess culminates in a moral program defined by the practice of restraint, the Puritans did not see it that way. The penultimate restraint that they encouraged in the moral life was motivated by and in service to a more ultimate experience of excess, the promised spiritual fellowship with God in the perfect commonwealth. Considered this way, restraint, while a major characteristic of Puritan morality, was not its end. Restraint was simply a means to an excessive end—"to glorify God, and to enjoy him forever."[64]

Notes

1. Deirdre McCloskey, "The Prehistory of American Thrift," in this volume.

2. See, e.g., Augustine, sermon 355, sermon 356, and letter 209.

3. R. A. Markus, "Augustine: A Defense of Christian Mediocrity," in Markus, *The End of Ancient Christianity* (New York: Cambridge University Press, 1990), 45–62.

4. Augustine, sermon 306e (D.18), 7–8, in *The Works of St. Augustine*, pt. 3, *Sermons*, ed. John E. Rotelle, O.S.A., trans. Edmund Hill, O.P. (Hyde Park, NY: New City Press, 1997), 11:277–78.

5. Augustine, sermon 4.9.9, in *The Works of St. Augustine*, pt. 3, *Sermons*, ed. John E. Rotelle, O.S.A., trans. Edmund Hill, O.P. (Hyde Park, NY: New City Press, 1997), 1:189.

6. Peter Brown, *The Cult of the Saints: Its Rise and Function in Latin Christianity* (Chicago: University of Chicago Press, 1982).

7. For more, see Charles Mathewes, "Augustinian Anthropology: *Interior intimo meo*," *Journal of Religious Ethics* 27 (June 1999): 195–221.

8. For more, see Charles Mathewes, "The Career of the Pelagianism Controversy," *Augustinian Studies* 33 (Summer 2002): 201–12.

9. For more on cosmology and politics in this era, see Hal Drake, *Constantine and the Bishops: The Politics of Intolerance* (Baltimore: Johns Hopkins University Press, 2000).

10. Kate Cooper and Conrad Leyser, "The Gender of Grace: Impotence, Servitude, and Manliness in the Fifth-Century West," *Gender and History* 12 (November 2000): 536–51; more generally, Conrad Leyser, *Authority and Asceticism from Augustine to Gregory the Great* (Oxford: Clarendon, 2001).

11. See also John Cavadini, "Simplifying Augustine," in *Educating People of Faith: Exploring the History of Jewish and Christian Communities*, ed. John Van Engen (Grand Rapids, MI: Eerdmans, 2004), 63–84.

12. See, e.g., Peter Miller, *Peiresc's Europe: Learning and Virtue in the Seventeenth Century* (New Haven, CT: Yale University Press, 2000).

13. Diogenes Laertius, *Lives of the Eminent Philosophers*, 7.148; see also 7.134.

14. John Calvin *Institutes of the Christian Religion* 1.5.5; hereafter, this work is cited in the text. Quotations taken from John Calvin, *Institutes of the Christian Religion*, ed. John T. McNeill, trans. Ford Lewis Battles (Philadelphia: Westminster Press, 1960).

15. In general, on Calvin's theology of nature, see Susan Schreiner, *The Theater of His Glory: Nature and the Natural Order in the Thought of John Calvin* (Grand Rapids, MI: Baker, 1995).

16. On Renaissance materialism, see Simon Schama, *The Embarrassment of Riches: An Interpretation of Dutch Culture in the Golden Age* (New York: Knopf, 1987); Lisa Jardine, *Worldly Goods: A New History of the Renaissance* (New York: Norton, 1996). On self-fashioning and rhetoric, see Stephen Greenblatt, *Renaissance Self-Fashioning: From More to Shakespeare* (Chicago: University of Chicago Press, 1980); Serene Jones, *Calvin and the Rhetoric of Piety* (Louisville, KY: Westminster John Knox Press, 1995). For the centrality of grace to Calvin's piety, and the centrality of that piety to his theology, see B. A. Gerrish, *Grace and Gratitude: The Eucharistic Theology of John Calvin* (Minneapolis, MN: Fortress, 1993). The common failure to understand Calvin in light of what Greenblatt has called Renaissance self-fashioning lamentably limits the understanding of Calvin's relationship to the Renaissance.

17. Our essay takes a transatlantic view of the Puritans and their theology. That is, we assume that American Puritanism, while significantly influenced by its context in New England, remained fundamentally the same theological system as that practiced and preached by Puritans in England. Thus, in order to understand the Puritan mind and its influence on American culture, it is instructive to attend to sources from both English and American Puritanism and to treat Puritanism of both continents as an ideological whole. For a rare but remarkable example of this approach to the study of Puritanism, see Francis Bremer, *John Winthrop: America's Forgotten Founding Father* (New York: Oxford University Press, 2003). Given the emphasis Innes places on the New England context in "Thrift and Prosperity," a transatlantic approach to Puritan studies justifies our heavy reliance on English Puritans William Ames and Richard Baxter to explicate the role of thrift in Puritan thought.

18. Richard Baxter, *A Christian Directory* (1673; Ligonier, PA: Soli Deo Gloria Publications, 1990), 217.

19. Ibid., 851.

20. Contrary to widespread assumptions, Calvinists did not assume that Christians alone were capable of moral performance. The moral capacity of non-Christians was historically documented, empirically obvious, and theologically explainable through concepts like Calvin's common grace. The Puritans shared his basic assumption that God enabled even non-Christians to know basic right from wrong, to experience self-conviction when they committed a moral error, and to achieve a basic level of moral accomplishment and social coexistence. In fact, they tended to be slightly more optimistic about this capacity than Calvin, though they tended to prefer the language of natural morality or natural law to that of common grace. In particular, the Puritans believed that the value of time

and timeliness was written on the canvas of creation itself, and thus, no one—regenerate or otherwise—had any excuse for sloth or idleness. For a discussion of Puritan conceptions of natural morality, see James Calvin Davis, *The Moral Theology of Roger Williams* (Louisville, KY: Westminster John Knox Press, 2004), chap. 3.

21. See Gerrish, *Grace and Gratitude*.

22. For example, see *The Poems of Edward Taylor*, ed. Donald E. Stanford (Chapel Hill: University of North Carolina Press, 1989).

23. Max Weber famously suggested that this uncertainty around election was also responsible for the Puritans' work ethic and, by extension, for the evolution of capitalism in the West. While Weber may have overestimated the energy of the Puritan anxiety and its responsibility for Puritanism's role in the development of capitalism, he was right to point out that the Puritans did emphasize "proving" the faith—or "working out one's salvation," as the Puritans alternatively called it (adopting a biblical phrase)—through the imposition of moral disciplines like thrift.

24. Baxter, *Christian Directory*, 224.

25. Ames used two different terms for the general concept of thrift. *Parsimony* he defined as "the virtue of spending on what is worthy and necessary," whereas *frugality* "is the virtue of conducting our affairs with profit and benefit." See William Ames, *Marrow of Theology*, trans. John Dykstra Eusden (1629; Grand Rapids, MI: Baker, 1997), 324. While these two terms always occur in tandem in Ames's major writings, it is not always easy to see how he distinguished one from the other. His definitions from *Marrow of Theology* might suggest that parsimony is preoccupied with the expenditure of money specifically, while frugality refers to more general conduct with our material possessions. In other words, parsimony provides a minimalist dimension to thrift while frugality represents a fuller sense of the concept—except that in book 5 of his *Conscience with the Power and the Cases Thereof* (1643; Norwood, NJ: Walter J. Johnson, 1975), Ames seems to reverse this assignment. There *parsimony* is defined as the caution to "not idly lavish those things, which can be employed either in profitable or honest uses," while frugality consists of the avoiding "vaine and unprofitable" uses of money (254–55). In the end, how Ames parses the distinction between parsimony and frugality may be less important than that together the two virtues represent the importance of thrift as a virtue governing the use of all material possessions, including money. Baxter treated the two terms as synonymous, yet he also insisted that "Christian parsimony cannot be defined by a mere negation of active wastefulness," but rather it included the positive obligation to use one's material wealth as purposely as possible to serve God and the common good. Baxter, *Christian Directory*, 851.

26. Ames, *Conscience*, 254–55.

27. Baxter, *Christian Directory*, 853–54.

28. Ames, *Conscience*, 258.

29. Baxter, *Christian Directory*, 851.

30. Ibid.

31. Ibid.

32. For another example of this Puritan theme, see *The Works of Richard Sibbes* (Aberdeen: n.p., 1812), 3:424. Of course, defining excess, and thus the vice of prodigality, in terms of social rank implies that a higher level of wastefulness or extravagance might be tolerable among the elite than it is among the lower ranks, a disparity that may violate a contemporary sense of fairness but that struck most Puritans as common sense.

33. Baxter, *Christian Directory*, 226.

34. Ibid., 854.

35. The Westminster Confession 4.1, in *Creeds of the Churches*, 3rd ed., ed. John Leith (Louisville, KY: John Knox Press, 1982), 199.

36. Baxter, *Christian Directory*, 215.

37. Ibid.

38. Ibid.

39. Ibid., 851.

40. Ames, *Conscience*, 222–23.

41. Ibid., 255.

42. For a thorough treatment of the economic implications of the Weberian thesis, see Innes, "Thrift and Prosperity," as well as Stephen Innes, *Creating the Commonwealth: The Economic Culture of Puritan New England* (New York: Norton, 1995).

43. Ames, *Conscience*, 253.

44. See, e.g., ibid., 253–54; Baxter, *Christian Directory*, 219.

45. Ames, *Conscience*, 254. See also Sibbes and Baxter: "[God] never gives [his children] anything, but he gives them grace to make a sanctified use of it. They are sanctified to all things, and all things are sanctified unto them—use the world, as not abusing of it" (*Works of Richard Sibbes*, 2:419); "Riches may enable us to relieve our needy brethren, and to promote good works for church or state. And thus also they may be loved; so far as we must be thankful for them, so far we may love them; for we must be thankful for nothing but what is good" (Baxter, *Christian Directory*, 214).

46. Baxter thought that both the practical and the symbolic usefulness of wealth in the hands of political leaders could, on rare occasion, justify giving priority to maintaining that wealth even at the expense of the basic needs of poor members of the community, when those needy persons in question were judged to be of significantly lower communal worth: "But yet it must be confessed, that some few persons may be of so much worth and use to the commonwealth, (as kings and magistrates) and some so little, that the maintaining of the honor and succors of the former may be more necessary than the saving the lives of the latter. But take heed lest pride or cruelty teach you to misunderstand this, or abuse it for yourselves." Baxter, *Christian Directory*, 854.

47. "I know that if God put riches into your hand, by your birth, or his blessing on your honest labors, you must not cast away your Master's talents . . . but by a holy improvement of them, you may further his service and your salvation. But this is no reason why you should over-love them." Ibid., 219.

48. See n. 56, below.

49. Baxter, *Christian Directory*, 854.

50. Ibid., 236.

51. Ibid., 378.

52. Ibid., 379.

53. Ibid., 380.

54. Ibid.

55. Ibid., 386–94.

56. Ibid., 245.

57. Ephesians 5:15–16 (KJV); see also Colossians 4:5 (KJV): "Walk in wisdom toward them that are without, redeeming the time."

58. Baxter, *Christian Directory*, 382–84. According to Baxter, zeal is a disposition of character, an enthusiasm with which a Christian approaches his or her duties and the opposite of sloth. To be sure, Baxter acknowledged that not all zeal is virtuous; zeal can be misguided and energize sinners to "do much evil in a little time." He was careful to distinguish holy zeal from that destructive enthusiasm that arises from a different set of motives or intentions, such as revenge, factiousness, malice, or selfishness.

59. "Even about your lawful, worldly business, it is a time-wasting sin to be slothful. If you are servants or labourers, you rob your masters and those that hire you; who hired you to work, and not to be idle. Whatever you are, you rob God of your service, and yourselves of your precious time, and all that might get therein." Ibid., 242.

60. Ibid., 384.

61. Ibid., 230.

62. Ibid., 245.

63. See Ames's discussion of fasting in *Conscience*, 46–48.

64. The Westminster Shorter Catechism (1646), Q1.

5 }

Thrift and Prosperity

Stephen Innes

Thrift and the Weberian Thesis

When we ask what is thrift, and where did it come from, and what are its cultural analogues and antinomies, some surprising answers emerge. Although we in the twenty-first century regard thrift as akin to frugality or even stinginess, in its original Middle English *thrift* meant prosperity (from the Old Norse *thrifask*, "to thrive"). The very first definition of *thrift* in the *Oxford English Dictionary* is "the fact or condition of thriving or prospering." This meaning rather makes the title of this essay tautological, at least in the eyes of the seventeenth-century New Englanders it studies, but it does not render the connection illogical. Max Weber was famously the first theorist to link Puritanism to prosperity, and in so doing he showed how it was in the seventeenth-century Anglophone world that a thrift ethos first took root. He coined the expression "inner-directed worldly asceticism" (*innerweltliche Askese*) to explain the shift from the conspicuously unthrifty splendor of Renaissance humanism to the "rational calculating" ethic of sixteenth- and seventeenth-century English Calvinists.[1] The gravamen of Weber's argument was that anxiety over salvation drove Calvinists to seek assurance in unrelenting work and enterprise, all the while eschewing the temptations of luxury and enjoyment. He declared that "when the limitation of consumption is combined with [a] release of acquisitive activity, the inevitable practical result is obvious: accumulation of capital through ascetic compulsion to save."[2] For Weber, the Puritans' doctrine of improvement led to the functionalist bourgeois-directed economy in which nature becomes transformed into the means for satisfaction of human needs, which inexorably multiply and diversify and therefore can no longer be understood as "natural." The unending process by which one generation's "luxuries" become the next generation's "necessities"—the inexorably creative and destructive process in which wants become needs—was set in train.[3]

Rational calculation was, for Weber, the great touchstone for the evolution of functionalist capitalism. He declared that even large-scale demesne during the medieval era was not capitalist because it lacked an "estimate beforehand of the chances of profit from a transaction."[4] For Weber, a capitalistic action was "one which rests on the expectation of profit by the utilization of opportunities for exchange, that is, on (formally) peaceful chances of profit." The most important fact is always that "a calculation of capital in terms of money is made, whether by modern book-keeping methods or in any other way, however primitive and crude. Everything is done in terms of balances: at the beginning of the enterprise an initial balance, before every decision a calculation to ascertain how much profit has been made." Weber was adamant that the historically discrete phenomenon of capitalism *not* be equated with mere cupidity. The "impulse to acquisition, pursuit of gain, of money, of the greatest possible amount of money," he famously declared, "has in itself nothing to do with capitalism."[5] Such cupidity "exists and has existed among waiters, physicians, coachmen, artists, prostitutes, dishonest officials, soldiers, nobles, crusaders, gamblers, and beggars . . . [among] all sorts and conditions of men at all times and in all countries of the earth."[6]

At the same time, one of the striking features in Weber's celebrated Protestant ethic of methodical activity informed by purpose and self-denial—which Weber attributed almost entirely to English Calvinism—was the spread of the long-condemned acquisitive ethos. The drive to accumulate wealth, and by extension to save and reinvest it, served as an unintended consequence of the new cultural dominance of a secularized version of the Protestant notion of the calling. Weber began the main section of his essay *Protestant Ethic* by asking, "Now, how could an activity [methodized acquisitiveness], which was at best ethically tolerated, turn into a calling in the sense of Benjamin Franklin?"[7] It was Reformed Protestantism's dual emphasis on the positive merit of hard work and on the duty of *all* men and women, highborn and lowborn alike, to perform it, as Weber intuited, that signaled a real break with the past. In contrast to the Renaissance gentlemen who were numbered among Virginia's first colonists, the Puritan settlers who founded Franklin's Boston were drawn overwhelmingly from what John Locke called the "industrious sort"—men and women whose self-disciplined, striving behavior had already marked them off from what the Puritans described as the "mixed multitude." When institutionalized in the New World, their behavior, and the ideology that underwrote it, bequeathed to the American tradition a social priority on thrift.

Democratized Vocation and the Protestant Ethic

New England's was a new form of asceticism. It looked forward to the time-and-profit calculus of commercial and industrial society rather than backward to the flesh-mortifying desert hermits of Western monasticism. Ascetic

Protestantism in colonial New England, when accompanied by the unparalleled economic opportunities for the "middling sort" brought by New World colonization, did in fact foster the cultural analogues of the thrift ethos: the personal traits of frugality, industriousness, diligence, and temperance; the desire for material betterment; and, perhaps most important, the capacity for deferred gratification. As Perry Miller famously wrote of early New Englanders, "Devotion to business, accumulation of estates, acquisition of houses and lands: these were the duties of Christians." The need to improve one's talents led to the inescapable imperative to employ one's estate "so that it should become a larger estate," while the Puritan concept of redemptive community simultaneously demanded that one was obligated to remain ascetic in the midst of this prosperity.[8]

At the heart of this dedication to productivity was the Calvinist desire to glorify God in pursuing one's daily work, motivated by the theological doctrine of vocation. The Protestant Reformers' abandonment of ethical dualism, which separated humankind into either the religious orders or the sinful masses, eliminated the distinction between the higher morality of the monastery and the lower morality of the everyday world. With the elimination of the intercessory class, living the godly life became the vocation of every woman and man, not the prerogative of the cloistered few. Universalizing the obligation to work, sacralizing the workplace, and rationalizing time, the Reformers both spiritualized labor and collapsed the ancient and Scholastic bifurcation between workers and thinkers. Regardless of station, every Christian's principal obligation was now the glorification of God through earthly labors, or what was referred to as the "particular calling" of one's life. The calling was strikingly democratic in its implications; it made all humankind's work God's work.

For the first time in the West, *ordinary* work was celebrated. One of the foundational doctrines of the Roman Church, *conceptio culpa*—original sin—defined work in penal terms, as a punishment for Adam's disobedience. Labor became the "curse of Adam," at once proof and punishment for man's original sin, condemning postlapsarian men and women to toil all the days of their lives and to earn their bread "by the sweat of their brows." The Reformers' dignification of labor turned such attitudes on their head. Martin Luther advised his congregation, "Even though [your work] seems very trivial and contemptible, make sure you regard it as great and precious . . . because it has its place within that jewel and holy treasure, the Word and commandment of God."[9] The Protestant notion of calling, then, made cobblers, smiths, and farmers "consecrated priests and bishops." It applied to ruling-class males the same strictures against idleness and self-indulgence that had traditionally been directed in a discriminatory fashion only at the laboring classes. It provided an inner compulsion to maximize labor and the returns from labor, producing a zeal for work unlike anything Christendom had yet seen.

The rise of time consciousness required by the Reformed doctrine of the calling demanded not only that all citizens work but that they labor in a profoundly novel fashion: continuously, conscientiously, and enterprisingly. Charles and Katherine George have contended that the "work-in-the-world calling occupies the center of English Protestant attention—so much so that the particular calling comes very close to becoming the spiritual, salvation-working calling as well as the moral, socially utilitarian vocation."[10] If the calling was the belief that God had called every person to serve him, and the community, by working at some useful and productive occupation, then before entering an occupation, craft, or profession, a person was required to discern (initially this option was reserved for males) whether he had a calling to undertake it, an assessment that considered one's talents and inclinations as well as one's status in the community. What was *not* acceptable was a life of leisure, a life of nothing but prayer, or a life devoted to "vicious" luxury—in other words, any life that was unproductive, that failed to contribute to the common good. Idleness, sloth, and shoddy workmanship were to be shunned, as were such unproductive and morally suspect professions as acting, fortune-telling, and making playing cards. The doctrine of stewardship—the belief that all earthly possessions were temporary gifts from God—demanded a rational, systematic expansion of one's resources, and while production was encouraged, consumption beyond the level of moderate comfort was discouraged. Self-indulgent, luxurious living meant fewer surplus goods available for supporting church and community, and thereby this dishonored God. Thrift, time consciousness, and frugality were to be encouraged, as was rationalized planning in all facets of one's work and life.

In his 1657 "farewell sermon," the Puritan Richard Mather instructed members of his Dorchester congregation that "you must perform your religious duties" amid "your eating and marriage . . . your buying and selling, your plowing and hoeing, your sowing and mowing and reaping, your feeding cattle and keeping sheep, your planting orchards and gardens, your baking and brewing, your building houses or outhouses, your fencing in ground of [what] other business ever."[11] Nowhere else in the Reformed world was the rhetoric of the calling so all-pervasive in public and ecclesiastical discourse as it was to be in Puritan New England. Until the mid-eighteenth century, far longer than in England, the calling remained a mainstay in the New Englanders' conception of work. In the place of the old need-based and legal compulsions to work, the Puritans substituted a sense of duty and a force of habit. During a time when coercive forms of labor mobilization such as slavery and indentured servitude were taking root elsewhere in British America (and of course within European New World colonies generally), New England Puritans relied on what the Italian Marxist theorist Antonio Gramsci dubbed "reciprocal persuasion." Seventeenth-century New England can well be described, in Gramsci's formulation, as "a state where the working masses are no longer subject to coercive pressure from a superior class and where new methods of production and work have to be acquired by means of reciprocal persuasion and by convictions proposed and accepted by each individual."[12] At the heart of this process lay the religious injunction, based on the probational nature of the federal covenant, the imperative to be thrifty amid the temptations brought by prosperity.[13]

Indeed, in early New England it is unlikely that mere greed could ever have equaled the ideological (and almost inhuman) demand that every man or woman "improve every moment" with pious industry—a willful effort to glorify an inscrutable God through pious activity. This said, New England's ascetic Protestantism proved to be a splendid instrument for coping with the risks and uncertainties of early modern capitalism. Its social psychology, no less than its religious institutions and social networks, provided seventeenth-century saints with advantages others did not have. It fostered ambition and enterprise within the context of an overriding obligation to share the fruits of one's enterprise with one's church and community. In preaching the fundamentally irreconcilable doctrines of unconditional election and the autonomy of the willing self and by upholding the dialectical foundation of the Reformed tradition, New Englanders created the living contradiction of an ethos of personal responsibility in a providentially destined cosmos. In one of Puritanism's apparently inexhaustible store of ironies, the New World settlers most openly disdainful of "works-righteousness" ended up creating a work regime more rigorous and psychologically taxing than was found in those societies believing that work *could* be meritorious (i.e., it could lead to salvation). Protestant salvation theology helped create the ethically autonomous (male) individual even as it rooted all labor and enterprise in communal and otherworldly obligation. This, one must emphasize, was empathetically not the case of individualism rising at the expense of a declining communalism. The New England individual was imbedded in community. Inner-worldly individualism emerged as a consequence of, not at the expense of, a revived collective identity and social solidarity within the community of the elect. It was in mythologizing themselves as an "embattled people of the Word" who needed to "behave themselves in War-like Discipline" in order to uphold a sacred, exclusive covenant—in creating a "we"—that the Bay colonists created the core of the American thrift ethos.[14]

The "Reformation of Manners" in a Puritan Politics of Virtue

The Puritan development of collective identity and discipline notably occurred during a highly distinctive period in European confessional history. By the late sixteenth century, in England no less than on the Continent, the reformation of doctrine accomplished by Martin Luther, John Calvin, Martin Bucer, and Huldrych Zwingli was followed by demands for a second reformation, a "reformation of manners." From the time of the Presbyterian movement in the 1590s onward, dogmatic positions within confessional groups became less important than the improvement of the practical conduct of one's daily life. Disciplinary measures needed to be taken to educate and indoctrinate the faithful, aided by the mass production of devotional literature and the systematics and polemics of Reformed apologists. Within Calvinist populations these tendencies were quickened by a new mythistory (the dominant public myth around which a citizenry organizes its sense of identity and sense of purpose) predicting that the "End Time" was at hand, that the age-old conflict between Christ and Antichrist had reached its climactic phase.[15] As the originally derogative term *Puritan* suggests, many in their ranks indeed hoped to escape into the end-time purity promised by the scriptures. The Reformed movement's recovery of the true gospel was said to herald the final defeat of the beast of the Apocalypse (the pope), an event in sacred time that was expected to usher in the 1,000-year rule of the righteous. Such eschatological speculation became especially pronounced in England with the outbreak of the Thirty Years' War in 1618, and it led to intensification of popular fears of "popery" (expansionist, Counter-Reformation Catholicism) in the realm.[16]

With Protestants on the Continent afflicted by war, famine, persecution, and the forcible reconversion of some 6 million of their members between 1580 and 1640, the absolute need to work hard and eschew vice and luxury seemed self-evident to New England's Puritan founders. For the Reformed, the fulfillment of the millennial prophecies of Isaiah and Revelation depended on prevenient grace and on the preparationalist self-discipline of the individual believer. Those confessional groups like the English Puritans that embraced the theology of the probational covenant placed renewed emphasis on the need for personal discipline, humility, and self-denial as measures necessary to restore the favor of an angry God toward his chosen people.

The Reformers' demand for a reformation of manners, for a politics of virtue, of course had a long genealogy. All important philosophers from Plato through Locke had most heartily championed the personal traits of austerity, frugality, activity over sloth, and, most fundamentally, the mastery of one's passions and lusts. The Stoic ideal of *autarkeia*, self-rule, led to a revival of Stoicism during and after the Reformation. (Indeed, the comportment of founders George Washington and Thomas Jefferson almost certainly owed more to the reviviscence of Stoicism than to Reformed apologetics.) Self-mastery was the key for both Reformers and Stoics. Satan, the hero-villain of Milton's *Paradise Lost*, is a tragic figure precisely because of his lack of self-mastery, leaving him "enslaved" by his passions. Likewise, Locke, sounding more like a Puritan clergyman than the founder of modern liberalism, wrote in his *Letter on Toleration*:

> He who wishes to enlist under the banner of Christ must first of all declare war upon his own vices, his own pride and lusts, otherwise,

> without holiness of life, purity of manners, benignity and meekness of spirit, it is vain for him to seek the name of Christian. . . . For if the Gospel and the Apostles are to be believed, no man can be a Christian without charity, and without the faith which worketh [its ends] not by force, but by love.[17]

What made New England distinctive was that it got to implement the politics of virtue de novo. It was the only place where ascetic Protestantism served as the governing cultural model. While the continued existence of pre-Reformation practices blocked the full implementation of the Reformed principles in the Old World or elsewhere in the New, Massachusetts Bay Colony was afforded the opportunity to build an entire society on such principles from the beginning. Whereas in England, low-country Scotland, Holland, the German principalities, and the Swiss canton the culture of discipline could only be imposed selectively on individual congregations, New England was founded on such principles from the outset. In New England, the creation of a religiously based "culture of discipline" fostered industrious and striving behavior, individual and communal responsibility, and a high ratio of savings to investment by its limitations on idleness and leisure.[18] In purging the old calendar of its red-letter days, the Massachusetts Bay colonists substituted for the historically normative 2:1 work-to-rest ratio a 4:1 ratio. They declared a virtual cultural war on idleness and enforced this disciplinary regime by enlisting in the battle families, churches, towns, and the General Court, not to mention publicly funded schools, colleges, and printing presses. New England's founders created a rhetoric of discipline *and* the religious and civil institutions to enforce it. They took emergent trends within the parent country and pushed them to their logical conclusions. Puritan lecturers, exhorters, and pamphleteers between the 1580s and 1640s constructed both an ethical code for the conduct of daily life and the communal institutions necessary to compel obedience among the faithful. In New England, the reliance on testified regeneration membership (based on the conversion narrative) put this code into practice in congregational churches, which reached 720 in number in Massachusetts by the end of the colonial period. The culture of discipline endowed the standard virtues with a religious imperative, as important in their six days of the week as were prayer, sermons, and the sacraments on the seventh.[19]

The New England politics of virtue—although emphatically not Machiavelli's innovatively amoral conception of *virtu*—harkened back to the ancient Greeks, Romans, scholars, Christian humanists, and "Commonwealth" writers of the English Civil War period. Where the British revolution's Calvinism, which gave birth to Locke's political theory, broke new ground was in its marriage of the Protestant ethic with the newly created sovereign nation-state (the covenant-based Christian republican polity) and the church, both of which were dependent no longer on a long hierarchy of civil and ecclesiastical officials to enforce dictates, but rather on the self-gathered and self-governing community of saints. In colonial New England, both the family and the magistracy were responsible for the vigor or slackness of discipline. As John Milton declared, "Nor is there any sociable perfection in this life, civil or sacred, that can be above discipline. . . . Discipline is . . . the very visible shape and image of virtue."[20] Milton, like the early New Englanders, knew that there was an economic as well as a religious rationale for the culture of discipline. Since the 1540s, population growth, the price revolution (a fivefold rate of inflation within a century), enclosure, the increasing commercialization of agriculture, swelling numbers of masterless men, growing social inequality and want, and a series of bad harvests in the last decade of the sixteenth century put a new premium on self-disciplined behavior.[21]

In addition to being conscious of time, the culture of discipline was also preoccupied with eliminating destructive public vices. Again, it is important to recall that English Puritanism (and the Reformed movement in general) began as a countercultural revolt. Reformers were exercised not only over transubstantiation, communion rails, stained-glass windows, tithes, annates, and Crusaders' and Peter's pence but also over the public tolerance of vice—as typified by the notorious "alehouse culture" of early modern England. The personal vices that were most relentlessly denounced from the pulpit and in the House of Commons during the late sixteenth and early seventeenth century, as William Hunt has brilliantly shown in his study of the pre-Jacobean county of Essex, "were those that caused poverty: avarice and oppression on the part of the propertied; envy, sloth, and sensuality on the part of the poor."[22] Individual believers, churches, boards of selectmen, town meetings, county courts, and the General Court itself worked to free colonists from the slavery to sinful *and* impoverishing addictions. The saints were enjoined to throw off all debilitating addictions—to drink, luxury, idleness, sex, and social envy—so often that Hunt is drawn to describe the Puritan notion of sanctification (i.e., the manifestation of godly outward behavior, as opposed to justification, the actual possession of grace) as "an elaborate problem of detoxification."[23]

Although a fear of illicit sexual behavior is commonly viewed as the quintessential Puritan obsession, drunkenness was for them a far greater preoccupation, with few vices more destructive of the formation of "human capital." Many sixteenth-century observers—Reformed and Catholic alike—believed that drunkenness was becoming an increasingly acute and even dangerous social problem in late Elizabethan England. The availability of cheaper, more potent beer, along with a trend toward more public and less socially regulated drinking, helped produce the alehouse culture that so alarmed the saints. Such a culture, many Reformers declared, was about to bring England to ruin not only because it invited the wrath of God but also because it systematically undermined the personal discipline requisite for survival in difficult economic times. This was particularly true for the laboring poor. Not to put too fine a point on it, Reformers believed that spiritual impoverishment led to material impoverishment.[24] Families needed to socialize their children to work hard and respect the rights of others if they hoped to succeed as adults. (Revolutionary-era Americans believed that the success of democracy also depended on such household-acquired self-mastery). And the ability to plan, to consider alternative views of the future, to assign probabilities—in short, to calculate rationally—depended on a mind unclouded by alcohol. This linkage between what we would less judgmentally dub substance abuse and economic hardship has remained a home truth for reformers from the early modern period onward. During the 1820s, Philadelphia officials, after a tour that included Baltimore, New York, Boston, Providence, Hartford, and Salem, averred that "from three-fourths to nine-tenths of the paupers in all parts of our country, may attribute their degradation to the vice of intemperance."[25] The *U.S. Commercial and Statistical Register* found only one of the sixty-nine paupers receiving public relief in Portland, Maine, in 1841–42 were there for any other reason than "intemperance."[26]

For the Puritan preachers in both Old and New England, drunkard and saint came to represent the opposite poles of the human spectrum. It was widely believed in both societies that the alehouses were dangerous to the poor themselves, and there can be no doubt that alcoholism dragged many folks down from moderate hardship to utter destitution. The Puritans—in sharp contrast to today's cultural elites with their fondness for what Robert Bellah calls "expressive individualism" (the Whitmanesque freedom to express oneself, against all constraints and conventions)—knew that for the day laborer, cottager, or poorer artisan the surest route to an improved economic as well as spiritual condition was to "stay out of Mother Tibbald's alehouse."[27] Not surprisingly, it is with crimes of drunkenness, not of fornication, that we find among the early New England authorities the *Scarlet Letter*–like shaming punishments so offensive to post-Enlightenment sensibilities. In 1634, Roxbury's Robert Cole, "oft punished for drunkeness" (three times in the past year), was "ordered to weare a red D: about his neck for a yeare."[28] Underscoring the perceived linkage between intemperance and wasting time, the General Court also fined Timothy Hawkins and John Vauhan twenty shillings for "misspending their tyme in company keeping [carousing], drinkeing stronge water, and selling other."[29] After the wife of Springfield cooper John Mathews was killed in an Indian attack on the town during King Philip's War, leaving Mathews demoralized and frequently inebriated, the town meeting "voted and Agreed [that] the Select men shall take Care of John Mathews and have an inspection over him, that hee [shall] follow his employment and make improvement of his time: and to settle him in a way that he may doe it."[30] In an economically (and often socially) tumultuous period, the man or woman who was thrifty, diligent, and sober and who could think clearly and work hard was more likely to make it than those who were drunken and feckless. Character counted, something no one within a Puritan society was likely to forget.[31]

The Institutionalization of Puritan Thrift

The Puritan concept of redemptive community found institutional expression in the distinctive civic ecology of New England. This consisted of what might be termed the institutional and cultural detritus of the Protestant Reformation. It consisted of values *and* institutions, although the latter frequently are slighted in scholarship on the Puritan work ethic. Meditations on the alleged socioeconomic effect of Weber's Protestant ethic of hard work, enterprise, and deferred gratification—by privileging the "spirit" or individualized nature of such an ethos—have tended to tilt toward essentialism and (always invidious) macro comparisons with Catholic populations. The civic and institutional consequences of the Reformation are subsequently ignored, an oversight eighteenth-century commentators did not make. When in 1782 John Adams explained to a French correspondent the reasons for the then-evident American victory in the War of Independence, he pointed not to the colonial soldiers' bravery or to Washington's leadership (or, one should note, to France's substantial military and financial contributions) but rather to towns, schools, churches, and the militia.[32]

A robust thrift ethos requires an appropriate institutional context. It seems fair to argue that absent, first, a link between work and property ownership and, second, an appropriate legal and institutional framework, a robust thrift ethos is impossible.[33] Experiments with tenancy and communal landownership on Providence Island and in early Virginia and Plymouth showed that severing the link between work and landownership was doomed to failure in colonies dependent on attracting English immigrants. Making this point with respect to Plymouth Plantation's three-year experiment with communal landholding, Governor William Bradford distilled the major imperatives of the Protestant ethic, including its application to young and old, male and female alike:

> The experience that was had in this common course and condition, tried sundry years and that amongst godly and sober men, may well evince the vanity of that conceit of Plato's and other ancients applauded by some of later times; that the taking away of property and bringing in community [of ownership] into a commonwealth would make them happy and flourishing; as if they were wiser than God. For this community (so far as it was) was found to breed much confusion and discontent and retard much employment that would have been to their benefit and comfort. For the young men, that were most able and fit for service, did repine that they should spend their time and strength to work for other men's

> wives and children without any recompense. The strong. . . had no more in division of victuals and clothes than he that was weak and not able to do a quarter [that] the other could; this was thought injustice. The aged and graver men, to be ranked and equalized in labours and victuals, clothes, etc., with the meaner and younger sort, thought it some indignity and disrespect unto them. And for men's wives to be commanded to do service for other men, as dressing their meat, washing their clothes, etc., they deemed it a kind of slavery.[34]

A government that respects the rule of law was also an essential prerequisite for the sustenance of a thrift ethos. Confiscatory taxation and arbitrary law enforcement, the hallmarks of European "traditional" society, make a thrift ethos impossible because they sever the link between enterprising labor and security of property. The Catholic Church declined to endorse the legitimacy of private property until the twelfth century, and canonists and theologians thereafter continued to display a pronounced wariness regarding its potentially corrupting influence. English Protestants during the Elizabethan period were among the first Western Christians to directly challenge the ancient church notion that "the earth is the Lord's and the fullness thereof" meant the fruits of creation belong to all God's creatures in common. The thirty-eighth article of religion of the Church of England, promulgated in 1563, openly legitimated private property. It declared that "the Riches and Goods of Christians are not common, as touching the right, title, and possession of the same, as certain Anabaptists do falsely boast."[35] Only a state that respects the rule of law and taxes by consent can both legitimate and protect the activities, institutions, profit seeking, and property that make possible a capitalist society.[36] Writing at virtually the same time as Bradford, Puritan magistrate Nathaniel Rich led the county of Essex's resistance to King Charles's forced loans by linking security of property to both personal industry and national security: "If no propriety," Rich averred, "there will be no industry, and then nothing will follow but beggary, and if no propriety there will follow no valor."[37]

During its first two decades of existence, the Massachusetts General Court enacted a series of progressive legislative decrees that secured property rights—including the right to sell one's labor freely—and minimized arbitrary or confiscatory actions by the government. As a result of the General Court's decrees, the acts of buying and selling land, labor, and goods were, in ordinary circumstances, "lefte at liberty to be solde [at such prices] as men can agree." Large-scale trading monopolies, along with merchant and craft guilds, were likewise deemed against "the public goode and the liberty of free men."[38] Breaking new ground in the history of state building, the Massachusetts Bay Colony leaders used the state to promote economic performance by both legitimizing certain enterprises and demanding specific behavior from individuals. Fifteenth-century Venice had done the first without the second, while Calvin's holy commonwealth had required the second but not provided the first. In seventeenth-century Massachusetts, the developmental ethic of the mercantilist state was conjoined to the pious industry of the Protestant ethic. This combination provided the institutional backdrop, the civic ecology, for the Protestant elevation of secular callings over monasticism and clericalism, and it resulted in the striving ethic, the sacralization of the workplace, and the obsession with time.

Seventeenth-century New Englanders evidently understood the connection between individual thrift and collective fiscal probity, between security of property and work and productivity patterns. While Virginia's corrupt and spendthrift government during the second half of the seventeenth century compensated its burgesses with 4,000 to 5,000 pounds of tobacco per session (which typically lasted roughly a month) plus expenses for travel and a servant, "the inhabitants of New England," Edmund Morgan notes, "starved their representatives on two or three shillings a day (equivalent to twenty or thirty pounds of tobacco) from which they had to pay all expenses, including travel." In Massachusetts, the elected governor was paid £120 per year; in Connecticut the amount was £80; democratic Rhode Island won the prize for parsimony by paying its governor £10 per annum.[39] The connection between individual thrift and an encouraging political climate became even more apparent with the reassertion of royal control over the New England colonies in the last decades of the seventeenth century. On April 21, 1691, agents for Massachusetts, in seeking to justify to the Lords of Trade and Plantations the bloodless overthrow of the arbitrary Dominion of New England government in April 1689, insisted:

> It is true [that] Massachusetts and the other Colonies in New England are in a Distressed Condition, which was first Occasioned by putting them under an Arbitrary and despotick power, who disposed of their Persons and Estates, Imprisoned and Fined at their Will and Pleasure, to the terrour and Amazment of the Inhabitants and threatened yet much more, which made People careless in Business, and not solicitous to earn more [than] the supply of their Absolute necessityes. By means whereof Trade soon failed, Rents fell at least one third Part and the land greatly Impoverished.[40]

Massachusetts leadership drew a direct link between the colonists' declining work and productivity habits under the Dominion of New England and the loss of security of property that had been provided by their old, quasirepublican government.

The political benefit for a culture of thrift that came from a representative government at the top was complemented by a vibrant civic society at the local level. In today's parlance, civil society in colonial New England was animated by the principle of "subsidiarity," the belief that social tasks should be performed in the smallest available unit, from the family through the church, to the town government, to the central government.[41] The New England town—being, after the church, the central local institution during the colonial era—was not a simple carryover from the parent country, where local civic life was organized into boroughs and parishes. It was instead a wholly new institution: part borough, part joint-stock company, part land company, and part village. New England towns were the core institution of the culture of discipline because they were almost entirely locally controlled. Elected selectmen were responsible for carrying out the will of the people as expressed in town meetings, and thus local control in colonial New England was much more important than the central government's control in the day-to-day lives of the population. The New England town, as Alexis de Tocqueville declared, was a "little nation," and it was clearly with the New England town in mind that Tocqueville offered what would become one of his most famous pronouncements: a country "may establish a free government, but without municipal institutions it cannot have the spirit of liberty."[42]

The Puritan Paradox and the Evolution of American Thrift

At the core of this institutionalized Puritan ethic was a potent admixture of self-discipline and self-criticism. The central tension within the rhetoric of the calling—indeed, some believe it to be the central tension within Puritanism itself—was the need to show diligence in worldly business and yet deadness to the world. The Reverend John Cotton, the leading light in the Bay Colony's first generation of clergymen, told his congregation to be "busy like ants, morning and evening, early and late, and labor diligently with their hands and with their wits, and [every] which way soever as may be to the best advantage." Yet, and here was the rub, the believer's "heart and mind and affections" always had to be directed above.[43] The Massachusetts inhabitants were told by five generations of ministers that they could remain God's New Israel only by restraining avarice and cupidity. In no other colony could the most industrious men and women, who throughout their lives had striven to "improve [their] Time and Talents for God's glory," daily lacerate themselves with accusations of "selfishness, sensuality, unbelief, inordinate love to creatures, etc." and the overwhelming conviction that they were—"and ever have been"—the most "unprofitable" of the Lord's servants. No other colony was so obsessed with God's "controversy" with its settlers, devouring tracts on the impending "Day of Doom" or accepting at face value ministers' and civil leaders' pronouncements that "Degeneracy" was "a greater Evil in us than any other people." Only in Massachusetts, a scant nine years after the colony's founding, could its General Court be found lamenting that its population was rife with "novelties, oppression [price gouging], atheisme, excess [of apparel], superfluity, idleness, [and] contempt of authority."[44]

Despite the primacy placed on industriousness by the theology of vocation, then, the Puritans managed to create a self-critical ideology that effectively interpreted material success as spiritual failure. No more poignant expression of this self-indictment existed than the jeremiad, the Puritan preacher's lament for a colony that had strayed from its culture of discipline and its commitment to God's ways. If, as Sacvan Bercovitch has written, the New England jeremiad can indeed be seen as a mode of public exhortation designed to "join social criticism to spiritual renewal, public to private identity," then the clergy's and civil leaders' continuous admonitions to return to the purported moral rectitude of the founding generation both reaffirmed civic identity and reanimated the colonists' work and reinvestment ethics.[45] It was the Puritans' special devotion to the first half of the book of Jeremiah, the book of Daniel, and Revelation (to the typology of the Sinai covenant) that made self-accusation the central trope of New England literature. The belief that they were acting according to providential design gave New Englanders their identity and much of their sense of purpose. Like the Old Testament prophets, New England clergymen railed against the hegemony of commercial values, because of *both* the potency of such values in their society and the moral leaders' conviction of the need to set their face against them. The same religious precepts and civil institutions that systematized and amplified the virtues of unrelenting enterprise and thrift likely to produce commercial success checked New Englanders' free play on behalf of church and community, on behalf of the common good. Clergymen never tired of reminding their charges that selfishness and self-indulgence, along with hard dealing and bad workmanship, were not reconcilable with a properly formed Christian conscience. As Miller observed, it was only "by remaining ascetic in the midst of prosperity" that the saints could "abide their covenant."[46]

An ethic that enjoined men and women to labor incessantly with their hands as well as their wits, that told them to improve every talent to the best advantage—and all the while eschew the temptations of worldliness—made psychological demands of a wholly new order on New World Protestants. As Stephen Foster declares, "If Christians had been under orders to die daily for sixteen hundred years before a European even set foot in New England, at least they had not always been told to pursue their mundane affairs with a truly holy violence in the process." The right thing, as Miller noted, was simply too close to the wrong thing. The difference between "covetous affection" and "diligent zeal," writes Foster, "could be grasped only by a mental contortionist." To all outward appearances, the diligent saint (working for God's glory alone) was indistinguishable from the diligent worldling (working for himself alone). Given that each Puritan had to judge his attitude by a standard that "almost always required him to bring in a verdict of guilty," it is not difficult to account for the answering calls the clergy's jeremiads invariably provoked.[47]

As a result, one of the social and psychological consequences of the Protestant ethic was that, despite New England's manifold accomplishments—the virtual elimination of outright pauperism, the early achievement of middling-rank prosperity, including landownership and the right to vote for more than 80 percent of adult males, and the like—it suffered from what I have elsewhere described as the "Protestant dilemma." The central irony of the Protestant dilemma was that it was inescapable; industry, thrift, and self-discipline might well lead to the temptations of wealth and worldliness, but a Puritan who foreswore the virtues of productivity in fear of these temptations was no longer a Puritan. Sloth, indolence, and idleness within the workforce could not be countenanced, and neither could a lack of striving in the marketplace. Increasing material expansion after 1650 may well have signaled that New England was "deserting the ideals of its founders" (becoming a "plantation of trade" rather than a "plantation of religion"), but the congregational clergy "would have deserted them even more had they not also exhorted diligence in every calling—precisely the virtue bound to increase estates, widen the gulf between rich and poor, and make usury inevitable." The celebrated jeremiads of the clergy, upbraiding second-generation New Englanders for their worldliness, told the story of a "society which was founded by men dedicated, in unity and simplicity, to realizing on earth eternal and immutable principles—and which progressively became involved with fishing, trade, and settlement." A growing chorus from the ministers lamented that economic growth brought "a decay of godliness, class struggles, extravagant dress, and contempt for learning." In a memorable passage, Miller summarizes the problem: "The more everybody labored, the more society was transformed. The more diligently the people applied themselves—on the frontier, in the meadows, in the counting-houses or on the banks of Newfoundland—the more they produced a decay in religion and a corruption of morals, a society they did not want, one that seemed less and less attractive." At base, Miller declares in a comment that continues to resonate today, the jeremiad represents "a chapter in the emergence of the capitalist mentality, showing how intelligence copes with—or more cogently, how it fails to cope with—a change it simultaneously desires and abhors."[48]

At the core of the Protestant ethic was a tension that was at once extraordinarily productive economically and tremendously difficult psychologically. The fundamental problem was something that the early modern world, with the notable exception of Virginia's founder, Captain John Smith, had not yet come to grips with: social mobility. Not until the publication during the 1750s of James Burgh's *Dignity of Human Nature* and the installments from Franklin's *Poor Richard's Almanack* would the upward mobility that was the almost inevitable result of the Protestant ethic in a New World setting be openly sanctioned. The concept of the calling, by demanding that every person pursue one's livelihood relentlessly and methodically, always tempted one to get out of one's place, to strive to grow richer, and eventually seek profit for oneself and not for God and community. The Protestant ethic of hard work and restraint, in other words, always threatened to turn into the calculative rationalism that Weber called the "spirit of capitalism."

The classic American jeremiads, from Cotton's through those from such twentieth- and twenty-first-century commentators as Reinhold Niebuhr, Daniel Bell, and Gertrude Himmelfarb, are all essentially variations on the Protestant dilemma. As usual, Miller said it best: it was "pious industry" that destroyed the city on a hill. Invariably, piety produces industry, which produces wealth, which produces status conflicts and an abiding discontent as well as a sense of anticlimax with one's material achievements (however considerable). This last consequence was best chronicled by Tocqueville, who described his hard-driving American subjects as "restless in the midst of their prosperity, . . . sad, even in their pleasures."[49] As Cotton Mather declared of Plymouth during the 1690s, "Religion begot prosperity, and the daughter devoured the mother."[50] In the mid-eighteenth century, John Wesley mournfully observed that "religion must necessarily produce both industry and frugality, and these cannot but produce riches. But as riches increase, so will pride, anger, and love of the world in all its branches."[51] In 1819, John Adams asked Thomas Jefferson, "Will you tell me how to prevent riches from becoming the effects of temperance and industry? Will you tell me how to prevent riches from producing luxury? Will you tell me how to prevent luxury from producing effeminacy, intoxication, extravagance, Vice, and folly?" This was an old refrain for Adams, one he directed against himself since his youth. On the eve of the Revolution, he admonished himself in his diary to "beware of idleness, luxury, and all vanity, folly, and vice."[52] By the twentieth century, this cycle of self-accusation and collective accusation would be secularized by Joseph Schumpeter as the process by which capitalism "destroys" the moral foundations on which it is built.[53]

What this represents could be classified as a form of collective neurosis. What many entranced by the Weber thesis overlook is that the German sociologist portrayed relentlessly striving, thrift-obsessed behavior as fundamentally unnatural—as a peculiar and historically contingent form of behavior. Skeptical over the presumed naturalness of "maximizing" behavior postulated, in their different ways, by both Marxists and neoclassical economists, Weber declared categorically that "a man does not *by nature* wish to earn more and more money, but simply to live as he is accustomed to live and earn as much as is necessary for that purpose."[54] Even Adam Smith averred with the ancients that rest, not work, was the natural and ideal human condition, synonymous with freedom and happiness.[55] Gramsci regarded as among the "weirdest" things about twentieth-century America the fact that tycoon Henry Ford, already among the richest men in the world, was still working sixteen-hour days late in life instead of retiring to a decadent existence on a country estate like any respectable European of his class. Workaholism has indeed produced fables of abundance in the Republic and at this writing shows no signs of abating, but there is no denying that these have come at a psychic cost. As the massive recent growth of psychopharmacology attests, a modern-day Tocqueville would still find many Americans sad amid their prosperity.

Conclusion

By the mid-eighteenth century, of course, a more secularized version of the Protestant ethic would famously be provided by Franklin: "Our time is reduced to a Standard, and the Bullion of the day [is] minted out into Hours . . . [so that] he that is prodigal of his Hours is . . . a squanderer of money."[56] For Franklin, "Lost time is never found again."[57] Indeed, in Franklin the equation of disciplined time and work with upward mobility reached its American apotheosis. In his autobiography, Franklin asserted what he called the "precept of Order requiring that every part of my business should have its allotted time"; therefore, "one page of my little book contain'd the following scheme of employment for the twenty-four hours of a natural day":

> 4:30 a.m.–7:30 a.m.: Rise, wash, and address Powerful Goodness! Contrive day's business, and take the resolution of the day; prosecute the present study, and breakfast.
> 8:00 a.m.–12:00 p.m.: Work.
> 12:00 p.m.–2:00 p.m.: Read, or overlook my accounts, and dine.
> 2:00 p.m.–6:00 p.m.: Work.
> 6:00 p.m.–10:00 p.m.: Put things in their places. Supper. Music or diversion, or conversation. Examination of the day.
> 10:00 p.m.–4:30 a.m.: Sleep.

By setting aside time for "music or diversion," Franklin showed himself to be no Puritan; but despite such lapses, along with his rejection of providentialist cosmology, Franklin retained the core of Puritan social ethics. Each of his mornings began with the question, "What good shall I do this day?" and evenings concluded with the inquiry, "What good have I done today?"[58] The discipline of thrift was alive and well.

At the same time, although hegemonic throughout the colonial and early national periods of New England history, the Protestant ethic—not least because of its very inhumanness—was never an uncontested value system. As far back as the early years of the Plymouth colony, Governor Bradford discovered how much the non-Puritan settlers bridled at the loss of the old calendar's many holidays. On December 25, 1621 (or, in the disapproving words of Governor Bradford, "the day called Christmas Day"), the clash between Merrie Old England and the culture of discipline erupted in the infant colony.

Expunged from the Puritan calendar as a pagan remnant, Christmas had long been a traditional day of revelry in Elizabethan and Jacobean England, especially among the laboring classes. When Bradford tried to lead a work detail into the woods that morning, he discovered that some recent arrivals wanted to honor this ancient tradition. They expressed "scruples" and, doubtless knowing that such language would answer in a Reformed settlement, declared that "it went against their consciences to work on that day." Declaring that "he would spare them till they were better informed," Bradford led the rest off to their tasks. But when the governor and his laborers "came home at noon from their work," they found that those who had been left behind were "in the street at play, openly; some pitching the bar, some at stool-ball and such like sports." Pitching the bar, stoolball, and shuffleboard, along with other traditional alehouse pastimes as "diceplaying, cards, tables, shovegroat, scales, dancings, hobbyhorses, and such unseasonable dealings," had been banned by the Plymouth General Court as sinful uses of God's precious time. Accordingly, Bradford "went to [the revelers] and took away their implements and told them that [their playing sports] was against *his* conscience, that they should play and others work." He informed them that "if they made the keeping of [Christmas a] matter of devotion, let them keep [to] their houses; but there should be no gaming or reveling in the streets." The governor followed this entry in his *History* with the wry observation that since that time, "nothing hath been attempted that way, at least openly."[59]

This may have been the first Kulturkampf in North America, but it would not be the last. From its inception the Protestant ethic bred contesting, mirror-opposite value systems. Piety versus worldliness, utilitarian individualism versus expressive individualism, the "party of reticence" versus the "party of exposure"—the nomenclature would change, but the nature of the underlying conflict would not. The Protestant ethic could never fully control or contain the counterideologies it invariably provoked. And, as Leszek Kolakowski has argued, in the end that may be the most important thing:

> Cultural momentum always has its source in a conflict of values which each side attempts, at the expense of the other, to claim exclusivity, but is forced under pressure to restrict its aspirations. In other words, culture thrives both on a desire for ultimate synthesis between... two conflicting elements and on being organically unable to ensure that synthesis. The achievement of synthesis would mean death to culture.[60]

In the twenty-first century, evidence abounds that what Weber called the "ascetic compulsion to save" is on the wane in the Republic. America's savings rate has dropped from 10 percent two decades ago to near 0 percent today. In 2004 Americans spent 99 percent of their disposable income, saving but 1 percent.[61] Trade deficits mushroom while foreign investors recycle our dollars into U.S. Treasury debt, "justifying our failure to be frugal," in the ironic characterization of the *Wall Street Journal*.[62] In the real estate section of the *Washington Post* of June 3, 2005, no less a paladin of the established order than Heather McElrath, spokeswoman for the American Banking Association, laments that "we're a society that prefers instant gratification—it's a short-term rather than a long-term focus."[63] (Countering that is the massive democratization of stock and equity investment since the 1970s, with now over half of U.S. households vested in securities and stocks listed on the New York Stock Exchange, suggesting that market investments have simply become a more rational option for those who wish to "lay up" a nest egg for the future.) As any child of a parent who lived through the Great Depression will know, the thrift culture was alive and well late into the twentieth century, but the spending and saving habits of baby boomers has long been an object of concern for their parents. Whether this concern is just a new incarnation of the old jeremiads, or whether it truly augurs a break with the American past, remains to be seen. Building on Kolakowski's insight, however, one is tempted to believe that as long as Americans continue to agonize about thrift—and the accompanying material abundance we simultaneously desire and abhor—the ethos will continue to shape our lives. As the history of the jeremiad from the seventeenth century onward suggests, perhaps the best way for a people to *avoid* actually going to hell in a handbasket is to have their principle spiritual and cultural commentators insist that this is precisely what they are doing.

Notes

Note to the reader: This article is being published posthumously. Thus we were unable to confirm some of Professor Innes's citations.

1. Max Weber, *The Protestant Ethic and the Spirit of Capitalism*, trans. Talcott Parsons (New York: Scribner, 1958), 140.

2. Ibid., 116.

3. Ibid., 17–18, 21–22; Max Weber, *General Economic History*, ed. Frank H. Knight (New York: Collier, 1961), 53; Alan Macfarlane, *The Culture of Capitalism* (Oxford: Blackwell, 1987), 223–27.

4. Max Weber, *The Theory of Social and Economic Organization*, trans. A. M. Henderson and Talcott Parsons (New York: Free Press, 1964), 267.

5. Weber, *Protestant Ethic*, xxxi.

6. Ibid.

7. Ibid., 74; quoted in Albert O. Hirschman, *The Passions and the Interests: Political Arguments for Capitalism before Its Triumph* (Princeton, NJ: Princeton University Press, 1977), 130, 9.

8. Perry Miller, *The New England Mind: From Colony to Province* (1953; Cambridge, MA: Harvard University Press, 1961), 52, 41.

9. Martin Luther, *Works* (St. Louis: Concordia, 1955–86), 44:189–90, quoted in Stephen Innes, *Creating the Commonwealth: The Economic Culture of Puritan New England* (New York: Norton, 1995), 113–18.

10. Charles H. George and Katherine George, *The Protestant Mind of the English Reformation, 1570–1640* (Princeton, NJ: Princeton University Press, 1961), 169.

11. Richard Mather, *A Farewell-Exhortation to the Church and the People of Dorchester* (Cambridge, MA: printed by Samuel Green, 1657), 11–12.

12. *Selections from the Prison Notebooks of Antonio Gramsci*, ed. Quintin Hoare and Geoffrey Nowell Smith (New York: International Publishers, 1971), 281, 300.

13. Miller, *New England Mind*, 42.

14. Harry S. Stout, *The New England Soul: Preaching and Religious Culture in Colonial New England* (New York: Oxford University Press, 1986), 7; Innes, introduction to *Creating the Commonwealth*.

15. William H. McNeill, *Mythistory and Other Essays* (Chicago: University of Chicago Press, 1986), 3–42. According to McNeill, "A people without a full quiver of relevant agreed-upon statements, accepted in advance through education or less formalized acculturation, soon finds itself in deep trouble, for, in the absence of believable myths, coherent public action becomes very difficult to improvise or sustain." Ibid., 23.

16. Antipopery dominated English public and popular life for an astonishing length of time, almost three centuries. It was the dominant popular prejudice from the time of the Armada year of 1588 and the Gunpowder Plot in 1605 to well after the Reform Bill debates of the 1830s. The same could be said for the American colonies, especially those dominated by dissenter populations, like New England. As late as 1768 Massachusetts patriot Samuel Adams could be found (writing in the *Boston Gazette* as "A Puritan") declaring that there was much more "to be dreaded from the growth of POPERY in America, than from the Stamp-Acts or *any* other Acts destructive of men's *civil* rights." Regarded by both friend and foe as the most effective political agitator during the Revolutionary crisis, Adams spent much of his energy during those years ruminating on "the probable causes of POPERY in a land [Massachusetts] of so much light and knowledge." As Adams's musings suggest, the binary opposition between Reformed Protestantism and English liberty on the one hand and popery and arbitrary government on the other was the dominant political trope in the Anglophone world for more than two centuries. Jonathan Scott, *England's Troubles: Seventeenth-Century English Political Instability in European Context* (New York: Cambridge University Press, 2000), 1–39; *The Writings of Samuel Adams*, ed. Harry Alonzo Cushing, 4 vols. (New York: Octagon Books, 1904–8), 1:203–7.

17. John Locke, *A Letter on Toleration*, trans. J. W. Gough (Oxford: Putnam's, 1968), 59, 99.

18. William Hunt, *The Puritan Moment: The Coming of Revolution in an English County* (Cambridge, MA: Harvard University Press, 1983), 79–81.

19. Innes, *Creating the Commonwealth*, 117.

20. John Milton, *Reason of Church-Government* in *Complete Prose Works*, ed. Don M. Wolfe (New Haven, CT: Yale University Press, 1953), 1:751.

21. Steve Hindle, *The State and Social Change in Early Modern England, c. 1550–1640* (Basingstroke, UK: Macmillan, 2000).

22. Hunt, *Puritan Moment*, 83.

23. Ibid, 79.

24. Alan Ryan, "Waiting for Gordon Brown," *New York Review of Books*, June 23, 2005, 35.

25. Marvin Olasky, *The Tragedy of American Compassion* (Washington, DC: Regnery Gateway, 1992), 46. The *American Quarterly Review* reported that the 90 percent figure was more accurate; *American Quarterly Review* 14 (1833): 90, quoted in Olasky, *Tragedy of American Compassion*, 46.

26. *U.S. Commercial and Statistical Register* 6 (1842): 363, quoted in Olasky, *Tragedy of American Compassion*, 42.

27. Robert N. Bellah et al., *Habits of the Heart: Individualism and Commitment in American Life* (Berkeley and Los Angeles: University of California Press, 1985), 34; Hunt, *Puritan Moment*, 70–129.

28. *The Journal of John Winthrop, 1630–1649*, ed. Richard S. Dunn, James Savage, and Laetitia Yeandle (Cambridge, MA: Harvard University Press, 1996), 111. Cole's punishment was remitted at the next meeting of the General Court. Nathaniel Bradstreet Shurtleff, ed., *Records of the Governor and Company of the Massachusetts Bay in New England, 1628–1686*, 5 vols. (1853–54), 1:118, hereafter referred to as *Mass. Recs.*

29. *Mass. Recs.* 1:112; see also 1:213; 2:195.

30. Henry M. Burt, ed., *The First Century of the History of Springfield: The Official Records from 1636–1736*, 2 vols. (Springfield, MA: H. M. Burt, 1898–99), 2:147–48, 152–53.

31. James Davison Hunter, *The Death of Character: Moral Education in an Age without Good or Evil* (New York: Basic Books, 2000), 31–53.

32. Theodore Draper, *A Struggle for Power: The American Revolution* (New York: Knopf, 1996), 476.

33. Hirschman, *The Passions and the Interests*, 18.

34. William Bradford, *Of Plymouth Plantation, 1620–1647*, ed. Samuel Eliot Morison (New York: Knopf, 1952), 120–21.

35. Thomas Rogers, *The Catholic Doctrine of the Church of England: An Exposition of the Thirty-nine Articles* (Cambridge: University Press, 1854), 352.

36. Thomas Rogers, *The Faith, Doctrine, and Religion Professed and Protected in the Realm of England, and Dominions of the Same, Expressed in Thirty-Nine Articles* (Cambridge: printed by John Hayes, 1675), 51.

37. Nathaniel Rich, *Common Debates, 1628*, ed. Robert C. Johnson (New Haven, CT: Yale University Press, 1977), quoted in Hunt, *Puritan Moment*, 213.

38. *Mass. Recs.* 1:115.

39. Edmund S. Morgan, *American Slavery, American Freedom: The Ordeal of Colonial Virginia* (New York: Norton, 1975), 208.

40. Robert Earle Moody and Richard Clive Simmons, eds., *The Glorious Revolution in Massachusetts, Selected Documents, 1689–1692*, Publications of the Colonial Society of Massachusetts 64 (Boston: Colonial Society of Massachusetts, 1988), 484–85.

41. Michael Novak, *The Catholic Ethic and the Spirit of Capitalism* (New York: Free Press, 1993), 80–81, 260; Shelley G. Burtt, *Virtue Transformed: Political Argument in England, 1688–1740* (New York: Cambridge University Press, 1992); Paul Halliday, *Dismembering the Body Politic: Partisan Politics in England's Towns, 1650–1730* (New York: Cambridge University Press, 1998).

42. Alexis de Tocqueville, *Democracy in America*, ed. Phillips Bradley, trans. Henry Reeve, 2 vols. (New York: Knopf, 1945), 1:63.

43. John Cotton, *Puritans in America: A Narrative Anthology*, ed. Alan Heimert and Andrew Delbanco (Cambridge, MA: Harvard University Press, 1985), quoted in Innes, *Creating the Commonwealth*, 124.

44. *Mass. Recs.* 1:253.

45. Sacvan Bercovitch, *The American Jeremiad* (Madison: University of Wisconsin Press, 1978), xi.

46. Miller, *New England Mind*, 42.

47. Stephen Foster, *Their Solitary Way: The Puritan Social Ethic in the First Century of Settlement in New England* (New Haven, CT: Yale University Press, 1971), 122; Innes, *Creating the Commonwealth*, 122–25.

48. Quotations from Miller, *New England Mind*, 40, 49–51; Innes, *Creating the Commonwealth*, 27.

49. Tocqueville, *Democracy in America*, bk. 2, chap. 13.

50. Mather, *Farewell Exhortation*, quoted in Innes, *Creating the Commonwealth*, 26.

51. John Wesley, quoted in Robert Southey, *Life of Wesley; and the Rise and Progress of Methodism* (New York: Duyckinck and Long, 1820), 2:308.

52. *The Works of John Adams*, ed. Charles Francis Adams, 10 vols. (Boston: Little, Brown, 1850–56), 2:304. Suggesting the neurotic dimension of such behavior, Peter Shaw points out that Adams "truly believed that his choice lay between dissipated indolence and stern self-discipline." Peter Shaw, *The Character of John Adams* (Chapel Hill: University of North Carolina Press, 1976), 38.

53. Innes, *Creating the Commonwealth*, 25–26.

54. Weber, *Protestant Ethic*, 60.

55. Adam Smith, *Wealth of Nations*, ed. Andrew Skinner (Oxford: Clarendon Press, 1980), 120.

56. Benjamin Franklin, *Poor Richard's Almanack*, January 1751, in *The Papers of Benjamin Franklin*, ed. Leonard W. Labaree and W. J. Bell (New Haven, CT: Yale University Press, 1961), 4:86–87, quoted in Innes, *Creating the Commonwealth*, 132–59.

57. Benjamin Franklin, *The Political Thought of Benjamin Franklin*, ed. Leonard W. Labaree (New Haven, CT: Yale University Press, 1904), 150, quoted in Bellah et al., *Habits of the Heart*, 32.

58. *The Autobiography of Benjamin Franklin*, intro. by Lewis Leary (New York: Macmillan, 1962), 86. The belief that such daily regimentation was *the* key to worldly success subsequently became a staple of American middle-class and even elite culture. In 1880, Gifford Pinchot's mother, Mary, admonished her fifteen-year-old son that "I greatly fear you do not systematize your time sufficiently, and for the present, I wish you to write me every day what you have done the preceding day—from breakfast to bedtime." She urged young Gifford always to heed Saint Paul's admonition (Romans 12:11) to be "not slothful in business; [but] fervent in spirit; serving the Lord." Mary Pinchot to Gifford Pinchot, October 17, 1880, Family Correspondence, Gifford Pinchot Collection, Library of Congress. I am grateful to Professor Brian Balogh for bringing this passage to my attention.

59. Bradford, *Of Plymouth Plantation*, 145–46.

60. Leszek Kolakowski, *The Presence of Myth*, trans. Adam Czeriawski (Chicago: University of Chicago Press, 1989), 135.

61. Robert J. Samuelson, "Time to Toss the Textbooks," *Washington Post*, June 22, 2005, A21. Samuelson ascribes such low savings rates to the "wealth effect": "In the 1990s higher stock prices caused Americans to spend more; now higher home values (up 55 percent since 2000, to $17.7 trillion) are doing the same. So consumer spending increasingly depends on 'asset markets'—stocks and homes—and not just income."

62. Paul B. Farrell, "MarketWatch: Ten Ways to Win the Loser's Game," *Wall Street Journal*, July 10, 2005.

63. Interview comment quoted in Kirstin Downey, "Market Driving Ricky Mortgages," *Washington Post*, June 3, 2005, D1.

6 }

Moderation in the First Era of Popular Consumption

Joyce Appleby

In the eighteenth century, sustained prosperity undermined many of the habits of thrift and introduced an entirely new dialogue about economic behavior. The disapprobation of spending and other forms of self-indulgence did not disappear, but it mutated from moral strictures to shrewd advice. A breakthrough in the production of goods changed forever the relations of human beings to the fruits of their labor. Population growth began its long ascent, and secular ideas about social well-being promoted a new matrix of modern attitudes.

The idea of moderation was well embedded in both classical wisdom and Christian homilies, but developments in material culture posed a new challenge to the old virtue of restraint. For the first time in history an array of goods to comfort and adorn body and home became available well outside the exalted circles of the upper class, spreading to the middling families of farmers, artisans, shopkeepers, and clerks. The "carrots" of purchasable goods could now be added to the "sticks" of private fears to secure the disciplined labor that ministers, magistrates, and parents had so long sought in their charges. A new tension appeared between the employing and laboring classes. With the market enabling workers to spend in new and pleasurable ways, their social superiors struggled to retain the social control that the old virtue of thrift had helped maintain.

Because the site of this dramatic transformation took place in Great Britain, the North American continental colonies felt its full brunt. Although religious motives had stirred many colonial founders, survival of the European settlements in the New World required finding a niche in the emerging imperial economy. The initial planting of people and land in Virginia and Massachusetts coincided with the conversion of the English economy, which was replacing its traditional emphasis on supplying food and clothing with a focus on growth and expansion.

Traditional statutes had enjoined employers to retain workers even when they did not need them. They also regulated the grain trade in deference to feeding the populace rather than bringing returns to farmers. Slowly over the course of the seventeenth century, the moral economy embodied in these laws yielded to the demands of enterprise. Regulations fell into desuetude as landlords and masters caught the ear of the nation's leaders with their lesson that husbanding their capital in lean times was essential if the base of employment were ever to expand.

Agricultural productivity pushed English men and women across a barrier that divided them from their own past and from every other contemporary society. Somewhere around 1650 the country moved beyond the threat of famine, even if few were aware of it. Innovations in farming, combined with the capability of bringing grains from other places in times of shortages, drove one of the four horses of the apocalypse from England's shores. Chronic malnutrition lingered on for the bottom 20 percent of the population, but famine was gone. In the future there would be food shortages, skyrocketing bread prices, distress, and dearth, but never again would poor harvests go hand in hand with rising mortality rates.

A powerful reason for maintaining strict control over economic activities had unobtrusively disappeared, leaving behind a set of social prescriptions whose obsoleteness had to be discovered one by one in the course of the next century and a half. It would be hard to exaggerate the effect that freedom from famine had on the lives of the English. Even more impressive was its influence on the imagination. Options, alternatives, and choices opened up for all but the destitute. And in the process the rigid demarcations of status gave way to the more fluid lines of class, to the great concern of conservatives among the elite.

With food in greater abundance, the English population began to grow. The world's population had expanded and contracted over three millennia, but in the eighteenth century a vital revolution was in the making. Unlike the old accordion-like pattern that had characterized previous European population fluctuations, the increase in people this time laid a base for future growth, with each generation forming a kind of springboard from which world population still continues to soar. The 20 million French citizens Louis XIV ruled in 1700 became the 40 million French citizens who couldn't be wrong in 1914. The English population increased at an even faster clip. And in England's North American colonies—that catch basin of surplus people from northwestern Europe—the number of people doubled every twenty-five years, an unheard of rate first detected by the curious Benjamin Franklin.

Just as the second third of the eighteenth century marked the beginning of population growth, so the end of famines smoothed out the cyclical ruptures of lean and fat years, leaving more and more of farmers' earnings to purchase the goods that manufacturers would turn out if there were buyers. Neither development banished poverty; contemporaries estimated that half of the

English population had to resort to some form of charity to get through each year. What made England conspicuously prosperous was the ability of the state and private philanthropy to meet this social need without interrupting economic growth. In the colonies, the absence of poverty was striking, but there too towns taxed themselves to take care of the disabled poor.

The variety of goods that people wanted grew even faster than the number of people. By the end of the seventeenth century, England had formed a unified market, the largest circulation of food, wares, and services in the world. No longer could local regulations interrupt the flow of goods churning through the English countryside. Private cultivation squeezed out common fields. The market rewarded efficiency. Even landed nobles and gentry found themselves forced to acquire new skills. Efficiencies led to a drop in nationwide prices, punishing those tied to old ways of caring for their crops.

At the same time, England's expansion across the Atlantic and into the Indian Ocean created great profits for the new trading companies. The growth of the thirteen continental colonies that stretched from Georgia to New Hampshire provided a strong market for English-manufactured items, even as colonial tobacco, rice, indigo, fish, grains, lumber products, and rum found ready sales in Europe. Great Britain controlled the commerce of certain enumerated articles like tobacco, but the colonists shipped grains and lumber regularly to the West Indies, the Netherlands, and Spain.

The dialogue about thrift had to insert itself into public discussions and private conversations addressing new inquiries about the nature of the economic transformation taking place before the very eyes of contemporaries. At no time was the call for moderation, restraint, and self-discipline silenced, but the assigned motives for acquiring sound and sober habits took on an instrumental quality. As standards of living rose for an enlarged middling section of professionals, merchants, tradespeople, and artisans, the English gentry and nobility felt the loosening of their social authority. Upwardly mobile groups saw thrift less as an arrow in the quiver of social control and more as a self-adopted habit of pleasures denied in deference to capital accumulation.

An enormous amount of intellectual energy went into understanding the phenomena of global trade, profit-oriented farming, the cumulative innovations in marketing goods, and the intricacies of making payments over long distances. To the old distinction of new and old was added the more compelling one of modern and old-fashioned.

A peculiar dynamic of the emerging world commerce revealed itself most strikingly in England's first colony, that fragile outpost of Europe established by the Virginia Company on the far side of the Atlantic in 1607. Because this settlement was explicitly made to find or produce vendible commodities, it is not surprising that one of its first settlers, John Rolfe, experimented with hybridizing a tobacco strain that could compete with the much-esteemed Spanish Orinoco leaf. Rolfe's successful effort triggered a boom in Virginia.

Tobacco fetched a price abroad high enough to encourage Virginia Company shareholders to pour money and men (and a few women) into their plantations. Cultivation spread along the tidal rivers emptying into the Chesapeake Bay. The volume of exports surged.

When the inevitable bust of oversupply followed this expansion in cultivation, prices dropped. So low did they become that a whole new crowd of poorer consumers could afford to smoke and chew tobacco. This fresh demand in turn created an incentive to find ways to cut production costs so as to make a profit from supplying this larger body of consumers with cheap tobacco. Slave labor and economies of scale sustained the expansion of tobacco cultivation for the next century and a half, even though prices never approached those of the boom.[1] A similar phenomenon occurred in the 1630s with tulip bulbs only to be repeated over and over again in less spectacular episodes with cutlery, calicoes, pottery, pewter, and pepper.

Ordinary people joined their social superiors in the pursuit of the pleasures of spending, and their numbers changed the character of the enterprise. Retrospectively we can see that this boom-and-bust cycle unintentionally widened the market for new goods. Investors responded to the profits of the boom, ordinary people to cheap prices during the bust. This dynamic enabled commerce—a feature of human society as old as the Bible—to move out of the interstices of the traditional social order and impose its imperatives on the culture as a whole. The enormous augmentation in the volume of goods when ordinary people became consumers meant enormous augmentations in the wealth and power of those nations and persons who participated successfully in supplying to the new tastes. At the same time it upset the traditional relations among the strata of society, undercutting the social authority that the wealthy had long enjoyed over their inferiors. The extolling of thrift became more prominent as it slowly lost relevance to most consumers.

We are, of course, used to hearing the litany of new products entering European markets from the sixteenth century onward—first from New World mines and the fabled East India trade, then from the British colonies, next from the homely shops of ingenious artisans, and finally the prodigious outputs of the marvelous machines of the factory age. Rattling off the names of new condiments, textiles, and inventions has served as the incantation for summoning the spirits that presided over the rise of the West. These details of early modern enterprise with its cumulative revolutions of technology and human adaptations have supplied the factual grist for the mill of material progress.

What was profoundly unsettling, even shattering, about the gains in material culture whose permanence became manifest by the eighteenth century was that they made it evident that human beings were the makers of their world. A peculiarly intense form of curiosity in Western culture drew countries along the path of innovation that grew ever wider as the path breakers pushed against a comparatively weak attachment to customary practices. On this broad avenue of human inventiveness Europeans encountered themselves as the creators of their own social universe. But this discovery took place while the actual social arrangements of their world still reflected traditional assumptions about divine punishments, fallen human nature, and the inherent frailty of civil society.

In this essay, I want to avoid anticipating the events in the familiar history of progress and instead look at the influence of this transformation on the idea of thrift and its associated values of moderation, discipline, and solvency. Looking ahead, I shall explore the reevaluation of economic behavior that began in the seventeenth century and climaxed with the publication of Adam Smith's *Wealth of Nations*. No longer castigated as self-indulgence, spending was finally given a positive role in the economy. A political discourse developed that entwined individual economic rights with political liberties, leaving the core Protestant beliefs about thrift more admonitory than practical. And the idea of thrift became entangled in the accompanying efforts of the elite to maintain control over working people.

As is often the case in times of change, economic novelties outpaced social sensibilities. Early in eighteenth-century England—in the so-called Augustan age—a new discourse stigmatizing the new buying patterns as evidence of moral degeneration gathered force. Particularly addressing the spending habits of ordinary people, like housemaids and plowmen, these authors tried to wrest economic discussions from empirical analysis. Next a new kind of civility blossomed with the emergence of coffeehouses, literary journals, self-improvement societies, and scientific associations. Consumption became a part of a burgeoning, urban middle-class culture. Less attention was paid to improving morals and more to creating a participatory society of readers, discussants, and political reformers. Serious effort to explain social change passed to the North, where Adam Smith, David Hume, and their circle of fellow Scottish moralists laid the foundation for the social sciences.

As we shall see by following this story of successive discourses about thrift and its nemesis consumption, England and its colonies were knit together with both tangible and intangible links. English books and pamphlets appeared in the colonies, and lesser pieces were also reprinted in their newspaper columns. The writings of Franklin and a few other colonial authors found their way into print in Great Britain. Travelers, going in both directions, exchanged reports when they returned home. British officials maintained a presence in the colonies, their numbers always augmented during the many wars with France, which began in 1689. Colonists made long stays abroad when they sought education, like Benjamin Rush going to medical school in Edinburgh, Gilbert Stuart working in the art studios of Benjamin West, and Franklin mastering the printing trade in London. Not a single cultural unit, as the Revolution would reveal, the Anglo-American connection was very much alive.

New Thinking about the Economy

The greatest threat to the habit of thrift came with the waves of new objects to buy that appeared in English shops: colorful calicoes from India, tobacco from Virginia, and maps, prints, and furnishings from hundreds of British ateliers. The avidity of buyers prompted new reflections about human nature. "The Wants of the Mind are infinite," one contemporary observer noted. "Man naturally Aspires, and as his Mind is elevated, his Senses grow more refined, and more capable of Delight; his Desires are inlarged, and his Wants increase with his Wishes, which is for everything that is rare, can gratifie his Senses, adorn his Body and promise the Ease, Pleasure and Pomp of Life."[2]

More challenging to the actual practice of thrift was the observation that "the main spur to Trade, or rather to Industry and Ingenuity, is the exorbitant Appetites of Men which they will take pains to gratifie, and so be disposed to work, when nothing else will incline them to it; for did Men content themselves with bare Necessaries, we should have a poor World."[3] Clearly a human response had come into view that needed to be described, understood, and perhaps controlled.

The rise in consumption led to social theories that moved well beyond clerical moralizing and beggar-thy-neighbor prescriptions for maintaining national wealth. The economic dynamism, evident in England as the eighteenth century began, had created a plateau of prosperity that changed the spending habits of men and women at all levels of society in the Anglo-American worlds. The enhanced productivity of farmers and manufacturers created sufficient returns for capital investments as well as personal spending. The significance of colonial imports of British-manufactured goods that could be easily measured through custom receipts gave colonists a new status as customers. As hostilities among European countries discouraged trade across the English Channel, British merchants increasingly turned to the kingdom's colonies in the New World.

In the initial writings on commercial activity, a clear divide emerged between those who continued to think in Aristotelian terms and those who broke entirely with that intellectual tradition. The Aristotelians composed aphorisms for traders and tradespeople; they spoke in essentialist terms of fixed prices and standard rates. New entrants into the discussions about trade preferred to talk about increasing rather than regulating it. They offered more analysis than advice. Their first task was to isolate economic elements from their social and political entanglements, all the better to avoid patrimonial intrusions from the king and his minister. Soon they differentiated causal factors from contingent ones.

Slowly the idea that the economy was an autonomous system of exchange built up, in defiance of the older view that the economy had to be directed from the political center. The traditionalists looked to royal authority to regulate commercial relations, particularly the exchange rate. The pragmatic acceptance of fluidity and individual judgment in commercial life offended them deeply, but no one could stop commerce from moving into uncharted geographic and conceptual waters.[4]

One nearly intractable problem grew even worse in the early modern period: that of controlling labor. Manufacturers who had to deal with the dissolute habits of their employees thought in punitive terms, insisting on the necessity of low wages to impose thrift on the working class, while merchants, especially those who sent their ships overseas, began to connect greater purchasing power with high wages. As with the opposing essentialists and pragmatists, the manufacturing representatives relied more on truisms about personal behavior than abstract models of the economy. Those less involved in the day-to-day work of producing goods began to envision an ethos of productivity that would dramatically change the very nature of society. Among John Locke's papers is a scrape upon which Locke scribbled, "If all the people in the world worked, the world's work could be done in half a day." The social leveling implicit in such a reflection is as startling as the advocacy of a functional society to replace the existing one honeycombed with customs, statuses, privileges, and prescriptions.[5]

Consumption—the active seeking of personal gratification through material goods—was the force that had to be reckoned with. Like other social activities, consumption had first to be named before it could be discussed. As long as thrift and its associated values of restraint and moderation dominated moral discussion, there was no room for a positive evaluation of spending. Yet writers began to formulate one that continued to win advocates decade by decade despite the renewed call for curbed appetites.

Research has demonstrated that it was domestic consumption, not foreign trade, that sustained England's manufacturing expansion in the eighteenth century.[6] But social concerns trumped economic knowledge in the early eighteenth century. The critics of material abundance seized the discursive high ground in England, appealing to classical republican texts to stigmatize novelty as the harbinger of social unrest. Using the essay form to inveigh against the new consuming tastes, these social critics identified the goods they saw in haberdashery shops and food stalls as dangerous signs of corruption and degeneration. Against the delights of consumption they pitted predictions of social disintegration. The only antidote was frugality and simple living for the people and austere civic virtue in their leaders—in short, a return to thrift. The rubric under which they rallied was luxury.

Luxury, Civil Society, and the Scottish Intervention

Worries about consumption did not go away; they appeared in new guises in the revival of classical wisdom about luxury. Later, Smith and his circle of fellow Scottish moralists reacted against these literary lamentations with their excursions into the social sciences. In the closing years of the century, those exhilarated by the French Revolution found their intellectual Waterloo in Malthus's mordant rebuff to optimism about the future.

Luxury was not a thing but a concept. The Greek view of luxury complemented the biblical view. Luxury in the Old Testament represented a complex of evils moving from the personal and inveterate propensities of humankind to the ethical tendencies of the nation. The gravest feature of the repeated lapses was evidence of disobedience. When a people ignores the law of necessity, it undermines the established hierarchy between lawgiver and subject. Necessity sets limits, and happiness, according to this view revived in English letters, consists in having the rational capacity to abide by those restraints. Luxury brings disorder because it destroys harmony and prevents human beings from fulfilling their nature.[7]

In both Christian and classical thought the central unworthiness of human beings stems from their desiring things that are unnecessary. Taking control of this endemic envy, vanity, gluttony, and lust requires both draconian laws and God's redeeming grace. Augustan essayists, political figures, novelists, and journalists contributed to an unrelieved depiction of the horrors awaiting England if the nation did not mend its luxurious ways. Luxury was not a personal indulgence; it was a national calamity, as the biblical account of the ravages of luxury offered in the books of Samuel and Kings so powerfully demonstrated.

Hebraic tradition, which gave English Puritans so rich a rhetorical resource for vivifying sin, identified luxury with desire and desire with disobedience. Eve indulged in luxury when she unnecessarily ate the fruit of the tree of knowledge. The Israelites persisted in the most serious of human errors in their yearnings for things that they neither needed nor had the right to claim. When represented anthropomorphically, luxury, of course, is a woman—sometimes a powerful evoker of desire carrying the comb and mirror of cupidity and self-love, at other times an abject, naked woman under attack from toads and snakes.

Depicted as a constant psychological drive, the attraction to luxury, Augustine said, could never be more than suppressed, but the act of suppressing it constituted the reason and justification for the minute control of the status, duties, and privileges of all members of society. England had failed dramatically to do that during the political upheavals of its civil war. In the eighteenth century it risked becoming as Socrates described Athens when it was acquiring "a multitude of callings which are not required by any natural want; such as the whole tribe of actors, of whom one large class have to do with forms and colours; another will be votaries of music—poets and their attendant trains of rhapsodists, players, dancers, contactors; also makers of diverse kinds of articles, including women's dresses." Athens might be visited by economic development as England had been.[8]

Writers fell over themselves declaiming against luxury and the loss of thrifty habits. Henry Fielding spoke of a "vast torrent of Luxury which of late Years hath poured itself into the nation . . . almost totally changed the Manners, Customs, and Habits of the People, more especially of the lower Sort." Even more dangerous, he explained, was the stirring up of desire among the poor, "a desire for things they may not and cannot have, hence their wickedness, profligacy, idleness, and dishonesty."[9]

Of course the presence of shops bulging with cheeses, sweetmeats, coffee, tea, table linens, dry goods, gadgets, pictures, and prints gave the lie to Fielding's assertion that the lower sort desired things they could not have. It was exactly their increasing ability to buy what was being made available in ever-cheaper forms that created the crisis of social leadership. Popular attraction to the sensual pleasures of eating, entertainment, adornment, and comfort—made manifest in actual consumption—gave proof of the need for strictly enforced hierarchies of authority in the home, the shop, the street, the town hall, and the church.

The disjuncture between the jeremiads on luxury and the source of prosperity in the conspicuous behavior of ordinary people cried out for clarification. Bernard de Mandeville, a Dutch physician living in England, captured the confusion in this discourse about luxury when he pointed out that it was vice, not virtue, that stoked the engine of commerce. Mandeville's goal, however, was to point up the hypocrisy in the outcry against luxury, not to endorse the abandonment of society to the consuming impulses of the least-discerning members of society.[10]

Closely attuned to the writers and moralists who worried about how new vanities threatened old customs were political leaders who criticized the king and his advisers for corrupting Parliament. Looking back to classical texts for lessons in political stability, these opposition leaders taught a kind of classical republicanism in which men—and it was only men—realized their full human potential by participating in civic affairs. Supported by a substructure of laboring men and all women, this idealized citizenry of landowners, in the prescriptive literature, would achieve moral autonomy because of its independence from pecuniary concerns. Capable of disinterested reasoning, they would deliberate within a community of peers.

A highly artificial construct, classical citizenship elevated the citizen above things crass, mundane, earthy, and vulgar. Commerce reeked of all these unattractive qualities, linking men and women together in new systems of interdependence while exploiting physical needs, worldly tastes, undisciplined wants, and preposterous yearnings. Rather than try to understand the economic changes transforming their society, parliamentary reformers like Lord Henry Bolingbroke looked backward like the Augustan essayists to the ancients. What their writings pointed up was how menacing prosperity was to a social order that relied on deference and dependence for its ties. In subtle ways, the suggestion that thrift was not necessary raised questions as well about the necessity of submissiveness from the lower classes.

The Augustans were conspicuously unsuccessful in stemming either the tide of popular spending or the rush of entrepreneurs to meet the new demand for goods. By midcentury the profits from commerce, banking, and manufacturing were paying for city amenities like coffee shops, lecture halls, and meeting rooms. Within the many new forms of public sociability, consumption began to appear less threatening. As Thomas Paine wrote enthusiastically, "Commerce works to cordialize mankind."[11] More impishly, Samuel Johnson explained that "there are few ways in which a man can be more innocently employed than in getting money."[12]

Not forced to overthrow an oppressive old regime like their neighbors across the Channel, prosperous English men and women settled down to enjoying the affability afforded them by urban life. Sipping coffee, displaying new forms of politeness, relishing the wit and wisdom of their enlightened age, they bent their minds to figuring out how individuals could pursue life, liberty, wealth, and happiness while maintaining the social solidarity and order that all agreed were essential. Thrift might still be a good policy for the poor, but the middle classes had conspicuously joined the gentry and nobility in displaying both their taste and their purchasing power.

The more serious conversation about economic development and social change took place among Hume, Smith, and their friends, who moved the discussion about thrift and luxury onto an entirely different plane.[13] Building on a century of commentary, Smith produced a magisterial study of how nations grow wealthy. Slowly, he explained, habits of thrift had created the stored wealth of savings, which made it possible to organize labor better. With more employees, manufacturers increased output by breaking the production process down into minute steps. Applying the division of labor took capital for hiring more workers and then for marketing the increased output, and hence this development awaited the accumulation of savings.

These mechanisms, Smith argued, could sustain a momentum of ever-increasing productivity that eventually would push all countries into the niche where they would have a natural, comparative advantage. Fed with ever-renewed freshets of capital, the modern commercial system would escape the cycle of luxury, corruption, and decline because it enlisted the self-improving energies of most members of society.

Following Hume, Smith saw that in the much-lauded primitive societies where men and women retained the whole of their produce, there was material equality but lives of misery and want. In commercial societies, with their flagrantly unequal distribution of wealth, the laboring poor prospered as well. Smith's description of how nations grow wealthy through commerce—ingeniously detailed as it was—would not have answered the moral question posed by their contemporaries had not he and Hume before him considered human morality from the new perspective of the great sympathies and sociability enlisted in commercial society.

Smith attributed to all human beings the propensity to truck and barter, as well as the incessant drive to improve their condition. From these promptings human beings were drawn to each other's company. Here in the marketplace, not the political assembly of classical times, modern men and women developed the capacity to reflect on themselves in society, to excel by emulating virtue and shunning dishonor. In the concourses of commerce, human beings acquired their notion of probity and justice.

It was also a feature of the modern entrepreneurial economy that ordinary laborers were independent. They fed themselves through their wages and thereby participated in what Smith called the system of natural liberty. By shifting investigations of human character from politics to economics, the Scots were creating a conceptual universe that included the lower classes. Modern commerce had made it possible for all to be independent and thus cut the critical link in classical theory between independent citizens and dependent, disenfranchised workers. Within the realm of independent men—wage laborers, merchants, manufacturers, and landlords—the natural operation of the invisible hand of the market could regulate affairs better than the legislator's, thus adding to the freedom from servile dependency a freedom from overweening political authority.

Although it took him until book 4 to say it, Smith placed buying at the heart of modern market society: "Consumption is the sole end and purpose of all production and the interest of the producer ought to be attended to, only so far as it may be necessary for promoting that of the consumer. The maxim is so perfectly self-evident, that it would be absurd to attempt to prove it."[14] Yet Smith was far from happy with the human propensity to consume, characterizing it variously as a fascination for "baubles and trinkets," a passion for accumulating objects of "frivolous utility," and, worse, a vehicle for deception with the false promise that wealth would bring happiness.

Money will, at best, "keep off the summer shower," Smith said, "but not the winter storm," leaving humans more exposed than before to anxiety, fear, and sorrow, and to disease, danger, and death.[15] Thus, even as a new mastery of economic phenomena was being achieved, the older rationale for thrift reappeared. Buying and spending, as William Wordsworth wrote, "we lay waste our powers." Economic development had arrived, but dissatisfaction with the habits it promoted persisted.

Among the strengths of the Scottish moral philosophers was their ability to build on human nature as they found it and to discern the springs of moral action from the close observation of men and women in their own society. Probing for the causes of the avidity so evident in his society, Smith concluded that it was envy and admiration for the rich and powerful and fearful contempt of the poor that drove men to seek wealth. And since in modern society, with its striking inequality of condition, where the prods from above and beneath were omnipresent, the material wants of man would be insatiable. In the "uniform, constant and uninterrupted effort of every man to better his condition," Smith found the greatest grounds for hope.[16] For this was the human disposition that prompted men to defer pleasure, to save, to compete, and to shun prodigality.

The most sophisticated analyses of the modern commercial society that blossomed in the eighteenth-century Anglo-American world came back to thrift. Only this time thrift was connected not so much to the well-regulated life as to the great engine of productivity. The desire for goods was no longer seen as a sign of disobedience to God or as the deformation of a fine-tuned character but rather as a requisite part of modern society. At their best, the delights of consumption would push people to work harder. The new ethic shunned waste, fraud, and idleness but not well-earned spending. The word *comfort* began to figure as the happy mean between biting necessity and indulgent luxury.

Mary Wollstonecraft elaborated on the notion of comfort when she explained that the French people had never acquired an idea of that independent, comfortable situation in which contentment—rather than happiness—is sought, because the slaves of pleasure or power can be roused only by lively emotions and extravagant hopes. In fact, she went on to observe that the French did not even have a word in their vocabulary to express comfort, "that state of existence, in which reason renders serene and useful the days which passion would only cheat with flying dreams of happiness."[17] However, the concept stretched across the Atlantic. Working over a draft treaty sent to him from John Adams in 1787, Thomas Jefferson replaced the word *necessities* with *comforts*. The new American nation would establish commercial treaties on the basis of exchanging comforts, not just necessities.[18]

The passions evoked by the French Revolution challenged the benign optimism of those making their peace with Smith's market society. Across the Channel it became apparent that competitive self-interest could translate quickly into violent clashes of interest. The discreet skepticism of Hume flowered into the open irreverence of Paine, which was promulgated to ordinary people through mass printings. If labor, instead of being God's curse on Adam, created value, what was the position of the laborer? Even liberty and equality looked different when the economy, rather than the polity, became the preeminent social system. What need was there of the talented few whose extraordinary virtue and rectitude alone preserved the constitution if it was the economy that provided stability?

The century's last word in economic theorizing in England went to Robert Thomas Malthus, who put forward a population theory that interpreted abundance as spurious and pernicious. He sidestepped the debate about human predispositions and socializing influences, arguing instead that human beings were ruled by a set of inexorable equations. Consumption was at the center of his theory. Abundance created cheap food. In good times, men and women married early and had lots of children. Without the checks of war and disease, human population would grow geometrically, swiftly outpacing the incremental increases of harvests that brought forth the surplus births.[19]

Unequivocal about the immediate relevance of his mathematical discovery, Malthus wrote, in his first essay on population growth, which appeared in 1798, that the "period when the number of men surpass their means of subsistence has long since arrived, has existed ever since we have had any histories of mankind, does exist at present, and will for ever continue to exist."[20] The possibility of easy living demonstrated to Malthus that only biting necessity got human beings to exert themselves. Thus while the fear of famine was evil, it was only a partial evil because it acted for the greater good by teaching men and women their true situation, inculcating the lessons of thrift and restraint through hunger pangs.

Since Malthus did not believe that either deferred marriage or family limitations could relieve this parlous human condition, he consigned human beings to a new determinism, the one inflicted by nature. The crucial issue became whether men and women could regulate their numbers and thereby avoid the evils of population pressure. Malthus said no, and for the rest of his life refined his explanation of nature's great catch-22 about plenty and poverty.

The American Setting

In many ways, the eighteenth century is an anomalous period in the history of thrift in its American setting. As the essays on the seventeenth and nineteenth centuries by Stephen Innes and Daniel Walker Howe in this volume emphasize, the Puritans and their descendants drew their ideas about thrift from Puritan theology and homiletics—what became known later in the scholarly world as the Protestant work ethic, explicated by the German sociologist Max Weber.

The advice and bromides that filled colonial almanacs carried the venerable wisdom about self-disciplined moderation, as did the columns of newspapers, but in the eighteenth century, as we have seen, a competing set of tastes and values emerged. An urban culture sprang up. Like men and women in provincial cities throughout the rest of the empire, those in Boston, New York, Philadelphia, Williamsburg, and Charleston eagerly sought to imitate the architecture and fashions of London.

Although the American social structure was a pyramid without an apex, there were enough well-off families to be able to fill the ships outbound from Great Britain with crates of china, fabric, clocks, mirrors, utensils, and jewelry. Wishing to set themselves off from ordinary people, the gentry put their servants into livery. Merchants built grand townhouses, while southern planters decorated the streams and rivers of the South with the handsome plantation houses they built to replace the region's original, modest structures.

For the upper classes, restraint seems to have become passé as they rushed to copy the clothes and furnishings of the British officials who came with their families to take up posts in the colonies. Through much of the century, returns on southerners' rice, tobacco, and indigo crops were large enough to encourage English merchants to extend a long line of credit. By midcentury most planters who could had committed a substantial part of their next year's crop to paying last year's bills.

Fashionable consumption entered the colonies very quickly in the middle third of the eighteenth century. The craze for decorative items like china tea services reached well down into the middle class. Within a generation comforts were calibrated as necessities, and luxuries had been redesignated as comforts. Archaeological digs and surveys of probate inventories have turned up a surprising quantity of English goods owned by middling families.[21] What had happened so quickly had been a rejection of the plain style that had been conspicuous during the first generations of settlement. With the abandonment of the simple and unostentatious came a scramble for adornments and possessions that could distinguish one stratum of society from another.

Like the Augustan writers who raised the alarm about luxury in England, the colonists produced their own Cassandras. Reflecting traditional wisdom, almost all writers accepted the spending of the rich and shuddered at the social upheaval only when the poor followed suit.[22] Here imitation seems more influential than reality, for America's distinguished families had not been around long. The flourishing economy of the eighteenth century produced not only a high level of prosperity but also a lot of new wealth as well, yet colonists were well aware of the importance of social distinctions in Great Britain.

For those not involved in a contest for social position, a significant part of disposable income went to upgrading amenities like furniture and table settings. Nothing so marked the eighteenth century as the building and refurbishing of residential space. Men and women seized the opportunity to shelter their informal, personal acts from outside scrutiny, first by simply adding partitions to close off rooms and subsequently by creating privacy for the daily acts of sleeping, eating, bathing, entertaining, and reading, with appropriate rooms for each. These domestic innovations introduced the ubiquity of the parlor, where special possessions could be showcased.

Lessons of thrift, learned at their parents' knees, still resonated among colonists, particularly those in the working class. If a man aspired to pass from being a journeyman in a craft to becoming a master, savings were critical. With marriages still carrying a dowry to the husband, selecting a mate became partly a business calculation. The expenses of marriage also got attention, with hackneyed stories about wives hankering after expensive tea sets making their way repeatedly into the newspapers.

What changed in the eighteenth century was the migration of homilies about moderation from a religious context to that of prudential advice. The life of Franklin, which spanned the eighteenth century, conveys this transformation perfectly. Franklin detailed in his autobiography, begun for the benefit of his son, the many canny ways he cultivated relationships with important people, moved up in his craft, nurtured his savings, and secured loans. Often the impression of seeming busy was enough, in his view, to achieve the end of building that reputation for rectitude so crucial to a rising businessman. Franklin could not gauge accurately which contributed more to his success, his spectacular talents or his well-honed discipline; we are inclined to think the former, but he probably credited his own character and efforts.

A clever writer as well as a successful printer and publisher, Franklin created the character of Poor Richard to fill his popular almanacs with shrewd taglines. A colonial favorite, Poor Richard admonished readers to "remember, that *time* is money." He also announced that credit was money and that "money is of the prolific, generating nature." Poor Richard advised borrowers that "the most trifling actions that affect a man's credit are to be regarded," explaining that "the sound of your hammer at five in the morning, or eight at night, heard by a creditor, makes him easy six months longer." Sayings like these delighted Weber, who was looking for proof of changing values in early modern Europe and its colonies. Franklin's Poor Richard columns epitomized this radical ethic, which Weber made into the linchpin of his study of capitalism.[23]

Weber's *Protestant Ethic and the Spirit of Capitalism* shocked readers when it was published in 1904 because it suggested that religious doctrine, faith, and piety had been central to the emergence of capitalism. Going against the grain of the accepted belief that techniques like the division of labor had made the entrepreneurial economy possible, Weber insisted that it took a change of habits and thoughts before the kind of rational, disciplined effort required of economic development could take place.

In asking about a new ethic supportive of capitalist growth, Weber concerned himself with something that did not much interest his fellow scholars, most of whom took the modern imperatives of capitalism for granted. He stated his premise quite clearly: "A man does not 'by nature' wish to earn more and more money, but simply to live as he is accustomed to live and to earn as much as is necessary for that purpose." In precapitalist times, Weber maintained, men and women—whether employers or employees—preferred to work less than earn more.[24] This being the case, how were early modern men and women ever shaken out of the customary routines that clogged work with holidays, naps, personal idleness, long lunches, and irrational attachment to inefficient techniques?

Weber's answer was the Protestant religion in the full flush of its break with Rome. Under the tutelage of John Calvin, English and Dutch Protestants claimed the mundane world as a field of Christian labors. They introduced reason into the organization of work tasks and celebrated each person's calling as sacred in the eyes of God. They viewed disciplined workdays as security against the snares of the devil. The thrift associated with moderation and restraint in classical and biblical texts now took on a more totalizing aspect, demanding the control of impulse and the application of unceasing effort.

Calvinism did not promote capitalism per se, but it produced the kind of men and women who would upend old ways of doing things and make way for the new. They cultivated in their devotional life the kind of attitudes and behavior that would encourage the accumulation of profits and the reinvestment of savings into yet greater production systems. This assiduous application of thought, time, and savings revolutionized the traditional economic order. In choosing Franklin's Poor Richard as an exemplar of the spirit of capitalism, Weber was as interested in Franklin's lack of piety as he was in his aphorisms, for he wanted to show how over time the original religious impulse had been recalibrated as practical wisdom.

The actual experience of the middling classes in England and the colonies substantiated Weber's belief that the titanic fight against profligacy and the constant inculcation of good work habits were critically important to the progress of capitalism. In America, the classroom was the farmhouse, in which 80 percent of the colonists lived. In shops and factories as well, children grew up under the eye of an interested relative. Parental attention focused on adolescent boys, who were deemed most at risk to the temptations of idleness, drinking, and sexual adventures.[25] Mixing humor with practical caution, Poor Richard no doubt seemed the appropriate guide in thousands of colonial households where parents were shepherding the young across the bridge of adolescence to secure manhood and womanhood.

Poor Richard's strictures about borrowing point up the capitalist element Franklin took for granted. His favorite sage did not advise against borrowing; rather, he was in favor of creating the kind of reputation that greased the wheels for getting loans. People raising money for business ventures commonly sought loans from friends and relatives or asked them to countersign as surety in getting money from a stranger. The demonstrations of thrift and moderation that Poor Richard recommended proved credit worthiness within one's community. Equally obligatory was making prompt and regular payments to sustain one's reputation and to enhance the possibility of getting additional loans as need arose.

Indebtedness was an inevitable component of colonial society, with its scarcity of capital and its abundance of petty entrepreneurs. Even the smallest farmers had occasions to invest in crops for future sales, once the needs of the family had been met. The grand plantation owners of the South were deeply in debt, with the value of their tobacco, rice, and indigo harvests being high enough to spring open generous lines of credits with the British merchant houses that handled their crops. Producing, spending, and borrowing formed a circle that usually only death or bankruptcy could interrupt.

Thrift, or the lack thereof, became a potent element in the polemics that led up to the American Revolution.[26] Much of the fighting of the Seven Years' War took place on the North American continent, where New France and its Indian allies confronted colonists along a long border extending from Pennsylvania through New York and New England. It was an intercolonial war effort, bringing Virginians like George Washington into the Pennsylvania battles to secure dominance on the North American continent. When Prime Minister William Pitt decided to invest heavily in the American sector of the war front, which extended to Europe and the Caribbean, he poured in army and navy personnel and a host of civil servants to administer the campaigns. After the war, the English officials returned home to tell their countrymen and country women about the colonial society of which the British public had little awareness, much less knowledge.

What struck the English soldiers and civil servants most was the level of prosperity in the colonies. Where earlier British visitors had noted the quality and quantity of food enjoyed by American colonists and the paucity of beggars, these later observers gushed about the imported English luxuries that ordinary colonists possessed. Teapots, printed cottons, prints, mirrors, and books appeared in the homes of artisans, shopkeepers, and lawyers in addition to those of wealthy merchants, they said. Paid for in part by the money Great Britain was pouring into the colonies to mount the war effort against New France, these purchases provoked indignation among the English. Somehow, in their imagination, the designation of *colonial* carried with it a due subordination in material possessions as well as in political power. After the war was won, the British attempted to shift their share of the war's cost to the colonists, thus launching the chain of events that led to colonial independence.

That the American colonists were lightly taxed compared with the English furnished a rationale for reforming the imperial tax system, a fateful initiative that led to a decade of protests capped off by the colonists' Declaration of Independence and the successful prosecution of a war to secure it. As the political leader John Dickinson lamented, "An opinion has been industriously propagated in Great Britain, that the colonies are wallowing in wealth and luxury." The colonists insisted that English writers were totally misrepresenting the true state of the modest colonial living standards even as they accused the British of wanting to keep them poor.[27]

Thrift acquired a powerful new support in the decade of resistance that preceded the outbreak of hostilities. Americans' buying habits became a double-edged sword. They justified new taxation to the British, but they also suggested to the colonists ways to oppose the taxes. In sending boatloads of textiles, tools, and decorative items to the colonies, the British had also delivered hostages to the colonies. Boycotting the importing of British goods became an effective device used from the resistance to the Stamp Act in 1765 to the Continental System prohibiting all trade with Great Britain nine years later. When British merchants urged members of Parliament to repeal the Stamp Act, they handed the colonists a weapon forged by their own importing patterns.

The several nonimportant agreements that bound merchants not to import British goods severely strained the colonists' capacity to continue resistance. Merchants, inclined by their wealth to be conservative, became targets of the crowds' wrath when they continued to import those tempting commodities from England, and, one suspects, also for being so wealthy.[28] Colonial housewives scorned imported fabrics and returned to the frugal taste of an earlier day. Wearing homespun became a badge of honor that even as elegant a dresser as Washington observed.

In England, some observers saw that American consumption had been a mighty engine for England's own economic train, but the compatible economic relations between the mother country and the continental colonies foundered on the rock of assertions of indivisible sovereignty. After six years of fighting, Great Britain gave up the richest part of its first empire, and the thirteen colonies, successfully independent, had to weave themselves into a nation.

The successful conclusion of the American War for Independence left the new Americans woefully deep in private and public debt. The necessity of thrift did not need to be stressed; few had any alternatives but to restrain their purchases and make do with what they had. Unable to exact sufficient requisitions from the thirteen states that had signed the Articles of Confederation, the Continental Congress prosecuted the war on loans, confiscations, and paper money. Printed with abandon, the paper money began to depreciate the minute it came off the press, leaving behind the expression "not worth a Continental dime." Franklin ingeniously suggested that the rapidly depreciating bills acted as a kind of tax that each holder paid during the time he or she held the note.

Peace reversed the fortunes of the northern and southern states of the new United States. The staple-producing areas of the South lost their privileged position within the empire, whereas the more entrepreneurial, commercial northern cities found themselves liberated from British restrictions. Able to strike out with their ships and cargoes to any place in the world, it took them less than ten years to reach India! And foreign trade was but one facet of an independent economy that moved in new directions in farming, manufacturing, and marketing.

The eighteenth century closed with America on the cusp of a great religious revival. Actually comprising dozens of local revivals, the Second Great Awakening brought American culture back to the simple tastes that reigned at the beginning of the century. Methodist and Baptist clergymen followed American families as they moved westward. They preached a powerful, personal message about salvation. Unencumbered by the costly seminaries of the older churches, the sects could easily increase the number of their preachers. The colonial Congregational and Anglican establishments became American denominations, seeking voluntary support alongside the new sects. The older churches, mainly located along the Atlantic seaboard, did not escape the influence of evangelizing Christianity.

The older ideals of living without ostentation, dressing simply, and rearing children to modest behavior dominated again. The Federalists, governing under Washington and John Adams in the closing decade of the century, tried to establish a national elite with all the elegance and conspicuous consumption implied by the term, but the coming century was to belong to America's ordinary men and women. Even southerners acquired a deeply felt faith that curbed extravagant living styles. Sweat equity and family loans financed hundreds of new ventures like these. Few colonial estates made it through the Revolution. Innovation-averse in an age of dramatic change, the wealthy yielded economic leadership to ordinary Americans, who succeeded in gaining political power as well with the election of Jefferson. Thrift, initially imposed by necessity, became more culturally powerful when endorsed by members of the rapidly expanding middle class.

No longer restrained by royal edict, families poured into, and beyond, the western parts of Virginia, New York, Pennsylvania, Tennessee, and Kentucky. Poor men had the rare opportunity to turn their labor into capital by preparing claimed land for cultivation, selling it in an improved state, and moving on. By 1810, one-third of Americans lived beyond the Appalachian Mountains. Their capacity for productive labor astonished all. Rejecting the grim conclusions of Malthus, Jefferson wrote with some hyperbole that the fertility of American soil produced crops that grew exponentially, thus springing the citizens of the new United States from the population trap.[29]

The novelty of consumption in the eighteenth century had come from the inclusion of more and more people in the spending spree. Elite groups had always consumed, and they had used consumption for self-gratification and to establish their identities. Ordinary people had to brave the ridicule of others and buy beyond their station. This impinged on every social and political relation. Coming to terms with popular consumption as the driving force behind the new productive system was not easy for members of the elite, who had to give up many of the visual cues of their superiority. More important, they had to accept—however grudgingly—that ordinary people were self-activating agents, masters of their own dollars, if not their destiny.

The urban conviviality that commercial prosperity introduced into the eighteenth-century Anglo-American world narrowed to a family-based respectability in nineteenth-century America. More new farms came into existence even than stores and shops; the country remained rural. Evangelical Christians reclaimed the public sphere from the sophisticates who previously set tastes. Increasingly, the desire to better oneself became associated with the motive of providing for one's family. Novelists gave respectability a distinctly material embodiment in the cleanliness and cut of clothes, the privacy afforded in the home, and the accoutrements required for the round of domestic rituals.

Thrift acquired more champions at the end of the century, though its champions would have distinguished it from parsimony and an inability to appreciate the niceties of living. The love of refinement stirred personal ambitions, but the restraint imposed by good manners was more important to a reputation for being refined than was the mere acquisition of beautiful objects. And the long train of speculations about the workings of the new economy passed, unmissed, into the newly forming "dismal science" of economics. The eighteenth century, with all its temptations to chase after what Smith had called "baubles and trinkets" of "frivolous utility," had been weathered. A new generation, confident of its capacity for self-government, both personal and political, moved onto the national stage.

Notes

1. Sidney Mintz explores these booms in *Sweetness and Power: The Place of Sugar in Modern History* (New York: Viking Press, 1985).

2. Nicholas Barbon, *A Discourse of Trade* (London: printed for J. Johnson, 1690), 15.

3. Dudley North, *Discourses upon Trade* (London: printed for J. Johnson, 1681), 114. This body of literature is discussed in Joyce Oldham Appleby, *Economic Thought and Ideology in Seventeenth-Century England* (Princeton, NJ: Princeton University Press, 1978).

4. Appleby, *Economic Thought and Ideology*, 42–48.

5. Lovelace Collection of Locke Papers, Cambridge University Library.

6. Neil McKendrick, "Home Demand and Economic Growth: A New View of the Role of Women and Children in the Industrial Revolution," in *Historical Perspectives: Studies in English Thought and Society in Honour of J. H. Plumb*, ed. Neil McKendrick (London: Europa, 1974).

7. John Sekora, *Luxury: The Concept in Western Thought, Eden to Smollet* (Baltimore: Johns Hopkins University Press, 1977). See Joyce Appleby, "Consumption in Early Modern Social Thought," in *Consumption and the World of Goods*, ed. John Brewer and Roy Porter (London: Routledge, 1993), 162-176.

8. Sekora, *Luxury*, 44.

9. Henry Fielding, quoted in ibid., 5.

10. Bernard de Mandeville, *The Fable of the Bees; or, Private Vices, Public Benefits* (London: printed for J. Roberts, 1714).

11. Thomas Paine, *Rights of Man, Being an Answer to Mr. Burke's Attack on the French Revolution* (London: J. S. Jordan, 1791), 99.

12. James Boswell, *Life of Samuel Johnson*, ed. George Birkbeck Hill (1791; Oxford: Clarendon Press, 1887), 2:323.

13. Istan Hont and Michael Ignatieff, "Needs and Justice in the *Wealth of Nations*: An Introductory Essay," and Nicholas Phillipson, "Adam Smith as Civic Moralist," both in *Wealth and Virtue*, ed. Istan Hont and Michael Ignatieff (Cambridge: Cambridge University Press, 1983), 79-202.

14. Adam Smith, *An Inquiry into the Nature and Causes of the Wealth of Nations* (New York: Modern Library, 1937), 623, hereafter referred to as *Wealth of Nations.*

15. Adam Smith, quoted in Hont and Ignatieff, "Needs and Justice," 10.

16. Smith, *Wealth of Nations*, 324–25. See also Samuel Fleischacker, *On Adam Smith's Wealth of Nations: A Philosophical Companion* (Princeton, NJ: Princeton University Press, 2004), 61–70.

17. Mary Wollstonecraft, *An Historical and Moral View of the Origin and Progress of the French Revolution and the Effect It Has Produced in Europe* (London: printed by Thomas Dobson at the Stove-house, 1795), 511.

18. Thomas Jefferson to John Adams, November 27, 1785, in *The Adams-Jefferson Letters: The Complete Correspondence between Thomas Jefferson and Abigail and John Adams*, ed. Lester J. Cappon (Chapel Hill: University of North Carolina Press, 1959), 1:103.

19. Robert Thomas Malthus, *An Essay on the Principle of Population* (London: printed for J. Johnson in St.-Paul's Church-Yard, 1798).

20. Ibid., 272.

21. Cary Carson, "The Consumer Revolution in Colonial British America: Why Demand?" in *Of Consuming Interests: The Style of Life in the Eighteenth Century*, ed. Cary Carson, Ronald Hoffman, and Peter J. Albert (Charlottesville: University of Virginia Press, 1994), 494–99.

22. Ibid., 521.

23. Max Weber, *The Protestant Ethic and the Spirit of Capitalism* (1904–5; New York: Scribner, 1958), 48–50. All these sayings of Poor Richard appear in Weber's book.

24. Ibid., 60.

25. Margaret R. Hunt, *The Middling Sort: Commerce, Gender, and the Family in England, 1680–1780* (Berkeley and Los Angeles: University of California Press, 1996), 47–56.

26. T. H. Breen, *The Marketplace of Revolution: How Consumer Politics Shaped American Independence* (New York: Oxford University Press, 2004).

27. John Dickinson, quoted in ibid., 11; see also ibid., 14.

28. Gary Nash, *The Urban Crucible: Social Change, Political Consciousness, and the Origins of the American Revolution* (Cambridge, MA: Harvard University Press, 1979), 351–56, 350–57.

29. Jefferson to J. B. Say, February 1, 1804, in *The Writings of Thomas Jefferson*, ed. A. A. Lipscomb and A. E. Bergh, 20 vols. (Washington, DC: issued under the auspices of the Thomas Jefferson Memorial Association of the United States, 1903–4), 11:2–3.

7 }

Spreading the Gospel of Self-Denial

THRIFT AND ASSOCIATION IN ANTEBELLUM AMERICA

Kathleen D. McCarthy

"Americans of all ages, all conditions, and all dispositions constantly form associations," marveled Alexis de Tocqueville in 1840. "As soon as several of the inhabitants of the United States have taken up an opinion or a feeling which they wish to promote in the world" they unite, and "from that moment they are no longer isolated men, but a power seen from afar . . . whose language is listened to."[1] Beginning in the 1790s, American voluntary associations preached the gospel of thrift to men, women, and children of every station. Three waves of associational activity helped to forge the antebellum thrift ethic's dual emphasis on parsimony and upright behavior: a growing crop of urban charities that began to appear in the 1790s; the reformist organizations of the Benevolent Empire after 1810; and the efforts of mutual aid societies and lodges such as the Washingtonians and the Sons and Daughters of Temperance in the 1840s. The result was a complex web of initiatives that ultimately helped to recast the parameters of virtuous behavior, individual piety, public sin, and "moral" consumption.

These campaigns were fueled by a variety of concerns. Protestant proselytizing was the driving engine behind the Benevolent Empire—the network of Bible, tract, Sunday school, and temperance societies (among others) that emerged in the early national and Jacksonian years. However, reformers were also inspired by a secular desire to aid impoverished women, reduce pauperism and tax rates, enhance working-class solidarity, and combat racism.

Although religion was important, economic considerations, rather than religious proselytizing, were the common thread that united these efforts, all of which needed money to operate and grow. As a result, almost all of these campaigns engaged in commercial transactions, which drew them into the antebellum scramble for profits.

These groups not only encouraged Americans to adapt to the profound economic changes of the antebellum years through their moral injunctions but were deeply enmeshed in the market economy themselves, simultaneously preaching the interrelated doctrines of thrift, investment, abstemious behavior, and consumerism for social causes and self-improvement. Moreover, just as the consumption ethic helps to drive the American economy today, the nineteenth-century thrift ethic provided surplus cash for economic development, binding associations and their adherents to the expanding capitalist economy in a variety of ways. In the decades before the Civil War, the market and moral reform were inextricably linked.

Charities

The associational redefinition of public vice and virtue was marked by widening circles of philanthropic influence, as well as by moralizing and market values, beginning with the urban poor. A smattering of charities appeared in seaboard cities in the late eighteenth century, including a number of organizations founded by and for women, beginning in the 1790s. Most underscored the need for industry and thrift, while placing the needs of impoverished women and children on public agendas for the first time. As the trustees of New York's Society for the Relief of Poor Widows with Small Children (SPRWC) explained, "Almost every class of mechanics live not only plentifully, but luxuriously; an evil too general to be cured. Our poor widows have been partners in the evil, and now sustain the whole of the punishment. They must now learn economy from adversity, and to their credit . . . they do."[2]

Groups such as the SRPW sought to recast the social construction of acceptable working-class female behavior by refusing aid to supplicants who were deemed immoral, who sold "spirituous liquors," or who were seen "begging publicly."[3] They also promoted what they considered to be more virtuous forms of female industry by buying and distributing cloth to be sewn into shirts, replenishing stocks for female vendors, or providing spinning wheels so their recipients could work at home—efforts they often coupled with advice on frugal housewifery and material aid.

While many of these ventures sought to supplement working women's transition into the wage economy, they also brought their founders and trustees into the public economic sphere, as employers, vendors, and investors. Surplus cash was limited in the early national years, and donations small. As a result, charities habitually cobbled together mixed portfolios of public and private donations and income generation to sustain their operations. Philadelphia's Female Society is a case in point. The Female Society often employed well over a hundred impoverished women in spinning and sewing in its offices and in the women's homes. It then sold the resulting sheets, table linens, comforters, fabric, and clothing, dividing the profits between the women and its own operations; this generated a substantial portion of its annual organizational budgets. In 1819, for example, the Female Society received $626 ($7,074 in "constant" 2000 dollars) in donations, $342 ($3,865) in interest from stocks and loans, and $1,182 ($13,357) in sales receipts.[4] Charitable investments in property, savings banks, and stocks provided liquid capital for urban development and public works, broadening the economic roles of elite women and drawing them into the profit-making economy while garnering interest to fund their organizational operations. In the process, women's charities forged an enduring template for the symbiotic relationship between the market and the voluntary sphere, coupling charity and commerce in the pursuit of moral regeneration and communal ends.[5]

THE SOCIETY FOR THE PREVENTION OF PAUPERISM AND THE SAVINGS BANK OF NEW YORK

Both male and female elites founded charities, particularly after the War of 1812, which introduced a far more critical tenor into private efforts to remold the behavior of the poor. In the war's aftermath many eastern cities grappled with a severe depression borne of changing trade patterns and monetary policies that sent poor rates spiraling. Estimates placed the number of impoverished New Yorkers at 8,000 in 1819; this situation was exacerbated when the state legislature cut the city's poor-relief allocations, hobbling its ability to distribute relief on the eve of a major financial panic at decade's end.[6] Groups of prominent male professionals sought to supplement government funds with private donations to deal with the emergency and to find ways to cut costs in the future. Rather than examining the wage structure or the impact of broader economic trends, they blamed the "improvidence and viciousness" of the poor for the city's plight, which led them to champion moral reform.

As the founders of the New York's Society for the Prevention of Pauperism in the City of New York (SPP) explained, "Public energies had much better be directed at saving individuals from poverty than in raising funds to support them in it."[7] Although pauperism had been an enduring fact of European urban life, that "the same calamity to any considerable extent should be found" in America was deemed "a matter of astonishment and regret."[8] Because the problem was still in the early stages, the society's managers agreed that it could be cured through careful investigation of the causes and prudent programs to redress the underlying ills. Created in 1817, the SPP vowed to direct "the poor to the paths of morality and industry" in order to save them—and the city—from "beggary and crime."[9]

The SPP also set out to catalog the social and personal factors that contributed to growing poor rates, including (among others) intemperance, lotteries, and a host of commercial ventures, from pawnbrokers to taverns and houses of ill repute. Drunkenness headed its list of vices. "It consumes every virtue," the SPP trustees snarled, and "dissolves every social tie," souring "industry, honesty, and self-regard" into "crime and outrage."[10] It also consumed a considerable amount of cash. As they explained, the estimated $1.9 million spent by New Yorkers on ardent spirits in 1820 was evidence of a "fatal prodigality."[11] The managers noted disapprovingly that 1,630 licenses had been granted for the sale of ardent spirits, spawning "an average of one tippling house to every fourteen houses in the metropolis" where patrons could purchase West India rum, whiskey, homemade rum, and apple brandy for two to three cents per glass.[12] Laborers were deemed particularly incorrigible patrons, swilling a glass or two in the morning, with two to three more before noon, and a like amount before the end of the day—which in the trustees' opinion gave rise to widespread drunkenness. This in turn led to lawsuits for assault and battery. Generally, the "lowest orders" were deemed the most likely to overindulge, wasting the money needed to feed their families on liquor, fighting, and clogging the courts with wasteful and needlessly expensive trials.[13]

Pawnbrokers added to the woes and weaknesses of the poor, often charging as much as 25 percent interest on loans under twenty-five dollars. Gambling houses were culpable as well, posing a dual threat to industry and morality. "Let the votary of the practice consider the unprofitable consumption of time" spent gambling, the society's managers advised. "Let him add up the moments which are squandered here, without benefit to soul, to body, or to society."[14] Like drinking, gaming led invariably to ruin, in their opinion, creating "an excitement in the mind . . . [that] obliterates the last trace and vestige of moral principle."[15] Even if begun as an innocent pastime, games of chance inevitably led to betting and moral decline. "Around the gambling table, all vices cluster . . . intemperance, profanity, fraud and falsehood," they ominously warned.[16] Even public lotteries to help fund the city's charities and schools harbored the malignant seeds of corruption "by exciting in the mind of the person interested, an improper dependence upon pernicious contingencies."[17]

Savings banks were conceived as an antidote to these practices, providing a means of diverting laborers' meager holdings into safe investments rather than the coffers of the taverns, lotteries, and gambling dens. They also helped to ensure that money saved from sin would fund civic ends, a theme that later temperance advocates—both black and white—repeated. Whereas gambling rested on vague probabilities, banking guaranteed a safe and steady return. Created under the SPP's auspices in 1819, the Savings Bank of New York (SBNY) set the threshold for deposits at a minimum of one dollar, with a 5 percent yield culled from investments in state bonds and public works such as the Erie Canal. The idea for the initiative originated in Europe, part of a transatlantic movement to encourage savings among people of modest means as a way of encouraging thrift. Developed in the late eighteenth century and introduced in London under the auspices of the Society for Bettering the Condition of the Poor in 1816, the model was quickly transferred to the United States, where a number of mutual savings banks (including the SBNY) were founded in New England and the Middle Atlantic states between 1815 and 1820.[18]

Like its European counterparts, New York's bank was initially devised as a charitable venture—run by the society's trustees, who volunteered as tellers—and designed expressly to instill habits of economy among members of the working class as a means of eradicating pauperism and enabling them to save for sudden catastrophes and the demands of old age in an era of limited government. To quote the founders, it was rooted in a desire "to encourage and promote industrious and provident habits among the poor" by making its depositors modest stakeholders in the emerging capitalist economy.[19]

Banks like the SBNY aggressively worked to attract savers of modest means, often with considerable success. When the bank opened, approximately 25 percent of its depositors were listed as unskilled workers. By 1839, the proportion had risen to 51 percent, many of whom were female domestics, a pattern replicated in most of the other charity banks as well.[20] Similarly, 43 percent of the women depositors at Philadelphia's Saving Fund Society in 1850 were domestics, and another 13 percent of the bank's passbook holders were listed as porters and laborers, suggesting that the thrift ethic made considerable inroads among a diverse swath of urban laborers during the antebellum years.[21]

Backed by growing ranks of passbook holders, the SBNY quickly (and somewhat unexpectedly) became one of the country's leading financial institutions, further linking moral reform to economic growth. Even the bank's promoters were stunned by its early success. SPP leader John Pintard had optimistically predicted that the venture would draw $50,000 ($565,000) in deposits its first year; instead, it accumulated $150,000 ($1.7 million) in its first six months. By 1825, the bank had $1.4 million (≈ $16.8 million) in accounts; a decade later that sum had risen to $3 million ($39 million) deposited by 23,000 small investors. "By 1860, three New York City mutuals (the Bank for Savings, the Bowery and the Seamen's) ranked among the ten largest business organizations in the country."[22] Limited to investing in state and federal bonds by its charter, the SBNY quickly became "the single most important financier of the Erie Canal," providing liquid capital in an era when few individuals had comparable resources to invest.[23] Eventually these institutions would become commercial ventures, but in the beginning they provided highly visible models for the ways in which philanthropy and commerce could be combined to promote savings and thrift among the working poor while yielding badly needed capital for investments. They left a complex legacy, encouraging some of the most abstemious workers to save, popularizing an investment mentality that underscored the ties between moral reform and economic growth, and ultimately bankrolling a crucial segment of America's transportation revolution with the savings of the working poor.

The Benevolent Empire

Economic development also helped to stoke the religious revivals of the Second Great Awakening, as Americans turned to the church to make sense of their changing world. The country's first charities developed a thrift ethic for the laboring poor; antebellum moral reform societies cloaked these ideas in the language of salvation, sanctity, and sin. In the 1820s and 1830s, when the revivals reached their peak, growing numbers of settlers were moving into the new territories of the Louisiana Purchase and the western reaches of the old colonial states. Towns like Rochester, New York—one of the flash points of the Second Great Awakening—grew up almost overnight thanks to the newly opened Erie Canal. While westward migration sundered familial ties, other traditional anchors such as household production began to weaken and give way to small-scale manufacturing, winnowing former masters, journeymen, and apprentices into new and unsettling class divides. Jacksonian politics introduced another new strain and allowed thousands of propertyless white males to vote in national elections for the first time. The market revolution played a role as well, drawing citizens into a burgeoning national cash economy. The uncertainties generated by these changes helped to fuel the revivals, beginning with the frontier camp meetings of the 1790s and culminating in the massive Finneyite campaigns across the "burnt over district" in upstate New York in the 1820s and 1830s.[24]

Theology was equally important. The language of Evangelical Protestantism was the language of hope. While earlier, Calvinistic strains had preached the doctrine of predestination, urging parishioners to labor in their calling and pursue upright behavior in the hope of being among God's chosen, revivalists promised more immediate gains. For them, the conversion experience was a tangible sign of grace, the moment at which the convert's sins were washed away, clearing the way for a new life. It also cleared the way for reform, as new converts were urged to share their good fortune with others through moral suasion and the eradication of sin. The doctrine of human perfectibility that undergirded these activities provided the ideological framework for the Benevolent Empire's ambitious campaigns to reshape American behavior and norms.

Beyond championing theological tenets, Evangelical Protestantism provided a second important contribution to antebellum reform. While some strains of Protestantism, such as Episcopalianism, are sacerdotal sects that place rituals at the heart of the religious experience, and while many other denominations relied heavily on the ministrations of an educated clergy, Evangelicalism was more accessible, privileging reading the Bible as the central religious rite. As a result, the promotion of literacy became a vitally important component of the Evangelicals' mission, spurring the growth of networks of Sunday schools and of tract and Bible campaigns and paving the way for efforts to widely market new values, mores, and ideals to national audiences. The activities of the American Sunday School Union (ASSU) and both the American Temperance Society and its successor, the American Temperance Union, illustrate the ways in which the Benevolent Empire wedded religion and reform to the imperatives of moral consumption.

SUNDAY SCHOOLS

Like savings banks, Sunday schools were a European import. Begun by British Evangelicals in the eighteenth century, the Sunday school movement was transplanted to the United States in the 1790s. It continued to spread, in part because of the work of organizations like New York's Female Union Society for the Promotion of Sabbath Schools, which created a network of female-run auxiliaries stretching from Connecticut to North Carolina by the 1820s. The advent of the ASSU in 1824 knit these efforts into a national framework, combining local activities with national marketing, missionary, and publication campaigns. By 1832, the ASSU boasted more than 8,000 affiliated schools in every state, echoing the rapid expansion of its sister societies in the Benevolent Empire.[25]

This was a notable achievement in an era when the mails were often unreliable, the roads were impassable, and travel was not a pastime for the faint of heart. One of the ways in which the ASSU held its network together was through publications such as the *American Sunday School Magazine* for teachers (1824–30), *Youth's Friend* (1824), and *Infant's Magazine* (1826). Its most popular products, however, were its booklets for class instruction, which were sold via ASSU bookstores (or depositories, as they were known); hawked by ASSU missionaries, who doubled as sales clerks; and highlighted in advertisements in national children's magazines. Commercial transactions played a central role in these designs, placing consumption at the heart of the ASSU's crusade to evangelize the country. Auxiliaries were entitled to buy these publications at a discount, while unaffiliated schools paid full price for the society's primers and five to ten dollars for sets of "Sunday School Libraries." Even the smallest outposts, such as the auxiliaries in Halifax County, North Carolina, seem to have been avid consumers of the ASSU's wares, collecting dozens and sometimes hundreds of ASSU publications. Backed by an expanding market, ASSU sales topped the $10,000 (≈ $122,000) mark in 1826, reaching a peak of $235,000 ($3 million) on the eve of the Civil War.[26]

Missionaries also played a role in expanding the ASSU's reach and the number of its adherents, as did the application of what would later become standard business techniques such as market and evaluative research. In 1830, for example, the parent society tapped its auxiliaries and local churches for information on the perceived benefits that the schools conferred "to teachers themselves, or to children, parents, or society at large." Data were gathered on the character and number of schools, students, teachers, and subscriptions to ASSU publications in each community; on how the ASSU might improve the sale and circulation of its publications; on the role of the clergy; and on how the society's work might be "increased, extended and perpetuated." In the process, the association gleaned information not only about existing schools but also about the roadblocks to future development and opportunities for continued sales.[27]

The ASSU's professed aims were twofold: to teach literacy skills and to inculcate moral values, including temperance and thrift. As its charter explained, "It is no less a maxim in politics than in morals, that the strength and glory of a nation consist in the virtue and intelligence of its members." In effect, it sought to spark "a moral revolution in the mind and conduct" of the nation's youth and, if possible, among their parents as well. Although much of the ASSU's effort was aimed at the children of the poor, its programs also reached adults and children of other classes, making this the mainstay of public education in communities without more formal schools and marking a considerable expansion beyond earlier charitable efforts to reform the habits of the urban poor.[28]

Sunday school publications emphasized abstemious behavior, adopting a decidedly moralistic cast. For example, one pamphlet entitled "The Glass of Whiskey" outlined the dangers of intemperance; another underscored "the folly and sin of fighting." More general treatises like *Youth's Friend* blended brief essays on subjects ranging from the workings of the Congress to scriptural passages and moralistic stories on correct behavior.[29]

The perils of liquor were stressed in tales of drink and gambling that led straight to the grave. In one story, a young boy from a pious family is injured at work and takes a job as a bartender in Philadelphia. For the first four years, liquor never crosses his lips, but from the first drop, he is doomed. Several years later he kills a man in a drunken barroom brawl and is hanged. Gambling, the story explains, is fueled by the "love of obtaining other people's money, without earning it by honest industry"—echoing the themes of the SPP. Gamblers drink to keep each other engaged, they quarrel, and some quarrels end in murder or with "some miserable wretch, who has made himself and his family poor," taking his own life.[30]

Other sinners were consigned to the asylum. One essay features a vignette of Philadelphia's House of Refuge, warning readers that it is filled with youngsters who have lied, stolen, and disobeyed their parents. Another essay, "Miseries of the World," paints a bleak picture of the city's asylums—from the House of Refuge, where "boys and girls" are "kept in confinement for their bad conduct," to the almshouse, where "you will see such wretchedness, as will make you sick."[31] The moral is clear: those who behave badly or fall into poverty will face a miserable existence. "All the troubles of men are the consequence of sin," the article confidently concludes.[32]

As was the case of charities, women such as the managers of New York's Female Union Society played a prominent role in the development of the Sunday school models and auxiliaries. By 1847, women made up an estimated 61 percent of the teaching force. However, while upper- and middle-class "benevolent ladies" generally ran their own charities, Sunday school women worked primarily under male supervision, particularly after the demise of the Female Union Society in 1828. On the other hand, women's participation in the Sunday school movement was widespread, stretching into the hinterland even into the rural South, which was often notably resistant to public moralizing.[33]

Concerted efforts were also made to spread the gospel of good behavior to African Americans. Many catered to the educational needs of African Americans, including some Sunday schools in the South before Nat Turner's bloody slave uprising in 1831. Some northern organizations, like the Female Union Society, taught integrated classes for black and white children and adults, and free blacks also ran their own Sunday schools in the North. Although the ASSU initially encouraged the development of schools for African Americans, its policy changed in the 1830s, in the wake of the Turner rebellion, after southern legislators passed laws forbidding whites to teach blacks basic literacy skills. Afterward, the society seeded black schools only where they could be created with the consent of local whites.

Other tensions began to simmer within the organization as sectional rifts widened with the tariff debates and the Nullification Crisis, which brought southern states into direct confrontation with the federal government, presaging the tensions that led to the Civil War. Some of the complaints centered on the ASSU's economic policies. Before 1832, ASSU auxiliaries were required to pay dues to the parent organization and to raise funds for their own operations. Sometimes, the society's missionaries were treated as economic interlopers when they tried to raise funds from southern congregations. By the early 1830s, some auxiliaries in the South were beginning to complain that they were "a mere colony in the benevolent empire," subjected to "spiritual swindling" because the national societies were "siphoning off the hard-earned donations from earnest southerners and diverting them to projects in the North."[34]

Certainly, organizations like the ASSU and, especially, the American Bible Society (ABS) were lucrative financial operations. According to historian Charles Sellers, between 1816 and 1830 the combined revenues of the thirteen largest Benevolent Empire societies reached an estimated $2.8 million (≈ $36.8 million), a sum that compared favorably with the $3.6 million that the federal government had spent on internal improvements since the country's inception.[35] The ABS was among the wealthiest, drawing approximately half of its $50,000 budget from sales in 1824 alone. By 1826, more than 450,000 Bibles had been distributed, many of them through sales by volunteer auxiliaries. Like the ASSU, the ABS engaged in market research, staging local house-to-house surveys through churches and auxiliaries. By the 1830s and 1840s it had begun to invest as well, including an account with Massachusetts Hospital Life, a trust company that transferred the holdings of some of the country's wealthiest nonprofits into New England's burgeoning textile industry—practices that lent credence to southern complaints.[36]

There were other points of regional contention. Many of the Benevolent Empire societies came under increasing suspicion after the birth of abolitionism in the early 1830s, particularly because prominent antislavery advocates such as Gerrit Smith and brothers Lewis and Arthur Tappan were among their major backers. Even before the rise of abolitionism, ASSU missionaries complained that "strange prejudice, and deep ignorance" impeded their work in southern states. Local Sunday school advocates sometimes bemoaned their failure to strike a spark among what they termed "tenants of the lowest grade in society who disregard the Sabbath [and] have no inclination whatsoever to have their children educated in any way, least of all in Sabbath schools."[37]

Undeterred, the ASSU mounted a major campaign to evangelize the South in 1833. Backed by both northern and southern contributions, these efforts were expressly designed to counter the region's "defiance of evangelical Christian norms" that Daniel Walker Howe and Patrick Rael describe in their contributions to this volume. Toward this end, the Southern Enterprize, as it was termed, sought to develop Sunday schools "in every neighborhood, (where such schools may be desired by the people, and where in other respects it may be practicable)" within a five-year period, marking a major campaign to blanket the region with auxiliaries for moral reform.[38] Following its penchant for market research, the ASSU began with a survey of the current state of education in the South, including both public and Sunday schools. Maryland had the largest number of Sunday schools (243), with Virginia running a respectable second (203), while Florida (4), the District of Columbia (37), and Georgia (43) fell at the bottom of the list.[39] In total, 52,192 out of an estimated 500,000 white children attended ASSU Sunday schools, with an additional 20,000 in unaffiliated ventures.[40]

Educational efforts were particularly important in this region because there were few common schools, which may account for the generosity of southern donors in helping to launch the enterprise. For example, the survey found that as of 1828, fewer than 13,000 of Virginia's children were receiving publicly funded educations.[41] This finding increased the importance of the ASSU schools and their ability to make moral uplift a central aspect of southern educational fare. Other states such as North Carolina and Georgia had substantial sums in their state literary funds, "but nothing has yet been actually done."[42] Perhaps inspired by the gap between public educational facilities and public needs, Virginians were particularly generous backers, donating $4,000 ($52,400) in Richmond, more than $2,200 ($28,280) in Petersburg, and $280 ($3,668) in Alexandria to launch the southern Sunday school campaign.[43]

The history of the ASSU provides important insights into the question of who participated in spreading the gospel of abstemious behavior in the antebellum period. Initially, scholars emphasized the role of the clergy and the wealthy elites who managed the headquarters of the Benevolent Empire societies from their offices in Philadelphia, Boston, and New York. By the 1980s, the emphasis had shifted to what might be termed "men on the make": the northern merchants and fledgling manufacturers who benefited most directly from the country's wrenching transition to a market economy. Women's historians also emphasized the role of middle-class white women's groups, particularly in New York. Since then, scholars have begun to examine activities in other regions as well. But what emerges from the records of the ASSU is a truly national effort grounded in grassroots mobilization, much of which was fostered by the society's agents, but some of which emerged spontaneously outside ASSU networks—providing literacy training and moral education for children, parents, and even grandparents in towns and hamlets across the nation. Although these developments were uneven and fraught with challenges, what began as a trickle of elite reforms in the eighteenth century had become a nationwide, mass-based drive to promote thrift and upright behavior under the banner of Protestantism by the 1830s.[44]

THE EVANGELICAL TEMPERANCE MOVEMENT

While the ASSU sought to promote the "moral" consumption of its wares, the temperance movement attacked the "immoral" commerce in liquor. The movement's history is well known. Between 1810 and 1850s it passed through four stages: (1) local efforts in the wake of the War of 1812 that were influenced by many of the same sorts of civic concerns that inspired the SPP; (2) the creation in 1826 of the American Temperance Society (ATS), a national organization promoting moderation in the use of "ardent spirits" (hard liquor); (3) the push for total abstinence and stronger local and state regulation under a successor organization, the American Temperance Union (ATU), founded in 1836—efforts that culminated in passage of a number of statewide prohibition laws in the 1840s and 1850s; and (4) a groundswell of working-class and cross-class activity in the 1840s under the auspices of the Washingtonian movement, the Sons and Daughters of Temperance, and related mutual benefit groups.[45]

One of the movement's premier spokesmen, Lyman Beecher, outlined the thrust of the campaign in a series of sermons in 1825. According to Beecher, alcohol abuse was bankrupting the country by siphoning public dollars into spiraling taxes to care for the criminals, brawlers, and paupers that tippling spawned in its wake. It shortened lives and stunted the quality of labor. It diverted public and private funds from more civic ends, draining away dollars more aptly spent on the maintenance of government, colleges, schools, and religious institutions. And it undermined morality. "Intemperance," he thundered, "is a national sin." Absolution resided in the market. For Beecher, nothing less than "THE BANISHMENT OF ARDENT SPIRITS FROM THE LIST OF LAWFUL ARTICLES OF COMMERCE" would win the battle against Demon Rum.[46]

Beecher's sermons neatly summarized the movement's rationale, which blended an array of religious, scientific, statistical, and civic arguments to make the case for moderation and abstention. Following Beecher's call to concentrate on "the business of collecting facts" about "the height, and depth, and length of this mighty evil," temperance advocates cobbled together data on everything from the cost of caring for dependents and deviants to revenues lost from competing economic and civic pursuits.[47] They also tallied the social and political costs. While northern advocates stressed the toll of alcohol consumption on laborers and production, southerners bemoaned its influence on slaves, politics, and the sons of the rich. Thus, "once honest and faithful" servants became "corrupted and depraved" and, once they succumbed to the lure of the bottle, were no longer capable of performing the work on "which depend so much of our comfort, safety and happiness."[48] Moreover, drinking drew freemen into debt and polluted elections, corrupting the political process. Slavery metaphors abounded in both sections of the country, with inveterate tipplers habitually cast as "the bound slaves of that insidious Habit."[49]

Commentators roundly denounced the volatile link between liquor and politics. In the North, much of this animus focused on tavern keepers, who allowed local politicians to use their establishments as rallying points for working-class political mobilization. Liquor greased the workings of southern politics as well. The free-flowing liquor at preelection barbeques and other political rallies threatened "the subversion of our liberties," according to one southern temperance group, by tempting men to sell their votes "for a drink of grog." In this milieu, temperance was deemed "the work of the patriot as well as the philanthropist," casting the Revolutionary equation of independence, liberty, and the need for a virtuous citizenry in a fresh idiom.[50]

In addition to cleansing political processes, temperance was hailed as the springboard to social mobility. Testimonials were regularly invoked to document the positive economic benefits of abstention. As one author recalled, when he opened his country store in rural Alabama in 1824, he was selling about 100 barrels of hard liquor each year to the area's impoverished residents. By 1831, that figure had dropped to five barrels, and the savings diverted into local economic development, enabling many residents to become independent planters.[51] Northern manufacturers were tapped for testimonials as well. The ATU began its operations with brief survey of northern factory owners, asking them whether they allowed their workers to drink on the job and what they had learned from their policies concerning on-the-job temperance or tippling. The response from a mill owner in Lowell, Massachusetts, was emphatic: no liquor was allowed in his factories, and any worker caught drinking was immediately dismissed. "All our male and female operatives, with very few exceptions, lay up money every year," he confidently concluded. "Since we adopted the principle of entire abstinence, our business has been conducted more profitably for ourselves and our workmen have laid up more property," explained another manufacturer. "Some have come to work for us in very embarrassed circumstances, and have, while in our employ, paid up their debts, and are now acquiring property."[52] Commentaries such as these underscored the notion that temperance, investing, and economic advancement went hand in hand.

The task of translating these ideas into action initially fell to local elites, the churches, and the temperance societies. Backed by funding from wealthy donors like Stephen Van Renssalaer, the ATS's executive committee outlined an ambitious plan to spark meetings "in all of the cities, towns and villages throughout the United States" in 1833, mirroring the comprehensive designs of the ASSU's Southern Enterprize.[53] To achieve its goals, the ATS sent out a circular calling on temperance societies and local ministers to coordinate meetings and on newspaper editors to publicize them. It also sent circulars to households across the country, enjoining "each family in the United States to furnish themselves with some temperance publication," such as the ATS's tract *On the Immorality of the Traffic in Ardent Spirits*.[54] By the 1830s, the society had sent millions of temperance tracts, reports, and convention proceedings to spark the creation of new auxiliaries; these figures continued to grow under the ATS's successor, the ATU. More than 12 million pieces of literature were distributed in the ATU's first year alone, including copies of its national *Journal of the American Temperance Union*, which were distributed to every congressman on a monthly basis, as well as to subscribers, postmasters, and editors who might reprint its stories.[55] By 1839, sales accounted for over 60 percent of the ATU's operating funds; five years later, the ratio had risen to over 75 percent, echoing the financial operations of the ABS and the ASSU.[56]

In addition to using the pulpit, the press, and the postal service to advance their aims, temperance Evangelicals also conscripted political leaders into their ranks. President Jackson's secretary of war, Lewis Cass, was an active member of the American Congressional Temperance Society in Washington, as were a number of congressmen and senators from both northern and southern states. Cass's participation was pivotal in the campaign to curb the distribution of liquor to army troops and on naval ships, which was considerably bolstered by the secretary's 1832 order banning ardent spirits from every "fort, camp, or garrison of the United States."[57] Temperance society members were also encouraged to shun political candidates who were heavy drinkers, and they lobbied for state and local option legislation to stem the granting of liquor licenses, efforts that culminated in the passage of seventeen statewide "Maine laws" prohibiting the sale of liquor by the mid-1850s.

Historians such as Ian Tyrrell have depicted the Evangelical phase of the temperance movement primarily as a northern phenomenon, but more recent scholarship suggests that, like the Sunday school movement, it made significant inroads into the South, spreading the crusade to national dimensions. Virginia listed 113 ATS auxiliaries in 1831, which compared favorably to the 140 chapters in Maine, and New Hampshire's tally of 96.[58] Southern political leaders such as South Carolina's William Pinckney and Senator Felix Grundy from Tennessee were active in the American Congressional Temperance Society, and Kentucky formed its own Legislative Temperance Society under ATS auspices, headed by the state's governor and lieutenant governor in 1834. Similarly, Governor Wilson Lumpkin of Georgia was an early leader in the crusade against what he termed "distilled damnation."[59] Georgia's state university went dry under his watch by 1834, and at least one county voted to deny the granting of liquor licenses.

Although rarely in positions of leadership, women played a significant role in the temperance movement in both the North and the South. While temperance arguments were cast in a resoundingly male idiom rooted in science, economics, and political concerns, women were accorded a voice by virtue of their authority as moral guardians and as the frequent victims of liquor-related domestic abuse. Most estimates place female participation at roughly 40 to 50 percent.[60] In addition to joining mixed societies, northern women formed at least twenty-five female auxiliaries of the ATS by 1831, and there are scattered references to female temperance societies in the South.[61] However, because the temperance movement sought to regulate male behavior, southern women's roles tended to be carefully circumscribed and were primarily confined to mixed associations.

African Americans were active in the temperance movement as well. While southerners organized societies for current and former slaves, northern freemen developed a wide network of local, state, and national societies, paralleling the work of the ATS. Beginning with the creation of the New Haven Temperance Society of the People of Color and the New York Temperance Society in 1829, the movement grew to include scores of chapters with hundreds of members, culminating in the creation of the Colored American Temperance Society. Initially, the movement was cast as a counterpoint to both the efforts of the American Colonization Society to deport free blacks to Liberia and the society's claims that blacks could never be fully free in the United States because of racism, which were used to justify these programs. African American temperance advocates viewed moderation and abstention as tools for combating racist stereotypes and the society's deportation programs. At first, their efforts paralleled white temperance campaigns, but by 1836 they were increasingly linked to abolitionism, blending a variety of reformist concerns within individual organizations.[62]

Themes of thrift, waste, and civic expenditure figured prominently in the rhetoric of black temperance advocates, just as they did in that of the white associations. African American reformers linked intemperance to prejudice, to lost opportunities for communal self-help, and to abolitionism. As one observer noted, thousands of dollars were wasted annually on liquor, money that might have supported schools, literary societies, and libraries where African Americans could "acquire useful scientific and practical knowledge" to counter racial prejudice.[63] The squandered funds could also have built churches and schools. Because civic institutions were regarded as visible indices of racial progress, communal achievement, and—as Rael points out later in this volume, black agency—these arguments were undoubtedly compelling.

By the 1830s, both the temperance movement and the Sunday school movement had reached national dimensions, mobilizing a wide variety of white and black women and men across the country in their campaigns. The popularization of the gospels of individual thrift and abstemious behavior—along with larger economic, social, and political reforms—lay at the heart of their activities. They also sought to distinguish moral from immoral consumption, condemning gambling and the liquor trade while urging consumers to use the monies saved from sin for self-improvement, civic ends, and associational wares. The push to popularize the thrift ethic witnessed several permutations after the turn of the century, expanding from elite white men's and women's urban charities to national networks of grassroots auxiliaries spearheaded by middle-class merchants, manufacturers, professionals, and their wives. In the 1840s, working-class organizations appeared as well, drawing the movement once again into more secular realms.

Mutual Aid Societies and Lodges

While middle-class activists worked through churches to build their empires for reform, Washingtonian Societies and the Sons and Daughters of Temperance preached the tenets of abstemious behavior through secular mutual aid, drawing on long-standing traditions of ethnic, class, and racial self-help dating back to the eighteenth century. Like their middle-class charitable counterparts, many of these groups imposed moral criteria—including prohibitions concerning liquor consumption and public displays of immorality and inebriation—in return for financial assistance. They imposed these criteria, in part, to protect their resources from members seeking benefits for afflictions they had caused themselves through drink or other forms of disorderly conduct. Like more affluent, middle-class charities, mutual aid societies were magnets for capital formation, amassing and depositing their holdings in banks, loans, and other investments.

The Sons and Daughters of Temperance built on these precedents, offering mutual benefits as well as temperance advice; the Washingtonians provided rescue and charitable services to recovering alcoholics. Launched in 1840 in Baltimore, "Washingtonianism" is often depicted as a predominantly working-class crusade, encompassing significant numbers of skilled and unskilled workers. Members embraced teetotalism and borrowed techniques from revivalists, political stump speakers, and commercial culture to bolster their ranks. Most combed their cities seeking inebriates to reform; and once the pledge was signed, charges were given clothing, food, and help in finding jobs to set them on the road to recovery. To subsidize their efforts, Washingtonians staged concerts and temperance fairs, as well as vending highly popular volumes of temperance melodies. The cold-water groceries and boardinghouses that began to dot both black and white neighborhoods also provided safe consumer alternatives for the redeemed.

These institutions directly challenged the livelihoods of other working-class men, and women, in the liquor trade—the small entrepreneurs who ran the groceries, taverns, and grog shops where liquor was dispensed. Antebellum saloons were lively centers of working-class male sociability, the locus not only of political rallies but also of a variety of pastimes that many reformers abhorred, such as prostitution, bare-knuckle prize fighting, rat-baiting contests, and dogfights. While temperance societies promoted a vision of manhood based on saving and self-restraint, saloons offered an alternative version of masculinity, one rooted in bravado, treating, and contests of chance. In these domains, prowess and physical courage—rather than sobriety and frugality—were the earmarks of local leaders and the currency of social esteem.[64]

Many of the women who joined Martha Washingtonian societies were doubtless already familiar with the culture of the grog shop and the saloon as the wives or daughters of drunkards or as recovering alcoholics themselves. Although the temperance movement was cast in a decidedly male idiom, tippling also was rampant among women. According to historian Bruce Dorsey, "Criminal court records in Philadelphia or New York show that women drank as frequently as men and appeared nearly as often on charges of public intoxication"—patterns reflected in the pages of women's temperance journals.[65] "Over two hundred females were arrested for drunkenness in this city last week!" exclaimed the *Pearl*, a New York temperance magazine.[66] The *Pearl* was particularly critical of the wealthy women who stopped on their "shopping excursions to drink intoxicating liquors" in the "elegant confectionary establishments" in the fashionable shopping area on Broadway. "The class of female tipplers, who daily take their drams at these places, is daily increasing," the journal warned. These "grog shops for ladies" joined saloons on the Martha Washingtonians' list of proscribed institutions.[67]

In addition to aiding their husbands' recovery efforts, female Washingtonians visited female tipplers in their homes, encouraging them to sign the pledge, and one group even established an asylum for "previously inebriate widows." Female Washingtonian auxiliaries also published their own newspaper (the *Olive Plant and Ladies' Temperance Advocate*), created juvenile temperance societies, and placed a strong emphasis on philanthropy in their programs. Both members and the redeemed inebriates who signed the pledge were encouraged to participate, paying an initiation fee and a small amount each month to support charitable works. Moreover, like their middle-class counterparts, they engaged in a variety of profit-making ventures to raise funds for their charitable endeavors, including cold-water entertainments to counterpoint the lure of the saloon.

Their picnics, concerts, and boat rides drew mixed audiences of men and women, emphasizing the temperance movement's role in keeping families together, in contrast to the saloon, which drove them apart. Not content just to siphon off business, some auxiliaries staged protests in saloons, publicly begging the owners to "desist from prosecuting their ruinous traffic."[68] To quote historian Ruth Alexander, the Martha Washingtonian movement "marked the first time that American women of relatively low rank joined and played a prominent role in reform," bringing a working-class perspective to efforts to encourage thrift and reorder the entertainments of the poor.[69]

Despite widespread popularity in both the North and the South, Washingtonianism began to decline after 1843 due to backsliding among its members, competition from Evangelical temperance groups, and the movement's loosely structured organizational form. Many Washingtonians, especially the women members, gradually transferred their loyalties to temperance lodges and mutual benefit societies such as the Daughters of Rechab and the Daughters of Temperance, a female counterpart to the Sons of Temperance. These new groups blended the appeal of fraternal lodges and teetotal pledges with insurance services, charging initiation fees and weekly dues in return for health and burial benefits. They also became investors, advertising their benefits and investment policies in temperance papers like the *Pearl*. Thus, the members of the Original Purity Tent Number One of the United Daughters of Rechab pointed out that they had placed their deposits in "the Savings Bank, for which they draw 6 percent interest," in order to boost consumer confidence and attract new members.[70] In the process, these organizations emphasized their role in cultivating "social virtues," including thrift, to enable their "members, while in health and prosperity, to provide for the hour of sickness and adversity." The female auxiliaries were extremely popular, with "at least fifty-eight mutual benefit societies in Manhattan and Brooklyn alone," counting thousands of women among their members by 1847.[71] Backed by a blend of moral, social, and economic imperatives, the Sons and Daughters of Temperance quickly became a national movement, drawing more than a quarter of a million members, more than 40 percent of whom hailed from the South.[72]

While the Daughters of Temperance and similar lodges continued to attract working-class women, the movement's male auxiliaries were increasingly dominated by professionals and artisans, marking a break with the Washingtonians. In addition to promoting benefits, rituals, and teetotalism, these associations preached the gospels of charity, industry, frugality, and sobriety, urging their members to "be industrious, and attentive to [their] occupation—frugal in all [their] affairs . . . and sober in [their] deportment."[73] They also amassed impressive amounts of cash. Pennsylvania's Grand Division of the Sons of Temperance was one of the wealthiest statewide auxiliaries, with 21,000 contributing members in 1847 and $76,000 (≈ $1 million) in dues, $32,000 (≈ $428,000) of which was available for investment.[74]

The Washingtonian societies and temperance lodges of the 1840s secularized the task of promoting thrift and shifted it to working-class constituencies and mutual concerns. They also provided a different window into the issue of associational commerce and capital accumulation. Like their middle-class counterparts, most of these organizations were tied to the market in some way, either by vending entertainments and goods to raise funds for their programs or through their investments and quasi-business activities in providing health and burial benefits. In effect, many of the lodges operated as proto-insurance companies, which was undoubtedly a significant part of their appeal. In the process, the cold-water entertainments of the Washingtonians provided another slant on the notion of moral consumption, affording alternatives to commercial entertainments where liquor, gambling, or prostitution were often part of the fare. Similarly, the mutual benefit societies stressed the virtues of thrift and investment for the future as alternatives to the immediate gratifications offered by the saloon. And they influenced public behavior. Echoing Tocqueville's dicta, the *Pearl* reassured its readers that "the voice of a single individual may seem weak and powerless, but the combined voices of thousands make the expression of public opinion, which is all powerful."[75] In the process, organizations such as the Washingtonians and the Daughters of Temperance wed working-class missionaries for teetotalism to the market economy in the name of moral uplift, following the path of earlier elite charities and middle-class Evangelical campaigns. They also drew an ever-widening array of Americans into national movements for reform.

Conclusion

The crusade to spread the gospel of abstemious behavior was highly heterogeneous, blending a variety of perspectives and aims. While the first women's charities sought to get women out of the almshouses and off the public till by promoting industry and thrift, antebellum female reformers often cast their campaigns in the idiom of religion and of hearth and home, ideas that transcended regional boundaries. Although some scholars have argued that southern ruralism and class structures discouraged women's participation in associations, female charities began to appear in the South in the early 1800s, and both urban and rural female Sunday schools and Bible societies were operating throughout the region by the 1820s.[76] Clearly, there was a distinctive ecology of southern reform, with the greatest autonomy allotted to female charities and benevolent societies, and the least to activities that sought to regulate male pastimes such as drinking. Unlike their northern counterparts, southern women promoted reforms that were carefully circumscribed by topic and generally limited to mixed-group societies under the watchful supervision of their spouses, sons, and sires.

While antebellum white women cast their efforts in the idiom of motherhood and the home, middle- and upper-class white male reformers focused on political and economic themes. Many of their earliest endeavors were grounded in the notion that social pathologies could be nipped in the bud before they became endemic problems. Prominent reformers helped to marshal support for temperance by arguing that the country was producing a drunken underclass with, as Beecher put it, "no right in soil, and no capital at stake, and no moral principle," providing ready tinder for demagoguery and revolt.[77] Projects like the SBNY sought to counter these developments by giving even people of limited means a stake in the country's economic future, and Sunday schools and temperance crusades sought to regulate antisocial behavior. Temperance had political implications as well. If a man's vote could be bought with drink, temperance advocates argued, the future of the Republic was in peril.

Working-class initiatives tended to be more inward-turning and less inclined to use the ballot to regulate behavior. But they were no less enthusiastic in their promotion of temperance and the virtues of thrift. For the recovering alcoholics who joined groups like the Washingtonians, charities and lodges provided an abstemious alternative to the raffish camaraderie of the grog shop and the saloon. African Americans, on the other hand, often endorsed temperance and educational ventures as counterweights to racism and discrimination.

An undercurrent that ran through all these activities was the notion that self-restraint would serve both civic and individual ends. Antebellum America was steeped in an economy of scarcity. Liquid capital was often difficult to obtain, and public monies were severely limited by the ethos of circumscribed government and taxation. Within this milieu, charity advocates and social reformers stressed self-support as an alternative to reliance on the public till, underscoring the notion that the monies saved from the dens of iniquity, unnecessary litigation, jails, and poor relief could be spent on families, churches, schools, and economic advancement.

As the essays by Lawrence Glickman and Kiku Adatto in this collection make clear, the notion of moral consumption resonated throughout the country's history. In effect, the people who bought Sunday school and temperance tracts, patronized antislavery fairs, or purchased war bonds were diverting their surplus funds from personal gratification to public ends. Similarly, the donors who supported the charitable causes described by Olivier Zunz (also in this collection) were essentially buying services for others with their contributions, providing another iteration of moral consumption. Seen in this light, both thrift and consumerism were civic imperatives, as moral consumption provided a mechanism for turning spending into the handmaiden of a growing array of charitable, reformist, and civic ends.

Nonprofits such as the ASSU and the Sons of Temperance played economic roles as well by virtue of their ability to attract and invest capital and the commercial activities they used to bankroll their campaigns. Economic imperatives, rather than Evangelical religion or legislative reforms, were the common denominator that distinguished these groups. Indeed, the entire infrastructure for moral reform was predicated on the acceptance—and the skillful exploitation—of the emerging commercial and capitalist economy. In the process, these associational efforts became engines for investment and nonprofit entrepreneurship, as well as for the promotion of upright behavior, delineating parallel economies of vice and virtue under the rubric of reform.

Notes

1. Alexis de Tocqueville, *Democracy in America*, tr. Henry Reeve, 2 vols. (1835–40; New York: Modern Library, 1981), 2:403, 407.

2. Society for the Relief of Poor Widows with Small Children, *Annual Report* (New York: J. Oram, 1800), 18.

3. Society for the Relief of Poor Widows with Small Children, *Annual Report* (New York: J. Seymour, 1812), 8.

4. Female Society of Philadelphia for the Relief and Employment of the Poor, *Annual Report* (Philadelphia: W. Fry, 1819), 4. Throughout the text, I have converted nineteenth-century "current" dollars into "constant" dollars for the year 2000 to indicate the approximate value of these sums today; equivalents that appear in parentheses throughout the text. These figures, which should be used with care, have been added to give a reasonable sense of the present value for purposes of comparison. I am indebted to Professor Thom Thurston, the chairman of the economics department of the Graduate Center, City University of New York, for his help in determining the formula for changing current to constant dollars. The multipliers are 9.1 for 1810, 11.3 for 1820, 13.1 for 1830, 12.6 for 1840, 14.2 for 1850, and 12.8 for 1860. For dates that fall at middecade, I have averaged the decennial markers, indicating this by the use of the ≈ sign before the parenthetically noted amounts.

5. What distinguished these activities from those in the for-profit arena was their distribution of the society's earnings, which were plowed back into the programs rather than distributed to the subscribers and trustees.

6. Society for the Prevention of Pauperism in the City of New York (SPP), *Second Annual Report* (New York: E. Conrad, 1819), 17.

7. Society for the Prevention of Pauperism in the City of New York (SPP), *Sixth Annual Report* (New York: M. Day, 1823), 3.

8. Society for the Prevention of Pauperism in the City of New York (SPP), *Fourth Annual Report* (New York: E. Conrad, 1821), 5.

9. SPP, *Sixth Annual Report* (1823), 3.

10. SPP, *Second Annual Report* (1819), 6.

11. Ibid., 7.

12. SPP, *Fourth Annual Report* (1821), 7.

13. SPP, *Second Annual Report* (1819), 17.

14. SPP, *Fourth Annual Report* (1821), 26–27.

15. SPP, *Second Annual Report* (1819), 36.

16. SPP, *Fourth Annual Report* (1821), 23. For an interesting discussion of antebellum gambling, see Ann Fabian, *Card Sharps and Bucket Shops: Gambling in Nineteenth-Century America* (New York: Routledge, 1999).

17. SPP, *Fourth Annual Report* (1821), 26.

18. For the history of British savings banks, see Oliver H. Horne, *A History of Savings Banks* (London: Oxford University Press, 1947).

19. For the bank's history, see Alan L. Olmstead, *New York City Mutual Savings Banks, 1819–1861* (Chapel Hill: University of North Carolina Press, 1976).

20. Ibid., 50–51, 61.

21. George Alter, Claudia Goldin, and Elyce Rotella, "The Savings of Ordinary Americans: The Philadelphia Saving Fund Society in the Mid-Nineteenth Century," *Journal of Economic History* 54 (December 1994): 742.

22. Olmstead, *New York City Mutual Savings Banks*, 157–58. I have converted nineteenth-century "current" dollars into "constant" dollars for the year 2000 to indicate the approximate value of these sums today; these equivalents that appear in parentheses throughout the text. The multipliers are 9.1 for 1810, 11.3 for 1820, 13.1 for 1830, 12.6 for 1840, 14.2 for 1850, and 12.8 for 1860. These figures should be used with care but were added for purposes of comparison. Figures for dates that fall at mid-decade average the decennial rates, as indicated by the ≈ sign.

23. Ibid., 4.

24. See, e.g., Paul E. Johnson, *A Shopkeeper's Millennium: Society and Revivals in Rochester, New York, 1815–1837* (New York: Hill and Wang, 1978).

25. Anne M. Boylan, *Sunday School: The Formation of an American Institution, 1790–1880* (New Haven, CT: Yale University Press, 1988), 31, table 5.

26. Ibid., 85.

27. "American Sunday School Union Circular," March 1, 1830, in reel 15, American Sunday School Union Manuscripts, Library of Congress, Washington, D.C.

28. American Sunday School Union, *The Charter; Being a Plain Statement of Facts in Relation to an Application to the Legislature of Pennsylvania to Grant a Charter to the American Sunday School Union* (Philadelphia: American Sunday School Union, 1828), 8.

29. American Sunday School Union, *Descriptive Catalogue* (Philadelphia: American Sunday School Union, 1838), 8.

30. *Youth's Friend* (Philadelphia: American Sunday School Union, 1839), 95.

31. Ibid., 29.

32. Ibid., 26.

33. Boylan, *Sunday School*, 115. See, e.g., Elizabeth R. Varon, *We Mean to Be Counted: White Women and Politics in Antebellum Virginia* (Chapel Hill: University of North Carolina Press, 1998), 27; and John W. Quist, *Restless Visionaries: The Social Roots of Antebellum Reform in Alabama and Michigan* (Baton Rouge: Louisiana State University Press, 1998), 81–89.

34. Barbara L. Bellows, *Benevolence among Slaveholders: Assisting the Poor in Charleston, 1670–1860* (Baton Rouge: Louisiana State University Press, 1993), 35.

35. Charles Sellers, *The Market Revolution: Jacksonian America, 1815–1846* (New York: Oxford University Press, 1991), 217.

36. American Bible Society, *Annual Report* (New York: American Bible Society, 1825), 6.

37. Joseph Bruce Adams of Lawrence County, Alabama, to Frederick W. Porter, October 24, 1831; unknown (author's signature illegible) of Monroe County, Virginia, to Frederick W. Porter, April 9, 1830, both in reel 15, American Sunday School Union Manuscripts, Library of Congress, Washington, D.C.

38. *The Southern Enterprize* (Philadelphia: American Sunday School Union, 1833), 4.

39. Ibid., 6.

40. Ibid., 4, 6.

41. Ibid., 5.

42. Ibid.

43. Ibid., 24–25.

44. For the literature on male Evangelicals, see Clifford Griffin, *Their Brothers' Keepers: Moral Stewardship in the United States, 1800–1860* (New York: H. Wolff, 1960). The theme of "men on the make" is exemplified in Ian Tyrrell's *Sobering Up: From Temperance to Prohibition in Antebellum America, 1800–1860* (Westport, CT: Greenwood Press, 1979); and Johnson's *Shopkeeper's Millennium*. For interpretations by women historians, see Nancy A. Hewitt, *Women's Activism and Social Change: Rochester, New York, 1822–1872* (Ithaca, NY: Cornell University Press, 1984); Christine Stansell, *City of Women: Sex and Class in New York, 1789–1860* (New York: Knopf, 1986); Lori Ginzberg, *Women and the Work of Benevolence: Morality, Politics, and Class in the Nineteenth-Century United States* (New Haven, CT: Yale University Press, 1990); Anne M. Boylan, *The Origins of Women's Activism: New York, 1797–1840* (Chapel Hill: University of North Carolina Press, 2002). Southern trends are discussed in Varon, *We Mean to Be Counted*; Cynthia Kierner, *Beyond the Household: Women's Place in the Early South, 1700–1835* (Ithaca, NY: Cornell University Press, 1998); and Quist, *Restless Visionaries*.

45. Tyrrell's *Sobering Up* offers a particularly useful overview of the temperance movement, while Robert H. Abzug's *Cosmos Crumbling: American Reform and the Religious Imagination* (New York: Oxford University Press, 1994) provides an incisive analysis of the religious aspects of reform (including chap. 4, which deals with temperance); and chap. 3 of Bruce Dorsey's *Reforming Men and Women* (Ithaca, NY: Cornell University Press, 2002) examines the gendered aspects of the temperance campaign.

46. Lyman Beecher, *Six Sermons on the Nature, Occasions, Signs, Evils, and Remedy of Intemperance*, 6th ed. (Boston: T. R. Marvin, 1828), 61–65.

47. Ibid., 71.

48. Temperance Society of South Carolina, *Proceedings of the Temperance Society of Columbia, South Carolina, Together with Their Constitution and Report of Their Committee on the Influence of the Intemperance upon the Health, Morals, and Prosperity of the Country* (Columbia, SC: McMorris and Wilson, 1829), 20–21.

49. Lucian Minor, *Reasons for Abolishing the Liquor Traffic: Address to the People of Virginia* (Richmond, VA: H. K. Ellyson, 1853), 5.

50. Temperance Society of Columbia, South Carolina, *Proceedings*, 37.

51. American Temperance Society (ATS), *Sixth Annual Report* (Boston: American Temperance Society, 1833), 105.

52. American Temperance Union (ATU), *First Annual Report* (1837), in *Permanent Temperance Documents of the American Temperance Union* (New York: American Temperance Union, 1852–53), 18.

53. ATS, *Sixth Annual Report* (1833), 6.

54. Ibid., 93.

55. ATU, *First Annual Report*, 26.

56. American Temperance Union, *Third Annual Report* (1839), 6, in *Permanent Temperance Documents of the American Temperance Union* (New York: American Temperance Union, 1852–53); ATU, *Sixth Annual Report* (1843), 5.

57. ATS, *Sixth Annual Report* (1833), 8.

58. American Temperance Society, *Fourth Annual Report* (New York: American Temperance Union, 1831), 38.

59. American Temperance Society, *Seventh Annual Report* (New York: American Temperance Union, 1834), 48.

60. Tyrrell, *Sobering Up*, 68.

61. Varon, *We Mean to Be Counted*, 32. Douglas W. Carlson notes that statistics gathered by the Georgia Temperance Convention in 1844 indicate that women constituted 43 percent of the members in a survey of eighty-nine of the state's temperance groups and were in the majority in twenty-five of those groups. Douglas W. Carlson, "'Drinks He to His Own Undoing': Temperance Ideology in the Deep South," *Journal of the Early Republic* 18 (Winter 1998): 682.

62. For a fuller discussion of these trends, see Donald Yacovone, "The Transformation of the Black Temperance Movement, 1827–1854: An Interpretation," *Journal of the Early Republic* 8 (Fall 1988): 281–97.

63. "Prostitution of Our Means," *Colored American*, May 18, 1839, quoted in Louis Filler, *The Crusade against Slavery, 1830–1860* (New York: Harper, 1960), 144.

64. For a particularly interesting discussion of working-class commercial pastimes, see Elliott Gorn, *The Manly Art: Bare-Knuckle Prize Fighting in America* (Ithaca, NY: Cornell University Press, 1986).

65. Dorsey, *Reforming Men and Women*, 101.

66. *Pearl*, October 10, 1846, 141.

67. *Pearl*, August 8, 1846, 76.

68. *Pearl*, June 27, 1846, 29.

69. Ruth Alexander, "'We Are Engaged as a Band of Sisters': Class and Domesticity in the Washingtonian Temperance Movement, 1840–1850," *Journal of American History* 76 (December 1988): 764.

70. *Pearl*, July 25, 1846, 62.

71. Alexander, "'We Are Engaged,'" 777.

72. Carlson, "'Drinks He to His Own Undoing,'" 668.

73. Abel Fletcher, *The History, Objects, and Principles of the Order of the Sons of Temperance: An Address Delivered in Richmond, Virginia, December 2, 1844* (Philadelphia: Gihon and Porter, 1845), 17.

74. Samuel Ellis, *The History of the Order of the Sons of Temperance* (Boston: Stacey, Richardson, 1848), 106.

75. *Pearl*, October 3, 1846, 140.

76. See, e.g., Elizabeth Fox-Genovese, *Within the Plantation Household: Black and White Women of the Old South* (Chapel Hill: University of North Carolina Press, 1988), 80–81.

77. Beecher, *Six Sermons*, 58.The Emergence of Thrift in Early America, 1630–1880

8 }

African Americans, Slavery, and Thrift from the Revolution to the Civil War

Patrick Rael

Notions of thrift have played a vital role in the history of race in the United States. The young nation, founded on the principle of universal human equality, struggled with the fate of peoples it defined as nonwhite. The discourse of thrift deeply informed these anxious discussions. To many Americans, the virtues of thrift—industriousness, discipline, and self-control—offered a measure of civilization by which nonwhites were frequently found deeply wanting. The history of the nation from the Revolution to the Civil War documents the ways that freedom and civic inclusion came to be defined largely in terms of a racialized discourse of thrift. Those thought to embody thrift's antitheses—laziness, improvidence, and profligacy—often found themselves on the margins of a civilization defined in terms of industry and frugality.

This process was most pronounced among Americans of African descent, as black people assumed the preeminent role in discussions of thrift and race in nineteenth-century America. Unlike Native Americans, who were almost universally excluded from American society, African Americans challenged the boundaries of inclusion by their very presence. Enslaved African Americans lived among whites, who forced them to perform the menial tasks required by the cash-crop economy of the plantation South. Even nominally free African Americans—particularly those who lived in the northern states before the Civil War—raised troublesome questions over the limits of citizenship and national inclusion.

The place of African Americans in the nation became a question of central importance in the decades following the nation's birth. The market revolution—the great engine of capitalist transformation that fostered both the bourgeois work ethic of the industrializing North and the "precapitalist" social order of the antebellum South—deeply exacerbated differences among the sections of the country. These economic changes fostered disparate visions of American society. Whereas many in the northern states idealized a social order predicated on the middle-class market values associated with industrialization and urbanization, plantation society in the South developed its own ideal, rooted in capital-rich slaveholders' benign but efficient control over the labor of black slaves and poor whites. These competing ideals of thrift emerged as mutual antagonists; regional identities dialectically defined themselves in opposition to economic and social worlds each saw as inimical to the good society. The Civil War resulted from these tensions and largely resolved them—in favor of the market-oriented values of the industrializing North. But while northern visions of market-oriented thrift triumphed over southern paternalism, the war did very little to extirpate the racial inequalities inherent in them.

Thrift and Race in the Age of the Revolution

At the time of the American Revolution (1775–83), the thrift ethos lay at the heart of the Founding Fathers' anxious deliberations over the prospects for a new American democracy. The presence of slavery and the example of an oppressed race on American shores combined with notions of thrift to shape revolutionary discourse in powerful ways. American radicals easily equated England's treatment of its American colonies with the practice of enslavement. As the Declaration of Independence put it, king and Parliament had pursued policies toward the colonies evincing "a design to reduce them under absolute Despotism." Chattel bondage offered more than a compelling metaphor for colonists' experience; American revolutionaries struggled against slavery as an actual political condition that was, in their estimation, a startlingly near political possibility for white American colonists. Patriot Josiah Quincy conceded as much in 1774, declaring, "Britons are our oppressors . . . *we are slaves*."[1] Countless other revolutionaries explicitly equated the oppressions of the British with those endured by slaves—degradations known all too well to the slaveholding fathers of the American republic. No less a patriot than George Washington, himself the owner of several hundred human beings, warned his fellow colonists that to "submit to every Imposition that can be heap'd upon us . . . will make us as tame, & abject Slaves, as the Blacks we Rule over with such arbitrary Sway."[2]

Values associated with thrift stood at the opposite end of slavery's dependence and degradation and, hence, associated thrift with freedom. America's founders were anxious revolutionaries who posed themselves as custodians of a tradition of English rights that coveted both liberty and social order, and they viewed habits associated with thrift as vital to the preservation of both. For them, the opposites of liberty were, on the one hand, luxury, effeminacy, and wastefulness, and, on the other, poverty, servility, and dependence. John Adams put it well in a letter to his wife, Abigail, in 1774, worrying that a decade of parliamentary depredations had created a "universal Spirit of Debauchery, Dissipation, Luxury, Effeminacy and Gaming" in the colonies. "How much servility, Venality and Artifice and Hypocricy, [*sic*] have been introduced among the Ambitious and Avaricious by the british Politicks of the last 10 Years?" he asked.[3] Thrift stood with liberty in the virtuous center between the extremes of luxury and servility, tyranny and anarchy. Benjamin Franklin advocated thrifty values among his famous "thirteen virtues" to cultivate, which included temperance, frugality, industry, and moderation. Such virtues were personal in character but collective in their effects. Wrote one American Revolutionary, "The public good is not a term opposed to the good of individuals; on the contrary, it is the good of every individual collected."[4] Particularly in a self-governing republic, self-restraint and independence were the watchwords of civic health. "It is easy to see that when republican virtue fails, slavery ensues," Thomas Paine wrote in *Common Sense*.[5] Adams echoed this sentiment succinctly in a letter to Thomas Jefferson: "Without virtue, there can be no political liberty."[6]

The racial import of these values of civic virtue became clear as a consequence of the inexorable logic of the Revolution. For if all mankind were created equal, and if government was to serve the interests of those governed, were not African-descended people entitled to the right of self-governance—the precious fruit of equality? How could a nation that had founded its bloody nascence on the principle of universal human liberty deny that liberty to any among its ranks? No one raising a hand for American liberty could ignore these deep conundrums. British critics spared no opportunity to point out the apparent hypocrisy of the colonials' stand on slavery. "How is it," quipped Samuel Johnson, the English writer and satirist, "that we hear the loudest yelps for liberty among the drivers of Negroes?"[7] The colonists themselves were far too committed to their revolutionary ideology to miss the point. The great paradox of the Revolution was not lost on founders such as John Jay, the New York attorney who penned some of the most eloquent defenses of the young nation. "To contend for our own liberty and to deny that blessing to others," he wrote in 1785, "involves an inconsistency not to be excused."[8] This attitude was more common in the northern colonies and states, where the mercantile economy relied on slavery, but was less apparent in the declining tobacco regime in the Chesapeake and the expanding rice and cotton plantations farther south, in low-country Carolinas and northern Georgia.

The consequence of revolutionary ideology on the practice of slavery was profound, if inconsistent. Between 1777 and 1827 every state north of the Mason-Dixon Line provided for the gradual, compensated abolition of slavery. Those such as Vermont prepared constitutions that prohibited slavery, while Massachusetts ended slavery through legal fiat. The most important slaveholding states in the North—Pennsylvania, New York, and New Jersey—passed a series of legislative half measures that, collectively and over time, provided for the complete freedom of their enslaved populations. Even in the nominally "free" North, however, African Americans confronted grave questions about their characters. The principles of the Revolution might have dictated the inadvisability of continuing slavery in a land of freedom, but they left plenty of room for debating the wisdom of granting freedpeople political equality. Here values associated with thrift assumed great significance, for it was precisely blacks' alleged failings in this realm that seemed to justify their continued enslavement or exclusion. In New Jersey, where slavery was particularly entrenched, arguments against black freedom asserted that African Americans' "deep wrought disposition to indolence and laziness" went hand in hand with their "general looseness of passions and uncontrovertible propensity to gratify and satiate every thirst . . . without attending to the consequences."[9] To unleash such people on the body politic would be the height of civic irresponsibility.

The pattern in the North, by which slavery fell hardest where the economy depended on it most, was even more evident in the South, where the institution itself weathered considerable disruption in the course of the Revolution but did not die. The Upper South states of Virginia, Maryland, and Delaware witnessed a spate of voluntary manumissions. Some slaveholders sought to put their revolutionary principles into practice through such actions; others simply wished to rid themselves of the burden and expense of an aging slave population in a declining economy. Regardless of the motives for manumission, the free black population of the Upper South exploded in the postwar years, increasing threefold from 1790 to 1810.[10] Such, though, was slavery's hold on the agricultural economy of the Chesapeake that revolutionary ideology and economic expedience were insufficient to extinguish slavery. And farther south, where the cash-crop economy was expanding, the Revolution inspired no efforts to, for example, trade slaves their freedom in exchange for military service. Instead, slaves took it upon themselves to strike a blow for freedom.

As the war shifted to the southern theater in the early 1780s, slaves availed themselves of the opportunities offered by the chaos of war and fled the plantations. Once the conflict was over, Lower South slaveholders moved quickly to reconstitute their control over their bound laborers. With but few exceptions, they paid little heed to calls for gradual abolition. Instead, they defined southern interests in terms of slaveholding and championed their region's right to own slaves. In the Constitutional Convention of 1787, so ardently did they argue their position that they nearly scuttled the fragile national compact.[11] William Loughton Smith of South Carolina argued that "slavery was so ingrafted into the policy of the Southern States, that it could not be eradicated without tearing up by the roots their happiness, tranquillity, and prosperity."[12] The result of delicate sectional negotiations, the final Constitution included clauses permitting an end to the international slave trade and counting three-fifths of the slave population for purposes of representation in the House of Representatives.

Ideas of thrift played a critical role in the fate of slavery during the periods of the American Revolution and Early Republic. Slavery's most ardent apologists claimed that African-descended people lacked the qualities necessary to include them among the group of "all men" to whom the Declaration of Independence applied. The innate characters of Africans, it was argued, unfitted them for the critical responsibilities of self-rule. The most well-respected natural philosophers of the day had ascribed to this view before the Revolution. David Hume, for example, suspected that Africans were "naturally inferior to the whites," for they had never attained the features of "civilization"—"no ingenious manufactures amongst them, no arts, no sciences."[13] According to such influential views, Africans' innate inadequacies amounted to shortcomings in their personal characters. On the eve of the Revolution, an American naturalist proclaimed of Africans that "treachery, theft, stubbornness, and idleness . . . are such consequences of their manner of life at home as to put it out of all doubt that these qualities are natural to them and not originated by their state of slavery."[14] There was little room for the virtue of thrift in such a formulation. Indeed, pre-Revolutionary ideas tended simply to echo the perspectives of European travelers back to the sixteenth century, who had long listed Africans' lack of foresight and frugality among the many deficiencies that rendered them uncivilized.

The social, cultural, and intellectual changes that attended the Revolution raised new possibilities for Africans. The Enlightenment that had spawned the natural rights philosophies of the Age of Democratic Revolution helped create an ambivalent science of race. On the one hand, European philosophers' mania for classifying the natural world placed white people at the top of nature's hierarchy, relegating Africans to a position somewhere between civilized man and savage nature. Eighteenth-century anthropologists regularly claimed, for example, that "the *Penis* of an African is larger than that of an European" and that "apes and baboons menstruate less than negresses, monkeys still less."[15] Meanwhile, the Enlightenment's stress on the role of environment in the formation of human character—nurture rather than nature—offered Africans some potential means of redemption. True, Africans' characters were largely deficient of all qualities that defined the "civilized," but circumstance rather than color may have determined this; under benign circumstances Africans might conceivably be uplifted to a level of equality with whites. Revolutionary doctor and abolitionist Benjamin Rush attributed the characteristic degradation of slaves not to Africans' innate natures but to the abuses of slavery itself. Prominently referencing such nonthrifty character defects as idleness and thievishness, Rush argued that "all the vices which are charged upon the negroes . . . are the genuine offspring of slavery."[16] The Revolution thus represented a qualified respite from an already-long history of inveterate racial denigration, but it was one deeply qualified by the presumption of white superiority and by the looming question of blacks' emancipatability—the potential for their release into a free and self-governing republic.

In the Revolutionary and early national periods, the discourse of thrift intersected with the discourse of universalism to contest the boundaries of national inclusion. Through the concept of civic virtue, the discourse of the Revolution racialized thrift, just as thrift helped racialize Revolutionary discourse. Thrift offered a template for considering not simply the question of slavery but the question of race as well. Thrift thus lay profoundly at the center of the great paradox of the American Revolution, and perhaps of American history itself: How could a liberty-loving nation become a bastion for racial oppression? Many of the founding generation believed sufficiently in the Revolution's universalism to liberate African-descended people from the galling yoke of slavery. But just as many believed that slaves lacked the qualities necessary to exercise their freedom in ways conducive to the public weal. The racialized discourse of thrift excoriated servitude as dangerously antirepublican, but at the same time it rendered those who had been slaves unfit to wield the precious right of self-rule. In the end, the Revolution's discourse of thrift helped make slavery an institution "peculiar" to the South but racism a practice common to the nation.

Thrift and Race in the Market Revolution

The full significance of the racialization of thrift became clear during the period of the market revolution in America, which stretched roughly from 1820 to the Civil War. This era witnessed the confluence of several mutually reinforcing processes that amounted to the birth of the modern industrial order. It began with the emergence in America of technological changes that had begun in Great Britain and western Europe as new materials and new refining processes led to a revolution in manufacturing. New materials and technologies, in turn, led to a revolution in the transportation of goods, people, and ideas across the nation. And the transportation revolution fostered the development of new goods, which were manufactured by new methods.

As production moved from individual homes to centralized establishments, new systems of labor emerged to maximize productive efficiency. Mechanized production, interchangeable parts, the specialization of labor in new manufactories—all had vast social consequences. The most fundamental of these was urbanization. As sites of manufacturing activity and markets for goods and labor, cities grew in size and number. The prevailing system of artisanal manufacture gave way to a new workforce composed of largely unskilled laborers, increasingly supplied from the ranks of displaced craftsmen, rural folk attracted to the urban economy, or European immigrants. Apprentices once destined to learn their entire craft and open their own shops now stayed in their unskilled or semiskilled occupations for life. Entrepreneurial artisans, who once took part in every part of the manufacturing process, became nascent capitalists who managed the labor of others or hired others to do so. Industrialization thus led to the emergence of modern social classes. Workers began to identify themselves through a cultural style that jealously guarded their few workplace privileges and set them apart from the growing middle class, while a rising middle class just as assiduously sought to distance itself from "rough" laborers through "respectable" comportment and conspicuous display of elevated class status.

The rise of this new middle class transformed the discourse of thrift, supplanting the Revolutionary era's republican concern for civic virtue with the market revolution's liberal regard for individual economic virtues. The market revolution celebrated bourgeois life and endowed it with potent cultural authority. Economic development became the progress of civilization, of national material and moral well-being, and whatever tended to aggrandize the one was valued as enhancing the other. Popular literature—the articles and stories offered in a spate of new weekly and monthly serials—captured the new ethos. For example, an antebellum history of the Illinois frontier modeled the civilizing process of economic expansion in describing what it saw as the enterprising young people of the state. Whereas an older generation of settlers had been satisfied to live in "old log cabins, go bare-footed, and eat hog and hominy," the Illinoisans of the 1830s were impelled to enterprise by "a desire to gratify artificial wants." These wants—better clothing, a new horse, something to display in the home—led people to learn "new notions of economy and ingenuity in business" in order to fulfill them. A self-reinforcing cycle of economy and progress ensued: "This again led to settled habits of enterprise, economy and tact in business, which once acquired and persevered in, were made the cause of a thriftiness unknown to their fathers and mothers."[17] It was, then, the desire to consume—to improve the material circumstances of life within appropriate moral bounds, a phenomenon that French observer Alexis de Tocqueville called "interest rightly understood"—that led the wise to save; and these personal habits of thrift fostered the economic and, hence, moral well-being of all.[18]

Antebellum paeans to the virtues of responsible consumption knew few bounds. Commentators pictured thoughtfully directed desire as the guarantor of political liberty and as the cement that would bind up the social divisions created by industrialization. Satisfying "the sharp necessities of life," argued Unitarian divine William Ellery Channing, might "chain man to toil," but it could also "wake up his faculties, and fit him for wider actions." The thrift required to satisfy human desires responsibly enhanced the social order by fostering self-control. "Thus freedom," Channing wrote, "is the end of all just restraint."[19] According to the *American Whig Review*, thrifty habits would best serve the laborer, who even while engaged in menial work requiring no exercise of intellect may instead use his mind "in digesting and arranging its accumulated treasures" and thus be carried "onward in the path of eternal progress."

The *Review* closed with a wish, repeated often in the bourgeois literature of the antebellum North, that "industry, diligence, [and] thrift" would grant "every true laborer, whether with head or hand, an honored place as a vital, worthy, [and] precious member of the body politic."[20] Thrift, then, if properly directed, promoted a degree of political and social harmony that would enhance progress and foster the virtues of civilization.

But the virtuous regulation of desire required a delicate balance, for if wrongly directed the impulses that led Americans to thrifty behavior could lead to the corruption of desire, or vice. In his popular 1856 work *The Elements of Morality*, British philosopher William Whewell remarked that "habits of care, with regard to sparing and spending, as may tend toward Poverty and Privation, are reckoned as Virtues: such virtues are *Economy, Frugality*. By these, a man *thrives*, or grows in his possessions; he is *thrifty*." But overzealousness or neglect could transform any virtue into a vice: "Though wealth may be desired for ends which make the Desire virtuous; the progress of men's habits is such that, when sought at first as a means, it is afterwards desired as an end. The Desire to acquire money is then unlimited; and is *Covetousness, Avarice*."[21] Antebellum moral advisers suggested the dangerous proximity of healthy desire, which drove men to thrifty lives, to unhealthy desire, which produced immorality. The *United States Magazine and Democratic Review*, for example, distinguished "high ambition" from "mere idle vanity," declaring that while the former produced "great and noble deeds," the latter led only to "indolence and sloth."[22] This was the great moral crime of the Industrial Revolution: idleness threatened the entire civilization built on market values. Work, its opposite, was not "a mere provision for animal wants," as *Harper's New Monthly Magazine* put it in 1858. Rather, labor was "a great auxiliary to the moral and spiritual interests of life," the means through which human beings could exercise their "higher attributes" in a manner "ordained by the Creator." In short, the work that led to thrift reflected the highest spiritual aspirations of humankind: self-culture.[23]

By these bourgeois standards of thrift, African Americans were doomed to, at the least, obsolescence in the industrial economy. Nearly completely free by 1827, northern blacks once deemed too deficient in civic virtue to participate equally in the political life of the North were now frequently deemed too deficient in market virtue to participate equally in the economic life of the North. Carrying forward older generalizations about blacks' inherent natures, respectability's standard-bearers found free blacks deeply wanting in their capacity to properly regulate their desire. According to white critics, free blacks simply failed to respond rationally to the market's system of incentives and rewards. "The negro," complained a Connecticut newspaper, "can supply all his physical wants without industry, and beyond the supply of his immediate physical wants, he has little inducement to look."[24] Rather than seek the self-culture necessary to improve their lives, blacks were charged with being satisfied with the minimum. In 1837, delegates to a state constitutional convention in

Pennsylvania argued for the disfranchisement of blacks on these grounds, declaring that northern African Americans were "engaged in no business that requires even ordinary capacity, in no enterprizes [*sic*] requiring talents to conduct them. The mass are improvident, and seek the lowest avocations, and most menial stations."[25]

Some ascribed African Americans' alleged aversion to the material benefits of bourgeois life to a consequence of their time in bondage. "Those who have just emerged from a state of barbarism or slavery have few artificial wants," declared some Connecticut whites in 1834. As a result, blacks were "regardless of the decencies of life, and improvident of the future."[26] Tocqueville agreed, writing that for the freed slave "independence is often . . . a heavier burden than slavery," for in freedom, "a thousand new desires beset him, and he has not the knowledge and energy necessary to resist them." As Tocqueville intuited, virtue in market culture required internal discipline, but masters maintained order through external controls. Desire and passions were "masters which it is necessary to contend with," he wrote, but the slave "has learned only to submit and obey." As a consequence, "liberty destroys him."[27]

Unsurprisingly, free African Americans bristled at this depiction of the race. Throughout the northern states, wherever black people enjoyed sufficient liberty and opportunity to organize themselves to resist oppression, they issued streams of counterspeech designed to refute the calumnies uttered against them. The result was a rich body of protest thought that fueled the efforts of white abolitionists and polarized the national debate over slavery. In newspapers, sermons, pamphlets, public celebrations, and conventions, prominent African Americans in the antebellum North responded directly to the claims of blacks' detractors, arguing that African Americans were indeed capable of imbibing the civilizing influences of the market economy.

They spoke in terms deeply reminiscent of antebellum apostles of market virtue. "Commerce is the pioneer of civilization and intelligence," declared a national convention of African Americans in 1853. "It gives a field apace for essential, refined morality."[28] Like Channing, they spoke of the great significance of self-improvement. An earlier national convention of African Americans in 1847 put it eloquently: "Mental culture"—the "growth," "expansion," and "development" of intellect—was a "primeval duty" that had been "bestowed upon us by the Almighty."[29] In literally thousands of similar utterances, African American leaders urged their people to embrace the virtues of bourgeois life. Black newspapers like *Freedom's Journal*, the nation's first, promised to "dwell . . . upon the general principles and rules of economy," frequently running didactic essays on the subjects of thrift and industry.[30] A later New York newspaper, the *Colored American*, typified these calls to embrace market virtues, urging readers to "cultivate honesty, punctuality, propriety of conduct, and modesty and dignity of deportment," as well as "untiring habits of industry, the dint of perseverance," and "rigidness of economy."[31]

The virtues of bourgeois life held special resonance for African American public figures. These were precisely the qualities blacks were claimed to lack, and it was on the basis of this deficiency that prejudicial social policies—slavery in the South, disfranchisement and exclusion in the North—were justified. Antebellum blacks' analysis of their dilemma and its solution stemmed directly from understandings of thrift they shared with whites. The core of their complaint was that black people were too frequently viewed as inherently and irrevocably degraded. Black leaders conceded that African Americans were merely human and that as poor and excluded people they confronted their own moral challenges. But they charged prejudiced whites with exaggerating the immoral conduct of a few. Wrote one black commentator of free African Americans, "Every indecorous act on their part is used as a weapon by the pro-slavery spirit of the age against the cause of freedom, . . . to show that the colored people are not fit for freedom."[32] The worst consequence of this phenomenon was that all African Americans became tainted with the vices of the minority. Wrote another: "Any exhibition of vice or folly on the part of a single individual among them, is often taken as an evidence of the moral degradation and inferiority of the whole people."[33] Furthermore, prejudice in this form contradicted the promises of a marketplace presumed to be neutral, and thus imperiled market culture as a whole. "Vice and virtue are . . . treated with equal disfavor by our oppressors," charged Frederick Douglass. "In many of the Northern States of the Union, a low, idle, vicious white man stands higher in the social and political scale of society, than the most refined and virtuous colored man can do."[34] To black abolitionist Charles Remond, such a system—wherein "virtue may not claim her divinely appointed rewards"—seemed "well calculated to make every man disregardful of his conduct, and every woman unmindful of her reputation."[35]

The solution most antebellum black leaders proffered relied deeply on the workings of the market economy. If the charge against blacks was that they lacked market virtues, then the answer was that they must provide "practical evidence to the contrary."[36] To black leaders, a bourgeois concern with self-regulation offered the most potent means of breaking the cycle of oppression and returning the nation to (what they presumed to be) its race-neutral first principles. The values of thrift, economy, and gratification delay—in short, everything encapsulated by the word *thrift*—resonated among black leaders precisely because they offered individual character as a space of uncontested authority that could help change white minds. "We have to act an important part, and fill an important place . . . in the work of emancipation," intoned black editor Samuel Cornish. "On *our* conduct and exertions much, very much depend."[37] Through their own actions, behavior, and comportment, African Americans could rebut the racist claims that held them back. "I think," wrote Austin Steward, "that our conduct as colored men will have a great bearing on the question that now agitates this land. . . . Let it be shown that we as a people are religious, industrious, sober, honest and intelligent, and my word for it, the accursed system of Slavery will fall, as did Satan from Heaven."[38]

If prejudice constituted a violation of market principles, only proper market behavior could offer a solution. The discourse of thrift offered African Americans a means of changing white minds that lay within the market order itself. The key was to work properly—to conserve blacks' energies, only to invest them in aims likely to produce the highest returns in liberty and equality. "If we would be men and command respect among men, we must strike for something higher than sympathy and perpetual beggary," wrote one black editor. Charity did not foster elevation and independence in men, but rather "has a tendency to make them indolent and stupid."[39] Blacks had to change their relationship to the market, African American leaders said; they had to attain a position of power within the market that would let them command the equality they were owed. "Society is a heard-hearted affair," wrote Frederick Douglass. "The individual must keep society under obligation to him, or society will honor him only as a stranger and sojourner."[40] Time and time again, prominent African Americans called for blacks to act in such a way as to make whites as dependent upon blacks as blacks were upon whites. Wrote one black editor: "Self-respect induces all equals to respect those who belong to their order, interest impels them to cultivate good understanding with those whose assistance may at any moment be necessary to preserve life or property."[41] In practice, this strategy meant rising up out of the lowest rungs of the economy and scaling the hierarchy of labor. The Colored National Convention of 1853, which dedicated an entire committee to this very problem, loudly proclaimed that "commerce leads to respectability."[42] Others echoed the claim over and over again, urging nonelite blacks to move from the vice-filled cities into the countryside, to take up skilled trades, and become cogs in the machinery of American business.

Black leaders' reliance on the discourse of thrift as a strategy for obtaining equality offered one commanding benefit: agency. For African American leaders, the great value of moral reform lay precisely in the promise of agency it offered every single African American, regardless of status or condition. "Each one for himself, must commence the improvement of his condition," wrote Cornish. "It is not in mass, but in individual effort and character, that we are to move onward to a higher elevation."[43] As a class, African Americans might not control much, but they could always control themselves. "I possess nothing but moral capability," Boston's Maria Stewart once said.[44] God, wrote one black minister, "holds man responsible only for his moral conduct in the formation of his moral character, and on nothing more in his own existence has he control."[45] While liberal ideology may have inhibited blacks from developing a more sophisticated understanding of the structural economic forces underlying their plight, it offered the individual as an uncontestable space for exercising personal agency. Ultimately, this was the best the discourse of thrift could offer. While self-cultivation may or may not eradicate prejudice, it was worth pursuing as its own reward.

Thrift and Race in the Critique of Slavery

The political abolitionists of the 1840s and 1850s—those who developed into the Republican Party of Abraham Lincoln—molded a potent critique of slavery out of their faith in the virtues of the liberal marketplace. Black activists and white abolitionists operated on the margins of public culture, vilifying southern slavery as above all sinful—a message that resonated among some Evangelical reformers of the age but was more likely to earn its adherents the title of "crack-brained fanatics." Later generations of political antislavers employed the values of thrift to fashion critiques of slavery that could appeal to the moderate center of the northern electorate. Thrift framed the issue of slavery in such a way that an entire, mass political party could rise and even thrive with an antislavery message. With the election of Lincoln to the presidency in November 1860, this came to pass. And of course it was the election of Lincoln, an antislavery Republican, to the White House that spurred southern fire-eaters to their victorious campaign to launch a preemptive revolution against the incursions of liberal democracy and the free market and to secede from the Union. But the success of Republicans' thrift-based ideology was predicated on an appeal to masses who were overwhelmingly prejudiced. And while Republicans successfully portrayed slavery as a threat to the self-interest of white northerners, they did little to root out the innate racism of American life—a problem that became all too apparent after the Civil War was over.

By standards of northern thrift and industry, southern society appeared backward and antiprogressive. Unitarian minister Elhanan Winchester Reynolds described the difference between the free and slave states, the former displaying "thrift, refinement, intelligence, order, and the tender charities that spring from Christian culture," while the latter manifested "indigence, brutality, ignorance, incipient anarchy, and heathen cruelty."[46] Historian Eric Foner, in his study of free labor ideology in antebellum America, has documented the myriad counts on which antebellum Republicans found the South wanting in prosperity.[47] William Seward, through his southern travels, found "exhausted soil, old and decaying towns, wretchedly-neglected roads, and, in every respect, an absence of enterprise and improvement."[48] Other Republicans spoke of the South's "lack of invention and resource," its "inefficiency and irresolution," and the "sameness of poverty and unthrift" that beset the region.[49] Few left any question as to the source of the South's retrograde economy. "Such has been the effect of slavery," pronounced Seward, while New Hampshire jurist Nathaniel Upham attributed the South's poverty to its "thriftless, improvident system" of labor.[50] Slavery's critics emerged even in the South, where a few outspoken dissidents like Hinton Helper ascribed the region's backwardness "to the same cause that has impoverished and dishonored us in all other respects—the thriftless and degrading institution of slavery."[51]

Economic critiques of slavery, infused as they were with the discourse of thrift, owed slavery's blighting effects to its violation of principle tenets of market society. Most obviously, slavery offered little positive incentive for the slave to labor industriously. The lash kept slaves at work but did little to enhance their morals. In a work on political economy, George Tucker, the Virginia politician and philosopher, stated the case clearly: "The slave, not being stimulated to industry by the expectation of receiving the fruits of his own labor, is likely, from the love of ease so natural to man, to work less willingly, with less energy, and to avoid the toil when he can."[52] The slave simply had no stake in the system he labored under. "However much of revenue he may produce," wrote one Republican, "his own share will be strictly limited to the necessities of life."[53] In such a system, why should anyone labor? The moral degeneration of slaves followed directly from slavery's failure to offer positive incentives to labor. "The instinctive feelings of the slave," continued Tucker, "impel him to extraordinary expense and waste. He is therefore generally thievish, careless, and improvident."[54] Slavery thus made blacks incapable of participating responsibly in market society, instead rendering them improvident, thievish, and thriftless. Wrote Helper, "Where a system of enforced servitude prevails, it is very apt to beget loose notions about the obligations of paying for anything."[55] According to this view, the consequence for masters was just as grave as for the slave. Slavery produced "pride, indolence, luxury, and licentiousness,"[56] consigning the slave owners themselves to "idleness" and "vicious indulgences."[57]

Most distressing, according to economic critiques of slavery, were the effects of the peculiar institution on laboring white men. If slavery led planters to become idle aristocrats and slaves to become shiftless and indolent, it brought nonslaveholding whites to the very brink of barbarism. The *North American Review*, lauding Irish economist John Elliot Cairnes's treatise *The Slave Power*, agreed that the poor whites of the South were "an ignorant, restless, vagrant class, and add almost nothing to the material prosperity of the country," and that this was "the necessary result of the system, social and industrial, under which they live."[58] Maine Republican George Weston agreed, arguing that the poor whites of the South "live a semi-savage life, sinking deeper and more hopelessly into barbarism with every succeeding generation." Those who had migrated to the North had "brought more ignorance, poverty, and thriftlessness, than an equal amount of European immigration."[59] The point was that because it was cheaper and neglected, slave labor would always outcompete free labor, and where the two competed, free labor would always decline as a result. Wrote one Republican ideologue, "Free labor languishes and becomes degrading when put in competition with slave labor, and idleness, poverty, and vice, among large classes of non-slaveholders, take the place of industry and thrift and virtue."[60] It was not a far leap to conclude that the slavery that debased nonslaveholding whites in the South also threatened laboring whites in the North. The Republican Party found its most appealing message in delineating the menace that slavery allegedly posed to the northern rank and file. Many agreed with the Iowa Republican who declared slavery "a curse upon the poor, free, laboring white man."[61]

Conspicuously absent in this brand of Republican antislavery were the interests of the enslaved themselves. Abolitionists, in championing the cause of the enslaved, had long earned the ire of a prejudiced society, which often labeled them "nigger lovers" who wished for "amalgamation," or racial intermarriage. Given the pervasive racism of the day, no mass political party could ever hope to develop a broad-based appeal on the basis of such perceptions. While Republican ranks included some of the earliest and most ardent of the political abolitionists, all were practically minded enough to understand that only through appeal to the self-interest of the majority of northern whites was an antislavery politics possible. The Republican coalition succeeded precisely because it embraced a wide range of views on slavery and race, which cohered only in opposing the extension of slavery into the West. This left considerable room for men such as Kentucky's Cassius Clay, who sought "the highest welfare of the white, whatever may be the consequences of liberation to the African,"[62] or Pennsylvania's David Wilmot, who in opposing slavery wished to "preserve for free white labor a fair country" where those of his "own race and own color" could "live without the disgrace which association with negro slavery brings upon free labor."[63]

The North that elected Lincoln in November 1860 had, in general, little love for black people. To most who voted for it, the Republican Party stood not for racial equality or humanitarian sentiment but for the constellation of personal character virtues associated with the market liberalism of the Industrial Revolution in America—with, in a word, thrift. And it was to preserve this racial inheritance of free white men that so many voted for Lincoln—a man who had openly declared his white supremacist principles during his famous debates with Stephen Douglas in 1858. "I am not, nor ever have been in favor of bringing about in any way the social and political equality of the white and black races," he had said, averring that he was "as much as any other man . . . in favor of having the superior position assigned to the white race."[64] Yet this Lincoln was also the Lincoln who would not, when the great conflict came, yield to the fire-eaters of the South. "I believe this government cannot endure permanently half slave and half free," he had stated in his famous "House Divided" speech of June 1858, predicting that "it will cease to be divided. It will become all one thing, or all the other."[65]

Thrift and Race in the Defense of Slavery

Lincoln's words reflected just one side of the polarizing political rhetoric of the 1850s. The Republicans were not alone in issuing strident denunciations of those they saw as corruptors of coveted American values like thrift. From the start of the abolitionists' campaigns of the 1830s, the slaveholding South had produced a powerful group of intellectuals dedicated to defending the peculiar institution. Defenses of plantation servitude took many forms, such as the argument that slavery was an ancient human institution sanctioned by Christianity's sacred texts. But Republican critiques of the economic aspects of chattel bondage challenged proslavery apologists to respond in kind. These ideologues reflected the deeply conservative outlooks of the southern economic aristocracy, but to a remarkable degree they relied on the basic presumptions of market society—and particularly its understandings of thrift.

The argument began with a claim that most white northerners would have accepted: black people innately lacked thrift and hence were characterologically incapable of participating equally in society. George Fitzhugh, the Virginian whose proslavery works included elaborate economic defenses of slavery, noted blacks' alleged thriftlessness as an intrinsic quality of the race: "The negro is improvident; will not lay up in summer for the wants of winter; will not accumulate in youth for the exigencies of age." This thriftlessness was not without larger consequences, for left without direction, "he would become an insufferable burden to society."[66] Proslavery southerners like Fitzhugh delighted in looking to the free North for evidence of the inadvisability of mass emancipation. According to them, northern experience demonstrated the unelevatability of blacks. David Christy, in the introduction to his proslavery anthology, *Cotton Is King* (1855), typified this argument, pointing to "the slow progress made by the great body of the free blacks in the North" and absence "of any evidences of improvement in industry, intelligence, and morality."[67]

From such evidence Edmund Ruffin, the fire-eating Virginian who wrote *The Political Economy of Slavery* in 1857, broadly theorized about society's need to regulate the poor. "The lower that individuals are degraded by poverty and want, the lower do they descend in their appreciation of actual and even natural wants," he argued, echoing the popular economic idea that the reasoned pursuit of desire inspired men to virtue, industry, and civilization. Ruffin magnified the dangers posed by those "in the lowest grade" who preferred a "wretched existence to the alternative of steady labor." Enslavement offered the solution, as it would compel the poor to develop "habits of labor" while at the same time uplifting them "not only physically, but morally and intellectually."[68] In sum, the regulation of those who by choice or innate deficiency refused to participate in the market's system of incentives and rewards would relieve society of the burden of their nonmarket behavior, secure their labor for those who could make the most of it, and offer the best means of inculcating, to the extent possible, market habits in the poor. Clearly, in this view, slavery was best for Africans. As John C. Calhoun, South Carolina's fierce proslavery orator and politician, declared before the U.S. Senate, "Never before has the black race of Central Africa . . . attained a condition so civilized and so improved, not only physically, but morally and intellectually."[69] Fitzhugh argued that the slave trade removed "the negro" from Africa (and "every brutal vice and crime that can disgrace humanity") to America, where slavery "christianizes, protects, supports and civilizes him."[70]

While antislavery northerners found it incredible that the brutal institution of slavery depicted by abolitionists could actually civilize the slaves, proslavery apologists had a ready defense, again fashioned from the values of the North's own market culture. The very system of incentives and rewards that made market culture a civilizing force—rational and moderated self-interest, or Tocqueville's "interest rightly understood"—made slavery a humane and civilizing influence in the lives of the slaves. Fitzhugh put it most crassly, writing that "when slaves are worth near a thousand dollars a head, they will be carefully and well provided for."[71] Ruffin's subtler formulation had it that slaves' "general good treatment" was "induced by the self-interest of the owners."[72] In short, thrifty masters treated their slaves humanely. The thrift of masters served as a proxy for the thrift lacking in slaves. According to proslavery ideologues, slaves' isolation from the market was not simply a social necessity but a great boon to the slaves themselves, who would be protected from the vicissitudes of a market culture all too often grasping, competitive, and ruthless. Fitzhugh, for example, contrasted the economic climate for enslaved blacks who "luxuriate in corporeal and mental repose," with that for the white northerners he addressed, whose "capital would soon vanish, if you dared indulge in the liberty and abandon of negroes."[73]

Rooted in this contrast of cultures was a profound critique of northern market society. Slavery's defenders viewed the free labor economy of the North as a hideous and inhumane alternative to the benevolent paternalism of plantation slavery. As James Henry Hammond remonstrated with northern capitalists, "Your whole hireling class of manual laborers and 'operatives,' as you call them, are essentially slaves."[74] Fitzhugh repeated this observation in his 1857 treatise, *Cannibals All! or, Slaves without Masters*, the subtitle of which referred directly to the free white workers who supplied the labor for northern industry.[75] Whereas Tocqueville complained that desire and passion were "masters" with which slaves had not learned to struggle, Ruffin argued that "extreme want" was for free laborers a far less benevolent overlord. Whereas slavery insulated slaves from the inevitable misfortunes of market society, in the North "the laboring class . . . feels the first and heaviest infliction" of such crises.[76] Fitzhugh, too, argued that slavery was more humane than free labor, on the basis that the former provided a haven from the buffets of the market economy: "Capital exercises a more perfect compulsion over free laborers than human masters over slaves; for free laborers must at all times work or starve, and slaves are supported whether they work or not."[77]

Paradoxically, in their malign view of free labor southern conservatives found common cause with antebellum socialists of the North, who began experiments in communal living as alternatives to the competitive individualism of market society. Ruffin, for one, thoroughly endorsed the socialist conclusion "that the productive labors of all, if associated, . . . might be made much more productive." What was lacking in the socialists' experiments—which had all met "with signal, and also speedy, failure"—was hierarchy and authority, in the form of "one directing mind, and one controlling will." Add this will, Ruffin wrote, and the utopian community "is thereby converted to the condition of *domestic slavery*."[78] And utopian the vision was, for it promised an antidote to "the eager pursuit of gain" and the "passion" of "avarice" that conservatives feared was overspreading the nation. The unbridled market did incite invention and industry, but in making man "regardless of his soul" led to a social order that was "low, selfish, atheistic and material."[79]

The alternative to the North's hyperindividualism offered by proslavery conservatives did not negate thrift but merely reposed it. Thrift remained a central, if fluid, ideal; it was the *content* of thrift that slavery's defenders appropriated and reformulated. Free labor advocates posed the South as thriftless and thus antiprogressive; the fire-eaters claimed that they properly tempered thrift with benevolence, thus avoiding the avarice that made market society so hellish for free laborers. In the North, wrote Fitzhugh, free laborers enjoyed "no domestic affection" from their employers; "no kind mistress, like a guardian angel, provides for them in health, tends them in sickness, and soothes their dying pillow."[80] At the same time that slavery "provides for sickness, infancy and old age" and ensures "homes, food and clothing for all," it also "makes all work" and "permits no idleness."[81] As a result of slaveholders' benign intervention into the political economy, the social tensions that divided northern society were said to be nonexistent in the South. According to Calhoun, the South was exempt from the "conflict between labor and capital" produced by industrial civilization.[82] Fitzhugh believed that "it is impossible to place labor and capital in harmonious or friendly relations, except by the means of slavery."[83]

Two benign consequences flowed from the social harmony allegedly achieved by slavery. First, and in direct answer to free labor arguments, fire-eaters argued that slavery dignified the labor of whites. Slavery "does not bring all industry into disrepute," argued Fitzhugh, because blacks—assumed to be naturally unfitted for "all skillful pursuits"—were denied all but the lowest reaches of the hierarchy of labor. The rest were left for whites.[84] "We need never have white slaves in the South," he wrote, "because we have black ones."[85] The second benefit was political stability and, perversely enough, political democracy. The fire-eaters argued that slavery was "the most solid and durable foundation on which to rear free and stable political institution."[86] In the herrenvolk democracy of the slave South, all free white men shared a fundamental level of freedom made possible by the existence of an unfree caste beneath them. So wrote Alexander Stephens of Georgia, who went on to become vice president of the Confederate States of America: "With us, all of the white race, however high or low, rich or poor, are equal in the eye of the law."[87]

Thrift and Race in the Civil War and Reconstruction

From 1861 to 1865, these two basic visions of American society clashed. On the one hand was an emerging industrial society committed to a thrift ethos that extolled the potential of the individual to "rise" in society through the cultivation of personal virtues that would create success in the marketplace and the good society for all. On the other was a plantation society, similarly dedicated to a culture of thrift, but which viewed market liberalism with a suspicion bred from the latter's rejection of slavery as a legitimate and progressive form of labor control. Both sides participated in and relied on liberal markets for their economic lifeblood. Where they clashed was not in their estimation of African Americans—whom a majority in each section regarded as hopelessly deficient in the qualities necessary for economic, civic, and social equality—but in their vision of thrift and its benefits and of how society ought best be ordered to achieve them. The Republican Party that swept into the White House in March 1861 had long declared its opposition to the expansion of a system of labor that it viewed as inefficient and retrogressive. And the southern fire-eaters who led eleven slaveholding states out of the Union that spring had long declared their willingness to stake all in defense of the social order and social harmony they saw as threatened by the free labor society of the North.

The contest that ensued demonstrated the might of northern market society in a long-drawn-out military struggle. The Union boasted a free population almost three times the size of the Confederacy's, with more than ten times as many industrial workers, over twice as many miles of railroads, 110,000 manufacturing establishments to the Confederacy's 10,000, well over ten times as much banking capital, nearly as great a preponderance of capital investment, and almost ten times as great a value of annual production. Economically, then, the Union was a powerhouse against which the Confederacy could not hope to compete. Unfortunately for those on whom the "hard hand of war" fell, the Union initially lacked skilled generals and an effective army in the eastern theater of the war. In addition to general inexperience and widespread command incompetence, Civil War soldiers also confronted the fruits of the Industrial Revolution in the form of new rifled muskets, which rendered existing military tactics not simply obsolete but often suicidal. Decisive battlefield actions became rare, and the war stalemated into a protracted struggle of economies and societies, wherein the Union's vast advantages eventually prevailed. But the effort was not simple; on both sides it involved the consideration of revolutionary measures no one would have contemplated before the start of hostilities.

The exigencies of war led both combatants to consider the use of emancipated slaves in their armies, despite pervasive concerns on both sides that thriftless blacks would prove to be worthless soldiers. The Confederacy's stronger ideological commitment to white supremacy delayed its dalliance with emancipation beyond the point at which it could have aided the Confederate cause. The Union embarked on such a path much sooner. As early as 1861, African Americans themselves were turning the tide in favor of black freedom by escaping to Union lines, much as they had taken advantage of the chaos of war during the Revolution to seek their own freedom. Their efforts put the question of slaves' role in the conflict squarely before Union policy makers, who had to decide between violating the sanctity of private property by "confiscating" the slaves and risking defeat through a lack of critical manpower. As Lincoln eventually became convinced, "We must free the slaves or be ourselves subdued." The result was Lincoln's Emancipation Proclamation and Congress's Confiscation Acts, which collectively liberated millions of enslaved African Americans during the war. The recruitment of nearly 200,000 African Americans into the armed forces of the Union proceeded apace, and black soldiers demonstrated in action after action their capacity to fight with or against the best white troops. More important, once slaves were freed, it became nearly impossible to imagine the reimposition of slavery. When asked if he would consider revoking his proclamation in order to bring the war to a speedy, victorious conclusion, Lincoln replied: "I should be damned in time and in eternity for so doing. The world shall know that I will keep my faith to friends and enemies, come what will." In December 1865, the Union made good on its wartime promise to African Americans: the Thirteenth Amendment to the Constitution was ratified, thus ending slavery in America.

It was critical for the fate of African Americans that emancipation happened as a result of military exigency rather than a revolution in racial sentiments. Though undoubtedly the sectional crisis and the Civil War helped "abolitionize" some of the northern public, little had happened to disrupt the racial prejudice that pervaded both sections of the country. An enormous victory over the sinful and inefficient institution of slavery had been won, but blacks themselves remained mired, it was thought, in their thriftless, slavish habits. Could they become part of a market-oriented society? Would they continue to labor to produce the agricultural products like cotton that were so vital to the industrial economy? The reconstruction of southern labor was a complex affair involving unequal negotiations between many parties: former slaveholders, the Union government, and the freedpeople themselves.

Concerned primarily with securing for themselves an exploitable labor force, landholders sought to reconstitute southern agriculture on terms as close to slavery as they could. Meanwhile, the Union government, eager to convert plantation society to free labor, incanted its mantra of market virtues to slaves with no experience of or desire for them. Most slaves sought only autonomy from the market order that had fueled their enslavement, preferring to work in families and produce food for their own subsistence rather than cotton for the textile market. The resulting compromise—sharecropping, which permitted them to live in families but forced them to work cotton—initially reflected the freedpeople's capacity to exert their agency in a cash-starved and labor-poor economy. As time went on, though, and the federal government's commitment to racial justice gave way to political expediency, sharecropping became little more than a system of debt peonage, with credit and capital firmly in the hands of local whites who were as committed to the exploitation of labor as they were to white supremacy.

All of this happened with only minimal questioning of the capitalist order that had produced the racialized discourse of thrift. Reconstruction had failed, but defenders of liberal capitalism—who in general had always been willing to sacrifice racial equality for faith in their economy—tended to view the resulting racial inequity as a confirmation of blacks' inherent deficiency rather than as an inherent flaw in capitalism itself. Blacks had been given a chance, it was reasoned; if they had failed to make the most of it, then they themselves must bear the blame. So Thomas Huxley, a British disciple of Charles Darwin, concluded in the aftermath of Reconstruction, "Whatever the position into which the laws of social gravitation may bring the negro, all responsibility for the result will henceforward lie between Nature and him. The white man may wash his hands of it, and the Caucasian conscience be void of reproach evermore."[88] The ex-Confederates who swept back into power in the aftermath of Republican rule in the South thus gained in defeat what they had lost in war. Deprived of their slave labor, they nonetheless remained the South's master race. And their justifications for the campaign of racial terror they were about to unleash recalled an unreconstructed discourse of thrift all too familiar to black ears. "So long as negroes are *contented*," wrote Fitzhugh during Reconstruction, "they will have no property, no useful arts, no separate ownership of lands, no law, little or no government, and indeed none of the institutions of civilized life. . . . Yet, properly taken care of and provided for by the white, and educated to proper industrial pursuits, they become the most valuable part of every population, because the most productive." Fitzhugh proposed that the slaves be returned to their "natural" place, as the forced laborers of thrifty masters who would treat them with their characteristic benevolence. He concluded, "Let not our Northern friends, then, fear to turn the freedmen over to us."[89] To African Americans' great misfortune, and to the nation's great shame, that is almost precisely what they did.

Notes

1. Josiah Quincy, *Memoir of the Life of Josiah Quincy, Jun., of Massachusetts: By His Son, Josiah Quincy* (Boston: Cummings, Hilliard, and Company, 1825), 451.

2. George Washington to Bryan Fairfax, August 24, 1774, in *The Papers of George Washington: Colonial Series*, ed. W. W. Abbot and Dorothy Twohig (Charlottesville: University Press of Virginia, 1995), 10:155.

3. John Adams to Abigail Adams, July 5–6, 1774, in *Adams Family Correspondence*, ed. L. H. Butterfield (Cambridge, MA.: Belknap Press of Harvard University Press, 1963), 1:135.

4. Thomas Paine, *Dissertations on Government; the Affairs of the Bank; and Paper Money* (1786), quoted in Gordon S. Wood, *The Creation of the American Republic, 1776–1787* (Chapel Hill: University of North Carolina Press, 1969), 69.

5. Thomas Paine, *Common Sense: On the Origin and Design of Government in General, with Concise Remarks on the English Constitution; Together with the American Crisis, 1776–1783* (New York: Putnam's, 1912), 83.

6. John Adams to Thomas Jefferson, December 18, 1819, in *Adams to Jefferson/Jefferson to Adams: A Dialogue from Their Correspondence*, ed. Richard K. Arnold (San Francisco: Jerico Press, 1975), 330–31.

7. Samuel Johnson, "Taxation Not Tryanny," in *The Yale Edition of the Works of Samuel Johnson* (New Haven, CT: Yale University Press, 1977), 10:454.

8. William Jay, *The Life of John Jay: With Selections from His Correspondence and Miscellaneous Papers* (New York: J. and J. Harper, 1833), 1:231.

9. New Jersey Journal, quoted in Arthur Zilversmit, *The First Emancipation: The Abolition of Slavery in the North* (Chicago: University of Chicago Press, 1967), 143–44.

10. Ira Berlin, "The Revolution in Black Life," in *The American Revolution: Explorations in the History of American Radicalism*, ed. Alfred F. Young (De Kalb: Northern Illinois University Press, 1976), 359.

11. *The Debates in the Federal Convention of 1787, which Framed the Constitution of the United States of America, Reported by James Madison*, ed. Gaillard Hunt and James Brown Scott (Buffalo, NY: Prometheus, 1987), 2:443–51.

12. William Loughton Smith, *Annals of Congress*, 1st Cong., 2nd sess., 1508, quoted in Winthrop D. Jordan, *White over Black: American Attitudes toward the Negro, 1550–1812* (Chapel Hill: University of North Carolina Press, 1968), 326.

13. David Hume's Essays, *Moral and Political* (1742) appends these racist comments to his essay "Of National Characters." See Emmanuel Chukwudi Eze, ed., *Race and the Enlightenment: A Reader* (Cambridge, MA: Blackwell, 1997), 33.

14. Bernard Romans, *A Concise Natural History of East and West Florida* (New York: n.p., 1775), 105, quoted in Jordan, White over Black, 305.

15. Charles White, *An Account of the Regular Gradation in Man, and in Different Animals and Vegetables; and from the Former to the Latter* (London: n.p., 1799), iv, 1, quoted in Thomas F. Gossett, *Race: The History of an Idea in America* (Dallas: Southern Methodist University Press, 1963), 48.

16. Benjamin Rush, *An Address to the Inhabitants of the British Settlements in America, upon Slave-keeping* (Philadelphia: J. Dunlap, 1773), 2.

17. Thomas Ford, *A History of Illinois, from Its Commencement as a State in 1818 to 1847* (Chicago: S. C. Griggs, 1854), 95.

18. Alexis de Tocqueville, *Democracy in America* (New York: Vintage, 1945), 2:129.
19. William Ellery Channing, *A Selection from the Works of William E. Channing* D. D. (Boston: American Unitarian Association, 1855), 21.
20. "How Shall Life Be Made the Most of?" *American Whig Review.* 1 (April 1845): 423.
21. William Whewell, *The Elements of Morality, Including Polity* (New York: Harper, 1856), 178, 177.
22. "Fame and Its Accessories," *United States Magazine and Democratic Review* 20 (May 1847): 433.
23. "Enjoying Our Work," *Harper's New Monthly Magazine*, October 1858, 664.
24. *African Repository* (1828), 4:118, quoted in Leon F. Litwack, *North of Slavery: The Negro in the Free States* (Chicago: University of Chicago Press, 1961), 156.
25. *Proceedings and Debates of the Convention of the Commonwealth of Pennsylvania* (Harrisburg, PA: Packer, Barrett, and Parke, 1837–39), 9:364, quoted in Litwack, *North of Slavery*, 155.
26. Edward S. Abdy, *Journal of a Residence and Tour of the United States* (London: Murray, 1835), 3:246–47, quoted in Litwack, *North of Slavery*, 161.
27. Tocqueville, *Democracy in America*, 1:344.
28. *Proceedings of the Colored National Convention, Held in Rochester, July 6th, 7th and 8th, 1853* (Rochester, NY: Office of Frederick Douglass' Paper, 1853), 27.
29. "The Colored Convention, Report of the Committee on Education," *North Star* (Rochester, NY), January 21, 1848.
30. *Freedom's Journal*, March 16, 1827.
31. *Colored American*, May 6, 1837.
32. John W. Lewis, "Essay on the Character and Condition of the African Race," in John W. Lewis, *Life, Labors, and Travels of Elder Charles Bowles, of the Free Will Baptist Denomination* (Watertown, CT: Ingalls, 1852), 252–53.
33. "Cushing" and "Means of Elevation.—No. II," *Colored American*, June 22, 1839.
34. Frederick Douglass, "A Few Words to Our Own People," *North Star*, January 19, 1849.
35. Charles L. Remond, "Address to a Legislative Committee in the Massachusetts House of Representatives, 1842," *Liberator*, February 25, 1842.
36. "Cushing" and "Means of Elevation."
37. Samuel Cornish, in *Colored American*, March 4, 1837.
38. Austin Steward, in *Colored American*, June 2, 1838.
39. Voice of the Fugitive, March 26, 1851, in *The Black Abolitionist Papers Collection, 1830–1865*, ed. George E. Carter and C. Peter Ripley (Sanford, NC: Microfilming Corporation of America, 1981), reel 6, frame 855.
40. "Learn Trades or Starve," *Frederick Douglass' Paper*, March 4, 1853.
41. Pacific Appeal, July 12, 1862, in *The Black Abolitionist Papers Collection, 1830–1865*, ed. George E. Carter and C. Peter Ripley (Sanford, NC: Microfilming Corporation of America, 1981), reel 14, frame 392.
42. *Proceedings of the Colored National Convention* (1853), 27–28.
43. Samuel Cornish, in *Colored American*, June 2, 1838, and April 22, 1837.
44. Maria W. Stewart, "A Lecture by Maria W. Stewart, Given at Franklin Hall, Boston, September 21, 1832," in *Early Negro Writing, 1760–1837*, ed. Dorothy Porter (Boston: Beacon Press, 1971), 136.

45. Lewis, "Essay on the Character and Condition of the African Race," 228, quoted in *Pamphlets of Protest: An Anthology of Early African-American Protest Literature, 1790–1860*, ed. Richard Newman, Patrick Rael, and Philip Lapsansky (New York: Routledge, 2001), 192.

46. Elhanan Winchester Reynolds, *The True Story of the Barons of the South; Or, the Rationale of the American Conflict* (Boston: Walker, Wise, 1862), 161.

47. Eric Foner, *Free Soil, Free Labor, Free Men: The Ideology of the Republican Party before the Civil War* (New York: Oxford University Press, 1970), 41.

48. William Seward, quoted in ibid.

49. ibid., 50.

50. Seward, quoted in ibid., 41; Nathaniel Gookin Upham, *Rebellion—Slavery—Peace. An Address . . . Delivered at Concord, N.H., March 2, 1864* (Concord, NH: E. C. Eastman, 1864), 27.

51. Hinton Rowan Helper, *The Impending Crisis of the South: How to Meet It* (New York: A. B. Burdick, 1857), 77.

52. George Tucker, *Political Economy for the People* (Philadelphia: C. Sherman and Son, 1859), 83–84.

53. New York Republican George Opdyke, quoted in Foner, *Free Soil*, 46.

54. Tucker, *Political Economy*, 84.

55. Helper, *Impending Crisis*, 398.

56. Foner, *Free Soil*, 69.

57. Tucker, *Political Economy*, 84.

58. "Cairnes on the Slave Power," *North American Review* 96 (April 1863): 479.

59. George Weston, quoted in Foner, *Free Soil*, 47, 50.

60. Wisconsin Governor Alexander W. Randall, quoted in ibid., 57.

61. ibid., 42.

62. Cassius Clay, quoted in ibid., 63.

63. *Appendix to the Congressional Globe*, 29th Cong., 2nd sess., 1847, 317.

64. Abraham Lincoln, "Fourth Debate with Stephen A. Douglas at Charleston, Illinois" (September 18, 1858), in *The Collected Works of Abraham Lincoln*, ed. Roy P. Basler (New Brunswick, NJ: Rutgers University Press, 1953–55), 3:145–46.

65. Abraham Lincoln, "A House Divided," in *Ibid.*, 2:452–53.

66. George Fitzhugh, *Sociology for the South, or, The Failure of Free Society* (Richmond, VA: A. Morris, 1854), 83.

67. David Christy, *Cotton Is King: Or, the Culture of Cotton, and Its Relation to Agriculture, Manufactures, and Commerce; To the Free Colored People; And to Those Who Hold that Slavery Is in Itself Sinful* (Cincinnati: Moore, Wilstach, Keys, 1855), 21.

68. Edmund Ruffin, *The Political Economy of Slavery; or, The Institution Considered in Regard to Its Influence on Public Wealth and the General Welfare* (Washington, DC: Lemuel Towers, 1853); reprinted in *Defending Slavery: Proslavery Thought in the Old South, a Brief History with Documents*, ed. Paul Finkelman (Boston: Bedford/St. Martin's, 2003), 61–64.

69. John C. Calhoun, "Speech in the U.S. Senate, 1837," in *Defending Slavery: Proslavery Thought in the Old South, a Brief History with Documents*, ed. Paul Finkelman (Boston: Bedford/St. Martin's, 2003), 58.

70. Fitzhugh, *Sociology for the South*, 84.

71. George Fitzhugh, *Cannibals All! or, Slaves without Masters* (Richmond, VA: A. Morris, 1857), 48.

72. Ruffin, *Political Economy of Slavery*, in Finkelman, *Defending Slavery*, 70.

73. Fitzhugh, *Cannibals All*, 31.

74. James H. Hammond, "Speech on the Admission of Kansas, Under the Lecompton Constitution, Delivered in the Senate of the United States, March 4, 1858," in *Selections from the Letters and Speeches of the Hon. James H. Hammond*, of South Carolina (1866; Spartansburg, SC: Reprint Co., 1978), 319.

75. Fitzhugh, *Cannibals All*, 31.

76. Ruffin, *Political Economy of Slavery*, in Finkelman, *Defending Slavery*, 67, 71.

77. Fitzhugh, *Cannibals All*, 49.

78. Ruffin, *Political Economy of Slavery*, in Finkelman, *Defending Slavery*, 73–75.

79. Calhoun, "Speech in the U.S. Senate, 1837," in Finkleman, *Defending Slavery*, 60; Fitzhugh, *Sociology for the South*, 90.

80. Fitzhugh, *Sociology for the South*, 85.

81. W. J. Gray, "The Hireling and the Slave," *Debow's Review, Agriculture, Commercial, Industrial Progress and Resources* 19 (August 1855): 209.

82. Calhoun, "Speech in the U.S. Senate, 1837," in Finkleman, *Defending Slavery*, 59.

83. Fitzhugh, *Cannibals All*, 48.

84. Ibid., 297.

85. Fitzhugh, *Sociology for the South*, 93.

86. Calhoun, "Speech in the U.S. Senate, 1837," in Finkleman, *Defending Slavery*, 59.

87. Henry Cleveland, ed., *Alexander H. Stephens, in Public and Private: With Letters and Speeches, before, during, and since the War* (Philadelphia: National Publishing, 1866), 722.

88. Thomas H. Huxley, "Emancipation—Black and White," in *Science and Education: Essays* (New York: D. Appleton, 1897), 3:67.

89. George Fitzhugh, "The Freedman and His Future: A Rejoinder," *Lippincott's Magazine* 5 (February 1870): 191–97.

PART } II

The Modernization of Thrift: Years of Transition and Transformation, 1880–1950

9 }

The Modernization of Thrift

T. J. Jackson Lears

Despite superficial changes in style, American moralists remain wedded to the tradition of the Puritan jeremiad: the lament for lost virtue is a default setting. The virtue of thrift is no exception to the rule. Generations of Jeremiahs have lamented its disappearance. It has become one of those "traditional values" that have always just been eclipsed by a "revolution in manners and morals." The problem with this formula is that—with respect to thrift as well as to other allegedly lost virtues—the cultural transformation is never as complete as either the would-be revolutionaries or their critics claim. The revolution is not as liberating, nor the tradition as constraining, as the formula implies. We will never understand changes in moral values unless we first separate ourselves from linear notions of progress and decline. This is as true of the history of thrift as it is of the history of sex.

American attitudes toward thrift reflect the tensions at the core of our Protestant, capitalist culture—between frugality and extravagance, a drive for rational self-control and a longing for magical self-transformation. Participation in the market demanded discipline but promised the possibility of sudden wealth and sensuous luxury. And from the outset, market exchange rewarded guile as well as diligence. The self-made man was haunted by his shadowy double, the confidence man. In his autobiography, Benjamin Franklin brilliantly deployed both personae—he presented himself as both a list-making moral bookkeeper and a clever manipulator of appearances. The division between self-made man and confidence man characterized American capitalist culture throughout the nineteenth century and beyond. It marked a shifting but unmistakable boundary between the respectable bourgeoisie and a heterogeneous sporting crowd of gamblers, speculators, and schemers: those on the lookout for the main chance, who doubted that diligence was the only path to success.

In a land of abundant opportunities, where fortunes could be made or unmade overnight, thrift remained an embattled ideal. Like the other virtues that constituted the Protestant ethic, it was supposed to be nurtured in the home, that paradoxical institution that provided refuge from the corrupt world but also training for success in it. The inculcation of thrift was part of the broader bourgeois agenda of character formation; like other virtues it was difficult to achieve. To absorb it into one's conscience, to make it part of one's moral being involved a struggle—both with one's own impulses toward extravagance and with temptations in the larger society. With respect to money, thrift was never the only game in town. The sporting crowd was ever present. So were the votaries of fashion, who posed an even more seductive challenge for women as well as men. Like chastity, temperance, and other elements of the ethos of self-control, thrift was defined in opposition to a world of lawlessness and license.

Still, throughout most of the nineteenth century, the Protestant ethic remained the dominant architecture of the self, and thrift was a key part of its foundation. The morality of saving cemented the smallholder economy of farms and shops, undergirding the petit bourgeois mentality and scarcity psychology that supported capitalist development in its accumulationist phase. To be sure, as Lendol Calder's essay in this volume shows, local networks of credit made indebtedness a way of life in many villages and farming communities—or at least a way of cushioning the unpredictable cataclysms in weather and commodity prices. But even though thrift was sometimes more honored in the breach than the observance, the preaching of financial prudence remained essential to the official view of life, the outlook of the respectable classes. The Franklin who made it into the McGuffey Readers was not the manipulator of surfaces but the spouter of aphorisms: Poor Richard.

There was a third Franklin as well: neither a confidence man nor a self-made man but a republican citizen for whom the avoidance of waste was a means of enhancing the commonweal. Thrift, from this view, was not merely a prescription for individual or familial prosperity. It could also be a strategy for stewardship, a way of sustaining or enlarging resources in the service of a larger community or cause. A number of essays in this collection explore the public uses of thrift—by mutual aid societies, philanthropic fund-raisers, and reformers ranging from opponents of slavery to environmentalists. Still, what was striking about the dominant discourse of thrift, well into the twentieth century, was its narrow preoccupation with private monetary concerns. The public dimensions of the topic were nearly as absent from moralists' pronouncements as the public man Franklin was from the McGuffey Readers.

By the mid-twentieth century, the McGuffey Readers had become anachronisms and the world they evoked a mere memory. But the Protestant ethic they embodied did not disappear; it survived in forms more appropriate to an advanced capitalist society dominated by large corporations. Thrift was reconfigured, modernized for a managerial age. From the 1890s through the 1940s, success ideologues, advice givers, and other custodians of cultural values developed a new idiom to orchestrate the familiar tensions between release and restraint.

Rather than the triumph of "hedonism" over self-discipline, the emerging managerial ethic epitomized a more demanding discipline, rooted in a more fluid and malleable conception of self that gave rise to ever more comprehensive strategies of social control. The ethical heart of the new managerial order was "personal efficiency." This was hardly hedonism. On the contrary, the gospel of efficiency—spread by Frederick Winslow Taylor and other apostles of "scientific management"—was originally intended to squeeze maximum productivity out of workers by eliminating wasted time and motion in the workplace. The aim was not pleasure but peak performance, and as Taylorism seeped beyond the shop floor into the society at large, peak performance became a personal moral imperative.

The performance ethos was energized by a subtle shift in conceptions of the individual psyche: a movement away from a psychology of scarcity, which counseled the careful husbanding of psychic resources, toward a psychology of abundance, which emphasized "how you can *do* more and *be* more" by drawing on an apparently bottomless reservoir of hidden energies. Expanding possibilities for self-manipulation reinforced a more expansive attitude toward consumption—a new tolerance for spending, a new insouciance toward saving. In 1907, the economist Simon Nelson Patten announced that the new basis of civilization was abundance rather than scarcity and that Americans should set about learning to enjoy the new world of goods. Circulation, not accumulation, was the order of the day. As installment plans proliferated, the old horror of debt receded. Henry Ford became an icon of the emerging corporate system: he dismissed the preoccupation with saving as an outmoded obsession, paid his workers the unheard-of sum of five dollars a day, and flooded the landscape with cars that epitomized the possibilities of liberation through consumption.

Yet the release from old constraints was balanced by powerful countertendencies. There was, first of all, the ballast of nostalgia for the past—a sentiment often felt most strongly by the most fervent devotees of progress. Ford himself became obsessed with reconstructing replicas of preindustrial village life. Attachment to old ways was more than merely a pose. More important, though, were the inextricable ties between the rhetoric of release and the underlying reality of control, which remained at the core of the managerial ethos. Patten predicted that corporate-sponsored abundance could reinforce and regularize the work ethic; good consumers, Patten realized, made good producers (or, as a contemporary bumper sticker has it, "I owe, I owe, so off to work I go"). Responsible borrowing underwrote labor discipline. Indeed, the managerial drive for peak performance tuned the work ethic to a higher pitch. The emerging preoccupation with personal growth (which paralleled the managerial dream of economic growth) raised the stakes in the race for upward mobility far higher than they had been in the days when success in life meant the accumulation of a "competence" and the attainment of "respectability."

Against that static ideal of success, managerial ideologues proposed an endless process—part status striving and part self-creation, though neither part was ever done. The pursuit of personal efficiency redefined thrift, redirecting its focus from saving money to saving time. It's not that money management was not part of the picture; it's just that it was put in a denser and more dynamic context than the cookie jar or the string drawer. By the early twentieth century, thrift was becoming assimilated to the hierarchical organization of capital: investment banks and brokerage firms for the rich, "thrift institutions" (savings banks) and installment plans for the rest.

This concentration of capital in fewer and fewer hands alarmed the middle- and upper-class reformers who called themselves Progressives. They wanted to represent (in Woodrow Wilson's words) "the men on the make" rather than the "already made" men—the corporate executives and white-shoe bankers who ran the Steel Trust, the Oil Trust, the Sugar Trust, and the Money Trust (of Wall Street insiders). The Progressives turned to managerial solutions for the problems posed by unregulated monopoly power. They challenged familiar notions of economic individualism, redefined poverty as a social responsibility, and laid the foundations for the American version of the welfare state. In the process they began to chip away at established laissez-faire assumptions about thrift, such as the notion that personal savings alone were enough to build security and avert catastrophe.

But the incipient Progressive challenge to laissez-faire thought did not develop fully until the economic collapse of the early 1930s. World War I marked the culmination but also the exhaustion of Progressive managerial policy. During the 1920s, a corporate-sponsored version of managerial thought came to the fore, combining fantasies of economic and psychic abundance with a rhetoric of efficient performance and social service.

The crash of 1929 and its aftermath reconfigured the relationship between private and public responsibility. As part of the general turn toward cultural conservatism in the 1930s, personal habits of thrift evoked renewed admiration from public moralists. Yet the severity of the crisis made it clear that frugality alone was not enough to protect an individual, no matter how thrifty, from the accidents of economic fate. From this new and more realistic perspective, thrift could no longer be conceived as a panacea or a simple criterion for distinguishing the deserving from the undeserving poor. The conclusion was inescapable: government had a responsibility to protect people from economic catastrophes beyond their control. Public thrift reappeared in the discourse of policy.

How the government was to protect its citizens remained an open question, and the answers to it revealed the redefinition of thrift in both the public and private household during the midcentury decades. The Depression encouraged economists, led by John Maynard Keynes, to stress the importance of increasing aggregate consumer demand as a way of smoothing out the business cycle and reviving prosperity. World War II provided a proving ground for Keynes's vision. Americans had cash in their pockets for the first time in years, and there were not that many things they could spend it on—but advertisers made clear that the country after the war was going to be a consumers' paradise.

Yet the model consumer who emerged from economic depression and war was not (or not often) a free-floating individual pursuing his or her desires. On the contrary, the typical advertised consumer was embedded in social obligations and family ties. The ethos of peak performance was adjusted to fit the demands of the corporate workplace and the resurgent domestic ideal. As in the 1920s, spending was under the supervision of mothers who were now celebrated (at least in the advertisements) as much for their managerial skills as for their moral example. In the mainstream rhetoric of consumer desire, acquisitive households frequently replaced acquisitive individuals. Consumer credit and installment plans did not mean the end of thrift; there were still car payments, furniture payments, refrigerator and washing machine payments—all the payments for all the big-ticket items that had become part of the middle-class family's standard package, all of which could be stabilized and sanitized by their association with domestic life. The unprecedented power of labor unions ensured widespread job security and reduced the risk of long-term indebtedness. Patten's hope—that good consumers would make good producers—was finally fulfilled. Thrift was alive and well among mid-twentieth-century Americans, although as practiced then, it would scarcely have been recognizable to their grandparents.

Scrimping and Saving: The Victorian Synthesis

Poor Richard's principles flourished during the decades after the Civil War. Old counsels of thrift preserved a comforting familiarity amid the unpredictable lurches of the business cycle. While dreams of overnight wealth fired the speculator's imagination, middle-class housewives and their husbands were continually urged to scrimp and save. Thrift was a cardinal rule of the Victorian self-help synthesis. When Samuel Smiles, the English author of *Self-help* (1859), published *Thrift* in 1875, the book was warmly praised by American reviewers. "Half the domestic quarrels" of the day would be ended, *Harper's* observed, if couples embraced the habit of saving by "grading desires according to the means of honestly gratifying them," as Smiles recommended. *Thrift* was "emphatically a book for hard times," one that suited the bleak aftermath of the crash of 1873, yet the "moral tone which pervades its pages prevents the thrift which it recommends from degenerating into sordidness or its economies into niggardliness."[1]

This was the balancing act that moralists had to perform: they urged middle-class folk to live within their means and to trim wants to meet circumstances, yet they also recognized that decency demanded that one keep up appearances—and that cost money.

There was a deeper conflict as well, one that illuminated the complexities of class privilege in a country officially committed to denying that class even existed. Thrift had different meanings for those in the poor and working classes, who were expected to accept their lot in life, than it did for the those in the middle class, who were expected to be moving up in the world, and for those in the upper class, who were pressed into high expenditures to maintain their social position. Matching one's desires to one's social station was all very well for working stiffs, but it was more problematic for those who wore white collars to work.

Contradictory assumptions emerged in journalistic commentary on the less fortunate—those kept low by ill luck, hard times, or their own profligate ways. Through the business downturn following the panic of 1873, advocates of thrift considered the plight of the working-class majority. In 1879, the *Atlantic Monthly* surveyed the situation of "workingmen's wives." What emerged was a portrait of resourceful women who had borne the "anxiety and suffering" of the long business downturn with more patience and courage than their "depressed and injured" husbands had been able to muster. These women were often knowledgeable and pragmatic. They pointed out the difficulty of saving when there was no safe repository, when banks frequently failed and securities were likely to decline in value. But they also upbraided other working people for their inability to live within their means.[2]

Some were as hard on members of their own class as any bourgeois moralist could be. Indeed, one wife wondered, maybe working people simply were not fit to accumulate wealth the way their economic superiors did. Interest on savings and investment might be fine for businesspeople, she said, "but for working people it does harm, and not good. Many of our class are excited and dazzled by the thought of their money increasing, and as they say, 'piling up while they sleep,' so that they often risk losing the whole of it by lending it to men who are not to be trusted, or venturing into wild speculations." The dream of easy money gives workers "unreasonable hopes for the future, and leads them to desire above all things to escape from the necessity [of work]." Better to be useful and happy as we are, doing the necessary work of the world, than to try "to rise to positions which are not suited to us" by going into debt for expensive pianos and clothes for our children and teaching them to want what they cannot have. Another was asked what working people need and replied,

"They need discipline, the power and habit of self-restraint and self-direction in nearly everything, but especially in their use of money." In a country like ours, full of resources, "they might all be rich, but they are so impulsive and extravagant that most of them are in debt, and are often pressed and harassed by their inability to pay their notes."[3] Systemic indebtedness kept the poor under, but the root of their woe was personal improvidence—so it seemed to moralists of varying backgrounds.

And so it seemed especially to the bourgeois moralists who filled the pages of *Good Housekeeping* during the Gilded Age. "The best the market affords is good enough for them, and by their constant demand for what they wrongly consider the choice cuts of meat, they maintain the present high prices," a columnist in the magazine complained in 1887. A year later another observed that there was more true economy among the rich than among the poor, but the middle class were the most accomplished managers of all. With a dollar a middle class woman will make twenty loaves of bread, while a poor woman will buy bread and beer. "The poor do not understand economy and do not care to learn, hence they are poor."[4] This sort of sweeping dismissal typified the class blinders worn by devotees of thrift throughout much of the late nineteenth century.

Within the middle class the prospects for implementing thrift were more promising. The key site was the home, especially the kitchen, where the housewife skilled in what the women's advice writer Christine Herrick called "the dainty utilization of scraps" could quickly learn that "it is in the minor economies that true savings consists." Once committed to a plan, the housewife could see immediate savings, "the penny on this, and two cents on that." Franklin had said "A fat kitchen makes a lean will," but *Good Housekeeping* writers were unwilling to sacrifice appetite to purse. "Why should we think it savors of stinginess to look after odds and ends, and thus beneath our dignity, when our lives are so largely made up of trifles?" a columnist asked in 1887. Old corned beef, underdone brown bread, stale cookies—"Everything can be used to the last crumb, if one is not afraid of trouble, and like the joiner we dovetail one in the other to make all fit."[5] Making do in the kitchen was honest labor, a craft as honorable as carpentry.

If the household was where middle-class women learned and practiced thrift, it was also where they passed the virtue on to their children, who, it was hoped, would learn similar lessons at school. Sometimes those lessons were explicit and highly organized. In 1885, for example, J. H. Thiry, school commissioner for Long Island City, New York, decided that the way to stop cigarette smoking among boys and gum chewing among girls was to offer an alternative use for their money—a school savings plan like the ones in his native Belgium. Enlisting local banks, Thiry arranged for children to deposit money weekly. When they reached a dollar they received a bankbook; they could withdraw only with the permission of parent, teacher, and principal. Looking back on the experiment after eighteen years, the *Outlook* pronounced it a huge success, noting that similar plans had been adopted in over 1,500 schools nationwide. What particularly impressed the *Outlook* was the larger purpose of the scheme: "to foster the habit of saving, of providing for the future, of teaching [children] that a coin given or earned is not to be spent for the gratification of the moment, but represents a power to be rightly used; that the self-denial and self-control which savings indicates are the basis of all manhood, all citizenship, all right living."[6] Thrift was the keystone of the Protestant ethic and the basis for creating an independent self.

This was true especially if the self in question was male. Ideals of autonomy assumed masculinity. Thrift was important for both sexes, but for men it was—at least according to its advocates—the key to affirming one's identity as an economically free man. The prerequisite for economic freedom was freedom from debt. Throughout the nineteenth century and into the early twentieth, one could still be imprisoned for debt in many places, including New York City. The horror of debt arose not merely from the prospect of imprisonment but also from the tendency to equate debt with dependency and even slavery, with loss of the self. Indebtedness was the opposite of independence, and the chronic debtor had been an emblem of failure since the days of the early Republic. If profligacy led to debt, setting the spendthrift on the slippery slope to social death, then thrift reversed that process, keeping the prudent man on the hard path of full manhood.[7]

Only in the United States was it "comparatively easy" for a middle-class man to achieve pecuniary independence, observed a *Harper's* contributor in 1894. To do so, "a man must steadily earn an excess of what will provide for his daily wants; he must employ his mind, be commonly educated, capable of some self-discipline. He must be, in short, what the mass of Americans are in intelligence and enterprise, and what they are not in thrift and monetary appreciation." Slow accumulation was preferable to sudden riches, which were likely to turn business into passion and passion finally into monomania. A "manly man" does not fear poverty or disaster except as it affects his wife and children—for their sake, investments had to be chosen conservatively. The bottom line was to underwrite the larger aim of independence: "No man can be otherwise independent who is not pecuniarily so." The dependent man "must smile on those he hates, he must extend his hand where he would strike, he must speak pleasantly with a curse in his throat, because he is ever seeking work. . . . He wears dependence like a yoke." Independence, in contrast, kept a man "dignified and self-respecting, above the need of asking for favors, above all the inevitable meannesses of poverty." Thrift and forethought, in other words, were necessary (if not sufficient) to manliness.[8]

Nevertheless, men and women both were entangled in issues of saving and spending. Couples struggled with each other over money. Generally the struggle was unequal, given the typical (though not universal) male control over the money supply. Still it was a struggle, and both sides had accusations to make. Imprudent investments as well as improvident housekeeping could start the family on the road to ruin. Cigars and stag outings could waste as much money as ball gowns and silver slippers. From either partner's point of view, the citadel of thrift—the bourgeois household—was under siege.

Thrift faced challenges from several social quarters. In most cities, the sporting crowd was a constant presence, tempting family men away from their firesides to fritter away small fortunes with cards and dice. This at any rate was the great fear shared by custodians of conventional morality, and there was no doubt much truth to it—sharpers fleeced many men of whole paychecks or more, with ruinous consequences for the men and their families. Beyond the opulent casinos of Saratoga and similar watering holes, vernacular gambling could be an innocuous, feet-on-the rail night out with the boys, but (according to its critics) a fundamental ethical problem remained embedded even in this apparently harmless recreation. "The desire to acquire what is another's without paying for it is the gambler's demon," wrote a *Harper's* contributor in 1895, and that desire was "inexorably at war with the Divine economy." Gambling was part of a larger fascination with getting rich quick—the same instinct that drove men to join the speculative frenzy of the stock market in search of overnight wealth or to crowd into Nevada gold camps in search of a "lucky strike." The most flagrant exploitation of this impulse was the lottery, which demoralized the poor with its false promises of instant success, encouraging their "neglect of business and general shiftlessness." Hence by the 1890s, lotteries had been forbidden in all enlightened nations and every state in the Union except Louisiana, from which it continued to extend its appeal. The siren song of something for nothing was never completely silenced.[9]

The appeal of fashion was equally seductive and equally injurious to thrift. Since the eighteenth century, republican moralists had railed against the noxious influence of extravagance in dress. By the post–Civil War era, the misogynist assumptions of this critique had become explicit. Chuckleheaded women, piling up frivolous purchases, taken in by "the shams of the shops," had become stock figures in the male humor and the (often female) criticism of the late nineteenth century. But fashion was more than a symptom of female silliness. It was part of a larger social picture, an increasingly fluid and mobile society, with 500 classes instead of 4 (as one observer put it, glancing across the Atlantic to England)—a society where people were constantly seeking advance through the clever deployment of display.[10]

For advocates of thrift, upward social mobility (or the desire for it) was a complex and ever-present menace to frugal ways. Status striving was pervasive. It was by no means confined to women; though they were often blamed for it, they often claimed in response (with justification) that by organizing fashionable entertainments and attending charity balls they were only doing what their husband's position required them to do. Whether the husband in question was an executive or a shipping clerk, status striving was a temptation for husband and wife, and it was held responsible for busting many a family budget.

By the late nineteenth century the high cost of appearances was having dire consequences. In 1886, journalist C. S. Messinger compared the expenses of five families in varying economic circumstances "to arrive at a clear estimate at what might be cut out of our expenditure and not interfere with comfort or health." An alarming number of men he knew—"brain workers"—had died in early middle age, succumbing to "the strain of trying to live at an expensive rate, and at the same time to make savings against old age." They made the savings all right, but they did not live long enough to use them. Their frantic lives and early deaths were becoming a typical pattern among "our nervous ambitious American race." What Messinger claimed to discover was that no matter what their income, all five households were sufficiently nourished and decently dressed; the increase in expenditure as one went up the economic scale was due to the expense of higher social position. This was the burden of the well-to-do, or the would-be well-to-do—it was an unnecessary "source of much anxiety to breadwinners" at the upper end of the income scale. While fretting primarily about the rich, Messinger expanded his findings to an all-encompassing conclusion. The lesson was clear, he said: "We want too much."[11]

It was one thing to lament excessive wants among the working class, who were supposed to be cultivating contentment with their lot, and quite another to find the same fault among the middle class, who were supposed to be improving themselves. The critique of middle-class desire posed potentially subversive questions about the dynamic of dissatisfaction at the core of market culture, about the very possibility of sustaining a stable sense of self in a society given over to perpetual jostling for personal advantage. The ruinous results of status striving led advocates of economic thrift to advocate psychic thrift as well.

By the 1880s, the need to conserve scarce psychic resources was a commonly voiced priority among the educated and affluent. George Miller Beard's *American Nervousness* (1881) had identified "the disease of the age" as neurasthenia, or "lack of nerve force." Neurasthenia and nervous prostration became catchall terms for a constellation of symptoms that today would be characterized as signs of chronic depression: anxiety, irritability, nameless fears, listlessness, loss of will. In a Protestant culture where effective exercise of will was the key to individual selfhood, the neurasthenic was a kind of antiself—at best a walking shadow, at worst a bedridden invalid unable to make the most trivial choices or decisions. Beard and his colleagues—neurologists, psychiatrists, and self-help writers in the popular press—all agreed that nervous prostration was the price of progress, a signal that the psychic circuitry of "brain-workers" was overloaded by the demands of "modern civilization."[12]

While some diagnoses of this disease deployed electrical metaphors, the more common idiom was economic. Popular psychology, like popular economics, was based on assumptions of scarcity: There was only so much emotional energy (and only so much money) to go around. The most prudent strategy was the husbanding of one's resources as a hedge against bankruptcy and breakdown. "The sufferer from nervous prostration has not kept his books balanced with the minute care which Nature always employs in the management of her accounts," wrote a *Harper's* contributor in 1891. "He has hoped . . . that she was at least as careless, or as weakly indulgent as he, and that some few things might be overlooked or happily forgotten. But Nature's ways of business are not . . . the curving and yielding lines of benevolence and charity, but the rigid and straight ones of truth and justice." The key to contentment was not the satisfaction but the reduction of overblown wants—to the point where we take "a positive pleasure . . . in seeing shops loaded with innumerable things that we do *not* want and wouldn't have if we could." Psychic thrift promised relief from the endless cycle of dissatisfaction and desire.[13]

This more capacious notion of thrift encompassed emotional, aesthetic, and intellectual as well as monetary matters. It also suggested a broader critique of late-Victorian culture—a middle-class, mainstream version of the assault on conspicuous consumption conducted by Thorstein Veblen, and of the dissent from modernity developed by such thinkers as John Ruskin and William Morris. The most common form of this critique was a plea for simplicity in material and mental life. By 1900, the gospel of the simple life had found its Saint Paul in Edward Bok, the crusading editor of the *Ladies' Home Journal.* Bok railed constantly against bric-a-brac and accumulations of cheap stuff, arguing that cluttered homes embodied cluttered minds. "We must get to the point where we will allow nothing in our homes except those things for which we have an actual use," he wrote in 1900. "This does not mean that our homes will be 'too plain,' as many will object. Simplicity is not plainness. It is, I repeat, the highest form of good taste. Nothing can improve the beauty of a simple line. No one can quarrel with it. It is beyond criticism. . . . We seem to lose sight of the fact that we are most comfortable when we are most natural." The evocation of "the natural" was a recurring rhetorical strategy in American paeans to simplicity, from Henry David Thoreau to E. F. Schumacher, but its meaning varied with its context. In Bok's case the context was the overloaded lives of the late-Victorian bourgeoisie and the search for a simplified alternative.[14]

By 1900 the "simple life" had become a cause célèbre among educated and affluent Americans, who, as always, tended to project their own experience and views onto society at large. "From every class in American life," an "American Mother" wrote in *Ladies' Home Journal*, "there comes the same cry for a simpler, more rational way of living. . . . The way to bring about a more rational social order throughout the Union is to begin it in your own house—in your parlor and your kitchen." This was not simply a matter of tossing out clutter; it required a rethinking of our obsession with status ascent. "There are no real distinctions of caste among us, and there cannot be unless we change our republic into a monarchy. Rank is a real possession of the Englishman's, but we do not own it, and never did, and in trying to set up a sham, pinchbeck imitation of it we are losing the solid strength, and repose, and wealth out of our lives." Democracy and simplicity were twinned.[15]

The quest for the simple life merged psychic and economic thrift, as the self-help writer Annie Payson Call made clear in her advice about how to avoid "money strain."

> If we think quietly and stop worrying about what we are unable to buy, and try to separate our real needs from our superficial desires,—if we try to cultivate the art of really satisfying our wants in the best way possible, no matter what our conditions in life, it will be surprising to see how much we can have, and how much enjoyment we can get out of the things that are within our reach.[16]

For the comparatively comfortable readers of the *American Magazine*, where Call's advice appeared, the gospel of simplicity was more than a mere prescription to know one's place in life—as it would have been for a working-class audience. While the distinction between needs and desires remained as elusive as the difference between necessities and luxuries, Call's advice suggested a humane alternative to frenetic getting and spending. The truly subversive aspect of simplicity was the suggestion that genuine leisure was more than the purchase of prepackaged entertainment, that it was in fact at the center of what a later generation would call "the quality of life." Indeed, advocates of the simple life wanted to reduce time spent on housework, even at the cost of unswept floors or an extra nickel, to increase time available for cultivating one's self or one's relationships with family and friends. The gospel of simplicity fostered an ideal of thrift more capacious than mere scrimping and saving.

But that hopeful leitmotif was largely lost in the broader transformation of thrift that took place around the turn of the century. Aesthetic and ethical ideals were assimilated to an emerging managerial synthesis. The dream of a home stripped of Victorian clutter found fulfillment in the functionalist designs of Frank Lloyd Wright, Richard Neutra, Charles Eames, and other modernists, though in most American homes, modernism never got beyond the kitchen. The vision of a more leisurely, simplified life disappeared in the managerial culture created by advertising, mass media, and other institutions through the early decades of the twentieth century. Time-thrift remained essential to the well-managed life, but this was in order to promote productivity and personal efficiency rather than opportunities for repose. Familiar notions of thrift, the clever stratagems of the frugal farmer or housewife, began to seem old-fashioned in a society where people were increasingly surrounded by seductive images of elegant consumers enjoying luxury goods. After 1900, as Susan Strasser has shown, a make-do ethic of scarcity, one that encouraged the creative bricolage of reuse and recycling, gradually gave way to a throwaway economy of disposable goods and planned obsolescence.[17]

An economy of mass-produced abundance depended on consumers who were willing to go into debt, to keep trading up whenever they could, to stay on the ever-accelerating treadmill of earning and spending in the name of personal growth and self-development. In some ways one needed more thrift-discipline than ever to maintain this new regime, to borrow responsibly, and to meet payments regularly. One also needed more energy, given new managerial standards of peak performance. All of this meant that the transformation of thrift under corporate capitalism was accompanied by a broader transformation of the American self—or at least the ideas about it that predominated among the middle and upper classes. An economy of abundance was intertwined with (perhaps even dependent on) a psychology of abundance.

Managerial Thrift: The Formative Years

In cultural history, nothing changes all at once. Familiar admonitions to thrift persisted well into the twentieth century. Chautauqua lecturers promoted Franklinesque plans for turning every spare moment to self-improvement. Public figures urged postal savings banks for the poor, so that (as Postmaster General James Gary said in 1901) "those who have been improvident in little things and have not learned from experience that money makes money, would be educated slowly but surely to save a surplus over and above their living expenses." When prices rose and wages failed to keep pace, or when Wall Street panic wiped out the dividend income of temporarily fortunate families, advice givers proposed familiar strategies for living less expensive lives—fire the cook, use the scraps, skip dessert. The horror of debt survived as well, at least in some quarters. In 1909, a frugal minister from Ohio was still telling *Good Housekeeping* readers that the secret of living on $600 a year was simple: "Never go in debt. Pay as you go or do without." As late as 1914, "The Autobiography of a Stingy Man" appeared in the *American* magazine, authored "By One Who Is Proud of the Fact." He wondered: "Why is it that we teach our children that thrift, proper economy, and the saving spirit are akin to the cardinal virtues; that wastefulness is near to sin,—and then laud the spendthrift as a 'good fellow' and ridicule the stingy man?" Having put his finger on a fault line in American culture, the author proceeded to recount his rise to riches through saving his own and his employers' money, ending up as a manager and shareholder of a western stockyard. Stinginess, he concluded, was the cure for the high costs of business and domestic living. Stinginess was not miserliness or loving money for itself—though he regretted the loss of every dime; it was simply "chronic objection to waste."[18]

Recoil from waste was the common reflex joining Victorian and managerial thrift. The rhetoric of corporate advertising subsumed spending into "scientific purchasing"—well-informed consumption was a key to personal efficiency.

Advertisers, seeking to shed their snake-oil past, claimed to be educators rather than hucksters and struck a heroic pose on the cutting edge of cultural change. The vision of the good life presented in national advertisements was perfectly consistent with the scientifically managed society promoted by Taylor and his colleagues in the "efficiency movement." It was only a short step from the factory to the kitchen, according to advertisers and to those in the new field of "domestic science" (soon to be known as "home economics").[19]

Adopting the language of the shop floor to the middle-class home could produce unintentional self-parody, as Martha Bensley Bruere revealed in 1913. Writing on efficiency methods in the home in *Good Housekeeping*, she announced that "the success or failure of a matrimonial firm depends on the product it turns out, and the product is of three kinds: happiness, public service, and children of the right sort. That firm is most successful which turns out the largest and best product in the shortest time for the least cost in muscle, money, and brains." It was all about time-thrift. The test of good management was not "the amount of work one is able to do" but "one's ability to get the largest product for the least work." Consider the Gordons—husband, wife, daughter, all professionals, no servant—who "believe that their home factory is for the making of only such things as commerce has proved herself unequal to." They served the author a "delicious" dinner of canned soup, canned asparagus, purchased roast chicken, boxed potato chips, and purchased "merangue [*sic*] glace." Only the lettuce was prepared at home. One could hardly ask for a meal more suited to the tastes promoted by corporate advertisers, who joined domestic scientists in redefining household thrift for a managerial age.[20]

As managerial thrift was assimilated to the agenda of peak performance, a new atmosphere of dynamism enveloped old moral prescriptions. After the turn of the century, money was less often seen as an inert commodity, to be gradually accumulated and tended to steady growth, and more often seen as a fluid and dynamic force. To Americans enraptured by Theodore Roosevelt's panegyrics to the strenuous life, energy became an end itself, and money was a kind of energy. Success mythology reflected this subtle change. In the magazine hagiographies of business titans—as well as in the fiction of writers like Theodore Dreiser and Frank Norris—the key to success frequently became a mastery of Force (as Dreiser always capitalized it), of raw power. This reflected an economy dominated by combinations of capital more powerful than any ever seen before. Whatever their actual stature, the "trust builders"—Andrew Carnegie, John D. Rockefeller, and their kin—seemed larger than life. Their long shadows put the earnest plodders of Horatio Alger's day in permanent eclipse.[21]

The new emphasis on money as Force paralleled and reinforced a new economy of the self. The neurasthenia epidemic among the middle and upper classes provoked a broad rethinking of assumptions about the human psyche—a growing awareness of the interplay between mind and body, of subconscious mental powers that had been tapped by mystics and healers in the past but overlooked by mainstream medicine and religion in more recent times. Liberal Protestants lacked the firm theology of their Calvinist forebears but preserved old habits of inwardness; without clear supernatural justification, self-scrutiny became "morbid introspection," the breeding ground for neurasthenia. No wonder some began to question the rigidities of orthodox Christian dualism, turning toward the possibilities of mental healing offered by Mary Baker Eddy, whose Christian Science teachings had (according to one *Good Housekeeping* writer) recalled the churches to a "forgotten truth—the message of the gospel of the body."[22]

The irony, of course, was that Christian Science's "gospel of the body" denied its reality altogether. Nevertheless, Eddy's teachings were the first trickle of what became a powerful current in American Protestant thought—an outlook (unlike Christian Science) that did take the body into account by considering its interaction with mental and spiritual life. Pastors of more educated and affluent flocks, especially in the urban Northeast, began to discover the healing powers of the subconscious mind, powers that could be released through hypnotism, psychoanalysis, or other forms of "autosuggestion." Ministers and therapists began to work along parallel paths.

The neurasthenic posed the toughest task for mental healers. For him, concerned observers agreed, "waste is going on in useless and unproductive channels." Tormented by sleeplessness and restlessness, "he never has any reserve energy but lives from hand to mouth on his capital." The task of renewing energy, as Eddy understood, was blocked by "fear-thought." Fear was often the "first knot" healers needed to unravel; as Charles Tuckey pointed out in *Good Housekeeping*, "Fear is largely the outcome of morbid self-suggestion and must be overcome by healthy suggestion applied from without but acting from within." Pastors and psychologists alike began to think that, amid unprecedented abundance and opportunity, perfectly healthy people were leading pinched and fearful lives for no good reason.[23]

This perception suggested the need to rethink certain doctrines of traditional Christianity, such as the admonition to voluntary poverty. As the *Outlook* observed soon after the turn of the century, American society seemed to be opening up inexhaustible sources of wealth through the application of organized science and capital. The danger of prosperity was that new economic freedoms might reveal a poverty of spirit; the danger of adversity was that it might promote meanness and brutality. This was no time for the church to urge a reduction of energies for the sake of greater spirituality; rather, "the work of the church today is not to preach poverty, but a more vigorous and commanding spiritual life; men cannot be helped by being made poor; they can only be saved by being made strong." The search for strength energized new Protestant efforts at "mind-cure," among them the Emmanuel Movement in Boston, spearheaded by the Reverend Elwood Worcester. He too was alarmed by the rise of American nervousness and traced it to the demands of modern civilization. The remedy was "increasing the strength of the individual and the race," not cutting back our demands on ourselves; lightening the burdens of modernity would involve reversing progress, which was unthinkable. "Following upon the introduction of steam came electricity, with its incredible marvels; the next step is the unlocking of untold spiritual forces," Worcester said. "We seem to be on the verge of vast discoveries in this direction." For Worcester and his contemporaries, the subconscious mind was a reservoir of benign energy that—if properly tapped—would heal the body and soothe the soul.[24]

Outside the churches, William James was the leading advocate of releasing untapped psychic forces from the subconscious. He was fascinated by the unrealized power embodied in "second wind," by mental and physical phenomena "beyond the very extremity of fatigue-distress, amounts of ease and power that we never dreamed ourselves to own, sources of strength habitually not taxed at all, because habitually we never push through the obstruction, never pass those early critical points." James was convinced that "as a rule men use only a small part of the powers which they actually possess and which they might use under appropriate conditions." The question was, How to get at those powers?[25]

Many contemporaries joined James in pursuit of revitalization. The desire to draw on hitherto undreamed-of psychic resources led many Americans (including James and his brother, author Henry James) to embrace such fads as "Fletcherism"—Horace Fletcher's method of slowly and thoroughly chewing one's food, savoring every bite, and never eating more than one's appetite demands. This system brought Fletcher "back from death's door to a richer and intenser life," he claimed. The economist Irving Fisher advocated Fletcherism on grounds of national efficiency—national health equals national wealth, he reasoned. "In brief," Frances Bjorkman summarized in *Good Housekeeping*, "Fletcherism is one of the many forms under which one of the most dynamic ideas of our time finds expression: the faith in the power of man to make himself what he will through the use of powers which, up to the present time, have lain dormant within him."[26]

If chewing one's food carefully could accomplish all this, imagine what regular exercise could do! And, indeed, "physical culture" became a popular obsession among desk-bound men during the early twentieth century, making heroes out of the muscle builder Eugene Sandow and even the magician Harry Houdini, whose "magical" escapes involved a great deal of strenuosity and struggle. Nor was this an entirely male phenomenon: women doffed corsets, jumped on bicycles, and in general displayed the same passion for renewed vitality that one finds among middle- and upper-class men.[27]

In this strenuous atmosphere, old prescriptions for neurasthenia lost legitimacy. The rest cure, it appeared, could be a positive danger. So Richard Cabot claimed in *Good Housekeeping* in 1909. If nervous prostration were due to overwork, rest might be indicated, but "the vast majority of cases" were due not to overwork but to "overemotionalism, distraction, worry, and fear. Many neurasthenics were born tired and have been getting more tired the more they rest. Nothing will ever rest them but work." So Cabot preached in his article "The Healing Power of Work," insisting that "soul and body alike, we are creatures made and meant *to react to a need*, to answer to a stimulus from without. We do not carry our energy like a storage battery. We run on a trolley responding to currents of energy supplied from without, by our fellow-men, by nature and by God," each of us responding in his individual way.[28]

Whether energy came from within or without, it was as limitless as electricity apparently was. The obstacles to access were not material—class barriers or economic deprivation were never mentioned by devotees of abundance psychology—they were mental and emotional. And the most debilitating emotion was fear, which cropped up constantly as the core problem in diagnoses of neurasthenia. The preoccupation with freeing oneself from internal constraints undermined the older, static ideal of thrift at its psychological base. As one observer noted in 1902, "The root cause of thrift, which we all admire and preach because it is so convenient to the community, is fear, fear of future want; and that fear, we are convinced, when indulged overmuch by pessimist minds is the most frequent cause of miserliness." Freedom from fear meant freedom to consume.[29]

And consumption began at the dinner table. The nutritionist Woods Hutchinson identified the new ideal of the modern biological engineer in 1913: "to induce the individual human machine to consume as much rich, nourishing food as it can eat with zest and appetite and thus develop the highest possible 'horsepower' of which its boiler and engines are capable, regardless of the expense." Despite the cavalier disregard of economic actuality embodied in that last phrase, Hutchinson claimed that the nutritionists' newfound enthusiasm for calories was entirely appropriate to a mobile, democratic society. The old "stagnation" theory of diet merely sought to maintain the level of health and vigor; it was a diet for slaves or serfs, for men who were not supposed to rise above their station. "The new diet theory is based on the idea of progress, of continuous improvement, of never resting satisfied with things as they are," Hutchinson wrote. "No diet is too liberal or expensive that will . . . yield good returns on the investment." Economic metaphors for health persisted into the twentieth century, but they focused on growth and process rather than stability, on consumption and investment rather than savings.[30]

The turn toward dynamism in the language of the self paralleled trends in economic thought. Professional economists focused increasingly on the generative powers of consumption, criticizing Eugen von Bohm-Bawerk's "Positive Theory of Capital," which held that savings forms capital, and arguing instead that capital is formed by the immediate demand and the conditions that determine general purchasing power. Twentieth-century capital was the result not of savings but of reinvested or surplus earnings. This proto-Keynesian position challenged the familiar assumption that thrift was an instrument of working-class ascent. In fact, spending was more effective than saving in raising the standard of working-class life, as *Gunton's* observed in 1902: "The real propelling force that keeps up and raises wages is not the number of laborers, nor the amount of work the laborers perform, but the cost of living as determined by the character of their social surroundings and customs." Whatever is customary will be insisted upon, by strikes if necessary. The standard of living that has become habitual "is the most irresistible quality in human life." Once workers have carpets they don't return to bare floors. The developing self demanded an escalating standard of living.[31]

The economist who did the most to popularize this new way of thinking was Simon Nelson Patten, whose book *The New Basis of Civilization* (1907) argued that the United States had passed from an "era of scarcity" to an "era of abundance" based on the unprecedented availability of mass-produced goods. Patten predicted that workers' desires for things would not undermine their capacity for disciplined achievement, as generations of moralists had claimed; rather, the multiplication of wants would become part of the civilizing process, as workers would broaden their horizons and take pride in their accumulating possessions. "In the course of consumption expanding by orderly processes the new wants become complex, oppose each other, project themselves into the future, and demand forethought in their balances," Patten wrote. "The worker steadily and cheerfully chooses the deprivations of this week in order to secure the gratifications of a coming holiday. From this motive the virtue, abstinence, at length emerges and is a motive for activity. Men idealize the future and depreciate the present; they advance into a period of restraint and morality, puritan in essence but various in form." Status striving, from this view, was not a threat to the work ethic but a new and secular way of reinforcing it. Installment buying, far from demoralizing workers, kept them on the path of steady ascent.[32]

Patten's vision depended on a well-paid, economically secure working population; without job security, one could hardly be expected to become a responsible consumer or borrower. These conditions did not come into existence, even imperfectly, until the rise of industrial unions and the comparative prosperity of the post–World War II era. But Patten captured the essential feature of the modernization of thrift—its assimilation to a managerial version of the Protestant ethic amid unprecedented mass-produced abundance and tolerance for spending. Patten in effect foresaw the way thrift would be refashioned to fit the hamster cage of earning, spending, and borrowing that would characterize everyday life in an expanding consumer economy. The history of thrift from the 1920s through the 1950s is part of the larger history of Americans' efforts to implement Patten's vision (whether or not they had even heard of him): that is, to sustain steady progress through the gradual increase of purchasing power, to use consumption as an agent of civilization. The first such effort was conducted under corporate managerial auspices during the 1920s. But the prosperity the managers created was unstable in its very essence, based on a weak foundation of inadequate and narrowly distributed consumer demand, as well as on inflated capital markets.

Prosperity, it appeared, demanded the democratization of consumption. Since the early twentieth century, Progressive reformers and maverick economists had groped toward models of social democracy that depended at least in part on consumer-based prosperity. They began the other major effort to realize Patten's vision, the one that depended on a government-business partnership rather than business alone. The Progressive ideal of a managerial state—supplementing personal thrift with social security—was stillborn in the 1920s, revived fitfully during the New Deal in the 1930s, and at least imperfectly fulfilled during the wartime and postwar prosperity of the 1940s. By midcentury, the pattern of disciplined consumption had taken hold among the working class, the more fortunate of whom (thanks largely to union power) could depend on steady wages that allowed them to pay off big-ticket items over time. Eventually, the cars and boats in the driveways of their brick ranch houses would keep industrial workers in harness, year in, year out. Patten would have been pleased. It would take nearly half a century, but his vision would finally be realized.

Managerial Thrift: Progressive and Laissez-Faire Strains

The background to the rise of Progressive reform was a quarter century of labor strife and Populist insurgency. Much of this conflict was characterized, at least by the threatened bourgeoisie, as a struggle between thrift and extravagance. This was especially true of the "money question"—the Populist demand for democratic control of the money supply and for deliberate inflation of the currency to ease the circumstances of desperately indebted farmers. The election of 1896 pitted William McKinley and the Republican advocates of "sound money" against William Jennings Bryan and the Democrats, who had coopted the Populist principles into a demand for the free coinage of silver. In citadels of eastern privilege, one would have thought the barbarians were at the gates. Bryan, a quintessential petit bourgeois, was reviled as an "agrarian revolutionist." The *Atlantic Monthly* took a more moderate view, hoping that the campaign would educate the public to the follies of cheap money: "Besides the necessity of sound money another lesson is forcibly taught [by the campaign],—a larger corollary of the same proposition, that financial honesty is the basis of character,—the lesson, namely, of the intricate workings and supreme value of credit." The link between character and credit led to a moral critique of cheap money, as a crutch for thriftlessness and moral sloppiness.

Indeed, it was "more than coincidence that the menace to property and credit is most determined" in the South and West, two regions that have "nothing in common but a lack of thrift." There and elsewhere, "it is not by saving, but by 'booming,' that fortunes are thought to be made." This assumption led the less prudent to "borrowing with only a speculative opportunity to pay," a serious sin against the trust required to maintain the credit system.[33]

Fortunately for frightened Republicans, McKinley defeated Bryan handily, and for six years after the election, as one observer noted, Wall Street investors sustained a "tremendous bull market." The turn of the century was characterized by "a carnival of speculation, and an unexampled rush to form combinations of industrial or railroad interests or trusts," enormous capitalizations in excess of real value, creating stock that the public was "crazy to buy." It quickly became apparent that Wall Street traders and investors were more entranced by the dream of overnight wealth (and more able to cash in on it) than discontented farmers and workers had been.[34]

Besides inflating stock prices, the merger wave of 1897–1903 had other, more lasting consequences. Most important, it created a new generation of industrial behemoths: United States Steel, United Fruit, American Tobacco, American Sugar, Northern Pacific Railroad, and their kin. When the bubble burst in 1903, elite conservatives like Ellery Sedgwick applauded the moral renewal they imagined would take place. ("Are not three billions of dollars a modest price to pay for buying back our old ideal of American manhood and American citizenship?" he asked. "Isn't it a dirt cheap return for the realization that honesty—exact, absolute, unqualified honesty—is the single corner stone of current business success?") The rise in stock prices was temporary, ephemeral. The trusts were more permanent installations, and their economic and political power was unprecedented—virtually uncontested in some industries and legislatures.[35]

The specter of corporate lawlessness combined with sharpening perceptions of working-class life and deepening sensitivity to the poor to intensify the impulse toward Progressive reform. Humanitarian sentiments reinforced old-fashioned republican concerns about concentration of power. Settlement house workers like Jane Addams led the more humane Progressives to acknowledge the impact of material deprivation on the supposedly universal beneficence of thrift—the sort of insight that led to a broader rethinking of charity. A scrupulous charity worker might well suspect "that in holding her poor family so hard to a standard of thrift she is really breaking down a rule of living which they had formerly possessed: that saving, which seems quite commendable in a comfortable part of town, appears almost criminal in a poorer quarter, where a next-door neighbor needs food," Addams wrote in 1899. Confronted with communal alternatives, "she feels the sordidness of constantly being obliged to urge the industrial view of life." The more one learned about the lives of the poor, the more platitudes were overturned; consider the "horrors of the saloon," which to the poor may be a place of kindness, free lunch, treating, loans, and warmth in hard times. The ethos of systematic self-control was not adaptable to all social circumstances.[36]

Much of the literature of reform that flourished in the first two decades of the twentieth century involved the detailed reconstruction of the lives of the poor and the working class for an affluent audience, people who really did not understand and could hardly imagine households like those described in Ida Tarbell's "Where Every Penny Counts." Sympathetic biographies of factory girls, shop girls, day laborers, and the like proliferated; whatever else these stories taught, they made plain that maxims about thrift were risibly inadequate to the lives of the working poor. Social conditions, not character defects, were the primary cause of poverty.[37]

This momentous insight affected social workers, social scientists, and even economists like Patten. It was "not that the creation of a favorable environment will itself transform character," an *Atlantic* writer argued in 1908, "but that the normal man, who is now crushed, will, under favorable conditions, rise unaided, and that poverty and destitution will know him no longer." This was Patten's view, and it promoted a dramatic new perspective on charity. "When the social worker accepts this creed, he soon finds that regeneration is prevented, not by defects in personality, but by defects in our environment, and that the subjective tests of character to which he has been accustomed must be replaced by objective standards which test the environment." The shift from character to conditions marked a Copernican revolution in social work, one that reconfigured thrift for generations of managerial Progressives.[38]

One of the economic conditions that struck Progressives with particular force was the increase in the cost of living during the early twentieth century. *"Do you realize that in this country to-day nourishing food is becoming a luxury?"* Elizabeth Hewes asked in *American* magazine in 1910. Wages had not kept pace with prices, and somehow an increasing share of the national wealth had to be secured for the laboring classes, as well as the lower white-collar classes of clerks and shop workers who were being forced down the social scale by high prices. The question was how to accomplish this project of economic betterment. Gradually a managerial consensus emerged. Progressives recoiled from revolution, and most rejected redistribution as well. The trick was to make the pie larger, not cut the slices more equally. By the early twentieth century, Patten and other economists had begun to undermine the old Malthusian assumption that wages must be kept low to avoid depleting a static "wages fund." On the contrary, they argued, wages should increase as productivity increased—and productivity had indeed increased dramatically during the decades since the Civil War, largely through the development of technology and the exploitation of natural resources. The abolition of poverty was a problem no longer of production but of distribution. That was where the Progressive preoccupation with efficient management came into the picture.[39]

Among the many kinds of reformers who called themselves Progressives, a horror of waste coexisted in varying proportions with humanitarian sentiments and a passion for justice. For some, efficiency became a kind of philosopher's stone, the key to ending the wasteful war between capital and labor and to promoting an abundant, harmonious society based on scientific principles. The passion for organization, practically as an end in itself, led Progressives to strange enthusiasms—strange, at least, for those who professed fealty to democratic ideals. The economist Richard Ely, for example, announced in 1903 that "the organization of the Mormons is the most nearly perfect piece of social mechanism with which I have ever, in any way, come in contact, excepting alone the German army." Ely, like other Progressives, was a humane man, but he believed that humanitarian aims could be achieved only by perfecting the "social mechanism." Efficiency and morality merged.[40]

From the managerial Progressive view, employers who knew how to eliminate waste and increase productivity could be counted on to raise wages accordingly. The prototype seemed to be Henry Ford, who announced his five-dollar day in 1914, soon after his successful introduction of assembly-line production. But the most vigorous champion of scientific management, Frederick Winslow Taylor, based his system on piecework—workers who followed the procedures laid down in the Planning Department would increase output and be rewarded handsomely (though not commensurately) for the increase. Progressives like Louis Brandeis believed that Taylorism could be used to discipline corporations, keeping railroad rates in line, for example, by basing them on more efficient management: managerial thrift created savings that could be passed along to consumers. Taylor himself claimed that his system would realize the Progressive dream, solving class conflict through science and promoting abundance for all.[41]

What actually happened was something else. Taylorism intensified class conflict. Workers resisted the loss of autonomy on the job, the destruction of craft traditions, the submission to arbitrary and pseudoscientific rules fashioned by "efficiency engineers." But ultimately, over decades, workers yielded control over the pace and process of their work in exchange for higher wages and the things higher wages could buy. Work was reduced to its instrumental value. Fulfillment was to be found off the job, through the purchase of commercial goods and entertainment. Taylorism, like Fordism, underwrote Patten's vision of a dynamic consumer culture and so became a key component in the modernization of thrift. It offered a parody of abundance psychology for the working class, showing workers how they could "do more and be more," but only on the managers' terms. The dream of never-ending "personal growth" remained largely a possession of the affluent.

World War I brought partial fulfillment to the managerial redefinition of thrift: steady work, well-paid workers, an ascending spiral of production and consumption. To be sure, some cultural conservatives welcomed the war as a "great discipline" that would revive habits of economy, especially with respect to food. "There is not enough food in the world for the people," a commentator warned in 1917. In the coming "war of starvation," our duty would be to raise and save all we can, not wasting so much as a crust of bread. Others welcomed "the new simplicity" the war would force on the genteel middle class, even as (alas) it enriched parvenu plutocrats and skilled workers. The purchase of Liberty Bonds could also be characterized as a form of saving, of postponing gratification until some future point, in order to serve a selfless purpose in the present.[42]

Still, the overall effect of the war was to put more cash in a lot of people's pockets and to provide new possibilities for spending and risk taking. Though Ernest Hemingway, E. E. Cummings, and other literary figures were as disillusioned as the Europeans by the war, a more typical American reaction was the airheaded abundance psychology epitomized by Lieutenant W. R. Gayner, who told *American* readers about the lesson learned by men who had been injured and could have honorably quit but who chose instead to return to fighting. "War has shown them that there is almost no limit to human endurance and human achievement, if the will to endure and achieve is strong enough." The author himself "cracked" on a flying mission over France and had to be hospitalized. He was never allowed to fly again, but "the will, the determination to fly was persisted in so long that it is still there in spite of everything." Here the Victorian ideal of will was detached from any moral framework and made an end in itself, an expression of personal vitality and a rebuke to prudence. Why be frugal with one's emotions if one could experience the fine, careless rapture of self-affirmation through self-sacrifice?[43]

After the war, during the 1920s, abundance psychology returned to peacetime projects. Lillian Gilbreth brought scientific management into the domestic sphere, calling for "a *fatigue-eliminating home* for the entire family, in line with progressive industry, an efficient industrial plant, PLUS!" Corporate advertising hammered home the message that women were the purchasing agents and managers of this domestic "industrial plant." Ads for everything from oatmeal to disinfectant reminded housewives of their responsibility to keep the home free of germs and its inhabitants full of vim. This involved rigorous saving less than informed spending, keeping up with the latest advances in toilet paper and vacuum cleaner bags. The throwaway economy was an expression not of careless pleasures but of a managerial agenda meant to minimize disease and maximize human control over the biological world. Dixie Cups and Kleenex, according to their advocates, were primarily instruments of sanitation—as was the packaging that routinely enwrapped nationally advertised brand-name goods. The new empire of mass consumption advanced not in the name of "hedonism" but under the banner of scientific efficiency. Even cigarettes were brought into the picture, as quick smokes more compatible with the managerial pace of life than the leisurely old cigar had been. The horror of waste did not disappear, but it focused less on material things than on that most evanescent of commodities: time.[44]

Outside the fantastic universe of corporate advertising, other panegyrics to mass-produced abundance employed an idiom more exalted than empowerment through purchase. In 1922, the self-help writer Ralph Waldo Trine, author of *In Tune with the Infinite* (1897), made a pilgrimage to Dearborn, Michigan. He sat at the feet of Ford, seeking insight into the secrets of "divine supply" and trying to puzzle out how ordinary folk like his readers might tap into it. The scene was characteristic of the age. The Progressive partnership between business and government had peaked during World War I, and the managerial ethos that dominated the 1920s developed a boosterish tone. Corporate advertising systematically blurred the boundaries between luxuries and necessities. If the kitchen became the nerve center of an efficient industrial plant, the dining room remained an arena for social performance, where elegant ladies and gentlemen dressed for dinner and never let the servants see them sweat. Advertising for luxury goods (or pseudoluxury goods) created the images that dominated popular culture, promising to usher in the utopian reign of "obsolescence, free spending and creative waste"—as the industry spokesman J. George Frederick put it at the end of the decade.[45]

The automobile industry pointed the way to planned obsolescence, based not on technical improvements but on nothing more than superficial changes in styling. Ford was fervently attached to the Model T, available in "any color as long as it's black." But by the mid-1920s, his company was losing huge chunks of market share to General Motors, which under Alfred Sloan had introduced colors and instituted the annual model change. The obsession with novelty was appropriate to an era when thrift was comparatively devalued, spending was increasingly sanctioned as the key to prosperity, and getting rich quick was all the rage. Speculation on Wall Street, once scorned as little more than gambling, became a part of the pursuit of serial sensations that increasingly characterized middle- and upper-class life. The bull market sparked a sanitized Dionysian frenzy that swept through affluent suburbs. Here was abundance psychology run riot.[46]

Yet for most Americans speculation remained a spectator sport. As Lendol Calder has shown, a more popular pastime among ordinary folk was using installment plans to buy furniture, appliances, and cars. The General Motors Acceptance Corporation made its new models more affordable by popularizing the use of consumer credit. The corporation's title was more than an ironic euphemism—to have credit extended to oneself was a sign of acceptance into consumer society, a privilege extended only to those who earned it (and could continue to meet the payments).[47]

Still, families could get in over their heads, and household finances could provoke tension between husbands and wives. By the 1920s, public discussion of marital monetary policy took place in a psychological rather than a moral framework. Dr. G. V. Hamilton, reporting the results of his research in "Marriage and Money" in *Harper's* in 1928, concluded that "friction over money is usually a symptom of something else wrong with the marriage." He assumed (with Sigmund Freud) that the major sources of marital dissatisfaction were "the things that your mother and father did to you while you were putting your first six birthdays behind you." It was hard to keep moral indignation aflame in such an atmosphere.[48]

Nevertheless, critics continued to warn against the dangers of the get-rich-quick mentality, the susceptibility to swindlers and high-pressure sales tactics. A few even worried that prosperity was built on the flimsy basis of overvalued stocks and inadequate consumer demand. And General Electric, along with a few other corporations, implicitly acknowledged the inadequacy of undiluted laissez-faire, devising workmen's compensation and social insurance schemes that became the prototypes for Social Security and similar government programs. Corporate managers really did believe they had entered a New Era, one personified not by the old-fashioned robber baron but by the great engineer Herbert Hoover, who fed the starving millions of war-torn Europe and epitomized the managerial ethos. In 1928, when Hoover was elected on a tide of unprecedented prosperity, few American could sense just how brief the New Era would be.[49]

Depression, War, and Fulfillment

As the stock market crash and its aftermath reverberated through the culture of the thirties, the cheerful assumptions of abundance psychology began to seem a cruel joke. The supposedly bottomless reservoir of benign energy, the source of endless personal and economic growth, turned out to have a bottom (and an end) after all. When the bottom dropped out, middle-class Americans felt it most acutely. Many white-collar proletarians and blue-collar aristocrats had temporarily cashed in on the promise of the New Era, and then they lost everything. Feelings of insecurity were sharper among the formerly secure than among those who had never known even temporary relief from economic anxiety. No wonder, then, that the popular culture of the Depression years was pervaded by longings for security, emotional as well as economic.

One might think that, in such an atmosphere, scarcity psychology and Victorian notions of thrift would make a comeback, and to a certain extent they did. Among editorialists and moralists, there was—quite understandably—much gnashing of teeth about the evils of irresponsible speculation and the get-rich-quick mentality. There was also much talk about how "we" Americans had been rebuked for our spendthrift ways and reminded of our dependence on basic values embedded in work, family, and community. At its best this impulse could lead to a revaluation of leisure (making a virtue of necessity for the jobless) and a brief revival of the Progressive Era vision of the "simple life." More commonly, nostalgic yearnings to recover the virtues of an imagined past pervaded popular culture, persuading advertisers to associate their products with pseudotraditional settings (the Southern plantation, the New England village), hoping that I. W. Harper whiskey or Campbell's pork and beans would resonate with folkish virtues—including the virtue of thrift. Depending on the product (e.g., margarine), the value of thrift could simply be embedded in the increasingly shrill appeals to price that characterized Depression advertising. Sometimes more elaborate rhetorical contortions were involved. The apparent indulgence of an electric refrigerator, for example, could point the way to more systematic economies in the food budget over time.[50]

As this example suggests, though, the practice of managerial thrift in hard times could be more complicated than scrimping and saving. The transformation of thrift in the 1930s was not just a matter of continuing its reconfiguration in accordance with managerial norms; it also involved a refocusing of attention from individual to collective strategies for saving. Longings for security focused less on the separate self than on the self in the larger context—of family, community, or nation. Indeed (as Warren Susman noticed years ago), the Depression-bred longing for security was at bottom a longing to belong, to make a shattered self whole again by immersing oneself in a warm bath of transcendent, collective identity. In Europe these sorts of desires led to fascism and Nazism; in America they led to more benign fantasies, mythologies of "the past," "the people," and the American "way of life." This pseudopopulist nationalism, which animated everything from the film version of *Grapes of Wrath* to the songs of Irving Berlin, has been vastly overpraised by "traditionalists" in our own time. But for all its fatuities, the bland, classless, and monochromatic vision of the American way of life served up by Broadway and Hollywood in the 1930s and 1940s was infinitely preferable to more sinister forms of collectivism flourishing elsewhere.[51]

The longing to belong reshaped the impulses toward self-fulfillment in abundance psychology and redefined notions of psychic health. Personal growth was still a mandate, but now it increasingly involved fitting in, cooperating, and getting along. Dale Carnegie's *How to Win Friends and Influence People* (1936) was the characteristic success manual of the age. In a society increasingly preoccupied with group identity, psychological health more and more was a matter of "adjustment"—a word that became a litmus test of normality in the decades to come.[52]

Of course it would be a stretch to overemphasize the collectivization of values. Men still blamed themselves for being out of work, despite the overwhelming and undeniable evidence was that unemployment was due to circumstances beyond any individual's control. But among policy makers and in public discourse generally, there was a broad recognition that social conditions played a more decisive role than personal character in keeping people poor. From this perspective, thrift was no longer the all-sufficing protection from want that moralists had once deemed it to be. The specter of starvation, impossible to ignore by the early 1930s, revived the Progressive insights of a quarter century before. The introduction of Social Security, Unemployment Compensation, Aid to Families with Dependent Children, and other forms of federal and state relief all underscored the inadequate protection provided by personal savings in an era when joblessness lasted years and banks failed daily.

While the emergent welfare state acknowledged the insufficiency of thrift, the persistent consumer culture sustained a hunger for stuff. Corporate advertisers may have donned overalls and rolled up their sleeves to show their solidarity with the plain folk, but Hollywood still lionized luxurious consumption. Indeed, the movies of the thirties may have begun a cultural tendency that has become particularly pronounced in our time: the tendency to redefine class in cultural terms, to focus satire on the stuffed shirt rather than the plutocrat. This initially harmless but eventually insidious practice developed in screwball comedy and the sentimental narratives perfected by Frank Capra. Being rich was OK, if you weren't too snooty about it. Luxury still fascinated.

Family desires for comfort and even luxury could still be met (if one was able) through the installment plan. Well into the Depression, in 1932, the journalist Roy Helton complained that the aspiration to provide a better life for their children led parents to sacrifice the present to the future. The home, filled with items bought on the installment plan, was no longer a refuge from this obsession with advancing the next generation: the homeowner "no longer has possessions but only obligations." Running faster to stay in the same place, the consumer under economically depressed conditions was hardly a model of liberation.[53]

Yet consumer debt was increasingly acceptable, as popular economics made a virtue of necessity. "Do you need some money?" asked Alliston Cragg in a book with that title in 1941. "If you do it is no longer a matter for apology or concealment. The almost universal experience of needing some money during the past ten years has no doubt contributed much toward breaking down old fetishes. After centuries of disgrace, borrowing has at last become reputable." Borrowing allowed people to keep up appearances, not necessarily to rise but simply to fit in.[54]

And fitting in sometimes meant buying expensive things, especially cars. "There are a good many reasons why the automobile industry is happier than most industries these days," Bernard DeVoto observed in 1936 from his "Editor's Easy Chair" at *Harper's*, "but one vital reason is that it is doing its job. It is giving the consumer good value for his money, it has done so over a long period of time, and it has improved its products as circumstances and the rigid limits of the possible allow." Despite occasional fussiness in design, based on the mistaken assumption that "women buy the cars in America and buy them on the basis of the ash-trays and arm-rests," auto manufacturers were giving the consumer "a square deal and a lot more. The man who buys his car is getting what the pulpits used to call a miracle of modern progress—is getting not only the usufructs but also the stock dividends of the machine age." Such brave talk aimed to articulate a consumerist redefinition of thrift. Buying a well-engineered product of the machine age was neither frivolous nor extravagant; it was plain common sense that technology could revitalize capitalism by rendering it transparent and rational, purging it of fraud, delivering quality products that men as well as women (who were supposedly indifferent to technology) could admire. This sanitized and rationalized version of consumption played a major role in extending consumer culture to men.[55]

It is tempting to say that once Americans had had a taste of mass-produced consumption, there was no going back. But that would be conjecture. What is more certain is that the revival of consumer demand became known as a public necessity during the 1930s—not just within the advertising industry, whose interest it served directly, but among policy makers in general. Not until 1936, though, did Keynes's *General Theory* make a systematic case for using government fiscal or monetary policy to stimulate aggregate demand. By the late 1930s a few of the younger and more venturesome New Dealers were itching to implement a Keynesian agenda, which was part of a broader shift in economic thought toward recognizing the importance of purchasing power to prosperity. The subtitle of *Do You Need Some Money?* was *Consumer Credit as a Means to Economic Stability*, and the author argued that the "new economics" had shown that capital investment was not curtailed by consumer debt.

All of these intellectual changes helped ease the transition toward a managerial version of thrift, one more consistent with spending and borrowing than with scrimping and saving.

But institutional change proved decisive in securing that transition. In 1938, the Congress of Industrial Organizations (CIO) won the right to represent workers in steel, automobiles, and other basic industries. The social contract between labor and management, the implicit agreement that would underwrite the midcentury managerial consensus, was falling into place. The terms were simple: steady work and higher wages in exchange for acceptance of management work rules and a minimum eight-hour day.

The war and its aftermath allowed management to keep its side of the bargain, for a while.[56] Even before Pearl Harbor, basic industries geared up to wartime production, as Franklin Roosevelt committed his government to supporting Britain through the lend-lease policy ("Take these battleships, pay for them whenever"). Double-digit jobless figures shrank, and by 1941, national income soared past 1929 levels to $90 billion. And that $90 billion was more equitably distributed than ever before. The immediate consequence of war-built prosperity was a rapid rise in consumer spending on durable goods: a 40 percent rise in auto purchases, 35 percent in refrigerators, 50 percent in stoves, 20 percent in vacuum cleaners. The coming of an "all-out" war economy, commentators observed, would mean prosperity "in terms of business activity and employment" but not "consumer goods and satisfactions." Success would depend on "the little man" and his willingness to sacrifice gratification in the present for the good life in the future.[57]

In advertising, government propaganda, and public discourse generally, the sacrifice demanded by the war was always presented in precisely those terms, as a temporary expedient required during a national emergency. War bond drives revived traditions of public thrift, as Kiku Adatto shows elsewhere in this volume; throughout the war years, Americans dutifully cultivated thrifty habits in everyday life—eating it up, wearing it out, making it do, doing without. They saved mountains of scrap metal, rubber, paper, and rags, all to be recycled for industrial purposes; even wasted kitchen fats could be retrieved from oblivion and turned into a source of nitroglycerin for bombs. Rationing suppressed the outward signs of class distinctions and (as many observers noted) prevented people "from spending their 'excess' money for which no consumable goods have been produced." There were only so many wristwatches and movie tickets one could buy. But General Motors, Kelvinator, and other corporate advertisers who had converted to wartime production bombarded Americans with images of the prosperity that would be coming after the war, reminding everyone that scarcity was only to be endured "for the duration."[58]

Outside the advertising industry, Americans were less sanguine about postwar economic prospects. Many feared the return of depression within months or years after peace broke out. But gradually such anxieties subsided. Despite a postwar strike wave, antiunion legislation like the Taft-Hartley Act, and other strains between labor and management, the social contract survived—largely because the United States had been uniquely insulated from the ravages of the war and had emerged from it as the richest country in the world. American economic supremacy meant that American corporations did not face overseas competition; their managers were willing (though reluctantly) to provide job security, health insurance, retirement pensions, and other benefits demanded by unions—which by the late 1940s represented an unprecedented 34 percent of the private sector workforce. The American government, meanwhile, rhetorically committed itself to Keynesian principles in the Full Employment Act of 1946; with the onset of the Cold War and the arms race, it embraced a military version of Keynesian policy. As in Keynes's theory, government fiscal policy could be used to put people to work and increase or sustain aggregate demand. But the only major public works that Congress was willing to pay for were projects conducted by military contractors, designing things that blew up.

Though postwar fiscal policy departed from Keynes's hopes for peacetime social democracy, it nonetheless set the stage for the fulfillment of Patten's earlier, blander vision. Barriers of race and class still prevented many Americans from participating in postwar prosperity, but by 1950, the more fortunate American industrial workers were using their newfound job security to surround themselves with an unprecedented cornucopia of mass-produced, durable goods. Much of this was "plant equipment" for the domestic household—kitchen appliances and cars sanitized by service to the family. And much of it was financed on the installment plan or with the assistance (in the case of home mortgages) of such government agencies as the Veterans Administration and the Federal Housing Administration. Debt was respectable, "adjustment" remained the benchmark of psychological normality, and a consumerist version of thrift was transformed into a key component of the midcentury managerial consensus.

The consensus survived until the early 1970s, when overseas competition became impossible to ignore, and American business ended the implicit social contract with unions by seeking cheap labor in overseas markets. The fulfillment of Patten's vision, far from being the outcome of inevitable laws of progress, began to seem the product of temporary, anomalous conditions—the global economic supremacy that underwrote job security and corporate social responsibility. The era of "leaner and meaner" corporations and resurgent laissez-faire was already on the horizon in 1973, when the Organization of the Petroleum Exporting Countries (OPEC) oil boycott signified the shattering of the managerial consensus. Whether thrift would survive that breakup remained to be seen.

Notes

I want to thank fellow contributors for their advice and comments on this essay. I owe a special debt of gratitude to Virginia Gilmartin for her brilliant and indefatigable research assistance.

1. "*Thrift* by Samuel Smiles," *Harper's New Monthly Magazine*, May 1875, 602.

2. "Workingmen's Wives," *Atlantic Monthly*, January 1879, 59–71.

3. Ibid., 64, 70.

4. "Economy of Food," *Good Housekeeping*, 1887, 130; Ida Branch Mills, "Economy That Doth Not Tend to Poverty," *Good Housekeeping*, 1888, 276–77.

5. Christine Terhune Herrick, "The Wastes of the Household," *Good Housekeeping*, 1885, 6; E. P. K., "Still Another Chapter in Economy," *Good Housekeeping*, 1887, 280.

6. "To Parents and Teachers," *Outlook*, 1903, 14–16. See also "Penny Wisdom," *Charities Review* 10 (1900): 59–60.

7. Milo Maltbie, "Pawn Shops," *Municipal Affairs* 2 (1898): 747–52; William Roe, "New York's Marshalsea," *Arena* 23 (1900), 31–39; "Bankrupt Wage-earners and Wives," *Harper's Bazar* [*sic*], 1900, 210–11.

8. Junius Henry Browne, "Pecuniary Independence," *Harper's Monthly*, 1894, 903–6.

9. John Bigelow, "What Is Gambling?" *Harper's Monthly*, February 1895, 470–80; Thomas McIntyre Cooley, "Federal Taxation of Lotteries," *Atlantic*, April 1892, 523–35. Also see Jackson Lears, *Something for Nothing: Luck in America* (New York: Viking Press, 2003).

10. Helena Rowe, "Family Fashions and Fancies," *Good Housekeeping*, 1886, 73–74.

11. C. S. Messinger, "Family Expenses," *Good Housekeeping*, 1886, 73–74.

12. George Miller Beard, *American Nervousness* (New York: Putnam, 1881). I have discussed neurasthenia at length in chap. 1 of *No Place of Grace: Antimodernism and the Transformation of American Culture, 1880–1920* (New York: Pantheon Books, 1981)

13. Anna C. Brackett, "The Technique of Rest," *Harper's Monthly*, June 1891, 53. Also see, e.g., Frances Dyer, "Economize Your Strength: A Reserve Force," *Good Housekeeping*, 1885, 5–6.

14. Edward Bok, "Is It Worth While?" *Ladies' Home Journal*, November 1901, 18. Also see David Shi, *The Simple Life: Plain Living and High Thinking in American Culture* (New York: Oxford University Press, 1983).

15. "How We Can Lead a Simple Life: By an American Mother," *Ladies' Home Journal*, 1900, 18. Also see, e.g., "The Simple Life," *Outlook*, 1902, 214–16; Ellen Talbot Lane, "Mother's Sacrifices to Baby," *Good Housekeeping*, 1907, 213–14.

16. Annie Payson Call, "Every Day Living: V. Money Strain," *American Illustrated Magazine*, 1905, 112–14. Also see Mary Heaton Vorse, "Our Expensive Daughters," *Good Housekeeping*, 1907, 265–71; Rebecca Harding Davis, "The Disease of Moneygetting," *Independent*, 1902, 1457–60; Eliot Gregory, "Social Stilt-walking," *Harper's Monthly*, 1905, 555–58; Christine Terhune Herrick, "Pound Foolishness," *Independent*, 1901, 2227–29.

17. Susan Strasser, *Waste and Want: A Social History of Trash* (New York: Henry Holt, 1999), chaps. 3 and 4.

18. Herbert Horwill, "Utilization of Time-Waste," *Chautauquan*, 1902, 178–80; "Postal Savings Banks," *Independent*, 1901, 2791–92; "Better Living on Less Money," *Good Housekeeping*, 1907, 428–29; "From $3500 to $1200 a Year," *Good Housekeeping*, 1908, 336–37; "That Six Hundred a Year," *Good Housekeeping*, 1909, 224–25; Call, "Every Day Living," 112; "The Autobiography of a Stingy Man," *American Magazine*, 1914, 46–51.

19. Frederick Winslow Taylor, *The Principles of Scientific Management* (New York: Harper, 1911); Samuel Haber, *Efficiency and Uplift: Scientific Management in the Progressive Era, 1890–1920* (Chicago: University of Chicago Press, 1964); Robert Kanigel, *The One Best Way: Frederick Winslow Taylor and the Enigma of Efficiency* (New York: Viking Penguin, 1997).

20. Martha Bensley Bruere, "Efficiency Methods in the Home," *Good Housekeeping*, 1913, 253–58. Also see Elizabeth Billings, "A Revolution in Advertising," *Atlantic*, 1912, 782–85; and Jackson Lears, *Fables of Abundance: A Cultural History of Advertising in America* (New York: Basic Books, 1994), chap. 6.

21. Earl Mayo, "The Trust Builders," *Frank Leslie's Popular Monthly*, 1901, 56–65; Charles Gleed, "Captains of Industry: Andrew Carnegie," *Cosmopolitan*, 1901, 297–301.

22. Charles Lloyd Tuckey, "How Suggestion Works: A Chapter from the Experience of a Famous London Physician," *Good Housekeeping*, 1909, 639–42. For more on this phenomenon in general, see Jackson Lears, "From Salvation to Self-realization: Advertising and the Therapeutic Roots of the Consumer Culture, 1880–1930," in *The Culture of Consumption, 1880–1980: Critical Essays in American History*, ed. Richard Wightman Fox and T. J. Jackson Lears (New York: Pantheon, 1983).

23. Tuckey, "How Suggestion Works," 641–42. Also see Donald Meyer, *The Positive Thinkers: Religion as Pop Psychology from Mary Baker Eddy to Norman Vincent Peale* (1965; New York: Pantheon, 1980).

24. "Not Poverty but Strength," *Outlook*, 1902, 111–12; "An Evening at Emmanuel Church," *Good Housekeeping*, 1908, 200–201.

25. William James, "The Powers of Men," *American Magazine*, October 1907, 57–65.

26. Michael Williams, "Fletcherizing with Fletcher," *Good Housekeeping*, 1908, 502–5; Frances Bjorkman, "The Philosophy of Fletcherism," *Good Housekeeping*, 1909, 504–6. Also see H. Addington Bruce, "Bending the Twig," *American Magazine*, 1910, 691.

27. John Kasson, *Houdini, Tarzan, and the Perfect Man: The White Male Body and the Challenge of Modernity in America* (New York: Hill and Wang, 2001); John Higham, "The Reorientation of American Culture in the 1890s," in his *Writing American History* (Bloomington: Indiana University Press, 1973).

28. Richard Cabot, "The Work Cure," *Good Housekeeping*, 1909, 296–98; Cabot, "The Dangers of Rest," *Good Housekeeping*, 1909, 730–32.

29. "Motives of Misers," *Current Literature*, 1902, 428–29.

30. Woods Hutchinson, "The Joy of Eating," *Good Housekeeping*, 1913, 673.

31. L. G. Bostedo, "The Function of Saving," *Annals of the American Academy of Political and Social Science* 17 (January 1901): 95–99; James Henry Hamilton, "Savings and Savings Institutions," *Gunton's*, 1902, 518.

32. Simon Nelson Patten, *The New Basis of Civilization* (1907; Cambridge, MA: Harvard University Press, 1968), 141.

33. "The Political Menace of the Discontented," *Atlantic*, October 1896, 447–51.

34. Henry Clews, "Wall Street's Wild Speculation," *Cosmopolitan*, 1904, 404–10. Also see "The Degradation of Wall Street," *Frank Leslie's Popular Monthly*, December 1903.

35. Ellery Sedgwick, "Promoters and Morals," *Frank Leslie's Popular Monthly*, 1903, 225; Charles Conant, "Recent Economic Tendencies," *Atlantic*, June 1900, 736–48.

36. Jane Addams, "The Subtle Problems of Charity," *Atlantic*, February 1899, 163–78.

37. Ida Tarbell, "Where Every Penny Counts," *American*, 1909, 437–39, and "The Golden Rule in Business: Making the Hire Worthy of the Laborer," *American*, February 1915, 25–29, 66.

38. Edward T. Devine, "The New View of Charity," *Atlantic*, 1908, 136–44.

39. Elizabeth Hewes, "Some Dangers from High Prices," *American*, 1910, 346–47 (emphasis in original); Jacob Hollander, "The Abolition of Poverty," *Atlantic*, 1912, 492–97.

40. Richard T. Ely, "Economic Aspects of Mormonism," *Harper's Monthly*, April 1903, 668. Also see Atherton Brownell, "Business Reduced to a Science," *World's Work*, 1904, 596–601; Robert Thurston, "Engineer as Financier," *Cassier's*, 1902, 332–45.

41. Frederick Winslow Taylor, "The Gospel of Efficiency," *American*, 1911, 570–81.

42. E. S. Martin, "The Great World Movie: Give Us This Day Our Daily Bread," *Good Housekeeping*, 1917, 36–37; Katherine Fullerton Gerould, "The New Simplicity," *Harper's*, 1918, 14–24; Charles A. Beard, "A Call upon Every Citizen," *Harper's*, 1918, 655–56.

43. Lieut. W. R. Gayner, "Doing More Than You Ever Dreamed You Could Do," *American*, 1919, 44–45, 74–82.

44. Lillian Moller Gilbreth, "Have You a Restful Home?" *Good Housekeeping*, 1926, 158; Lears, *Fables of Abundance*, chap. 6; Strasser, *Waste and Want*, chap. 4.

45. Ralph Waldo Trine, *The Power That Wins* (Indianapolis, IN: Bobbs-Merrill, 1928), 5, 18–19; J. George Frederick, "Obsolescence, Free Spending, and Creative Waste," in his *A Philosophy of Production* (New York: Bobbs-Merrill, 1930). See also Ralph Waldo Trine, *In Tune with the Infinite* (New York: Thomas Y. Crowell, 1897)

46. Steve Fraser, *Every Man a Speculator: A History of Wall Street in American Life* (New York: HarperCollins, 2005), chap. 11.

47. Lendol Calder, *Financing the American Dream: A Cultural History of Consumer Credit* (Princeton, NJ: Princeton University Press, 1999), esp. chaps. 4–5.

48. Dr. G. V. Hamilton and Kenneth MacGowan, "Marriage and Money," *Harper's*, 1928, 437.

49. Keyes Winter, "Fools and Their Money," *Harper's*, 1927, 361–71; Jesse Rainsford Sprague, "Prosperity without Profit," *Harper's*, 1928, 83–91.

50. Lears, *Fables of Abundance*, 236–47, 381–87; Strasser, *Waste and Want*, 209–11.

51. Warren Susman, *Culture as History* (New York: Pantheon, 1984), 150–210.

52. Dale Carnegie, *How to Win Friends and Influence People* (New York: Simon and Schuster, 1936).

53. Roy Helton, "Sold Out to the Future," *Harper's*, 1932, 129–42.

54. Alliston Cragg, *Do You Need Some Money? Consumer Credit as a Means to Economic Stability* (New York: Harper, 1941), 3. Also see Calder, *Financing the American Dream*, chap. 6.

55. Bernard DeVoto, "The Consumer's Automobile," *Harper's*, 1936, 717–20.

56. Lizabeth Cohen, *Making a New Deal: Industrial Workers in Chicago, 1919–1939* (New York: Cambridge University Press, 1991), esp. chaps. 3, 6–8; Nelson Lichtenstein, "From Corporatism to Collective Bargaining: Organized Labor and the Eclipse of Social Democracy in the Postwar Era," in Steve Fraser and Gary Gerstle, eds., *The Rise and Fall of the New Deal Order, 1930–1980* (Princeton, NJ: Princeton University Press, 1989), 122–52.

57. Irwin Ross, "Labor, Capital, and Co.," *Harper's*, 1941, 414–21; Frank Hanighen, "Defense Begins to Hurt," *Harper's*, 1941, 561–71.

58. Katharine Fisher, "You're in the Army, Too," *Good Housekeeping*, 1942, 110–11; Kurt Solmssen, "Ration Book vs. Pocketbook," *Harper's*, 1942, 143–47.

10 }

Thrift and Moral Formation

James Davison Hunter

In 1849, Daniel C. Eddy, a twenty-seven-year-old pastor of the First Baptist Church in Lowell, Massachusetts, published his first of many books on moral guidance. Eddy was already well known as a public orator in the region, and *The Young Man's Friend* extended his renown and the reach of his influence. His book, as described on the cover, contained "admonitions for the erring, counsel for the tempted, encouragement for the desponding, and hope for the fallen."[1] Eddy reached the crux of his argument in chapter 5, "The Fast Young Man," the title of which was taken from a term of derision popular at the time. Here he described the antimoralist of this age. The fast young man, for Eddy, applied to "one who is breaking away from restraints, defying by his recklessness the common sentiment of the community, and displaying an uncommon haste in learning vicious habits and becoming acquainted with depraved men. It is a term of reproach, and courted only by those who are 'void of understanding.'"[2] A "fast young man" typically followed a progression downward, "fast in getting away from home and beyond the wholesome restraints of the fireside," "fast in forsaking the sanctuary," and "fast at learning bad habits." This slide would typically begin with smoking, move to swearing, lead to theatergoing and "cotillion parties," and then move to drinking. Not least in all of the fast young man's tendencies was being *"fast in making and spending money."* The danger, Eddy argued, was that most of these fast young men "have just enough income for frugal living." Because they "cannot see how they can lay up a dollar for the future" and continue in such bad habits, they would become vulnerable to "the demon of speculation" who would lead them invariably to "gambling, forgery, embezzlement." Eddy makes it clear that he was not advocating a "miserly disposition": "Let a young man enjoy as he goes along in life; but, aside from all the reasonable enjoyments, how much is spent for the mere gratification of lust!" The point was that if fast young men were more frugal, they could support their families, including their "widowed mothers," and could buy stocks, make deposits, and "save multitudes from degradation and ruin, and make them ornaments to virtuous society."

For Eddy, the best advice to the young men of his day was to invest their greatest God-given assets—their intellect, conscience, affections, hope—in the truth of Jesus Christ, rather than in property, literary or military pursuits, or pleasure.[3] Christ was Eddy's "perfect model" for the young man. Among other things, Christ was "*a perfect guide in all the bargainings and traffickings of life*" on account of his honesty in all matters.[4]

Curious as it may seem, the cautionary tale about the fast young man was one of the earliest and, in fact, one of only a very few efforts to explicitly encourage the "virtue" of thrift to children and young adults prior to the late nineteenth and early twentieth centuries. Yet the story quietly signals an important shift that was just beginning to take form—a shift not just in the moral and spiritual education of the young but in American culture more broadly. In this chapter, the moral formation of the young provides a window into the nature and direction of that shift in the meaning of thrift and the culture of capitalism.

Locke, the Calvinists, and the Cultivation of Restraint

Though primarily known for his political theory, John Locke made one of the most significant contributions to the literature on moral formation in the late seventeenth and early eighteenth centuries. His essay *Some Thoughts Concerning Education*, published in 1693, had its origins in a series of letters he wrote to a friend, Edward Clarke.[5] When published, this work became highly influential—in some respects, it was a seventeenth-century equivalent to Benjamin Spock's *Baby and Child Care*.[6]

Though this was a long treatise, the word *thrift* did not appear once. The elaboration of a moral culture of restraint, however, was prominent and integral to his views of both a virtuous life and a virtuous society. "He that has not a Mastery over his Inclinations, he that knows not how to *resist* the Importunity of *present Pleasure or Pain*, for the sake of what Reason tells him is fit to be done, wants the true Principle of Virtue and Industry, and is in danger never to be good for any Thing."[7] At the heart of restraint was the capacity to deny the self its whims and impulses. "The Principle of all Virtue and Excellency lies in a Power of denying our selves the Satisfaction of our own Desires, where Reason does not authorize them."[8] This capacity, "so contrary to unguided Nature," was not innate and only to be coaxed out of the child, but had to be cultivated early in life. "Children," Locke said, "should be us'd to submit their Desires, and go without their Longings even *from their very Cradles*."[9] Locke was not in favor of frequent beatings or chidings for the simple reason that he judged them ineffective at best and, often, counterproductive.[10] He also rejected reasoning with children beyond what was appropriate to their age: "Long discourses, and Philosophical Reasonings, at best, amaze and confound, but do not instruct Children."[11] For Locke, the proper technique for cultivating restraint was shaming the child. "Ingenious *Shame*, and the Apprehensions of Displeasure, are the only true Restraint. These alone ought to hold the Reins, and keep the Child in Order."[12]

A mastery over the self had as its object control over vice in its multiple expressions. The seeds of vice "are not to be suffer'd to take any Root, but must be carefully weeded out, as soon as ever they begin to shew themselves in him."[13] Among the vices that concerned Locke were those relating to time and money. Occasions for idleness in children were to be avoided, and industriousness in all tasks was to be encouraged. Locke complained of "pastimes" or diversions such as gaming, cards, dice, and drinking. Too many "throw away their spare Hours in them. . . . They cannot bear the dead Weight of unemployed Time lying upon their Hands nor the Uneasiness it is to do nothing at all: And having never learned any laudable manual Art wherewith to divert themselves, they have recourse to those foolish or ill Ways in Use to help off their Time, which a rational Man . . . could find very little Pleasure in."[14]

Children, or more precisely the children of the gentlemen of whom Locke was speaking, should also learn the skills of the accountant. At an early age, a child should learn to keep an account of his income and expenses, for no one who "has constantly under the Course of his domestick Affairs, lets them run to ruin."[15]

Yet while a culture of restraint surrounded the handling of money, thrift was not exactly encouraged. In fact, what came to be known as thrift had a vague resemblance to the vices of covetousness and of hoarding. As Locke put it, "The Desire of having in our Possession, and under our Dominion, more than we have need of, being the Root of all Evil, should be early and carefully weeded out, and the contrary Quality of a Readiness to impart to others, implanted."[16] A person, he admonished, "loses nothing by his *Liberality*."[17] "As to the having and possessing of Things, teach them to part with what they have, easily and freely to their Friends, and let them find by Experience that the most *liberal* has always the most Plenty, with Esteem and Commendation to boot, and they will quickly learn to practice it."[18]

Though these examples taken from Locke's essay emphasize the primacy of personal autonomy and secular rationality, his views on authority and its relation to the moral life were rather traditional. Most strikingly, Locke argued both that virtue could not exist without reverence for God and that there could therefore be no morality without God:

> *As to the Foundation of* [*virtue*], there ought very clearly to be imprinted on his [the child's] Mind a true Notion of *God*, as of the independent Supreme Being, Author and Maker of all Things, from whom we receive

> all our Good, who loves us, and gives us all things. And consequent to this, instill into him a Love and Reverence of this Supreme Being.[19]

This was not empty rhetoric. Locke encouraged levels of spiritual discipline unimaginable today, advising parents and masters to keep "Children constantly Morning and Evening to Acts of Devotion to God, as to their Maker, Preserver and Benefactor, in some plain and short Form of Prayer, suitable to the Age and Capacity," as well as to teach children "to *pray* to Him, and *praise* Him as the Author of his Being, and of all the God he does or can enjoy."[20] To this end, it was "necessary he should learn perfectly by heart" the Lord's Prayer, the creeds, and the Ten Commandments.[21]

In sum, the moral life is defined by, and emanates from, the authority of God, which in turn is mediated by the authority possessed and exercised by parents. The loving yet stern authority parents exercised would be the means by which children would come to understand God's sovereign love and judgment. Obedience and respect for one's parents were thus an expression of obedience and reverence for God.

Though Locke's own faith tended toward a minimalist and rationalist Anglican theology, his views of the religious foundations of the moral life and the importance of the authority vested in parents put him in greater sympathy with Calvinist thinking than one might have supposed.[22] Beyond this, the themes Locke stressed—restraint, the productive use of time, industry and generosity—were precisely those emphasized in the literature on moral formation in Puritan New England, and in Calvinism more generally, through the early decades of the nineteenth century.[23]

As it was for Locke, piety was the definitive foundation of the moral life for Calvinists from the early eighteenth century to the middle of the nineteenth century.[24] Of course, true piety had implications for how one lived. The divines, however, rarely mentioned the virtue and practice of thrift; and when they did, it was usually as a passing reference.[25] For example, in *The New England Primer*, first published in 1690 and by far the most commonly used textbook in the colonies for the century that followed, there is just a single reference. The extent of the primer's advice on such matters was found in its exegesis of the eighth commandment: "to get our goods honestly, to keep them safely, and spend them thriftily."[26]

In the practical affairs of household economy, the emphasis was never on the management of money, much less on saving. Rather, emphasis was placed on the moral obligations that surrounded those affairs. One fundamental duty was industry. In the context of eighteenth-century and early nineteenth-century America, industry meant more than busyness in various activities. In *The Mother's Friend*, the distinction is explained:

> The exertions which are occasionally extorted from us, by the exigency of circumstances, or those to which we are impelled by vanity, deserve

> not the name of industry; for they are perfectly compatible with laziness. That change of unmeaning occupations, in which some loiter away their time, that bustling activity about trifles, that volatile disposition, which prompts some to begin many things, but never allows them to perfect or complete any thing—all this is but idleness.
>
> Industry is activity under the regulation of moral principle; it is the application of power, to the attainment of an aim established by reason and conscience; it precludes evil thoughts and evil desires; it increases our powers by giving them due and wholesome exercise; and renders us more fit for our vocation on earth, and our destination beyond it.[27]

Industry was not only "the positive duty of everyone" but also "a means of preservation from the dangers and temptations of life."

> Mark the characters and histories of those who have sunk into the most abject and deplorable circumstances, and you will generally find that they have failed, not from the want of opportunity to improve their condition in life, but from the absence of industry and care.[28]

Implied in the pursuit of industry was a duty to use time prudently. "Be diligent to improve Time," exhorted Eleazar Moody in his 1775 book *The School of Good Manners*. "Suffer not precious Hours to run away without improvement."[29] The prudent use of time was, in many ways, more important at this time than the thrifty use of money. "No economy is so essential as the economy of time; . . . [as] by squandering pence we are very soon deprived of pounds, so by wasting minutes we shall lose not only hours, but days and months."[30] The point was not just to encourage self-improvement but to eliminate opportunities for indolence. As Enos Weed put it in 1803, "Children should be kept busy, for if they are not employed so as to obtain good to themselves or in doing good to others, they will be employed in doing evil."[31] The consequences were always potentially catastrophic.[32]

In the affairs of household economy, a third duty was that of justice. Benjamin Wadsworth, in his popular 1712 treatise, "The Well-Ordered Family," never says that children should practice thrift in order to support their parents in old age. Rather, he focuses on children's duty to do so as the most important obligation they have toward their parents. And in the exercise of that duty, "Children should not be covetous and niggardly in supplying their Parents; but (if able) they should readily afford what may suffice, be enough and sufficient for them," as a reflection of the love and support the parents gave the children themselves growing up.[33] As to the poor, justice also required generosity. Thus, in *The New England Primer*'s exegesis of the eighth commandment, mentioned earlier, children were also encouraged to be charitable to those in need, to "impart your portion to the poor, in money and in meat."[34] And in the affairs of commerce, most counseled instruction in arithmetic and bookkeeping as a useful skill, yet the more important lesson was honesty and fairness. In Weed's words, "Children should be taught to be just in their dealings, one with an other . . . and they should be instructed how to obtain property lawfully, and how to use those things which they need, after they are in possession of them."[35] Here, again, the virtue of thrift goes unmentioned but implied.[36]

Yet insofar as Calvinism appropriated the moral ideals of the monastics for the common person, it could be said that thrift was in some ways implied in the purposive rational controls on everyday behavior—where *restraint* is another word for ascetic self-control over worldly affairs, *industry* is another word for hard work and the efficient use of time, and *temperance* is another word for moderation in the satisfaction of personal appetites. And yet the discourse was not merely a form of means-ends rationality. It was, rather, overwhelmingly moral in character, tied in direct ways (especially for the Calvinist) to their spiritual calling on earth and their fate in eternity. Only in this way did it provide the elements necessary for the idea of thrift to emerge in popular discourse as a virtue necessary to a good life and the common good.

Industrialization, Pragmatism, and the Emergence of a Discourse of Thrift

The factors that account for the change in the discourse were suggested by the Reverend Eddy himself in his discussion of the "fast young man." "We live in an age of progress," he said,

> Men eat fast, work fast, travel fast, and live fast. A man's life is measured by the speed at which he goes, and steam seems to be the propelling power in all the movements of our race. . . . There is a progress downward as well as upward; progress in error, crime, shame, and ruin. . . . Men of science have invented machines to tunnel through gigantic mountains; they have discovered various processes for breaking and working bars of iron; they have agents for draining marshes, turning the course of rivers and bowling out the contents of the sea. So there have been invented machines, in the moral world to tunnel through characters that men deemed impregnable; processes for breaking the heartstrings, draining the breast of man of all its generous impulses and filling up the waste with the most ruinous passions and lusts; agencies for turning the affections into new courses, away from home, away from truth, away from God, into channels the banks of which are strewed with wrecks of the lost.[37]

Science, steam, machines, iron, the transformation of the world all in the name of progress—it is of no surprise that the factors Eddy laments are those of the early stages of industrial capitalism.

Up to the mid-nineteenth century, the economy was mainly agrarian and mercantile, and for most people it was an economy of scarcity. Whether it was articulated as thrift or simply implied, the prudential use of money, materials, and any accumulated wealth was a given, a prerequisite of subsistence and, during hard times, survival. So too in the early decades of industrialization, wealth generated by manufacturing depended on a reliable, hardworking workforce willing to put in long hours. Profit making served the growth of industry, the industrialists who owned and directed these firms, and, to a lesser extent, the growing middle class who managed them. Moreover, the expansion into new realms of profit making—such as steel production, the construction of railroads, and the like—required large quantities of capital, some of which would come from the savings of ordinary people. Scarcity remained a fact of life especially for the urban working classes and for the expanding middle classes; without inherited wealth, insurance, retirement programs, and higher wages, frugality remained the principle and only honest means for managing one's finances.

Corresponding to changes taking place in the economy were changes taking place in the moral culture. Though the virtue of thrift may have been rarely mentioned in the literature on moral formation before the Gilded Age, a rich, consistent culture of restraint had been articulated. The idea of thrift was, in many ways, both alien to and derivative of that culture. It was alien because thrift was a negative virtue, emerging as it would against the affirmations of justice and generosity. It was derivative because while compatible with the moral controls of Reformed Protestantism, thrift by itself was never sanctioned by it theologically. In matters of money, thrift was prudence minus justice. To the Puritan mind, this would look much like greedy accumulation. Thrift could only emerge by a dilution of the Calvinist culture of restraint by the kind of pragmatism presaged a century earlier by Benjamin Franklin.

Franklin is important to the story for several reasons. His approbations of thrift were moral in character, but they were derived primarily by pragmatic concerns. In the eighteenth century, one could be imprisoned for debt; in fact, Franklin's prospective patron as a young man (a governor of Pennsylvania) was imprisoned for this reason. Thrift was a safeguard against such consequences. "He that goes a borrowing goes a sorrowing," said Poor Richard. The moral meaning of frugality for Franklin was the preservation of personal freedom and the possibility of changing one's lot in life. In his tract "The Way to Wealth," he wrote, "The borrower is a slave to the lender, and the debtor to the creditor, disdain the chain, preserve your freedom; and maintain your independency: be industrious and free; be frugal and free."[38] This logic and its application were well ahead of their time. The idea that ordinary people could achieve freedom and self-sufficiency through industry and thrift was, in critical respects, revolutionary.[39]

Yet in the late nineteenth century, Franklin's virtue of thrift, rooted in the pragmatism of individual independence, had become commonplace.[40] The complications and exigencies of industrialization and urbanization for ordinary people created conditions in which thrift was completely plausible. What is more, popular myth celebrated the individual who, having started with nothing, had accumulated enormous fortunes due to the disciplined practice of saving his or her hard-earned money.

Thus, while the tendency of people to be careful with their possessions and money had not changed much on the surface, a subtle but important change had taken place. A discourse of thrift emerged as the larger Calvinist culture of restraint receded. What had always been more or less implicit became explicit; what began as the fruit of piety increasingly became a strategy of personal well-being.

Thrift Education

It was in this way and in this sense that thrift became an explicit part of the common culture in late nineteenth-century America. With the expansion of free public education, it was only natural that the teaching of thrift would become a part of the educational mission.

In 1902, James Hamilton, a professor of sociology at Syracuse University, made a case for saving as a matter of state educational policy.[41] This was an idea whose time was about to come. Savings institutions proliferated in the late nineteenth and early twentieth centuries—in banks, of course, but also within post offices and at places of employment. Hamilton argued for their establishment in the schools as a means of inculcating habits of thrift in the children. Children would learn thrift by practicing thrift. Indeed, this had already been established successfully in England—with the creation of more than 7,000 "penny banks" by the first decade of the twentieth century—and their educational effect had proved considerable.[42] Though one can find their existence in America as early as 1885, school savings banks did not catch on until the first decade of the new century. Established by local banks in the schools, the school savings banks enabled students to bring money they had earned or had been given by their parents on banking days and give it to a representative from the bank, who would then deposit it into personal savings accounts.

By 1910, Massachusetts passed the first law requiring school banking programs. Not long after, New York, New Jersey, California, and Minnesota did the same.[43] In 1915, a total of 1,925 schools in 280 cities, representing nearly 400,000 students nationwide, had savings banks.[44]

Youth organizations also took up the cause. The Boy Scouts of America was founded in 1908 as an institution committed to transforming boys into men.

Among the laws memorized by every Scout was the rule that "a Scout is thrifty." As the 1908 Boy Scouts' manual explained, a Scout "saves every penny he can, and puts it into the bank, so that he may have money to keep himself when out of work, and thus not make himself a burden to others; or that he may have money to give away to others when they need it."[45] The YMCA and the YWCA followed suit, warning young men and women of the grim consequences of squandering time and money and teaching thrift as an alternative. They too established "thrift clubs" to encourage boys and young men to make regular deposits.

Importantly, thrift education was not just a movement of the white middle classes. At Tuskegee Institute at the turn of the century, Booker T. Washington regularly lectured students on the building of character. Thrift was a theme he returned to from time to time, and, as he made clear, thrift was essential to progress for the race. In "A Penny Saved," Washington reminded his students of the many times he had urged them "to economize your time, to save your time, . . . to make the most of every minute and hour of your existence."[46] This was to stand against "the hurtful reputation which a large proportion of the people of our race get in one way or another because of this seeming inability to put a proper value upon time, or a proper value upon the importance of keeping one's word in connection with obligations." "The people who succeed," he argued, "are, very largely, those who learn to economize time, in the ways I have referred to, and those who also have learned to save, not only time, but money." Against the accusation of materialism, Washington argued that "in order to get hold of the spiritually best and highest things in life there are certain material things that we are compelled to have first"—among these, a "decent house" and "good nourishing food, well-cooked." Money "enables a person to become a good, steady, safe citizen," "develops foresight," and "gives us a certain amount of self-respect." What is the means of acquiring wealth? "People cannot get hold of money—or at least cannot keep hold of it—who have not learned to exercise self-control. They must be able to say, 'No.' I want you students, when you go out from here, to be able to say 'No.'" Concluding his remarks, Washington declared, "We cannot get upon our feet, as a people, until we learn the saving habit; until we learn to save every nickel, every dime and every dollar that we can spare."[47]

Two important events launched thrift education into a national phenomenon. The first was the financial panic of 1907, when the nation's gold shortage triggered a run on the undercapitalized trust banks. While the most significant result of this crisis was the establishment of the Federal Reserve Bank, ordinary people were encouraged to do their part as well, which meant putting their savings into banks.

In response, initiatives were taken up in many quarters, but one of the more ambitious was the formation of the American Society for Thrift in 1914. Its chief aim was to devise a strategy "to promote thrift among the people of the

United States" through "education in the principles of thrift and economy."[48] Within a year its founder, Simon Straus, a successful businessman from Chicago, had announced a "national thrift movement" that would, among other things, press for the enactment of laws mandating the teaching of thrift in all public schools.[49] The society took its case to the National Education Association (NEA), which responded with a national thrift education plan whose capstone was two essay contests. Adults were given the challenge to create the best outline for a curriculum in thrift, while children were to write about the importance of thrift. In 1916, 20,000 children submitted entries, and in the following year there were more than 100,000 entries. Textbooks followed—at least fifteen published between 1915 and 1919.[50] And, as important, the lessons of thrift became integrated into the larger moral educational agenda of the time.[51]

The second catalytic event was world war. Thrift became a national priority for the simple reason that the war effort required citizens to make sacrifices. In this setting, the National Education Association made thrift education among its highest priorities, devoting speeches and workshops to the topic at every major assembly.[52] Conservation of resources was encouraged—civic organizations of all types joined a thrift campaign to ration food and to collect clothes, scrap metal, rubber, and the like—and so too was the purchasing of savings bonds as a means of financing the war effort.[53] By the end of the war, Straus could conclude:

> The war did more to teach thrift to mankind than any event in history. The victory which we won was not alone one of right and justice; it also was a victory of thrift. And the peace that has come to the world, glorious alike it in its realities and its possibilities of human betterment, must be a peace of thrift.[54]

Indeed, the war did galvanize opinion around the importance of thrift, but it also fundamentally transformed the meaning of thrift. Thrift had now become a republican virtue. On the surface, the conspicuous practice of thrift through the war was one way for citizens to demonstrate their patriotism.

But this view extended beyond the war. In the most widely respected and widely circulated civics textbooks of the period, Arthur Dunn wrote:

> Thrift is necessary. . . for good citizenship. It is by thrift that CAPITAL is accumulated with which to carry on the world's work. The citizen who saves and invests his savings in a home, in business enterprises, in bonds or savings stamps, not only makes his own future secure, but becomes identified with the community and takes a greater interest in it. The thrifty citizen inspires the confidence of the community, and acquires an influence in community affairs that the unthrifty citizen does not enjoy.[55]

Even more, thrift was the key to nation building. As Straus put it, "America today stands in the position in which all her economic problems must be solved through thrift. . . . Unless our people gain a deep, sincere appreciation of the absolute necessity for thrift, we cannot hope to hold the proud position we occupy as the flag bearer of nations."[56]

But above all, Dunn argued, thrift "is the very essence of democracy. For democracy means freedom, equality of opportunity, 'self-determination.' There is nothing in the world that will so establish one's faith in the future and that will, therefore, give that freedom of spirit upon which democracy depends, as the wise use of today and of today's resources."[57] There are echoes of Franklin's pragmatism here; however, the freedom intended was not the freedom of personal financial independence but the political freedom achieved by a democratic nation against its enemies.[58]

Dunn's work reflected not only the change in the meaning of thrift common to the time but also the breathless optimism for what its practice among all Americans might achieve. He was not alone in this. Dunn's text was part of a larger wave of thrift education at the start of the 1920s. The Lippincott Company's Thrift Text series, designed to supplement the reading in elementary and secondary school courses, was one important effort. The U.S. Treasury Department also took an active role by producing and distributing booklets such as *Ten Lessons in Thrift*.[59] Along with the numerous civic organizations involved in the wartime thrift effort, the Treasury Department issued a statement articulating its highest hopes: in the future, "thrift education [must] be made a part of the course of study in all school systems."[60]

Indeed, the expectations were great right through the 1920s. At this point, there were more than 12,000 schools with savings banks in them. One educator, writing at the end of the decade, put it this way: "With such a universal interest in the subject, the implications for the future of thrift education in the United States are tremendous."[61] As it turned out, however, she could not have been more mistaken, for this was just the moment when thrift education in any traditional sense lost traction.

THE NEW AND "TRUE" MEANING OF THRIFT

Technological, managerial, and bureaucratic advances in manufacturing and finance in the early decades of the twentieth century combined to accelerate productivity and lower costs as never before. The Great War only crystallized these trends. As Stuart Chase observed, the same number of workers were employed in 1929 as in 1919, but they were turning out roughly 40 percent more goods.[62] As a Department of Labor report claimed, America was "experiencing what is perhaps the most remarkable advance in productive efficiency in the history of the modern industrial system."[63]

It was not long before popular scholarship and polemics were beginning to emerge to explain the implications of mass production to the American public: Thomas Carver's *Present Economic Revolution in the United States* (1925), Rexford Guy Tugwell's *Industry's Coming of Age* (1927), Paul Mazur's *American Prosperity* (1928), as well as Chase's *Prosperity* (1929) and *The Economy of Abundance* (1934). In all of this, one can see the sentiment surrounding traditional notions of thrift shifting and shifting quickly. For example, in Chase's view, "when the formula of capitalism sags, due to excess plant capacity, saving, hoarding, thrift, operate to freeze economic activity, forcing it to ever lower levels. What was once a virtue becomes in these circumstances a vice. The moral duty rests with the spender, not with the hoarder; turning traditional doctrine upside down."[64] His point, and the argument of an increasing number of observers, was that energetic spending by the masses, rather than their saving, was the key to the nation's future prosperity.

This is not to suggest that consumption was ignored in the education of the young prior to the quarter-century mark. As early as 1909, the American Home Economics Association announced that "education for consumption" would be one of the goals of the field.[65] Indeed, the topic was a growing concern within the profession through the second decade of the century. Yet in these early years, consumer education was regarded as complementary to the virtue and habits of thrift. This was a consumption oriented toward the interests of thrift; a consumption that aimed to be intelligent and parsimonious. It was not until the 1920s that the idea of spending itself—as distinct from saving—came to be viewed as the means by which the economy might be energized.

So what was it? "Is a nation . . . that spends freely more or less prosperous than a nation which restricts consumption, lives simply and saves thriftily?" Who holds the answer, the "thrift school" or the "spending school"?[66] The economist Alvin Hansen posed this question in 1920; by the early 1930s, enlightened opinion had answered it in favor of the "spending school." By 1929, home economist and marketing expert Christine Frederick could proclaim in her book *Selling Mrs. Consumer* that "consumptionism is the name given to the new doctrine; and it is admitted today to be the greatest ideal that America has to give to the world; the idea that workmen and masses be looked upon not simply as workers and producers but as consumers. . . . Pay them more, sell them more, prosper more is the equation."[67] Frederick's was not a lone voice but one echoing and echoed by others in books such as Hazel Kyrk's *Theory of Consumption* (1923), Elizabeth Hoyt's *Consumption of Wealth* (1928), and Paul Nystrom's *Economic Principles of Consumption* (1929).[68] Even in the early years of the Great Depression, when few had money to spend, education in spending became a high priority in the schools.

However the Depression affected people economically, it had a considerable impact on the conventional wisdom on thrift for it revealed the utter inadequacy of individual saving. Individual thrift simply could not provide protection and security against disaster—whether economic collapse or mere illness. Against these kinds of misfortune, the idea of a rainy-day fund was nonsensical. Besides, the establishment of Social Security and unemployment benefits on the part of the government and health insurance plans and retirement plans on the part of more and more businesses meant that thrift was being collectivized; individuals did not have to save for themselves in the same way as they might have before.

Of even greater significance was the subtle redefinition of thrift from saving to "wise spending" and "proper use," and from personal restraint in financial matters to prudent and efficient release. This was thrift "in its true light." Americans, it was said, need to be "less concerned about saving per se, [and] more concerned about conservation, and proper utilization as a means to greater service, greater welfare and greater happiness."[69] In this way, average Americans were encouraged to be more businesslike in the way they managed their money, where income could be regarded as capital and expenses could be seen as investment. Carver, an economist from Harvard, went further than this. "The thrifty person," he argued,

> is not a miser. He is one who spends money just as freely as the extravagant man, but he spends it wisely instead of unwisely. He spends it for durable things, instead of for transient things. . . . When we realize that thrift consists in spending money wisely, instead of unwisely, we shall very easily see that the thrifty man spends exactly as much money as the thriftless man, provided he has as much money to spend. Moreover, in the long run, the thrifty man will spend more, because he will have more to spend than the thriftless man; and the thrifty community will be a community in which more money is spent than in the thriftless community.[70]

Thrift, he concluded, "consists in buying, but in buying wisely. Urge every one, if you please, to buy and to buy now, but URGE HIM TO BUY THINGS THAT WILL GIVE HIM MORE BUYING POWER NEXT YEAR AND EVERY YEAR."[71] Through this redefinition, the older moral vocabulary had become mostly obsolete.

The field of education trailed behind these trends by about a decade. It was not until the mid-1930s that education as a profession began to make these adjustments in the curriculum. This was reflected in the greater presence of consumption as a topic or theme in professional journals, textbooks, and curricula.[72] At this point, consumer education was confined, by and large, to "home economics" classes with the goal of encouraging practical and efficient everyday use of one's income in securing goods and services in the marketplace.

Perhaps the most wide-ranging means for teaching the new meaning of thrift to children at this time was the practice of giving children a regular allowance. Though the practice of giving allowances extends back at least to the seventeenth century among the privileged and titled, it did not become a practice among middle-class families until the turn of the twentieth century when, as Viviana Zelizer observes, the meaning of childhood shifted from "useful" to "priceless"—when children moved from the agricultural or industrial workplace to the schools.[73] It was not until the 1930s that the practice became embedded with the logic and practice of consumerism.

From the beginning, the idea was that allowances would provide children with hands-on experience learning good "business methods," among which were how to understand values in the marketplace and how to "buy judiciously."[74] While some part of the allowance should be earmarked for specific purchases like school supplies, Sunday collection, and club dues, advocates argued, part of it should be unrestricted, and parents should exercise little control over this unrestricted portion. The dominant theme in this literature was that "money is for spending."[75] "The primary object," as one advocate put it, "is to teach [the child] how to spend money rather than to save it."[76] When saving was discussed, it was not saving for the rainy-day fund but rather "saving up" in order to make larger purchases. Many of the popular-magazine authors tell parents to teach children about money management by taking them shopping. For example, "Take your children with you when you shop—not just because you must but to involve them in the process of shopping. Explain to small children that you buy a particular brand of cereal because it is more nutritious than other brands, and a particular size package because of the saving. Don't assume they're too young to understand."[77] Moreover, parents are told to "involve your child in somewhat larger money decisions,"[78] and that "it is vital to take children along on shopping trips so that they learn how to squeeze value from a dollar."[79] "The next time you go shopping," parents are advised, "tell your child to bring her money if she thinks she might want to purchase something."[80] Zelizer summarizes the change succinctly: "In the new consumer society of the twentieth century, the old lessons of thrift and saving were no longer sufficient. By teaching how to spend wisely, the allowance would train children as efficient shoppers."[81]

While allowances were clearly meant as tools to teach children about money management, wise spending, and, to a lesser degree, giving, the moral logic is thin. At this point, psychologists and educators had become the chief moral advocates for the young. From their perspective, an allowance would inculcate self-reliance and responsibility and provide a way for the child to express his or her autonomy. Surely the child would make mistakes in the process, but he would learn from them and become, over time, savvier in the marketplace. In this way, the growing practice of giving allowances provided an education into the new culture of consumerism.

In sum, by the mid-1930s, thrift education had become embedded in a growing culture of consumerism. Whatever remained of thrift education, traditionally understood, after the advent of mass production disappeared with the shift from an industrial to a service economy.

Culture and Moral Formation

In any generation, the moral sensibilities of the young are acquired and cultivated in early socialization through the acquisition of language and in the natural participation in everyday life. Language itself provides horizons for the moral imagination. Yet primary socialization is also that stage of life when moral instruction is articulated, deliberately so. Not only are children told plainly what is right and wrong or good or bad, but they are also often offered reasons why they should behave in such a way or avoid behaving in other ways. The whats and whys of the moral life, then, are made explicit for the young by parents, teachers, clergy, and others in ways that eventually become taken for granted when the young become adults. Even if these lessons are not learned well or their truths are regularly violated, they provide a measure against which acts and episodes and life itself are considered and weighed.

Yet morality does not just exist outside of children (or anyone else, for that matter) as an impersonal set of rules and regulations or abstract ideals. It is through the formal and informal means of formation that the moral demands of a community—both positive and negative—are appropriated into consciousness. In other words, it comes to be received by the individual, internalized into subjective consciousness, and soon enough, experienced as the basic ordering categories of life. Morality demands, requires, expects of people, but in a way that makes sense. It prompts, prods, and encourages people, but in a way that seems natural and logical to them. The tension between release and restraint is first experienced in these early years as children negotiate their personal and subjective relationship with a culture that presents itself as external, objective, and coercive.

And so, while the moral formation of children is interesting in its own right, it is also a prism into a larger social world.[82] By looking at the ways in which moral understanding is mediated to children, one can learn much about the moral ideals that prevail at a particular time and place.[83] It mirrors the moral culture that adults prize and thus seek to pass on to succeeding generations; at the same time, it provides a prism through which the particular tensions of release and restraint are worked. When all is said and done, it is for this reason that moral education is always more a reflection of the culture in which it is found than a source of that culture's transformation.

Where does this leave us in the case of thrift and the changing culture of the market?

If the moral admonition of the young is any measure, frugality and thrift were undoubtedly practiced in the seventeenth and early eighteenth centuries among ordinary people, but this was of necessity and, from all indications, not self-consciously for its own sake. Franklin notwithstanding, thrift was certainly no virtue. It only had intelligibility in a moral culture of restraint that was framed by the higher virtues of justice and benevolence. It was not until the second half of the nineteenth century, when industrialization began to generate surplus wealth, that thrift became a virtue celebrated as such and explicitly taught to the young.

What is remarkable is how quickly thrift emerged into popular discourse, was utterly transformed, and then, as quickly as it came into being, mostly evaporated from public consciousness. When the Reverend Eddy wrote, thrift was embedded within admonitions of spiritual well-being. For him and for thrift's other clerical promoters, salvation was at stake. By the end of the nineteenth century, thrift was taught for the moral purposes of financial independence and self-improvement. What was at stake now was the security of the family and the possibility of improving one's lot in life at a time when upward social mobility was possible. By the 1920s, thrift had become regarded as a civic duty—an expression of devotion to the nation and its role as leader of the free world. Democracy itself was at stake. By this time, the educational establishment had excised the language and perspective of religious faith from the discussion of thrift. Religion did not exist either as a framework for understanding thrift's moral meaning or as a source of personal motivation. The incentives were now drawn from psychology. The necessity of thrift, as the renowned educational psychologist Edward Thorndike put it, was simply a matter of "rational insight." In matters of money, "children and adults of uncritical minds" now must be taught to inhibit their "instinctive appetites" and "esteem prudent behavior."[84] Within a decade the meaning of thrift had changed yet again from "saving" to "wise spending." The educators and psychologists, the arbiters of moral admonition, changed their message accordingly, now telling parents that lessons in financial responsibility were an aspect of moral development. Absent of religious, civic, or practical significance, thrift—as wise spending—had become the cultural segue into a new culture of consumption. In any traditional sense, the ideals and practice of thrift had now become obsolete.

In matters of money, it would seem that little has changed since then. In the moral formation of the young, the word *thrift* is rarely if ever used, but it does retain some popular understanding in the realm of time management. As we have seen, the need to "improve" how one spends time—or, at the least, to not waste time through idleness—has been a solid plank in the Protestant ethic for centuries. In earlier centuries, idleness was to be avoided because it was linked to a variety of vices—gambling, fornication, drinking, and the like. To be sure, it still is linked to the vices that teenagers are susceptible to (premarital sex, drug use, theft, and vandalism), but its moral meaning has changed with the times—neither salvific, nor civic, nor personal improvement is at stake. Rather, the imperative to learn how to manage time wisely now points to the development of skills that are essential for success in the professional labor force. The readiness to break away from restraints, a willingness to take financial risks through speculation, the ability to be "fast in making and spending money"—these attributes, characteristic of the "fast young man" that the Reverend Daniel Eddy castigated in 1849, do not appear so objectionable 150 years later. With the exception of the vice of smoking, the fast young man would seem to be an exemplar of precisely the qualities our society now prizes—qualities essential for success and social mobility in the fast-paced, high-demand, and rapidly changing commercial republic.

Notes

1. Daniel C. Eddy, *The Young Man's Friend*, 2nd ed. (New York: Hurst, 1865).
2. Ibid., 126. Additional quotations in this paragraph are taken from pp. 126, 134, 136, 140–44 (emphasis in original).
3. Ibid., 169.
4. Ibid., 260 (emphasis in original).
5. John Locke, *Some Thoughts Concerning Education* (Cambridge: Cambridge University Press, 1880).
6. Mary Cable, *The Little Darlings: A History of Child Rearing in America* (New York: Scribner, 1975), 51.
7. Locke, *Some Thoughts*, 29 (emphasis in original).
8. Ibid., 25. See also 21.
9. Ibid., 29.
10. There was one exception: "There is one, and but one Fault, for which, I think Children should be beaten, and that is, *Obstinacy* or *Rebellion*." Yet he goes on to say that "the Shame of the Whipping, and not the Pain, should be the greatest Part of the Punishment." Ibid., 56–57.
11. Ibid., 61.
12. Ibid., 36 (emphasis in original). Elsewhere, he writes, "Shame of doing amiss, and deserving Chastisement, is the only true Restraint belonging to Virtue." Ibid., 57.
13. Ibid., 89.
14. Ibid., 181. See also 109ff.
15. Ibid., 182.
16. Ibid., 89.
17. Ibid.
18. Ibid.
19. Ibid., 116 (emphasis added).
20. Ibid..
21. Ibid., 134–35.
22. It is not insignificant that Locke's parents and siblings were Puritans. His father even served in a cavalry company on the Puritan side in the early stages of the English civil war.
23. For example, Locke insisted that the child's habits be shaped in accordance with the virtues of piety, loyalty, industry, and temperance. Cotton Mather argued that children were

to be taught to "remember four words . . . and attempt all that is comprised in them: obedience, honesty, industry and piety." Cotton Mather, *Essays to Do Good* (1710; New York: American Tract Society, n.d.), 46–47.

24. As implied previously, the meaning of piety for Locke was somewhat, though not altogether, different from the meaning held by the Calvinists. The theme of piety was articulated in good Puritan form by Benjamin Wadsworth in 1712: "Tis absolutely necessary for your Children to be truly Religious. They're Children of wrath by Nature; they can't escape Hell, without true Faith and Repentance. . . . Twould be barbarous, inhumane, worse than brutish, if you should neglect the Bodies of your Children; and thro' sloth and carelessness suffer them to starve and die: how much greater then is your barbarity and wickedness, if you take no care to prevent the everlasting ruine of their Souls?" Benjamin Wadsworth, "The Well-Ordered Family," in *The Colonial American Family: Collected Essays*, ed. David J. Rothman and Sheila M. Rothman (New York: Arno Press, 1972), 71. Needless to say, the social and spiritual pressure on parents was great. "Amazingly great will your guilt and danger be," Wadsworth argued, "if you neglect the Religious Education of your Children" (ibid., 74). To this end, parents were to "see to it that [they] instruct every one of [their] children in the things of God," to "take [their] children with [them] to God's publick worship," and to "indevour [*sic*] that [their] children may rightly understand the great truths and duties of religion" (ibid., 59, 60, 62).

25. In Enos Weed's supplement to the *Educational Directory*, he includes "Twenty Mixed Precepts," nine "Directions for Children's Behavior While at Home," and twenty-eight "Directions for Children's Behavior While in Company." None of these lists mentions thrift, although there is a warning against idleness. Enos Weed, *Educational Directory* (Morristown, NJ: Johnson, 1803).

26. *The New England Primer* (Boston: Benjamin Harris, 1690). The first edition was printed in 1690 and was still in use in 1900. Its purpose was to teach children to read through rhyme, poetry, prayer, creeds, and exhortation.

27. The full title of this work is *The Mother's Friend or Familiar Directions for Forming the Mental and Moral Habits* (Cooperstown, NY: H. and E. Phinney, 1843). The original American publication was in 1834, but even at that time, it was a republication of an English work published earlier, which cited neither an author nor a date. This selection is taken from chap. 7, "Activity and Industry," 77–78.

28. Ibid, 90.

29. Eleazar Moody, *The School of Good Manners: Composed for the Help of Parents in Teaching Their Children How to Carry It in Their Places during Their Minority* (Boston: Boyle, 1775), 32. This was first printed in the Americas in 1715.

30. *Mother's Friend*, 80.

31. Weed, *Educational Directory*. See also David J. Rothman and Sheila M. Rothman, eds., *The Colonial American Family: Collected Essays* (New York: Arno Press, 1972), 55.

32. In *Mother's Friend*, the dangers are elaborated. "It is . . . owing to idleness, that so many boys begin gaming in the streets, and are led on from pitch-farthing, &c., to better, swearing, and other pernicious habits. It is, in most cases, owing to idleness, that young people of both sexes are tempted to go into bad company and to proceed from step to step, till our penitentiaries and prisons are crowded with wretched inhabitants, who, but for the want of good training in their early years, might have lived with present comfort and a well grounded hope of future happiness" (90–91).

33. Wadsworth, "Well-Ordered Family," 101–2.

34. *The New England Primer*, 40. Likewise in Samuel Phillips, *A Child Well Instructed in the Principles of the Christian Religion* (Boston: S. Kneeland and T. Green for D. Henchman in Corn-Hill, 1738), where in the discussion of the eighth commandment, the argument is made "that it is our Duty, not only to shun and avoid the gross act of stealth and robbery; whether by sea or land, in the house or by the way; as also that we do not, in a way of commerce and trading, overreach, or defraud, any person whatsoever: But, on the other hand, that we unfeignedly wish our neighbour's prosperity, and promote the same together with our own, as there shall be opportunity; as also that we cheerfully devote a suitable proportion of our incomes (a tenth at least) to pious and charitable uses."

35. Weed, *Educational Directory*, 50.

36. In addition to the other works referenced, see Isaac Watts's *Discourse on the Education of Children and Youth*, first published posthumously in 1754; and John S. C. Abbott, *The Mother at Home* (New York: American Tract Society, 1833).

37. Eddy, *Young Man's Friend*, 127–28.

38. Benjamin Franklin, "The Way to Wealth," 1758, first appeared in the 1758 preface to *Poor Richard's Almanack* (Philadelphia: B. Franklin, 1758); http://www.swarthmore.edu/SocSci/bdorsey1/41docs/52-fra.html (accessed July 21, 2006).

39. See the interview with Franklin scholar J. A. Leo Lemay in "Interview: Benjamin Franklin," *In Character* 1 (Fall 2004): 24–31, and at http://www.incharacter.org.

40. The growing acceptance of this take on thrift was partly seen with the publication in 1838 of the fourth of the McGuffey Readers, William McGuffey, *The McGuffey Fourth Eclectic Reader* (New York: Clark and Maynard, 1866). In it were stories such as "Waste Not, Want Not" (reading 21), "The Consequences of Idleness" (reading 39), "The Advantages of Industry" (reading 40), and "Hugh Idle and Mr. Toil" (readings 79 and 80). It is true that not all concerned with the moral formation of the young included thrift in their list of virtues to be learned. For example, Kate Douglass Wiggin and Felix Adler, in two important books, made no mention of it. See Kate Douglas Wiggin, *Children's Rights: A Book of Nursery Logic* (Boston: Houghton Mifflin, 1896); Felix Adler, *The Moral Instruction of Children* (New York: D. Appleton, 1892).

41. James Henry Hamilton, *Savings and Savings Institutions* (New York: Harper, 1902).

42. As put in the 1911 *Encyclopedia* (Cambridge: Cambridge University Press, 1911). "Although the financial result is not large, the educational effect of these banks is considerable. It has been found that many children open accounts at outside penny banks in preference to going to those carried on at their own schools, but it is probable that the idea of so doing is often suggested by the school savings bank." This is available at http://www.1911encyclopedia.org.

43. See Carobel Murphey's history of thrift education in *Thrift through Education* (New York: A. S. Barnes, 1929).

44. George Zook, "Thrift in the United States," *Annals of the American Academy of Political and Social Science* 87 (January 1920): 208.

45. In 1911, the explanation was revised as follows: "A Scout . . . does not wantonly destroy property. He works faithfully, wastes nothing, and makes the best use of his opportunities. He saves his money so that he may pay his own way, be generous to those in need, and helpful to worthy objects. He may work for pay but must not receive tips for courtesies or good turns." The 1908 and 1911 Boy Scout Laws can be seen at http://www.inquiry.net/ideals/scout_law /chart.htm (accessed July 21, 2006).

46. Quotations here are taken from Booker T. Washington, *Character Building: Being Addresses Delivered on Sunday Evenings to the Students of Tuskegee Institute* (New York: Doubleday, Page, 1903), 267–78.

47. In the address titled "The Virtue of Simplicity," Washington repeated this theme that students make sure "that in no department is there wastefulness. We must try to make every dollar go as far as possible." Ibid., 37.

48. Simon Straus, *The Greater Thrift* (Philadelphia: Lippincott, 1919), 68.

49. Ibid., 103ff.

50. Roy Blakey, "The New American Thrift," *Annals of the American Academy of Political and Social Science* 87 (January 1920): 1–3.

51. One interesting indication of this was "The Children's Morality Code." This code, conceived by William J. Hutchins, was awarded the $5,000 Donor's Prize, for the best children's code of morals, in the 1916 National Morality Codes Competition. Every state participated, and the competition was under the auspices of the Character Education Institution. "The Children's Morality Code" was intended to "express intelligent public opinion as to the moral ideas which ought to be inculcated in the minds and hearts of children." These are laws that "the best Americans have always obeyed." The fourth item under the first law, "The Law of Self-Control," is "I will control my actions. I will be careful and thrifty, and insist on doing right." The rationale for the law of self-control is that "those who best control themselves can best serve their country." The seventh law, "The Law of Reliability," has this as its first item: "I will be honest in every act, and careful with money. I will not cheat, nor pretend, nor sneak." The fourth and final item under the tenth law, "The Law of Team-Work," states, "When I have received money for my work, I will be neither a miser nor a spendthrift. I will save or spend as one of the friendly workers of America." William J. Hutchins, "The Children's Morality Code," *Journal of the National Education Association* 13 (November 1924): 292.

52. Lee Moore Hunter, "Learning to Spend: From Thrift to Consumer Education in the Era of Emerging Mass Consumption" (Ph.D. diss., Boston University, 1983), 21.

53. It is significant that the Liberty War bonds were advertised primarily through posters showing images of German soldiers destroying villages, murdering children, or capturing nuns. The implication was clear: the only way to survive the wrath of the wicked Hun was to purchase Liberty Bonds.

54. Straus, *Greater Thrift*, 21.

55. Arthur William Dunn, *Community Civics and Rural Life* (Boston: Heath, 1920), chap. 13; see http://www.pos1.info/c/cmmcv (accessed July 21, 2006). This message is repeated in all the versions of this text: see Arthur William Dunn, *Community Civics for City Schools* (Boston: Heath, 1921), and later editions of Arthur William Dunn, *The Community and the Citizen* (Boston: Heath, c. 1914).

56. Simon W. Straus, "The Patriotism of War Savings," in "Thrift," National Education Association pamphlet, 1918, quoted in Dunn, *Community Civics and Rural Life*, chap. 13. See also Thomas Nixon Carver, "The Relation of Thrift to Nation Building," *Annals of the American Academy of Political and Social Science* 87 (January 1920): 4–8.

57. Dunn, *Community Civics and Rural Life*, chap. 13.

58. See William Mather Lewis, "Freedom through Thrift," *Annals of the American Academy of Political and Social Science* 87 (January 1920): 9–10.

59. Murphey, *Thrift through Education*, 13.

60. U.S. Treasury Department statement, quoted in Leo Day Woodworth and American Banker's Association, *School Savings Banking* (New York: Ronald Press, 1923), 65. The hope was that thrift would be not simply a separate subject left to the discretion of the individual teacher but rather a central part of the general school curriculum.

61. Murphey, *Thrift through Education*, 19.

62. Stuart Chase, *Prosperity: Fact or Myth* (New York: Charles Boni Paper Books, 1929), 136.

63. Quoted in Rexford Guy Tugwell, *Industry's Coming of Age* (New York: Harcourt Brace, 1927), 2–3.

64. Stuart Chase, *The Economy of Abundance* (New York: Macmillan, 1934), 275.

65. Claud Charles Thompson, "The Influence of Social Conditions and Curriculum Trends on Consumer Education before World War II" (Ph.D. diss., University of Wisconsin, 1970), 1.

66. Alvin H. Hansen, "Thrift and Labor," *Annals of the American Academy of Political and Social Science* 87 (January 1920): 44.

67. Christine Frederick, *Selling Mrs. Consumer* (New York: The Business Bourse, 1929), quoted in Hunter, "Learning to Spend," 43.

68. Hazel Kyrk, *A Theory of Consumption* (New York: Houghton Mifflin, 1923); Elizabeth Hoyt, *The Consumption of Wealth* (New York: Ronald Press, 1928); Paul Nystrom, *Economic Principles of Consumption* (New York: Macmillan, 1929).

69. Blakey, "New American Thrift," 3.

70. Carver, "Relation of Thrift to Nation Building," 5. See also Lewis, "Freedom through Thrift," 9.

71. Carver, "Relation of Thrift to Nation Building," 8 (emphasis in original).

72. Hunter, "Learning to Spend," 94–104.

73. See Viviana Zelizer, *Pricing the Priceless Child* (New York: Basic Books, 1985), 103–12. The wages of working-class children prior to the start of the twentieth century were regarded as part of the family income. Wages were not theirs to spend.

74. Carlotta Ford, "Shall I Give My Child an Allowance?" *Ladies' Home Journal*, June 1930, 94; cf. Benjamin C. and Sidionie Matsner Gruenberg, "Teaching Children the Use of Money," *Parents*, December 1931, 50; Gladys Denny Shultz, "Their Own Christmas Money to Spend," *Better Homes and Gardens*, December 1930, 54. The consistency of the advice from the 1930s to the present is remarkable. In 1956, an allowance "is a method by which your child can learn to handle money in a sensible manner, and with a good sense of values." Julius Segal, "Your Child Has Financial Problems, Too," *Better Homes and Gardens*, January 1956, 90. In 1986, an allowance trains children "to budget and to make decisions," and "to be more careful shoppers." Grace W. Weinstein, "'My Own Money': An Allowance Is a Perfect Tool for Teaching Your Child Money Management," *Parents*, November 1986, 56. Even the language used by the authors is virtually unchanged over more than fifty years.

75. The allowance also should never be used as a bribe, nor should it be withheld as punishment. It is the child's "share of the family income," an entitlement. Mary Robbins, "Learning to Spend and Save," *Parents*, December 1935, 82; Jeannette Eyerly, "What Should You Do about Allowances?" *Better Homes and Gardens*, March 1951, 150; Jeannette Eyerly, "What's Wrong with This Family?" *Better Homes and Gardens*, June 1951, 249. See also Don Dinkmeyer and Gary D. McKay, *Raising a Responsible Child: Practical Steps to Successful Family Relationships* (New York: Simon and Schuster, 1973), 225.

76. Shultz, "Their Own Christmas Money," 30. See also Jerome Beatty, "A Budget Plan That Works," *Parents*, October 1936, 72; Marion M. Miller, "Learning about Money," *Parents*, May 1942, 77; C. G. Moser, "Making the Most of the Money They Have," *Parents*, April 1946, 101; Grace W. Weinstein, "My Own Money," *Parents*, November 1986, 56–61.

77. Grace W. Weinstein, *Teaching Children about Money*, Public Affairs Pamphlet 593 (New York: Public Affairs Committee, 1981), 5.

78. Francis Roberts, "Are Allowances Obsolete?" *Parents*, February 1981, 90.

79. Weinstein, *Teaching Children about Money*, 27.

80. Pamela Kramer, "Little Spenders," *Parents*, September 2000, 262.

81. Zelizer, *Pricing the Priceless Child*, 105.

82. Émile Durkheim argued that by examining a phenomenon at its incipient stages of development, one has the opportunity to learn about the phenomenon as a more complex reality. So it is, I would contend, with moral development and moral instruction.

83. "Character," as Ralph Waldo Emerson put it in his classic essay on this topic, is "this moral order seen through the medium of individual nature." It is for this reason that he viewed "men of character [as] the conscience of the society to which they belong." Ralph Waldo Emerson, *Character* (Philadelphia: Henry Altemus, 1896), 10–11.

84. The vocabulary comes from Edward L. Thorndike, "Psychological Notes on the Motives for Thrift," *Annals of the American Academy of Political and Social Science* 87 (January 1920): 212–18.

11}

The Virtue of Consumption

CHALLENGING THRIFT IN AN AGE OF TRANSITION

Lawrence B. Glickman

Contemporary Americans view thrift as quite literally old-fashioned, a forgotten (and, to some, irrelevant) virtue from a bygone era. "We've gone from . . . sacrifice to self-indulgence," asserts the pundit Cal Thomas, echoing an observation that many columnists before him have made, particularly the large number who compared what they saw as the consumerist patriotism following the tragic events of September 11, 2001, with the sacrificial patriotism of the home front during World War II. "Sacrifice is out. Self-indulgence is in," wrote Marie Coco of *Newsday* in response to the call from President George W. Bush and other politicians for Americans to buy, buy, buy as a means of demonstrating their patriotism. "Our mothers had to give up their silk stockings. We're being asked to make a national trip to the shopping mall." Whereas once, it is believed, thrift was the country's defining social value, many Americans now understand it to be, in the words of one popular commentator, the editor of the *Tightwad Gazette*, an "alternative lifestyle."[1] Although Phillip Longman hoped to "reawaken" this virtue in his 1996 book, *The Return of Thrift*, many Americans believe it to be a lost virtue and a fringe value, held dear by a small cadre of voluntary simplifiers and cultural conservatives but largely abandoned by the majority, whose personal savings rate is at an all-time low (zero, according to an August 2005 report by the U.S. Department of Commerce) and whose borrowing capacities are seemingly unlimited.[2]

When did thrift lose its cultural dominance? Many scholars point to the New Deal era as the key turning point in a long-term renunciation of thrift, a time when both public policy, embodied in Keynesianism, and popular culture, embodied in mass production and consumption, demonstrated that thrift far from being the solution to the nation's problems was in some ways a fundamental cause of them. Others point to the postwar years when, in what Lizabeth Cohen has called the Consumers' Republic, consumption was defined as both a private pleasure and a patriotic duty.[3] Historians of these periods sometimes assume that the diagnosis of one of the nation's economic problems as underconsumption and these eras consumerist solutions were new.

The roots of the assault on thrift, however, extend much farther back in history, to the post–Civil War period and even in some cases to the antebellum era. The "traditional assumptions" of "thrift, restraint, and self-denial" were "beginning to erode" well before the Depression decade, as Alan Brinkley has noted.[4] Urging patrons to buy goods on behalf of what they deemed to be moral causes, abolitionists, Sabbatarians, and other antebellum Americans developed a philosophy of moral consumerism. And a half century before New Dealers rejected Say's law—the doctrine that production creates its own purchasing power—many working-class leaders had already done so. Long before John Maynard Keynes coined the phrase "the paradox of thrift," consumer activists, proponents of labor's "consumer turn," and many Progressive reformers had developed similar arguments about the dangers of excessive thrift. Indeed, New Deal and postwar theories and policies of underconsumption are best thought of as a culmination of patterns of action and ideas that had been germinating for the prior two generations. The era of what some historians have called the New Deal Order, from the 1930s to the 1980s, was critical not because intellectuals and politicians invented a new anti-thrift consciousness but because in this period such a worldview, which had roots in the late nineteenth and early twentieth centuries, was consolidated and popularized. Even in this period, it must be pointed out, thrift was not entirely abandoned; indeed, practices of thriftiness were part of the folklore (and even the reality) of both the Great Depression and the World War II home front. They remained a continuing, if less noted, aspect of postwar American culture as well.

Yet even if thrift has not been abandoned, it has been displaced. The story of the displacement of thrift is complex, containing many strands. This essay will take up several significant elements of anti-thrift thought and practice that emerged between the Civil War and World War II. It will examine, in roughly chronological order, consumer activists and working-class intellectuals in the nineteenth century, as well as a group of Progressive Era activists and New Deal planners. The essay will conclude by turning again to consumer activists, this time in the twentieth century.

Other groups, it should be emphasized, participated in this early reevaluation of thrift. In the late nineteenth century, the antithrift message, articulated in distinct and not always consistent ways, manifested itself in almost every conceivable arena, from the labor movement (which underwent a "consumerist turn"), to politics (where the tariff, the currency question, and the question of maintaining and expanding the so-called American standard of living all became an important part of public rhetoric and policy), to domestic furnishings and architecture (where, as Michael McGerr notes, "the homes of the rich suggest how the old standards of restraint and frugality had decayed").[5] As Jackson Lears has demonstrated, post–Civil War middle- and upper-class

Americans in search of authentic experience also contributed to the acceptance of consumption as part of the modern landscape.[6] African American practitioners of what Evelyn Brooks Higginbotham has called the "politics of respectability" did so as well. By insisting on their right to dress well, furnish homes in comfort, and participate in respectable amusements, these African Americans made claims to the fruits of American consumer society—claims that, notes Higginbotham, "invariably held subversive implications" in a society bent on white supremacy.[7] Finally, as various groups of Americans were reevaluating thrift in practice, a group of economists, mostly outsiders too, were in the process of reconsidering it in theory. Simon Patten and his followers as well as a new group of marginalist economists (who challenged both producerism and the labor theory of value, replacing them with consumerist understandings of the creation of value) began, in different ways, to understand consumption as the fulcrum of economic activity and health.[8]

While a complete history of the reevaluation of thrift would need to consider each of these challenges, the five episodes treated in this essay—covering roughly the century-long period from the antebellum era through the Great Depression—convey the central elements of that history: namely, the de-moralization of thrift and the concomitant moralization of consumption. Early nineteenth-century consumer activists, though hardly advocates of conspicuous consumption, held that spending, especially in the context of the "buycotts" that they invented in the 1820s, could serve moral purposes. Proponents of what I have elsewhere called labor's "consumerist turn" in the late nineteenth century argued that consumption was an instrument of solidarity and a cornerstone of civilization.[9] The Progressive reformers associated with the National Consumers League (NCL) challenged the notion that the thrifty shopper was necessarily a virtuous one. Many New Dealers came to the conclusion that at the macroeconomic level, thrift was bad public policy. Contemporaneously, another group of consumer activists who called for a boycott of Japanese silk in the late 1930s promoted the idea that consumption could serve not only the cause of virtue but also that of beauty and pleasure.

Cumulatively, these challenges amounted to a repudiation of what I call the reigning "ideology of thrift," defined as a belief that thrift was not only a highly important moral attribute but the essence of individual well-being, as well as social and political health. In addition to challenging the primacy of thrift, members of these groups began to articulate (tentatively in some cases, fiercely in others) a vision in which thrift's opposite, spending, served, under the right conditions, as an important means toward the ends of justice and morality—and eventually pleasure and beauty—previously associated with thrift. Many, perhaps most, Americans in this period continued, as they do today, to value thrift. Nonetheless, these distinct but reinforcing strands of thought and practice undermined the claim that thrift was virtuous in and of itself. For different reasons, these groups argued that in cases where spending could bring about justice, consumption should be embraced. In rejecting the automatic association of thrift with virtue, then, they also posited something new—a morality of spending.[10]

It is important to note that none of these groups was unambiguous or unambivalent in its praise of consumption, and for the most part they continued to hold thrift in high regard. In this sense, they were transitional figures, situated between what we can call America's Age of Thrift and the era of the Consumers' Republic. Reflecting their debt to the older ideology of thrift, the consumer and labor activists and the Progressive and New Deal reformers continued to tether morality to spending. But they also poked holes in the ideology of thrift, taking it to be not only out of date but also a conduit for injustice and inequality. Some of them began to highlight other positive consequences of spending, focusing increasingly on the public policy benefits and the ways in which consumption could be allied with aesthetics. Although none were ready to accept William Whyte's 1956 claim that "thrift is now un-American" by denying thrift its privileged position as an end in itself and instead redefining it as a means to an end, they introduced an alternative moral economy, one that, in turn, laid the roots for the Consumers' Republic of the postwar years.[11]

These assaults on thrift were both a reflection and a cause of a broader shift in American liberalism, which, in this period, transformed from a philosophy of laissez-faire to a philosophy that authorized state intervention in the economy. They were also both a reflection and a cause of new understandings of morality—one espoused by advocates of the Social Gospel and one that lay at the root of the Progressive enterprise—in which the metric shifted from a focus on individuals to a focus on the broader society. While not denying the ethical importance of individual action to the moral well-being of the individual agent, the groups discussed in this essay argued that, in an increasingly interdependent, market-connected world (a time in which "interdependence has replaced independence," as the economist John Bates Clark declared in 1899), the only way to measure the morality of individual actions was to determine their impact on the broader society.[12] Thrift, like all other practices, they believed, had to be understood in social context. For different reasons, each of these groups came to the conclusion not only that thrift did not in all circumstances serve the body politic but that consumption could be a powerful instrument of moral improvement.

This history of the reevaluation of thrift between the Civil War and World War II, then, is best interpreted not as an abandonment of basic morality, or as a weakening of traditional values (or even a rejection of the value of the personal virtue of thrift itself), but as part of a complex process by which social virtues were redefined. Those who condemned thrift in this period did so because they came to believe, as Brinkley puts it, "that indulgence was a greater social good than abstinence."[13] The word *social* is key: almost all the reformers, activists, and politicians who challenged thrift's hegemony did so because they believed that society no longer benefited from an ideology of thrift. These debunkers of thrift agreed that in a Jeffersonian society of individual producers (artisans, farmers, and other small producers), thrift was a necessary value—good for families and the broader society. The welfare of society, these groups began to argue, depended in good measure on what I call "moral mass consumption," in which citizens exercised the power of the purse not only to pursue private pleasures but also to ensure the well-being of the producers of the goods they bought. Articulators of the critique of thrift posited that America had entered a new era in which interdependence had replaced self-sufficiency and so necessarily required new kinds of solidarities, many of them market-based. Chief among these new solidarities was the claim that consumers, whether they were aware of it or not, had an obligation to those who made the goods or services they bought (or did not buy). Moral consumption, they believed, contributed to the good society.

Part of what makes the story of the reevaluation of thrift complex is that the term *thrift* itself has had, and continues to have, many meanings. Although *thrift* is often thought of as a synonym for *frugality*, *saving*, and *economical management*, the first of many definitions in the revised *Oxford English Dictionary* is "the fact or condition of thriving or prosperity." These meanings, seemingly antithetical, have long been related to each other. In the Victorian era, as the critique of the ideology of thrift developed, the promotion of thrift did not disappear. Indeed, champions of thrift were among the most prominent Americans, and they disseminated their ideas in part by combining the two opposing meanings of the term. In the late nineteenth century, advice books, Algeresque fiction, and the homilies of leading industrialists, including Andrew Carnegie, promoted thrift as a virtue. But these late nineteenth-century defenders of thrift revalued its meaning by defining it both as the practice of economy and as the condition of wealth resulting from that practice. For its champions, thrift was both the mark of virtuous character and a means to an end. Thrift was a habit that they sought to instill, but it was also an instrumental value. This conception of thrift as a means to wealth goes back at least as far as Benjamin Franklin, but it reached new heights of popularity in the Gilded Age and was fundamentally opposed to those Christian teachings which saw poverty as ennobling. These Victorian popularizers did not wish thrift to be understood as the serene acceptance of doing without. As Theodore Munger, one of the army of religiously inspired thrift pamphleteers of the Gilded Age, wrote, "I wish I could fill every young man who reads these pages with an utter dread and horror of poverty." Carnegie, too, proposed thrift as sacrifice, not because sacrifice was good in and of itself but because it was the path to capital accumulation.[14]

For these Victorian proponents, thrift was not merely a way to wealth but the basis of civilization itself. Munger wrote that "a spendthrift or idler is essentially a savage," and "the chief distinction between civilization and barbarism turns on thrift."[15] The most popular text of this sort—by the Scottish author of nineteenth-century books of virtue, Samuel Smiles—simply titled *Thrift*, claimed that "thrift began with civilization." The reason for this, according to Smiles, was that "every thrifty person may be regarded as a public benefactor, and every thriftless person as a public enemy." Thrift was a public good because public virtue was simply the agglomeration of individual private ones. As Smiles wrote, echoing the American proponents, "Thrift means private economy. . . . While it is the object of Private Economy to create and promote the well-being of individuals, it is the object of Political Economy to create and increase the wealth of nations. Public and private wealth have the same origin."[16]

But was political economy simply private economy writ large? And was thrift the measure of civilization? Many Americans answered in the negative. Such claims would be true if the political economy was, as Smiles believed, simply the agglomeration of private family economies. But, as opponents of the ideology of thrift were beginning to argue, in a system in which each economic transaction affected many people in the chain of production, distribution, and consumption, private economy could result in widespread poverty and other forms of immorality in the public sphere, including the sanctioning of unfree labor. Many workers and reformers adopted the term *social economy* to describe the social nature of economic life and to challenge Smiles's once-commonsensical claims. As Jessica B. Peixotto, whose title was professor of "social economics" at the University of California, Berkeley, noted in 1927, for many Americans the doctrine of "wise spending" had replaced "older canons of thrift through going without."[17]

These debates about thrift were in part a clash of different meanings of civilization or, more precisely, a clash of different understandings of the relationship between thrift and civilization. What better served the cause of civilization, thrift or spending? For its advocates, thrift was a bulwark of civilization itself. But for thrift's challengers, civilization rested on a very different base: consumption. Moreover, these challengers took thrift to lead to the very opposite of civilization. Rather than accepting an automatic linkage between thrift and civilization, these challengers focused on the social consequences of thrift in order to evaluate its virtuousness.

It was precisely this orientation to the social consequences of thrift that led a group of antebellum consumer activists, and their postbellum descendants, to be among the first to challenge its hegemony. Consumer activists, often famously thrifty themselves, would seem to be unlikely challengers of the thrift ideology. The boycott tradition up to that time, and indeed well beyond the nineteenth century, was not opposed to the tradition of thrift. Dating back to the American Revolution, consumer activists had associated sacrifice with virtue, and consumption (especially of immoral British goods) with effeminacy. Thousands of Anglo-American boycotters in the 1790s had urged citizens to abstain from slave-made goods, such as cotton and sugar. All these groups valorized sacrifice and denial as the essence of morality. The abolitionist-led "free produce" movement of the 1820s in some ways extended the association of virtue with sacrifice. Establishing what they labeled an "abstention movement," many free-producers held up the "straightforward path of self-denial" as the highest ideal. By refusing to buy altogether, one refused to collude in slavery. A number of boycotters linked self-sacrifice and virtue and paired these with a general criticism of aesthetic goods as immoral. Many free-produce activists accordingly took it as an article of faith that "the natural wants of man are few, whilst his artificial wants are manifold."[18] The movement, they believed, should discourage people from developing an interest in beauty and fashion, which stimulated such bogus wants.[19]

But the free-produce movement also portended a new model of consumer activism in which consumption, not withdrawal from the market, was the key to promoting virtue. Organizing alternative means of moral commerce (so-called free-labor stores sprang up in eight states and in England), free-produce activists encouraged concerned citizens to exercise moral prerogatives through shopping. Patronizing these stores, they argued, promoted the antislavery cause even more than eschewing slave-made goods because such acts of consumption would directly reward farmers and manufacturers who relied on free labor. Shortly after the launch of the free-produce movement, other groups, sometimes with very different agendas, embraced the idea that consumption could serve moral ends. Urging shoppers to "buy for the sake of the slave," a group of abolitionists organized antislavery fairs, which raised money for antislavery organizations. A group of wealthy Sabbatarians in upstate New York, discouraged by the ineffectiveness of their boycott campaign, organized the Pioneer Line, a shipping company meant to compete with their Sabbath-breaking competitors. In the South, white advocates of "nonintercourse" with the abolitionist North urged their fellows to punish opponents of slavery by buying only goods made and sold by southerners. This range of activities suggests that campaigns for moral consumption used similar techniques in the service of radically different, even contradictory, causes. It also shows that, leaving aside the obvious differences in how they defined morality, diverse groups of Americans, even before the Civil War, were beginning to associate spending with morality. Consumption was a means of social change that, unlike traditional and largely ineffective means of moral suasion, offered an opportunity to effect change "through the medium of their pockets," as a group of nonintercourse advocates claimed. In the postwar years, even as the causes of southern economic nationalism, abolitionism, and Sabbatarianism faded, the technique of shopping (or boycotting) for social change continued to be an oft-used tool in campaigns for social justice.[20]

If consumer activists challenged the hegemony of thrift by showing that spending, even more than abstinence, could foster morality in the increasingly national and global web of market relations, another group of activists in the late nineteenth-century labor movement rebutted the ideology of thrift more directly by challenging the equation between thrift and civilization itself. One way that thrift's opponents established this claim was through a form of rhetorical jujitsu first employed by the labor reformer and intellectual Ira Steward. Reversing the commonly accepted meaning of the terms, he and his many followers in the labor movement argued that, under certain conditions, thrift was wasteful and spending productive, that thrift was in fact a form of barbarism, and that consumption formed the new basis of civilization. With the technique of linguistic inversion, they frequently associated thrift with terms that its proponents took to be antonymous, calling it "wasteful" and "indulgent." Moreover, *pace* Carnegie and company, they associated thrift not with civilization but with savagery. What was really wasteful and socially unproductive, they believed, was an unthinking thrift whose consequences were borne by society's least fortunate. These leaders invented the inverted vocabulary that many Progressives and New Dealers borrowed, in which the term *thrift* was often modified by its opposite. By 1931, when the economist Thomas D. Eliot claimed that "an individual or a community may indulge in false thrift" and that "it may be most thrifty and economical to spend," he was invoking a well-established trope.[21]

Thrift, according to the labor intellectual Ira Steward, led not to civilization but to barbarism. It was spending, the quality most demonized by the sermonizers of thrift, that made social and moral improvement possible. Steward especially resented the manner in which the rich, who spent freely, lectured the laboring poor on the virtues of thrift. "The laboring classes are taught that 'economy is wealth' and that it would be 'extravagant' to increase their expenditures and luxuries," he wrote in his uncompleted magnum opus, *The Political Economy of Eight Hours*. "If every body had always economized as much as possible in consuming wealth, there could have been no progress. And all mankind would have remained savages."[22] Middle-class moralists, he charged, defined scrimping as a virtue and spending as a vice: in this view, economy was prudent, extravagance wasteful. For Steward, the two were reversed: spending was far more socially productive than saving. "Economy," he wrote, "is the real extravagance." Unnecessary saving, not extravagance, was the economically wasteful act.[23]

The charge of extravagance and the promotion of the duty of thrift were, in Steward's mind, elements in the arsenal of those engaged in class warfare. When "a more expensive style of living . . . is denounced as 'extravagant,'" he wrote, it "is another way of saying that the laborer must accept less wages." Similarly, he wrote that "the charge of extravagance is made to sustain the claim that wages ought not to be any higher."[24] Steward insisted that the praise of economy as a social good signified the desire of the rich to prevent workers from enjoying the fruits of their labor.

Working-class proponents of what Steward called an "American Way of Living" (and soon became known as an "American Standard of Living") challenged the belief that restraining their desires was necessarily a good thing for workers or for the broader society. As the historian Richard Schneirov has noted, "By the 1880s Steward's ideas had evolved into an analysis widely shared by labor leaders, prolabor political economists, and Republican party tariff advocates focusing on the need to maintain or raise workers' standard of living and implying an underconsumptionist analysis of crisis."[25] In 1886, for example, a labor reformer criticized the worker "who indulges in unnecessary and niggardly economy," thereby depriving "some brother producer of a proper market for the products of his labor." By using *indulge* to connote excessive frugality, the author demonstrated the need to rethink moral categories: thrift was indulgent; a better, more socially useful goal, he claimed, was to "spend liberally" because to do so was to "radiate employment" to other workers.[26] There was a point to this linguistic subversion: it emphasized the connection between frugality and slavery on one pole and consumption and freedom on the other. As Steward wrote, "When the working classes are denied everything but the barest necessities of life, they have no decent use for liberty."[27] Another worker-intellectual, A. S. Leitch, prepared a similar paean to extravagance in 1887:

> The wage workers' extravagance is the wage workers' salvation. . . . Suppose all workingmen of the United States . . . at a certain time conclude to squander no more of their earnings in the purchase of tobacco—thousands of tobacco workers would soon go hungry. Or beer: the brewers would be ruined. To shut down on "superfluous luxuries" of books and papers, the printers would get a tough deal.[28]

Drawing on Steward's ideas, he concluded with an attack on the critics of working-class "extravagance." "It is what press and pulpit term the extravagance of workingmen," wrote Leitch, "that keeps money in circulation . . . and gives employment to thousands of our brother wage-slaves by means of which they gain a livelihood." The same year, the freethinking radical Robert Ingersoll made a similar argument, condemning the employer who "tells the workingman that he must be economical," since "under the present system, economy would only lessen wages." Rather than championing the thrifty worker, Ingersoll vilified him: "Every saving, frugal, self-denying workingman is unconsciously doing what little he can to reduce the compensation of himself and his fellows."[29] Shopping was not simply a means of satisfying oneself and one's family but also a way of assisting fellow workers. As a union-label organization in Philadelphia declared in 1901, "You are your brother's keeper to the extent of your purchasing power."[30] In this view, there was nothing moral about thrift, which impoverished workers, limited possibilities for solidarity (which, as the last quotation suggests, was now best pursued through consumption), and prevented workers from fully developing their capabilities.

For these working-class opponents of thrift, consumption was a civilizing force, not a license for hedonism. For them civilization had a progressive, not a static, meaning. It was a term of movement; the preamble of the Knights of Labor platform, for example, spoke of "advancing civilization." George Gunton, a labor intellectual who finished Steward's uncompleted opus, used the phrase "the lever of civilization."[31] As the Knights' preamble put it, "industrial and moral worth, not wealth," should be "the true standard of individual and national greatness." Unlike other critics of capitalism, however, these working-class proponents of civilization conceded that there was a close relation between wealth and civilization: wealth in itself did not necessarily lead to civilization, but lack of wealth surely harmed the prospects for achieving it. Civilization, in this view, was characterized by a vibrant public sphere, a large number of what Gunton called "social wants" (which were both made possible and propelled by a high-wage, high-consumption economy), and a culture of solidarity, which linked the welfare of citizens to each other and to the commonwealth. Consider these passages from George McNeill's popular collection of essays by labor leaders and reformers, *The Labor Movement: The Problem of To-day* (1887), a work whose chief point was that reclaiming civilization required recognizing that consumption could be paired with virtue:

> Civilization is measured, not by the wealth, power or culture of the few, but by the quantity and quality of the opportunities possessed by the many.
>
> Civilization simply means, materially, the highest purchasing power of a day's labor.
>
> To reduce wages is to turn civilization backwards; to advance wages is to lift civilization to a higher level.
>
> Civilization is but another name for progress in the direction of better distribution of the material comforts and mental and moral opportunities of mankind.[32]

In these passages, we do not see the republican opposition between virtue and commerce or the equation of virtue with thrift; rather, we see a conception of virtue through commerce. This faith in the market was tempered by a deep suspicion of pure laissez-faire, especially as it was expressed in the late nineteenth century by the accumulation of immense wealth among a small number of people. In this way, social economy straddled moral economy and political economy: it was neither antimarket like the moral economy nor free market like political economy. Like moral economy, social economy measured the health of society by its level of consumption.[33] But whereas moral economy was concerned with maintaining a minimum level of subsistence (e.g., in the form of affordable prices for bread and other staples), social economists adopted the idea that an ever-increasing standard of living was necessary. In solving the "labor problem," McNeill urged Americans to consider that "the remedy will not come through making people live cheaper, but by making them live dearer." In this context, Samuel Gompers's famous demand for "more more" appears less as the origination of an asocial pure and simple unionism than as the continuation of the laborist view that consumption made civilization possible.[34]

These proponents of an American standard of living also criticized what Terence Powderly, the grand master workman of the Knights of Labor, called "the sin of cheapness." Quoting the Scottish clergyman Dr. Donald Macleod, Powderly wrote that "the craving for cheapness and the hunting after bargains, is not only economically false, but a cause of great suffering to thousands of men, women, and children."[35] Understanding purchasing power as the fulcrum of economic life, labor leaders believed that to buy cheap goods was not only to endorse but also to indirectly *hire* low-paid labor. In this consumption-driven understanding of political economy, there was nothing ethical about following the dictates of thrift. Rather, the cause of morality was best served by increased leisure and higher wages, the rudiments of the American standard of living.

After the dawn of the twentieth century, the consumerist understanding of economy and society put forth in the nineteenth century by consumer activists and labor leaders (as well as the economic marginalists) found a hearing among a group of reformers, politicians, and religious leaders. The historian Meg Jacobs aptly labels this diverse group the "purchasing-power progressives."[36] Analogizing the consumer to the citizen, rather than seeing them as opposites, many Progressives argued that consumption was a key (perhaps *the* key) activity of citizenship because of its social impact. Progressives so closely identified consumption with citizenship that they often described the two in overlapping terms. In the modern world, "you cannot be a citizen without being a consumer as well," said the Reverend Henry Potter, the Social Gospel promoter and bishop of the Episcopal diocese of New York, who considered the two words to be "copulative not antithetical."[37] Progressives believed the reverse was true as well: if citizens were consumers, consumers were also citizens. Consumer power was a double-edged sword, however, because if consumers acted selfishly or ineffectually, their actions would inevitably diminish citizenship and impoverish society. As the economist Arthur Hadley declared, "Reform is likely to come through the agency of the consumer rather than from any other source."[38] This was so, according to Maud Nathan of the National Consumers League (NCL), because the consumer had become "the lever . . . which controls . . . the great forces of the industrial world"; or, as Potter claimed, "in the hands of the discriminating consumer rests finally the settlement of the gravest issues in the whole industrial problem."[39]

No group made these consumerist claims more forcefully than the NCL, which in many ways should be considered the first Progressive organization. (The first Consumers League, in New York City, was established in 1891, and the NCL was founded in 1899.)[40] To help solve the problem of low-wage labor, NCL activists and many other Progressive reformers called on the state to assist poor, female workers via minimum-wage legislation. As the first line of the constitution of the NCL stated, "The interest of the community demands that all workers should receive not lowest wages, but fair living wages."[41] Minimum-wage laws, which were enacted in twelve states after Massachusetts passed the first one in 1912, hardly promoted conspicuous consumption among low-paid workers. But they were justified in part because of the benefits to the economy of broad working-class consumption and because of the need for even the poorest workers to have a decent standard of living.

The NCL suggested that consumption, too often misconstrued as private, was in fact a profoundly public act whose powerful and far-reaching effects were little understood. Its primary mission was to convince shoppers "to do their buying in such ways as to further the welfare of those who make or distribute the things bought," wrote John Graham Brooks, the organization's first president.[42] The NCL, which acknowledged that few consumers viewed shopping in these terms, harbored no illusions about the difficulty of inculcating such a vision; Florence Kelley, the executive director and heart and soul of the organization, called the job of the NCL "our never ending task," and Nathan declared the "work of the Consumers League will never be fully accomplished."[43] When Walter Lippmann wrote that "the art of consumption is uncultivated," he in effect described the raison d'être of the NCL.[44]Cultivating the "art" of ethical consumption (NCL members preferred to see it as a science) required imbuing consumers with a new sense of civic duty. "Consumers can abolish sweatshops," declared an NCL pamphlet, revealing the vast potential it assigned to shoppers.[45] Consumers, in other words, were capable of making the Great (complex, distended) Society (the phrase that American Progressives borrowed from the British social theorist Graham Wallas) a good (just, ethical) society. This was a variation on Steward's claim that increased consumption advanced the cause of civilization.

Drawing on the claims of the consumer activists about the moral responsibility of shopping and of the labor activists about the need to express solidarity through purchases, all shoppers, as Nathan put it, "had a direct moral responsibility" to workers, since, whether they were aware of it or not, they "were the employers."[46] While not rejecting the benefits of stretching the family budget through the search for inexpensive products, the NCL constantly warned of "the high cost of cheap goods," as one of its pamphlets was titled.[47] Because consumption was a market-based activity, shoppers pondering what Nathan called "the ethics of the bargain hunter" had to weigh the benefits of buying cheap alongside the impact of the "brutal side of the bargain" on those who made the goods. "Without bargain hunters and bargain counters there would be no sweatshops," declared a writer for the *American Woman's Home Journal*, who condemned thrift in a manner reminiscent of Steward's "ill-judged economy."[48] "Mere cheapness is not the end of life," said Potter; Brooks decried a "cheapness which is bound up with dangerously low surroundings" for workers.[49] The NCL regularly dismissed what it called the worship of the "almighty bargain counter" and the "almighty 99 cents," and its constitution condemned "consumers who persist in buying in the cheapest market, regardless of how cheapness is brought about."[50] Unlike later consumer organizations, such as Consumers' Research or Consumers Union, whose core mission was understood as finding bargains for shoppers, the NCL stood against bargain hunting.

"False thrift" was a related bugbear to purchasing-power progressives. "Thrift emphatically does not consist in hoarding money," wrote the economist Thomas Nixon Carver in 1920. "In these days that is one of the most thriftless things one can do with money."[51] If, as Lippmann wrote, the "consumer is trying to redeem his helplessness in the complexity of the newly organized industrial world," many Progressives saw it as their duty to overturn older ideas about thrift and consumption.[52]

In the 1920s, the purchasing-power progressives turned their attention to the problem of underconsumption. In "Old King Cole in Trouble," William Trufant Foster and Waddell Catchings interpreted the nursery rhyme as a metaphor for the problem of underconsumption. As a result of the king's orders to be thrifty, "the warehouses were bulging with lumber and leather, wheat and wheelbarrows . . . and no end of other things that nobody would buy." All of the king's advisers are stumped by this problem until the fool and chief jester provide the answer: "When they have the cash to pay, / They'll quickly take the goods away."[53] Elsewhere Foster and Catchings, whose popular books *Business without a Buyer* (1927) and *The Road to Plenty* (1928) summarized the arguments of the purchasing-power progressives, held that "'more pay and less work,'—the aim which organized labor has often been censured for pursuing—should, indeed be the aim of society."[54] A corollary of this view was that spending served important social functions. Not only could it be used at the microeconomic level to help workers, but at the macroeconomic level, aggregate consumption provided the key to a full-employment economy. When Robert Lynd claimed in 1936 that "men have not stopped to examine their institutional hair shirt of Scarcity," he joined a long line of thinkers in rejecting the equation of thrift with civic and moral health.[55] Stuart Chase's 1932 book, *A New Deal*, foreshadowed Roosevelt's New Deal by, like Lynd, claiming that thrift ill served an "economy of abundance."[56] (Chase believed that America had left behind an "economy of scarcity" to which thrift was better suited.) Chase and many others, including FDR himself in his 1932 Commonwealth Club of San Francisco address, diagnosed "underconsumption" as chief among the nation's ills.[57]

Understood in the context of a history that included consumer activists' labeling certain forms of consumption as virtuous, working-class proponents of labor consumerism, and Progressive Era efforts to decry bargain hunting and promote consumption, New Deal economic thought—or at least that branch of it that diagnosed underconsumption as the nation's number one ill—can be seen as an extension of a longer tradition of thought and action. As Alan Brinkley has noted, far too much credit for the diagnosis of a pathology of underconsumption has gone to the British economist John Maynard Keynes. To an extent that even Brinkley may not recognize, however, many of the American politicians, bankers, and brain trusters who urged the promotion of mass consumption drew on the theories and practices of earlier generations of reformers. For example, Brinkley highlights the rejection of Say's law as a key to the new economic thought of the New Deal era. While it is true that Leon Henderson called it "bunk," labor intellectuals going back to Steward had been debunking Say's law since the 1870s.[58]

When President Roosevelt encouraged American women to "buy now under the blue eagle"—that is, to patronize only those stores that complied with minimum wages and maximum hours guidelines—he was extending a technique that dated back to working-class practitioners of consumerist solidarity and continued through the NCL's recruitment of shoppers in the service of morality. Noting that the "real power of the recovery campaign lies with the consumers," the National Recovery Administration, as had previous generations of politicized consumers, encouraged that targeted spending be considered a form of political power.[59]

What was new about the rejection of thrift and concomitant embrace of spending during the New Deal era (keeping in mind that New Dealers, including FDR himself, were deeply divided about whether the consumerist solution was the right one) was that it marked the first time these calls came from mainstream and powerful voices and that it entered into public policy. It is notable that New Deal consumerist thinking was less tethered to morality than were its predecessors. The consumer activists, labor reformers, and National Consumers League members who called for virtuous consumption were outsiders, able to affect policy only insofar as their activism was effective. The New Dealers who embraced consumers generally did so from positions of power. Moreover, their justifications for consumerism had more to do with macroeconomic health than with ethics. "Our depression was not brought about as a result of extravagance," Marriner Eccles, the Utah banker and future chair of the Federal Reserve, noted in June 1932. "The difficulty is that we were not sufficiently extravagant."[60] In this way, the consumerist New Dealers were transitional figures on the road toward the postwar Consumers' Republic.

During the New Deal period another challenge to the ideology of thrift emerged, this time from a boycott of Japanese silk called by a loosely affiliated set of women's, labor, student, and community organizations and other advocates, which lasted from 1937 to 1940.[61] The tactics employed by the silk boycotters departed from the rhetoric of renunciation that had been a staple of most previous episodes of consumer activism. They extended the claims of their consumer activists forebears that consumption could be moral, and they added a dimension about which, until that point, most consumer activists had been either silent or hostile: aesthetics and pleasure. Consumers, the sociologist Zygmunt Bauman has written, are "guided by aesthetic interests, not ethical norms." By placing aesthetics in the service of virtue, the silk boycotters challenged such a dichotomy.[62]

Despite the deadly seriousness of their charges against wearers of silk, the boycott movement aimed to link aesthetics and politics, not to force people to make a choice between fashion and virtue. As they put it, "We are boycotting silk, not fashion." Rather than demanding sacrifice from American women, they encouraged them to engage in a simultaneously playful and serious process of creative refashioning. Stressing the importance of "making it a fashion to wear cotton, wool, or rayon clothes," they emphasized the congruence between good politics and good fashion. Urging women to "put silk in the doghouse," Leonard Sparks and Mississippi Johnson called on "women of means, working women, housewives, students, and professional people" to "start boycotting fashions which will not only keep the figurative blood and bones of Chinese babies from around their legs, but which will give them pleasure and artistic satisfaction." This was perhaps the first consumer movement that placed "pleasure" on a par with virtue—in part because, unlike most boycotts, the emphasis was not on doing without but on finding pleasurable means to outdo silk fashions. Boycott supporters argued that renunciation was not good politics.[63]

Despite the chastened wartime message of many consumer activists, the quest for a politics that was both pleasurable and ethical continued during the war. As Robert Westbrook has demonstrated in his ingenious analysis of the wartime cult of the "pin-up," rather than defining their military or civilian service as sacrificial, many Americans understood themselves, and their comrades, to be fighting for erotic, if domesticated, pleasures.[64] In the postwar years, some consumer activists continued to promote a socially oriented, pleasure-centered consumerism that was evocative of the silk boycotters. It is notable that in these years, *Consumer Reports*—now chiefly seen as a bargain-hunting bible—included regular columns on design, fashion, and sexuality. Other branches of the consumer movement, as Lizabeth Cohen has documented, maintained an asceticism that was increasingly "out of step" with the zeitgeist of the postwar years. In the Japanese silk boycott, however, they contributed another less-widely heeded model, what we might call virtuous aestheticism—a form of consumer activism that sought nonexploitative pleasure and socially conscious fashions and that challenged the view that responsible consumption should not automatically be equated with self-denial.

By the time America joined the fighting in World War II, the prevailing understanding of thrift was very different from the one that reigned at the start of the Civil War. Although Americans continued to admire the virtue of thrift and even, at times, to display it themselves, it no longer stood unchallenged as the nation's dominant ethos. In the post–World War II years, in part due to the legacy of the five groups examined in this essay, many Americans saw in consumption the path toward happiness and national strength, destinations previously deemed attainable only through sacrifice and self-denial.

Many of those who reevaluated thrift did not see their actions as an abandonment of morality. Rather, they understood their actions as a necessary revision of economic thinking and practices in order to maintain moral standards. Whereas once thrift seemed to be a necessary component of individual virtue and economic life, a large number of Americans in the age of transition between the Civil War and World War II came to question these associations. In this period, consumption replaced thrift as the key to individual morality, solidarity, and macroeconomic health.

In the postwar years, and even more so in recent times, the link between mass consumption and morality has been attenuated. While it is doubtless true that the link to morality, critical for members of the groups examined in this essay, has been sundered for the majority of modern consumers, many Americans, consciously or not, have continued the practices of moral consumption invented by these predecessors. From contemporary "buycotters," to protesters of Wal-Mart's labor practices, to promoters of municipal "living wage" ordinances, to those who seek to merge style with morality through purchases of sweatshop-free (or animal-cruelty-free or fair trade) goods, many Americans continue to practice moral mass consumption.[65] In so doing, they evoke the pioneering challengers to thrift in the century between the 1830s and the 1930s, the first groups to posit consumption, rather than thrift, as the means to a moral life and a good society.

Notes

Some of the material in this essay is drawn from my books *A Living Wage: American Workers and the Making of Consumer Society* (Ithaca, NY: Cornell University Press, 1997) and *Buying Power: A History of Consumer Activism in America* (Chicago: University of Chicago Press, 2009).

1. Cal Thomas, "Gas Was Cheap, People Were Valued," *State*, August 19, 2005, A9; Marie Coco, "It'll Take More Than Shopping to Heal America's Wounds," *State*, September 29, 2001, A11; and Amy Dacyczyn, *The Tightwad Gazette: Promoting Thrift as a Viable Alternative Lifestyle* (New York: Villard, 1992). See also *The Complete Tightwad Gazette*, published in 1998, which carries the same subtitle as the 1992 volume.

2. Phillip Longman, *The Return of Thrift: How the Coming Collapse of the Middle-Class Welfare State Will Re-awaken Values in America* (New York: Free Press, 1996). As Longman writes, "While Newt Gingrich has been busy trying to reinvent the orphanage, another

Victorian idea is in even greater need of rehabilitation: middle-class thrift and self-reliance" (ibid., 7). For an analysis of reactions to September 11, see Lawrence B. Glickman, "'Make Lisle the Style': The Politics of Fashion in the Japanese Silk Boycott, 1937–1940," *Journal of Social History* 38 (Spring 2005): 573–608. Jonathan Franzen calls thrift one of our "unfashionable values" in "My Bird Problem: Loss, Grief, and a Change in the Weather," *New Yorker*, August 8 and 15, 2005, 59. On the Commerce Department's report about the nation's zero personal savings rate, see Robert J. Samuelson, "No Savings? No Problem," *State*, August 20, 2005, A9.

3. Lizabeth Cohen, *A Consumers' Republic: The Politics of Mass Consumption in Postwar America* (New York: Knopf, 2003).

4. Alan Brinkley, *The End of Reform: New Deal Liberalism in Recession and War* (New York: Knopf, 1995), 67.

5. Michael McGerr, *A Fierce Discontent: The Rise and Fall of the Progressive Movement in America* (New York: Free Press, 2003), 11–12.

6. T. J. Jackson Lears, *No Place of Grace: Antimodernism and the Transformation of American Culture, 1880–1920* (New York: Pantheon, 1981).

7. Evelyn Brooks Higginbotham, *Righteous Discontent: The Women's Movement in the Black Baptist Church, 1880–1920* (Cambridge, MA: Harvard University Press, 1993), 188.

8. Simon Nelson Patten, *The New Basis of Civilization* (New York: Macmillan, 1907); see also James Livingston, *Pragmatism and the Political Economy of Cultural Revolution, 1850–1940* (Chapel Hill: University of North Carolina Press, 1994).

9. Lawrence B. Glickman, *A Living Wage: American Workers and the Making of Consumer Society* (Ithaca, NY: Cornell University Press, 1997).

10. As understood by most of the thinkers in Daniel Horowitz's book *The Morality of Spending: Attitudes toward the Consumer Society in America* (Baltimore: Johns Hopkins University Press, 1985), the phrase "morality of spending" usually connoted moral problems associated with consumption, not the moral good that can result from spending, which is how most of the thinkers discussed in this essay understood it.

11. Cohen, *Consumers' Republic*, 121.

12. John Bates Clark, "A Modified Individualism," *Independent*, May 1, 1902, 1066–68, quoted in James L. Huston, *Securing the Fruits of Labor: The American Concept of Wealth Distribution, 1765–1860* (Baton Rouge: Louisiana State University Press, 1998), 361.

13. Brinkley, *End of Reform*, 69.

14. Theodore Thornton Munger, "Thrift," in *On the Threshold* (Boston: Houghton Mifflin, 1883), 81; Andrew Carnegie, "Thrift as a Duty," in *The Empire of Business* (New York: Doubleday, Page, 1902), 95–99. For a similar viewpoint, expressed from a religious perspective, see Rev. E. V. Tenneycke, "New Year's Choice: Frugality or Prodigality," *Christian Recorder*, January 11, 1883.

15. Munger, "Thrift," 82, 83.

16. Samuel Smiles, *Thrift* (London: John Murray, 1888), Quotation 13.

17. Jessica B. Peixotto, *Getting and Spending at the Professional Standard of Living* (New York: Macmillan, 1927), excerpted in *American Standards and Planes of Living: Readings in the Social Economy of Consumption*, ed. Thomas D. Eliot (Boston: Ginn, 1931), 566.

18. Unsigned letter, *Pennsylvania Freeman*, May 28, 1840, 4.

19. On self-denial, see "Abstinence from the Fruits of Unrequited Toil," *Pennsylvania Freeman*, August 30, 1838, 1. On the self-denial of the movement's progenitors, including John Woolman, Benjamin Lundy, and Elias Hicks, see Elizabeth M. Chandler, "John Woolman," in

The Remembrancer (Philadelphia: T. Elwood Chapman, 1841), 27–30; "Biography of Benjamin Lundy," *Pennsylvania Freeman*, October 5, 1839, 3.

20. See Lawrence B. Glickman, *Buying Power: A History of Consumer Activism in America* (Chicago: University of Chicago Press, 2009).

21. Thomas D. Eliot, introduction to *American Standards and Planes of Living*, 6.

22. This passage is found in Ira Steward, "Consumption and the Hours of Labor," a chapter in his uncompleted magnum opus, "The Political Economy of Eight Hours" (ms.), Ira Steward Papers, Historical Society of Wisconsin, Madison.

23. Ira Steward, "Economy and Extravagance," in "Political Economy of Eight Hours," 6.

24. Ibid.

25. Richard Schneirov, *Labor and Urban Politics: Class Conflict and the Origins of Modern Liberalism in Chicago, 1864–97* (Urbana: University of Illinois Press, 1998), 187.

26. "Economy as a Virtue and Otherwise," *John Swinton's Paper*, September 11, 1886.

27. Ira Steward, "A Second Declaration of Independence," in *We, the Other People: Alternative Declarations of Independence by Labor Groups, Farmers, Woman's Rights Advocates, Socialists, and Blacks, 1829–1975*, ed. Phillip Foner (Urbana: University of Illinois Press, 1976), 115–19, Quotation 117.

28. A. S. Leitch, "Wage Slavery as Viewed by a Wage Slave, III," *John Swinton's Paper*, May 29, 1887, 2.

29. "Col. Ingersoll on Labor," *John Swinton's Paper*, March 13, 1887, 1.

30. Robert Hunter, "Unionism and Union Labels," *Shoe Workers' Journal*, April 3–4, 1916; "Trade Unionists of Philadelphia," *Vindicator and Union Label Advertiser*, n.d.; "Collection of Material Regarding Union Labels Dated from Late 1800s to Mid-1900s," unnumbered file, State Historical Society of Wisconsin Library, Madison.

31. George Gunton, "Feasibility of an Eight-Hour Workday," *American Federationist*, July 1894, 92.

32. George E. McNeill, *The Labor Movement: The Problem of To-day* (Boston: A. M. Bridgeman, 1887), 464, 472, 475, 483.

33. E. P. Thompson writes, "Economic class-conflict in nineteenth-century England found its characteristic expression in the matter of wages: in eighteenth-century England the working people were most quickly inflamed to action by rising prices." Thus the consumerist concerns of social economists paralleled—in the context of the new economy—those of eighteenth-century workers. E. P. Thompson, "The Moral Economy of the English Crowd in the Eighteenth Century," in *Customs in Common: Studies in Traditional Popular Culture* (New York: New Press, 1993), 189.

34. McNeill, *Labor Movement*, 480. Certainly, many nineteenth-century social economists would have agreed with Martin J. Sklar's suggestion that "consumption is the quintessential proletarian principle." Martin J. Sklar, "Some Political and Cultural Consequences of the Disaccumulation of Capital: Origins of Postindustrial Development in the 1920s," in *The United States as a Developing Country: Studies in U.S. History in the Progressive Era and the 1920s* (New York: Cambridge University Press, 1992), 144.

35. Terence Powderly, quoted in McNeill, *Labor Movement*, 583.

36. Like many twentieth-century historians, Meg Jacobs does not sufficiently acknowledge the nineteenth-century roots of purchasing-power progressivism or of labor consumerism. Meg Jacobs, *Pocketbook Politics: Economic Citizenship in Twentieth-Century America* (Princeton, NJ: Princeton University Press, 2005), 74–76.

37. Henry C. Potter, "The Citizen and the Consumer," in *The Citizen in His Relation to the Industrial Situation* (New York: Scribner's, 1902), 125–26.

38. Arthur Hadley, quoted in John Graham Brooks, "The National Consumers League," National Consumers League Pamphlet (Cambridgeport, MA: National Consumers League, 1899); quoted too in Kathryn Kish Sklar, "The Consumers' White Label Campaign of the National Consumers' League, 1898–1918," *Getting and Spending: European and American Consumer Societies in the Twentieth Century*, ed. Susan Strasser, Charles McGovern, and Matthias Judt (New York: Cambridge University Press, 1998), 25.

39. Maud Nathan, *The Story of an Epoch-Making Movement* (Garden City, NY: Doubleday, Page, 1926), 125; Potter, "Citizen and Consumer," 155–56.

40. There is not agreement about either of these dates. Some date the Consumers' League of New York to 1888 and the NCL to 1898.

41. Nathan, *Story of an Epoch-Making Movement*, 25.

42. John Graham Brooks, *The Consumers' League*, 3.

43. Florence Kelley, quoted in Sklar, "Consumers' White Label Campaign," 27; Nathan, *Story of an Epoch-Making Movement*, 124.

44. Walter Lippmann, *Drift and Mastery: An Attempt to Diagnose the Current Unrest* (1914; New York: Henry Holt, 1917), 67.

45. "Consumers Can Abolish Sweatshops" (Boston, n.d.), in Consumers League of Massachusetts Early Publications, box 16, folder 253, Consumers League of Massachusetts Papers, Schlesinger Library, Harvard University.

46. Nathan, *Story of an Epoch-Making Movement*, 23.

47. "The High Cost of Cheap Goods" (n.p., n.d.), in Consumers League of Massachusetts Early Publications, box 16, folder 253, Schlesinger Library, Harvard University.

48. "Do Bargain Hunters Encourage . . .," *American Woman's Home Journal*, scrapbook excerpt, Maud Nathan Papers, Schlesinger Library, Harvard University. In 1892, Kelley made a similar point: "If the people would notify Marshall Field, Henry King, and others that they would buy from them no clothing made in sweatshops, the evil would be stopped." Florence Kelley, "Denounced from the Pulpit: All Souls' Church Congregation Hears of the Sweating System," *Chicago Tribune*, May 9, 1892, 6.

49. Potter, "Consumer and Citizen," 152; Brooks, *Consumers' League*, 16–17.

50. Nathan, *Story of an Epoch-Making Movement*, 25.

51. Thomas Nixon Carver, "Thrift and the Standard of Living," *Journal of Political Economy* 28 (November 1920): 782–86, Quotation 785.

52. Lippmann, *Drift and Mastery*, 75.

53. William Trufant Foster and Waddell Catchings, "Old King Cole in Trouble," *Atlantic Monthly*, July 1926, 94–100, in *American Standards and Planes of Living*, 231–39, Quotation 239.

54. Note the explicit recognition by the "purchasing-power progressives" of the laborist roots of this idea. William Trufant Foster and Waddell Catchings, "Cash for Consumers," in *Profits* (Boston: Houghton Mifflin, 1925), in *American Standards and Planes of Living*, 240–45, Quotation 242.

55. Robert Lynd, "Democracy's Third Estate: The Consumer," *Political Science Quarterly* 51 (December 1936): 483–86, quoted in Brinkley, *The End of Reform: New Deal Liberalism in Recession and War* (New York: Knopf, 1995), 300n6.

56. Stuart Chase, *A New Deal* (New York: Macmillan, 1932).

57. Brinkley, *End of Reform*, 70.

58. Ibid., 83; David Montgomery, *Beyond Equality: Labor and the Radical Republicans* (1967; Urbana: University of Illinois Press, 1981), 253; Schneirov, *Labor and Urban Politics*, 185–86.

59. Jacobs, *Pocketbook Politics*, 111.

60. Marriner Eccles, *Beckoning Frontiers: Public and Personal Recollections* (New York: Knopf, 1995), 83, quoted in Brinkley, *End of Reform*, 80.

61. For a detailed account of the boycott and its aftermath, see Glickman, "Make Lisle the Style."

62. Zygmunt Bauman, *Work, Consumerism, and the New Poor* (Philadelphia: Open University Press, 1998), 31.

63. Leonard Sparks and Mississippi Johnson, "Put Silk in the Doghouse: A Review of Fashions and Their Origins Proves That It Is Possible to Start a Big Swing for China and against Japan," *New Masses*, September 20, 1937, 13.

64. Robert Westbrook, "'I Want a Girl, Just Like the Girl That Married Harry James': American Women and the Problem of Political Obligation in World War II," *American Quarterly* 42 (December 1990): 587–614.

65. For an analysis that places these contemporary practices in historical perspective, see Lawrence B. Glickman, "Boycott Mania," *Boston Globe*, July 31, 2005, D12.

12 }

Thrift and Advertising

Jennifer Scanlon

No industry could appear, at first glance, more antithetical to values associated with thrift than the advertising industry. American advertising in the late nineteenth and early twentieth centuries effectively communicated the increasing availability of the expanding range of consumer goods that, in many ways, improved the lives of those able to purchase them. It also promoted an American identity that appears only contradictory to the value of thrift. Advertising helped shape an identity marked most prominently by desire, by the valuing of release over restraint, excess over moderation, accumulation over use. As advertising thrived as an industry, it also became—in a wide range of media and through a wide range of methods—a visible and verbal backdrop for the nation's conflation of want with need. The story of advertising's ascendance, nevertheless, is complicated precisely by the tensions it could not erase. As is true of the other cultural practices and industries explored in this volume, advertising emerged, grew, and thrived in a "transitional" culture in which thrift maintained a place in the American mind and in practices of daily living, even as it was tempered by other forces, values, and practices. As Jackson Lears demonstrates in *Fables of Abundance*, countering his own influential earlier work, advertisers, the "point men of modernization," sought to replace thrift not with reckless consumerism but rather with modern notions of efficiency and self-control, themselves analogues for thrift.[1]

Central to this transformation rather than simple negation of thrift—and to advertising's role in it—were two groups of people whose motivations, practices, and interactions form the core of this essay: the first generations of "professional" advertisers and their most important clients, female consumers.

Following a discussion of the development of advertising in this period of transition, this chapter explores the worlds of the advertising professionals and the female consumers they courted. Part educator, part preacher, part newly minted professional, the advertising agent furthered a national consumerist agenda in ways both planned and accidental—or at least unconscious. Our contemporary difficulty in thinking beyond commodity culture, paired with the very real, monumental growth of the advertising industry in the late nineteenth century, might encourage us to believe that as early as the turn of the twentieth century thrift had been abandoned, relegated to the dustbin of quaint, decidedly nineteenth-century practices. Those who promoted consumerism so purposefully and artfully, we might add, must have led the shift in values with nary a look back. These practitioners, however, were products of a changing society, not merely producers of change. They shared with others in the growing middle class a belief that a modern world demanded a managed self, one neither wholly liberated nor wholly regulated through the marketplace.[2] And if, as others in this volume argue, notions of thrift during this period in American history changed from the saving of money to the saving of time, advertisers provided thrifty answers to the needs of manufacturers and consumers alike.

Similarly, the actions of female consumers, who increasingly came to define themselves and each other first by their role as purchasers and then by the brand names they selected, seem to suggest a repudiation of thrift and an embrace of things, of goods, of excess. Through the thrifty practice of informed consumerism, however, they not only met the needs of their families but also secured for themselves time away from the daily grind of household work. Accordingly, these same people who have come most to exemplify consumerism as the antithesis of thrift provide telling tales of continuity, accommodation, and complexity in a gradual and bumpy process of change.

The Emergence of National Advertising and Professional Advertisers

In 1930, John Dewey argued that thrift, that "old-fashioned ideal," had been rendered obsolete by people's increased purchasing, which had become the nation's economic "duty."[3] The process he noted, however, began decades earlier and remained incomplete at the time of his observation. In the years between the Civil War and the turn of the century, the nation's productive capacities increased tremendously. Manufacturers sought, at home and abroad, new markets for their products. On the home front, purchasing increasingly came to be equated not only with social mobility and middle-class status but with the very notion of citizenship. "By the end of the century," writes historian Kathleen Donohue, "the nation's phenomenal productive capacities had convinced all but the most recalcitrant that the real threat to a capitalist economy was not too much consumption but too little."[4]

Manufacturers and advertisers had the support of other institutions, including the U.S. government, in furthering an American identity steeped in participation in the culture of consumption. And that Americans viewed foreigners as consumers suggests the degree to which they felt secure in that definition themselves. "What is the process of civilizing," argued Josiah Strong in an 1886 religious tract, echoing an increasingly common sentiment, "but the creating of more and higher wants?" The "arts and habits of civilization," shared by missionaries and manufacturers alike, included by the late nineteenth century the habit of consumption. White, native-born, middle-class Americans, positioned at the apex of civilization, shouldered the responsibility of demonstrating their place through consumer activity so that "Others" at home and abroad could and would emulate these behaviors.[5] As one early twentieth-century advertiser put it succinctly, "All over the world, people can be educated, and are daily being educated, to want more and more of the things which their ancestors never even dreamed of possessing."[6]

In fact, during this time period large numbers of consumers at home could for the first time make purchasing decisions based on considerations other than price.[7] In addition, with the implementation of a shorter workweek, many citizens had more time to spend both thinking about consumer goods and actively acquiring them. The role of advertising changed in response to this constellation of shifting economic, social, and cultural conditions. John Kenneth Galbraith later described this process as the "dependency effect," in which "wants are increasingly created by the process by which they are satisfied." Advertisers played a significant role in encouraging consumers to meet the needs if not of themselves, then certainly of the manufacturers.[8] Over time, professional advertisers came to be seen as those individuals best suited to this task: they would identify ways to marry consumers with products by promoting the qualities of goods and, increasingly, by recognizing that mass production required, among other things, "greater skill in mass seduction."[9] What advertising historian Roland Marchand identified as the "consumption ethic"—a complex dance performed by manufacturers, advertisers, and of course consumers—celebrated not only goods but also gratification through consumer items, citizenship through consumption, the desire to desire.[10]

As the nineteenth century closed, advertising had also reached a considerable level of professional respectability, having created a "strategic niche" in the expansion of merchandising, credit, and corporate development.[11] As was true of other enterprises, advertising agencies of the twentieth century were populated with more educated, affluent, and trained practitioners than had been true in the nineteenth century. Advertising professionals, who were part of the expanding middle class that historians credit with creating both modern work culture and efforts to reform it, assumed an influential role in American life partly through self-promotion, as did their peers in a multitude of corporate projects around the nation.[12] The industry founded its first professional association, the Advertising Federation of America, in 1904. Immense growth both resulted from and furthered this increasing professionalization. In the 1880s, only two copywriters of any significance had plied their trade; by the late 1890s, hundreds, and by 1915, thousands, had secured employment in the field.[13]

Certain trends marked this growth. The development of national advertising accounted for a good deal of the change. In 1906, the Kellogg Company launched the first national ad, in the *Ladies' Home Journal*, and national brands and national advertising grew rapidly in the following decades. Accompanying this trend toward nationalization was a trend toward specialization, as the "modern" specialists, advertising agencies, took over where a variety of trades and relationships had existed. By 1917, 95 percent of all national advertising was handled by agencies, and the big agencies increasingly dropped smaller and local clients in the interest of servicing large ones.[14] Industry trends in this era of transition favored national branding, specialized agency development, large manufacturing, and urban activity: by the 1920s much of the country's advertising activity took place in either New York or Chicago, and by 1923 Madison Avenue had come into usage as shorthand for the advertising world.

The growth was facilitated as well by changes in technology and in the industry's ability to brand itself as technologically advanced, research based, psychologically savvy, and successful. Technology proved one of the earliest and most significant advancements. By the late 1890s, the visual elements of women's magazines, including advertising, came to rival editorial copy in sophistication; this had enormous implications for an industry steeped in visual appeals. Advertising agencies formed art departments in the first decade of the twentieth century, even before they organized research departments. Improvements in color printing continued into the 1920s, resulting in particularly effective ads for food, textiles, and automobiles.[15] The movement in commercial art away from complex Victorian styles and toward a modernist aesthetic accompanied these technological developments and demanded a more organic relationship between advertising images and copy.[16] Technological advancements in other media, namely, radio and film, both facilitated advancements in print advertising and helped educate the advertising profession about the necessity of finessing relationships with and appeals to audiences. Radio, according to Marchand, "impressed advertisers most forcefully with the public craving for personal relationships through the media."[17] The silver screen, particularly by the 1920s, furthered consumer desires for identities heroic, sensual, sophisticated, urban, and wealthy, and it provided clear evidence of consumers' aspiration potentials.[18] Advertisers carried both the technological and the ideological lessons of these other cultural media over to print, outdoor, and electric advertising.

In addition to technology, advertising agencies of the early twentieth century touted their advancements in research capability. The J. Walter Thompson Company, one of the earliest and most successful of the national and then international agencies, began market research early in the twentieth century and rapidly assumed leadership in the field. The agency began working with census data in 1912 and by 1915 had organized a research department. Within a year, the research department boasted a 650-volume library of trade publications, agency portfolios, samples of work, files on clients and competitors, and other data.[19] The status of research in the profession grew, and by 1919, the J. Walter Thompson Company had both a planning department and a statistical investigation department.[20] Some in the industry would go so far as to declare advertising a science, but even those less certain of advertising's rigor willingly spent money on research to enhance success and to move away from the dubious reputations of many of their predecessors. Touting the research base of advertising lent credence to a profession that many remembered primarily for its harboring of hucksters and charlatans.

At the same time that they compiled data on spending habits and brand preferences, the J. Walter Thompson Company and other national agencies developed psychological approaches to understanding the consumer, attempting to reach above and beyond the lessons of radio and film. In this arena, advertisers seem to move most clearly and deliberately away from the values of thrift, away from advancing practical relationships between consumers and the world of goods. Indeed, these early advertisers increasingly recognized that consumer participation was not only about gratifying needs but also about engaging with desire, about fully experiencing the means as well as the ends of consumer participation. Certainly they understood that consumers purchased only a fraction of what they were invited to buy. Although they often claimed that their role was limited to claiming the merits of one brand over another, advertisers' larger role, as we look back, was to help "fix our desires out there, beyond where we are."[21] But even in this, the process was mixed. The J. Walter Thompson agency, for example, hired behavioral psychologist John B. Watson, whose very presence elevated the notion that advertising could make effective use of psychological insights. Nevertheless, the end goal of using psychology, for Watson and others, was to manipulate consumers in particular ways, namely, to regulate them and shape them into efficient, even thrifty practitioners of modern life.[22]

Historians of market research have concluded that most advertising research through the 1920s, including psychological research, provided more effective means of studying the wallets than the minds of consumers. And many, if not most, individual advertisers themselves still believed they were selling products, not a way of life that would or even could rapidly run amuck. Nevertheless, the ethos of consumption these professionals worked within and furthered both responded to and helped to fuel the recently popular Freudian notion that happiness was as an episodic state of mind rather than a permanent state of being.[23] One of the most popular advertising approaches of the 1920s, scientific advertising, attempted to combine a variety of the latest approaches through the use of clear, precise, and adequately descriptive language; psychological entreaties; and a consumer "hook," such as a coupon. Such an approach demonstrates the variety of tools advertisers would enlist to reel in consumers; it also reveals the transitional and formative nature of the process of consumption, as an emotionally rewarding purchase was packaged simultaneously as a practical and thrifty one.

Assessments of advertising's impact on American life—specifically on its ability to displace values of thrift and cement values of excess—varied widely, even wildly, in the first decades of the new century. Advertisers occasionally admitted to each other that they felt at the mercy of the consuming public; but their own public commentaries, paired with those of their friends and foes, made them appear omnipotent forces in an increasingly corporate, consumerist, anti-thrift world.[24] "Advertising has a thousand principles, one purpose, and no morals," wrote Samuel Hopkins Adams in *Collier's* in 1909.[25] Equally bombastic but with a different twist, William Allen White addressed the Advertising Club of New York in 1927 and argued, "The real revolutionist is the advertising man, whose stimulation of mass desire and demand results in mass production and buying. Could I control the advertising publications of this country I could control the entire land."[26] Importantly, however, for this discussion, others saw in advertising, quite simply, a thrifty ally to business, a shortcut among the myriad choices of contemporary life. Advertising "has revolutionized business," argued one turn-of-the-century proponent, "and made it possible to accomplish in a few years what otherwise would have taken generations to compass."[27] A 1909 editorial in *Profitable Advertising* captured this same sentiment. Manufacturers might believe in investing in buildings, workers, and equipment, but these "cannot guarantee the man a market for his proposed product. Advertising can."[28] Like their counterparts who were implementing scientific management methods in business, advertisers promoted efficiency as a mainstay of their work. They did not waste. Instead, they wove nineteenth-century values of efficient practice into twentieth-century business environments. They remained producers while they touted consumption, thrifty workers while they advocated excess. They also practiced their craft with a constancy smacking of nineteenth-century religious devotion while they claimed for themselves twentieth-century innovative and secular identities.

In their efforts they held a great deal in common with their peers in the professions and in academia in the first decades of the twentieth century, when middle-class values helped shape workplaces and notions of the good life grew increasingly tolerant of corporate involvement and influence. And although much of the professionalization of the advertising industry had already taken place by the onset of World War I, the efforts of advertisers to shape public opinion in support of the war, to create links to other professions engaged in war work, and to continue to mark national identity through purchasing paid off in further dividends. Similar processes would come into play during the Second World War as well, but even by the end of the First World War, national advertising, by all accounts, provided the nation's "characteristic cultural expression."[29]

Ad Agents: Advertising Professionals and Secular Religiosity

> Advertising has nothing to do with literature.
> It is instead closely related to preaching.
> —HELEN WOODWARD, *IT'S AN ART*

Advertising developed through the efforts of a wide range of individuals and a wide range of emerging professions and practices, including artists, job printers, publishers, copywriters, account executives, and professional managers, but many of those individuals and occupations became merged in the popular imagination in the form of the "ad-man" or advertising agent.[30] This composite individual—whom I will call an *ad agent* in respect to the women who, while a minority, populated the field—increasingly came to stand in for the industry and, in a number of cases, for many of the significant cultural changes of the day.[31] These symbols of salesmanship and commerce provided, through their ads, the "usual person's high school."[32] They simultaneously participated in the everyday life of the nation, operated in the business world, populated the self-help literature, and appeared in popular fiction. For those who approved of or even celebrated their work, advertising professionals were responsible for helping to create a higher standard of living for all. This was no mean contribution. In 1928, Frenchman André Siegfried wrote that for Americans, the standard of living was "a somewhat sacred acquisition," suggesting the merging of religious with secular, even business, practices.[33]

Yet for Siegfried and for many critics at home and abroad, the very sacredness of this standard of living proved its inevitable sinfulness. For Americans, Siegfried continued, "This means that they would be ready to make many an intellectual or even moral concession in order to maintain that standard."[34] For advertising's harshest critics, participation in consumer culture on the terms laid out by advertising presupposed a negative gain. Ad agents in this reading purposefully and nefariously shrouded the public in what Karl Marx, continuing the religious metaphor introduced by Woodward, called the religious fog of commodity culture. While purely Marxist analyses of consumer culture fail to offer the kinds of explanatory power they once seemed to promise, the notion of "religious fog" is worth pursuing further. To what degree did the advent of corporate, capitalist consumerism move religious practice out of houses of worship and into what Walter Benjamin called "palaces of consumption"?[35] Did these advertising professionals, in their attempts to sell products, practices, and models of consumer behavior, purposefully and successfully transform thrift to excess? Was consumerism, quite simply, modernity's religion? Arguably, what marks the change from religiosity to secularism, and from thrift to consumption, is not overthrow but accommodation. Ad agent Bruce Barton, himself famous for "conflating the pulpit and the sales counter," attempted through advertising both to secularize Jesus and to sanctify the world of business.[36] The following profile of three of his cohorts demonstrates the nature of continuity in the process.

The first generation of ad agents, with some exceptions, were a homogeneous group marked by race (white), religious background (Protestant), and ethnicity (Anglo), as well as gender (male). They entered and became successful in professional life by embracing the set of cultural values Lears identifies in this volume as operating simultaneously: secular, scientific, and managerial. As the following examination of the lives of three of advertising's early professionals suggests, however, it was through a reformulation rather than rejection of core nineteenth-century values—including religious faith, adherence to hard work, and the practice of thrifty behaviors—that these advertisers developed professional identities, accommodated themselves to the demands of modernity's changing cultural and economic marketplace, and, importantly, legitimated consumption on moral grounds. Several of the most successful of this generation of ad agents, in fact, came from strict religious families, firmly grounded in nineteenth-century values; their professional lives provide apt portrayals of the kinds of accommodation others inside and outside of advertising would likely have experienced in this era of transition. Precisely because they maintained values of thrift and hard work, these individuals would have been hard pressed to view consumer participation, or their own role in promoting it, as behaviors antithetical to moral life. And perhaps consumer directives were more akin to religious tradition than we are inclined to think, as they were, even in this early period, not simply about gratification but about longing, about a search for something at once concrete and intangible, even otherworldly.[37]

CLAUDE C. HOPKINS

Claude C. Hopkins, one of the earliest and highest-paid professional ad agents of the late nineteenth and early twentieth centuries, grew up among strong religious figures and later claimed to have rejected not only their brand of religion but religious practice altogether. Hopkins was born in the small town of Hillsdale, Michigan, in 1866. His paternal grandfather was a minister, a founding member of the Freewill Baptist Church, and a cofounder of the church-affiliated Hillsdale College. His father, who graduated from Hillsdale College, jettisoned family tradition and became printer and then part-owner of a newspaper. He died or, more likely, abandoned the family when Hopkins was a young child, placing the boy in a position of economic responsibility. From age ten he worked for pay, and by the time he graduated from high school, as historian Rob Schorman puts it, he was left with "a flinty, unsentimental view of life and labor and [was] utterly unfazed by the prospect of a sixteen-hour workday."[38] In the company of his mother, a Christian so devout that, as he recalled later, "every joy in life was a sin," Hopkins attended weekly services that might last throughout the day on Sunday.[39]

In keeping with his mother's wishes, or possibly demands, Hopkins started to preach at age seventeen, yet he made a break within a year not only from Baptist preaching but also from his mother. He abandoned religion wholesale, he later declared, because he could not reconcile himself to the notion that "people who danced, played cards or attended the theater belonged to the devil's ranks."[40] Nevertheless, scholars of advertising have argued convincingly that his religious zeal and deterministic outlook factored importantly in his success in the advertising world. Hopkins argued that he found in the secular world more support for his life and work. His beliefs in hard work, the predictable if disappointing nature of human beings, and faith in something larger than himself became manifest in a professional life that promoted the secular over the sacred, and excess over thrift, but his advertising contributions, like his approaches to work, suggest both continuity and contrast.

For many, Hopkins is the greatest copywriter in American advertising history. He invented the "hard-sell" technique of using direct language and research-based approaches. One of the outcomes of his research-based initiatives was the preemptive claim, in which an advertisement highlights a particular quality of a product and suggests its resulting uniqueness and superiority. For a Schlitz beer account, Hopkins discovered that the beer bottles were steam cleaned in the factory prior to bottling. He used this fact to claim the merits of Schlitz, a company sophisticated enough to offer consumers bottles "washed with live steam."[41] For Pepsodent toothpaste, Hopkins introduced a new discovery, plaque, arguing that Pepsodent could erase this harmful substance from teeth. That other breweries steam cleaned their bottles, and that other toothpastes too could eliminate plaque, Hopkins saw no reason to acknowledge. His 1923 book, *Scientific Advertising*, spelled out these and other hard-sell, research-based approaches in detail.

Some considered Hopkins's approach unscrupulous; others found it inspiring. It certainly encouraged consumers to buy goods, and Hopkins became one of the highest-paid copywriters in the business. Yet his contribution to consumer culture was not simply to usher in rampant consumerism, to displace thrift with excess. Hopkins spoke of his own "conspicuous conservatism," and, as Stephen Fox points out, his devotion to work was so strong that, ironically, his entry into advertising effectively denied him the joys he had left the church to experience.[42] He wanted consumers to consume, but he understood the material realities of their lives. He had grown up poor and found salvation in hard work and in the world of business. He was a salesman, but he would hardly have approved of ordinary people's spending themselves into penury or even spending beyond their means. Hopkins walked each morning through Grant Park in Chicago, stopping to preach the rewards of hard work to the men he found residing on park benches. Frugality remained his practice and his doctrine, even as he helped shift the consciousness of the American consuming public.

Hopkins's mother and grandfather had offered him nonmarket ways to meet human needs, and these seemed incongruous with both the world he saw before him and the world he wanted to live in. Advertising offered market ways to meet human needs, and Hopkins's religious background, transplanted to the emerging world of business, pushed him to become enormously successful. It provided him, in an uncertain world, with job security, professional identity, and a middle-class existence, things he lacked as a child bound in part by the rules he consciously rejected. This background also provided him with a second role as preacher, ostensibly serving but also clearly hoping to influence both of his constituencies—clients and consumers.

EARNEST ELMO CALKINS

Earnest Elmo Calkins, born two years after Hopkins, was raised in another small midwestern town, Galesburg, Illinois, under somewhat similar circumstances. The town of Galesburg and its central institution, Knox College, were founded by a revivalist preacher who offered young men missionary training at the college in exchange for manual labor. It was the presence of the railroad, however, rather than the college, that eventually defined Galesburg: within twenty years of the arrival of the railroad in 1854, the town's population had increased from 860 to 10,000. It was in this environment, one of the sacred in direct competition with the secular, that Calkins grew to adulthood. Calkins's mother, having accepted the Baptist training of her father, promoted the idea that "whatever was pleasant was wrong."[43] But Calkins had an alternative influence, or at least an alternative model, in the person of his father, who worked as a clerk and delivery agent by day and attended law school at night. Childhood illness also played a profound role in Calkins's life: a bout with measles at age six started a decline into deafness, which would be almost complete for him by age fourteen.[44]

Calkins had his first experience with advertising while a student at Knox College. As editor of the student literary publication, the *Coup d'Etat*, Calkins received an invitation from George Rowell, founder of *Printer's Ink*: Rowell sent the *Coup d'Etat* a complimentary copy of *Printer's Ink*, offering a free subscription in exchange for an endorsement in print. In his subsequent editorial, Calkins proclaimed *Printer's Ink* the "Messiah" that would take advertising and "elevate it to an art and reduce it to a science."[45] This one experience did not influence his early professional direction, however, and he later more or less stumbled into advertising. Nevertheless, he too became one of its most influential early professionals. While Hopkins believed that his journey from the world of religion to the world of business was an absolute move, Calkins acknowledged the dual influences, as well as his lifelong inability to cast off one identity in pursuit of the other. His legacies, as he put it, left him a "human cocktail, with a jigger of rock-ribbed Puritanism and a jigger of irresponsible liberalism."[46]

Calkins's imperfect acceptance of religious values mirrored his similarly imperfect rejection of values of thrift. While Hopkins developed the hard sell, for which statistics, focus groups, and observation of real behaviors determined advertising approaches, Calkins would make his mark promoting the "soft sell," in which creativity, a feeling for the work, and artistic expression predominated. This aesthetic approach facilitated the move for advertising art into modernity and away from some of the most pronounced Victorian uses of artwork.[47] Earlier advertising artwork had included busy images, even sexually lurid images, which drew the attention of viewers but did little to link the image to the product, the image to the text, or the image to the consumer. Using emerging principles of graphic design and soliciting the work of enormously talented artists, Calkins provided an important counterpart to Hopkins and helped further the centrality of advertising as a form of visual and cultural communication. Yet Calkins's enormous success as a business professional did not require that he abandon a sense of mystery. Even studying psychology, he maintained, could not "make a good advertising man out of one who has not a certain feeling for the work, any more than a study of prosody and versification will make a poet."[48]

Before he promulgated the soft sell, Calkins had a successful career writing advertising jingles; even when his design work took hold, he never lost sight of the importance of language, of advertising copy. For the most part, however, Calkins is remembered for his aesthetics. For an Arrow Collar campaign, he included artwork that showed not only the collar but also an attractive young man wearing the collar. For Wesson Oil, Calkins's ads included beautifully painted images of salads. Calkins's contributions would, in important ways, link aesthetics and consumption and, as Lears puts it, "dematerialize" desire.[49] With the soft sell, participation in consumer culture transported consumers to alternate identities and realities. Calkins's approach helped further an ideology of daily life, particularly in its consumerist elements, that moved away from thrift and toward excess, or at least novelty. Nevertheless, it also helped define thrifty business practice not by stripping advertising down to its most basic elements but by asserting the necessity of beauty, of artwork, of aesthetics in so practical a "science" as advertising. What marked Calkins as so enormously influential was his ability to convince clients to invest in artwork not as a luxury but as an essential element of advertising. His concerns were linked more closely to the material realities of business than those of consumers, and his form of preaching during this period of transition served to elevate art and aesthetics to the level of thrifty business practice.

HELEN LANSDOWNE RESOR

A third member of this early advertising community was Helen Lansdowne Resor, an outsider because of her gender but a "preacher" nonetheless.[50] Born in 1886 in the mountains of northwestern Kentucky, the youngest of nine children in the Lansdowne family, she also grew up with religious influences, although hers were more liberal than those of Hopkins or Calkins. Her maternal grandfather was a Presbyterian minister who had spent three years at Princeton Theological Seminary, and her mother practiced a faith that was progressive and gendered. When Lansdowne was four years old, her mother left her father and moved herself and the children to Covington, Kentucky, where she began paid work. "You're never going to get caught the way I was," she told her daughter. "You're going to learn how to work."[51] She demanded devotion to hard work and success, gender considerations aside—or perhaps made central. Lansdowne graduated as valedictorian from Covington High School and then went to work, for the World Manufacturing Company. Several jobs later she began to write advertising copy for the Street Railways Advertising Company, which controlled much of the nation's streetcar advertising.[52] Eventually she would marry Stanley Resor, and together they would build the J. Walter Thompson advertising agency into one of the world's most powerful.

Lansdowne Resor was one of the first women to write advertising copy, and she later claimed that this "women's view" not only became valued in the advertising world but also made the J. Walter Thompson Company the industry's leader. "The success of the J. Walter Thompson Company has been in large measure due to the fact that we have concentrated and specialized upon products sold to women," she wrote.[53] One of her most significant contributions to the field was the illustrated feature story, which effectively combined the direct talk and research-based copy of Hopkins with the visual appeals of Calkins. She and the women copywriters who worked for her in the gender-segregated women's editorial department at the J. Walter Thompson Company created ads that increasingly looked and felt like editorial copy. This advance in advertising's ability to make a virtually seamless connection between consumer products and other elements of women's magazines had an enormous impact on the field of advertising and on the role of consumerism in women's daily life. Lansdowne Resor is also credited with initiating the use of sex appeal in advertising through her famous campaign for Woodbury's Soap, "The Skin You Love to Touch." Moving away from sexually lurid advertising, these advertisements suggested sensuality and linked the performance of that sensuality directly to a consumer product. These two contributions—the illustrated feature story and the use of sex appeal in advertising—certainly helped to naturalize consumption, to make of it something utterly ordinary and simultaneously something almost otherworldly. In this regard, Lansdowne Resor helped usher in an era of women's consumerism in which excess would eventually trump thrift.

Nevertheless, Lansdowne Resor, in her personal and professional life, demonstrates the lingering nature of thrift in this period. She achieved wealth and enormous professional success, yet she lived and advocated a life for her employees and her consumer clients that included hard work and the thrift that, in her particular twist, would allow women greater financial independence from men (for her employees) and greater household independence (for female consumers). Described in a company newsletter as "a brainy, quietly competent woman of great charm," who dressed conservatively and plainly, wearing no makeup, Lansdowne Resor modeled a demeanor in which work outranked glamour. When she hired women to write copy, she demanded not that they have any advertising experience but, rather, that they be smart and, importantly, value women consumers and themselves. For her, the thrifty ad agent, like the thrifty housewife, could make progress in the world by engaging with consumer culture in ways that validated all women as more complex than nineteenth-century and early twentieth-century American society allowed. In her mind and in her advertising practice, thrift was feminized as gendered service. Professional advertising women provided a shortcut to help consumers make decisions that would simultaneously improve their home lives, give credence to their multiple identities, and acknowledge that many women had goals that included but went beyond the boundaries of domesticity.

Lansdowne Resor encouraged her employees to influence female consumers; she also encouraged them to listen to these consumers. In a staff meeting in 1916, the women discussed the frustrations they heard female consumers express about the *Ladies' Home Journal*, their flagship publication. The *Journal* encouraged passivity among women, censored its fiction, and failed to move forward with women readers. When the staff secured an endorsement by feminist Alva Belmont for Pond's Cold Cream, they celebrated what they saw as an enormous step forward in advertising. For these women, consumer participation was a thrifty way to free women up for more broadly defined activity. The preaching that occurred from the halls of the women's editorial department, under the direction of Lansdowne Resor, favored greater consumption accompanied by greater independence, by womanhood defined as both domestic and public. In this reading, participating in consumer culture provided modern women thrifty avenues to liberation from onerous elements of daily life.

A writer for the J. Walter Thompson Company newsletter argued in 1925 that advertising is "in itself a non-moral force, like electricity, which not only illuminates, but electrocutes. Its worth to civilization depends upon how it is used."[54] Hopkins, Calkins, and Lansdowne Resor, with a zeal that spilled over from their religious upbringings and with a faith in business that mirrored their parents' and grandparents' faith in God, believed that advertising had a great deal to contribute to civilization. As Lears argues about early advertising executives as a group, these individuals merged "professionalism and postmillennial Protestantism," maintaining faith in progress and casting themselves in a redemptive role.[55] Through this faith, they helped further an ethos they understood, arguably, only in part. Caught in a transitional period, these preachers embraced the new and practiced the old, encouraged consumerism and practiced thrifty lifestyles, welcomed change and feared its excesses. Like the female consumers they approached in ways calculated and experimental, sheepishly and with authority, they were both conscious and unconscious arbiters of enormous change.

Women Consumers and Advertising

Edward Bok, longtime editor of the *Ladies' Home Journal*, the most successful women's magazine of the early twentieth century, would articulate in straightforward terms how these advertising professionals simultaneously promoted the values of thrift and postthrift culture. "Make home happy," he wrote, "hold loved ones first in your heart; leave off fussing over fashionable ways of living; be natural, and you will be living the simple life, though you ride in a motor car, clean house by electricity, entertain at the country club, and have every convenience known to man. The quality of the individual is what determines the simple life, never his surroundings."[56] One could, in this world of goods, be thrifty and have it all—and have it all in part by exercising thrift. For Bok and the *Ladies' Home Journal*, for the pioneering advertising professionals profiled earlier in this chapter, and for the culture at large, however, it was no easy task to promote the primacy of consumer goods while praising or at least acknowledging the culture's reliance on women's supposed innate preference for home and family above all else. Nor was it easy to praise women's independence from household tasks, which theoretically if not practically resulted from their participation in consumer culture, while defining home in large part by women's presence in it. It was no easier to promote the breathtaking array of consumer goods available to ordinary Americans while praising women's responsibility for the thrifty maintenance of homes and the modeling of thrifty civic behaviors. It was no easy task, but this transitional group of individuals and organizations did just that; and the women consumers they addressed responded positively on the terms set by advertisers and, in many cases, on terms of their own design.

In a now-famous phrase, an ad agent wrote what by 1929 seemed pure common sense: "The proper study of mankind is man . . . but the proper study of markets is women."[57] Industry estimates stated that women purchased at least 80 percent of the total goods accumulated in families.[58] The middle-class woman, darling of the advertisers, had to be courted by the advertisers and magazine publishers who approached her alternately as her confidant, friend, minister, critic, advocate, and teacher.[59] Just as ad agents were being influenced by changes in advertising technology and by increasing professionalism in their field, so too they were looking to women consumers for important lessons about, as well as proving grounds for, exploring which cultural values could be abandoned, which maintained, and which transformed in the movement from values of scarcity to surplus, thrift to excess.

By the turn of the twentieth century, advertisers increasingly turned to mass-market periodicals as the primary vehicles within which to ply their trade. Women's magazines quickly became dominant, drawing together mass, class, and gender. At the same time that women's magazines began quite effectively to develop a national community of women in their pages, advertisers inserted themselves as central to any developing definitions of community, even family, for women. They did this in two significant ways: by moving advertisements forward in the magazines and by mimicking editorial content in language, imagery, and tone. Early advertising, even in women's magazines, was limited to the margins, specifically to the back pages. The most significant development in the early decades of the twentieth century, perhaps surprisingly, is not that ads became so much more numerous (this had happened by the end of the nineteenth century) but that they moved forward, forming by 1929 a "prodigious labyrinth" of editorial and advertising matter from the front pages of the magazines through to the back covers.[60] At the same time, as described previously, the insights of Hopkins, Calkins, and Lansdowne Resor merged in the advertising profession so that a more integrated approach to advertising copy, images, and appeals meant that it was at times difficult to distinguish advertising from editorial matter. Women's roles as consumers became naturalized even as they were extraordinarily carefully crafted. The "emergent managerial culture" that fostered the gendered advertising played a dual role as well, simultaneously offering myriad promises and providing professional, scientific, rational advice about women's work in the home.[61]

There is no doubt that female consumers responded positively to the developing consumer ethos. Their enthusiastic responses, in fact, ensured the success of the two industries that, mutually dependent, also fully depended on that female consumer: advertising and women's magazines. Women's magazines play a particularly important role in this, as they reveal the give-and-take process with which women's magazine readers and consumers engaged. Because the magazines had a larger role in addressing many facets of women's lives, some of which existed outside of consumer culture, readers developed more intimate relationships with these publications than they did with the more anonymous, although often authoritative, advertisements. Women's magazines offered an increasingly complex web of consumerist values. Advertisements mirrored editorial pieces in language and imagery, but the magazine as a whole offering complicates the question of who mocked whom. Editorial columns on healthy eating increasingly relied on the advertisements that bordered their texts for reinforcements of food-related messages, as well as for visual accompaniments to more simple presentations. Fictional pieces began to rely on the trope of the consumption of goods as solution to a protagonist's search for fulfillment in work or family life. Readers' voices found in letters to the editor, when considered together with a resistant reading of both editorial and advertising content of the magazines, complicate the sense that this change in cultural ethos, even to the degree to which it was successful in a time of transition, was simply as predatory for women as the notion of an abandonment of thrift and embrace of excess suggests.[62]

In women's magazines, as well as in other arenas of advertising, ad agents found new ways to seduce consumers into new cultural patterns. But to do so effectively, they had to give credence to the complaints consumers voiced about modern life, with its excesses, indulgences, anonymity, and isolation—some of the very constraints that emerged from the loosening of ideals of thrift and its accompanying cultural practices. They did so by promoting a community of women bound together by domestic responsibility, as well as through a certain consumer camaraderie. They promised consumer goods as the link that would strengthen rather than weaken family relationships, allow movement to modernity even for those not at the top of the economic ladder, and provide shortcuts to onerous daily tasks through branding and nationalization of consumer goods. Consumerism, in this reading, was thrifty action that facilitated happier, more connected, more efficient household arrangements in a time of uncertainty. The dual voices of authority—the women's magazine writers and editors and the advertisers—ensured, in fact, that women, through consumer participation, finally got the respect they were due.

To go even further, though, and capture the imaginations, wallets, and loyalties of female consumers, women's magazines and advertisers had to acknowledge the limits on women's freedoms that remained firmly in place regardless of changing economic or cultural patterns. Advertising did this more effectively than did the culture at large, laying the groundwork not only for the compensatory exchange of consumer participation but also for the gendered, liberatory possibilities of that same participation.[63] Nineteenth-century and early twentieth-century women remained largely embedded in the domestic. They managed and supported families, sometimes within increasingly less restrictive economic constraints, sometimes not. The contribution of advertising was that it encouraged women to do all this by acknowledging them as citizens who had suffered the injurious nature of some nineteenth-century values. Thrift, in many ways, had relegated at least middle-class women to the private sphere. Consumerism not only promised thrifty approaches to cooking, cleaning, and caring; it also promised leisure time for women and an acknowledgment that women yearned for ways to satisfy their "inarticulate longings" for independence, intimacy, sensuality, personal autonomy, self-worth, and social recognition.[64] Female consumers responded to advertising and its transformation of values of thrift not by abandoning their roles as homemakers but rather by expanding them—by putting thrift to the service of their gendered identities rather than putting their gendered identities to the service of thrift. For women, this embrace of thrift paired with consumerism was a means not simply of accommodating dislocation but, to some degree, of embracing it.[65]

Advertising Thrift

In 1916, the YMCA initiated Thrift Week, a national weeklong celebration commencing annually on the birthday of Benjamin Franklin, the nation's standard-bearer for frugal living. Emphasizing the importance of both saving money and using it wisely, Thrift Week activities initially supported preparedness activities leading up to World War I. Following the war, however, thrift education seemed no less pressing to many, since, according to one national report, the postwar period brought a rejection of thrift and an ethos of excessive consumption, an era of "almost reckless expenditure." In every walk of life, the report continued, "it was the same. Money before saved and invested was spent lavishly and unwisely, time was frittered away and energy and effort dissipated."[66] Interestingly, at the same time that the nation engaged in war and in national attempts at thrift education and practice, the J. Walter Thompson Company advertising agents developed the following advertisement for the Willys-Overland Motor Company (Figure 12.1). The ad provides an apt example of the themes of this essay: the transitional nature of thrift in the culture and in advertising; the ways in which language and imagery worked together to sell products and new ways of participating in twentieth-century life; and the ways in which appeals to women relied, for their effectiveness, on acknowledging the role of women as actors in this social and cultural transition. For advertisers and for female consumers, thrift remained a viable selling point, a compelling cultural value, even as the ad evokes other, competing practices and values.

In imagery, language, and overall cultural message, the Willys-Overland advertisement, which appeared in the April 1918 issue of *Ladies' Home Journal*, acknowledges and even celebrates the transitional nature of thrift in early twentieth-century American advertising and culture. The advertisement's targets—the white, middle-class American housewife and the woman who, although less well off, aspires to such status—are not expected to abandon (at least not altogether) traditional values, even as they embrace new ones. This Overland vehicle will help the female consumer negotiate the demands of a changing world while she retains responsibility for the recreation, health, and busy schedules of her family members. The car's driver does not drive off into

The Thrift Car

WOMAN'S time and ability never were demanded as now.

Never was her need of a motor car so great.

The Overland is known as an ideal woman's car—easy-to-handle, comfortable and dependable.

In hundreds of thousands of homes women are saving time and money, providing recreation and building up health with the thrifty Overland.

Couldn't *you* do more with one?

Appearance, Performance,
Comfort, Service and Price

Willys-Overland Inc., Toledo, Ohio
Willys-Knight and Overland Motor Cars and Light Commercial Cars
Canadian Factory, West Toronto, Canada

FIGURE 12.1[67]

the sunset, abandoning hearth and home. Instead, the multitasking housewife, like the corporate businessman using advertising, recognizes that the tools of consumer culture have become her tools, her assistants as she moves ahead as a modern, consuming, thrifty citizen.[68] As Marchand put it, "Civilization had become its own redeemer."[69]

This advertisement, created by the women in the J. Walter Thompson Women's Editorial Department, provides a compelling example of the ways in which the contributions of Hopkins, Calkins, and Lansdowne Resor helped shape advertising culture and consumer culture. While the language of the advertisement does fix its target on the woman's domestic responsibilities, the image suggests the promise of the car as a vehicle not only for transportation but also as a means to an identity that is classy, sophisticated, independent, sensual, even powerful. The text identifies the car's driver as a housewife, but the image suggests otherwise. This woman may be inextricably tied to children and a husband, but she sits alone in the front seat. The ad as a whole suggests not only a grounding but a launching, not only for a wife but for a woman, not only for a thrifty mother but for a daring adventurer. With the help of Overland, the modern woman can have it all. The ad promises what it can deliver: a more efficient way to accomplish the tasks demanded by an increasingly busy, time-bound society. It also promises what it cannot deliver: autonomy, respect, mystery, and power. The Overland car facilitates rather than threatens women's traditional roles. At the same time it promises more and demonstrates the transitory power of thrift in the face of consumer culture, as images outweigh text, promises outweigh concrete realities, and aspirations outweigh practicalities.

Between 1910 and 1924, not a single product introduced by the J. Walter Thompson advertising agency failed.[70] Advertisers managed, successfully, not only to "stir up" but also to "manage" desire.[71] The J. Walter Thompson Company and its many peers in the growing industry would never have reached such levels of success without a winning combination of appeals: research-based, artistic, psychological, grounded, fanciful, gendered. Neither advertising's practitioners nor its target markets, however, were ready to or required to abandon nineteenth-century values entirely as they moved into twentieth-century practices. On one level, it was difficult by the early twentieth century to view participation in consumer culture as antithetical to thrift; in fact, it was increasingly difficult to even tease one practice out from the other. The efficient housewife would buy ready-made clothes rather than make her own in an effort to live both industriously and in keeping with modern mores. The manufacturer who needed to be convinced of the efficacy of advertising would receive instruction about its inherent thriftiness. Thrift and consumption were paired, twinned, mutually supportive rather than mutually exclusive.

A celebration of National Thrift Day in the town of Malvern, Arkansas, declared that during its subsequent follow-ups to thrifty practice, "all merchants will be expected to offer some unusually attractive bargains." If, as Lawrence Glickman argues in this volume, thrift was both a mark of virtuous character and a means to an end, the end increasingly included participation in consumer culture, and consumption became mass and remained moral. The emerging consumerism that accompanied or prompted this transformation of thrift from a standing value to a tool for effective, modern living went hand in hand with the professionalization of advertising, the development of corporate capitalism, and the modernization of the American middle-class woman.

Notes

1. Jackson Lears, *Fables of Abundance: A Cultural History of Advertising in America* (New York: Basic Books, 1994), 139. In this work, Lears revisits his own earlier work, including in particular arguments he made in "From Salvation to Self-Realization: Advertising and the Therapeutic Roots of the Consumer Culture, 1880–1930," in *The Culture of Consumption: Critical Essays in American History, 1880–1980*, ed. Richard Wightman Fox and T. J. Jackson Lears (New York: Pantheon, 1983).

2. Like economist Simon Patten, many advertisers viewed their "era of abundance" as compatible with moral living. In fact, as Patten argued, this same abundance could facilitate citizenship. See Simon Nelson Patten, *The New Basis of Civilization* (New York: Macmillan, 1907); and Daniel M. Fox, *The Discovery of Abundance: Simon Nelson Patten and the Transformation of Social Theory* (Ithaca, NY: Cornell University Press, 1967).

3. John Dewey, *Individualism Old and New* (New York: Minton, Balch, 1930), 43–44.

4. Kathleen G. Donohue, *Freedom from Want: American Liberalism and the Idea of the Consumer* (Baltimore: Johns Hopkins University Press, 2003), 81.

5. On the discourse of American overproduction and its varied political, diplomatic, and economic manifestations, see Matthew Frye Jacobson, *Barbarian Virtues: The United States Encounters Foreign Peoples at Home and Abroad, 1876–1917* (New York: Hill and Wang, 2000). Josiah Strong, *Our Country: Its Possible Future and Its Present Crisis* (New York: Baker and Taylor, 1886), 14–15, quoted in Jacobsen, *Barbarian Virtues*, 17.

6. A. L. Reinitz, "Research: The Approach to Export Advertising," *Export Advertiser*, November 1929, 30. Similarly, Calvin Coolidge wrote, "The uncivilized make little progress because they have few desires. The inhabitants of our country are stimulated to new wants in all directions. In order to satisfy their constantly increasing desires they necessarily expand their production power. They create more wealth because it is only by that method that they can satisfy their wants. It is this constantly enlarging circle that represents the increasing progress of civilization." Calvin Coolidge, address to American Association of Advertising Agencies, 1926, quoted in "President Coolidge Sees in Advertising a Great Educational Force," *J. Walter Thompson News Bulletin* 126 (January 1927): 26–27, J. Walter Thompson Company Archives, Duke University Library, Durham, North Carolina.

7. Susan Strasser, *Satisfaction Guaranteed: The Making of the American Mass Market* (New York: Pantheon, 1989), 28.

8. John Kenneth Galbraith, *The Affluent Society* (Boston: Houghton Mifflin, 1969), 158, 140. On Galbraith's critiques of American abundance, and their cultural influence, see Daniel Horowitz, "Critique from Within: John Kenneth Galbraith, Vance Packard, and Betty

Friedan," chap. 4 of *The Anxieties of Affluence: Critiques of American Consumer Culture, 1939–1979* (Amherst: University of Massachusetts Press, 2004).

9. William Leach, *Land of Desire: Merchants, Power, and the Rise of a New American Culture* (New York: Vintage Books, 1993), 298.

10. Roland Marchand, *Advertising the American Dream: Making Way for Modernity, 1920–1940* (Berkeley and Los Angeles: University of California Press, 1985), 158.

11. Ibid., 32. On the development of consumer credit, see Lendol Calder's contribution to this volume and his *Financing the American Dream: A Cultural History of Consumer Credit* (Princeton, NJ: Princeton University Press, 1999).

12. On changes in the advertising industry in particular, see Lears, *Fables of Abundance*, 110; on the formation of corporate culture in a number of industries, see Olivier Zunz, *Making America Corporate, 1870–1920* (Chicago: University of Chicago Press, 1990).

13. Leach, *Land of Desire*, 43.

14. Daniel Pope, *The Making of Modern Advertising* (New York: Basic Books, 1983), 144.

15. Neil Harris, *Cultural Excursions: Marketing Appetites and Cultural Tastes in Modern America* (Chicago: University of Chicago Press, 1990), 185.

16. See Pamela Walker Laird, *Advertising Progress: American Business and the Rise of Consumer Marketing* (Baltimore: Johns Hopkins University Press, 1998), 272–73.

17. Marchand, *Advertising the American Dream*, 353.

18. On Hollywood, see George Cotkin, *Reluctant Modernism: American Thought and Culture, 1880–1920* (New York: Twayne, 1992), 28.

19. The J. Walter Thompson Company Archives are in the John W. Hartman Center for Sales, Advertising, and Marketing History, Duke University Library.

20. Strasser, *Satisfaction Guaranteed*, 153.

21. Vincent Miller, *Consuming Religion: Christian Faith and Practice in a Consumer Culture* (New York: Continuum, 2004), 124.

22. See Kerry W. Buckley, *Mechanical Man: John Broadus Watson and the Beginnings of Behaviorism* (New York: Guilford Press, 1989).

23. Sigmund Freud visited the United States for the first time in 1909 and found himself a virtual unknown person, but by the 1920s his theories of psychoanalysis would have taken a firm hold in the American psyche and influenced the advertising world. See Miller, *Consuming Religion*, and Marchand, *Advertising the American Dream*.

24. On the dual performance of advertising agents, see Marchand, *Advertising the American Dream*, 49. Making use of Erving Goffman's theory of "benign deceptions," Marchand argues that advertising agents performed, in trade journals, their expertise and professionalism. With each other, however, they performed a backstage routine in which they acknowledged the uncertainties of their professional lives in general and their ability to sway behaviors in particular.

25. Samuel Hopkins Adams in *Collier's*, May 22, 1909, quoted in Steven Fox, *The Mirror Makers: A History of Advertising and Its Creators* (New York: William Morrow, 1984), 66.

26. William Allen White, *New York Times*, January 13, 1927, quoted in Fox, *The Mirror Makers*, 101.

27. Oscar Herzberg, "The Century's Achievements in Business," *Printers' Ink* 28, no. 2 (1899): 17–19, quoted in Laird, *Advertising Progress*, 338.

28. "From P.A.'s Point of View," *Profitable Advertising* 18, no. 12 (1909): 1180–81, quoted in Laird, *Advertising Progress*, 350.

29. On advertising during World War I, see Pope, *Making of Modern Advertising*, 6, 12, 30; and Fox, *Mirror Makers*, 74–77; Lears, *Fables of Abundance*, 218–25.

30. Although Walter Friedman's recent work focuses on the salesman, not the ad agent, his historical analysis sheds light on social and economic changes that parallel those in the world of advertising. See Walter A. Friedman, *Birth of a Salesman: The Transformation of Selling in America* (Cambridge, MA: Harvard University Press, 2005).

31. When Marchand published his history of the field in 1985, he reported that the ratio of men to women working in advertising in the early twentieth century was approximately ten to one. He also argued that women played a more influential role in advertising than in any other industry except publishing, movies, and department store retailing. Marchand, *Advertising the American Dream*, 33. Following up on Marchand's suggestive tidbits about women in the field, other historians have explored the lives of advertising women. See, e.g., Jennifer Scanlon, *Inarticulate Longings:* The Ladies' Home Journal, *Gender, and the Promises of Consumer Culture* (New York: Routledge, 1995).

32. Alex Osborn, "Advertising, the Life of a Nation—Used Wisely, It Leads to the Pot of Gold," *Newspaperdom*, September 9, 1915, quoted in Richard M. Fried, *The Man Everybody Knew: Bruce Barton and the Making of Modern America* (Chicago: Ivan R. Dee, 2005), 52.

33. André Siegfried, "The Gulf Between," *Atlantic Monthly*, March 1928, 289–96, quoted in Leach, *Land of Desire*, 266.

34. Ibid.

35. On Walter Benjamin and the arcades of nineteenth-century France, see Susan Buck-Morss, *The Dialectics of Seeing: Walter Benjamin and the Arcades Project* (Cambridge, MA: MIT Press), 1989.

36. Fried, *The Man Everybody Knew*, 89. Although Bruce Barton is not profiled here, his life in many ways, particularly concerning issues of religion, mirrors those of Hopkins, Calkins, and Lansdowne Resor. Fried's recent biography sheds a great deal of new light on Barton and his work.

37. See Peter H. Sedgwick, *The Market Economy and Christian Ethics* (Cambridge: Cambridge University Press, 1999), 83.

38. Rob Schorman, "Claude Hopkins, Earnest Calkins, Bissell Carpet Sweepers and the Birth of Modern Advertising," unpublished paper, 2005.

39. Claude C. Hopkins, *My Life in Advertising* (New York: Harper, 1927), 9, quoted in Fox, *Mirror Makers*, 53.

40. Hopkins, *My Life*, quoted in Schorman, "Claude Hopkins," 4.

41. Hopkins, *My Life*, quoted in Fox, *Mirror Makers*, 54.

42. Ibid., 53.

43. Earnest Elmo Calkins, "The Natural History of the Soul," *Atlantic Monthly*, November 1925, 625, quoted in Schorman, "Claude Hopkins," 6.

44. Lears, *Fables of Abundance*, 308.

45. Editorial, *Coup d'Etat*, April 8, 1891, 4, quoted in Schorman, "Claude Hopkins," 16.

46. Earnest Elmo Calkins, "And Hearing Not—," in *Annals of an Adman* (New York: Scribner's, 1946), 11, quoted in Schorman, "Claude Hopkins," 7.

47. See, in particular, Jackson Lears, "The Courtship of Avant-Garde and Kitsch," chap. 10 of *Fables of Abundance*, 299–344.

48. Earnest Elmo Calkins, *The Business of Advertising* (New York: D. Appleton, 1915), 202–3, quoted in Laird, *Advertising Progress*, 277.

49. Lears, *Fables of Abundance*, 313.

50. For a more thorough discussion of Helen Lansdowne Resor, see Scanlon, *Inarticulate Longings*.

51. Gar Schmidt, obituary of Helen Lansdowne Resor, *JWT News*, n.d., J. Walter Thompson Company Archives, Duke University Library.

52. Helen Lansdowne Resor, Stockholder's Affidavit, March 20, 1924, Bernstein History: Officers and Staff, box 4, file 26, J. Walter Thompson Company Archives, Duke University Library.

53. Ibid.

54. "A Radical's View of Advertising," *JWT Newsletter* 84 (June 11, 1925): 6, J. Walter Thompson Company Archives, Duke University Library.

55. Lears, *Fables of Abundance*, 154.

56. Edward Bok, "The Simple Life amid Plenty," *Ladies' Home Journal*, November 1905, 18, quoted in David Shi, "Edward Bok and the Simple Life," *American Heritage*, December 1984, 102. See Horowitz, "Critique from Within," 161.

57. *Printer's Ink* 7 (November 1929): 133, quoted in Marchand, *Advertising the American Dream*, 66.

58. *News Bulletin* 191 (December 1, 1927): 497, J. Walter Thompson Company Archives, Duke University Library.

59. Kathryn Weibel, *Mirror, Mirror: Images of Women Reflected in Popular Culture* (Garden City, NY: Anchor Books, 1977), 158.

60. Sally Stein, "The Graphic Ordering of Desire: Modernization of a Middle-Class Women's Magazine, 1914–1939," *Heresies* 18 (January 1985): 9.

61. On the male and female professionals who urged efficiency in women's lives, see Lears, *Fables of Abundance*, 177–92.

62. On fiction in women's magazines, see Scanlon, *Inarticulate Longings*, 137–68.

63. Fredric Jameson, "Reification and Utopia in Mass Culture," in *Signatures of the Visible* (New York: Routledge, 1990), 9–35.

64. See Scanlon, *Inarticulate Longings*.

65. Women posited that their thrifty behaviors, which combined home work with consumer participation, particularly during wartime, made them ideal candidates for involvement in public life. See ibid., 126–27.

66. "Thrift Education: Being the Report of the National Conference on Thrift Education, Held in Washington, D.C., June 27 and 28, 1924, under the Auspices of the Committee on Thrift Education of the National Education Association and the National Council of Education," in *Prosperity and Thrift: The Coolidge Era and the Consumer Economy, 1921–1929*, Library of Congress, American Memory Project, http://memory.loc.gov/ammem/coolhtml/coolhome.html (accessed January 3, 2011).

67. Source: *The Ladies Home Journal* (April 1918). (This image is in the public domain).

68. Similarly, male automobile workers who lived up to Henry Ford's demands and operated thriftily with their wages and expenses could themselves purchase the automobiles they manufactured.

69. Marchand, *Advertising the American Dream*, 223.

70. Scanlon, *Inarticulate Longings*, 20.

71. Lears, *Fables of Abundance*, 10.

13 }

Hard Payments

CONSUMER CREDIT AND THRIFT

Lendol Calder

Consumer credit has been hard on thrift, most people would say. Historian David Tucker, in *The Decline of Thrift in America*, goes so far as to claim that an American "culture of thrift" was dismantled in the 1920s and 1930s and that it was consumer credit that "killed the concept."[1] It is a familiar equation, this notion that more credit equals less thrift. But a more subtle calculus is necessary. To advance our understanding of the relation between credit and thrift, we must resist nostalgia and ground the history of credit and thrift in evidence beyond the reach of popular memory.

The letter to President Calvin Coolidge is dated January 4, 1929. "Does the policy of Instalment Buying encourage thrift?" a high school student wants to know. The young man asks whether the president has given any speeches on the subject.

No, the president's secretary replies, he has not. The secretary has seen this request before. Since taking office, Coolidge has received hundreds of inquiries from bankers, retailers, credit men, school principals, social workers, ministers, and other interested citizens soliciting the White House for an edict on what the newspapers call "the instalment question." Many are concerned that consumer installment debt has tripled since the end of the Great War. As more and more Americans buy their automobiles, radios, furniture, washing machines, and other big-ticket items "on time," saving before purchasing seems old-fashioned and useless, like sleeping on corn-husk mattresses or observing the formalities of social calling. Even so, the twenties are thrift-haunted times. Not since the American Revolution has thrift been promoted so vigorously. Coolidge is tireless on the thrift front, endorsing campaigns by the Girl Scouts, the Boy Scouts, the YMCA, churches, public schools, the National Thrift Week movement, and others who believe with the president that thrift is "the foundation of civilization." For this reason, those with an interest in the rising popularity of installment buying want to know what

Coolidge, the country's leading exemplar of frugality and self-restraint, thinks about "buy now, pay later." The high school student is canny—all he asks the president to do is simply answer the question "with a yes or a no." "Does the policy of Instalment Buying encourage thrift?" Yes or no?[2]

Yes or no, either-or—this is the way the problem of thrift and consumer credit has always been defined. Most have answered the student's question with an emphatic no. No, said Herbert Hoover, who in 1920 compared a person who buys goods on the installment plan to "a man walking around with a hole in his pocket." No, exhorted a sermon distributed at about the same time for National Thrift Week: "Thriftlessness—debt—mars and stains the soul." No, journalist William H. Whyte Jr. reiterated three decades later as he surveyed the debt loads of suburban households in the fifties, concluding, "Thrift now is un-American!" No, agreed John Kenneth Galbraith in an obituary for thrift included in *The Affluent Society* in 1958: "People have changed their view of debt. . . . There has been an inexplicable but very real retreat from the Puritan canon that required an individual to save first and enjoy later." No, Daniel Bell famously asserted twenty years later in *The Cultural Contradictions of Capitalism*: "The greatest single engine in the destruction of the Protestant ethic was the invention of the installment plan, or instant credit." No, echoes contemporary political commentator David Frum, claiming in a history of the 1970s that when credit cards were democratized in the "Me Decade," "self-denial became downright irrational."[3]

Thrift, one can see, has died a thousand deaths, and every generation since the twenties has believed it was witnessing its final days. The alleged thrifticides have changed over time. At first, people blamed the unregulated loan sharks; then it was the "easy pay" retailers; today, fingers are pointed at credit card issuers and payday lenders. But always the deed is said to have been done with a form of consumer credit, a lethal dart to the heart of the erstwhile thrifty American who—in the twenties? fifties? seventies? nineties?—collapsed in a heap, a victim of the moral poison of instant gratification.

This chapter examines what the rise of modern consumer credit meant for the idea and practice of thrift—the student's question in 1929, more or less. Did consumer credit encourage thrift? The trick will be to escape the inertia of yes-or-no analyses—both the *yes* of the credit industry's view of its service, which is a mythic story about the democratization of credit, and the *no* of the jeremiad tradition, with its equally fantastic belief in a lost golden age of economic virtue, a prelapsarian era when few went into debt and everyone lived within their means. My aim is not to prove the conventional wisdom wrong. Rather, it is to strike out in a wholly new direction, this time attending carefully to unmined historical evidence that challenges popular memories of how credit and thrift operated for previous generations. Serious thought on the problem of what consumer credit has meant for thrift must break away from ahistorical understandings of its subjects.

For example, talk about thrift often assumes it has meant the same thing to all people at all times and in all places. Many think that abstinent saving is the sum total of thrift. But we should not mistake a particular version of thrift for thrift's essential nature. "It is so delightful," opined *Harper's Bazar* in 1890, to budget "systematically, now in a wise outlay, now in a glorious extravagance, now in a sturdy self-denial."[4] From the golden age of thrift comes a statement whose sentimentality does not take away from what it discloses about the essential motion of thrift—how it has ever been less of a straight march to the savings bank than a zigzag trek between spending and saving, destroying and conserving, living for today and taking care for tomorrow. What is thrift really but the coaxing of wealth from scarcity? Time has revealed it to be a supple ethos, demonstrating a large capacity for incorporating new ideas and adapting to changed economic conditions.

Bearing in mind, then, that thrift has a history, and its meaning and application have changed over time, the rise of consumer credit appears in a different light. Credit cannot be said to have killed thrift so much as it transformed it. Whatever else it may signify, the introduction of buying goods "on time" marks a historic moment in what Eugene McCarraher terms "the moral economy of selfhood," the moment in late capitalism when people became convinced that time is more valuable than space or material resources. In this new order of perception, credit emerges as thrift applied to a new commodity: time. The years ahead are uncertain and few—who knows whether we will ever get to spend the money we save on the goods we long for? The tacit prospect of death, sickness, injury, and catastrophe makes waiting for something a chancy affair. But the rise of new forms of credit solves this problem by making it possible to import future satisfactions into the present. From this point of view, there are times when the delay of gratification can be considered unthrifty, a waste of time, our most precious resource.

If common understandings of thrift suffer from a historical amnesia, then the same is true for the way we think about debt and credit—indeed, here many drift into a kind of fantasia. Thinking that consumer credit meant the death of thrift usually assumes that before the invention of credit cards or the installment plan people never went into debt. It assumes that yesteryear's prescriptive sermons on thrift described a thrifty people, too. But the presence of a robust thrift ethos in a historical period tells us little about how people actually handled their finances, about whether people then were very thrifty at all.

President Coolidge knew this much. In 1926, three years before the high school student inquired whether consumer credit encouraged thrift, Coolidge was asked the very same question by reporters. Caught off guard, the president allowed that he disagreed with his secretary of commerce, Herbert Hoover, who had recently described installment buying as a menace to national prosperity. Sensing that reporters were surprised by his response, the nation's foremost apostle of thrift enlarged on his opinion with a statement that made front-page headlines across the country. Coolidge said he viewed the method of having definite obligations to pay at stated intervals far preferable to what he observed in his neighborhood as a boy, "the old way of running up a bill at the store" and "perhaps never paying it at all."[5] The old way of never paying at all? Here is a good place for a history of thrift and consumer credit to begin.

Beautiful Credit! The Foundation of Modern Society

Reconstructing how people lived with debt before the rise of modern consumer credit will help to show in what ways consumer credit was and was not new and also how it could spring up so quickly in the face of what is usually remembered, not very accurately, as a debt-averse culture.

Consider the case of Walter T. Post, a late nineteenth-century railroad clerk whose letters offer an unusually transparent window into the money management of a household that aspired to middle-class respectability in the era before consumer credit.[6] Born on a farm in Michigan in 1867, Post attended a Detroit business college and then landed a job in 1889 as an accountant with the Northern Pacific Railroad in St. Paul, Minnesota. From the day he arrived in St. Paul until the week he lost his job with the railroad seven years later, Post wrote weekly letters to his parents, providing a detailed record of his thoughts, activities, and personal finances. Many of the letters offer monthly budget figures, with outlays recorded down to the penny. The young man revealed in these letters was no spendthrift. He was a man who liked to do right, whose one great passion in life was evangelical religion. But on a clerk's salary of fifty-five dollars a month, Post still had a hard time making ends meet. While a single man, he did all right. Though he regularly bought goods on credit from local retailers and traveling salesmen, and though he occasionally obtained loans from friends, some months saw him in the black and lending money to coworkers or sending a surplus home to his folks.

But once Post got married in 1894, balanced budgets were a thing of the past. The remaining two years of letters show him and his wife, Lilly, deeply in debt. It began the month after they were married. Having rented a house, the Posts felt it necessary to fill the bare rooms, floors, and walls in a manner befitting a middle-class couple expecting to entertain guests. After some comparison shopping and some whittling down of their original wish list, the young couple purchased furniture and carpets from Schuneman and Evans department store on terms of two-thirds down and the balance in sixty days. For the kitchen, Post bought a used stove from a friend for $6 down and $15 later. As the debts mounted higher, it turned out to be *much* later. By the spring of 1895, the Posts owed money to the dentist, the doctor, the grocer, the butcher, a tailor, the hardware store, and a sewing machine agent. They also still owed money on the furniture and stove, extending these loans several times over. As the creditors became insistent, Post borrowed from Peter to pay Paul, tapping his brother Charlie for a loan. After rent, groceries, ice, fuel for the stove, and other fixed expenditures, Post's disposable income that spring was about $10 a month; the Posts' debts totaled $78.50. "Has not the middle class its poverty?" asked labor leader Ira Steward twenty years earlier. "Very few among them are saving money. Many of them are in debt, and all they can earn for years, is, in many cases, mortgaged to pay such debt."[7]

In 1896, when Post lost his job with the Northern Pacific during a period of corporate reorganization, he still owed money to the doctor, dentist, sewing machine agent, and his brother. Reading Post's letters adds sense and meaning to a saying attributed to Artemus Ward, the mid-nineteenth-century humorist, who was fond of telling audiences, "Let us live within our means, even if we have to borrow money to do it."[8]

We may wonder whether the Posts were exceptional. Post seemed to think so. In his letters, he portrayed himself as the thriftiest of the dozens of clerks who worked in the St. Paul office, clerks who were occasionally fired for drunkenness, for gambling, and for having their wages garnished by persistent creditors. Perhaps Post was kidding himself. But his letters put a human face on the U.S. Census Bureau's estimate that in 1890 the average American household owed $880 (about $16,000 today), an estimate of recorded mortgage debts that almost certainly undercounted the kinds of obligations carried by the Posts.[9]

Close observers of the American scene like humorists Artemus Ward and Mark Twain got closer to the truth about American household finance in this period than the census takers could. "Beautiful credit!" observed Twain in 1873, was "the foundation of modern society." He said this in *The Gilded Age*, a satire of the lustful acquisitiveness and greedy speculation of the postbellum era, both in the world of commerce and in the homes of the "thousands of families in America" obtaining "prosperity and luxury" the same way, through the formula of "Charge it!"—the first time this phrase appears in American literature.[10] Twain implied that once it was not so, that earlier Americans knew better how to live within their means. But this is doubtful. Just before the Civil War, the celebrated orator and statesman Edward Everett observed everywhere around him a "natural proclivity to anticipate income, to buy on credit, to live a little beyond our means." Putting aside business debt, Everett estimated the nation's total household indebtedness in 1858 to be $1.5 billion, or $300 per household. The figure was conjectural, based solely on Everett's observation and experience, but Everett felt it could hardly be denied that the entire country was trying to go forward under "a mountain load of debt."[11]

Reliable data on personal indebtedness only became available many decades later, so estimates of debt before 1920 are soft. But they all point in the same direction, toward the conclusion that it is a mistake to think that nineteenth-century Americans lived in a golden age of thrift, when people always saved up for the things they wanted or did without. It is generally recognized that nineteenth-century producers—farmers, say, or shopkeepers, or entrepreneurs—floated on a vast sea of credit. Credit made it possible to buy land, conduct business, put in crops, and start new enterprises. But nineteenth-century consumers depended on credit, too—credit obtained from a vast, subterranean network of formal and informal lending sources.

It is easy to forget this earlier credit system because its transactions were conducted mostly away from the public eye. Before 1915, credit for individuals was capillary-like and hidden. It was disorganized, decentralized, poorly capitalized, socially stratified, and disreputable in some of its forms. Most credit was an arrangement between private individuals. If it was necessary to go outside the circle of family and friends for a loan, where a person went depended to a great extent on whether one was male or female, white or black, foreign- or native-born, Jewish or Catholic, a resident of New York City or of San Francisco. How gender, race, ethnicity, and region mattered for obtaining credit would fill volumes. Here, I will briefly sketch the difference made by social class.

"I buy everything on credit until I get no more, then I go to another store and do the same there," a German American housewife wrote to the *New Yorker Volks-Zeitung* in December 1882, when the second largest German American daily in New York City asked its working-class readers to comment on the costs and expenditures of their family budgets. From the discussion that followed it became clear that most of the readership was barely scraping by, and many were in debt.[12] Their stories were not atypical for late nineteenth-century workers' households. Families at the broad base of the working-class pyramid struggled daily to make ends meet and stood desperately in need of credit assistance. Budget studies conducted in the early years of the twentieth century show that at least half of working-class families in large cities waged a constant, teetering effort to match income with expenses and that a little over a quarter experienced deficits at some point in a year.[13] The slightest disturbance in the balance between income and expenses, whether brought on by illness, unemployment, injury, or simply the desire to help a relative in need, sent families looking for money. They easily found it from pawnbrokers and small-loan lenders, or "loan sharks," operating outside the legal limits on usury. Also, as the German American housewife testified, by the 1880s working-class families made regular use of retail installment credit from peddlers and low-quality borax stores, so-called because their overpriced goods and high-pressure selling "cleaned a person out."

If working-class households were driven into indebtedness mostly by poverty, middle-class households were similarly affected by prosperity. By the late nineteenth century, much of what it meant to be middle class lay in a style of living that required ownership of a home and an array of commodities to adorn it. But homes and household goods did not come cheaply. Consequently, many families with bourgeois aspirations resorted to purchasing the symbols of middle-class life out of their future earnings. We have already seen what this practice looked like in the case of the Posts. Their experience was typical, since nineteenth-century middle-class households satisfied their credit needs with book credit from local merchants; installment credit from merchants such as high-grade department stores, furniture dealers, piano companies, and booksellers; and cash loans obtained from friends and family. "There is a poverty of which no man heareth," observed investigators of the standard of living in Boston in 1870, whose study of middle-class homes resulted in a report on what they called "the poverty of the middle class." The middle-class worker had a higher income than the low-paid unskilled worker, but, as the investigators pointed out, "the wage of the one, though double, it may be, of that of the other, is consumed in his necessary cost of living."[14] Middle-class homes called for the satisfaction of a thousand wants. The net result of higher incomes and higher expenses was that middle-class people had need of credit just as much as lower-class families.

But for everyone who was not rich, both workers and professionals, what required the most credit was the house itself. "About everyone that lives in what he calls his own house, is in debt!" observed a Massachusetts shoe leather cutter in 1870.[15] In fact, in the late nineteenth century, home mortgages accounted for the largest single portion of household debt.

The ideal way to buy a home was to save money first and then find or build a house later. But then as now life was too short to wait to pay cash for a home. In the last third of the nineteenth century, houses for low- and moderate-income families ranged in price from $1,000 to $4,500. Thus, in order to buy a modest home of $1,500, a family earning $1,000 a year—about the average salary of white-collar clerical workers—would have to save one-tenth of its income per year for fifteen years. Not willing to wait that long, most acquired their houses with funds borrowed from relatives, from public and private building and loan associations, from previous owners, from individuals loaning their savings at interest, and from a variety of banks. Nationwide, the typical arrangement for home financing was a mortgage for 69 percent of the sales price, obtained from individual savers with money to lend, savings banks, or building and loan associations, at 5 to 6 percent interest, for five years. But this should not be allowed to obscure the creative diversity in the sources, methods, and terms of home financing. The 1890 U.S. census found that mortgages were taken out on 29 percent of the homes in the United States, with an average debt of $1,139 per home.[16]

Mortgage buying compelled homeowners, except those from the wealthiest families, to practice strategies of economy over a long period of time. Letters sent to a 1903 *Ladies' Home Journal* survey on house financing spoke of the joys of home ownership but also of the "close calculation" and the "struggle, toil, and labor" needed to pay off such large debts. Mortgagees often reported that debt for the home required them to pay cash for everything else, to cut out nonessential consumption, and to adopt strict budgeting procedures. "It was all a question of management," a man from Virginia wrote, explaining how he and his family paid off their loan:

> Bless me, how we did economize. . . . The lifetime of a garment extended far beyond the allotted span for such things. We walked, disdaining street cars. It was good exercise and saved the nickels which were needed to pay interest on our mortgage. We bought the high-priced articles less often; the lower-priced more frequently. I was my own bootblack and barber. Indeed we might almost call our house the house of small economies, for it certainly was only by saving in small matters that we were able to secure it.[17]

The financial discipline imposed by purposeful indebtedness left its mark on people. "So deeply was the habit of saving rooted within us," reported a homeowner from Missouri who had recently retired the mortgage on his house, "we have continued to save, to some extent, and now . . . have bought and paid for several other houses."[18] In this way did millions of Americans discover that credit could be used to make distant dreams present realities. In the process they also learned that debt could be a hard master.

It was a lesson in discipline even renters could learn—the Posts, for example. "I have to do some awful close figuring to make ends meet," Walter Post wrote to his brother Charlie, "and then they don't meet." To his father, he complained, "We were paid off today but all the money is spoken for before I get it almost."[19] Nevertheless, Post felt that the debts he had incurred were helpful for achieving the life he wanted. Comparing the costs of keeping house as renters versus as boarders, he conceded that a few more years of boarding would have enabled him and Lilly to put aside $150 of his salary at a savings bank. "But now we have $202.80 worth of furniture," he answered himself. "And we might have had to use some of the money in the Bank so you see we are ahead a good deal."[20] It is an interesting logic: though they owe money on their tables and chairs, Post regards their furniture as a form of savings. He recognizes that the liquidity of a bank savings account is to him a constant temptation to spend money on more insubstantial expenditures. Here are the core ideas for a developing ethos of thrift that, thirty years later, will figure prominently in public justifications of new kinds of consumer credit. But Post did not come to these ideas on his own. He found them latent in the ethical norms governing money management he learned from his parents, teachers, and community leaders—norms that are worth looking at if we want to understand how consumer credit became morally plausible as a form of thrift.

The claim so far is that, contrary to popular myths of lost economic virtue, a river of red ink runs through American history. This is easily forgotten because this indebtedness flowed mostly underground, hidden away in the grocer's book and the pawnshop ledger, on the butcher's tablet and in the memory of friends. But this is not to say that nineteenth-century Americans failed to live up to reigning ideals of thrift. The surprise is that the money management ideals they were given to live by were more flexible about indebtedness and spending than people later remembered. When a 1915 survey asked people to describe their early training in money management, one respondent replied, "My financial training at home was not very extensive. . . . I was taught, however, to be strictly honest and was never permitted to go into debt."[21] The respondent's memory may have been accurate, but as a synopsis of nineteenth-century instruction on money management, it is an insufficiently rich version of the subject. The way to wealth in the Victorian era viewed judicious debt as a permissible method for turning poverty to plenty—in other words, as a case of thrift.

The Way to Wealth

"The Way to Wealth," of course, was Benjamin Franklin's omnium-gatherum of proverbs on industry and frugality culled from the pages of *Poor Richard's Almanack*, published in 1758. A thousand subsequent editions made it the nineteenth century's most popular single text of economic advice, creating a notional capital so immense that some of its sayings still resonate today: "Early to bed, and early to rise, makes a man healthy, wealthy, and wise"; "He who goes a borrowing goes a sorrowing"; and so on.[22] The popularity of this text and its hundreds of analogues indicates how nineteenth-century Americans took the measure of an expanding market economy. Living by making and spending a money income required mental and moral abilities of a kind not inculcated by older systems of exchange, and these abilities were far harder to acquire than we realize. It required new cultural disciplines that compelled people to become more calculating, more provident, and more intent on self-control, that is, to acquire what were called the "economic virtues": thrift, economy, planning, and saving.

As didactic literature, nineteenth-century money management advice often took a hard line on debt. Debt was portrayed as "a calamity," "an oppressive and degrading incubus," "an inexhaustible fountain of dishonesty," an "ally of the devil." The best lines belonged to Franklin's Poor Richard: "The second vice is Lying, the first is running into Debt"; "The borrower is a slave to the lender"; "Maintain your Independency, be frugal and free." But if advice-givers like Franklin had to shout against debt, one reason was because no one was listening. As Poor Richard notes at the conclusion of Father Abraham's antidebt homily in *The Way to Wealth*, "The People heard it, approved the doctrine, and immediately practiced the contrary."[23]

It was not simply that people lacked the discipline of their ideals. The fact is that nineteenth-century money management ethics proscribed debt and then winked at some forms of it. "Debt is an inexhaustible fountain of dishonesty," maintained Henry Ward Beecher. But on other occasions the minister also averred that "if a young man will only get in debt for some land, and then get married, these two things will keep him straight, or nothing will."[24] "One never becomes rich until he is in debt," ran a popular nineteenth-century epigram, which is similar to Twain's report of overhearing a man who said, "I wasn't worth a cent two years ago, and now I owe two millions of dollars."[25] P. T. Barnum was one of the century's great advocates for thrift, yet he told audiences the story of an old Quaker who said to his son, "John, never get trusted, but if thee gets trusted for anything, let it be for 'manure,' because that will help thee pay it back again."[26] General Benjamin Franklin Butler, when asked to summarize his financial advice for young men, offered rather prosaic advice: "Buy improved real estate, partly for cash, and partly for small notes."[27] Such evidence represents the thin end of a wedge in the didactic literature's prohibition of debt, a wedge that opened up space for at least certain types of borrowing.

As Philip Rieff has argued, all ethical systems of meaning employ a dialectic of complementary constraints and exemptions. Cultures build community and make sense of behavior by first organizing moral demands on people and then sanctioning appropriate releases from those demands. The moral demands make society a friendlier, more trustworthy place, while the approved releases give people relief from the strain of conforming to communal purposes.[28] This dynamic of restraints and releases is evident in the financial advice given by even the most famous hard-liners on indebtedness. Cotton Mather, the Puritan, and Benjamin Franklin, the Yankee, both recognized that debt could not be absolutely prohibited.[29] Although financial advisers generally took a dim view of debt, they also were ready, and sometimes eager, to make concessions to the opportunities of an advanced money economy.

Borrowed money was, after all, credit, which in nineteenth-century America was a valued necessity. Credit built communities; it got young people started in life. Credit staked the pioneer for a homestead, enabled immigrants to obtain a business, allowed business owners to enlarge their plans, and knit borrower and lender together in bonds of mutual dependency. "Credit to a man," declared business journalist Freeman Hunt, "is what cream is to a nice cup of coffee."[30] Hunt's jocular tone was made possible by attitudes toward credit he could take for granted, an ethos appearing a century earlier that viewed lending and borrowing as a barometer of public morality, the exact measure of the soundness of the social state. Examining writers as diverse as Mather, Franklin, Royall Tyler, Charles Brockden Brown, and Judith Sargent Murray, Jennifer Baker finds that "writers within all these social and intellectual circles [Puritan, Yankee, southern agrarian, revolutionary] imagined new modes of financial speculation and indebtedness as a means to build American communities and foster social cohesion." After the Revolution and continuing into the early twentieth century, credit was an emblem for the unity and coherence of society as a whole. In the language of the day, people did not "borrow money"; rather, they "got trusted."[31]

Credit was character, credit was trust, credit was good. Recognizing this truth, the money ethic allowed borrowing in certain circumstances. Negotiating the interplay between caution and opportunity, nineteenth-century Americans recognized a taxonomy of debt that distinguished proper from improper indebtedness, "getting trusted" from being "in debt." The crucial categories, taken from classical economics, were "productive" and "consumptive" credit.

Speaking to lenders, William Cunningham, in his 1891 book *The Use and Abuse of Money*, advised, "If a man burdens his estate not in order to enable him to make permanent improvements, but in order to maintain an extravagant expenditure, he is at least acting foolishly, and it is wrong to help him to make a fool of himself."[32] Productive credit put borrowed money to work in such a way that the debt repaid itself in full and turned a profit, too. If a borrower had good character and an opportunity arose requiring a loan but offering reasonable hopes that profits would liquidate the debt, then the attitude was to go ahead: "To borrow for genuinely productive purpose, for a purpose that will bring you in more than enough to pay off your debt, principle and interest, is a profitable enterprise. It shows business sagacity and courage, and is not a thing to be ashamed of. But it cannot be too much emphasized that the would-be borrower must calculate very carefully and be sure that it is a productive enterprise before he goes into debt."[33]

Indeed, it is doubtful whether nineteenth-century Americans considered productive debts to be debt at all. The conservative *Banker's Magazine* was explicit on this point, avowing in 1888 that indebtedness "for the creation of a valuable property . . . cannot be truly considered an indebtedness, inasmuch as the capital borrowed is still in existence, and has been the means of a new creation."[34]

It was productive credit that Calvin Colton (using the pen name Junius) praised when he wrote in 1840, "Credit has been the spring of our enterprise, the nurse of our prosperity, the cause of our greatness."[35] Productive credit's short list of legitimate and healthy purposes began with borrowing to start a business or to purchase land. But if the concept of productive credit established that "no man has a right to be a borrower who has not the most positive assurance of his ability to pay," then, by this criterion, Americans found increasing scope for borrowing money as the nineteenth century wore on.[36] Under this rubric, loans obtained for building or buying a house qualified as productive debt. "The installment mortgage . . . is a great incentive to saving, and a very popular method of borrowing money," the *Ladies' Home Journal* advised readers in 1898. By putting money in an investment that would increase in value, home mortgages guaranteed that the debt could be paid off. In addition, it diverted money that might have been spent on luxuries to a more productive purpose.[37]

This kind of thinking gradually put other items on the list of productive uses for debt. A contributor to one of the numerous published debates over installment buying in the 1920s remembered that while growing up on a "midwest wilderness farm," he had come into contact with the installment plan on five occasions: "first, when my mother bought her sewing machine; second, when my father bought his reaper; third, when the family purchased a piano; fourth, when I bought my first good suit . . .; and fifth, when I purchased my *Encyclopaedia Britannica* in place of the college education that was beyond my reach."[38] H. L. Reade's financial advice book *Money and How to Make It* described the sewing machine as "a business necessity," the piano as "a source of delight and perhaps (if needful) of revenue," and the mower as something that would "pay for itself." These examples indicate the manner of thinking when it came to defining prudent debts.[39]

The mirror image of productive credit was "consumptive debt." "Borrowing money is a strictly business transaction," said *Harper's Weekly*, "to which no reproach should attach, unless the borrower be a spendthrift, and merely raising funds for some reprehensible end."[40] The list of reprehensible ends was larger than the list of proper uses for debt. It included every object that consumed money without yielding a net addition to the balance sheet. The category included food, clothing, flimsy house furnishings, entertainments, and "the ordinary necessaries of life."[41]

But even so there were exceptions to be made. One was for those "honest debtors" who through no fault of their own found themselves in financial straits.[42] The other exception applied to reliable people who, for reasons of convenience, kept a tab running for groceries and other basic supplies. Debts of convenience were considered acceptable if accounts were settled on a regular basis.[43] Money moralists warned that book credit had its dangers. The picture hinted at by Coolidge in 1926 when he was reminiscing with reporters is filled out by Barnum: "Debt for what you eat and drink and wear is to be avoided. Some families have a foolish habit of getting credit at 'the stores' and thus frequently purchase many things which might have been dispensed with."[44] But particularly in rural communities where ready money was scarce, book credit was almost the only way to pay for goods.

If the hard line on thrift was never to go into debt, this was advice easier to commend than to live out. The more practical advice on money management opened a breach that, in the early decades of the twentieth century, entrepreneurs with money to loan easily stormed through.

The Credit Revolution

Between 1900 and 1940, in a highly uneven process that had begun long before and would continue down to the present time, household finance in the United States was remade by the creation of a modern system of credit for consumers.

By "modern" I mean that the older, subterranean, local system of credit was replaced by a new corporate system that was regulated by the state, widely publicized and promoted, democratic in aspiration (though not in execution, especially at first, when women in particular found it harder to obtain credit on their own, not easier), and so immensely popular or at least useful that living on credit became a notable feature of the American way of life.

The expansion of the nation's credit system involved so many changes in the infrastructure of finance that contemporaries agreed they were witnessing nothing less than a "credit revolution." From 1920 to 1929, outstanding loans for consumer goods soared 131 percent, from $3.3 billion to $7.6 billion. According to Martha Olney, the ratio of debt to income in American households in this period doubled, rising from around 5 percent to almost 10 percent.[45] By 1926, two of every three cars sold were bought on credit, and credit plans were powerful incentives for the sales of radios, refrigerators, vacuum cleaners, fine jewelry, and other consumer durable goods. A key to this development was the widespread adoption of the installment plan, which—more than open account credit—was suited to the regular pay schedules of industrial and salaried workers.

The expansion of the credit supply was channeled by a new system of lenders and creditors, principally installment sales finance companies, retail installment lenders, and licensed consumer finance companies. The latter waged a successful fight in state legislatures after 1917 to repeal restrictive usury laws that for years had essentially outlawed small-loan lending. Not every loan shark was interested in joining reform-minded colleagues to professionalize the small-loan business, but those who did joined with progressives in the Russell Sage Foundation and reversed the usual strategy of professional association by campaigning *for* state regulation of their industry. The resulting Uniform Small Loan Law became the legal foundation for small-loan lending in the United States. Joining the licensed lenders were "industrial" banks, remedial loan societies, credit unions, Morris Plan banks, and a few commercial banks ready to experiment with personal loan departments. These new institutions of credit brought capital, bureaucracy, rationalized procedures, and legal recognition to the growing business of consumption credit. Equally important, the new consumer lenders brought the blaze of publicity to a type of lending and borrowing that was formerly conducted in the shadows of public life. Household credit was one of the most heavily promoted consumer services of the 1920s. By the end of the decade, phrases such as "buy now, pay later" and "take advantage of our easy payment plan" had become standard in the vocabulary of consumership.

Snappy slogans would lure some into more debt than was good for them, but overall it seems evident that demand for credit preceded supply. This order is clearly apparent in the way that automobile credit developed.

In the beginning of the automobile trade, manufacturers and dealers sold cars only for cash. Credit seems to have been offered in the used-car market first, when private individuals took out classified ads offering "terms to suit." Later, starting about 1910, a few large dealers began offering credit plans. But most dealers were too busy scrambling to line up financing for themselves to be in a position to offer credit to their customers; manufacturers expected dealers to pay cash on delivery. To meet the credit needs of both customers and dealers, the first sales finance company was created in 1913. The immediate success of sales finance companies prompted Ford and General Motors to formulate business plans addressing the problems and opportunities presented by automobile financing. The plans they came up with could not have been more different. From 1923 to 1927, car buyers had the unusual prospect of a genuine choice between rival moral economies: one that valued money, the other that valued time. The winning plan would shape the contours of thrift for decades to come.

General Motors responded first to consumers' demand for credit, creating in 1919 the General Motors Acceptance Corporation (GMAC) for the purpose of financing GM automobiles on a company-sponsored installment plan. But Ford held back. That same year Edsel Ford estimated that at least 65 percent of Ford cars and trucks were being sold on a time-payment basis through independent sales finance companies. Henry Ford, though, believed his company had an obligation to the nation to encourage the character-building discipline of saving to buy a Ford automobile with cash. As GM installment sales rose from 33 percent of new cars sold in 1919 to 46 percent in 1923, and as GM gained ground in market share on Ford's leadership of the industry, Ford managers could see that customers welcomed monthly payment plans because such plans enabled them to buy expensive cars they would never be able to afford for cash. The Ford Weekly Purchase Plan, unveiled in April 1923, was Ford's remarkable alternative to the GMAC approach. The Ford plan sounded like a typical installment scheme, but it was actually more of the reverse. Under the Ford plan, a customer selected a body style at the local Ford dealer and then filled out papers with the salesman to begin a dealer-sponsored savings plan with a "down payment" of as little as five dollars. The dealer took the money and succeeding weekly payments to a local bank, where it was deposited in the purchaser's name and drew interest for the buyer. Depositors were allowed to skip deposits, and the money could be withdrawn in the event of emergencies. When the purchase price of the selected automobile had been accumulated, the customer took delivery on the car. A starker alternative to the idea of "buy now, pay later" would be difficult to imagine. The Ford Weekly Purchase Plan promoted the most conservative conceptions of thrift, savings, and delayed gratification.[46]

The "admosphere" of consumer societies makes it difficult to maintain the self-discipline required for a long obedience to abstinent saving. The Ford

Weekly Purchase Plan was intended to give people in the $1,000 to $2,000 income bracket the necessary external support they needed to save money over an extended period. Customers might simply have established their own savings account, but developers of the Ford plan observed that when this happened, most savers ended up frittering away their small accumulations "with nothing to show for it."[47] Ford executives became convinced their plan would work after studying the popular Christmas club plans organized by various banks across the country. In 1922 Americans had saved $190 million for Christmas presents this way.[48] Ford executives hoped that the Ford plan would appeal to thrift-minded people who believed that good things come to those who wait.

But most people no longer viewed the world in these terms, if very many ever did. The Ford plan was an embarrassing failure. In the first eighteen months of the program only 400,000 people enrolled. Of these, only 131,000 persevered to take delivery on cars (less than a month's regular sales). The Ford plan fell apart for several reasons. Because there was nothing in the Weekly Purchase Plan to interest the dealers, they had no reason to promote it. In addition, customers found it hard to stick with the plan. "We often had to refund [deposits]," explained one Ford dealer. "After people would get $50 or $75 they would want a vacation or something and they would withdraw it."[49]

But fundamentally the Ford plan failed because most car buyers entertained ideas about consumer finance considerably more sophisticated than the simple notions about thrift espoused by Henry Ford. What seemed like thrift to Ford seemed more like waste to others. In the minds of many, the costs and benefits of saving to buy a car were greater than those associated with buying expensive durable goods on credit. While saving to buy a house, one had to pay rent. While saving to buy a refrigerator, one had to pay the ice man. While saving to buy a ring, a suitor might lose his prospective fiancée. In the same way, while saving to buy a car, people either had to pay money for other forms of transportation or go without the benefits provided by an automobile. Why not, many reasoned, take advantage of a pay-as-you-use installment plan, thus avoiding the costs of not owning a car? This line of reasoning gained converts all through the 1920s, including eventually Henry Ford himself. The Ford Weekly Purchase Plan was such a miscalculation of what the public wanted in automobile financing that Ford later disclaimed any responsibility for the plan.[50]

With the failure of the Weekly Purchase Plan and the surrender of market leadership to General Motors for the first time in 1926, Ford was finally forced into the credit business. Introducing the long-awaited Model A in late 1927, Ford announced a few months later the creation of a company-sponsored installment sales finance company, the Universal Credit Corporation. Ford justified its belated entry into the consumer finance business as one more step in its long-range goal of integrating all aspects of automobile production "from the mines to the consumer." It was a step that came too late to help Ford regain the lead in its race with General Motors.[51]

From Consumptive Debt to Consumer's Credit

Spearheaded by automobile financing, the rise of consumer credit in the twenties inspired passionate debate among those who watched it grow, some with fascination, others with dismay. "The American family's plunge into debt for commodities during the last few years," wrote Harvard economist Franklin W. Ryan in 1930, "constitutes one of the most remarkable phenomena in modern history."[52] The biggest question for observers then—including the high school debater who wrote President Coolidge—was, what did it all mean?

The dominant view among cultural elites interpreted the rise of consumer credit as a significant departure from a thrifty past when, as Ryan remembered it, "most people 'never got into debt and always lived within their means.'"[53] "We are living in an age of credit," wrote George Horace Lorimer of the *Saturday Evening Post* in 1924, "or perhaps a more accurate delineation would be an age of debt. The firmly rooted aversion to debt in any form which prevailed a generation ago has almost completely evaporated."[54] Obviously, Lorimer had never read Twain's *Gilded Age*, which made the very same claim a half century earlier. But he was hardly alone in misremembering the way things used to be. In the urbanizing, industrializing, and socially fragmenting world of the early twentieth century, nostalgia for a lost golden age was widespread as Americans looked to sentimentalized reconstructions of the past to provide a baseline for measuring the extent of the rapid, overwhelming changes taking place about them. A tendency developed to view the past in romantic terms, remembering it as an untroubled pastoral era, a time when the moral lines were more clearly drawn and more faithfully followed. "In other and simpler days," recalled an editorialist in the *New York Times* in 1923, "debt was a thing dreaded as the worst of ogres."[55] This is what I have called the myth of lost economic virtue, a piece of nostalgia entirely in harmony with the times.[56]

Belief in the myth led many to hold installment borrowing and buying responsible for a breakdown in the moral nature of economic decision making. "Consumer credits," wrote the historian Preston William Slosson in 1930, put thrift "at a discount in all classes."[57] If this was true, it was no small development in the history of the United States. Thrift had long been deemed a core value of American citizenship, as well as a mainspring for national prosperity. This helps explain why credit then and later received so much abuse. Before consumer credit, it was possible to believe the average person was insulated from the temptations of affluence. "No nation was ever hurt by luxury," maintained Samuel Johnson, "for it can reach but to a very few."[58] For a century and more after Johnson, a dearth of disposable income functioned as a moat preventing most Americans from entering Vanity Fair. But consumer credit bridged the moat. When the millions stormed over, it seemed obvious to many that a moral revolution was in progress. Critics saw that consumer credit not only tempted people to sin but provided the means for them to do so.

As consumer debt came out from the shadows, attitudes about consumption debt began to change not just from shame to acceptance but, particularly among social scientists, away from the idea that debt was a moral issue to begin with. "Credit for consumers," observed Paul Douglass, an editor for the proceedings of one of the many academic conferences held on the subject in the 1930s, "has . . . expanded beyond the stage where it can be condemned or justified. Its existence is an almost universal reality."[59] By the end of the thirties, the old distinction between productive and consumptive debt had largely broken down, and value-freighted terms like *consumptive debt* and *getting trusted* were discarded for the brighter and thinner *consumer credit*.

The person most responsible for altering the older language of credit and debt was Edwin R. A. Seligman, chair of the Department of Economics at Columbia University. One of the most erudite economists of his generation, Seligman was a cofounder of the American Economics Association, editor of *Political Science Quarterly*, editor in chief of the *Encyclopedia of the Social Sciences*, and a chief architect of modern American public finance. In 1927 Seligman published *The Economics of Instalment Selling*, a massive, two-volume study of credit for consumption.[60] Seligman's treatment of the subject became the definitive vindication of credit for consumption, or, as Seligman termed it, "consumers' credit." The change from "consumptive" to "consumers'" credit is significant. Seligman's immediate success at introducing new idioms for credit and thrift suggests his gift for conceptualizing what many Americans already regarded as conventional.

In the old way of thinking about credit, credit for production was thrifty because it increased one's physical capital. Credit for consumption was said to be thriftless because it destroyed or used up material wealth. Seligman found three problems with this "ordinary, haphazard, slapdash" theory of credit.

First, he argued that the classical distinction between production and consumption was unclear and not finally sustainable. Acts normally considered to be "production" often result in a deficit of material utilities, as in the case of poorly run businesses. Conversely, many activities in the suspect category of "consumption" produce huge surpluses of social wealth, such as the furnishing of a comfortable home, the eating of a healthful diet, and the securing of "the finer wants that are developed by civilization." Seligman urged the replacement of the old consumption/production with a new theory of utilization recognizing the benefits of *immaterial* satisfactions. In his new theory, productive surpluses of utilities over costs could result in new goods, more income, or a surplus of "pleasurable sensations." All three types of utilization were equally legitimate. Spending money on a vacation was prima facie no more or no less justifiable than putting money in a savings account. "The real secret of life," Seligman counseled, was not to blindly pursue "production" while renouncing "consumption." Rather, it was to pursue "the productive utilization of wealth, as in the positive utilization of all our opportunities." This was the true road of moral progress in thrift.[61]

Second, Seligman questioned the deeply inscribed line of thinking that assumed a boundary had to be drawn between necessities and luxuries. Debate over installment credit almost always ended with attempts to establish the dividing line between needs and wants, with the automobile representing the ultimate test case. But the familiar claim that installment credit was "all right for necessities, but not for luxuries" was outmoded, argued Seligman, who saw himself as finishing the work of those who long ago had planted dynamite in the cracks of the classical and medieval view that luxuries were inherently decadent. Voltaire had famously wondered whether the first humans to make themselves shoes were guilty of luxury or industry. More recently Simon Patten had held up the relativity of luxury as a positive good, in the sense that the desire for costly things set in motion the wheels of ingenuity, capital, and production, resulting in higher wages, a higher standard of life, and the transformation of yesterday's luxuries into necessities for the masses. Seligman's new wrinkle on the problem was that the wisdom or folly of purchasing a costly or sensual commodity depended on whether the purchase maintained or increased the individual's surplus of utilities over costs, as opposed to diminishing or destroying the surplus. In the final analysis, Seligman added, a truly free society would let individuals decide for themselves.[62]

Finally, Seligman faulted critics of "consumptive" borrowing for misrepresenting the true nature of installment buying. Critics frequently complained that "buy now, pay later" elevated the charms of immediate gratification over the character disciplines of self-control and perseverance. Seligman met the criticism head-on, arguing that it was only under the credit system President Coolidge described as "the old way of running up a bill at the store" that consumers really postponed the act of repayment until *after* they have enjoyed the use of a good. But with the installment plan, Seligman pointed out, where a reasonable down payment was followed by periodic payments, consumers in actual practice pay *in advance* for the satisfactions they enjoy. Since all durable commodities possess a bundle of utilizations that consumers enjoy not all at once but a little bit at a time, "the ordinary purchaser really pays in each periodic installment for something which he will utilize in the future."[63] The pay-as-you-use concept seemed obvious once it had been said. Thus did Seligman rescue consumer credit for thrift.

The Economics of Instalment Selling was "a vindication for installment paying," wrote a reviewer for *World's Work*, while in the *New York Times* Evans Clark breezily pronounced installment buying "absolved by a high priest of the academy."[64] Years later, Alfred Sloan Jr. of General Motors, whose company had first approached Seligman with the idea for the study, credited Seligman for melting the opposition of bankers, businessmen, and the general public to installment selling.[65] The impact a text makes on readers is difficult to pin down, but it is hard not to agree with Sloan. After 1927 the number of articles published on the subject of installment buying dropped abruptly, as if the last word had been spoken and rearguard defenders of a hard line on debt had been driven from the pages of the popular press.[66] After Seligman's defense, the way people talked about debt, credit, and thrift was never the same again.

Seligman's formal, academic approach to consumer credit was quickly translated into popular idioms by the credit industry, which rejoiced to find an advocate on their side as eminent as the professor from Columbia University. This is most obvious in the way the terms *consumer credit* and *pay as you use* worked their way into general use. Finance companies and retailers multiplied countless "thrift plans" and "budget accounts" and pay-as-you-earn plans, legitimizing new forms of credit with the language of old thrift. In money management advice books, the terms *productive credit* and *consumptive credit* were replaced by a new set of core terms: *wise borrowing* and *foolish borrowing*.[67]

Building on the pay-as-you-use idea, Seligman advanced a redefinition of the concept of "savings" that in time became accepted wisdom among most economists. In classical economic theory, the discipline of saving referred to one thing: putting money in the bank. Seligman suggested there was a broader way to think about it. If it was true that consumers utilized a durable good not all at once but over an extended period, then it followed that income used to purchase at one time a good whose utilities would not be used up until a future date really amounted to a form of "saved" income. Viewed this way, buying an automobile was an act of saving just as much as putting the purchase money into a savings account. All that had to be considered was whether the automobile represented a wise investment for the consumer. It was the same reasoning Walter Post had followed a generation earlier.[68]

To this it could be objected of course that consumer borrowers hardly "save" money relative to cash buyers who save up for their purchases, if only because the former *pay* interest for the credit they use while the latter *earn* interest from their savings account. But with regard to savings, Seligman considered the psychological implications of consumer credit to be very important. He argued that installment credit increased not only consumers' capacity to save but also their desire to save. This had always been recognized as true for home ownership. Give a man a home mortgage, it was held, and he will work twice as hard. Now Seligman applied the same reasoning to credit for furniture, automobiles, and other durable goods. The family with car payments to make would be forced to work hard to make the payments and, presumably, would be less likely to fritter away paychecks on frivolous, nondurable expenditures.[69]

"Is installment selling thrift or spendthrift?" Seligman asked, raising the same question the student asked of President Coolidge.[70] Credit might ruin some consumers, he answered, but it rationalized others. For most people, living on credit led to looking ahead with more care, to more budgeting, to more purchasing of desirable durable goods and, consequently, to the augmenting of the capacity and desire to work steadily to pay for them. A striking visual depiction of Seligman's understanding of consumer credit appeared in a 1927 interview in *Collier's Weekly* with John J. Raskob, the first chairman of the General Motors Acceptance Corporation. In the artist's drawing, installment credit is represented as a bridge. Over the bridge march the masses, crossing over from a gray world of crowded tenements and wash hanging on the line to a splendid world of modern skyscrapers and tree-lined parkways. The tenements represent "Hand to Mouth Living." The bridge is labeled "Bank-Controlled Easy Payments." And the beautiful city is the land of "Regulated Abundance." Regulated abundance—thus did Seligman's "consumer's credit" coax wealth from scarcity.[71]

Regulated Abundance

Wanting an image to explain the nature of American wealth in the early 1960s, Randall Jarrell found one on the ceiling of the Sistine Chapel: "If anyone wishes to paint the genesis of things in our society, he will paint a picture of God holding out to Adam a check-book or credit card."[72] When Adamic consumers got credit, what became of them after that?

They went shopping, of course. But that is hardly the whole story. Consumerism as a way of being in the world is not without restraints of its own—mechanisms of control that enable commodity consumption to function as an integrating force for society. One of the most effective of these apparatuses has been consumer credit.

In 1924, an unnamed woman from Muncie, Indiana, described for anthropologists Robert and Helen Lynd how credit and debt affected her family's life. Forty-two years old, the wife of a pipe fitter and mother of two high school boys, the woman proudly ticked off her family's major assets, beginning with a $6,000 bungalow ("built . . . by a building and loan like everyone else does") and a $1,200 Studebaker ("with a nice California top, semi-enclosed"), which the family had just used for a vacation trip to Pennsylvania—taking in Niagara Falls along the way. It was clear in the interview that possessions such as these brought real pleasure to the woman and to her family, but pleasure exacted its payments—literally. When the monthly bills exceeded her husband's income, off to work the woman went, doing cleaning six days a week in one of the city's public institutions. "We had to meet payments on our house and everything else was getting so high," she explained. At first, "the mister" objected to her working outside the home, but the spur of regular monthly payments had a marvelous effect on his mind, and he eventually came around. So off to work she went. There were no regrets. "We have an electric washing machine, electric iron, and vacuum sweeper.... I bought an ice box last year—a big one," she told the Lynds. Like the Posts before her and millions since, this woman clearly believed that the best form of saving was paying back on loans.[73]

So in this family's life, did the policy of installment buying encourage thrift, yes or no? The question dissolves when one considers how, for most Americans, consumer credit works as an instrument of both cupidity and control.

Recalling Philip Rieff's analysis of how moral authorities operate, cultural orders consist of both releases and controls. Controls are moral demands used to interdict antisocial behavior; releases are carefully regulated permissions to bend and break the moral demands, so that individuals can bear the pressure of having to put communal purposes first. Writing in the mid-1960s, Rieff believed the era of traditional Christian controls had come to an end—"Religious man was born to be saved; psychological man is born to be pleased"—and that Western societies stood on the edge of a brave new culture that, for the moment at least, was composed almost entirely of releases. But Rieff had little doubt that "therapeutic" consumer culture would in time produce its own effective controls. It must, because no viable culture can preach only releases from the economic, social, and moral disciplines necessary for the survival and flourishing of society.[74]

Building on Rieff's provocative analysis, Jackson Lears has turned away from the view, which he helped to create, that sees the rise of modern American culture as a simple, linear shift from a society oriented around self-denying production to a society oriented around self-indulgent consumption. On the contrary, Lears now believes that consumer culture is "less a riot of hedonism than a new way of ordering the existing balance of tensions between control and release." Lears arrived at this view while studying the history of modern corporate advertising, an important social authority whose messages are commonly thought to emphasize fun, lust, sensuality, and materialism—in other words, hedonistic releases from traditional moral codes. But Lears finds themes of materialistic hedonism have been less predominant in corporate advertising than other messages of restraint, messages that amount to a "rhetoric of control" advising people to manage their desires in the interest of "personal efficiency": robust physical health, psychic well-being, productive relationships with others, and the like.[75]

The history of consumer credit provides a somewhat more concrete case for understanding the culture of consumption as a balance of tensions between permissions and restraints. On the side of permissions, consumer credit certainly enabled the American public to purchase expensive durable goods that, without credit, most of them could not or would not have bought. Credit made consumers of the millions.

But to stop here is to take a seriously truncated view of the significance of consumer credit. Jeremiads against easy credit focus exclusively on a single moment in time—the moment of purchase when desire is satisfied—and ignore the months and years following the day an installment contract is signed. Thus, they overlook an important and less obvious contribution consumer credit makes to American society: the way it enforces discipline, hard work, and the channeling of one's productivity toward durable consumer goods. Once consumers step onto the treadmill of regular monthly payments, it becomes clear that consumer credit is about much more than instant gratification.

In reality, it is about *budgetism*, a word coined in 1956 by *Fortune* editor William H. Whyte Jr. to describe "a person's desire to regularize his income by having it removed from his own control and disciplined by external forces." With the assistance of credit, Americans have learned to tie themselves to a tight regimen of enforced savings, budgeting themselves by means of various installment plans so that almost no unappropriated funds are left over to burn a hole in their pockets. As was evident in the lives of Walter and Lilly Post, the first generations to grow up in a full-fledged culture of consumption knew better than to trust their internal restraints. Enticed from all sides by inducements to spend, modern consumers know they need all the help they can get. Budgetism, said Whyte, is the "opiate of the middle class."[76]

In Whyte's budgetism we have a key for unlocking one of the great puzzles of the American way of life, one famously described thirty years ago by sociologist Daniel Bell. What prevents the acquisitiveness required of model consumers from sabotaging the discipline required of workers in the capitalist system of production? How has the consumer *economy* survived the subversive doctrines of consumer *culture*, a culture that would seem to wear down workplace productivity with its libertinism, its insatiable devotion to "wants," and its hedonistic concern with play, fun, pleasure, and leisure?

There is no single answer to this question, of course. But the most effective solution has been worked out in the domain of household financial management. Practically speaking, the resolution of the tensions inherent in consumer capitalism is most evident in how consumer credit has preserved and reformed the ethos of thrift. Far from causing the demise of thrift, consumer credit has actually worked to make most modern credit users at least as disciplined in their finances as the generations that lived before the credit revolution. The installment plan of repayment forces typical credit users to adopt disciplines of money management that would have impressed even Poor Richard. Poor Richard disapproved of indebtedness, but his creator, Benjamin Franklin, eventually came to wonder, "May not luxury therefore produce more than it consumes if without such a spur people would be, as they are naturally inclined to be, lazy and indolent?"[77] Indolence is not an option for people living with monthly credit payments. The fact is, "easy credit" is not all that easy. Consumer credit imposes on borrowers financial regimens requiring discipline, foresight, and a conscious effort to save income in order to make payments on time. "Easy payment!" exclaimed an immigrant housewife to a journalist in 1912. "Hard payment it is! Easy payment with everybody workin' their nails out!"[78]

Some borrowers have succumbed to the allure of "buy now, pay later" and become overloaded with debt. Historically, though, the numbers of those who are delinquent with payments or default on their loans have been very small compared with the numbers who pay their bills on time. Most installment borrowers, for the duration of their repayment periods, have been forced to cut out expenditures on momentary fancies, put aside money for the monthly installment bills, and work diligently at one or more jobs to guarantee a dependable supply of income.

Some find this version of the American dream to be not such a great way to live. In a 1998 survey of 827 workers at Atlanta's BellSouth, almost 70 percent of those polled wished to work fewer hours but felt they could not afford it. When asked why they could not cut back on their hours, the greatest single response was not that they were not paid enough or that their current spending was too high but that they had so many debts (53 percent).[79] So much for easy payments.

It might have been different. The original promise of industrialism was that it would bring people more time for leisure, not more money for goods. Goods we now have, but little time for leisure. Thus, consumer credit has done for personal money management what Frederick W. Taylor's scientific management theories did for factory work routines. It has imposed on consumers strict, exogenous disciplines to help with coaxing a plenitude of material goods from the triple scarcities confronting them: money, time, and personal discipline. To be sure, credit-driven consumerism offers moments of indulgence and excess. But the apparatus of credit ensures that consumerism is also a goad for more work. This has made American middle-class life today less a playground for hedonists than an extension of Max Weber's "iron cage" of disciplined rationality.[80]

In public life today, voices advocating thrift have faded to whispers. National Thrift Week is long gone, thrift education has vanished from the schools, and presidents call for consumer confidence, not cautiousness. The call to consume has not gone unheeded. In the twentieth century, Americans created an American dream of home ownership and durable goods consumption that would have astonished Walter and Lilly Post even as it has delighted and appalled observers from around the world accustomed to different forms of consumption. Homes, automobiles, boats, appliances, swimming pools, entertainment systems, electronic devices—the wealth of the American dream has been made possible by the installment plan. Thus, the history of consumer credit invites us to consider whether something like a "Laffer curve" might apply to thrift in American history. As Arthur Laffer demonstrated, lowered tax rates can, under certain conditions, actually increase government revenues. Have the disciplines of consumer credit made it possible to talk less about thrift while seeing more actual practice of it? Surely not, if it is traditional thrift we have in mind. But the history of consumer credit also shows that there is more to thrift than saving.

Thrift is the extraction of abundance from poverty. Patient saving is one way to be thrifty, but there are others. The new thrift imagined by Post and defended by Seligman extended the thrift ethos from land, soil, and resources—in other words, space—to time. When capitalism required that time be counted as money, the need for more time became urgent and the desire to manage time, with "time-payment plans," irresistible. But there was more at work in the development of new thrift than the dynamics of capitalism. No one knows how much time they really have. Hence, the desire to be thrifty with time, to turn its deficits into abundance, is at bottom a desire to cheat death, sickness, and debility of their inevitable victories. Traditional thrift recommends waiting and doing without, but in its obsession with space it ignores a truth about time that everyone feels: there may not be enough time to wait, and the postponement of gratification will have its own costs. "Buying on time" became popular because it removed the wait from wanting, producing surpluses of goods and time where before there had been scarcities. For this reason, the disciplines of consumer credit can be considered a special case of thrift.

Like traditional thrift, credit-based thrift poses its own problems and ironies. Time, even more than land and money, has proved difficult to manage, resulting in the harried lives of today's middle-class consumers. So-called easy payments have turned out to be hard indeed. But the irony is entirely in line with Americans' historic relation to thrift. Always there has been more praise of thrift than actual practice. With time no less than with land, soil, and natural resources, Americans find it all too easy to produce scarcity from abundance.

Notes

1. David M. Tucker, *The Decline of Thrift in America: Our Cultural Shift from Saving to Spending* (New York: Praeger, 1991), vii–ix, 99–155.

2. Frank Bugon to President Calvin Coolidge, January 24, 1929, reproduced in "Prosperity and Thrift: The Coolidge Era and the Consumer Economy, 1921–1929," Calvin Coolidge Papers, Credit—Installment Plan Buying 1926–29, Library of Congress, http://memory.loc.gov/ammem/coolhtml/coolhome.html (accessed August 21, 2006).

3. Herbert Hoover, quoted in "Thrift and American Women," *Ladies' Home Journal*, August 1920, 100; unattributed sermon, quoted in Tucker, *Decline of Thrift in America*, 68–69, 83–98. William H. Whyte Jr., "Budgetism: Opiate of the Middle Class," *Fortune*, May 1956, 133; John Kenneth Galbraith, *The Affluent Society* (Boston: Houghton Mifflin, 1958), 200; Daniel Bell, *The Cultural Contradictions of Capitalism* (New York: Basic Books, 1976), 21; David Frum, *How We Got Here: The 70's: The Decade That Brought You Modern Life—For Better or Worse* (Basic Books, 2000), 186.

4. *Harper's Bazar*, November 22, 1890, 910.

5. The Associated Press story is reprinted, with commentary, in *Industrial Lenders News* 10 (February 1926): 12. See also newspaper clippings in "Prosperity and Thrift: The Coolidge Era and the Consumer Economy, 1921–1929," Calvin Coolidge Papers, Credit—Installment Plan Buying 1926–29, Library of Congress, http://memory.loc.gov/ammem/coolhtml/coolhome.html (accessed August 21, 2006).

6. Letters of Walter T. Post, box P1040, Minnesota Historical Society, St. Paul, Minnesota.

7. Ira Steward, quoted in Massachusetts Bureau of the Statistics of Labor, *Fourth Annual Report* (1873), 414.

8. Artemus Ward [Charles Farrar Browne], *Artemus Ward in London* (New York: G. W. Carlton, 1867), 71.

9. U.S. Department of the Interior, Census Office, *Report on Real Estate Mortgages in the United States at the Eleventh Census, 1890* (Washington, DC: Government Printing Office, 1895), 102.

10. Mark Twain and Charles Dudley Warner, *The Gilded Age, A Tale of Today* (1873; New York: New American Library, Meridian Classic, 1985), 64, 193, 184–85. The Oxford English Dictionary first defined charging in relation to a credit purchase in 1889.

11. Edward Everett, *The Mount Vernon Papers* (New York: D. Appleton, 1860), 167–68.

12. Reader survey results from *New Yorker Volks-Zeitung*, December 14–15, 1882, quoted in Dorothee Schneider, "For Whom Are All the Good Things in Life? German-American Housewives Discuss Their Budgets," in *German Workers in Industrial Chicago, 1850–1910: A Comparative Perspective*, ed. Hartmut Keil and John B. Jentz (De Kalb: Northern Illinois University Press, 1983), 156.

13. Louise Bolard More, *Wage-earners' Budgets: A Study of Standards and Cost of Living in New York City* (New York: Henry Holt, 1907), 108, 268; Robert Coit Chapin, *The Standard of Living among Workingmen's Families in New York City* (New York: Charities Publication Committee, 1909), 236, 245–46; Frank Hatch Streightoff, *The Standard of Living among the Industrial People of America* (Boston: Houghton Mifflin, 1911), 24–25.

14. Massachusetts Bureau of the Statistics of Labor, *First Annual Report* (Boston: n.p., 1870), 185–87.

15. Ibid., 335.

16. D. M. Frederiksen, "Mortgage Banking in America," *Journal of Political Economy* 2 (December 1893): 204–10; Stephen Thernstrom, *Poverty and Progress: Social Mobility in a Nineteenth-Century City* (Cambridge, MA: Harvard University Press, 1964), 120; "How We Saved for Our Home," *Ladies' Home Journal*, January–October 1903; George K. Holmes, "The Concentration of Wealth," *Political Science Quarterly* 8 (December 1893): 590.

17. "How We Saved for Our Home," *Ladies' Home Journal*, July 1903, 27.

18. Ibid. For similar comments from other respondents, see "How We Saved for Our Home," in the following issues of *Ladies' Home Journal*, January 1903, 19; February 1903, 20–21; April 1903, 26–27; June 1903, 22; August 1903, 26; and October 1903, 22.

19. Walter Post to Charlie Post, January 20, 1896, and Walter Post to his father, April 2, 1895, Letters of Walter T. Post, box P1040, Minnesota Historical Society.

20. Walter Post to his father, April 2, 1895.

21. Edwin A. Kirkpatrick, *The Use of Money: How to Save and How to Spend* (Indianapolis, IN: Bobbs-Merrill, 1915), 20.

22. Benjamin Franklin, "Poor Richard Improved, 1758," in *Benjamin Franklin: Writings*, ed. J. A. Leo Lemay (New York: Literary Classics of America, 1987), 1294–1304. Lewis

J. Carey's count of the editions is cited in Louis B. Wright, "Franklin's Legacy to the Gilded Age," *Virginia Quarterly Review* 22 (Spring 1946): 273. Paul Leicester Ford, a nineteenth-century bibliographer of Franklin, listed fifty-six pages of various editions of "The Way to Wealth" and then gave up what was a hopeless task. He found it "impossible to find and note all the editions." See Paul Leicester Ford, *Franklin Bibliography: A List of Books Written by or Relating to Benjamin Franklin* (Brooklyn: n.p., 1889).

23. Franklin, "Poor Richard Improved," 1302.

24. Henry Ward Beecher, *Twelve Lectures to Young Men*, rev. ed. (New York: D. Appleton, 1890), 35–36, quoted in P. T. Barnum, *Dollars and Sense* (New York: H. S. Allen, 1890), 49–50.

25. Epigram quoted in Clarence Wassam, *The Salary Loan Business in New York City* (New York: Charities Publication Committee, 1908), 11; Twain and Warner, *Gilded Age*, 193.

26. Ward, *Artemus Ward in London*, 71.

27. General Benjamin Franklin Butler, quoted in "The Art of Making Money," *Nation*, September 15, 1887, 205.

28. Philip Rieff's functionalist interpretation of culture is put forward in *The Triumph of the Therapeutic: Uses of Faith after Freud* (Chicago: University of Chicago Press, 1987), 232–33.

29. See Cotton Mather, "A Christian at His Calling," in *The American Gospel of Success: Individualism and Beyond*, ed. Moses Rischin (Chicago: Quadrangle Books, 1965), 27–28.

30. Jacob Abbott, *Willie and the Mortgage* (New York: Harper and Brothers, 1854), 95; Freeman Hunt, *Worth and Wealth* (New York: Stringer and Townsend, 1856), 363; Junius [Calvin Colton], *The Crisis of the Country* (Philadelphia: T. K. and P. G. Collins, 1840), 4, 6, 12.

31. Jennifer Baker, *Securing the Commonwealth: Debt, Speculation, and Writing in the Making of Early America* (Baltimore: Johns Hopkins University Press, 2005).

32. William Cunningham, *The Use and Abuse of Money* (New York: Scribner's, 1891), 175–76.

33. Thomas Nixon Carver, "How to Use Farm Credit," quoted in Arthur W. Dunn, *Community Civics for City Schools* (Boston: Heath, 1921), 316.

34. "The Credit System," *Banker's Magazine* 42 (May 1888): 833.

35. Junius, *Crisis of the Country*, 4.

36. H. L. Reade, *Money, and How to Make It* (New York: John P. Jewett, 1872), 559.

37. Barton Cheney, "Buying a House without Cash," *Ladies' Home Journal*, April 1898, 28; Erastus Wiman, "The Hope of a Home," *North American Review* 156 (February 1893): 231–33.

38. Charles Connard Hanch, "The Case for Instalment Buying," *Forum* 77 (May 1927): 660.

39. Reade, *Money and How to Make It*, 570–76.

40. Jonathon Gilmer Speed, "Pawnbrokers and the Poor," *Harper's Weekly*, September 3, 1892, 862.

41. Ernest Walter Lyman, *Financial Independence* (Chicago: Perry, 1907), 120.

42. Ibid.

43. See Lewis E. Atherton, *The Frontier Merchant in Mid-America*, vol. 55 of University of Missouri Studies (Columbia: University of Missouri Press, 1971), 142–53.

44. Barnum, *Dollars and Sense*, 50.

45. Martha Olney, *Buy Now, Pay Later: Advertising, Credit, and Consumer Durables in the 1920s* (Chapel Hill: University of North Carolina Press, 1991), 86–91, 96.

46. "The Ford Plan," accession 6, box 296, Ford Motor Company archives, Dearborn, Michigan; Allan Nevins and Frank Ernest Hill, *Ford: Expansion and Challenge, 1915–1933* (New York: Scribner's, 1957), 268–69.

47. "The Ford Plan."

48. Reported in the Denver Colorado News, April 8, 1923; found in clipping file of accession 3, box 1, Ford Motor Company archives. Participants in a Christmas club plan have a set amount deposited into a special savings account each month and then use the accumulated funds for Christmas expenditures.

49. Quoted in Nevins and Hill, *Ford: Expansion and Challenge*, 268–69.

50. "Ford Says Output Is 6,700 Cars a Day," *New York Times*, May 30, 1923, 21.

51. "Universal Credit Corporation Educational Manual" and "Confidential Report of the Universal Credit Company," accession 33, box 95, Ford Motor Company archives; Arthur J. Kuhn, *GM Passes Ford, 1918–1938: Designing the General Motors Performance-Control System* (University Park: Pennsylvania State University Press, 1986), 312–13.

52. Franklin W. Ryan III, "Family Finance in the United States," *Journal of Business of the University of Chicago* 4 (October 1930): 415.

53. Ibid.

54. George Horace Lorimer, "Saving by Borrowing," *Saturday Evening Post*, January 12, 1924, 24.

55. "More People in Debt," *New York Times*, November 4, 1923, sec. 9.

56. On nostalgia in the 1920s, see Jacqueline Fear and Helen McNeil, "The Twenties," in *Introduction to American Studies*, ed. Malcolm Bradbury and Howard Temperley (New York: Longman, 1981), 195–96.

57. Preston William Slosson, *The Great Crusade and After, 1914–1928* (New York: Macmillan, 1930), 181.

58. James Boswell, April 13, 1773, in James Boswell, *The Life of Samuel Johnson, L.L.D.* Elibron Classics (Boston: Adamant Media Corporation, 2005), 207.

59. Paul F. Douglass, "Consumer Credit: A Critical Analysis of Credit Agencies and of the Development of Regulation," *Annals of the American Academy of Political and Social Science* 196 (March 1938): xi.

60. Edwin R. A. Seligman, *The Economics of Instalment Selling*, 2 vols. (New York: Harper and Brothers, 1927).

61. Ibid., 1:171–72.

62. Ibid., 1:222–25.

63. Ibid., 1:256.

64. Wilbur C. Plummer, Book Review, *Annals of the Academy of Political and Social Science* 137 (May 1928): 269; "A Vindication for Installment Paying," *World's Work*, January 1928, 242; Evans Clard, "Are 'Easy Payments' the Hardest?" *New York Times Book Review*, January 15, 1928, 11.

65. Alfred P. Sloan Jr., *My Years with General Motors* (Garden City, NY: Doubleday, 1964), 306.

66. Esra Christian Buehler, *A Debate Handbook on the Instalment Buying of Personal Property* (Knoxville: University of Tennessee Press, 1929), 1.

67. Reginald Heber Smith, "Performance Beats Propaganda," *Personal Finance News* 15 (October 1930): 12.

68. Seligman, *Economics of Instalment Selling*, 1:272–74.

69. Ibid., 1:277.

70. Edwin R. A. Seligman, "Economic Problems Involved in Installment Selling," *Proceedings of the Academy of Political Science in the City of New York* 12 (January 1927): 88.

71. W. G. Shepherd, "They Turn Your Promise into Cash: Interview with J. J. Raskob," *Collier's Weekly*, February 19, 1927, 8–9.

72. Randall Jarrell, *A Sad Heart at the Supermarket: Essays and Fables* (New York: Atheneum, 1962), 66.

73. Robert S. Lynd and Helen Merrell Lynd, *Middletown: A Study in American Culture* (New York: Harcourt, Brace, 1929), 28–29.

74. Rieff, *Triumph of the Therapeutic*, 14–27.

75. Jackson Lears, *Fables of Abundance: A Cultural History of Advertising in America* (New York: Basic Books, 1994), 10–11, 138, 159, 198, 206–7.

76. Whyte, "Budgetism," 172.

77. Benjamin Franklin, quoted in ibid., 134.

78. Unnamed immigrant housewife, quoted in Mary Fields, "The Drama of Wages," *American Magazine*, November 1912, 76.

79. Unpublished data from a survey conducted by Juliet Schor. Other results from the same survey are reported in Juliet Schor, *The Overspent American* (New York: HarperPerennial, 1999).

80. A good introduction to Frederick W. Taylor's ideas is Samuel Haber, *Efficiency and Uplift: Scientific Management in the Progressive Era, 1890–1920* (Chicago: University of Chicago Press, 1964). Max Weber's famous prediction that the future under capitalism would be "an iron cage" appears in the final pages of *The Protestant Ethic and the Spirit of Capitalism* (London: Unwin Hyman, 1930), 181.

14 }

Mass Philanthropy as Public Thrift for an Age of Consumption

Olivier Zunz

Saving and giving are not only important and widely shared American values, they are conceptually and institutionally tied together. In the eighteenth century, Benjamin Franklin promoted the dictum "A Penny sav'd is Twopence clear, A Pin a day is a Groat a Year. Save & have. Every little makes a mickle" in editions of *Poor Richard's Almanack*. But Franklin was a practitioner of philanthropic giving, as well as a theoretician of frugality. In modern parlance, he was the inventor of the matching grant, a device he masterminded in securing donations for his many associational ventures.[1]

Scholars, including many contributors to this volume, have shown how mass consumption was built in part by tapping the increasing savings reserves of the American population, often during periods when savings were vulnerable to inflation. In this essay, I want to show how these large reserves of untapped resources also became a source of giving during the early twentieth century—serving as the partial basis for the emergence of a modern mass philanthropy. By identifying saving and giving as complementary behaviors, promoters of this new mass philanthropy—whether fund-raising to fight diseases or to support the nation's involvement in World War I—cleverly called on the thrift ethos to expand the reaches of American giving.

Until the late nineteenth century, *charity* remained the predominant term for giving in America. This term *charity* reflected the religious motivations and mind-set of the givers; its usage revealed an emphasis on good works, almsgiving, and limited local aims, as well as organized religion's influence over civil society. In this context, the church and voluntary associations were the main mediators between saving and giving. But giving changed in the late nineteenth century with the simultaneous creation of big-money philanthropy, funded by the new business moguls, and a mass philanthropy, collecting the nickels and dimes of the many.

During the late nineteenth-century corporate revolution, a few wealthy donors broke away from the traditional charitable model. They replaced it with a philanthropic system meant to foster investigation and problem solving, sometimes independently, but more often in partnerships with government and civil institutions. The new philanthropy promoted systematic inquiry and became a critical partner in some of the most important scientific innovations and policy issues of the twentieth century.

American philanthropy was not limited to the largesse of the wealthy. During the early decades of the twentieth century, it rapidly democratized. A general rise in the standard of living and the use of mass-marketing techniques dramatically enlarged the number of philanthropic participants. In turn, a very large part of the American population came to contribute to philanthropic efforts *and* to view them as a means of life enhancement. The emerging new mass philanthropy developed, as I will show, as a form of public thrift for a new age. Mass philanthropy centralized America's tradition of small-scale, locally centered benevolence and channeled it toward relief on a broader scale. It often focused on social engineering projects such as fighting diseases or pressing for social reform. Mass philanthropy took many of its goals and ideas from the new big-money philanthropy, but its funding came from the savings of the American population at large. The same thrifty habits that allowed Americans to save for a rainy day led them to give outright to the new philanthropic institutions.

Thrift, Charity, and the Coming of a New Mass Philanthropy

In the traditional sense, the idea of thrift demands a constant personal effort aimed at staving off adversity. Thus fin de siècle developments in the Charity Organization Society movement and the first stages of the professionalization of social work promoted thrift as a means of personal improvement. Social worker Mary Richmond at the Russell Sage Foundation emphasized changing individual behavior, or "habits," through casework.[2] Fellow social worker Mary Wilcox Brown claimed in *The Development of Thrift* (1899) that the inculcation of thrift in the laboring classes via cooperative savings and building and loan associations, people's banks, forms of insurance, and other methods was succeeding. In addition to staving off the need for relief, thrift was also the way for rich and poor alike to participate in charity. Elaborating on the relationship between philanthropic activity and thrift, Brown wrote, "It is encouraging to learn on good authority that persons engaged in philanthropic work almost 'inevitably become more simple and frugal in their own way of living.'"[3]

By the turn of the twentieth century, social workers viewed thrift as a necessary "habit" through which the laboring classes could provide themselves with a minimum safety net, as well as a means of self-improvement. However, while social workers and economists believed that organized thrift was essential for the well-being of the common laborer, most Americans struggled to save. In a 1906 book on the living wage, Father John Ryan reported on the spending habits of 2,132 working-class families. From an average annual income of $687.02, workers paid out $6.42 for property insurance, $20.22 for life insurance, and $22.31 for the sickness and death benefits provided by a combination of fraternal associations and insurance companies. In total, these sums amounted to more than 7 percent of a family's annual earnings. Ryan, who would later become an important Catholic supporter of the New Deal, encouraged workers to eliminate the need for such expenditures by saving.[4]

As Father Ryan, Brown, and others encouraged habits of thrift among laborers and their families, they sought also to reshape habits of giving. By the turn of the century, these reformers could already look to a long-standing tradition of charitable giving among American workers. Father Ryan reported that workers gave $10.29 (or 1.5 percent) of their annual income to their church (for church maintenance as well as charitable causes) and $12.66 (or 1.8 percent) to labor and other organizations. They gave an additional $2.80 (0.4 percent) for informal charity, unmediated by church or lodge, usually to help neighbors and the local community. These modest figures, however, would soon grow significantly with the rise of a new mass philanthropy quite distinct from traditional giving through lodge and church.

The leaders of this new mass philanthropy openly counted on the savings ethos of Americans, but they promoted an important conceptual shift of saving for the common good. In soliciting donations for the American Red Cross, for the first national public health campaigns, and for the federation movement (which led to "community chests" and later to the United Way), they posited both collective and personal goals for individual savings. Philanthropic leaders increasingly looked to these savings as a potential source of gifts or, as social worker Lilian Brandt put it, "large subterranean pools of benevolence." This discovery prefigured the democratization of urban giving during the early twentieth century. If 3 percent of the population of a city contributed to philanthropic causes in 1900, the percentage likely jumped to 35 percent in the 1920s.[5] In limited cases, the results were even more staggering. Studies showed that among streetcar employees in San Francisco, the habit of giving to organized charity was almost universal by the 1930s. Even in 1933—at the very height of the Depression—an astonishing 93 percent of San Francisco streetcar men engaged in philanthropic giving. According to investigators, the habit of giving among these workers was so deeply engrained that their family budgets frequently included a line item for the Red Cross.[6]

One of the first efforts to organize and generate philanthropy of this sort on a mass scale was coordinated by the National Association for the Study and Prevention of Tuberculosis (NASPT, which was renamed the American Tuberculosis Association, or ATA, in 1918). In 1904, Danish-born reformer Jacob Riis (the author in 1890 of *How the Other Half Lives* and master of the infant art of photography) received a Christmas letter from Copenhagen bearing a peculiar seal. A Danish postal official had had the idea, embraced by his government, to sell the seals to raise money to build a local hospital for children with TB. As proof that mass philanthropy could work, the hospital was fully constructed by the time Riis recounted the story in a 1907 article for *Outlook*. In urging the duplication of this type of "penny subscription" in the United States, Riis noted that "no millionaire" had yet come forth "to endow" the fight against tuberculosis. Riis's larger point, however, was that "no millionaire" was "wanted" and that the job would be "far better done by the people themselves."[7] In sum, Riis called for a fund-raising campaign that matched the scale of the new big-money philanthropies yet relied on the traditional model of small-scale giving. And instead of tapping the wealth of a few corporate tycoons, Riis envisioned drawing on the "pools of benevolence" created by the thrift of ordinary Americans—that is, the nickels and dimes they usually kept in a savings box at home.

The seal idea was picked up by Emily Bissell, a young member of the editorial board of *Outlook* and the secretary of the Delaware Red Cross. Bissell, who was interested in helping a physician-cousin to support a TB sanitarium in Delaware, convinced the Red Cross to sell the seals for the NASPT.[8]

Teaming up with the Red Cross, which had been assuming an increasingly important role in the management of natural disasters—and later took the lead role in developing volunteerism and fund-raising during World War I—proved to be a smart move, and the marketing campaign aimed at the new form of giving paid off for the association. The campaign began modestly when Bissell posted a sign in her local Wilmington post office reading, "These stamps do not carry any kind of mail but any kind of mail will carry them."[9] Eventually, however, the fight against TB would grow into one of the most successful American fund-raising efforts in the twentieth century—the annual Christmas sale of stamps to fight TB. By the mid-1960s, the Christmas seals brought in $26 million from the mailing of 40 million letters. To be sure, the idea had originated in Denmark, but as Riis put it: "Denmark is a small country." By contrast, America was the country of mass marketing—a vast nation with a tradition of charitable giving—and it is thus no surprise that it was in the United States where the full potential of the seals campaign was realized.

Encouraging ordinary people to give small sums of money heretofore intended only for savings represented a significant innovation in fund-raising. The very same people who had been pushing ordinary Americans to save were now also pushing them to give to causes beyond their immediate community, especially to those causes that furthered social and scientific inquiry and, more broadly, the greater good of humankind. Public thrift for public programs thus became a form of democratic practice. While traditional thrift primarily benefited the giver or his or her immediate family, public thrift served the population at large.

In his landmark book *Fund Raising in the United States*, Scott Cutlip described the seals campaign as a turning point in the American population's acceptance of mass philanthropy.[10] The 1908 seals campaign, which raised $165,000, was a springboard from which to launch mass philanthropy, and within just eight years, seals receipts topped the $1 million mark. These efforts helped to generate rapid, impressive results in fighting the disease. Rates of TB in the United States dropped dramatically in the 1920s and 1930s, and monies raised by the association were critical to opening sanitariums and to developing the BCG vaccine.

In addition to contributing funds, the population at large played an increasingly important role in the act of fund-raising itself. Charles de Forest (brother of radio pioneer Lee de Forest), who ran the seals campaign for the NASPT, had the idea of using children as "crusaders" in their neighborhoods in 1915.[11] The more stamps they sold, the higher their rank as "crusaders" in the association's Modern Health Crusade. Elementary schools rapidly adopted the crusade as a system of health education, and by 1919 the effective campaign boasted 3 million "crusaders" in the United States. Thus American children became the first volunteers for national nickel-and-dime campaigns. In these same years, the pioneering professional fund-raisers Lyman Pierce and Charles Ward deployed the "Y" fund-raising and "every-member canvass" techniques in the service of the YMCA—strategies that helped to make fund-raising more efficient with intensive, "whirlwind campaigns."[12]

In fostering the belief that every American could and should give something, the NASPT, the Red Cross, and the YMCA embedded a strong sense of the public or collective side of thrift. Thus, thrift and the new mass philanthropy became increasingly related enterprises. As more Americans gave more to mass philanthropies like the Christmas Seals and Easter Seals programs, Americans were also *saving* more. In 1897, personal saving in the United States amounted to a paltry $410 million. The figure had skyrocketed to almost $4.5 billion by 1915. Even accounting for inflation, this represented a 900 percent increase in aggregate personal saving.[13]

The World War I Experiment in Public Thrift

The coming of World War I dramatically reinforced the changes under way for how Americans raised funds and conceived of giving. No longer just a new technique for expanding philanthropy's reach, fund-raising became a means to involve the whole nation in the war effort; in other words, giving was elevated to the level of national duty. In this regard, fund-raising served not only as a means of financing the conflict but also as a measure of each and every American's patriotism—and of the country's image abroad. The innovative ways in which the money was raised, the length of the effort, and the intensity of the pressure to give money all contributed to this drastic change.

Wartime fund-raising also penetrated deep into the population, producing an unprecedented level of giving among a broad cross section of Americans, including recent immigrants. Many overlapping institutions tapped a large reservoir of generosity to fund programs for soldiers, their families, and European aid. Most important, this type of nationalized personal fund-raising became part and parcel of the country's routine. As Americans contemplated sacrifice and savings, the term *thrift* became more prevalent, but so too did *giving*. The affinity between the two terms was such that wartime propaganda employed them almost interchangeably.

Having played an instrumental role in developing new forms of mass philanthropy, the YMCA responded to the wartime preparedness by launching a Thrift Movement on Ben Franklin's birthday anniversary on January 17, 1916. The movement encouraged thrift education during "thrift weeks" aimed largely at schoolchildren and also marketed interest-bearing "thrift stamps." These wartime efforts advanced an idea of thrift that included philanthropy. They also provided citizens serving the public good with a small gain.

The thrift stamps were the most explicit expression of the thrift ethos as both a commitment to national service and a means by which to reap a modest profit. These stamps—as well as the more elaborate campaigns for war savings certificates, loans, and bonds—represented an intricate combination of saving, investing, and giving. Not large or particularly ornate, they were roughly the size of a standard postage stamp and cost twenty-five cents each. With the first purchase of a thrift stamp, the purchaser was "given a card containing spaces for 16 thrift stamps, with the expectation that when the card was filled (for a total value of $4), it would be exchanged for a war savings stamp, or as it was sometimes called, a war savings certificate."[14]

Certificates issued as of January 2, 1918, cost $4.12 each, with the purchase price advancing at 1 percent per month. At maturity, on January 1, 1923, purchasers could go to any post office and redeem their certificates at $5 apiece. Not only was this a reasonable return on the original investment, but the ability to redeem at any post office (as opposed to a national, state, or federal bank) made this outreach truly national in scope—giving the stamps an appeal to rural and urban Americans alike.

Liberty Bonds and Victory Bonds, essentially government bonds issued to the public for coupon rates of between 3.5 and 4.5 percent, were conceived of and overseen by Secretary of the Treasury William McAdoo. Much like the emergent mass philanthropy, Liberty and Victory loan drives drew on local "precinct captains" and nonprofit groups such as the Boy Scouts to go door-to-door, soliciting funds through the purchase of these bonds. These drives also included payroll deductions and other means for average workers to ensure that their contributions and investments took place before attending to other costs of living.

The four Liberty loan campaigns (two in 1917, two in 1918) and the Victory loan campaign of early 1919 elicited a massive response from Americans from all walks of life. Surveying the sale of war bonds in January 1918, the president of New York City's National City Bank wrote of "an almost religious fervor that has been manifested in the sale of these bonds."[15] The thrift stamps, along with Liberty and Victory bond loan drives, also experienced astonishing success, engaging more than 66 million citizen-subscribers and raising roughly $25 billion for the war effort.[16] A 1918 editorial in the *English Journal* directed English schoolteachers to teach grammatical "conventions" "as the accessory of clearness and force in persuading one's hearers to buy Liberty Bonds or save for Thrift Stamps."[17]

American entry into the Great War in 1917 propelled the new mass philanthropy to a higher level as more intensive and more personal campaigns drew out of people's pockets the small amounts that would have otherwise likely gone into savings accounts.[18] Wartime fund-raising penetrated deep into the population. The number of Red Cross chapters in the nation leaped from 87 to 300—and then to more than 3,000—with membership growing from 250,000 members to more than 20 million. More than 8 million adults served as volunteer workers, and another 11 million youth claimed membership.[19]

With its public mandate, the Red Cross continued to expand into a quasi-governmental agency as the biggest mass American charity. President Woodrow Wilson appointed Henry Davison (of J. P. Morgan and Company) to head the "New Council" of financiers, politicians, and philanthropic leaders, and he launched the mass war campaign himself with a request for funds. Davison set a goal of $100 million to be raised June 18–25, 1917; he exceeded the goal by $15 million. A second campaign a year later raised $181 million. Like the wartime loan drives—as well as the earlier campaign against TB—these campaigns mainly solicited small sums from the population at large. An observer later called it the "most stupendous fund-raising effort by a voluntary relief society that the country had even known—and one which still has no real parallel."[20]

Although the Red Cross represented perhaps the most dramatic example of mass wartime philanthropy, during the war it seemed as though everywhere groups of citizens joined together for one cause or another: Armenian relief, Syrian relief, the Jewish fund, soldiers' comfort, and prisoners' camps.[21] The YMCA and Salvation Army multiplied their budgets and activities and kept in close contact with other American and Allied organizations on the front. Many of these organizations worked with the Red Cross, and nearly all collaborated with other associations in some way.

The United War Campaign (UWC), led by John R. Mott, was particularly remarkable in this regard. Initiated by Harry Fosdick of the Rockefeller Foundation at the request of President Wilson and spearheaded by Secretary of War Newton D. Baker, the UWC sought $170.5 million to aid prisoners of war and American troops abroad and to minimize civilian suffering where possible.

The wartime movement gained such momentum that it carried over well past the armistice. When the war ended on November 11, 1918—the day the drive was scheduled to open—the UWC's leaders remained undaunted. Mott, who was also a leader of the YMCA and the growing student volunteer mission movement, immediately redirected the purpose of the campaign to peace readjustment. In a famous telegram, he instructed all campaign workers "to prevent period of demobilization becoming period of demoralization." Only a few days later, the campaign had gone over the $200 million mark, largely exceeding the initial goal.[22]

Alongside these private nonprofit and federal government efforts at fund-raising, the "war chests" became the third way in which wartime conditions helped establish mass philanthropy as both public thrift and national duty. The war chests linked local and national giving in an unparalleled manner, reaching all the way down to virtually every American at the county and city levels. War chests acted as federated charitable combinations and were composed of virtually all of the local charities, churches, and many national charity branches (e.g., Knights of Columbus, Elks, YMCA and YWCA, Salvation Army). In addition to supporting the sale of Liberty Bonds and Victory Bonds and other federal initiatives, war chests themselves became the locus of billions of dollars in contributions between 1917 and 1918.

The war chests rapidly transformed prewar experiments in federated fund-raising into a national phenomenon, and by the summer of 1918 more than 300 cities had war chests. The forty-three principal war chests, covering an aggregate population of 7 million, reached 2,273,216 donors—fully 32 percent of their target population, or more than one donor per family. Coordinators dedicated their appeals to the war effort and distributed the collected funds to the various agencies involved in the local collections. "Sixty funds in one," said one poster; "humanity calls you," another.[23] In addition to funding war work, war chests included in their appeal the provision of funds for local welfare work. This was true in cities all across the country, from Cleveland—a pioneer in federated funds—to Detroit, Toledo, Indianapolis, and Rochester. These locally centered welfare expenditures prefigured the postwar shift from war chests to community chests.

The 1920s

The successes in local and national fund-raising during the war helped to routinize mass giving as public thrift for a *collective* rainy day. The YMCA's Thrift Movement birthed a national association that thrived through the 1920s and even published its own national newsletter, the *National Thrift News*. The YMCA, the United War Campaign, and the Red Cross reached out to an increasingly broad cross section of the American public. Thrift stamps,

Victory and Liberty loan drives, and other forms of public thrift turned saving and giving into complementary civic duties.

The transformation of the war chests into community chests provides the clearest illustration that Americans remained committed to collective causes after the charitable and patriotic appeals generated by the war had abated. With origins dating back before World War I—most notably in Cleveland in 1913—the community chests, also known as federations, firmly took hold in the 1920s. These chests appealed for American charitable dollars at the local level, calling on the fortunes of the few as well as the savings of the many, with the explicit aim of addressing an array of primarily local causes.

In *How Much Shall I Give?* (1921), social worker Lilian Brandt, who surveyed the rise of the community chests, argued that the federation of philanthropy and new techniques of mass fund-raising pioneered during the war democratized giving in important ways. Although skeptical at times, she concluded, "In the last year or two, with the shifting of what might be called the center of comfort from the professional classes and those whose income is derived from conservative investments to the wage-earning group, individual societies have been trying to get more support from the industrial classes, but this effort has not gone very far nor been general." The problem that many philanthropies continued to struggle with was that most Americans still regarded giving as a luxury item, "to be provided out of surplus." But according to Brandt, the community chest campaigns showed how a luxury might be transformed into an "essential element of living," complete with its own place in the family budget. "In cities where joint appeals have been made it has been demonstrated beyond any possibility of doubt that much larger sums and the substantial interest of a much larger proportion of the population can be assured, and that the support of social work can be made a genuine community responsibility instead of being left to a handful of the relatively well-to-do."[24] By building a "stimulus of suddenly intensified responsibility" not unlike a wartime atmosphere, federated fund-raising helped to transform mass giving from a matter of convenience—practiced only during emergency conditions or exceptional circumstances—into a regular habit enshrined in the family account book. In doing so, leaders of the new mass philanthropy finally gained access to the "subterranean pools of benevolence" Brandt so dearly coveted.

"What was once the task of the privileged few has become the job of the common man," a community-chest worker remarked in 1924, adding that

> the community chest plan has made possible scientific methods of molding public opinion. The centralization and unification of social work has provided funds with which to carry on constructive educational programs; money with which to bring to the attention of the entire community the social ills of that community. A student of community

> chests will find that there has grown in those cities the feeling on the part of the citizens that no one can be a true citizen, and measure up to the real responsibilities of citizenship, if he fails to identify himself with such a movement. Every citizen has it in his heart to give.[25]

Community chests, of course, raised more than individual charitable groups could alone. And they reduced the number of appeals to potential givers. Yet the real value of the chests may have been not in economies of scale but in advancing and broadening the ethic of giving.

Philanthropy as Public Thrift and the American Standard of Living

Giving to mass philanthropy also became an essential component of the standard of living. In *Why Is There No Socialism in the United States?* the German economist Werner Sombart defined this standard as the "material requirements of life" that a worker's wages could acquire. In 1906 Sombart's requirements included housing, clothing, and nutrition; money for "religious and charitable purposes" fell into the category of "free" or "surplus" income.[26] In the 1920s Brandt was contemplating how giving might "emerge above the margin of consumption."[27] Just as thrifty habits were expected from Americans, the ability to respond to the appeals of mass philanthropy came to be considered a part of the American standard of living, according to the experts who were measuring it.

Throughout the 1920s, professional fund-raisers and nonprofit administrators developed and refined the new mechanisms of mass philanthropy (e.g., community chests, various federated giving programs, door-to-door local and national "whirlwind" campaigns, Christmas Seals and stamps). Not coincidentally, during these years of economic prosperity—from the middle to late 1920s—a consumption-based ethos permeated American society. With new marketing techniques pushing an abundance of mass-produced goods into a market in which many Americans had more disposable income, consumerism profoundly influenced the way in which giving was incorporated into the idea of an American standard of living. Even as Americans continued to save during the twenties, prosperity also allowed them to consume more, invest more, and *give* more.[28]

In regional and national budget studies conducted during the 1920s, many economists recognized the relationship between saving, giving, and consuming. Charity was often placed under the rubric of "sundries," and measures of giving were prominent in the tables of what the American worker could "afford to give"—itself a frequently occurring phrase. Sombart himself had estimated that giving constituted 1.3 percent of the budget for workers' families, while economist Frank Hatch Streightoff had put this figure as high as 3 percent in his *Standard of Living among the Industrial People of America* (1911).[29]

Surveying the standard of living for farmers and their annual budgets in 1929, Ellis Kirkpatrick, an expert agricultural economist in the Division of Farm Population and Rural Life at the Department of Agriculture, found that "closely allied with the church contributions is the expenditure of $1.10 per family for Red Cross and other welfare, by the 2886 farm families" surveyed from eleven states across the nation.[30] Kirkpatrick characterized this as consumption of "advancement goods"—a category comprising "schooling, reading matter, organization dues, church, the Red Cross and other welfare."[31]

Postwar prosperity allowed people to give without dramatically altering their habits of consumption—or even drawing down their savings. Writing in 1920, Harvard political economist T. N. Carver asserted, "It is a common error among economists . . . to assume that there is something antagonistic between thrift and a high standard of living."[32] Others insisted that giving still involved an element of thrift. Carl Joslyn in a 1921 *American Economic Review* article, "What Can a Man Afford?" argued that Americans could manage to give more by saving on leisure pursuits like the movies and radio. He estimated that a single American making $10,000 a year could give 5.35 percent of his income, while a family of six with an income of $1,800 could give only 0.28 percent. The important point was that every American—regardless of income level—should embrace giving as both a civic obligation and one of the "elemental joys of life."[33]

In the end, the level of giving in individual households did not increase substantially during the 1920s. Mass philanthropy and local alliances did, however, bring about marked gains in both the number of givers and total philanthropic giving. From the biggest donors to the smallest of family contributions, individual giving was central to this process. By 1928, more than 100 million Americans were giving more than $2.5 billion per year for philanthropic causes, up from $2 billion in 1925 and $1.75 billion in 1921.[34] An ethic of giving had been embedded in the way that many Americans evaluated their family budgets.

Writing at the end of the 1920s, economist Willford King concluded that the trend toward the democratization of giving first observed by Joslyn had indeed continued through the rest of the decade. Surveying New Haven, Connecticut, in 1928, King discovered that the numbers of givers increased, while giving's role in the family budget was either constant or on the rise, depending on which measures were applied:

> The number of dollars contributed to philanthropic organizations in New Haven has grown very greatly from 1900 to 1925, the amount at the close of the period being about 4½ times as great as the former. In this city, at any rate, it is not true that all that has occurred has been a substitution of a few large organizations for many small organizations. . . . When contributions are reduced to terms of constant purchasing power, a decided growth in the total still appears.[35]

Community chests, as well as philanthropic organizations such as the Red Cross, confirm that the increase in the number of small givers represented a national trend. President Herbert Hoover, himself a former administrator of World War I philanthropic efforts at home and abroad, hoped to rely on these mass philanthropic organizations to stave off national calamity in 1929 and 1930. Hoover's response to the Depression was in part a logical reaction to the rise of mass philanthropy. During these early years of the Depression, the chests—built on the masses' commitment to public thrift—were able to meet a significant amount of the nation's needs. In some instances they even raised larger sums than they had in previous years, much of it donated by citizens who themselves remained vulnerable to economic calamity. Giving had indeed become a collective thrift. "In every city," according to the Association of Community Chests and Councils (the United Way of America) in November 1930, "a large part of the increase has come directly from job-holders—persons who may at any time have to turn to the chest for aid."[36]

Similar patterns of giving emerge in the results of a later study of Americans living on moderate incomes. For clerks and their families in the San Francisco Bay region in 1933, Emily Huntington and Mary Luck found that ninety-one out of ninety-eight clerks' families reported donating on average 1.5 percent of their annual earnings to church, charity, or other organizations during the hard years of the Depression in 1933. Eighty-six of these families donated to organized charity, while sixty gave to church.[37]

The public remained responsive to the overtures of mass philanthropy even as the economic downturn eventually drained personal saving. While personal saving accounted for almost $11.5 billion in 1929, by 1932 these savings had evaporated and many Americans were in debt.[38] Yet even as the model of personal thrift once promoted by the Charity Organization Society movement and social workers of the late nineteenth century became untenable, the commitment to public thrift—embodied by donations to community chests and, later, to the March of Dimes and the United Way—stayed firmly in place.

A "Big Wind" Sweeping the Country

In 1928 the magazine *American Mercury*, edited by H. L. Mencken, highlighted the rise of new professional fund-raising techniques and new forms of philanthropic management. Referring to a "Big Wind" sweeping across American philanthropy, the editors opined, "Where money-getters on the prowl once devoted themselves almost solely to the Big Money Boys, they now seek to be democrats, giving everybody, high or low, a fair chance to do his bit for the Worthy Cause." These changes represented not only the ongoing democratization of giving but also its professionalization. "Instead of chasing after fat checks of six figures, they snatch up whatever is offered—dimes and nickels, and even pennies. And what was once a simple art, practiced exclusively by amateurs, is now in the hand of Science and Organization. It has become, indeed, a Great Profession, with trained specialists who, for a fee and expenses, stand ready day or night to raise funds for any Great Cause."[39]

This "Big Wind" sweeping across philanthropy can be understood as public thrift. As a value, thrift had been a means of *personal* (or family) improvement. But through the advent of mass philanthropy during the early twentieth century, it was also transformed into a means of *collective* improvement. Public thrift as philanthropy emerged most prominently during the national war efforts from 1917 to 1918 and was amplified during the 1920s, when the economy increasingly centered on consumption. Thrift as a service to a wider public—rather than a form of the older, private form of self-improvement—became integral to the American standard of living during the 1920s, enduring even through the darkest days of the 1930s. During the Great Depression, personal savings disappeared, but the valorization of public thrift remained firmly in place.

Notes

I want to thank Christopher McKnight Nichols, Derek Hoff, and Christopher Loomis for exemplary assistance.

1. Benjamin Franklin, *Poor Richard's Almanack*, 1737 ed., in *Writings* (New York: Library of America, 1987), 1204.

2. Mary E. Richmond, *The Long View: Papers and Addresses* (New York: Russell Sage Foundation, 1930).

3. Mary Wilcox Brown, *The Development of Thrift* (New York: Macmillan, 1899), 7.

4. John Ryan, *The Living Wage: Its Ethical and Economic Aspects* (New York: Macmillan, 1906), 144–45.

5. Lilian Brandt, *How Much Shall I Give?* (New York: Frontier Press, 1921), 57.

6. Emily H. Huntington and Mary Gorringe Luck, *Living on a Moderate Income: The Incomes and Expenditures of Street-Car Men's and Clerk's Families in the San Francisco Bay Region* (Berkeley and Los Angeles: University of California Press, 1937).

7. Scott M. Cutlip, *Fund Raising in the United States: Its Role in America's Philanthropy* (New Brunswick, NJ: Rutgers University Press, 1965), 54–55; Jacob Riis, "The Christmas Stamp," *Outlook*, July 6, 1907, 511.

8. See undated clipping by Emily Bissell, "The Story of the Christmas Seal," Bill Frank Collection, box 11, folder 28, Historical Society of Delaware, Wilmington, Delaware.

9. Cutlip, *Fund Raising*, 55.

10. Ibid., 57–58.

11. Nancy Tomes, *The Gospel of Germs: Men, Women, and the Microbe in American Life* (Cambridge, MA: Harvard University Press, 1998), 122.

12. Cutlip, *Fund Raising*, 40–50, 81–93.

13. The first year for which data on saving are available is 1897. Personal saving includes saving by nonagricultural individuals, agriculture, and unincorporated businesses. Inflation calculated using the consumer price index (David-Solar-based); saving rate using both

gross domestic product (Millennial ed. ser.) and gross national product (Kendrick ser.). On national saving, see series F 540–51, "National Saving, by Major Saver Groups, in Current Prices: 1897–1945," in U.S. Bureau of the Census, *Historical Statistics of the United States: Colonial Times to 1970* (Washington, DC: Government Printing Office, 1975), 1:262. For all other data, see U.S. Bureau of the Census, *Historical Statistics of the United States: Earliest Times to the Present*, Millennial ed. (New York: Cambridge University Press, 2006), 3:25, table Ca10 ("Gross Domestic Product: 1790–2002; GDP—Millennial Edition Series"); 3:59, table Ca188 ("Gross National Product and Gross Domestic Product: 1869–1929; Kendrick; Gross National Product: Current Dollars"); and 3:158, table Cc1-2 ("Consumer Price Indexes, for All Items: 1774–2003; BLS-Based and David-Solar-Based").

14. *Scribner's Dictionary of American History*, "Thrift Stamps" (New York: Scribner's, 1940), 5:267.

15. Frank A. Vanderlip, "Financing with War Savings Certificates," *Annals of the American Academy of Political and Social Science* 75, no. 164 (January 1918): 33, 36.

16. Charles Gilbert, *American Financing of the War Effort* (Westport, CT: Greenwood Press, 1970), 139–40.

17. Editorial, *English Journal* 7, no. 6 (June 1918): 397.

18. From $4.72 billion in 1916, personal saving nearly doubled in 1917, then climbed to almost $13 billion in 1918 before falling back to $9.3 billion the following year. Even accounting for rampant inflation, saving nearly doubled between 1916 and 1918. See U.S. Bureau of the Census, *Historical Statistics* (1975), 1:262, table F 543 ("National Saving, by Major Saver Groups, in Current Prices: 1897–1945; Personal Saving: Total, Excluding Consumer Durables").

19. Foster Rhea Dulles, *The American Red Cross: A History* (New York: Harper, 1950), 151. See also American Red Cross, "World War I Accomplishments of the American Red Cross," American Red Cross Museum, http://www.redcross.org/museum/history/ww1a.asp (accessed July 26, 2006).

20. Dulles, *American Red Cross*, 148.

21. Merle Curti, *American Philanthropy Abroad* (1963; New Brunswick, NJ: Transaction, 1988), 245–47.

22. C. Howard Hopkins, *John R. Mott, 1865–1955: A Biography* (Grand Rapids, MI: Eerdmans, 1979), 535–44.

23. "1919 War Chest: Give Your Share" (n.p., 1919), http://www.trove.net/PATG0004/PATG0004_001136.html (accessed July 26, 2006); "Help Fill the War Chest: Humanity Calls You" (Philadelphia: Ketterlinus, c. 1914–18), http://docsouth.unc.edu/wwi/41913/50.html (accessed July 26, 2006).

24. Brandt, *How Much Shall I Give?* 56.

25. These comments were made by C. M. Bookman, executive secretary of Community Chest and Council of Social Agencies, Cincinnati, in "The Community Chest Movement—An Interpretation," in *The National Conference of Social Work Annual Proceedings, 51st Annual Session* (Chicago: University of Chicago Press, 1924), 22–23.

26. Werner Sombart, *Why Is There No Socialism in the United States?* trans. Patricia M. Hocking and C. T. Husbands (White Plains, NY: International Arts and Sciences Press, 1976), 61, 102–4.

27. Brandt, *How Much Shall I Give?* 2.

28. Aggregate personal saving between 1922 and 1929 was higher on average than personal saving between 1900 and 1915. The national saving rate was also higher, and personal

saving constituted a similar percentage of national saving as it did during the prewar years. Although statistics on giving before World War II are spotty, anecdotal evidence indicates an uptick in giving during the 1920s. For example, in 1919, annual private gifts and grants to higher education totaled $7,584,000. By 1929, this figure stood at $26,172,000. Personal consumption for clubs and fraternal organizations (a category that, unfortunately, also includes recreation) stood at $140 million in 1914, but this figure had more than doubled, to $302 million, by 1929. Finally, John Price Jones estimated in *The American Giver* that charitable contributions rose from less than $650 million in 1923 to more than $803 million in 1929. John Price Jones, *The American Giver: A Review of American Generosity* (New York: Inter-River Press, 1956), table 1. On national saving, see note 13. On giving, see U.S. Bureau of the Census, *Historical Statistics of the United States* (2006), 2:877, table Bg211 ("Higher Education Expenditures, Endowment Income, Receipts, and Voluntary Support, by Sources: 1919–1995; All Higher Education: Private Gifts and Grants"); 2:897, table Bg309 "Voluntary Membership Organizations—Number, Indicators of Economic Significance, Employment, Employee Consumption, Expenditures, and Income, by Source: 1909–2000; Personal Consumption Expenditures for Recreation, Clubs, and Fraternal Organizations"); and 2:923, table Bg591 ("Philanthropic and Charitable Giving, and Philanthropic Revenue of Nonprofit Organizations: 1900–1997; Charitable Contributions").

29. Sombart, *Why Is There No Socialism*, 104; Frank Hatch Streightoff, *The Standard of Living among the Industrial People of America* (Boston: Houghton Mifflin, 1911).

30. Ellis Lore Kirkpatrick, *The Farmer's Standard of Living* (New York: Century, 1929), 192.

31. Ibid., 183.

32. T. N. Carver, "Thrift and the Standard of Living," *Journal of Political Economy* 28, no. 9 (November 1920): 784, 786.

33. Carl Joslyn, "What Can a Man Afford?" *American Economic Review* 11, supp. no. 2 (December 1921): 114.

34. Robert Bremner, *American Philanthropy* (Chicago: University of Chicago Press, 1988), 133.

35. Willford Isbell King, *Trends in Philanthropy: A Study in a Typical American City* (New York: National Bureau for Economic Research, 1928), 74.

36. Bremner, *American Philanthropy*, 138.

37. Huntington and Luck, *Living on a Moderate Income*, 128–31, see also 166.

38. U.S. Bureau of the Census, *Historical Statistics of the United States* (1975), 1:262, series F 542.

39. R. J. Prendergast, "Raising the Big Wind," *American Mercury* 13 (1928): 464, cited in Roy Lubove, *The Professional Altruist: The Emergence of Social Work as a Career, 1880–1930* (Cambridge, MA: Harvard University Press, 1965), 215.

15 }

Immigrants and Thrift

David M. Reimers

They [immigrants] were all eager to save money. That was their main ambition.

—JOHN R. COMMONS

From the 1880s until 1940, 27 million immigrants entered the United States, most arriving before 1930. The restrictions enacted during the 1920s cut the flow by the end of that decade, and so did the lean years of the Great Depression, when visas were hard to come by. During World War II few were admitted. Overall, only 700,000 immigrants came to America from 1930 to 1945. This major influx between the 1880s and the 1920s stands out as one of three great waves of immigration, the last one beginning after 1970.[1]

The newcomers of the late nineteenth and early twentieth centuries arrived from nearly all corners of the globe, but Europeans by far amounted to the largest number. Before the 1880s, Germans, Irish, and persons from Great Britain dominated the statistics, and during the 1880s the largest number of Germans was recorded in a single decade. But a shift during the following decade brought a new pattern of European immigration. Irish and Germans still arrived after 1900, but their numbers fell while Italians, Russians, Poles, Greeks, Jews of various national origin, and immigrants from the Austro-Hungarian Empire accounted for the vast number of newcomers. At their peak, more than 300,000 Italians arrived annually in some years, compared with only a few thousand disembarking in New York City during the 1880s. Immigrants totaled over 1 million in the five years between 1900 and World War I; by 1910 nearly 15 percent of Americans were foreign born. In that same year approximately three-quarters of the population in New York, Chicago, and Detroit consisted of immigrants and their children.

Ellis Island, which opened in the 1890s and became the main receiving station for Europeans, was clearing several thousand persons daily by the early twentieth century. Other government stations also received immigrants, but in its heyday Ellis Island was the portal to America for more than two-thirds of European immigrants. In spite of growing restrictions, more than 98 percent of those steerage passengers who disembarked at Ellis Island were cleared for settlement within a few hours. These millions settled throughout the United States, but they generally avoided the South, where wages for labor were low. Thus only 5 percent of the southern population was foreign born in 1910. Yet New Orleans, Baltimore, and some of the emerging southern industrial cities attracted Europeans who found unskilled jobs in factories and extraction industries. And the cities had streets to be paved and transportation systems to be developed, so immigrants quickly found that their labor was needed.

While mining areas and industrial cities, large and small, were particularly attractive to immigrants, some Germans and Scandinavians managed to buy land and clear it for farming. Other immigrants were unable to accumulate enough money to purchase farms; hoping to own land some day, they worked as migratory laborers or as farm hands. Farmworkers moved with the crops, and others traveled as they built and maintained the railroads.

Anti-Semitism drove many Polish and Russian Jews to flee Europe, and some other immigrants found America tolerant of their religious or radical views. Yet economic motives drove most to leave home. The worst of the Irish famine was long past by the beginning of the twentieth century, and conditions improved for many Germans by then, too. But across Scandinavia and eastern and southern Europe, many still struggled to earn a living. There was simply not enough land to support the growing rural population. Thus many sought work in nearby cities. Once there, when conditions remained harsh, they took the next step: booking passage to America, where opportunities were supposed to be abundant. It was not the very poor who moved but rather those slightly above them with knowledge about America and sufficient funds for the journey.

Knowledge of the New World extended across Europe, reaching cities, rural areas, and small hamlets alike. Letters from America informed future emigrants of conditions there. Oftentimes the letters painted a rosy picture because those in America did not wish others to know of how hard life in the New World was or that they had failed to find the riches they expected. Jon Gjerde reported that letters home to Norway emphasized "bountiful land, high wages, and opportunity for enormous material wealth." One writer stressed, "'Here the food is overflowing and we get to drink as much sweet milk as we want; when the milk becomes sour, it is thrown out to the pigs,' a practice of waste unheard of in Norway."[2] Steamship lines, eager for new business, spread news of the United States (and South America, too), with their agents scouring for passengers in villages as far away as Russia.

The steamship companies offered more than information. By the 1880s, the days of long sailing voyages to America were past. The cost of travel from Europe to America dropped considerably, and the voyages now took only a few days instead of weeks. The "coffin ships" of the 1840s and 1850s, with their high en route death rates, were endured by those fleeing the Irish famine, as they had no choice. These ships were replaced by much better facilities, even if conditions in steerage, where most of the immigrants booked passage, were hardly ideal. From China a voyage that took several months during the heyday of the 1849 gold rush days consumed only two to three weeks by the late nineteenth century.

Impressive as the European migration was, Asians joined this search for a better life, particularly in Hawaii and the West Coast. Chinese laborers were legally banned in 1882, but some Chinese immigrants managed to gain entrance in spite of the restrictions. Erika Lee's careful study of Chinese immigration after 1882 demonstrated that thousands of Chinese entered, exempt from the restriction laws.[3] Japanese immigration to the United States picked up after 1880, and a few thousand Koreans and Indians also came to America in the early twentieth century, until they too were barred. After the American conquest of the Philippines, thousands of young Filipino men headed to labor in the United States.[4]

Another racially designated group was black immigrants. Some came from the Bahamas to harvest crops in Florida in the late nineteenth century; after 1900 they helped Miami grow as a tourist city. Their labor was important for building and staffing the city's hotels, where they could not stay as guests. Other West Indians, after helping build the Panama Canal, followed the banana boats north and settled in New York City.[5]

The era after 1890 also recorded the first substantial migration from the Middle East. Armenians and Syrian-Lebanese were the largest groups. They were mostly Christians, some of whom had heard the "good news" of the New World from Protestant missionaries who urged them to go to America.[6]

While Mexico today dominates U.S. immigration statistics, this most recent migration is by no means the first wave. Seventy-five thousand Mexicans joined the U.S. population following the annexation of the Southwest as a prize of the Mexican-American War in 1848. The border was only loosely patrolled after that, and thousands of other Mexicans headed north. The Mexican Revolution of 1910 added to the woes of Mexico and prompted many others to leave. Precise figures are not available because the border was so porous, but experts estimate that 1 million Mexicans settled in the United States from 1900 to 1930.

Immigrants did not settle in a random pattern. They frequently found employment with the help of friends and family. Indeed, those who had come before often paid the passage for others to follow. June Alexander reports that an astounding 98.4 percent of Slovaks entering in 1907 said they were "planning to join relatives or friends."[7] Similar tales could be told about other groups. Of Italians in Buffalo, Virginia Yans-McLaughlin notes that the evidence of settlement "tells us that kin played an active part in both immigration and settlement." Further, "The Italians who had arrived in Buffalo purchased hundreds of tickets for family members still in Italy."[8] Many immigrant letters contained tickets, and letters were huge in volume. Ewa Morawska reports that between 1900 and 1906 alone, "American sojourners sent 5 million letters to Russia and Austria-Hungary."[9] The U.S. Immigration Commission (the Dillingham Commission) concluded, "In fact, it is entirely safe to assert that letters from persons who have emigrated to friends at home have been the immediate cause of by far the greater part of the remarkable movement from southern and eastern Europe to the United States during the past twenty-five years." Finally, "The importance of the advice of friends as an immediate cause of emigration from Europe is also indicated by the fact that nearly all European immigrants admitted to the United States are, according to their statements, going to join relatives or friends."[10]

In some cases padrones, or labor bosses, found immigrants places of work for a hefty price. This practice was mostly confined to Italians and Greeks and became illegal when the Contract Labor Law was enacted in 1885. Theodore Saloutos explains that the agents often abused young Greeks eager to immigrate to America: "The prospective immigrant was also preyed upon by the labor agent, whose unethical practices were all too common."[11] Labor agents became less common after 1900, when immigrant networks brought their family and kin to America.[12]

Because most Mexican immigrants had historically been part of the Southwest, especially Texas, it might seem odd that by World War I Mexican communities had also been formed in the Midwest. Some of the first Mexicans were lured to the United States by contractors seeking section hands on the railroads across the Southwest, but eventually Mexicans journeyed to the Midwest, too.[13] The first to do so were usually young men who labored in the sugar beet fields or as contracted laborers; employers hoped they would return home after the harvest. However, some of the young men drifted to cities like Chicago, where they found jobs in industry. Such was the case during World War I when European immigration dropped sharply.[14]

No group was more controlled in its migration than the Chinese. Chinese moneylenders provided the funds for the journey to America, as well as placement in employment. The brokers collected money from the families of the potential immigrant and then, on American soil, collected additional money from the employees, such as those working on the railroads. The voyage was longer than that between Europe and America, and money was to be made in this lucrative business of human traffic. Madeline Yuan-yin Hsu reports that in 1877, Li Chudu, who became a moneylender, returned to Taishan County and persuaded more than 200 people to come to the United States to work on the railroad.[15] He was by no means the only successful creditor, and as a result thousands of immigrants found themselves in debt to the lenders under the "ticket credit" system. The Chinese who put up the funds to bring Chinese laborers to the United States also provided goods for the workers' consumption.[16]

In the case of Irish immigrants, mainly single women created the networks. Once here, Hasia Diner reminds us, "[Irish] women actively promoted migration and traveled along what might be seen as female chains. They made trips together, they helped finance one another, and they met and greeted one another. Although they certainly assisted male kin as well, particularly brothers, the primary emphasis focused on their sisters and other female relatives."[17] Even for those who chose a rural area, the patterns of kin, family, and friends dominated. Robert Ostergren has examined the case of several Swedish towns and farming areas in detail. Isanti County in Minnesota was the destination of more than 41 percent of those leaving Rattvik, Sweden. Letters from America told of the good life there compared with in Sweden, and as a result, "America fever" spread. They knew of those who had gone before. In the case of dissenting Baptists, they received more encouragement and aid to cross the Atlantic, no doubt because they were a tight-knit community.[18]

The immigrants changed America culturally and helped the nation industrialize and expand economically. Their labor in the mines and factories and on the streets and farms was essential to America's economic growth. Yet America changed and challenged the immigrants, too. Jackson Lears's essay in this volume points to the broad changes in the late nineteenth and early twentieth centuries. Lears notes that newcomers confronted a society in which moralists "remain wedded to the tradition of the Puritan jeremiad."[19] Yet there were also changes, as he notes. Lendol Calder has written about the rise of consumer credit, and Jennifer Scanlon tells us about advertising, both of which appeared in this era.

It was not possible for immigrants to be unaware of the society they confronted. But it is important to point out that the vast majority entered without speaking English, and many, especially women, did not master English after settling. As a result, they could not read American newspapers and magazines or comprehend the advertising. Often their workplaces and neighborhoods were shaped by a variety of ethnic groups, and not necessarily English-speaking ones. The immigrants turned inward and joined ethnic churches and fraternal organizations, not necessarily old stock American ones. Many of the first Irish conversed in Irish, but by the 1880s the new Irish immigrants were English speakers; even so, they largely kept to themselves, especially in their Catholic parishes. West Indians usually spoke English, but for black immigrants life was exceedingly difficult, and they were largely separated and isolated by color lines from the white population. Their contact with Americans was with African Americans as neighbors and as servants to white Americans.

For most of the others, a tangible world outside their neighborhood and workplace did not exist at first. Only with time, and especially with the second generation, did immigrants become aware of the broader social and economic changes taking place in the United States. Moreover, because so many of the newcomers were poorly educated and lacked skills, they were forced to take low-paying jobs.

The various credit schemes to fund ocean passage added to the expense of becoming an immigrant. Most no doubt hoped that life in the United States would improve their lot or at least that of their children; a few actually believed that the streets were literally paved with gold. Instead of riches, they found that the work was difficult indeed and the wages low. In studying Johnstown, Pennsylvania, Morawska writes, "Soon after arriving in this country, thousands of immigrants saw America for what it actually was. A promise, perhaps, but one to be redeemed at the price of terribly hard work, dismal living conditions, recurrent insecurity, and deteriorating health—a price much steeper than they had imagined in Europe."[20]

Just what wages enabled the unskilled newcomers to find decent housing, clothing, medical care, fuel, and food around the turn of the twentieth century? Various contemporaries suggested that at least $500 per year was needed to achieve a very modest standard of living, a figure that many immigrant families did not reach. Others used a higher figure of $600 per year.[21] Susan Glenn, in her book on Jewish immigrant women, claims that economists said a minimum of $800 per year was required for a "'normal standard of living'—food, housing, and transportation."[22] The Dillingham Commission found that post-1890 immigrant workers usually made less than $600 per year, which meant that many lived in poverty or on the edge of poverty. Practically all the new post-1890 immigrants earned less than white native-born Americans. The Americans made on average $666 annually, but for southern Italians, the figure was only $396. For immigrant Greeks annual income was $300; for Poles, $428; for Slovaks, $442; and for Croatians, $410. Wages did vary depending on the industry and location. Morawska notes that in 1911 the U.S. Immigration Commission found that immigrants from east central Europe averaged $573 annually in Johnstown, which was roughly $200 less than those in mills or mines or those with only one breadwinner.[23] By the 1920s these incomes had increased considerably, but inflation in World War I and high prices for goods still consumed most of newcomers' wages in the 1920s.[24] Moreover, employment was impacted by recessions and depressions, and injuries on the job were common at the turn of the twentieth century; good years could be offset by poor-earning ones.

In retrospect, it is amazing to see how so many survived on so little. To the immigrants, thrift meant watching each nickel and dime to provide for families. Sometimes, as noted, this started before the journey began as families saved to buy passage to America. Discussing Greek immigrants, Saloutos remarks, "The immigrant lived a hand-to-mouth existence. He needed cash and he needed it quickly in order to provide for himself, for his anxious parents or for the family he had left behind. Time and ready income were of the essence."[25] Slack times meant a loss of income, as did seasonal labor. When an industrial depression hit the United States in 1921 and 1922, Mexicans in the Midwest were among the first to be laid off, and thousands headed home or opted for employment in the beet fields, where the wages were considerably lower. Seasonal agricultural workers were paid $160 per year with little prospect of further employment until the next harvest. No wonder these immigrants preferred industrial jobs. The highest-paying positions were in the auto industry, which paid $6 per day. Other manufacturing paid somewhat less, and Mexicans usually held the lowest-paid and most onerous jobs. In 1911, the U.S. Commission on Immigration reported that Mexican immigrant men averaged only $379 yearly, one of the lowest figures for any group.[26]

In addition, many immigrants faced discrimination. Not only were Mexicans mostly confined to low-wage employment, but they also encountered prejudice when they attempted to find housing.[27] Signs saying "No Irish Need Apply" greeted many from the Emerald Isle. After World War I elite colleges restricted their admission of Jews, and firms openly advertised that job offerings were for "Christians only."[28] But perhaps no group encountered such blatant discrimination as the Chinese. Charles Crocker, who supervised the building of the Central Pacific Railroad, hired thousands of Chinese workers because he believed they were outstanding laborers and also because he could pay them less. The company paid white workers $35 per month plus room and board, whereas Chinese workers were given only $26 per month and nothing for room and board. White workers called the Chinese "Crocker's pets."[29] When the railroads were completed, Chinese workers left for cities; in San Francisco, where the largest number of them settled, they encountered still more discrimination, were driven out of particular trades both by law and by violence, and found themselves segregated into the Chinatowns of American cities.[30]

For many European immigrants, discrimination was not the primary handicap in the search for lucrative employment. The vast majority had arrived with little education and few usable skills and without the ability to speak or read English. In fact, the U.S. Immigration Commission found that only half of southern Italians who landed between 1899 and 1909 could read and write in their own language.[31] In time, with improved English-language acquisition, they found more opportunities, but during their first years in the United States they could not step into a high-paying white-collar job.

As for the skills of those who arrived around the turn of the twentieth century, 5.6 percent of the English were professionals and 29.8 percent were listed as skilled workers. But for the southern Italians only 0.3 percent were professionals and fewer than 12 percent were skilled workers. About one-quarter were farm laborers, and more than one-third were common laborers. While Italians were at the bottom of the occupational ladder for these New Immigrants arriving after the 1890s, most of the others had similar occupational backgrounds.[32] From Asia, Chinese immigrants were no more likely to be professionals or skilled workers than Italian or other New Immigrants from Europe. Those searching for "Gold Mountain" were mostly poor farmers who went into debt to pay their passage to America.[33]

To make ends meet, many immigrant families, which were on average larger than native-born white ones, had several wage earners. Most immigrant children did not stay in school long enough to finish high school; only one-third of all young persons finished high school by the time of World War I. Among immigrant children the figure was even less than one third.

Children's wages were needed at home. About one-fifth of immigrant households had child workers. Discussing Pittsburgh, several historians remark, "While most Italian parents expected support from their children, instances did exist where parents encouraged children to finish high school. A few second generation Italians completed twelve years of schooling, most did not."[34] They conclude that "like Poles, their desire to leave school early and assist their family was as likely to emerge from the child as it was from the parent."[35] It was also common for young unmarried women and men to live at home and turn most of their earnings over to their mothers, while keeping a small part for their own use.[36] As Susan Glenn reminds us, "The labor of daughters had been necessary to their families before migration to America and it became even more important after immigrants arrived."[37] For women who worked, their wages were lower than immigrant men's and native white women's.[38]

Married women usually did not leave the household to work. Immigrant women were busy enough caring for their large families. However, money could be made at home, perhaps sewing garments. More common and important was the extra cash that came with boarders. The boarders were often members of the extended immigrant family or persons from their villages in Europe, but some boarders were strangers. Given the fact that, during this era, the overwhelming majority of immigrants were males who needed a place to stay, boarders were easy to find. Some groups reported that more than half of immigrant households had boarders.[39] In Pittsburgh, historians found that young immigrant and black families were able to supplement their household income by approximately $12 to $16 monthly—not an insignificant sum in 1900. This meant the difference "between deprivation and starvation."[40] Oftentimes this meant that women had to prepare meals, do laundry, and clean the house for three to five additional persons. Little privacy was available under such conditions. Remarking on the burden boarders created, the one Slovak protagonist of Thomas Bell's novel *Out of This Furnace* tells her husband, "I hope we never have to take in boarders again. When I think of how I used to work I wonder how I ever did it."[41]

Yans-McLaughlin tells of another way that immigrant families made ends meet: "Thrifty Italians used . . . Old World devices to keep their families alive. Some kept small gardens behind their homes or in outlying city districts."[42]

Italians were by no means the only immigrants to have gardens to supplement their food. Frequently, Irish immigrants also cultivated the ground around their houses.

Given such low incomes, most immigrants had little to spend on consumer items or recreation. Yet historians have discovered that some newcomers were able to advance, if not from rages to riches, then at least modestly. From his study of Jews and Italians in New York from 1885 to 1915, Thomas Kessner concluded that this was the case, with Jewish mobility ahead of Italian.[43] Other studies have reported similar results. If they found America disappointing, "however limited and deprived their condition was in this country, as compared to what they had known at home, the immigrants perceived it as offering more promising grounds for sustained efforts to achieve a better life."[44] Some, such as Irish women domestics, had to measure their progress in small savings accounts.[45]

There are, of course, exceptions, and many failed and even returned home because they did not do well in America. Mexicans were usually hired to do menial work and could find no other employment. Once the Chinese were driven from the mines and helped to build the transcontinental railroad, they finally took up laundry work because little else was available except to return to China. Renqui Yu explains of Chinese laundries in New York City, "The Chinese chose to engage in the hand laundry business because they were excluded from most desirable occupations, and many rapidly expanding cities needed their cheap labor to fill the least undesirable unskilled job."[46]

In contrast, Andrew Heinze has argued that Jewish immigrants improved their lot substantially and became consumers of American culture and goods. He points to the role of the Yiddish press in attracting the advertising of national products.[47] He cites studies that show that members of households with budgets under $1,000 spent their money; they did not save it. Their spending included paying for basic necessities, but once these were paid for, they had additional money for "sundries," consumer items that were not absolutely essential. Once incomes hit $1,200 annually, they saved.[48] He also argues that installment buying for some products existed before its large-scale expansion after World War I. He identifies consumerism as becoming part of American culture in the early twentieth century. According to Heinze, "The practice of installment buying initiated newcomers into the possibilities of immediate acquisition and familiarized them with the impatient optimism that characterized the American consumer."[49]

Jews, he argued, incorporated the abundance of America into their religious observances and their secular life. Jewish women tended to pay attention to style and not simply the cost of a new dress. And, according to Heinz, Jewish women were not the only ethnic group to be so concerned about clothing. He notes that Irish women "seemed to pick up American habits more quickly than other non-Jewish newcomers."[50] Moreover, it was in this era that a vacation in the Catskill Mountains became a fixture for Jewish families. In 1883 about 70,000 people, mostly affluent Americans, enjoyed a summer vacation in the Catskill Mountains of New York. The number of vacationers had jumped to 400,000 by 1906, "an increase that owed much to the rapid acceptance of this custom by Jewish immigrants from New York City."[51] While not painting a picture of the rags-to-riches saga portrayed in Abraham Cahan's novel *The Rise of David Levinsky* (1917), Heinze's sketch is certainly a view of rapid social mobility and acceptance of consumerism.

Jewish immigrants did have advantages when they arrived because, compared with others, a larger share of these immigrants were skilled workers, many with experience as tailors in Russia. They fit easily into the garment factories of New York City. Moreover, proportionately more Jews than other immigrants of the post-1880s era were literate. They arrived in New York City when the garment trade was expanding rapidly and was largely run by the better-off Jews who employed the newcomers from eastern Europe. By the turn of the twentieth century, Russian Jews "had become the employers, having set up hundreds of small shops as contractors" and giving these Jews a head start.[52]

Yet it is important to recall that, in the early twentieth century, most immigrant households did not have annual incomes of $1,000, let alone $1,200. For the Jewish immigrants that Heinze studied, consumerism no doubt existed before World War I because they had more social mobility than others. But it is not always clear whether or not he is discussing an earlier German wave of immigration or the immigrant community of the Lower East Side, which returned a socialist to Congress. The poverty and poor living conditions there nurtured radicalism.

Speaking of New York's Germans, one historian writes, "Earlier, working-class German families likely had relatively little discretionary income: one study of seventeen such families in the 1880s found that for the most part 'trips to the theater, vacations, or other such extras were clearly out of reach.'" Not until 1910 were German families able to devote "between 4 and 10 percent of their budgets to 'recreation and pocket money.'"[53] Peter Connolly-Smith writes about a radical German paper's difficulty in attracting ads: "One reason for the newspaper's habitual lack of funds was its inability to attract significant advertising. According to the head of the advertising [of the paper], American companies were reluctant to advertise in the *Staats-Zeitung* as much because of its subversive politics as for the advertisers' lack of faith in the readership's purchasing power."[54]

Liz Cohen's masterful account of Chicago's workers from 1919 to 1939, many of whom were immigrants, suggests that such consumerism was not common, at least not in working-class neighborhoods in Chicago before World War I. Even in the 1920s, she argues, immigrants were not slavish consumers of everyday products. "Once again," she writes of the 1920s, "popular beliefs at the time do not hold up under close scrutiny. Industrial workers were not engaging in installment buying in nearly the numbers that marketers assume. First of all, workers had become savers during the 1920s, at least as much as spenders."[55] Just how they saved will be discussed later in this essay; it is important to realize that most immigrants were not heading off to summer vacations and accepting American consumer culture before World War I, even during the prosperity of the war and the 1920s.

The immigrant press generally reflected the immediate concerns of the editors and their readers. For many editors the foci were events at home and advice to readers. While some of the print media catered to upwardly mobile Jewish readers, most of the early foreign-language papers did not carry displays of consumer goods. As Robert Park notes, the immigrant press "is like a general store in a rural community. It offers to its public a multitude of things; but nothing distinctive, exotic, or stimulating except, perhaps, its radicalism—political or religious."[56] The services advertised ran from lawyers to doctors, employment opportunities, foreign-language books, and activities of immigrant fraternal organizations.

The first national advertisements appearing in these papers were for patent medicines. Such ads, "framed in a way to intrigue the readers of the local press, made patent medicines popular in the remote villages."[57] Park reports that only later did the immigrant press also carry ads for tobacco, gramophones, and other consumer products. And, of course, during World War I, the press appealed to readers to purchase Liberty Bonds to support the war effort.[58]

The immigrant press did feature many ads for shipping companies engaged in the process of bringing immigrants to America. This was, no doubt, of great interest to its readers, who wanted to learn about the cost of voyages to the United States from Europe. Such ads were also a sign that steamship lines owned a number of the papers and had a stake in their survival.[59]

While hardly reaching affluence, immigrant families did enjoy a higher standard of living the longer they labored in America, as wages increased and the length of the workday dropped. Studies have indicated that a more limited form of mobility did give immigrants some discretionary income that could be used for nonessential purposes. Roy Rosenzweig's study of working-class life in Worcester, Massachusetts, is a careful examination of working-class immigrants and leisure. The industrial development of Worcester began to change when the New Immigrants arrived after 1890. By and large the newcomers were confined to the unskilled job sector in the growing city. However, in the late nineteenth century, workers' incomes increased there as they did elsewhere in the United States.[60] These modest advances in income were accompanied by a decrease in the daily hours of labor. The steel industry remained on a twelve-hour day as late as World War I, but the workday for most other workers shortened between the 1880s and the 1920s. In Massachusetts the ten-hour workday was common by the end of the nineteenth century, and by the 1920s many skilled craftsmen were laboring only forty-eight hours per week.[61]

What did men, the family heads, do with a modest discretionary income? Rosenzweig points to the rapid growth of the saloon as a major focal place for men's spare time. While the city's reformers attempted to halt the spread of so many saloons, their efforts were not effective. The saloon proved to be attractive; as Rosenzweig notes, "drinking and the Saloon, then, offered recreational diversion well suited to growing, but still modest, working class incomes."[62] Saloons usually excluded women or placed them on the margin, but for the men the saloon provided more than drinking: "A man could get a free lunch with a five-cent beer and enjoy the good fellowship of the barkeep and patrons in the bargain. If he wanted a job, a loan, or simply the news, the working man headed for the saloon."[63] For reformers, mostly Protestants, the saloons were seen as centers of gambling, excessive drinking, and prostitution: places of vice that fed the social and political corruption of the city. They also saw the drinking places as wasteful, and they pointed to the number of women and families who were deserted by drunkard husbands.[64] Or, as one Chicago paper remarked of the saloons, "Men are drunkards, women are drunkards and the innocent looking at this get used to bad habits."[65]

While the Irish saloon has been a fixture in American fiction and popular reporting, other Worcester immigrant groups "developed their own drink centers."[66] Germans were well known for their beer gardens. For Greek men the gathering place was the coffee shop. Saloutos informs us that "the atmosphere of the coffeehouse, clouded with foul cigarette or cigar smoke, was hardly inviting for the public eye or nose. But this was the place to hear local gossip, who died or who was getting married."[67]

The men also joined trade unions, organized working-men clubs, and participated in the growing leisure of sports in the city's public parks.[68] Young men organized their own teams, but a variety of ethnic groups throughout the United States organized fraternal groups that encouraged the participation of the second generation in sports events.[69] For the second generation, participation in American sports was part of becoming American.[70] The parks catered to whole families and not just the immigrant men, for on hot days and nights public parks offered a brief rest from the tenements and other crowded houses of immigrants.[71]

Women on their own were also able to participate in increased leisure and consumption, albeit at a "cheap" level. Kathy Peiss, Susan Glenn, and Elizabeth Ewen, among others, have explored the world of immigrant women and consumption. "Since housing, food, and clothing consumed most of their income, the working-class family as a unit could afford only the cheapest of amusements," writes Peiss.[72] While men dominated most social activities outside of the home, married women spent their time cleaning, preparing meals, watching the children, or shopping for food and other necessities. Leisure for them meant conversing with other married women or socializing with neighbors. According to Ewen, "The streets of the Lower East Side [of New York] were constantly filled with women shopping, running errands, and exchanging news and gossip. To some social workers who had no street life of their own, this appeared to be idle activity."[73]

Peiss observes that even when the family ventured on an outing, it could mean more work for women. Picnics and parties, she noted, required preparation by the woman head of the household.[74] For young unmarried working women living with their families there was the possibility of leisure, but it required negotiation for them to keep part of their wages, usually about one-tenth of their earnings.

The possession of part of their wages enabled young unmarried women to experience some aspects of American consumerism and leisure. Of course a dollar or two could not buy much, but it did open possibilities of enjoyment outside of the home. Just what did these women do with their modest funds? A few joined social clubs for women, but perhaps more important was the attention given to clothing and style, which became "a major arena of contention between mother and daughter."[75]

The turn of the twentieth century also brought dance halls, boardwalks, and amusement parks, places that charged very little. Peiss believes that "of all the amusements that bedazzled the single working woman, dancing proved to be her greatest passion." In the New York City area, more than 500 dance halls had opened their doors by 1910.[76] The opening of Coney Island as a great amusement park offered another way to spend money and enjoy leisure. If dancing, says Peiss, "was the winter passion, Coney Island was the summer."[77] Glenn even reports that clothing of the working-class immigrant women could be purchased on the installment basis.[78]

Many of the conflicts generated by the wages of single women were differences between generations, with immigrant parents trying to instill the old ways while their daughters wanted to adopt American culture, with its growing emphasis on consumerism. And the conflicts were not limited to New York City. Vicki Ruiz's study of Mexican women found a similar desire to accept American culture. The young women protested against chaperones and eagerly sought to purchase the products that were advertised in both the English-language and the Spanish-language press. Such ads of one company promised that if "bleaching cream, hair coloring, and cosmetics were purchased, those with lighter more healthy skin tones will become much more successful in business, love, and society." Ultimately, Ruiz concludes, "Mexican-American women were not caught between two worlds. The Mexican-American generation selected, retained, borrowed, and created their own cultural forms."[79]

The immigrant theater and, later, vaudeville appealed to both the old and new generations, men and women. Rob Snyder reminds us that vaudeville originally was filled with stock ethnic characters and that its "creative roots lay largely in a world of tenements, immigrants, and street-corner wise guys."[80] As it broadened its appeal, it lost some of its ethnic flavor, but it produced some of the movie stars of latter years. The movies later expanded their audiences and became a major force in American culture. Yet in the early years, the movies flourished in immigrant neighborhoods where men and women could both attend.

Above all, movies were cheap, and it was easy to open a theater. Movies began as small storefronts in American cities. It almost appeared as if the early movies were made for immigrant America, and they quickly became popular in those neighborhoods. In Robert Sklar's words, they were "Nickel Madness."[81] The nickelodeons were short and they were silent, which could appeal to those immigrants with limited English comprehension. The early movies were bawdy and lowlife films, which made them even more popular with working-class immigrants.[82] To middle-class Americans bent on reforming urban culture, the nickelodeons were shocking; but to immigrants, here was a place where they could enjoy laughs and fantasy. Not until the 1930s, when sound took over, was English a requirement for enjoyment of movies, and by then the movies were being censored. Yet in all, whether nickelodeons, clothing, dance halls, or amusements, these forms of leisure and consumerism were indeed "cheap," as Peiss and others call them. They did begin the process of consumerism for many immigrants, but this was only a beginning. Immigrants (and their children) had other ways to spend a bit of cash from their meager earnings.

Especially important to the immigrant community were organizations that proliferated in immigrant neighborhoods. Some societies were for men and women, but gender segregation characterized others. The German immigrants and German Americans were renowned for the flourishing *Vereinwesen* in their neighborhoods. In 1900 a professor in Philadelphia characterized the German community as "a culture embodied in voluntary associations." A reader of German newspapers in 1892 would find coverage about "meetings, balls, concerts, fairs, festivals, and anniversary celebrations of a multitude of groups. Philadelphia had not fewer than 642 *vereine* in that same year."[83] They covered a wide range of activities, including athletics, singing, politics, and social occasions. World War I found the *vereine* under attack, and many closed their doors, including the largest national German organization, the National German Alliance.[84]

Germans were by no means the only immigrants to organize associations in their neighborhoods; wherever immigrants settled they organized groups. The Dillingham Commission only touched the tip of the iceberg when it examined fifty-eight societies among twenty-one ethnic groups. Many were religious, but others had secular purposes, such as encouraging political participation and aiding newcomers.[85] Among Jews and Italians the societies were often organized according to villages in Europe where they had lived. The associations sometimes had elaborate rituals, which in part aimed at providing places to gather and keep alive their Old World culture.[86]

Yet the associations were more than institutions to preserve ethnic culture: they offered concrete benefits for the newcomers and were an important source of aid at a time when the United States lacked significant governmental welfare programs. By 1920, writes Cohen, "Ethnic agencies offered their clients cemeteries, hospitals, dispensaries, orphanages, day nurseries, old people's homes, employment and some relief benefits."[87] In 1918, she reports, a high proportion of immigrants possessed life insurance offered by their nationality group. The amounts were usually for a few hundred dollars, but the policies were important for families.[88]

Dan Soyer's careful study of New York City's *landsmanshaftn* has provided us with a detailed look at how the associations worked. At its peak 3,000 associations existed with 500,000 members. They ranged in focus from politics, to religion, to charity and a great variety of monetary services to help newcomers. These mostly Yiddish-speaking groups charged about $4 to $6 per month to become and remain a member.[89] Regardless of their politics or origins, like the mutual aid societies in Chicago that Cohen describes, "*landsmanshaftn* of all types and persuasions offered essentially the same system of mutual aid. Each society met its members' basic material needs by providing a set of benefits that included medical care by an affiliated doctor, reimbursement for wages lost during illness, a form of life insurance, the cost of a funeral, and burial in the society's cemetery."[90] While the services offered were modest, so were the dues. And where else could immigrants find medical care? Soyer points out that the societies did not neglect the social or cultural aspects of immigrant life, even while providing aid.[91] While there would be trouble down the road with the Great Depression and a significant fall in immigration rates, they offered a great deal to the current immigrants. Indeed, they sometimes helped relieve the poverty of Jews crammed into the city's Lower East Side. Moreover, a special feature of the *landsmanshaftn*, as well as of many other fraternal orders, was the focus on events in their homeland. While money was short and the transfer of funds difficult, "*landsmanshaftn* managed to send some money to their hometowns and regions," especially during World War I.[92]

Another organization that both men and women supported was the immigrant church. For Roman Catholics, parishes already existed in the cities and neighborhoods where they settled. To form a new church required working with the diocese, and this was not simply raising funds for the building. Many of the New Immigrant Catholics wanted their own priests and churches and resented the Irish domination of the church that had been established before the 1880s. The American Roman Catholic Church did not approve of nationality-based parishes, but such parishes developed nonetheless.

No doubt a major reason for the nationality-based churches was a financial one. Immigrant Catholics formed committees to raise money, a new experience for them. In their homeland, Slovaks did not become involved in fund-raising, but in America the situation was much different; in the United States, with no established state church, voluntary action was required. Alexander notes of Pittsburgh's Catholics, "Fund-raising events became early features of Slovak Catholic parish life."[93] In 1904 Pittsburgh's bishop reminded the laity that "neglecting to donate money to one's church constituted a grievous sin."[94] "Still, even though Slovaks contributed goods and labor toward their pastors and perhaps contributed some money, they were not accustomed to being the church's chief financial backers."[95]

Even during the Great Depression, the contributions to Pittsburgh's Slovak Catholic churches remained steady. As a result, Catholic churches were able to distribute food and clothing during that decade. It is not known how much Slovaks contributed to the maintenance of individual congregations. But they were basically a working-class population, and they were subject to periodic recessions in the economy. Moreover, the church maintained a number of fraternal groups for men and women, and money was required for these groups to be successful. Tension arose when some priests charged fees for confessions and for the priest's salary.[96]

Pittsburgh's Slovaks were by no means unique. If anything, Polish immigrants were even more intense about their Catholicism, which led to sharp divisions in parishes where Poles were the dominant group.[97] Victor Greene reports this of Poles in the first decade of the twentieth century: "Polish laborers, although earning only a pittance, contributed a part of that hard-won income to their local parish." Further, "A 1905 observer judged the property value of Polish ethnic parishes and pastor maintenance at about $11,000,000. This figure, which excluded the cost of hospitals, orphanages, seminaries and the like, was the equivalent to over two weeks' wages for every adult immigrant."[98]

As the Catholic immigrant population grew and as public schools spread throughout the United States, Catholic leaders called for changes in the curriculum or state funds to support their own religious schools. State and local governments ignored these requests. As a result, the Roman Catholic Church in America attempted to build religious schools that would emphasize church teachings. A constant problem of parochial schools was money. Laypersons were expected to donate to the church's educational institutions. The schools certainly expanded. John Bukowczyk notes that "in 1921 511 schools operating in Polish America's 762 parishes taught 219,711, roughly two-thirds of 'Polonia' youth."[99] However, critics pointed out that the schools were often overcrowded, with students "'packed like herrings in a barrel.'"[100]

Many other immigrant Catholic groups were unable to match the development of parochial schools in Polish communities, in some cases because of the conflicts with the Irish-run church. At bottom, however, working-class immigrants did not have enough income to pay the tuition of the schools, even though the school budgets were limited because so many of the teachers were women, members of a particular order, who worked for low wages. If they lacked funds for the church "to participate in the communal life or to pay for the necessary services, or to preserve their self-esteem and reputation, they used the defensive tactic of making traditional payments in kind, offering the products grown in their gardens and made at home."[101]

Protestant immigrants of this era also turned to religion, attempting to re-create the world they left behind. Ostergren reminds us about Swedes in the Upper Midwest: "Settlers from Rattvik, and other parish or provincial groups who settled in county, moved early to establish their churches."[102] In the early years, too, some of the Lutheran churches operated without clergy. Funds were lacking to hire a minister or put up a building, so laymen ran the early churches and religious services were often held in homes.[103] Swedes also maintained schools that they hoped would preserve Swedish culture and language. In time, the congregations raised the money to build churches and employ ministers.

Competing with cheap amusements, consumerism, and support for ethnic organizations and churches was immigrants' desire to own a home in America. New Immigrants who hailed from a rural background were usually without land; if they possessed it, their holdings were dwarfed by the large landowners in eastern Europe. Three historians report that, based on the oral histories of immigrants, "homeowning was not a value that would-be Americanizers and middle-class reformers needed to impose upon immigrant Newcomers. It was a primary goal for families who decided to remain in America permanently."[104] In Bell's novel *Out of This Furnace*, the wife declares that her husband "wanted to live well, to live in a nice house away from the mill, and to give his boys a good education so they wouldn't have to work with shovel and wheel barrow like their father. He used to say, 'what was the use of coming to America if not to live better than we lived in the old country?'"[105] And in *The Fortunate Pilgrim*, Mario Puzo's novel about Italians in Manhattan's Hell's Kitchen, the mother laments, "Thousands of houses had been bought on Long Island by miserly thrift. But it would never work with her family. They would all be miserable, including herself. And it was her fault. She had not rubbed their noses in poverty as a good mother should."[106] According to Greene, "The building-and-loan societies of Baltimore were the Polish communities' outstanding features," and he quotes one authority as saying, "The Poles there were a thrifty people."[107]

But were immigrants able to purchase homes by "miserly thrift" instead of renting tenements or run-down single homes, often crowded with large families and boarders? In fact, a study of earlier Irish immigrants found they did. Stephan Thernstrom reports that in Newburyport, Massachusetts, real estate became "strikingly available to working class men (usually Irish) who remained in Newburyport for any length of time."[108] A later study of Irish miners in Butte, Montana, around the turn of the 20th century revealed similar results: "The key to home ownership among the Irish miners of Butte was the same as that for the entire working class in America. They had to stay in one place long enough to accumulate a psychological stake." David Emmons reports that of the Irish miners who had worked in Butte for four to seven years, 54 percent either owned their own home or were buying it with a mortgage. And the proportion of home ownership went up after that date.[109] Morawska reports that in Johnstown only a minority of newcomers were homeowners, but she found that a surprising number of families who persisted were able to buy home.[110] They were aided during the 1920s by prosperity and the use of banks and building and loan societies that helped Poles and Lithuanians finance their homes. In that decade, the associations, according to Greene, believed "Poles there were a 'thrifty people.' . . . They will go hungry and take their children out of school to work in order to secure money to purchase homes."[111]

The Dillingham Commission studied immigrant home ownership as one of the key variables of assimilation into American society. The commission did note that data were not entirely reliable, and historians have also found the data to be inconclusive. The commission's figures revealed that 21.6 percent of foreigners owned homes in the early twentieth century, compared with 21.8 percent of native-born whites.[112] Other data, based on the census, indicated a similar pattern.[113] The pattern of home ownership was especially remarkable in view of the fact that many were recent immigrants and that, in some industrial and mining towns, immigrants were effectively barred from owning a home. Isaac Hourwich, a staunch defender of New Immigrants, stated that results indicated that the immigrants had done quite well.[114]

However, those at the bottom of the income scale did not fare well. In 1924 only 18 Mexicans in Kansas City owned their own home. In Chicago, where industrial jobs were available, they did considerably better. In 1928, among autoworkers, 37 percent owned homes; but of the 15,000 Mexicans living in the city, only 100 to 200 families owned their own homes. In East Chicago as late as 1930 only 13 of 934 Mexicans owned their homes.[115] By and large Mexican workers rented housing and were more apt than other groups to take in boarders to make ends meet.[116]

The coming of World War I in April 1917 triggered a new nationalism and a new approach to immigrant thrift. As the war approached, immigrant (and older ethnic) groups were encouraged to become "loyal Americans." Home ownership was fine, but during the war whatever extra income the immigrants could spare should be plowed into the war effort. Once war was declared, they were told to forget the land of their ancestors and participate fully in the war effort against Germany and the Austro-Hungarian Empire. For Germans (and some Irish Americans) who opposed the policies of Great Britain, France, and

Russia before 1917, the declaration of war brought a marked shift in attitudes. The U.S. government—and various political leaders such as former president Theodore Roosevelt—insisted on absolute loyalty and patriotism. German Americans who were closely tied to German culture came under special attack, and German immigrants and German Americans supported the United States' war effort by ceasing to print newspapers in German. Moreover, many German American organizations closed their doors. German-language instruction was dropped in many public schools, and church services were no longer held in the German language.[117]

For German Americans especially, the war loan drives gave them a chance to demonstrate their loyalty to their new homeland and forget about German culture. Connolly-Smith explains that German American participation in these bond drives was encouraged—indeed, was expected and forthcoming—with New York's middle-class German-language press now conspicuously leading the charge. Whereas just a year earlier a German journal had published advertisements for "the Fourth German War Loan, the newspaper on May 4, 1917, began publishing large picture ads for the First Liberty Bond Drive free of charge," and other German publications followed suit.[118]

What of other ethnic groups? Many immigrants responded to the call by urging fellow foreign-born persons to naturalize, and naturalization rates did go up during the war. The federal government also published propaganda, distributed leaflets and posters, and held Loyalty Days celebrations in which ethnic Americans were urged to participate and demonstrate their firm commitment to the United States' involvement in the war.[119] They certainly did so. More important, perhaps, the government raised funds for the war by selling Liberty Bonds. The Liberty Loan drives told immigrants that by buying bonds they could demonstrate their Americanism. Alexander explains that "making immigrants demonstrate loyalty to the United States remained the all-out objective in wartime America. Nowhere was the pressure applied more than in the Liberty Loan drives."[120] Across the land posters appeared, one of which asked, "'Are You 100% American? Prove It! Buy U.S. Government Bonds.'"[121] The drives were often tinged ethnic appeals, especially aimed at those groups whose homelands were on the United States' side in the war.[122] The Treasury Department made special efforts to target immigrants, even publishing their messages in the foreign-language press.[123] According to press releases in Chicago the city's Greek subscription was $167.83 per capita, "which was said to be the highest of any national group."[124] The government's efforts paid off. "The ethnic strategy worked," writes Cohen. "During the Fourth Liberty Loan drive in September 1918, the peak of the bond campaigns, 46.5 percent of all subscribers were of foreign birth or parentage."[125]

Moreover, the Treasury Department, aware of immigrants' limited incomes, sold the bonds in small amounts. Cohen also explains that this was the first time immigrants were exposed to commercial banks, as compared with the storefront banks that thrived in ethnic enclaves.[126] Besides the patriotism and ethnic appeals, the normally cash-limited immigrant communities were aided by the wartime prosperity, which enabled them to buy bonds.

While meeting daily expenses, purchasing homes, engaging consumer culture with its cheap amusements, and buying Liberty Bonds, the post-1890 immigrants had another goal for saving and spending: the Old World claimed their attention and prompted many to return or send money home. In the contemporary United States an immigrant is a permanent resident alien. It must be kept in mind that many New Immigrants had no intention of becoming "permanent." A significant number of those immigrants worked for a few months or years in the United States and then returned home. They hoped to go back with money to buy a home in their native land or possibly open a business. The bulk of the New Immigrants were men—as high as 80 percent in some years. Others went back to bring their wives and children to America. Those who were single hoped to find a bride in their home village or city. One reported, "I came here [to Greece] to marry a woman who spoke the same language I did so I could lead a happier life." Another remarked, "One reason I came back was to get married. It was difficult to marry a Greek woman in the United States."[127] And for a few, patriotism compelled a flow back to Old World. Such was the case for those who returned to fight in the Balkan Wars and later in World War I.[128]

This return is no surprise; immigrants have always been interested in the land of their fathers and mothers. Irish immigrants, if not eager to resettle, still maintained great interest in the struggle of Ireland to be free from British colonialism, and they formed organizations to speed freedom for Ireland. Irish in Butte, Montana, sent money for the cause as early as 1881, and they continued to do so for years after.[129] Soyer found that the *landsmanshaftn* shifted its focus from local needs to those abroad: "From 1914 the immigrant Jewish community in America focused its attention on events in the old country, where the centers of Jewish population in Eastern Europe were being ravaged. . . . It became difficult to raise money for institutions in New York."[130]

How many returned? For some groups, such as Italians, the return rate was as high as 50 percent. However, some of these returned again to the United States for another spell, and some eventually settled in the New World.[131] United States officials estimate that between 1908 and 1923, 9,949,740 entered and 3,498,185 departed.[132] The return rates varied, with Italy and Poland having high rates of return, whereas Jews and Irish stayed in America. Indeed, there was little reason for them to go back. Understandably, Jews had the lowest return rate, only about 5 percent.[133]

Exact figures on how much money the repatriated immigrants brought with them are impossible to calculate. They often returned with their pockets filled with money and additional funds sewed into their clothes. Certainly enough had funds so that they could purchase businesses or buy homes, but owning land was their real passion. "Houses were important," Mark Wyman tells us, but "land was at the heart of the peasant's desire, the only investment he considered in most cases." Studies in Italy, Hungary, Galicia, Finland, and elsewhere in Europe document the "importance of land purchases. . . . Houses were generally second in importance."[134]

Some Americans regarded Italians who went home with hostility. Dino Cinel tells us that "the frugal habits of Italians in the United States and the substantial savings they were channeling to Italy were regarded as detrimental to the national [U.S.] economy."[135] Even among the Irish, who overwhelmingly stayed in the United States, there were returnees. Reportedly, 40 percent of the Butte Irish "between 1880 and 1890 were able to go back to Ireland, buy a farm, marry and settle down."[136] Yet it should be acknowledged that many did not take enough with them back to the Old World, which in some cases prompted them to head again for America for another attempt at riches.

Even when immigrants did not wish to return home, they could still maintain social, cultural, and monetary ties to their land of origin. Their letters from America often contained prepaid tickets for family members in the homeland, or they sent money home for the purchase of land or reunion with family and friends. Of these tickets, the Dillingham Commission reported in 1911, "just what proportion of the present immigration is assisted in this way [prepaid tickets] can not be determined. Some indication of this, however, is contained in the fact that about 25 percent of the immigrants admitted to the United States come with steamship tickets paid for in this country."[137] In other cases immigrant aid societies provided the necessary funds.[138] Some historians have accepted this estimate, but others believe the percentage is larger. Among the Chinese the vast majority of the early immigrants came with debts to the agents bringing them.[139]

Equally important were the remittances from the United States to Europe. Whether they were "frugal Italians" or members of other groups, the immigrants all sent substantial funds home to aid those kin and friends who remained behind. Again, precise data are not available, but the evidence that exists suggests a substantial flow of money. One historian calculates that the American Irish sent more than $260 million to Ireland during the latter part of the nineteenth century.[140] Not to be outdone, America's Greek community, although much smaller than the Irish, sent more than $100,000 in 1920, the most in any year. But it should be noted that the Greeks managed to remit funds home even during the Great Depression of the 1930s.[141] Cinel reports that a steady growth of lire was sent to Sicily, which peaked in 1920 when the figure hit £1 billion. At that time the dollar equivalent was roughly $250 million.[142] Overall, the Dillingham Commission estimated that remittances in 1907 totaled $275 million.[143] This figure was surely not accurate, for, as noted, many immigrants returned home with their savings on their persons and trunks filled with American goods.

Perhaps even more remarkable because of Chinese immigrants' low earnings were their remittances from the United States back to China. Chinese "working overseas," Hsu notes, "made it possible for their friends and families to build new houses and lead better lives." At the same time the hard-earned savings sent to China "encouraged waste and ostentation where previously there had been thrift and modesty."[144]

The remittances often substituted for a return home, and this meant long separation of families, stretching into years. Some immigrants had no desire to return, even if married; or if they returned, it was only temporary, and they once again migrated to the United States. For Chinese immigrants it was very difficult to bring one's family after the Chinese Exclusion Act passed in 1882, so they sent remittances to China and made occasional visits to their home villages; in effect, they became transnational families.

Purchasing tickets, remitting funds, and saving all required financial mechanisms. Steamship lines were busy selling tickets to the immigrants, and the post office was the mechanism used by countless others. But also important were vast numbers of banks appearing in immigrant enclaves, banks eager to become intermediaries, especially to those immigrants with poor English. Yet the banks were untrustworthy. Those operating hundreds of banks were "saloon keepers, labor agents, grocers, and boarding bosses." The Dillingham Commission said that the chief functions of the banks were to hold savings and send money abroad, that they were poorly run, and that they engaged in fraudulent practices.[145] Of course not all immigrant banks were small, poorly run affairs. The Irish Emigrant Society, founded in 1841, organized the Emigrant Industrial Savings Bank nine years later, and it became a major bank in the twentieth century. Many of the immigrant banks failed in the 1920s as immigrants turned to more carefully run banks.

The purchase of Liberty Bonds and the relatively good days of the 1920s eased the economic burdens of the New Immigrants and of their children, who were beginning to come of age during that decade. They also introduced immigrants to commercial banking and savings and loan associations. Yet even in those good times, many working-class immigrants struggled to make ends meet.[146] Whatever hopes existed for the good life in America were shattered by the onslaught of the Great Depression in 1929. Facing massive unemployment, immigrants were forced to cut back on their weekly expenses. Homes were lost, expenditures for consumer items were put on hold, and food budgets were stretched. As one historian notes, the immigrant households survived during the 1930s on "earnings from part-time jobs by family members; . . . by using up family savings and taking small loans from friends and relatives; by buying on credit at neighborhood stores; by using relief and government programs; and by reducing regular expenditures for food, clothing, and utilities."[147] The immigrant and ethnic organizations so important to immigrant life before the 1930s struggled to pay out benefits and collect dues.[148]

Yet another social trend unfolded during the 1930s. In that decade the children (and grandchildren) of the immigrants were coming of age and outnumbered the immigrant generation. The new generation was more exposed to the mass culture of movies, radio, and English publications, for they had learned English in American public and parochial schools.[149] Indeed, some of the new generation did not speak the language of their parents and grandparents. They had little interest in immigrant fraternal organizations and the foreign-language press, which was declining.[150] The fraternal groups ran short on funds and made special efforts to cater to the youth, but they were not always successful.[151] Where were the new members and programs to come from? As Soyer tells us,

> In the late 1930s, then, the *landsmanshaftn* still constituted an active and visible element in the Jewish community. . . . However, a number of factors were already apparent that would soon lead to their decline. The depression itself took its toll. . . . Most importantly, the end of mass immigration and the societies' inability to attract large numbers of the native-born meant that it was only a matter of time before membership began to fall.[152]

And this pattern of generational difference was repeated elsewhere, even among Poles, who represented a tight-knit community: "By the late 1920s typical young second-generation Polish-Americans in their late teens or early twenties might still speak Polish at home, might want to maintain Polish community life, and would not marry outside their group. But most differed from their immigrant parents in many other ways." Among those differences was whether or not to call themselves Americans or Polish Americans.[153]

World War II ended the Great Depression, and prosperity continued after 1945. In Puzo's description of the Italians of Hell Kitchen, "While the war raged over the world, the Italians living along the western wall of the city finally grasped the American dream in their calloused hands. Money rolled over the tenements like a flood. . . . The house on Long Island was bought for cold cash."[154] In addition, many of the children of immigrants (as well as some immigrants themselves) served in the military and for the first time came in contact with other ethnic groups. Millions migrated to the cities where defense jobs offered employment. After the war, the movement to the Far West continued, as did the growth of the Sunbelt. Along with prosperity came full-blown consumerism—with credit cards, the Internet, sprawling shopping malls, television, advertising, and a flood of consumer goods. All of this made for considerable mixing of the European ethnic groups and, to a lesser extent, Hispanic and Asian groups.

The triumph of the consumer society occurred just when the United States was receiving another wave of immigration. Immigration was low in the 1940s and 1950s, but Congress passed a number of laws—the Hart-Celler Act of 1965, the Cuban Adjustment Act of 1966, the Simpson Rodino Act of 1986, and the Immigration Act of 1990—that opened the golden door again to mass immigration. Beginning in the 1970s immigration increased substantially, averaging 1 million annually in the 1990s. The period from 1999 to 2002 recorded the highest number in any four-year period.[155]

There are differences between the newest wave and the old. First of all, the most recent immigrants are predominantly Asians, Latinos, Africans, and West Indians, whereas the earlier immigrants were overwhelmingly European. Second, today's immigrants are better educated than those in the past; among the new migrants are a large number of professionals, including physicians, nurses, and computer experts. Third, until 1990, the recent immigrants have been concentrated in six states. Then a wide dispersal took place, and unlike at the turn of the twentieth century, immigrants are now settling in areas where few lived before. For example, many of the post-1945 immigrants are settling in the South. A fourth difference is the role of women. Among immigrant families the women are much more likely to work outside the home for pay than did the women of 1900. Another difference is that among recent newcomers, women slightly outnumber men; at the turn of the twentieth century, a large majority of immigrants were men. In addition, most immigrants at the turn of the twentieth century passed through immigration stations and were legally entitled to remain, but after World War II, many unauthorized immigrants now lived in the United States. Experts place their number at over 11 million persons in 2005.[156] Finally, post-1945 immigrants are subject to more bureaucratic conditions than ever.

Yet there are also striking similarities between the new and old waves of immigration. Since World War II a large proportion of immigrants have been refugees, but whether then or now, most immigrants are drawn to the United States by economics; they wish to improve their lives and find greater opportunities in America. To be sure, immigrants today participate in mass consumerism, but then as now they work long hours to save and purchase homes. William Clark explains that "as immigrants arrive in the changing housing markets of the global gateway cities they often begin their lives in inexpensive rental housing, but . . . these immigrants in a few short years are successfully penetrating the housing markets in these cities and are becoming homeowners."[157] Among both the old and new the majority arriving are kin of those who came before. Indeed, since 1965, American laws preserved most of the allotments for family unification. Some 70 percent of all immigrants now enter under the family unification provisions of immigration policy. A higher proportion of immigrants at the turn of the century returned than do today, but even in recent years 20 to 30 percent of immigrants return to their land of origin. Immigrants in the past kept in touch with those left behind, though it is, of course, much easier to do so today, thanks to the telephone, Internet, and air travel. The days of long absences from China by Chinese immigrants have been replaced by frequent visits there to see family and friends.

One of the main ways to keep in touch in the past was through remittances, and this has not changed. Immigrants a century ago were frugal, saving so that they could send money home. These funds were often crucial for the people and communities receiving them and enabled those communities to survive. The remittances from the United States to Central America per migrant were $1,260 per person in 2001, a large sum for these low income immigrants living in the United States.[158] More than $9 billion was sent from the United States to Mexico in 2001; this amount increased to more than $13 billion in 2003.[159] Overall, Hispanic immigrants sent $32 billion to their homelands in 2005.[160] Then, as now, these remittances were vital to their homelands. It is fortunate for those left behind that immigrants in the last century have practiced thrift, willing to do without and saving money to send home.

Notes

1. Information on general trends in immigration can be found in Leonard Dinnerstein and David M. Reimers, *Ethnic Americans* (New York: Columbia University Press, 1999), and Roger Daniels, *Coming to America: A History of Immigration and Ethnicity in American Life* (New York: HarperCollins, 1990).

2. Jon Gjerde, *From Peasants to Farmers: The Migration from Balestrand, Norway, to the Upper Midwest* (New York: Cambridge University Press, 1985), 125.

3. Erika Lee, *Chinese Immigration during the Exclusion Era, 1882–1943* (Chapel Hill: University of North Carolina Press, 1994), esp. chaps. 3–7.

4. Ronald Takaki, *Strangers from a Different Shore: A History of Asian Americans* (Boston: Little, Brown, 1989), chaps. 7–10.

5. Philip Kasinitz, *Caribbean New York: Black Immigrants and the Politics of Race* (Ithaca, NY: Cornell University Press, 1992), 24–25; Marvin Dunn, *Black Miami in the Twentieth Century* (Gainesville: University of Florida Press, 1997), 13–19, and chaps. 2–3.

6. See David M. Reimers, *Other Immigrants: The Global Origins of the American People* (New York: New York University Press, 2005), 207–10.

7. June Granatir Alexander, *The Immigrant Church and Community: Pittsburgh's Slovak Catholics and Lutherans, 1880–1915* (Pittsburgh: University of Pittsburgh Press, 1987), 8.

8. Virginia Yans-McLaughlin, *Family and Community: Italian Immigrants in Buffalo, 1880–1930* (Ithaca, NY: Cornell University Press, 1971), 57, 58.

9. Ewa Morawska, "Immigrants, Transnationalism, and Ethnicization: A Comparison of This Great Wave and the Last," in *E Pluribus Unum: Contemporary and Historical Perspectives on Immigrant Political Incorporation*, ed. Gary Gerstle and John Mollenkopf (New York: Russell Sage Foundation, 2001), 182.

10. *Reports of the U.S. Immigration Commission* (Washington, DC: Government Printing Office, 1911), 4:57, 59. The commission is well known for its bias against the post-1890 immigrants, but these documents contain a wealth of information.

11. Theodore Saloutos, *They Remember America: The Story of the Repatriated Greek Americans* (Berkeley and Los Angeles: University of California Press, 1956), 4.

12. For passage to America, see *U.S. Immigration Commission*, 4:58–67.

13. Mario T. Garcia, *Desert Immigrants: The Mexicans of El Paso, 1880–1920* (New Haven, CT: Yale University Press, 1981), chap. 4.

14. Juan Garcia, *Mexicans in the Midwest, 1900–1932* (Tucson: University of Arizona Press, 1996), chaps. 1–2.

15. Madeline Yuan-yin Hsu, *Dreaming of Gold, Dreaming of Home: Transnationalism and Migration between the United States and South China, 1882–1943* (Stanford, CA: Stanford University Press, 2000), 32.

16. Sucheng Chan, *Asian Americans: An Interpretive History* (New York: Twayne, 1991), 30–31.

17. Hasia Diner, *Erin's Daughters in America: Irish Immigrant Women in the Nineteenth Century* (Baltimore: Johns Hopkins University Press, 1983), 38.

18. Robert C. Ostergren, *A Community Transplanted: The Trans-Atlantic Experience of a Swedish Immigrant Settlement in the Upper Middle West Community, 1835–1915* (Madison: University of Wisconsin Press, 1988), 114–17, 149–54.

19. See Jackson Lears, "The Modernization of Thrift," in the present volume.

20. Ewa Morawska, *For Bread with Butter: Life Histories of East Central Europeans in Johnstown, Pennsylvania, 1890–1940* (New York: Cambridge University Press, 1985), 112.

21. For a discussion of poverty and wages, see Robert H. Bremner, *From the Depths: The Discovery of Poverty in the United States* (New York: New York University Press, 1956), esp. chap. 9. Catholic economist John A. Ryan used a figure of $600. The Progressive generation made a number of investigations of living standards.

22. Susan Glenn, *Daughters of the Shtetl: Life and Labor in the Immigrant Generation* (Ithaca, NY: Cornell University Press, 1990), 64.

23. Morawska, *Bread with Butter*, 143.

24. Ibid., 198–203.

25. Saloutos, *They Remember America*, 12.

26. *U.S. Immigration Commission*, 19:120.

27. Garcia, *Mexicans in the Midwest*, 32–35, 56–60, 64–69.

28. The standard history of Anti-Semitism in America is Leonard Dinnerstein, *Anti-Semitism in America* (New York: Oxford University Press, 1994).

29. Peter Kwong and Dusanka Miscevic, *Chinese America: A History in the Making* (New York: New Press, 2005), 54.

30. Takaki, *Strangers from a Different Shore*, 239–45.

31. *U.S. Immigration Commission*, 19:360.

32. Ibid., 4:28.

33. Hsu, *Dreaming of Gold*, chap. 2.

34. John Bodnar, Roger Simon, and Michael P. Weber, *Lives of Their Own: Blacks, Italians and Poles in Pittsburgh, 1900–1960* (Urbana: University of Illinois Press, 1982), 96.

35. Ibid.

36. Glenn, *Daughters of the Shtetl*, 163.

37. Ibid., 79.

38. *U.S. Immigration Commission*, 9:61–64, 116, 122–23.

39. Ibid., 19:51, 75, 80, 149–54.

40. Bodnar, Simon, and Weber, *Lives of Their Own*, 104.

41. Thomas Bell, *Out of This Furnace* (Pittsburgh: University of Pittsburgh Press, 1941), 178. See also *U.S. Immigration Commission*, 19:149–50.

42. Virginia Yans-McLaughlin, *Family and Community*, 164.

43. For mobility in New York City, see Thomas Kessner, *The Golden Door: Italian and Jewish Immigrant Mobility in New York City, 1880–1915* (New York: Oxford University Press, 1977).

44. Morawska, *Bread with Butter*, 155.

45. Diner, *Erin's Daughters*, chap. 4.

46. Renqui Yu, *To Save China, to Save Ourselves: The Chinese Hand Laundry Alliance of New York* (Philadelphia: Temple University Press, 1992), 10.

47. Andrew R. Heinze, *Adapting to Abundance: Jewish Immigrants, Mass Consumption, and the Search for American Identity* (New York: Columbia University Press, 1990), chap. 9.

48. Ibid., 27.

49. Ibid., 47.

50. Ibid., 90–91.

51. Ibid., 126.

52. Nancy Foner, *From Ellis Island to JFK: New York's Two Great Waves of Immigration* (New Haven, CT: Yale University Press, 2000), 80.

53. Russell A. Kazal, *Becoming Old Stock: The Paradox of German-American Identity* (Princeton, NJ: Princeton University Press, 2004), 98.

54. Peter Connolly-Smith, *Translating America: An Immigrant Press Visualizes American Popular Culture, 1895–1918* (Washington, DC: Smithsonian Books, 2004), 69.

55. Lizabeth Cohen, *Making a New Deal: Industrial Workers in Chicago, 1919–1939* (New York: Cambridge University Press, 1990), 103.

56. Robert Park, *The Immigrant Press and Its Control* (New York: Harper and Brothers, 1922), 113.

57. Ibid., 309. See also Carl Wittke, *The German-Language Press in America* (Lexington: University Press of Kentucky, 1957); Sally M. Miller, ed., *The Ethnic Press in the United States: A Historical Analysis and Handbook* (Westport, CT: Greenwood, 1987); and Joshua Fishman, *Language Loyalty in the United States* (1966; New York: Arno Press, 1978).

58. Park, *Immigrant Press*, 374–75.

59. Ibid., 337–38, 369–76.

60. Roy Rosenzweig, *Eight Hours for What We Will: Workers and Leisure in an Industrial City, 1870–1900* (New York: Cambridge University Press, 1983), 46–47.

61. Ibid., 40–42.

62. Ibid., 47.

63. Kathy Peiss, *Cheap Amusements: Working Women and Leisure in Turn-of-the-Century New York* (Philadelphia: Temple University Press, 1986), 18.

64. Rosenzweig, *Eight Hours*, chap. 3; Diner, *Erin's Daughters*, 112–14.

65. Perry R. Duis, "The Ethnic Saloon: A Public Melting Post," in *Ethnic Chicago: A Multicultural Portrait*, ed. Melvin H. Holli and Peter d'A. Jones (Grand Rapids, MI: Eerdmans, 1995), 511.

66. Rosenzweig, *Eight Hours*, 50.

67. Saloutos, *They Remember America*, 24.

68. Rosenzweig, *Eight Hours*, 127–52.

69. June Granatir Alexander, *Ethnic Pride, American Patriotism: Slovaks and Other New Immigrants in the Interwar Era* (Philadelphia: Temple University Press, 2004), chap. 5.

70. See Peter Levine, *Ellis Island to Ebbets Field: Sport and the American Jewish Experience* (New York: Oxford University Press, 1992).

71. Peiss, *Cheap Amusements*, 14.

72. Ibid., 12.

73. Elizabeth Ewen, *Immigrant Women in the Land of Dollars: Life and Culture on the Lower East Side, 1890–1925* (New York: Monthly Review Press, 1985), 167–68.

74. Peiss, *Cheap Amusements*, 22–23.

75. Ewen, *Immigrant Women*, 197.

76. Peiss, *Cheap Amusements*, 88–89. See also Randy D. McBee, *Dance Hall Days: Intimacy and Leisure among Working-Class Immigrants in the United States* (New York: New York University Press, 2000).

77. Peiss, *Cheap Amusements*, 114.

78. Glenn, *Daughters of the Shtetl*, 164.

79. Vicki L. Ruiz, *From Out of the Shadows: Mexican Women in Twentieth-Century America* (New York: Oxford University Press, 1998), 57, 67.

80. Robert W. Snyder, *The Voice of the City: Vaudeville and Popular Culture in New York* (New York: Oxford University Press, 1989), 43.

81. Robert Sklar, *Movie-Made America: A Cultural History of American Movies* (1975; New York: Vintage, 1994), 18.

82. Ibid., 18–23.

83. Kazal, *Becoming Old Stock*, 30–32.

84. Ibid., 181–83.

85. *U.S. Immigration Commission*, 37:174–79.

86. Daniel Soyer, *Jewish Immigrant Associations and American Identity in New York, 1880–1939* (Cambridge, MA: Harvard University Press, 1997), chap. 3; Cohen, *Making of a New Deal*, chap. 2.

87. Cohen, *Making of a New Deal*, 60.

88. Ibid., 65–66.

89. Soyer, *Jewish Immigrant Associations*, chap. 2.

90. Ibid., 81.

91. Ibid., 103–12.

92. Ibid., 167. A considerable number of other associations became deeply involved in affairs abroad.

93. Alexander, *Immigrant Church*, 35.

94. Ibid., 50.

95. Ibid.

96. Ibid., 63–65.

97. John J. Bukowczyk, *And My Children Did Not Know Me: A History of Polish Americans* (Bloomington: Indiana University Press, 1987), 39–49.

98. Victor Greene, *For God and Country: The Rise of Polish and Lithuanian Ethnic Consciousness in America, 1860–1910* (Madison: State Historical Society of Wisconsin, 1975), 43.

99. Bukowczyk, *My Children Did Not Know Me*, 72.

100. Ibid., 73.

101. Morawska, *Bread with Butter*, 202.

102. Ostergren, *Community Transplanted*, 212.

103. Ibid., 212–13. Ostergren also notes that sectarianism marked the founding of many of the Swedish churches.

104. Bodnar, Simon, and Weber, *Lives of Their Own*, 153.

105. Bell, *Out of This Furnace*, 56.

106. Mario Puzo, *The Fortunate Pilgrim* (New York: Lancer Books, 1964), 94.

107. Greene, *For God and Country*, 41; quotation is from Mary Laura Swanson, "A Study of the Polish Organizations in the Polish Community of Baltimore" (master's thesis, Johns Hopkins University, 1925), 83.

108. Stephan Thernstrom, *Poverty and Progress: Social Mobility in a Nineteenth-Century City* (Cambridge, MA: Harvard University Press, 1964), 117.

109. David E. Emmons, *The Butte Irish: Class and Ethnicity in an American Mining Town, 1875–1925* (Urbana: University of Illinois Press, 1989), 80.

110. Morawska, *Bread with Butter*, 144–50.

111. Greene, *For God and Country*, 41. See also Bodnar, Simon, and Weber, *Lives of Their Own*, chap. 6.

112. *U.S. Immigration Commission*, 19:176.

113. Greene, *For God and Country*, 36–42; Morawska, *Bread with Butter*, 206–8.

114. Isaac A. Hourwich, *Immigration and Labor: The Economic Aspects of European Immigrants to the United States* (New York: Putnam, 1969), 274–83.

115. Garcia, *Mexicans in the Midwest*, 59.

116. Ibid., 59.

117. Connolly-Smith, *Translating America*, chaps. 7–9.

118. Ibid., 246.

119. Ibid.

120. Alexander, *Ethnic Pride*, 33.

121. Ibid.

122. Those ethnic groups whose native lands were under the domination of the Austro-Hungarian Empire hoped that the war would lead to the creation of their own country. With the dismembering of the empire, some of their dreams were realized when Slovaks and Czechs broke off from the empire with the creation of Czechoslovakia.

123. Christopher M. Sterba, *Good Americans: Italian and Jewish Immigrants during the First World War* (New York: Oxford University Press, 2003), 145–47.

124. Theodore Saloutos, *The Greeks in the United States* (Cambridge, MA: Harvard University Press, 1964), 165.

125. Cohen, *Making of a New Deal*, 77.

126. Ibid., 78–81; Sterba, *Good Americans*, 147.

127. Saloutos, *They Remember America*, 41.

128. Ibid., 37–41; Mark Wyman, *Round Trip to America: The Immigrants Return to Europe, 1880–1930* (Ithaca, NY: Cornell University Press, 1993), 109–13.

129. Emmons, *Butte Irish*, 301–9.

130. Soyer, *Jewish Associations*, 157.

131. Wyman, *Round Trip to America*, 11.

132. Ibid., 9–11.

133. Nancy Foner, *In a New Land: A Comparative View of Immigration* (New York: New York University Press, 2005), 66.

134. Wyman, *Round Trip to America*, 129.

135. Dino Cinel, *The National Integration of Italian Return Migration, 1870–1929* (New York: Cambridge University Press, 1991), 98.

136. Tim Pat Coogan, *Wherever Green Is Worn: The Story of the Irish Diaspora* (New York: Palgrave, 2000), 324.

137. *U.S. Immigration Commission*, 4:61.

138. Ibid., 4:65–67.

139. Hsu, *Dreaming of Gold*, 32–33.

140. Coogan, *Wherever Green Is Worn*, 285.

141. Saloutos, *They Remember America*, 120–21.

142. Dino Cinel, *From Italy to San Francisco: The Immigrant Experience* (Stanford, CA: Stanford University Press, 1982), 75.

143. *U.S. Immigration Commission*, 37:261.

144. Hsu, *Dreaming of Gold*, 41; *U.S. Immigration Commission*, 37:270–71.

145. *U.S. Immigration Commission*, 37:301–3.

146. Cohen, *Making of a New Deal*, 102–9; Morawska, *Bread with Butter*, 190–216.

147. Morawska, *Bread with Butter*, 216.

148. Alexander, *Ethnic Pride*, 168–75; Cohen, *Making of a New Deal*, 218–35.

149. See Cohen, *Making of a New Deal*, for an excellent discussion of the rise of consumerism during the 1920s and 1930s.

150. For the foreign-language press, see Fishman, *Language Loyalty*; and Miller, *Ethnic Press*.

151. See Alexander, *Ethnic Pride*, chap. 6.

152. Soyer, *Jewish Immigrant Associations*, 201.

153. Bukowczyk, *My Children Did Not Know Me*, 71.

154. Puzo, *Fortunate Pilgrim*, 282.

155. Information on post-1945 immigration is taken from Reimers, *Other Immigrants*; Roger Daniels, *Guarding the Golden Door* (New York: Hill and Wang, 2005); Frank Bean and Gillian Stevens, *America's Newcomers and the Dynamics of Diversity* (New York: Russell Sage Foundation, 2003).

156. Jennifer Van Hook, Frank Bean, and Jeffrey Passel, "Unauthorized Migrants Living in the United States: A Mid-decade Portrait" (Washington, DC: Migration Information Source, 2005).

157. William A. V. Clark, *Immigrants and the American Dream: Remaking the Middle Class* (New York: Guilford Press, 2003), 126.

158. Kevin O'Neil, *Remittances from the United States in Context* (Washington, DC: Migration Information Source, 2003).

159. Manuel Orozco, *The Remittance Marketplace: Prices, Policy, and Financial Institutions* (Washington, DC: Pew Hispanic Center, 2004).

160. Betsy Cummings, "Cash Flow across Border Starts to Get More Savvy," *New York Times*, July 28, 2005.

16 }

Saving for Democracy

THRIFT, SACRIFICE, AND THE WORLD WAR II BOND CAMPAIGNS

Kiku Adatto

The story of savings bonds during the Second World War is an intriguing episode in the saga of the thrift ethic in America. We often think of thrift in individualistic terms, but World War II provides a dramatic example of thrift collectively conceived. When Treasury secretary Henry Morgenthau initiated the savings bond program, one of the goals was to "instill into the minds of the American people the habit of thrift."[1] Yet thrift was not considered an independent virtue. It was saving for a greater good. President Franklin Delano Roosevelt emphasized that the defense bonds and stamps would be "the outward and the visible tokens of partnership through sacrifice," a way to "perpetuate democracy in the New World" and "aid embattled democracy in the Old World and everywhere else."[2]

Roosevelt spoke in a language that moved easily from high ideals to everyday life: "In this time of national peril what we all must realize is that the United States Government is you and I and all the other families next door all the way across the country and back again." Each family had the opportunity to share in the common defense "at the threshold of every home in America."[3]

The American people embraced this opportunity in record numbers even before the attack on Pearl Harbor. After Pearl Harbor, the defense savings bonds were renamed "war bonds," and saving for the national defense took on a new and urgent meaning. From May 1941 to December 1945, eight out of every thirteen Americans, 85 million people, invested $185.7 billion in war bonds.[4] Citizens were encouraged to save 10 percent of their income in bonds, and many did, usually through payroll savings plans at work.[5] Schoolchildren and newspaper carriers purchased an additional $1.5 billion of war savings stamps.[6]

After the war, the thrift ethic lost its civic force. Peace and prosperity ushered in a newly invigorated culture of consumption fueled in part by the pent-up savings of the war years. From the postwar years to the present, savings bonds have become a decidedly private affair, a strategy for individual investment.[7] Popular advertising slogans of recent times such as "Take stock in America" make the government sound more like a financial planner than a civic leader. Of all the reasons listed by the government to invest in U.S. savings bonds—easy to buy, safe and secure, market-based rates, liquid long-term investment, education savings, tax advantages—only the very last reason, "Good for America," makes a vague gesture toward civic goals.[8] Savings bonds have become so emptied of civic meaning that few Americans were even aware of the Patriot Bond, issued after September 11, 2001, because the government did so little to publicize it.[9]

The history of war bonds during World War II provides a perspective from which to ponder some questions about the ethic of saving and sacrifice today. After September 11, when the American people were eager to be summoned to sacrifice, President George W. Bush urged citizens to express their patriotism by consuming rather than conserving. In fact, there have been no major mobilizations to save and sacrifice during any of the conflicts after World War II—the Korean War, the Vietnam War, the Gulf War, the Iraq War, or the "war on terrorism." We seem to be living in an era when sacrifice is outsourced to a volunteer army, paid military contractors, and low-paid service workers at home and abroad.

Recalling the spirit of sacrifice that animated the war bond campaigns of World War II may help us remember that thrift is not a virtue in itself but a means to an end. The case for thrift always begs the question, "Thrift for the sake of what good?" The war bond campaigns offered a resounding answer: saving for democracy. This is not to suggest that American democracy during the war years was without deep flaws. It was marred most glaringly by the persistence of segregation and the Japanese internment camps. But the civic project of the war bond campaign left room for dissent and provided the opportunities for citizens to recast the campaign within their own culture, politics, and language. It did not demand a shallow patriotism or 100 percent Americanism. It espoused the ideals of unity in diversity.

The war bond campaigns were doubly democratic. They were fought under the banner of democratic ideals, and they were carried out in a way that promoted civic participation from the grassroots to the national level, bringing Americans together in common cause, across differences of class, ethnicity, and region.[10] When sacrifice is out of season and consumption is the balm for every ailment, it is important to recall the larger civic project that saving sometimes serves.

War and the Summons to Sacrifice

Seven months before the attack at Pearl Harbor, President Roosevelt prepared to address the American people. The world was at war. The Nazis had conquered much of Europe. Japan continued its conquest of Asia. A million

American men had already been conscripted in the first peacetime national draft. Congress had approved economic and military aid for America's allies. Yet the American public remained divided about entering the war. Strains of isolationism, pacifism, disillusionment with the idealism of the First World War, anticommunism, and the seeming security of two yawning oceans provided ample room for ambivalence.

Roosevelt wanted to animate the democratic energies of the American people in the fight against fascism and prepare for America's entry into the war. He had already delivered his annual message to Congress, in which he outlined the "four essential human freedoms": freedom of speech and worship, and freedom from want and fear. For Roosevelt, these freedoms formed the foundation of the "good society" and of a world "moral order" that would combat the forces of tyranny. To secure these freedoms, Roosevelt had asked the American people to accept the "sacrifice" of increased taxes to support defense spending.[11] Now, on April 30, 1941, as Americans gathered by their radios, Roosevelt announced a new campaign "to save and sacrifice in defense of democracy"—the defense savings bond and savings stamps program. The "character of the campaign," Roosevelt explained, would be "national and homey at the same time." It would "reach down" to "the individual and the family in every community." To show just what he meant, Roosevelt told the people that he was buying ten savings stamps for each of his ten grandchildren, and his first savings bond would name Mrs. Roosevelt as beneficiary.[12]

The U.S. government had vital economic interests at stake in encouraging the American people to save and invest in war bonds—financing the war and curbing inflation. Economic recovery from the Depression had already begun as the country prepared for war; now the economy had to operate in full gear. As millions of men left to fight the war, women replaced them in the plants, and men and women worked round the clock to meet production goals and generate the vast amount of military equipment and home-front goods needed to win the war.[13] Yet, "the paradox of wartime prosperity" was that although people had more money to spend, there were fewer goods to buy.[14] The demands of the wartime economy meant that vital goods and industries had to be used for the war effort. Companies that once produced cars, refrigerators, and washing machines were now producing tanks, Jeeps, and other military equipment. Gasoline, rubber, and food staples like sugar, meat, and coffee had to be rationed. The government's solution for all the new money in people's hands, colorfully labeled "wild money" or "dangerous dollars" by Treasury officials, was to encourage savings.[15]

War bonds were an ideal solution. Though the war bond campaigns did include appeals to individual economic interests—the benefits to the investor of saving for future purchases once peace and prosperity returned—the value of individual thrift was not the central feature of the war bond campaigns.

Thrift was nested within a constellation of values connecting the individual to the collective through work and savings, production and consumption, self-interest and the obligations of community. The war bond drives focused on savings as an obligation of citizenship, as a way of honoring the sacrifices of America's fighting men, and as an expression of national and intergenerational solidarity.

The war bond campaigns were not only animated by democratic ideals; they were democratic in practice. "I'm going to do it the hard way," Secretary Morgenthau announced in the first few weeks of the campaign, "which is the democratic way."[16] The democratic way meant tapping into every sector of society and conducting a grassroots campaign: "Nothing short of a savings crusade to reach every man, woman and child in the country would do."[17] A small, bipartisan team in the Treasury Department, many of whom were Washington outsiders with an antipathy to conventional bureaucrats, organized and coordinated the bond campaigns at the national level. The Treasury Department's strategy was to work through established national and local associations. To work with various constituencies, the Treasury Department created the Inter-Racial program, the Retail Stores Program, the Labor and Business Programs, the Women at War Program, the Schools at War Program, and even the Grandmothers' War Bond League.[18] State and local field organizations energized the campaigns from the bottom up, enlisting volunteer leaders from every walk of life and coordinating their efforts with a rich array of civic, business, labor, religious, educational, media, farm, ethnic, and immigrant associations—from the Boy Scouts to the B'nai B'rith, from the American Legion to the National Association for the Advancement of Colored People (NAACP), from the American Federation of Labor to the Farmers'Alliance. Half a million committee volunteers and 5 to 6 million local volunteers, called "Minute Men and Minute Women" and "Victory Volunteers," could be called into action for war bond drives.[19]

Campaigns for war bonds were waged person-to-person, door-to-door, neighbor-to-neighbor, and worker-to-worker. The most effective technique by far was being asked face-to-face. During the third war bonds drive, for example, surveys showed that while almost half the people who were asked bought bonds, only 17 percent of those who were *not* asked purchased bonds. This was a sobering statistic given the intensity of the national advertising and publicity campaign. In rural areas, the statistics were even more dramatic. Only 2 percent of farmers bought bonds because they responded to general promotion, but more than half bought bonds when personally asked.[20] This puts in context the national media campaigns of radio, ads, movies, and posters. The influence of the media was limited unless the message was mediated through conversations at the workplace, front door, or schoolyard. As Peter Odegard, a young political scientist and member of the Treasury Department's team, observed, "The experience of participation in a joint effort breeds community of purpose. . . . National unity is not so much the precursor as the product of united action."[21]

The war bond campaigns transcended the usual divisions between public and private life and civic and commercial space. People assembled in ballparks for "Baseball Defense Bond Day," in department stores for the "Four Freedoms War Bond Tour," on the Mall in Washington to witness military displays and hear testimonials of war veterans, and in their own town squares, meeting halls, and movie theaters to participate in war bond drives.[22]

The World War II war bond campaigns were designed to build unity through affirming diversity. "Instead of seeking to eradicate differences—of religion, race, class, section, or party," the Treasury Department wanted to make these differences a "source of strength and unity by finding a common cause in which all could work."[23] Affirming diversity meant opening up democratic discourse, even if it meant criticism of the government. A striking example of this was the "Double V" campaign organized by African American newspapers and civic organizations. A vigorous campaign to combat racism and segregation on the home front was matched by vigorous participation in the war bonds campaigns, victory gardens, rationing, recycling, and other civic activities.

Another great part of the success of the war bond campaigns was the way the government harnessed the power of popular culture and advertising. Advertisers, ardent purveyors of the culture of consumption, were enlisted as purveyors of the ethic of thrift and sacrifice as well. The Roosevelt administration encouraged the founding of the War Advertising Council—an independent, voluntary organization of advertisers, newspapers, and related business and media organizations that ran the entire advertising campaign for war bonds. Advertisers did not give up on promoting their own products or fostering dreams of future consumption. Many used the government's tax break for "goodwill" advertising to hawk their wares. Ads selling lipstick, stockings, china, liquor, and shaving cream sometimes displayed only pro forma patriotism—a small box inserted near the bottom of the ad urging the purchase of war bonds.[24] Yet volunteers from advertising agencies were enormously successful in promoting the government's aims using the power of their selling techniques. "Ironically, when advertising did go off to war," notes historian Frank Fox, "it went more resolutely, more evangelically, than all the entertainment media combined, and it wound up taking its morale-building responsibilities much more seriously."[25] In fact, the war bond campaign helped rescue the advertising industry from the financial doldrums of the Depression.

In coordination with the Office of War Information and the War Advertising Council, advertising firms saturated the country with compelling ads for war bonds in newspapers, radios, magazines, and movies and on billboards and the products people used in everyday life, like grocery bags, milk cartons, and chewing gum wrappers. In addition, the government enlisted artists to design thousands of posters encouraging Americans to produce, conserve, and save. Combining the power of art and advertising, posters were displayed in work spaces and public spaces where ads could not penetrate.[26] A huge mural in Grand Central Station in New York City, touted as the largest mural in the world, urged people to invest in savings bonds and stamps and quoted Abraham Lincoln's words from the Gettysburg Address: "Government of the people—Shall not perish from the Earth."[27]

Hollywood lent its full support to the war bonds campaigns, making newsreels and sending out its biggest stars—Humphrey Bogart, Carole Lombard, Spencer Tracy, Betty Grable—to lead war bond drives. All kinds of celebrities joined the war bond campaigns, from boxing hero Joe Louis to baseball great Joe DiMaggio. Albert Einstein donated the original copies of his manuscript on the theory of relativity for auction to raise money for war bonds.[28] Kate Smith, beloved for her rendition of "God Bless America," an Irving Berlin song written in 1938, which became an anthem of World War II, raised $39 million for war bonds in a single daylong radio marathon.[29] Bing Crosby crooned another popular Berlin tune from the radio hit parade, "Any Bonds Today?": "Buy a share of freedom today. . . . We'll be blest if we all invest in the U.S.A."

Beyond the explicit mention of war bonds, the core themes of solidarity and sacrifice that infused the war bond campaigns pervaded American popular culture during the war years. Sometimes it came in the understated voice of the maverick hero and ostensible cynic played by Bogart, who was willing to forgo his romance with Ingrid Bergman for the greater cause of the war resistance in the hit movie *Casablanca*. Other times, the movies spoke in the same democratic language of sacrifice as Roosevelt's fireside chats. As survivors gather in a bombed-out church in England to mourn the loss of their loved ones in the 1942 movie *Mrs. Miniver*, the vicar asks, "Why should they be sacrificed? I shall tell you why. Because this is not only a war of soldiers in uniform. It is a war of the people, of all the people. And it must be fought not only in the battlefield . . . but in the home and in the heart of every man, woman, and child who loves freedom. . . . This is the people's war. It is our war. We are the fighters. Fight it then!"[30]

The war bond campaign was conceived and run as a people's campaign. It enlisted the power of sentiment to inspire civic action and lifted sentimentality from its familiar habitation in private life and infused it with civic purpose. It was the most important home-front campaign to galvanize support for the war effort. The war bond campaign succeeded not only by galvanizing resources from every sector of American society but also by situating itself in the lived experiences of everyday life. It united the war front and the home front by making "home" and "hominess" central features of its symbolism and grassroots door-to-door campaigns. Even the so-called mass media was not some vast and distant presence. It too exerted a "homey" presence. Into the home came the voice of Roosevelt in his fireside chats. Into the home came the portraits of ordinary people—soldiers, workers, homemakers, parents, and children—featured in newspapers, magazines stories, and ads. Into the home came the necessities of everyday life: milk cartons, bags, and savings stamp books with patriotic pictures and slogans.

Home was not an entity distinct from civic life but a locus for civic engagement.[31] Norman Rockwell illustrated two of the "four freedoms" with images of home: "freedom from want" with a family gathered around a Thanksgiving dinner and "freedom from fear" with a mother and father standing by the beds of their sleeping children. These paintings were made into popular posters in the war bond campaigns. It was no accident that Roosevelt made home a central image in his radio address introducing Defense Bonds to the American people. "At the threshold of every home in America," Roosevelt reminded his listeners, "each family shared in the common defense."[32] The power of home and longing for home were expressed in the most popular song of the war years and a great favorite of soldiers on the war front, a song that made no mention of patriotism, country, or war bonds: "White Christmas."

The tangible and symbolic meaning of home and family unified the multiple, interwoven layers of savings that defined the war bond campaigns—saving and producing for the war, saving to honor the sacrifice of the soldiers, saving to preserve democracy, saving to defend freedom, saving for future consumption, saving for the family's security. By "saving for his individual future," noted a member of the Treasury Department's war bond staff, a purchaser of a savings bond guaranteed the "collective future." "National morale" depended on the "awareness that the future welfare of each member of the community is inextricably tied up with the future of the community as a whole."[33] This same collectively conceived thrift ethic pervaded the rationing, recycling, and victory garden campaigns.

Before exploring in greater depth how the war bond campaign brought diverse groups together in a common effort to save and sacrifice, it is useful to review briefly the historical role of war bonds, particularly the role they played in World War I.

Bonds and the Civic Project

The sale of government bonds goes back to the founding of the Republic. During the Revolutionary War, buying bonds was a risky venture. Unlike modern savings bonds, the government bonds were not guaranteed. When citizens of the colonies loaned the Revolutionary government money by investing in bonds, they realized they could lose their money if the British won the war. Nonetheless, private citizens purchased more than $27 million in bonds to help fund the Revolution, and the newly formed American government made good on these bonds.[34]

War bonds played a role in every war to follow. During the Civil War, the Treasury learned the value of person-to-person bond sales. The Spanish-American War demonstrated the popularity of small-denomination bonds.[35] Government bonds also offered Americans the opportunity to invest in public projects such as the Louisiana Purchase, the building of the transcontinental railroad, and, later, the construction of the Panama Canal and the acquisition of Alaska.[36]

It was not until World War I, however, that government bonds—called Liberty Bonds and later Victory Bonds—played a major role in the lives of American citizens.[37] The Liberty Bond campaigns were part of a broader ethic of thrift and sacrifice during the war years. Soon after Congress approved his declaration of war, President Woodrow Wilson emphasized: "This is the time for America to correct her unpardonable fault of wastefulness and extravagance. Let every man and every woman assume the duty of careful, provident use and expenditure as a public duty."[38] Herbert Hoover, Wilson's food administrator, reiterated the message, urging the "elimination of waste and actual and rigorous self-sacrifice on the part of the American people."[39] The government sponsored wheatless Mondays, meatless Tuesdays, and porkless Thursdays and Saturdays.[40] Banks also became apostles of thrift. The "Three Great Mottoes" espoused in a Bankers Trust Company pamphlet were "Know Thyself, Control Thyself, Deny Thyself."[41]

Yet, the Liberty Bond campaign differed in important respects from the World War II war bond campaign. First, the Liberty Bond campaign committees were controlled and directed by the Federal Reserve banks and dominated by bankers, brokers, and security dealers. Second, Liberty Bonds, like earlier government war bonds, were negotiable and tied to the fluctuations of the market.[42] If Liberty Bond holders needed cash before their bonds matured, they could not turn to the Treasury Department to redeem them. Instead, they had to sell them at market value, often at substantial losses because of higher interest rates. Professional security dealers made handsome profits at the expense of the ordinary citizens, and Liberty Bonds sold as low as eighty-two cents on the dollar.[43] Many citizens became disillusioned with government savings bonds when they realized after the war that the bonds were worth less than the original purchase price.

The Liberty Bonds campaigns were also more stridently patriotic, sensationalistic, and high-pressured than the World War II war bond campaigns. Slogans such as "Surely Your Patriotism Equals the Cost of a Bond" and "Are You 100% American? Prove It! Buy U.S. Government Bonds" exemplified this tendency.[44] Instead of encouraging immigrant and ethnic groups to express national loyalty through their distinctive languages, customs, and rituals, the Liberty Bond drives often defined Americanism as white, Anglo-Saxon, and Protestant. Government-sponsored patriotic groups included the Committee on Public Information, led by George Creel, which preached "100 percent

Americanism" and enlisted 75,000 "Four-Minute Men" to give speeches urging people to buy Liberty Bonds.[45]

Liberty Bond advertisements played more frequently on hatred and fear of the enemy than did war bond ads in the Second World War.[46] Even though the government declared that the purchase of war savings bonds and stamps was not compulsory, local groups sometimes resorted to overzealous shaming techniques to get people to participate. In Nebraska, a local "council of defense" called a meeting to reprimand farmers for failing to buy savings stamps. In other parts of the country, self-styled patriots painted people's homes and barns yellow if they failed to subscribe.[47]

The Liberty Bond campaigns do not, however, fully represent the thrift ethic of the World War I period. Civic and religious thrift movements sprung up around the country and gathered a large public following. One of the most prominent was the War Savings movement led by New York banker, Frank Vanderlip. The emphasis of the War Savings movement was on education and participation in civic life, not selling bonds. "Millions and millions are yearning for an opportunity to do something in this war, to deny themselves, to sacrifice," proclaimed a business leader affiliated with the movement. "The War Savings Movement is an answer to that yearning. It brings to every man, woman and child the opportunity to help."[48] The movement focused on reducing consumption, inculcating the habit of thrift, and sacrificing for the war effort.[49]

The War Savings movement of World War I respected and drew upon the distinctive languages and cultures of the participating groups, and it valued democratic organization. This more pluralistic approach became a prototype for the World War II war bond campaigns. The War Savings movement had a high-profile national committee and was directed by a well-run national organization based in Washington, but the movement was rooted in local civic, religious, and business associations, which formed their own War Savings committees.[50]

The War Savings movement also inspired the formation of school thrift programs and worked collaboratively with the National Education Association.[51] Lesson plans in the World War I school programs encouraged older children to write essays on such topics as "The First Time I Ever Admired Savings" and "History of Savings in Other Countries."[52] Teachers encouraged younger children to be frugal in their purchases of pencils, books, and clothes and to save their money for war stamps. Every student received a Thrift Card with sixteen squares to paste in their savings stamps, and each square contained a pithy saying of Benjamin Franklin's on the virtue of frugality. School plays and songs emphasized the virtues of thrift and patriotism:

> Save up your pennies for a rainy day.
> It's not always what you earn but what you put away.
> Uncle Sam has need of thrift.
> So do your best, and give him a lift.[53]

The thrift movement of World War I was also bolstered by religious organizations. The YMCA incorporated thrift into its "Christian Financial Creed," noting that it had come to see that "habits of wastefulness and extravagance rot character." A YMCA poster slogan reprised the words of Methodist minister John Wesley: "Make all you can. Save all you can. Give all you can." The Y sponsored a National Thrift Week and distributed sermon outlines for local congregations that included lines like "Thriftlessness—debt—mars and stains the soul."[54] Like earlier incarnations of the Protestant ethic, the Y's thrift ethic saw work and frugality as bulwarks against sin and pathways to salvation.

Despite the strong support for the thrift ethic during World War I, when the war ended "the mood of patriotic self-sacrifice quickly dissipated."[55] As one reformer lamented, "During the war we accustomed ourselves to doing without [but now] reckless spending takes the place of saving, waste replaces conservation."[56] Historian David Shi notes, "Such assessments have a familiar ring and a familiar hyperbole. Yet what differentiated the postwar buying binge from its predecessors was its scale, and the vigorous and imaginative support it received from public figures and business spokesmen."[57] New York City businessmen, for example, formed a National Prosperity Committee and condemned thrift: "Buy what you need now," their posters declared with a picture of Uncle Sam at the throttle of a locomotive.[58]

Even Henry Ford, once a member of the War Savings Division's Central Committee, announced that thrift was passé. "Economy is a waste: it is waste of the juice of life," remarked Ford. He urged young men to "spend your money on yourself, get all the experience you can. Don't try to save money and be a miser."[59] President Warren Harding espoused the value of thrift but promoted material prosperity, reminding his critics that America was "essentially a business country."[60] The government had other priorities than thrift education. The public schools remained a bastion of the thrift ethic, but funds for school savings programs were drastically cut back. "Every war brings after it a period of materialism and conservatism," observed Roosevelt, then a defeated vice presidential candidate; "people tire quickly of ideals."[61]

The stock market crash of 1929 and the bank failures during the Depression shook people's confidence in financial institutions. With millions out of work and widespread destitution, Americans had to do without. Yet thrift was more than a virtue of necessity. During the early New Deal, the thrift ethic took on a renewed civic dimension backed up by government reforms. Keynesian economics, with its rival paradigm of spending rather than thrift, would not take hold until the postwar period.[62] In 1935, in the midst of the Depression, the Roosevelt administration enacted some of its key and most enduring legislation that provided a new infrastructure for thrift—the Banking Act, the Social Security Act, and the modern savings bond program. These pillars of the New Deal were designed to renew confidence in financial institutions, provide unemployment insurance and old-age pensions, and ensure the savings of citizens.[63]

The U.S. savings bond program promoted thrift for the sake of an explicit civic purpose—to encourage the small investor to have a stake in America. First offered for sale in March 1935, U.S. savings bonds were designed to protect the small investor. They were safe, nonnegotiable, registered in the bearer's name, and replaceable if lost, damaged, or stolen, and they provided a reasonable interest rate. Individuals could invest in a savings bond for as little as $18.75 and redeem it in ten years for $25. Individuals could also redeem their bonds before they matured and recover their initial investment plus interest. At first, only post offices sold bonds over the counter. The government's promotion of savings bonds in magazine ads, posters, and leaflets was modest. The field organization was modest as well. One enthusiastic Treasury official became a "One-Man Chautauqua," traveling up and down the land "preaching the gospel of thrift" to any group that would listen.[64] By the late thirties, however, under Secretary Morgenthau's able direction, the savings bond program was well established. A Treasury survey of the first million bond buyers "framed a picture of national prudence and purpose and patriotism."[65]

As Roosevelt prepared the country for war in May 1941, the first series A savings bonds were reissued as series E defense savings bonds. They were renamed war savings bonds in June 1942. Savings stamps could be purchased for as little as ten cents and collected in a "Victory" booklet for a future bond purchase. No one in Treasury wanted to repeat the mistakes of the Liberty Bond campaign of World War I. Morgenthau wanted "no quotas . . . no hysteria . . . no appeal to hate or fear."[66] Citizens would never again be subjected to "the wicked devices of bond sharps and swindlers."[67] Some in government even lobbied for a mandatory savings program to avoid the problems of the World War I campaigns, but Roosevelt and Morgenthau insisted that the program be voluntary. As an early internal Treasury Department memo made clear, the new bond program would emphasize "participation rather than propaganda" and "local organizations" rather than the "creation of new machinery," and they would transform people from being "mere observers" to "active participants" in the national defense effort.[68]

Judged in purely financial terms, the participation of ordinary citizens in the war bonds program played only a small role in financing World War II. Of the $304 billion spent on the war, current taxation accounted for 45 percent of the bill, a much higher percentage than in either the Civil War or World War I, and borrowing accounted for the rest.[69] Most of the $185.7 billion raised in war bonds resulted from purchases by large investors—banks, insurance companies, and corporations. Individuals accounted for only 28 percent of the sales, and of the $43.3 billion sold to individuals, the small, investor-friendly E bonds accounted for $19.9 billion in sales.[70] These numbers, of course, are not the full measure of the story.

Unity in Diversity: A Civic Thrift Ethic

The war bond campaign was enormously successful in uniting and galvanizing the country. Between 1941 and 1946, well over half the population of the United States invested in war bonds and Victory Bonds during eight bond drives.[71] Yet the persistence of religious and ethnic intolerance, racism, and institutionalized segregation testified to how incompletely America had realized its democratic promise. The 1930s witnessed the growth of labor unions but also turbulent and bloody battles between labor and industry. The New Deal programs of the Depression did forge a renewed sense of social solidarity, and movies, radio, and advertising drew people from different regions, cultures, ethnicities, and classes into a common culture, but this did not erase profound social and economic inequalities.

Once the United States entered the war, the country united behind the war effort, despite the fact that all citizens were not treated equally. The war bond campaign contributed to this unity by waging a grassroots campaign that acknowledged and respected ethnic, cultural, and regional diversity. It brought rival groups together in a common cause by encouraging them to participate through their own organizations and associations. This is aptly illustrated by the highly successful war bond campaigns of organized labor and African American civic groups and newspapers. Despite school segregation, the war bond campaigns provided public schools with common material for young people to be schooled in democracy, sacrifice, and a renewed civic thrift ethic.

Labor's Leadership

In April 1942, women from three powerful rival unions—the CIO, the AFL, and the Railroad Brotherhood—met for a joint bond rally in New York City. Betty Hawley Donnelly of the New York State Federation of Labor declared, "We trade women recognize only three letters of the alphabet and those letters are not AFL or CIO—those letters are the U.S.A." Beatrice Abramson of the CIO emphasized, "Part of the job of defeating fascism is the regular, systematic saving of our pennies and nickels and dimes."[72] Two months earlier, the powerful leaders of these same unions had joined forces for Labor Defense Bond Week. "On this we are united," declared Allen Haywood of the CIO as he stood beside George Meany of the AFL. "Our country is in danger. Everything we have hoped for is in danger. The AFL, CIO, and the [Railroad] Brotherhood are behind MacArthur. . . . This is a people's war."[73]

The mission of working, saving, and sacrificing for democracy infused labor unions from the national to the local level. Workers saw in Adolf Hitler's doctrine of racial superiority a direct challenge to America's principles of equality. The Roosevelt administration's message of democratic inclusiveness also profoundly touched many union members. In the New England textile city of Woonsocket, Rhode Island, Catholic unionists declared, "We shall protect and amplify . . . democracy in America and in every peace-loving nation of the world, so that the soldiers of every race, creed and color . . . 'SHALL NOT HAVE DIED IN VAIN.'"[74] Historian Gary Gerstle compared war bond appeals made by labor and business in Woonsocket and discovered that while corporate and business groups emphasized financial or consumer benefits, labor unions appealed to democratic principles and civic solidarity.[75]

The outbreak of World War II revived labor by creating a huge demand for industrial production. Unions had made great gains during the 1930s, and labor saw President Roosevelt as a friend and ally. By 1937 and 1938, however, the economy had taken a downturn, slowing production and union organizing. Labor mobilized for the war effort by working around the clock in the war industries and by leading the country in war bonds investments, usually through payroll savings plans that regularly deducted 10 percent for bonds from the paycheck.[76] Workers in the war industries—steel, iron, ships, aircraft, electronic equipment, and automobiles—invested most heavily in bonds because they were acutely aware of war production needs, better organized, and relatively well paid.[77] By April 1943, CIO president Philip Murray announced on the radio that more than four-fifths of all industrial workers in the country regularly saved their money through the war bond program.[78] Rival unions engaged in spirited competitions to buy and sell war bonds, and union leaders also played prominent roles on state and local war bond committees.[79]

Labor also worked with management on joint war bond campaigns. Using the slogan "Banded Together to Bond-Bard the Axis," the United Rubber Workers formed a committee with the Firestone, Goodrich, Goodyear, and General Tire companies in 1942 and successfully enlisted full participation in the 10 percent payroll deduction plan.[80] A subsequent national government-sponsored study showed that among large corporations, those with joint labor-management committees led the nation in payroll-savings-plan bond purchases.[81] As one union president affirmed, "The joint labor-management effort follows the basic tenet of democracy. Dictatorship is the enemy of democracy and of the trade union movement which can function only in the free air of democracy."[82]

Despite highly successful joint campaigns for war bonds, tensions between labor and management remained. One issue was "equality of sacrifice."[83] To support the war effort, labor pledged not to strike, to work around the clock, and to forgo overtime and premium pay. Yet workers did not want management to exploit their sacrifices by war profiteering. Roosevelt was alive to the issue of equality of sacrifice before war broke out. It is "a damn sight simpler for all of us to appeal to [worker] patriotism," he noted, "if we say we are using exactly the same principle for the owners of industry as we are for the workers of industry."[84] The chairman of the National War Labor Board put the matter bluntly: "If you say to the boys, 'Why don't you make a sacrifice for your country?' they are going to say, 'That is fine . . . but I am not going to make it to increase the profits of General Motors.'"[85] To ease the fear of its members, the executive committee of the United Automobile Workers publicized a broad-based "Victory through Equality of Sacrifice Program," which included a government-controlled ceiling on profits and executive salaries and democratically controlled rationing and price controls.[86] Despite Roosevelt's support of core elements of the "Equality of Sacrifice Program," opposition by congressional conservatives and the antiunion bias of newly recruited wartime workers blocked its adoption.[87]

While the Treasury Department praised labor's "almost boundless" cooperation in war bond drives, Treasury officials acknowledged that even within its own national War Savings organization, the "promotional experts," drawn mostly from the business community, were "hostile to, or at least barely tolerant of, the increased importance of organized labor in national affairs."[88] Labor's war bond campaigns coexisted with flare-ups between labor and management, wildcat strikes, and protests over discrimination in the defense industries. Yet the persistence of these tensions did not stop labor leaders from organizing highly effective national and regional campaigns through the War Savings organization. Unions were highly effective in promoting their patriotic efforts. The Treasury's Film Section also featured movie shorts of union bond drives and war production, and Secretary Morgenthau "seized every opportunity to publicly praise labor's support of bonds."[89]

Treasury's war bond poster campaigns featured the worker as a "production soldier" and stalwart citizen in overalls. "Make Every Pay-Day BOND-DAY," declared an early bond poster with a smiling face of a workman holding up a bond framed in a red-white-and-blue background.[90] A later poster with the slogan "The Sky's the Limit: Keep Buying War Bonds" shows a woman working with two men to assemble part of a fighter plane, an unusual image before the war, but familiar once women entered the defense industries.[91] Rosie the Riveter, of course, was one of the most compelling images of the war years. Both labor and management generated and designed their own poster campaigns as well. Company posters blended the theme of workplace discipline with images of patriotism and sacrifice, while labor touted the patriotism of its unions with slogans like "A.F. of L. 100% for Defense."[92] After the war, the tensions between labor and management rapidly resurfaced. In 1946, labor unrest was higher than in all previous years, with 4,990 reported strikes involving more than 4.5 million employees. By 1948, the labor-management committees that had been so instrumental in fostering cooperation in war production and war bond drives had all but vanished.[93]

African American Support of Bonds and the "Double V" Campaign

In response to a request from a government press office, Walter White, head of the National Association for the Advancement of Colored People, sent a telegram in support of the fifth war bond drive on June 15, 1944. As on earlier occasions, the NAACP's enthusiastic support of war savings bonds was accompanied by a critique of the unfulfilled promise of American democracy for African Americans:

> Despite the fact that American Negroes so frequently are denied the democracy for which they are asked to fight and pay, it is imperative that all Americans, including thirteen million Negro Americans, make every sacrifice through the purchase of bonds.
>
> . . . We urge all Negro organizations and individuals to invest to the limit in democracy while they work to make that democracy real for all irrespective of race, creed, color, or national origin.[94]

In order to build national unity and a strong democratic coalition, the Treasury Department's War Savings Organization made it a priority to reach out to African American civic, religious, and business associations, as well as to other ethnic and immigrant associations. Immigrants often saw participation in war bond campaigns as a pathway to assimilation and Americanization. African Americans already had a long and noble history of fighting and sacrificing in American wars, but military and civilian sacrifices had not resulted in liberty and equality. During World War I, W. E. B. Du Bois urged blacks to "close ranks" with whites and "forget our special grievances." When liberty did not follow in the wake of war, the embittered Du Bois revised his slogan: "We *return*, we *return from fighting*, we *return fighting*."[95] For some the mismatch between democratic ideals and practice was a cause for cynicism, but for many it was a call to civic action, a call for America to be true to its deepest ideals. "America was never America to me," wrote the poet Langston Hughes in 1938. "And yet I swear this oath—America will be!"[96]

The espousal of democratic ideals by the War Savings Organization, however genuine and well intentioned, rested uneasily with the Roosevelt administration's policy of segregation in the military, segregated blood banks, lack of support for antilynching laws, and appeasement of southern Democrats. Under Roosevelt, Jim Crow segregation remained entrenched in the South, as did de facto segregation and racial prejudice in the North. How could African Americans reconcile support for the war as a fight for democracy when they were not experiencing full democracy at home? How could they give real substance to the war slogan "A Fight for the Four Freedoms"? The answer was to fight for democracy on two fronts.[97]

The *Pittsburgh Courier* summed up this idea in the symbol of the "double V": "Democracy: At Home and Abroad." The "Double V" campaign made a direct link between fascism abroad and segregation at home. It allowed African Americans to be patriots and critics of the government at the same time and provided African American civic organizations a way to galvanize support for war bonds and continue their fight for civil rights. Following the *Pittsburgh Courier*'s lead, the black press, the NAACP, churches, and civic groups took up the symbol of double V.[98] Whether or not the symbol was used, the commitment to fight for democracy on two fronts characterized African American civic activism during the war. "Now is the time *not* to be silent about the breaches of democracy here in our own land," editorialized the NAACP's main publication, the *Crisis*, after the United States entered the war.[99] "In the interest of national unity," declared A. Philip Randolph, labor activist and leader of the March on Washington Movement, "every law which makes a distinction in treatment between citizens based on religion, creed, color, or national origin" must be abrogated.[100] Beyond the statements of leaders, polls conducted by black newspapers and the government revealed a renewed militancy among many African American citizens. A poll reported in the *Pittsburgh Courier* found that "88.7 percent of those asked felt that the Negro should 'not soft-pedal his demands for complete freedom and citizenship.'"[101] African American soldiers were not fighting and dying for their country to return home to segregation and discrimination. A poem of a black soldier fighting oversees captured the prevalent sentiment:

> So while I fight
> Wrong over there,
> See that my folks
> Are treated fair.[102]

Just as labor unions invested in war bonds and pursued the cause of workers despite opposition, so African American organizations pursued their quest for equality and justice despite Roosevelt's attempts to quiet the "subversive language" of the black newspapers' "Double V" campaign.[103] After the Roosevelt administration sent the FBI to visit the *Pittsburgh Courier*, the paper cut by half the space devoted to the campaign.[104] The spirit of the "Double V" campaign, however, continued in black newspapers and in the publications of black civic organizations. A study published by Lester M. Jones in 1944 revealed that editorials in black newspapers devoted 50 percent more coverage to national and international aspects of race relations than they did during World War I.[105]

African American civic groups transformed the war bond campaign into another way to continue the fight to redeem democracy. Many of the most vociferous critics of the administration's failure to move rapidly enough on civil rights—such as Walter White of the NAACP—were also patriotic leaders in war bond campaigns. Similarly, Joe Louis, Duke Ellington, Marian Anderson, and other black sports figures and performers who spoke out against race discrimination also spoke out in support of war bonds.[106] Black newspapers promoting the "Double V" campaign devoted considerable space to promoting war bonds.

The war bond campaign conducted through the Inter-Racial Section of the Treasury's Defense Savings Program was a microcosm of the democratic organizing techniques that characterized the war bond campaign as a whole. The Treasury Department recruited William Pickens—a Yale graduate, dynamic public speaker, and field director of the NAACP—to coordinate the war bond campaigns in African American communities. Pickens traversed the country recruiting church leaders, college presidents, business leaders, and members of women's organizations and a range of other African American civic groups. From church pulpits, Pickens directly addressed the congregation's concerns about racial inequality, arguing that just as the church was the church for all its members, even the wayward and fallen, so America was still a democracy for all the people, despite intolerance and prejudice.[107] Churches in turn urged their members to buy bonds as a patriotic act and as a sound investment.

The backbone of support for the war bond program in many African American communities came from the Negro Savings Clubs. The idea for these came from P. L. Prattis of the *Pittsburgh Courier*, the same paper that had spearheaded the "Double V" campaign. The clubs, which were made up of members of the black middle and professional classes, worked closely with the Inter-Racial Section but were not part of the government. The clubs, particularly popular in the South, were led by a national organizing committee, which was composed of representatives from prominent African American organizations: the National Council of Negro Women, the Fraternal Council of Negro Churches in America, the National Urban League, the National Negro Land Grants College Presidents' Association, and the National Negro Housewives League.[108] The clubs focused on savings as a means of economic empowerment and civic virtue. The NAACP also linked liberty with economic power in encouraging its members to invest in bonds. In fact, the combination of thrift and work, of sacrifice and civic action, and of national unity and independent economic and political power was a central feature of the civic thrift ethic among African Americans during the war years.

Savings and Civic Virtue in the Schools

On September 25, 1942, 4,000 children carrying flags of the United Nations marched along Constitution Avenue to the Department of the Treasury to launch the Schools at War program. Eleanor Roosevelt was present along with Secretary Morgenthau, who told the assembled children that he could count on them "to enlist 100 percent in our fight for freedom—by buying War Savings Stamps and Bonds." Liberty Bricks were unveiled—saved from the renovations of Independence Hall in Philadelphia—and were offered as rewards for the best-performing schools in the war bond and stamp campaigns. The motto for the Schools at War program embodied core elements of the civic thrift ethic: "SAVE, SERVE, CONSERVE." Government officials urged students to "SAVE money to buy War Savings stamps and bonds"; "SERVE your school, community and nation"; and "CONSERVE all kinds of materials, service, and money" by recycling aluminum foil, paper, string, cloth, kitchen fat, and scrap metal, by "preserving Victory Garden foods," and by "wasting nothing."[109]

Children, like adults, were encouraged to see themselves as soldiers on the home front. "Boys and girls of the United States of America," declared a wartime book, "you are enlisted for the duration of the war as citizen soldiers. This is a total war, nobody is left out, and that counts you in."[110] School war bond campaigns made the link between war front and home front tangible and dramatic. Beginning in 1943, school children were encouraged to buy enough stamps and bonds to equal the price of a Jeep. The Triple Threat Jeep campaign captured children's imaginations: schools could sponsor the land-going Jeep, the amphibian Jeep, or the flying Jeep, called the Grasshopper.[111] Plaques were placed on the Jeeps with the name of the school, and sometimes servicemen wrote appreciative letters to the children from the war front. Patriotic songs sung to familiar folk tunes cemented the bond between the home front and the war front. Jerold Oldroyd of Utah remembered his favorite song as a boy:

> Buy Jeeps, buy Jeeps,
> Send thousands of Jeeps o'er the sea, the sea
> Buy Jeeps, buy Jeeps,
> And bring back my loved one to me.[112]

Children sponsored 40,000 Jeeps in the closing months of the school year and an additional 50,000 the following year.[113] The campaign was expanded so that children could sponsor other military equipment—parachutes, lifeboats, planes, and ships. In addition to Jeeps, schools financed 2,900 planes and 11,690 parachutes during 1944.[114]

However exciting it was to sponsor military equipment, the primary mission of the Schools at War program was "education for the preservation of democracy and good citizenship."[115] Educators and government officials built on the successful War Savings programs of World War I. They developed lesson plans in civics, thrift, and conservation across the curriculum and at every grade level. Knowledge was not simply top-down. Students had to act in the world—to gather scrap metal in the neighborhood, to buy war stamps, to encourage their parents and neighbors to conserve and save, to collaborate in recycling drives or cultivating victory gardens. During the summer and after school, children carried on their thrift campaigns through the Boy Scouts, Girl Schools, 4-H clubs, Campfire Girls, and other local and national civic and religious organizations.

Saving and conserving for democracy gave children an active role as citizens and a real sense of agency. "We built Mount Scrapmore," children declared, as they stood proudly atop a mound of scrap metal in Waterbury, Connecticut.[116] "Here's our answer, Mr. Roosevelt," proclaimed a banner held by two Boy Scouts as they led a parade of cars and trucks carrying spare tires for a rubber recycling drive in Stevens Point, Wisconsin.[117] Children took up broomsticks in New York City to defend a three-ton pile of scrap metal they had collected from sanitation workers who planned to cart it away. The standoff was resolved only when a sanitation driver promised the children they would receive "official recognition" and a police officer wrote down all their names.[118] When a war bond buy-a-Jeep campaign looked like it would not meet its quota in Philadelphia, children organized a "commando attack" to raise funds during the final week.[119] In fact, the survey research conducted after every bond drive discovered that children were just as effective as adults in person-to-person solicitations for war bonds.[120]

For adults and children alike, recognition and honor were important parts of the war bond campaigns. The government presented special flags to factories with high participation in the payroll savings plans, special certificates and medals to civic and business groups, and lapel pins for individuals who bought extra bonds or distinguished themselves in bond sales for their achievements.[121] Similarly, schoolchildren were honored with awards and certificates for their participation in war bond and other thrift campaigns. On occasion, they were even given the honor of naming a ship. New York City children named a ship *Lou Gehrig* after the late great baseball hero, and Florida children named a ship the USS *Colin Kelly* after an American pilot who was shot down in the Pacific after saving his crew.[122]

The Schools at War program knitted together the campaigns for war bonds, victory gardens, rationing, and recycling, and it provided a vital line between home, school, and neighborhood. The educators and government officials who designed the school curriculum hoped that through "thrift education" children would grow up to be "more substantial and financially secure citizens" once the crisis had passed, perhaps even be "prospective candidates for payroll savings plans."[123] The lessons of thrift would linger, but postwar consumerism would become a heady rival to the values of saving, sacrifice, and national unity, which formed the three pillars of the Schools at War program.

The Home-Front Media Campaign

Some historians have written about the patriotism of the war bond campaign as if it were just a form of government "propaganda," a campaign ultimately held hostage to "private values" or "consumerism."[124] This debunking view misunderstands the rich and varied uses of the media during the war, the range and depth of patriotic expressions, and the extent of grassroots involvement. The war bond media campaign consisted of far more than the shallow sell of Madison Avenue. The campaign was waged on both the national and local level, in big and small media: in Hollywood movies and newsreels and 35 mm slides used in local community organizing; in Roosevelt's fireside chats and local radio commentaries in towns and cities across the United States; in posters designed by renowned artists and posters produced by labor unions, schools, and community groups; in editorials in the *New York Times* and in local, ethnic, and immigrant newspapers. An essential part of the war bond media campaign included local coverage of community events, ceremonies, and drives: photos of African American children dedicating two Jeeps at Eliza Randall Junior High School in Washington, D.C., and photos of Poles, Czechs, Serbians, and Chinese in native costumes at the opening of their war bond booths in Pittsburgh.[125]

The government, members of the media, writers, and artists tapped into a wellspring of powerful symbols, images, and narratives that framed and defined the bond campaigns. Because the stakes were so high—uniting the home front and the war front for victory against fascism—little was left to chance. The Treasury Department, in coordination with the War Advertising Council and the Office of War Information, carefully outlined the themes of the national media campaign and the eight national bond drives.[126] Teams of social scientists and pollsters employed by the government and advertising agencies continually surveyed the public's responses and modified appeals accordingly. From 1942 through 1945, the Treasury used more than forty special surveys, many under the direction of Dr. Rensis Likert and known as the Likert surveys.[127] In addition, social scientists in academia published detailed studies of the war bond campaign during and immediately after the war. All this research, combined with more recent scholarly studies, provides an unusually rich empirical base from which to assess the home-front media campaign.

The Likert surveys tracked the multiple appeals made in the war bond campaigns ranging from savings as a "safe investment" to savings as a civic obligation. The first survey, based on interviews with workers in the city of Baltimore, Maryland, discovered that "most people felt they were buying bonds to help the Government win the war." A second reason was to "make a good investment for themselves."[128] Few people mentioned a concern about curbing inflation. As the war progressed, surveys identified the "paramount" motive for buying bonds as "patriotism."[129] Buying bonds provided citizens with a "tangible," "personal" way to be a part of the war effort and the fight to defend American freedom. War bond appeals contributed to "home-front morale" and "aroused patriotism and a spirit of sacrifice."[130] Surveys showed that ardent patriotism blended with a prudential view of long-term individual savings and investment. In a survey conducted after V-J Day, for example, people interviewed cited "the spiritual value of participation in a common national effort" and the "continuing advantages" and increased financial "security" to be gained from regular bond purchases.[131]

In his book *Mass Persuasion: The Social Psychology of a War Bond Drive*, published in 1947, Robert Merton argued that the spirit of sacrifice was a prime motive for buying bonds. Merton and a team of researchers studied in depth the public's response to Kate Smith's eighteen-hour war bond radio marathon on CBS on September 21, 1943. Surveys had shown that radio was the most powerful way of reaching citizens in the war bond campaigns.[132] Popular radio programs regularly made appeals for bonds, and stations ran marathons featuring celebrities. As noted earlier, the *Kate Smith Hour* radio marathon, which occurred during the third war bond drive, raised an astounding $39 million.[133] Aware of the findings of the Likert surveys, Merton was struck by the fact that Smith said *"nothing"* about "bonds as a sound investment, a nest egg of security, a promise of good things after the war."[134]

The keynote of Smith's appeal was the theme of sacrifice, primarily the sacrifice of the soldiers fighting overseas and the sacrifices of their families back home. Smith devoted fully half of her broadcast time to the theme of sacrifice, in addition to the related themes of civic participation (16 percent of the appeals) and the meaning of family (6 percent of the appeals): "It's not as if those boys are strangers to us. They are our sons . . . and our neighbor's sons," confided Smith in her homey voice.[135] "Now they are braving swamps and jungles, risking illness and wounds, pain and death, . . . staking their lives so that you and I may never know the horrors of a blitz or a bombing."[136] Over and over again Smith reiterated that by buying bonds her listeners could hasten the homecoming of the men fighting the war: "That's what war bonds are to every one of us, a chance to buy our boys back."[137]

Merton discovered that for many people, buying war bonds was not like a normal financial investment, such as buying railroad bonds or stocks. It was more analogous to a collection made in church, which congregants viewed as an "offering." As opposed to the "profane" realm of economic negotiations and interests, war bonds had a "sacred" quality. War bonds were associated with "blood and suffering and national unity," and "to tinge such contributions with commercialism would profane the sentiments centered on war bonds."[138] "You don't sell your patriotism," noted one woman interviewed at length. "I don't want any prizes for my money."[139] Another respondent observed, "What's patriotic in saving money and getting more for it? It's my duty. . . . The boys are doing the noble work."[140]

The themes of sacrifice, patriotism, civic participation, and the fight for freedom were given primacy in war bond slogans, posters, and ads as well.[141] Gordon F. Streib, a colleague of Merton's at the Bureau of Applied Research at Columbia University, analyzed the themes in war bond advertising in the *New York Times* for the first, third, and fifth war bond campaigns (a period that overlapped Merton's study) and discovered that most ads focused on the "sacred" values of patriotism, honor, and loyalty.[142] When he broke down the specific emphasis (using the same categories as Merton), Streib found that the majority of ads, 57 percent, appealed to civic participation, and only 20 percent of the ads specifically mentioned sacrifice.[143]

"Back the Attack" was one of the most popular slogans to rally support for the war. I analyzed war bond advertisements in *Life* magazine for the first, third, and fifth war bond drives (the same period studied by Streib) and discovered that 36 percent of the ads focused on this theme, stressing how companies supported the war through military production and how civilians could also support the military by investing in war bonds. The theme of "Back the Attack" was closely connected to two other major themes: civic participation and community (18 percent of the ads) and the sacrifice of soldiers or civilians (10 percent of the ads).[144] Nash-Kelvinator ads exemplify how companies interwove the themes of war production and civic participation. One full-page ad that appeared in *Life* during the first war bond drive, titled, "Nazi Nightmare," shows an U.S. Navy cargo plane built by Nash-Kelvinator flying over the ocean against a moonlit sky. "Let this be an example, Hitler, of how America is fighting the war," the text reads. "Men who yesterday made refrigerators and automobiles are now turning out more deadly, precise instruments of destruction than a Nazi mind ever dreamed. And we are *all* in this fight to win—buying War Bonds . . . bringing in scraps for victory. . . . The might of America is on the wing."[145]

War bond posters also took up the "Back the Attack" theme, showing soldiers charging a hill or airmen fighting enemy aircraft accompanied by slogans like "Let 'Em Have It—Buy Extra Bonds," "Keep Us Flying—Buy War Bonds," and "Buy That Invasion Bond."[146] Many posters portrayed the youth and humanity of the soldiers, with close-ups of their faces, creating the same bond that Smith evoked in her radio broadcasts—that the soldiers are "our sons" and "our boys." A 1942 "Buy War Bonds" poster shows a smiling soldier waving from the porthole of a ship with the words "Till We Meet Again" written in chalk above him.[147] A 1943 poster portrays Robert Deiz—a member of the elite Ninety-Ninth Pursuit Squadron of African American aviators established at Tuskegee College who flew ninety-three successful missions over North Africa and Italy—with the logo "Keep us flying!—BUY WAR BONDS."[148]

As the war progressed, the theme of sacrifice emerged more prominently accompanied by increasingly grim and gritty portraits of America's fighting men. The slogan for the second war bond drive, "They Give Their Lives—You Lend Your Money," set the tone.[149] Posters and ads depicted dead or wounded soldiers or poignant portraits of families that had lost a father or son, accompanied with captions such as "I Died Today . . . What Did You Do?" "His Patriotism Is Written in Blood," "I Gave a Man—Will You Give at Least 10% of Your Pay in War Bonds?," and "Remember Me? I Was at Bataan."[150] The cover of *Life* magazine on July 3, 1943, portrays two war-weary soldiers walking arm in arm, one supporting the other, who is wounded. Superimposed on the photograph is a picture of a war bond and the simple, bold message "Buy War Bonds."[151] A particularly powerful poster designed by Sergeant Ardis Hughes in 1944 pictures a soldier as a Christlike figure with crosses over his shoulder and a shovel in his hand, with the slogan "War Bonds—Are Cheaper Than Wooden Crosses."[152] A Nash-Kelvinator ad in the June 12, 1944, issue of *Life*, titled "The Church in the Jungle," depicts soldiers praying before battle with an accompanying first-person narrative: "I ask only this. . . . If we must die, let us be worthy to die. . . . If we must fall, let our fall be not unnoticed and alone."[153]

The danger and suffering faced by the soldiers fighting overseas loomed large in the public's imagination as millions listened to Edward R. Murrow's radio reports, read the dispatches of Ernie Pyle, and followed the course of the war in their local newspapers and popular picture magazines, like *Life* and *Look*. One out of three men between the ages of seventeen and thirty-five served in the armed forces, and approximately 16 million men were in uniform; 405,399 servicemen died during the war, 291,000 in battle, and more than 600,000 were left physically and psychologically wounded.[154] The war was far from home, but it was not emotionally distant. It was as close as the family, the neighborhood, the radio, the magazine, the newspaper, and the posters and ads that were everywhere. The July 5, 1943, cover of *Life* magazine, for example, pictures six soldiers in military fatigues carrying a simple wooden, flagged-draped coffin past a field of corn.[155] "Somebody has just kept his bargain with you," begins a war bond ad that appeared in the *New York Herald Tribune* in 1945 with a big picture of the helmet and rifle of a "kid" who died at the front. It was a "simple bargain," the ad continues. "He would fight, die if necessary. You would back him up."[156]

The strong identification with the sacrifices of the American armed forces and of America's European allies provided the impetus to sacrifice and save on the home front. Yet there was a general sentiment of modesty about what home-front "sacrifice" meant. When Roosevelt spoke to the American people about a "partnership through sacrifice," he gave primacy to the sacrifices made by the soldiers fighting the war. "Your Government is asking that you make this sacrifice," Roosevelt noted in announcing the bond program. "But is it a sacrifice? Is it a sacrifice for us to give dollars when more than a million of our finest young men have been withdrawn from civilian life to accept military life in defense of our country?"[157] Magazine and newspaper ads took up this theme as well. An ad for war bonds that ran in *Life* and *McCall's* sponsored by Vicks shows a downed American pilot stranded at sea with the caption, "and YOU Talk of 'Sacrifices'!" The text continues, "Is there any 'sacrifice' you can make to equal that of a man who gave his life? . . . To win this war we Americans Must buy War Bonds. . . . Let's forget the interest, the safety, and the security. LET'S

WIN THIS WAR! . . . Every dollar you put into War Bonds is life insurance for our boys. That's what counts!"[158]

The magnitude of the sacrifices made by America's allies was a theme emphasized as well. In a fireside chat, Roosevelt reiterated the importance of buying bonds in conjunction with participating in rationing and other forms of conservation: "I told the Congress yesterday, 'sacrifice' is not exactly the proper word with which to describe this program of self-denial. . . . Ask those millions who live today under the tyranny of Hitlerisms. . . . Many thousand of civilians all over the world have been and are being killed or maimed by enemy action. . . . Our own American civilian population is now relatively safe from such disasters."[159] Roosevelt, like the citizens who responded to Smith's radio marathon, cut home-front sacrifice down to size. Sacrifice was not a point of pride but the simple duty and obligation of citizenship. It could be demonstrated in small acts that taken together added up to a larger sense of solidarity. As Roosevelt noted during the sixth war bond drive: "We cannot all fight the enemy face to face. . . . But there is one front on which all of us—every man, woman, and child—can serve, and serve for the duration. We can all practice self-denial. We can all sacrifice some of our comforts to the needs of men in the service, and yes, even some of our needs to their comforts."[160]

Palimpsests of Patriotism

It is not possible to make sense of the media campaigns for war bonds without understanding how nimbly and adeptly they drew on familiar symbols and stories. The multiple overlapping appeals of the war bond campaigns formed palimpsests of patriotism. Like old manuscripts of papyrus or parchment that have been written on more than once, with earlier words still detectable among the new ones, or like cities and sites that bear the multiple imprints of their history, the themes of the war bond campaigns were continually reinscribed with multiple markers, symbols, images, and stories that "thickened" their appeal and connected them to resonant ideas and images of the past—particularly the fight for freedom and democracy. The Treasury Department chose Daniel Chester French's famous statue of the Minute Man as a logo and central icon.[161] Posters and ads blended images of the minutemen and World War II soldiers or featured scenes of the battles of Lexington and Concord with slogans such as "They fought for Freedom—We fight to keep it."[162] More than an image, the minuteman and minutewoman was an identity, the names given to the millions of volunteers in the war bond drives.

Abraham Lincoln emerged as an icon of equal or even greater power. Lincoln's words from the Gettysburg Address—"A Government of the people, by the people, and for the people, shall not perish from this earth"—appeared over and over again in giant banners, posters, and ads. Lincoln was the subject of documentary articles and feature pieces as well. Soon after Pearl Harbor, *Life* magazine ran a huge six-page picture spread of Lincoln titled "Lincoln in Wartime."[163] The accompanying text begins, "On January 5, 1862, as on January 5, 1942, the American people were engaged in a titanic war. Then, as now, the nation's existence, its territorial integrity, its destiny were at stake."[164] Lincoln's face and pictures of the Lincoln Memorial appeared with other famous quotes such as "This World Cannot Exist Half Slave and Half Free."[165]

Roosevelt's image was not used on war bond posters until after his death to avoid partisanship,[166] but excerpts from his "Four Freedoms" speech were rapidly incorporated into posters and ads, most prominently in Norman Rockwell's popular illustrations. Sober text-based ads sponsored by large corporations often incorporated the four freedoms theme or words from the Constitution. "This is the glory of democracy;" declares an ad sponsored by IBM in the January 1942 issue of *Life* magazine, "that a man may think as he will, speak as he will, vote as he will, and worship God in his own way."[167] Westinghouse sponsored a double-spread full-page ad in *Life* showing a painting of the Constitutional Convention with the words "Provide for the Common Defense" in bold letters.[168] As the war progressed, excerpts from Roosevelt's fireside chats quickly became captions for ads and posters with a range of patriotic images.

The American flag was a central and resonant symbol continually reconfigured in war bond posters and ads. One of the most popular poster and billboard designs of the bond campaign was a picture of a huge American flag with a tiny Minute Man logo on the side and a quotation from Roosevelt—"WE CAN . . . WE WILL . . . WE MUST!" The billboard industry displayed this poster at more than 30,000 locations in some 18,000 towns and cities across the county in 1942, and the Treasury brought back the billboard in campaigns in 1943. Public demand for copies of the American flag billboard was so great that the government printed 4 million small color reproductions.[169] Many ads and posters incorporated the flag as part of a patriotic pastiche or used the colors of the flag to deepen the patriotic appeal of pictures of soldiers, workers, and other citizens. The image of the U.S. Marines raising the flag on Iwo Jima was quickly incorporated in the seventh war bond drive, becoming one of the powerful images of the entire campaign. The logo for the flag raising on Iwo Jima read simply: "Now All Together."[170]

The phrase "Now All Together" captures the sense of collective purpose that animated the civic thrift ethic during the Second World War. This civic ethic reached beyond the war bond campaigns. It infused many aspects of community life—planting victory gardens, organizing recycling and scrap drives, canning and conserving goods, and rationing of scarce resources. Nearly 20 million Americans planted victory gardens during the war,[171] and more than 8 million tons of produce was grown on these plots in 1943 alone.[172] The Boy Scouts alone collected 109 million pounds of old rubber and 370 million pounds of scrap metal during the war.[173] Despite administrative problems, most people complied with the rationing of gasoline, rubber, sugar, meat, coffee, shoes, and other goods as a necessity of wartime.[174]

No civic ethic is so thoroughgoing as to command universal allegiance. Some people never bought war bonds. Others circumvented the rationing program by buying on the black market. One of the most intriguing features of the civic ethic of thrift during World War II is that it arose amid a rising tide of abundance. The war brought economic recovery and prosperity, and with it came new opportunities to buy goods, go to the movies, frequent clubs and ball games, and otherwise have a good time. Yet people saved, worked hard, and pulled together. As one popular logo of the food conservation campaigns put it, "Produce and Save, Share and Play Square."[175] The word *thrift* had not yet gone out of fashion, though Roosevelt rarely used it in his speeches and fireside chats, preferring instead the words *save*, *conserve*, and *sacrifice*. Thrift was not yet the hollowed-out virtue it has become. It was resonant with civic meaning—not as a virtue in itself but as a means to a greater good.

The waning of the civic thrift ethic in our times does not mean that it cannot be revived. It receded after World War I and rose again in World War II. The values of savings and sacrifice remain a reservoir of cultural values, buried below the surface, ready to be summoned again if the nation finds the will to produce, conserve, and sacrifice for the sake of the common good.

Notes

I would like to thank James Hunter for his intellectual vision and the way he has fostered a spirit of collegiality at every stage of this overall project; Josh Yates for helping guide the project from beginning to end; the contributors to this volume for their helpful comments on this chapter; Daniel Horowitz and Michael Sandel, especially, for a close reading of an earlier draft; and Meg Parekh, Matthew Cutler, and Amanda King for their able research assistance.

1. Lawrence M. Olney, *The War Bond Story* (Washington, DC: Government Printing Office, 1971), 2.

2. Quotations from Franklin D. Roosevelt, "Radio Address on the President's Purchases of the First Defense Savings Bond and Stamps (April 30, 1941)," in *The Public Papers and Addresses of Franklin D. Roosevelt* (New York: Random House, 1942), 10:138–41. For a complete set of Roosevelt's speeches online, see the American Presidency Project, University of California at Santa Barbara, http://www.presidency.ucsb.edu. (accessed January 26, 2006).

3. Ibid.

4. Jarvis M. Morse, *Paying for a World War: The United States Financing of World War II*, manuscript (Washington, DC: Government Printing Office, 1971), 269–86. Morse notes that the Treasury Department estimated that per capita sales of "E bonds" averaged $314 between May 1941 and January 1946. The E bonds were small-denomination bonds designed for the average investor.

5. At the peak of participation in the payroll savings plan, during the summer of 1944 and spring of 1945, 27 million Americans participated, with an average 76 percent participation in companies offering the plan. These statistics are cited in Lawrence R. Samuel, *Pledging Allegiance* (Washington, DC: Smithsonian Books, 1997), 30. A Treasury Department publication cites a slightly different statistic, noting that nearly 28 million workers participated in payroll savings plans by June 1944, with monthly deductions totaling $500 million. See U.S. Savings Bonds Division, Treasury Department, *The Book on U.S. Savings Bonds* (Washington, DC: U.S. Savings Bonds Division, Treasury Department, January 25, 1984), 92.

6. Olney, *War Bond Story*, 105–6; and Morse, *Paying for a World War*, 36–37.

7. See the U.S. Department of the Treasury, *A History of the United States Savings Bond Program* (September 1984), 26. The sale of U.S. savings stamps was discontinued on June 30, 1970, marking the end of the bond program's most successful programs—the school savings program and the newspaper carrier thrift plans.

8. U.S. Department of the Treasury, Bureau of the Public Debt, "Series EE/E: Seven Great Reasons," http://www.publicdebt.treas.gov/sav/savbene1.htm (accessed January 27, 2006).

9. The Patriot Bond was unveiled by the Treasury Department on December 11, 2001. See the press release at http://www.ustreas.gov/press/releases/po854.htm (accessed July 30, 2006). Information about the bond was largely confined to the Treasury Department's Web site, http://www.savingsbonds.gov. The Patriot Bond is actually a series EE savings bond inscribed with the words "Patriot Bond." According to the government's Web site, the Patriot Bond does not go directly to help pay for the war on terrorism or the Iraq War but to the government's general fund. "After the introduction of Patriot Bonds, there was a large increase in bond sales for the first three months," noted Stephen Meyerhardt, a spokesman for the Bureau of the Public Debt. "But since then there has been a noticeable blip in sales." The Treasury Department has not actively marketed the Patriot Bond, and Congress completely eliminated the marketing department for the Treasury Department, shutting down forty-one regional marketing offices across the country as of October 2003. No high-level member of the Bush administration has promoted the Patriot Bonds, and many financial planners are unaware of their existence. The preceding quotation and facts are reported by John Decker in "Neglected Patriot Bonds Still Make Sense," *Christian Science Monitor*, December 20, 2004, 14.

10. The argument I am advancing differs from some influential works by historians. John Morton Blum, in *V Was for Victory* (New York: Harcourt Brace Jovanovich, 1976), explores with a critical eye the failures of American democracy and provides an important corrective to the idealized portrayals of the home front during World War II. His discussion of war bonds, however, is flawed in several respects. In an attempt to debunk the importance of civic ideals, Blum's account focuses too narrowly on the role of advertisers and inflates their influence. He argues that the messages Roosevelt hoped to convey about "liberty and freedom" were undermined by the "technicians" and "copy writers" of the War Advertising Council, who were "trained to sell products rather than principles" (ibid., 19). Blum's assertion that "advertising sold the war as if it were fantastic gowns, flat silver, or bright-red lipstick" rests on an analysis of only three ads from *Glamour* magazine, which is not a systematic sample or representative of war bond advertising (ibid., 20, 344). Robert Westbrook argues that appeals to "private interests" and "private moral obligations" trumped appeals to civic obligations or the sense of "political community" in advertisements and posters during the war years (see

Robert B. Westbrook, "Fighting for the American Family," in *The Power of Culture*, ed. Richard Wightman Fox and T. J. Jackson Lears [Chicago: University of Chicago Press, 1993], 198). I admire Westbrook's works, but he, like Blum, does not provide any systematic analysis of advertisements to back his claims. For another influential study that examines the tension between writers and advertisers in the Office of War Information, see Alan M. Winkler, *The Politics of Propaganda: The Office of War Information, 1942–1945* (New Haven, CT: Yale University Press, 1978). In a later section, "The Home Front Media Campaign," I show that civic participation and sacrifice were central themes in the war bond campaign, drawing on studies of ads, posters, radio, and survey research conducted during and immediately after World War II; on contemporary studies; and on my own analysis of the war bond advertising in *Life* magazine and of war bond posters from archives and books. For an excellent, well-researched study of civic participation in the war bond campaigns, see Samuel's *Pledging Allegiance*, cited above. Recent works by historians that focus on in-depth studies of particular communities have stressed the importance of civic participation and patriotism in World War II home-front campaigns. See, e.g., Gary Gerstle, *Working Class Americanism: The Politics of Labor in a Textile City, 1914–1960* (Cambridge: Cambridge University Press, 1989); Amy Bentley, *Eating for Victory: Food Rationing and the Politics of Domesticity* (Urbana: University of Illinois Press, 1998); and Barbara McLean Ward, ed., *Produce and Conserve, Share and Play Square* (Portsmouth, NH: Strawbery Banke Museum, 1994).

11. Franklin D. Roosevelt. "Annual Message to Congress (January 6, 1941)," in *The Roosevelt Reader*, ed. Basil Rauch (New York: Rinehart, 1957), 272–74.

12. Roosevelt, "Radio Address (April 30, 1941)."

13. Alan M. Winkler, *Home Front U.S.A.: America during World War II* (Wheeling, IL: Harlan Davidson, 2000), 25.

14. Morse, *Paying for a World War*, 22.

15. Olney, *War Bond Story*, 60.

16. Samuel, *Pledging Allegiance*, 20.

17. Morse, *Paying for a World War*, 22.

18. Ibid., 155; Samuel, *Pledging Allegiance*, 33.

19. Morse, *Paying for a World War*, 272; Samuel, *Pledging Allegiance*, 43.

20. Olney, *War Bond Story*, 70–71; Morse, *Paying for a World War*, 262–66, 270, 274.

21. Peter H. Odegard and Alan Barth, "Millions for Defense," *Public Opinion Quarterly* 5 (Autumn 1941): 401.

22. Olney, *War Bond Story*, 26–29; Morse, *Paying for a World War*, 67–68.

23. Morse, *Paying for a World War*, 6.

24. In my study of war bond advertising during the first, third, and fifth war bond drives, I discovered that only 20 percent of the 244 ads that mentioned war bonds engaged in "pro forma patriotism" by focusing entirely on a product (e.g., watches, liquor, nylons) and simply placing a small logo or phrase, such as "Buy War Bonds" or "Back the Attack," at the bottom of the page. An example of such an ad is "Quality Is Economy—Be Wiser Buy Kayser," which suggests that Kayser's "Victory Stockings" will do "leg service on the home front" and ends by mentioning war bonds as an afterthought: "Kayser—Gloves, Hosiery, Underwear—Buy War Bonds Too!" *Life*, November 30, 1942, 6.

25. Frank Fox, *Madison Avenue Goes to War: The Strange Military Career of American Advertising 1941–45*, Charles E. Merrill Monograph Series in the Humanities and Social Sciences 4 (Provo, UT: Brigham Young University Press, 1975), 11.

26. William L. Bird Jr. and Harry R. Rubenstein, *Design for Victory: World War II Posters on the American Home Front* (New York: Princeton Architectural Press, 1998), 1.

27. Olney, *War Bond Story*, 29.

28. Samuel, *Pledging Allegiance*, 94.

29. Robert K. Merton, *Mass Persuasion: The Social Psychology of a War Bond Drive* (New York: Harper and Brothers, 1946), 3.

30. *Mrs. Miniver*, directed by William Wyler (Culver City, CA: Metro Goldwyn Mayer, 1942), quoted in Jordan Braverman, *To Hasten the Homecoming: How Americans Fought World War II through the Media* (Lanham, MD: Madison Books, 1996), 7.

31. Westbrook presents a different interpretation of Norman Rockwell's "four freedoms" posters, suggesting that Rockwell translated Roosevelt's universalistic moral language into a "particular moral language centering on private obligations and interests." Westbrook further argues that "this sort of translation is one of the most significant features of American propaganda during World War II" ("Fighting for the American Family," 207). Empirical studies of ads, posters, and radio programs show that the family theme as described by Westbrook is not prominent in war bond advertising. George F. Streib discovered that only 14 percent of war bond advertising dealt with the theme of the family (compared with 57 percent on the theme of civic participation), and Merton notes that only 6 percent of Kate Smith's appeals in her radio marathon focused on familial themes. When family is mentioned, it is often connected to the themes of civic participation and honoring the sacrifice of the men fighting overseas and their families at home. See George F. Streib, "Idealism and War Bonds: Comparative Study of Two World Wars," *Public Opinion Quarterly* 12 (Summer 1948): 272–79, and Merton, *Mass Persuasion*. Westbrook does argue that Rockwell's illustration for freedom of speech—a man standing up in a New England town meeting—evokes civic participation.

32. Roosevelt, "Radio Address (April 30, 1941)."

33. Odegard and Barth, "Millions for Defense," 402.

34. U.S. Department of the Treasury, *A History of the United States Savings Bond Program* (Washington, DC: U.S. Department of the Treasury, 1984), 2.

35. U.S. Department of the Treasury, *The United States Savings Bonds Program* (Washington, DC: U.S. Department of the Treasury, 1981), 13.

36. Department of the Treasury, *History of the United States Savings Bond Program*, 2.

37. Samuel, *Pledging Allegiance*, 3.

38. David E. Shi, *The Simple Life: Plain Living and High Thinking in American Culture* (Athens: University of Georgia Press, 2001), 215.

39. Ibid.

40. Ibid., 216–17.

41. Banker Trust Company, *Our United States* (New York: Banker Trust Company, 1917), 1.

42. Morse, *Paying for a World War*, 29–30.

43. Department of the Treasury, *United States Savings Bonds Program*, 13.

44. Samuel, *Pledging Allegiance*, 4, 6.

45. Ibid., 4; and Winkler, *Home Front U.S.A.*, 2–3.

46. Streib, "Idealism and War Bonds," 274–76.

47. David M. Tucker, *The Decline of Thrift in America: Our Cultural Shift from Saving to Spending* (New York: Praeger, 1991), 91; and Richard Polenberg, *War and Society: The United States 1941–1945* (Philadelphia: Lippincott, 1972), 29.

48. Tucker, *Decline of Thrift in America*, 86–87.
49. Morse, *Paying for a World War*, 32.
50. Ibid.
51. The antecedents of public school thrift programs go back to the common school movement. J. H. Thiry, an immigrant and successful businessman, established school banking programs in 1885, and mortgage banker Simon W. Strauss established the American Society for Thrift in 1914 to support school banks and school gardens.
52. Tucker, *Decline of Thrift in America*, 94–95.
53. Ibid., 89.
54. All the quotations in this paragraph are cited in ibid., 92–93.
55. Shi, *Simple Life*, 217.
56. Ibid., 216.
57. Ibid.
58. Tucker, *Decline of Thrift in America*, 96.
59. Ibid., 96–97.
60. Shi, *Simple Life*, 217.
61. Franklin D. Roosevelt to Mathew Hale, November 6, 1920, quoted in Kenneth S. Davis, *FDR: The Beckoning of Destiny: 1886–1928* (New York: Putnam, 1971), 642.
62. Alan Brinkley, *The End of Reform* (New York: Knopf, 1995); and Michael Sandel, *Democracy's Discontent* (Cambridge, MA: Belknap Press of Harvard University Press, 1996), 258–73.
63. David M. Kennedy, *Freedom from Fear* (New York: Oxford University Press, 1999), 242, 783.
64. Morse, *Paying for a World War*, 35.
65. John Morton Blum, *From the Morgenthau Diaries: Years of Crisis 1928–1938* (Boston: Houghton Mifflin, 1959), 341.
66. Kennedy, *Freedom from Fear*, 626.
67. Secretary of the Treasury Carter Glass had concluded in his 1919 annual report that among the factors causing the mass liquidation of Liberty Bonds after World War I were "the wicked devices of bond sharks and swindlers who take advantage of the inexperience of investors . . . whom the Treasury was, failing the necessary legislation, powerless to protect" (Morse, *Paying for a World War*, 23).
68. Ibid., 40.
69. Kennedy, *Freedom from Fear*, 625.
70. Morse, *Paying for a World War*, 284–86.
71. Ibid.
72. Samuel, *Pledging Allegiance*, 86.
73. Ibid., 87.
74. Gary Gerstle, "Interpreting the 'American Way': The Working Class Goes to War," in *The War in American Culture: Society and Consciousness During World War II*, ed. Lewis A. Erenberg and Susan E. Hirsch (Chicago: University of Chicago Press, 1996), 114.
75. Gerstle, *Working Class Americanism*, 291.
76. Samuel, *Pledging Allegiance*, 92.
77. Morse, *Paying for a World War*, 204.
78. Samuel, *Pledging Allegiance*, 89.
79. Morse, *Paying for a World War*, 202.

80. Samuel, *Pledging Allegiance*, 88.
81. Ibid., 88.
82. Ibid.
83. For an excellent discussions of the issue of "equality of sacrifice," see Mark Leff, "The Politics of Sacrifice on the American Home Front in World War II," *Journal of American History* 77 (March 1991): 1296–318, and Nelson Lichtenstein, *Labor's War at Home: The CIO in World War II* (Philadelphia: Temple University Press, 2003), 82–109.
84. Leff, "Politics of Sacrifice," 1302.
85. Ibid., 1302.
86. Ibid., 1301; Lichtenstein, *Labor's War at Home*, 99–103.
87. Lichtenstein, *Labor's War at Home*, 102.
88. Morse, *Paying for a World War*, 202.
89. Samuel, *Pledging Allegiance*, 92.
90. Bird and Rubenstein, *Design for Victory*, 21.
91. Derek Nelson, *The Posters That Won the War* (Osceola, WI: Motorbooks, 1991), 70.
92. Bird and Rubenstein, *Design for Victory*, 54, 78.
93. Ibid., 78.
94. Samuel, *Pledging Allegiance*, 158.
95. Neil A. Wynn, *The Afro-American and the Second World War* (New York: Holmes and Meier, 1976), 12.
96. Nelson, *Posters That Won the War*, 70.
97. For an excellent account of the experiences of African American soldiers during the war and how these experiences shaped African American home-front politics, see John Hope Franklin and Alfred A. Moss Jr., *From Slavery to Freedom: A History of Negro Americans*, 6th ed. (1947; New York: Knopf, 1988), 385–410. See also Roi Ottley, *New World A-Coming* (New York: Arno and the New York Times Press, 1968), 306–26.
98. Wynn, *Afro-American and the Second World War*, 100.
99. Ibid.
100. Ibid., 101.
101. Ibid., 100.
102. Ibid., 96.
103. Samuel, *Pledging Allegiance*, 138.
104. Ibid.
105. Lester M. Jones, "The Editorial Policy of Negro Newspapers of 1917–18 as Compared with That of 1941–42," *Journal of Negro History* 29 (January 1944): 24–31.
106. Samuel, *Pledging Allegiance*, 176.
107. Ibid., 142.
108. Ibid., 197.
109. All quotations and slogans are cited in U.S. Office of Education Federal Security, "Replacing School Life for the Duration of the War," *Education for Victory* 1, no. 15 (October 14, 1942): 7.
110. Angelo Patri, *Your Children in Wartime* (New York: Doubleday, Doran, 1943), 89.
111. Morse, *Paying for a World War*, 175; and William M. Tuttle Jr., *Daddy's Gone to War* (New York: Oxford University Press, 1993), 126.
112. Jerald Oldroyd, "Patriotic Fire Burned Bright in Boy's Heart," in *We Pulled Together . . . and Won!* ed. Deb Mulvey (Greendale, WI: Rieman, 1993), 42.

113. Morse, *Paying for a World War*, 175.

114. Jack Goodman, ed., *While You Were Gone* (New York: Simon and Schuster, 1946), 75.

115. Morse, *Paying for a World War*, 172; and Olney, *War Bond Story*, 20.

116. Frederick Chesson, "We Built Mount Scrapmore," in *We Pulled Together . . . and Won!* ed. Deb Mulvey (Greendale, WI: Rieman, 1993), 52.

117. Ronald H. Bailey et al., *The Home Front: U.S.A.* (Alexandria, VA: Time-Life, 1977), 126.

118. Tuttle, *Daddy's Gone to War*, 124.

119. Ibid., 126.

120. Morse, *Paying for a World War*, 266.

121. Ibid., 277.

122. Tuttle, *Daddy's Gone to War*, 123.

123. Morse, *Paying for a World War*, 172.

124. See Blum, *V Was for Victory*; Westbrook, "Fighting for the American Family"; and Winkler, *Politics of Propaganda*. Blum argues that "even sacrifice had a lesser part in the general experience of war than did temporary inconvenience" and that a "lack of idealism" characterized "government propaganda in general," but he provides scant evidence for these claims. I am surprised how frequently historians cite Blum's statement that among the great powers, only the United States was "fighting the war on imagination alone," since the source for this quotation, by Blum's own account, is one "rueful American" (see Blum, *V Was for Victory*, 16, 21). The hundreds of thousands of Americans who were killed or injured during World War II and the suffering of their families and friends signify an immediate, not an imaginary, form of sacrifice.

125. Samuel, *Pledging Allegiance*, 115–16, 199.

126. The Office of War Information (OWI) developed six themes to guide the production of all war posters: "(1) The Nature of the Enemy, (2) The Nature of Our Allies, (3) The Need to Work, (4) The Need to Fight, (5) The Need to Sacrifice, (6) The Americans—we are fighting for the four freedoms, the principles of the Atlantic Charter, Democracy, and no discrimination against races and religions, etc." This list was written by Alan Cranston, chief of the OWI's Foreign Language Division, to Norman Ferguson, November 17, 1942 (cited in Bird and Rubenstein, *Design for Victory*, 32–36). See Morse, *Paying for a World War*, 223–39, 260–86, 306–9, for a detailed discussion of the themes guiding the national and local grassroots media campaigns for war bonds.

127. Morse, *Paying for a World War*, 262.

128. Ibid., 262–63.

129. Ibid., 262–67. See also Rensis Likert, "Opinion Studies and Government Policy," *Proceedings of the American Philosophical Society* 92 (November 1948): 343. Likert noted that "when respondents were asked why they bought War Bonds, most of them gave a patriotic reason."

130. Morse, *Paying for a World War*, 262, 272.

131. Ibid., 267.

132. Ibid., 260.

133. Merton's study was based on detailed content analysis of what Smith said, on focused and open-ended interviews lasting three to four hours with a sample of 100 people who listened to Smith's radio appeal, and on survey data from 978 people. Smith had a huge audience: it was estimated that some 23 million people listened to Smith's daytime programs in a week. See Merton, *Mass Persuasion*.

134. Ibid., 45, 50.
135. Ibid., 57.
136. Ibid., 52.
137. Ibid., 58.
138. Ibid., 46–47, 76.
139. Ibid., 47.
140. Ibid., 46. As a matter of policy, the Treasury Department discouraged any prizes or monetary rewards for buying bonds.
141. Samuel identifies five broad themes in war bond posters: (1) back the attack (i.e., help the government to supply the military with equipment and material to win the war); (2) sacrifice; (3) community and national unity; (4) America's fundamental freedoms; and (5) save for the future (future security, future consumption, and, more compelling, future investment in American lives and the nation as a whole). See his discussion of America's fundamental freedoms in Samuel, *Pledging Allegiance*, 50–52.
142. Streib, "Idealism and War Bonds," 274. Streib notes that the data were analyzed in terms of the number of advertisements that carried a specific appeal. More than one appeal per advertisement was possible.
143. Ibid.
144. For this present essay, I analyzed all the war bond advertisements that appeared in *Life* magazine for the first war bond drive (November 30 to December 23, 1942), the third drive (September 9 to October 2, 1943), and the fifth drive (June 12 to July 8, 1944). There was a total of 244 war bond–related ads during this period. (The totals are as follows: first drive, 73; second drive, 91; third drive, 80.) Like Streib, I analyzed the major themes in each ad. The tally of ad themes reflected multiple appeals in ads: e.g., if an ad focused both on civic participation and on sacrifice, it was tallied in two categories. I wanted to be attentive to both the themes emphasized in Merton and Streib and the themes of consumerism raised by historians such as Blum and Westbrook.

My findings strongly support Streib's study of war bond advertisements in the *New York Times*. Streib discovered that 57 percent of the ads appealed to "participation," and I discovered that 54 percent of the ads appealed to this theme. Unlike Streib, I broke the "participation" category into two subcategories: backing the attack (supporting war production and financing the war through the purchase of bonds) and explicit mention of civic participation and community. The most prevalent theme, encapsulated by the slogan "Back the Attack," was generally found in advertisements by companies that had switched from peacetime to wartime production (36 percent). These advertisements reminded people of the war effort, describing how the companies were supporting the military and how, in turn, with the purchase of war bonds, civilians could also support the military. Civic participation, the second most common theme (18 percent), emphasized the importance of participation in the war effort for the sake of the community and the nation. The theme of sacrifice, either civilian or military, was less common, accounting for 9 percent of the total ads. Advertisements focused not on what people were giving up but rather on what they could do to help the war effort. References to purchasing bonds purely for the sake of economic benefit or the prospect of present or future consumption were even rarer, present in 6 percent of the total advertisements in *Life* during this period. Only 20 percent of the advertisements in my study focused on consuming a product with no rationale for buying a war bond other than affixing a war bond logo or stamp at the bottom of the ad.

These findings contradict the conclusions of historians, such as Blum and Westbrook, who argue that advertisers generally defined the advantages of war bonds in ways that emphasized consumption or private benefits.

145. The Nash-Kelvinator ad appears in *Life*, November 30, 1942, 53.

146. Bird and Rubenstein, *Design for Victory*, 36, 44–45; Olney, *War Bond Story*, 83.

147. Bird and Rubenstein, *Design for Victory*, 45.

148. Ibid., 36.

149. Olney, *War Bond Story*, 66.

150. Ibid., 83; and G. H. Gregory, *Posters of World War II* (New York: Gramercy Books, 1993), 42.

151. Cover, *Life*, July 3, 1944.

152. Nelson, *Posters That Won the War*, 87.

153. Nash-Kelvinator advertisement, "The Church in the Jungle," *Life*, June 12, 1944, 64.

154. The statistics on war dead and wounded are from a fact sheet titled "America's Wars," published by the Department of Veterans Affairs, http://www.va.gov/pressrel /amwars01.htm (accessed July 30, 2006). Similar statistics are cited in William L. O'Neill, *A Democracy at War* (New York: Free Press, 1993), 429.

155. Cover, *Life*, July 5, 1943.

156. Calvert Distillers Corporation, "Somebody Has Just Kept His Bargain with You," *New York Herald Tribune*, 1945. The ad is part of the archive of war bond advertisement of Duke University. For access to John W. Hartman Center for Sales, Advertising, and Marketing History, Duke University Rare Book, Manuscript, and Special Collections Library, see http://scriptorium.lib.duke.edu/adaccess/wwad-history.html (accessed July 30, 2006).

157. Roosevelt, "Radio Address (April 30, 1941)."

158. Vicks advertisement, "And YOU Talk of 'Sacrifices'!" *Life*, December 14, 1942, 6.

159. Franklin D. Roosevelt, "The Price for Civilization Must Be Paid in Hard Work and Sorrow and Blood—Fireside Chat to the Nation (April 28, 1942)," in *The Public Papers and Addresses of Franklin D. Roosevelt* (New York: Random House, 1942), 11:233.

160. Franklin D. Roosevelt, "The President Opens the Sixth War Loan Drive (November 19, 1944)," in *The Public Papers and Addresses of Franklin D. Roosevelt* (New York: Random House, 1944), 13:424.

161. Olney, *War Bond Story*, 8. Olney notes that the Treasury Department explored several symbols before deciding on the Minute Man, including representations of Roosevelt's "Four Freedoms" and the image of the Statue of Liberty. Peter Odegard came up with the idea of using Daniel Chester French's famous statue of the Minute Man, arguing that it was "definitely American," used widely in school textbooks across the nation, and familiar to the public, and that it was a civilian and not a military symbol.

162. Gregory, *Posters of World War II*, 40.

163. "Lincoln in Wartime," *Life*, January 5, 1942, 50–55.

164. Ibid., 50.

165. Gregory, *Posters of World War II*, 35, 39.

166. Treasury officials rejected a poster of Roosevelt sitting by a microphone framed by a flowing American flag. J. Walter Wilkinson, the painter who designed the poster, recalled that officials explained that picturing Roosevelt at the height of his power would open the war bond campaign to the charge that it was political propaganda (cited in Bird and Rubenstein, *Design for Victory*, 23).

167. International Business Machine Corporation advertisement, "The Glory of Democracy," *Life*, January 21, 1942, 20.

168. Westinghouse advertisement, "To Provide for the Common Defense," *Life*, February 2, 1942, 69.

169. Bird and Rubenstein, *Design for Victory*, 9. The source for these statistics is Outdoor Advertising Association, *Outdoor Advertising: A Channel of Communication in the War Effort* (Chicago: Outdoor Advertising Association, c. 1944).

170. Nelson, *Posters That Won the War*, 122.

171. Harvard Sitkoff, "The American Home Front," in *Produce and Conserve, Share and Play Fair: The Home Front Battlefield during World War II*, ed. Barbara McLean Ward (Portsmouth, NH: Strawbery Banke Museum, 1993), 43.

172. O'Neill, *Democracy at War*, 137.

173. Sitkoff, "American Home Front," 43.

174. See Bentley's chapter "Rationing Is Good Democracy," in *Eating for Victory*, 9–29, for a discussion of the strengths and weaknesses of the Office of Price Administration (OPA) rationing programs. The OPA promoted its rationing programs with the slogan "Use it up, wear it out, make it do or do without"; yet despite bureaucratic blunders and inefficiencies that annoyed the public, people generally complied with the rationing program (see Sitcoff, "American Home Front," 39).

175. Ward, *Produce and Conserve*, 173.

PART } III

Thriving after Thrift? Prosperity and Crisis since 1950

17 }

Why Do Americans Save So Little and Does It Matter?

Robert H. Frank

The paramecium is a single-celled animal about the size of the period at the end of this sentence. It is found in bodies of fresh water everywhere, but especially in quiet ponds that contain the decaying organic matter on which it feeds. Many species reproduce asexually, with each mature cell dividing into two identical daughter cells every day—in some cases twice a day.

In elementary schools around the world, this particular aspect of the paramecium's behavior has made it a favorite tool for illustrating the miracle of compound interest. Thus my third-grade teacher asked us to imagine that we started with one paramecium on the lower-left square of a checkerboard, then put its two daughters on the next square, the four daughters of those two on the square after that, and so on all the way to the sixty-fourth square. How many paramecia, she asked with a twinkle in her eye, did we think would be on that last square?

The answer, of course, is an incomprehensibly big number—something like 9,223,400,000,000,000,000. If we figure that 125 paramecia lined up elbow-to-elbow would span a distance of about an inch, this means that if the reproduction of a single paramecium were left unchecked for a mere sixty-four days, the result would be a string of paramecia spanning more than 1,164,600,000,000 miles—more than 6,000 round trips between the earth and the sun.

Needless to say, the miracle of compound interest plays out less dramatically when the relevant growth rate is substantially smaller than the paramecium's. Still, the results can be impressive with even relatively small growth rates. For example, money invested at an annual interest rate of 7 percent will more than double in only ten years, which means that a $1,000 deposit left in trust at that rate by Benjamin Franklin in the late eighteenth century would be worth more than $1 trillion today. Money invested in the U.S. stock market has grown at an inflation-adjusted after-tax average annual rate of 6.8 percent since World War II. So, $1,000 invested at that rate in 1945 would be worth more than $77,000 today.

An Opportunity Wasted

Given the miracle of compound interest, our ability to invest money at even modest rates of return represents an extraordinary opportunity. Consider two hypothetical individuals, each of whom earns an annual salary of $50,000. Each begins work at age twenty-one and retires at age sixty-five. Any money they save earns 5 percent interest each year. One ("High Saver") puts 20 percent of both her earnings and her interest income into savings each year. The other ("Low Saver") saves nothing. He also incurs $9,000 of credit card debt at age twenty-one, a revolving balance that he carries at 20 percent interest until just before retiring. At retirement, High Saver will have accumulated almost $565,000 in savings, whereas Low Saver will be forced to live on just his Social Security checks.

It is hardly surprising that thrifty people enjoy much higher standards of living during retirement. What many do not realize, however, is that higher savings rates

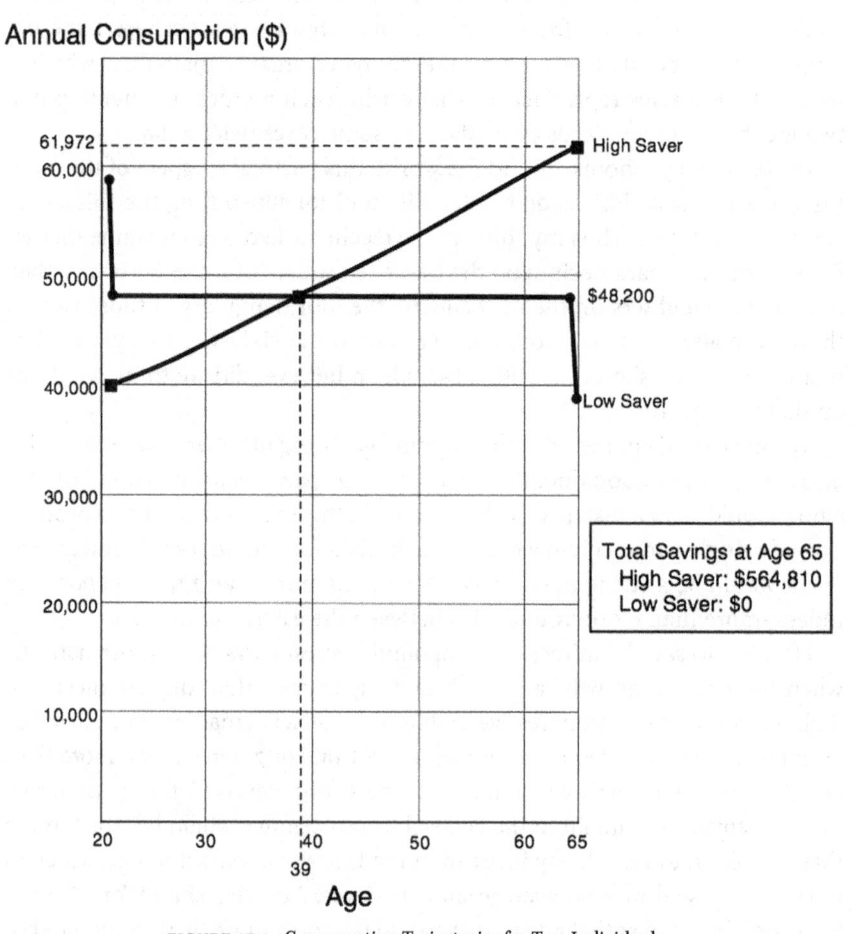

FIGURE 17.1 Consumption Trajectories for Two Individuals.

lead to increased living standards even well before retirement. Note in figure 17.1, which plots the consumption trajectories of the two individuals in the example, that High Saver's annual consumption shortfall is less than $5,000 by age twenty-nine and disappears entirely by age thirty-nine. From age forty onward, High Saver actually enjoys a steadily growing consumption advantage over Low Saver, an advantage that becomes even more pronounced during retirement.

If a compelling opportunity has been made available by the miracle of compound interest, it is one that most Americans have failed to seize. Our personal savings rate, always low by international standards, has fallen sharply in recent decades. Thus, according to U.S. Department of Commerce estimates shown in figure 17.2, the aggregate personal savings rate has fallen from an average of roughly 10 percent in the mid-1970s to near zero today. The personal savings rate in the United States was actually negative for the calendar year 2005, the first time that has happened since the Great Depression.

Almost one-fifth of American households have a net worth of zero or less.[1] Half of the respondents in one national survey reported life savings of less than $3,000, and another 40 percent said that it would be a "big problem" if they had to deal with an unexpected bill for $1,000.[2] A further indication that most middle- and low-income families save too little is that a majority of these families experience significant retrenchments in living standards when they retire.[3] To judge by the personal savings rates reported in figure 17.2, the typical American has essentially become Low Saver from figure 17.1.

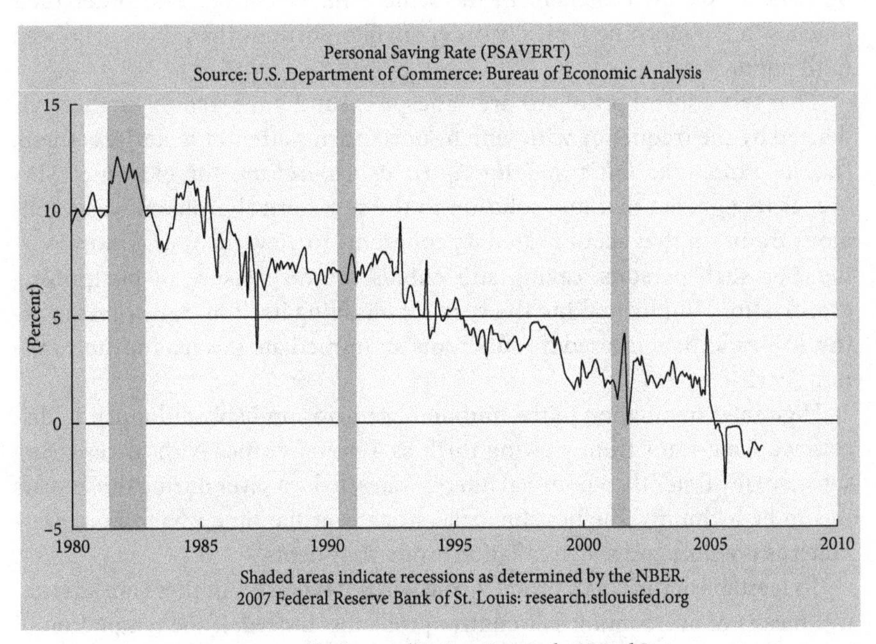

FIGURE 17.2 The Personal Savings Rate in the United States.

Why Do Americans Save So Little?

Why do we save so little, and is there anything we can or should do about it? Although numerous factors contribute to our savings deficit, I will mention only two and focus on one: First, we often find it difficult to summon the willpower to save. Second, we often confront pressures to keep pace with community spending standards. The self-control problem can be remedied by individual action, but the problem of keeping pace requires collective action.

THE SELF-CONTROL PROBLEM

Although the pain from reducing current consumption is experienced directly, the pain from diminished future consumption can only be imagined.[4] So the act of saving requires self-control. We might know exactly what is best for us and yet still have a hard time executing the right choices.[5]

George Ainslie has argued that human and animal nervous systems are simply hardwired to prefer the poorer but earlier of two goals when the earlier goal is close at hand.[6] Ainslie's hypothesis predicts preference reversals that are widely observed in everyday human behavior. Thus the dieter vows before dinner to forgo dessert but then changes his mind when the dessert trolley arrives. That his subsequent expression of regret at having done so is genuine is supported by the fact that he deliberately avoids keeping tempting desserts on hand in his own kitchen. In the same vein, executives who order their lunches in the morning typically order smaller portions than those who wait until noon.

That self-control problems are widespread and important is further evidenced by the frequency with which social norms attempt to address them. In *The Protestant Ethic and the Spirit of Capitalism*, for example, Max Weber recognized that one solution to the self-control problem was a religious tradition that acculturated its adherents to view thrift as a moral virtue. For such persons, saving still entails the displeasure of postponing gratification. But by making the very act of saving itself morally praiseworthy, Protestantism offered its adherents an immediate reward for their current sacrifice.

High rates of inflation in the mid-and late 1970s probably did much to discourage Americans from viewing thrift as a moral virtue. With prices rising substantially faster than nominal interest rates, to be a saver during those years was to be a chump. The best financial strategy at the time was to borrow as much as possible and watch inflation erode your debts.

To reestablish thrift as a moral virtue will not be easy. But there are alternative means of overcoming self-control problems. Indeed, if the temptation of current consumption were the only important source of our savings shortfall, individuals could solve the problem unilaterally—for example, by signing a contract to divert some portion of future income growth into savings until a target savings rate was reached.[7] Thus, if a family's income grew by 3 percent each year, it could commit itself to divert, say, one-third of that amount—starting *next* year—into savings.

THE COLLECTIVE-ACTION PROBLEM

Our savings shortfall also stems from a second source, one that is much harder to address by unilateral action. The following thought experiment illustrates the basic problem: If you were society's median earner, which of these two worlds would you prefer?

> You save enough to support a comfortable standard of living in retirement, but your children attend a school whose students score in the twentieth percentile on standardized tests in reading and math.
>
> You save too little to support a comfortable standard of living in retirement, but your children attend a school whose students score in the fiftieth percentile on those tests.

Because the concept of a "good" school is inescapably relative, this thought experiment captures an essential element of the savings decision confronting most middle-income families. If others bid for houses in better school districts, failure to do likewise will often consign one's children to inferior schools. Yet no matter how much each family spends, half of all children must attend schools in the bottom half. The choice posed by the thought experiment is one that most parents would prefer to avoid. But when forced to choose, most say they would pick the second option.

Context influences our evaluations not just of schools but of virtually every other good or service we consume. Looking good in a job interview, for example, simply requires that one dress better than other candidates. It is the same with gifts: "In a poor country, a man proves to his wife that he loves her by giving her a rose but in a rich country, he must give a dozen roses."[8]

The savings decision thus resembles the collective-action problem inherent in a military arms race. Each nation knows that it would be better if all spent less on arms. Yet if others keep spending, it is simply too dangerous not to follow suit. Curtailing an arms race thus requires an enforceable agreement. Similarly unless all families can bind themselves to save more, those who do so unilaterally will pay the price of having to send their children to inferior schools. Or they may be unable to dress advantageously for job interviews. Or they may be unable to buy gifts that meet expectations on important social occasions.

Temptation and collective-action problems may explain why Americans save too little, but why do we save so much less than other nations, which themselves confront the same problems? Inequality in income and wealth has always been more pronounced in the United States than in other industrial nations. As I will argue, that fact helps explain why our savings rate was lower to begin with, and the growth of the inequality gap in recent decades helps explain why the savings gap has grown.

How Income Inequality Affects Savings

In his 1949 book, James Duesenberry suggested that concerns about relative living standards help explain why people save too little. Thus, Duesenberry argued, people who find themselves among others with higher material living standards inevitably experience a sense of relative deprivation, which they then attempt to escape by saving less and spending more.[9]

Many economists, however, view this response as problematic because saving less now means experiencing even greater relative deprivation in the future. This objection may help to explain why most intermediate macroeconomics textbooks no longer even mention Duesenberry's relative income hypothesis. It is, of course, true that lower savings today usually means lower spending in the future. Yet concerns about current relative living standards may nonetheless reduce current savings if they operate with greater force than concerns about future relative consumption. Such a differential appears plausible for at least three reasons.

One is the general human tendency toward myopia mentioned earlier. Although the consequences of current relative living standards are immediate and vivid, those of future relative living standards can only be imagined. The press of daily business keeps most of us from thinking about our future circumstances very often, and evidence suggests that our attempts to imagine them are often wildly optimistic. More than 40 percent of survey respondents, for example, say they believe their heirs will pay estate taxes when in fact only about 1 percent of estates will be affected by this tax.[10]

A second reason that concerns about current relative consumption might affect savings is that many important outcomes depend much more on current relative consumption than on future relative consumption. Recall the thought experiment discussed earlier. Although most parents want to send their children to the best schools possible and also want to save enough to support a comfortable standard of living in retirement, these goals are squarely in conflict. Parents can spend more now for a house in a better school district, or they can save more now for retirement. Most view the first goal, which comes sooner, as more important.

These families may know full well that stretching their budgets to finance such a house will entail an unpleasantly low living standard during retirement. But the desire to avoid sending their children to a low-quality school in an unsafe neighborhood trumps that worry. Most parents opt for the better school now and hope for the best when it comes time to retire.

The aggregate effects of such choices, however, often turn out to be far from what people intend. Thus, when everyone spends more on a house in a better school district, the result is merely to bid up the prices of those houses. In the process, no one moves forward in the educational hierarchy, and yet parents end up having smaller savings for retirement. Acting as individuals, however, they have no real alternative except to send their children to less desirable schools.

A third reason for placing disproportionate weight on current living standards is that people who consume more in the present may actually enhance their future income prospects. Job seekers, for example, are told they should "look good" for interviews. Like a good education, however, a tasteful appearance is a relative concept. To look good means simply to look better than others who want the same job you do. The most direct means to this end is to spend more than other job seekers do on clothing. The catch is that this same calculus operates for everyone. The result is a fruitless escalation in the amount people have to spend merely to appear presentable. From a collective perspective, it would make sense to save more and spend less on clothing. But it would not be prudent for any individual, acting alone, to take this step.

To recapitulate, Duesenberry's relative income hypothesis is theoretically coherent if concerns about current relative living standards operate with greater force than concerns about future relative living standards. And it has long been clear that the relative income hypothesis does a better job than the competing life cycle and permanent income hypotheses of explaining important patterns in the savings data.[11] Before the recent sharp decline in personal savings rates, the stylized facts that any savings theory had to explain included these three: (1) as income grows over time, savings rates remain roughly constant; (2) consumption is more stable over time than income; (3) high-income persons save at greater rates than low-income persons.

The life cycle hypothesis explains facts 1 and 2 as consequences of the simple observation that families consume virtually all their incomes over the life cycle.[12] The permanent income hypothesis offers essentially the same explanation for (1), and it explains (2) by asserting that diminishing marginal utility of consumption leads people to smooth their consumption over time, saving when their incomes are above normal and dissaving when their incomes are below normal.[13] A specific implication of this argument is that the marginal propensity to consume out of windfall income should be very small—less than .05, say, for an individual in his twenties. But this implication has not stood up to empirical testing, which suggests a substantially higher marginal propensity to consume out of windfall income.[14]

The relative income hypothesis explains the long-run stability of savings rates by asserting that they depend on relative income, which cannot change in the aggregate over time; it explains the short-run stability of consumption by saying that each individual's consumption depends in part on a reference standard established by his past peak consumption level. The latter explanation is consistent with the observation that the rate at which consumption rises when income rises is sharper than the rate at which it falls when income declines. (Neither the life cycle hypothesis nor the permanent income hypothesis addresses this particular pattern.)

The life cycle theory makes no attempt to explain why the rich save at higher rates than the poor. In saying that all income is consumed over the life cycle, it predicts that rich families will save the same each year as poor families. The permanent income hypothesis addresses this problem by saying that the apparent pattern in the data is merely a statistical artifact. Thus, Milton Friedman argued that in any given year a disproportionate share of families with high current incomes will have incomes that are higher than normal; conversely, a disproportionate share of families with low current incomes will have incomes that are lower than normal. Because the propensity to consume out of transitory income is very small, according to Friedman, the result is that savings as a fraction of current income will be higher for families with high current incomes than for those with low current incomes.

This explanation has been subjected to empirical scrutiny numerous times, and each time it has come up short. One way to eliminate the influence of transitory income is to examine the average income levels for large groups of people, such as those who belong to a given occupation. Thomas Mayer examined the correlation between occupational income levels and occupational savings rates in different countries in different years. The permanent income hypothesis predicts zero correlation. But in twenty-eight of the twenty-nine cases examined by Mayer, that correlation was positive.[15] A 1984 study by Peter Diamond and Jerry Hausman found a similar positive correlation between incomes and savings rates of the same group of individuals over a multiyear period.[16] Numerous other authors have studied the relationship between savings rates and life cycle or permanent income. In his review of these studies, Thomas Mayer wrote that "of all the many tests which have been undertaken by friends of the [permanent income or life cycle] hypothesis, not a single one supports it. . . . I therefore conclude that the . . . hypothesis is definitely invalidated."[17]

Duesenberry's relative income hypothesis not only explains the three stylized facts in the historical consumption and savings data far better than the permanent income or life cycle hypotheses but also helps explain why middle-income families in the United States save much less now than in the 1970s. According to the permanent income and life cycle hypotheses, changes in income inequality will have no effect on how much a family with given income spends. By contrast, the relative income hypothesis predicts that a family with a given income will spend more if its relative position in the distribution of income declines. Recent changes in the distribution of income in the United States provide an opportunity to put these conflicting predictions to the test.

Changing Patterns of Income Growth

In the United States, income growth from 1945 until the end of 1970s was well described by the famous picket fence chart shown in figure 17.3. Incomes grew at about the same rate for all income classes during that period—a little under 3 percent per year. That pattern began to change at some point during the 1970s. During the twenty-four-year period shown in figure 17.4, the real purchasing power of people at the bottom income distribution remained essentially unchanged, and gains throughout the middle of the income distribution were extremely small. For example, median family earnings were only 12.6 percent higher at the end of that period than at the beginning. Income gains for families in the top quintile were substantially larger, and they were larger

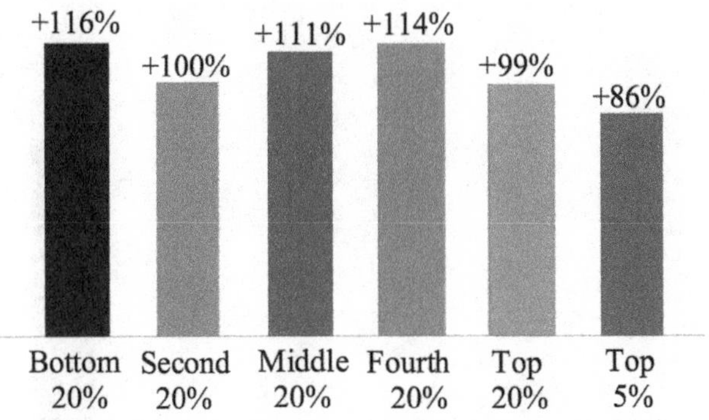

FIGURE 17.3 Changes in Before-Tax Household Incomes, 1949–1979.[18]

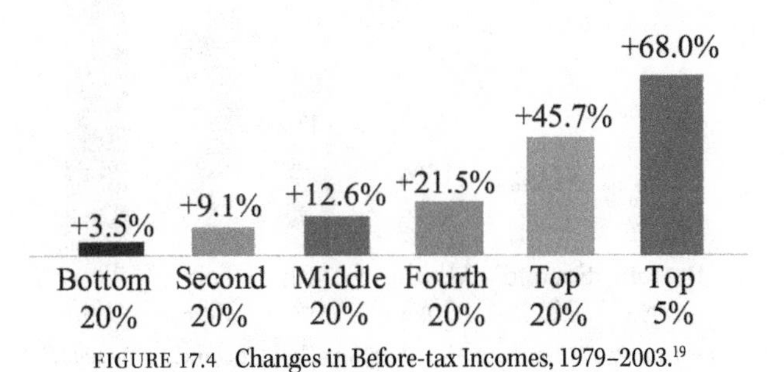

FIGURE 17.4 Changes in Before-tax Incomes, 1979–2003.[19]

still for those in the top 5 percent. Yet even for these groups, income growth was not as great as during the earlier period. The later period was thus one of both slower growth and much more uneven growth.

Income inequality has also increased in two important ways not portrayed in figures 17.3 and 17.4. One is that changes in the income tax structure during Ronald Reagan's presidency significantly shifted real after-tax purchasing power in favor of those atop the socioeconomic ladder, a change that was reinforced by additional tax cuts targeted toward high-income families during George W. Bush's presidency. A second change not reflected in these figures is the magnitude of the earnings gains recorded by those at the very top of the income ladder.

Figure 17.5 portrays some of the results of these two additional effects. Note that the bottom 20 percent of earners (net of both tax and transfer payments) gained slightly more ground than in figure 17.4, which shows pretax incomes (net of transfer payments). Note also that the gains accruing to the top 1 percent in figure 17.5 are almost three times as large as the corresponding pretax gains experienced by the top 5 percent. For people in the middle quintile, however, growth in after-tax incomes occurred at essentially the same modest pace as growth in pretax incomes.

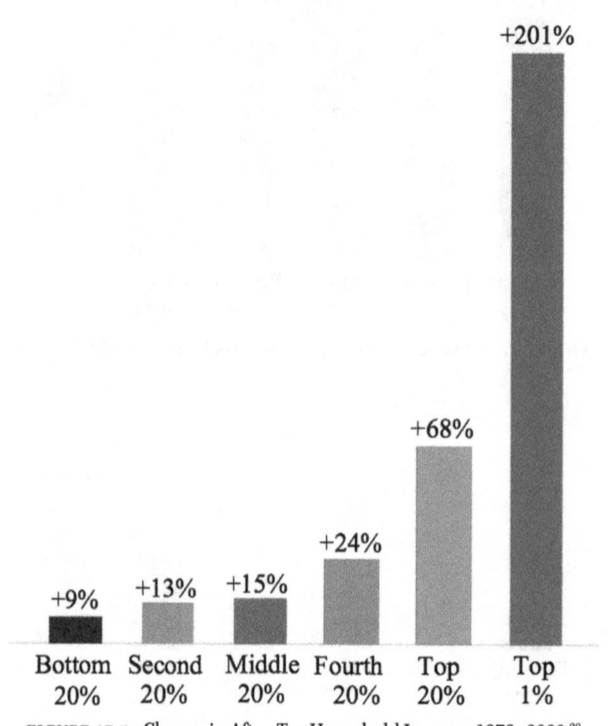

FIGURE 17.5 Change in After-Tax Household Income, 1979–2000.[20]

For our present purposes, an important feature of recent experience is that the aggregate pattern of income changes repeats itself in virtually every income subgroup. Thus, if we look at the top quintile of the earnings distribution, earnings growth has been relatively small near the bottom of that group and only slightly larger in the middle, but much larger among the top 1 percent. We see the same pattern again among the top 1 percent. In this group, the lion's share of income gains have accrued to the top 0.1 percent.

Although only fragmentary data exist for people that high up in the income distribution, a few snapshots are available. For more than twenty-five years, for example, *Business Week* has conducted an annual survey of the earnings of CEOs of the largest U.S. corporations. In 1980, these executives earned 42 times as much as the average American worker. But by 2001, American CEOs were earning 531 times the average worker's salary. There is evidence that the gains have been even more pronounced for those who stand even higher than for CEOs on the income ladder.[21]

A similar pattern of inequality growth is observed when we look across occupations and educational groups. It shows up, for example, among college graduates, dentists, real estate agents, and high school graduates.[22] *The upshot is that almost irrespective of the identities of the members of a person's personal reference group, income inequality within that group is likely to have grown sharply in recent decades.* Even among the wealthiest reference groups, for which average incomes have risen most sharply, most members are thus likely to have seen their incomes decline relative to those of their most prosperous associates.

Income inequality has been growing around the globe in recent decades, but not by nearly as much in most other countries as in the United States. For example, the ratio of a CEO's pay to that of an average worker has increased significantly in most countries, yet even today it is smaller in Germany and Japan than it was in the United States in 1980. Figure 17.6, which tracks movements in Gini coefficient values over the 1980s and 1990s, shows the inequality gap widening between the United States and each of the other countries shown except for the United Kingdom and New Zealand. As I argue in the next section, the patterns of inequality changes just discussed provide the most parsimonious explanation of the observed declines in savings rates, declines that are not predicted by traditional theories of savings.

Expenditure Cascades

I use the term *expenditure cascade* to describe a process whereby increased expenditure by some people leads others just below them on the income scale to spend more as well, in turn leading others just below the second group to spend more, and so on. As discussed earlier, income growth in the United

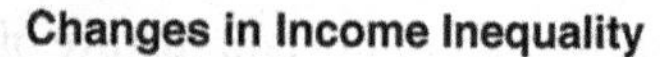

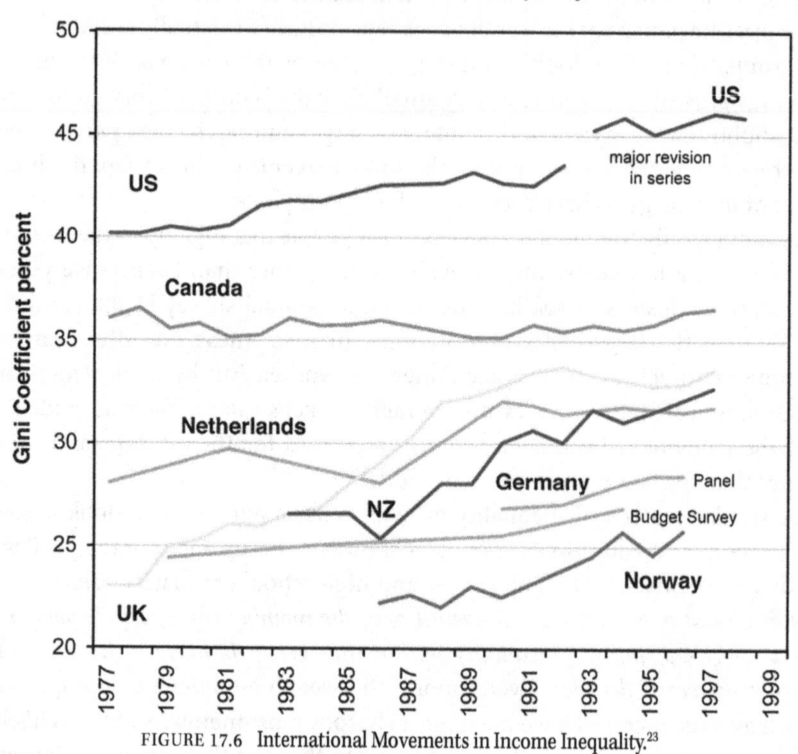

FIGURE 17.6 International Movements in Income Inequality.[23]

States in recent decades for almost all population subgroups has followed a pattern roughly like the one shown for the population as a whole in figure 17.5. People at the top of each subgroup have enjoyed robust earnings growth, whereas others have seen their incomes grow very slowly. The *expenditure cascade hypothesis* is that the new context created by higher spending at the top of each group largely has put pressure on others to spend more, thus accounting for the observed changes in savings.

In a recent paper, Adam Seth Levine and I attempted to test this hypothesis using U.S. census data on income inequality at the state and county levels.[24] Because reliable savings rate data do not exist at the state and county level, we actually tested a more general statement of the hypothesis, which is that families living in high-inequality areas will find it harder to live within their means than their counterparts in low-inequality areas.

Families respond to financial distress in multiple ways, some of which leave clear footprints in data available from the census or other sources. Beyond saving at lower rates, for example, they tend to carry higher levels of consumer debt, which increases their likelihood of filing for bankruptcy. In addition, families who cannot afford to carry the mortgage payments for houses in conveniently located neighborhoods with good schools often respond by moving to cheaper, more remote neighborhoods, thus increasing their average commute times. And like other forms of distress, financial distress may increase the level of stress in personal relationships, thus increasing the likelihood of marriages ending in divorce. We have found that for both state and county data, growth in inequality between 1990 and 2000 is positively linked with growth in each of these three measures of financial distress. For example, U.S. counties with larger increases in earnings inequality have experienced significantly larger increases in median house prices, personal bankruptcy rates, divorce rates, and average commute times.[25] Models that incorporate positional concerns predict these links.[26] Traditional models do not.

Although these findings contradict the predictions of traditional economic models of savings, they are part of a broader fabric of theoretical and empirical research that conveys a consistent message. On the theoretical side, our best current understanding of the conditions that molded the human nervous system lends no support to models in which individuals care only about absolute resource holdings. No serious scientist disputes the Darwinian view that animal drives were selected for their capacity to motivate behaviors that contribute to reproductive success. And in the Darwinian framework, reproductive success is all about relative resource holdings.

For example, frequent famines were an important challenge in early human societies, but even in the most severe famines, there was always some food. Those with relatively high resource holdings got fed, while others often starved. On the plausible assumption that individuals with the strongest concerns about relative resource holdings were most inclined to expend the effort necessary to achieve high rank, such individuals would have been more likely than others to survive food shortages.

Relative resource holdings were also important in implicit markets for marriage partners. In most early human societies, high-ranking males took multiple wives, leaving many low-ranking males with none. Even in contemporary societies, sexual attractiveness is strongly linked to relative resource holdings. So here, too, theory predicts that natural selection will favor individuals with the strongest concerns about relative resource holdings. The motivational structure expected on the basis of theoretical considerations is thus consistent with the expenditure cascade hypothesis but inconsistent with traditional models, in which only absolute consumption matters.

On the empirical side, our findings on the link between inequality and various measures of financial distress complement similar findings by other researchers. Using Organisation for Economic Co-operation and Development data across countries and over time, for example, Samuel Bowles and Yongjin Park found that total hours worked were positively associated with higher inequality, as measured by both the 90/50 ratio (that is, the 90th-percentile income divided by the median income) and the Gini coefficient.[27] Using specially constructed 2000 census data for a sample of 200 school districts in the United States, Bjornulf Ostvik-White found that median house prices were substantially higher in school districts with higher levels of income inequality, as measured by the 95/50 ratio, even after controlling for median income.[28]

The expenditure cascade hypothesis is also consistent with detailed patterns in cross-section data that are not predicted by the permanent income or life cycle hypotheses. For example, as James Duesenberry observed in his 1949 book, a black family with a given absolute income would have higher relative income in the segregated neighborhoods of the era than a white family with the same absolute income. And as Duesenberry predicted, the savings rates of black families with a given income level were higher than those of white families with the same income. The permanent income hypothesis and the life cycle hypothesis, both of which disavow any role for context in consumption decisions, predict that families will save at the same rate irrespective of where they stand in their respective local distributions of income.

The expenditure cascade hypothesis is also consistent with observed patterns in international savings rates that are not predicted by traditional economic theories. The aggregate savings rate, for example, was lower in the United States than in Europe in 1980, and the gap between European and American savings rates has grown larger during the ensuing years. One could invoke cultural differences to explain the initial gap, but the prevailing view is that cultures have grown more similar to each other with globalization, which leaves growth in the savings gap unexplained. The expenditure cascade hypothesis suggests, more parsimoniously, that the observed patterns in the savings data mirror the corresponding patterns in the inequality data. It thus suggests that Americans saved less than Europeans in 1980 because inequality was much higher in the United States than it was in Europe. It also suggests that the savings gap has grown wider because income inequality has been growing faster in the United States than in Europe in the years since then.

Finally, the expenditure cascade hypothesis suggests a plausible answer to the question of why aggregate savings rates have fallen even though income gains have been largely concentrated in the hands of consumers with the highest incomes. As noted earlier, formal versions of the permanent income and life cycle hypotheses predict no link between aggregate savings rates and differential rates of income growth across income classes. As a practical matter, however, modern specifications of these models have been forced to accommodate the fact that savings rates rise sharply with permanent incomes in cross-section data. If we take that fact as given, the observed pattern of income growth in recent decades would seem to imply a secular upward trend in aggregate savings rates. After all, the lion's share of all recent income gains have accrued to prosperous families with the highest savings rates. And yet, as noted, aggregate savings rates have fallen sharply.

The expenditure cascade hypothesis suggests that the apparent contradiction may stem from the fact that the patterns of income change within wealthy groups have mimicked those we observe for the population as a whole. As noted earlier, available evidence suggests that no matter how we partition the population by income or occupation, income gains are highly concentrated among top earners within each group. Again, the expenditure cascade hypothesis stresses that local comparisons matter most. So even though more income is now flowing to members of prosperous groups, most members of such groups have been losing ground relative to the most prosperous associates. If it is relative income that drives savings, and if local context is what really matters, the observed decline in aggregate savings rates is not anomalous.

The Political Economy of Thrift

Since Adam Smith's time, economists have argued that self-interested persons who trade with one another in competitive markets will be led, as if by an invisible hand, to make the most efficient possible use of society's resources. Although periodic downturns were an obvious fact of economic life from the eighteenth century onward, the prevailing view among economists during the century and a half after the appearance of Smith's *Wealth of Nations* was that market forces would quickly restore full employment.

The appearance of John Maynard Keynes's *General Theory of Employment, Interest and Money* led many economists to question that view. With the Western industrial economies mired in a deep and protracted depression, the intellectual climate was ripe for Keynes's argument that shortfalls in aggregate demand would not automatically be eliminated by market forces.

Before Keynes, the conventional wisdom regarding macroeconomic stability was summarized as Say's law—that supply creates its own demand. Then as now, all income must be either spent or saved. According to the French economist Jean Baptiste Say, capital markets would translate savings into investment, assuring that all income earned would end up getting spent on goods and services—and thus assuring full employment.

Keynes disagreed, saying that businesses would be reluctant to invest in new equipment when they already had sufficient capacity to produce more than people were willing to buy at current prices. The classical economist's rejoinder was that prices and interest rates would fall, in the process stimulating additional spending by increasing the real value of money held by people and firms. Keynes acknowledged that this might happen eventually, but he countered that prices and wages were often rigid for extended periods. The upshot was that economic downturns might not only not be self-correcting but could actually be self-reinforcing: fearing a loss of income, people might reduce their current spending, which would lead to further layoffs and further reductions in spending.

Keynes's prescription for economic stimulus—tax cuts and deficit spending—defied classical economic thinking about the role of thrift. Early economists had emphasized savings and investment as the driving forces behind economic growth. The more an economy saves, they argued, the more it will invest. And the more it invests, the more its capacity to produce additional goods and services will grow. Keynes did not challenge this view as applied to the long term, but he insisted that spending deficits could cause serious economic damage in the short run. In such situations, it was additional spending, not additional savings, that the economy really needed.

His prescription was that the government borrow or print money and spend it, thereby stimulating a self-reinforcing cycle of aggregate demand growth. Keynes's successors took delight in teaching their students about the paradox of thrift—whereby the effect of an increase in each individual's savings rate would be a shortfall of aggregate demand, resulting in lower incomes and savings than before.

The idea that economies might benefit from government stimulus during times of recession is now almost universally accepted by economists. But given our current willingness to use monetary and fiscal stabilization tools when needed, the empirical fact is that the U.S. economy has operated at very close to full employment during most of the years since World War II. And with near-full employment the norm, the logic of Say's law reasserts itself. Higher savings lead to higher investment, which in turn stimulates faster economic growth and higher incomes for all. It is thus no surprise that modern economics textbooks have again begun to emphasize the importance of long-run growth and to downplay the importance of short-run stabilization policy. Given our ability to manage economic downturns, savings is once again a good thing, not a threat to economic stability.

At the same time, we have seen a revival of faith in the efficacy of Smith's invisible hand—the idea that the self-seeking actions of individuals in private markets will lead, as if guided by an invisible hand, to the greatest good for all. It was Ronald Reagan's belief in the invisible hand that led his administration to enact large cuts in income tax rates and sweeping reductions in government regulation, policies that were pursued with even greater enthusiasm by the administration of George W. Bush. "It's your money," he and his advisers told us, "and you know how to spend it better than any bureaucrat does."

Smith's notion of the invisible hand assumes that people derive satisfaction primarily from the absolute quantities of goods and services they consume. Yet all available evidence from biology, psychology, sociology, and common sense tells us that absolute consumption is not the only, or even the most important, source of human satisfaction. In particular, there is compelling evidence that variations in satisfaction are much better explained by variations in relative income. In light of that evidence, there is simply no presuming that the spending decisions of self-seeking individuals will promote the greatest good for all. On the contrary, I have argued that there is a tendency for consumers to engage in wasteful spending races (such as bidding wars for houses in good school districts) that divert money from savings and other more pressing uses.

There is thus a measure of irony in the brief account I sketch here. The neoclassical resurgence of faith in the efficacy of private markets has led to deep cuts in personal income tax rates whose benefits have accrued mostly to high-income taxpayers. But the resulting increase in income inequality has led to expenditure cascades that have reduced aggregate savings to the detriment of all.

Now, it is not my claim that changes in income tax policy were the primary driving force behind recent growth in income inequality. On the contrary, inequality growth has been largely a consequence of the heightened influence of competitive forces in modern labor markets, as Philip Cook and I argued in *The Winner-Take-All Society*.[29] The fact remains, however, that federal tax policy has significantly exacerbated the pay disparities that have resulted from market forces.

Concluding Remarks

Some have argued that innovation, not thrift, has been the engine that drives economic growth. And true enough, without innovation, there would be clear limits on the extent to which additional capital could improve productivity.

Yet these observations do not diminish the importance of thrift. From the perspective both of the individual and of the economy as a whole, wealth grows over time as ownership of capital grows. The task of the capital market is to translate people's savings into investment. Money invested at a 7 percent annual rate of interest doubles every ten years. Over the past century, the real rate of return on equity investments has been greater than 7 percent. Innovation is an important factor in making this return so high. If a family or a nation saves and invests, its wealth will accumulate rapidly. But in the absence of investment financed by thrift, productivity advances from innovation will be smaller. Incomes will rise at a slower rate, and wealth will stagnate.

In short, the miracle of compound interest presents a remarkable opportunity for improved living standards. Without thrift, we completely squander this opportunity.

With the average family currently carrying almost $9,000 in unpaid credit card balances, it is difficult to second-guess the claim that Americans save too little. Evidence suggests that we do so in part because we find many consumption opportunities irresistibly tempting and in part because we face pressure to keep pace with escalating community consumption standards.

In principle, individuals can shield themselves from the temptation to spend too much by enrolling in payroll-deduction savings plans that place a portion of their earnings out of easy reach. Simple inertia appears to prevent many people from taking this step. Evidence from several studies suggests that people would be more likely to achieve their individual savings goals if participation in 401(k) and other employer savings plans were made the default option.

Savings shortfalls that stem from consumption "arms races" yield less readily to individual remedies. Curbing such arms races is likely to require either mandating higher savings directly (as by funding individual retirement savings accounts out of general tax revenues) or else rewarding higher savings by substantially increasing the price of current consumption (as by switching to a progressive consumption tax). Such policies clearly do constrain individual behavior (indeed, that is their aim). Yet even a steeply progressive consumption tax is not an especially intrusive measure. After all, we must tax *something*, and across-the-board consumption reductions do not appear to entail significant utility losses for upper-middle-income and high-income citizens, the only people who might experience a heavier tax burden under a progressive consumption tax.

Just as failure to save reduces an individual's standard of living over the life cycle, the aggregate effect of our failure to save is to make us much poorer as a nation. Recall the lifetime consumption trajectories of the two individuals discussed at the outset, reproduced here as figure 17.1.

Although our national personal savings rate was never as high as that of High Saver in figure 17.1, for much of the post–World War II period it was close to 10 percent. But now our aggregate savings rate is even lower than that of Low Saver in figure 17.1. Indeed, the aggregate savings rate was actually negative, −0.5 percent, for the calendar year 2005, the first time that has happened since the Great Depression. To finance our current spending binge, we have been borrowing from abroad at an annual rate of more than $700 billion. Once the world's largest creditor nation, we have become the largest debtor. And as our debt continues to mount, our interest payments to other nations will steadily erode not just our standard of living but also our political and diplomatic autonomy. Under the circumstances, we may wish to reconsider the wisdom of continuing to ignore our savings deficit.

Notes

1. Edward Wolff, *Top Heavy* (New York: New Press, 2002).

2. Robert Wuthnow, *Poor Richard's Principle: Rediscovering the American Dream through the Moral Dimension of Work, Business, and Money* (Princeton, NJ: Princeton University Press, 1996), chap. 1, n. 6.

3. See, e.g., B. Douglas Bernheim, Jonathan Skinner, and Steven Weinberg, "What Accounts for the Variation in Retirement Wealth among U.S. Households?" *American Economic Review* 91 (September 2001): 832–57.

4. A. C. Pigou, *The Economics of Welfare* (London: Macmillan, 1929), and, more recently, George Ainslie, *Picoeconomics* (New York: Cambridge University Press), 1992; David Laibson, "Life Cycle Consumption and Hyperbolic Discounting Functions," *European Economic Review Papers and Proceedings* 42 (May 31, 1998): 861–71; and Ted O'Donoghue and Matthew Rabin, "Doing It Now or Later," *American Economic Review* 89 (March 1999): 103–24.

5. Richard Thaler and H. Shefrin, "An Economic Theory of Self-Control," *Journal of Political Economy* 89 (April 1981): 392–405.

6. Ainslie, *Picoeconomics*, chap. 3.

7. Richard Thaler and Shlomo Benartzi, "Save More Tomorrow: Using Behavioral Economics to Increase Employee Savings," *Journal of Political Economy* 112 (February 2004): S164–87.

8. Richard Layard, "Human Satisfactions and Public Policy," *Economic Journal* 90 (December 1980): 741.

9. James Duesenberry, *Income, Saving, and the Theory of Consumer Behavior* (Cambridge, MA: Harvard University Press, 1949).

10. Larry M. Bartels, "Homer Gets a Tax Cut: Inequality and Public Policy in the American Mind" (paper presented at the annual meetings of the American Political Science Association, Philadelphia, August 2003).

11. See Franco Modigliani and R. Brumberg, "Utility Analysis and the Consumption Function: An Interpretation of Cross-Section Data," in *Post-Keynesian Economics*, ed. K. Kurihara (London: Allen and Unwin, 1955); and Milton Friedman, *A Theory of the Consumption Function* (Princeton, NJ: Princeton University Press, 1957).

12. Modigliani and Brumberg, "Utility Analysis and the Consumption Function."

13. Friedman, *Theory of the Consumption Function*.

14. See, e.g., Ronald G. Bodkin, "Windfall Income and Consumption," *American Economic Review* 49 (September 1959): 602–14; and Nissan Liviatan, "Tests of the Permanent-Income Hypothesis Based on a Reinterview Savings Survey," in *Measurement in Economics: Studies in Mathematical Economics and Econometrics in Memory of Yehuda Grunfeld*, ed. Carl F. Christ et al. (Stanford, CA: Stanford University Press, 1963), 29–59.

15. Thomas Mayer, "The Propensity to Consume Permanent Income," *American Economic Review* 56 (1966): 1158–77.

16. Peter A. Diamond and Jerry A. Hausman, "Individual Retirement and Savings Behavior," *Journal of Public Economics* 23 (February–March 1984): 81–114.

17. Thomas Mayer, *Permanent Income, Wealth, and Consumption* (Berkeley and Los Angeles: University of California Press, 1972), 348. See Christopher D. Carroll, "Why Do the Rich Save So Much?" in *Does Atlas Shrug: The Economic Consequences of Taxing the Rich*, ed. Joel Slemrod (New York: Oxford University Press, 1998), for a more recent study supporting the same conclusion.

18. (Source: U.S. Bureau of the Census, http://www.census.gov/hhes/income/histinc/f03.html).

19. (Source: U.S. Bureau of the Census, http://www.census.gov/hhes/income/histinc/h03ar.html).

20. (Source: Center on Budget and Policy Priorities, "The New, Definitive CBO Data on Income and Tax Trends," Sept. 23, 2003).

21. See, e.g., Paul Krugman, "For Richer: How the Permissive Capitalism of the Boom Destroyed American Equality," *New York Times Magazine*, October 20, 2002, 62–142. As Wolff, *Top Heavy*, has shown, the distribution of household net worth has also become more right-skewed in recent decades.

22. Robert H. Frank and Philip J. Cook, *The Winner-Take-All Society* (New York: Free Press, 1995), chap. 5.

23. (Source: Timothy M. Smeeding, "The Gap Between Rich and Poor: A Cross-national Perspective on Why Inequality Matters and What Policy Can Do To Alleviate It," prepared for the National Institute of Social Security Research, Tokyo, Japan, March 21, 2001; compiled from multiple sources).

24. Robert H. Frank and Adam Seth Levine. "Expenditure Cascades," Cornell University mimeograph, 2005.

25. Ibid.

26. These models also predict the observed negative relationship between income inequality and average happiness levels. See Alberto Alesina, Rafael Di Tella, and Robert McCulloch, "Inequality and Happiness: Are Europeans and Americans Different?" *Journal of Public Economics* 88 (August 2004): 2009–42.

27. Samuel Bowles and Yongjin Park, "Emulation, Inequality, and Work Hours: Was Thorstein Veblen Right?" *Economic Journal* 115 (November 2005): F397–412.

28. Bjornulf Ostvik-White, "Income Inequality and Median House Prices: An Analysis of 200 School Districts" (master's thesis, Cornell Institute for Public Affairs, 2003).

29. Frank and Cook. *Winner-Take-All Society*.

18 }

The Rise and Fall of "Collective Thrift"

SOCIAL INSURANCE, ECONOMIC PLANNING, AND THE DECLINE OF MODERN AMERICAN LIBERALISM

Steven Fraser

The Great Depression traumatized the United States. Its effect on the national psyche was second only to that of the Civil War. In contrast to the many Europeans who were disillusioned with capitalism, only a small number of Americans concluded the system was irreparable. Nonetheless, many, many more citizens called into question the viability of capitalism if left to its own devices. Economic breakdown so total and long-lasting indicted a bedrock faith in the compatibility of capitalism with democracy, in capitalism's egalitarian promise of opportunity for all, in its essential fairness, and in its capacity to provide for the general welfare. Even the association of capitalism with thrift—a character trait most people had for generations assumed constituted the genetic code of any capitalist economy—suddenly seemed not so self-evident.

Bread lines, relief rolls, homeless families, evicted farmers, tent cities, indigent old people, sickly children, and legions of the jobless made up a bill of particulars suggesting with overwhelming force that no matter how diligently people practiced an economical management of their daily lives, at the end of the day it didn't matter. Thriftiness was supposed to create a kind of capitalist homunculus, a miniature internal businessperson who directs optimizing behavior and secures, however modestly, future self-sufficiency. The Depression turned all that into a cruel joke. One horrific estimate had it that close to 90 percent of the population could not afford to go to a doctor. Thrift as the singular virtue of the prudent individual—already under assault by the newer maxims of consumer culture—now seemed a frustrating exercise in futility.[1]

Even more was at stake, however, than the survival of thrift as a core value of capitalism's moral economy. Thrift, after all, carried a social significance as well. Capitalism as a mode of production was assumed to be inherently thrifty. Its incentives for investment, technological innovation, and economic growth were presumably hardwired into the system. In America particularly, capitalism's defenders could point to an astonishing record of industrial progress, a prodigious set of technical and engineering accomplishments, and a general rise in the standard of living. This all constituted a prima facie case in favor of capitalism as a caretaker of the future, a husbander of resources and their wise, farsighted deployment. William Graham Sumner, the leading nineteenth-century evangelist for social Darwinism in America, noted that "captains of industry are as rare as great generals," because while "men of routine or men who can do what they are told are not hard to find . . . men who can think and plan and tell the routine men what to do are very rare."[2]

But the Great Depression made a mockery of this as well. Instead, capitalism as a system stood convicted of a tragic profligacy, irrational and planless. Its boast that it was the harbinger of progress turned out to be painfully too true, since—by lengthening the human life span and cutting people adrift from the land, tools, and familial networks that once afforded some independence—it vastly enlarged the population without any visible means of support, especially as that population aged. Idle men and idle machines, urban squalor and a devastated, depopulated rural landscape, a decaying infrastructure and shuttered workshops, exhausted and eroded farmland, millions of acres turned to dust—this all added up to a monumental wastefulness of human and material resources. If thrift, both as a lodestar of personal behavior and as a claim to economic preeminence, was supposed to be inseparable from capitalism, then what was its fate to be when capitalism died?

Turning to the state, the "public household," for an answer was something Americans instinctively shied away from. After all, Andrew Mellon, hailed in the 1920s as the greatest secretary of the Treasury since Alexander Hamilton, assured the country that the road to revival was self-evident: "Liquidate labor, liquidate stocks, liquidate the farmer, liquidate real estate." Thrift indeed! But in the teeth of an unprecedented calamity, such advice seemed not only callous but crazed, and even the most hardened inhibitions softened. If the private sector could no longer, all by itself, provide for the future—neither for the long-term material well-being of individuals nor for the prudent reinvestment of the nation's capital resources—then perhaps the commonwealth could, or at least could lend a hand. Could thrift somehow be collectivized, without provoking civil war? Perhaps, but it would be a delicate business to overcome an inbred aversion to such a démarche.[3]

As the financial sociologist Rudolph Goldscheid pointed out long ago, capitalism (and not just the American version) inherently seeks to keep the state weak and poor.[4] In noncapitalist societies that was not always so. The state was often not only powerful but heavily propertied, even if the line between public and dynastic resources was a hazy one. In such societies it was natural enough for the state to take up social obligations both with respect to provisioning against hard times and in directing the deployment of its public property. What Robin Blackburn has called "the pastoral role of the state as an instrument of social harmony" found a home even in some capitalist countries of Western Europe.[5] However, in America matters were quite otherwise. To try out some form of "collective thrift" would entail enriching and empowering the state, ceding to it both the material wherewithal and the political authority ordinarily considered best left untouched in the hands of private citizens. This was a daunting prospect indeed in a nation like the United States where the state had been deliberately kept on short rations, frail in its bureaucratic reach, without much property of its own, and starved for new sources of revenue. Yet the attempt was made. Out of the maelstrom of the Great Depression would emerge experiments in collective thrift, some still with us today, even if under siege.[6]

New Deal America defined security as the era's overriding dilemma. This too was extraordinary when measured against the main tidal currents of American culture. To be audacious, to welcome risky ventures into the unknown, to live surrounded by the dangers of the frontier (whether out west or back east in the ferociously competitive big city) was a widely celebrated feature of the American mythos. Jettisoning all that, admitting that self-reliance had reached a dead end, and embracing instead the notion that together citizens might have to collectively ensure their mutual security, resulted in a kind of culture shock. But there was no getting around it: capitalism had become intolerably risky. So it was that *security* became the watchword of the Roosevelt years. It hovered like a demiurge over every major piece of New Deal domestic legislation, laws as disparate in immediate purpose as the Banking Act of 1933, the Tennessee Valley Authority (TVA), and Social Security. At some even more exalted level, security encapsulated an ideology and a vision about the world to come, inscribed by Franklin Delano Roosevelt in his "Four Freedoms" speech as the reason men were being asked to fight and die.

In the quest for security, the New Deal ventured down two roads—converging paths of collective thrift—at once. Together they addressed the economy's failure to provide for the elementary material security of its workforce as well as its shortsighted misuse and waste of the country's capital inheritance. The first became a system of social insurance, most notably Social Security, unemployment insurance, and, decades later, government-subsidized medical care. Alongside that enlargement of the public household there developed a form of private-yet-collectivized thrift, also designed to provide long-term security, sponsored by American corporations and by the country's trade union movement. We live today with remnants of those twin systems of social insurance.

The second pathway to collective thrift turned out to be a much shorter one, leading nowhere. However, for a time people inside and outside the government experimented with and thought about various forms of economic planning. They sought to redirect the private sector away from misadventures in nearsighted redundancy and speculative excess. To do so might entail interfering with the normal structural configurations of property and power in a free-enterprise economy, a bridge not many proved willing to cross.

The survival of both social insurance and planning depended on an unusual coming together of social movements and political alliances whose life span turned out to be less than many expected. Both relied as well on the health of the state, on its robust growth and efficacy. That too was short-lived. Although the state bureaucracy would continue to expand, it did so in directions having less to do with social insurance or economic planning and much more to do with another kind of security, namely, the nation's military prowess. Meanwhile, its welfare apparatus would either atrophy or have to fend off assaults from a newly regnant political movement intent on resurrecting thrift as a function of the prudential individual and the free market.

Planning and the Free Market

Irving Fisher was perhaps the country's most famous economist in the 1920s. The Yale professor has come down to us as also being infamous for having articulated that era's most legendary expression of misplaced confidence in the stock market boom, remarking, on the very eve of the crash of 1929, that "stock prices have reached what looks like a permanently high plateau."[7] But Fisher was no free-market fundamentalist. He was instead a vigorous proponent of federal intervention, mainly through the Federal Reserve, to limit fluctuations in the business cycle that led inevitably to unemployed resources, bankruptcies, and wasteful speculation. If someone as essentially conservative as Fisher could entertain such ideas, it was because the notion of economic planning was already in the air even before the Depression descended. Herbert Hoover, the "Great Engineer," was its champion. As secretary of commerce in the Harding administration, Hoover chaired the President's Conference on Unemployment. The conference report declared that "the extremes [of the business cycle] are vicious, and the vices of the one beget the vices of the other. It is the wastes, the miscalculations, and the maladjustments grown rampant during the booms that make inevitable the painful process of liquidation."[8] Hoover and his co-thinkers in the business community did not envision government planning as a remedy (with the partial exception of countercyclical public works expenditures). Instead they imagined a system of business self-regulation—the trade association writ large—that would impose a corporatist discipline over the main sectors of industry and commerce, reining in their tendencies to overproduction, self-destructive competition, and speculative waste.[9]

Once the Depression established its grip, planning proposals multiplied, became more robust and radical than what Hoover had in mind, and radiated from all sectors of the political spectrum. *Business Week* asked a rhetorical question: "Do You Still Believe in Lazy-Fairness?" The editors concluded that "to plan or not to plan is no longer the question. The real question is who is to do it?" There were calls for national economic planning boards, five- and ten-year plans, Soviet-style plans alongside Hoover-inspired corporatist plans. Between 1930 and 1935 six major legislative proposals surfaced calling for a central planning body. Progressive politicians like Robert Lafollette offered one, as did Henry Harriman, president of the U.S. Chamber of Commerce. Labor leaders like John L. Lewis of the United Mine Workers of America and Sidney Hillman of the Amalgamated Clothing Workers chimed in, as did intellectuals like historian Charles Beard and political journalist George Soule. It was rather unclear what all of these schemes were suggesting—what powers a planning agency would have, who would exercise them, how they might be monitored, and so on.[10]

Bernard Baruch and William Gibbs McAdoo (President Woodrow Wilson's secretary of the Treasury) proposed a Peace Industries Board modeled after the War Industries Board that Baruch had chaired during World War I. The war was the occasion for the country's first real experience with planning, a process that included the rationing of capital resources as well as consumer expenditures. The shadow of the War Industries Board hung over those deliberating about what to do in this new crisis. Baruch conceived of its peacetime equivalent as an agency "whose duty it should be to encourage under strict Government supervision, such cooperation and coordination in industry as should tend to increase production, eliminate waste, conserve natural resources, improve the quality of products, promote efficiency in operations, and thus reduce the costs to the ultimate consumers."[11] Gerard Swope, head of General Electric, authored the most widely debated scheme for corporate-government planning. The Swope Plan envisioned a system of government-supervised trade associations to coordinate prices and production. A version of Swope's solution inspired the New Deal's first attempt at industrial recovery, the National Industrial Recovery Act.[12]

Indeed, although FDR ran a rather conservative campaign for president in 1932, he did suggest that "the problem of controlling through adequate planning the creation and distribution of those products which our vast economic machine is capable of yielding" might be necessary.[13] His first concrete foray in that direction, the National Recovery Administration, left the mechanics of planning in the hands of the country's peak corporations; it was, in effect, a kind of legalized cartelization. As such it invited heavy criticism. Influential circles both within and outside government were convinced that the government itself needed to play a more muscular role in husbanding and steering the investment of the country's capital resources. That was the way to make capitalism thrifty.[14]

Rexford Tugwell was perhaps the best-known proponent of planning within the inner councils of the New Deal. His work at the Agricultural

Adjustment Administration (AAA), his later work at other New Deal agencies, and his general approach to the problem of economic recovery all bear witness to this. The AAA sought to control agricultural output in a variety of ways: through acreage restriction, incentive payments, loans, and government purchases of surplus product. Its aim was to end waste and ruinously low prices. But it was rife with contradictions. Large cotton planters and agribusinesses tended to dominate the work and reap the benefits of the AAA; its controls and incentives generated more tenants than they eliminated. Tugwell, along with Mordecai Ezekiel and even Secretary of Agriculture Henry Wallace challenged this version of agricultural corporatism, standing up for the rights and interests of tenants and sharecroppers. For them the agricultural sector was a prime example of capitalism's thriftless irrationality. They sought to use the agency to reconfigure the southern social structure—its class as well as its racial dimensions.

Olympian planning of this sort, which tried to stand apart from the interests of powerful groups, would play itself out as well in the work of the Resettlement Administration, the TVA, the Farm Security Administration, and the Rural Electrification Administration. Tugwell ran the Farm Security Administration, established in 1937, and directed some of its efforts to create communal-cooperative farming projects and communities. Planning on this scale had many objectives, but central among them was the eradication of rural poverty and insecurity as endemic features of competitive agriculture. On the ground the results were meager, the political opposition vigorous. Having officials with considerable power advocating for the government to redirect the resources and sponsor the future economic development of a whole region opened a new avenue in American political life.[15]

Rural America was hardly the only sector to feel the imprint of government planning. Tugwell, Jerome Frank, and others envisioned an ordered economic world, one in which the government would create centralized institutions to coordinate the behavior of the nation's principal economic institutions. The Reconstruction Finance Corporation, an agency FDR inherited from Hoover, made overtures in this direction. Formed to bail out failing railroads and other vital corporations (prime exhibits of a thriftless capitalism), the Reconstruction Finance Corporation eventually extended its reach and altered its purpose. With immense financial resources, the agency could and did encourage the flow of credit into unconventional sectors needing development like housing, public works, and cooperative power plants. To some limited degree, therefore, it acted as a kind of development bank.

Later on in the 1930s, when the economy once again fell into severe recession, Ezekiel called for an industrial expansion program that would bring together business, agriculture, labor, and government in councils to supervise planned production. Adolph Berle, who, like Tugwell, was an original member of the Roosevelt "brain trust," and Gardiner Means, his coauthor of *The Modern*

Corporation and Private Property, the classic study of the corporation, similarly argued for some public intervention to end the chaos of the old order. Berle and Means thought supervision and coordination would serve all the constituents of the industrial corporation, including its shareholders, its labor force, its suppliers, its consumers, and the community at large by regulating capital flows and ensuring a balanced distribution of income.

Whatever their specific mechanisms, all these proposals shared a principal objective: the elimination of the waste that seemed to trail inevitably in the wake of competitive capitalism. Both efficiency and equity, planners were convinced, could best be served by some guiding intelligence. Tugwell put it bluntly: "We are resolved to recognize openly that competition in most of its forms is wasteful and costly."[16] According to a colleague, Tugwell wanted "the central planning of industrial activity, budgeting each year's national production and assigning it by quotas to individual producers."[17] Only such a public mechanism with real authority to coerce, if necessary, recalcitrant interests could ensure a thrifty deployment of economic resources, taking into account the long-term material well-being of the whole community. When President Roosevelt inaugurated the TVA, he reminded the country that "many hard lessons have taught us the human waste that results from lack of planning.... It is time to extend planning to a wider field."[18] In this connection, one of the purposes of the TVA was to establish a public "yardstick" when it came to prices and production—in this case through the generation of electrical power by publicly owned plants—that private companies would feel compelled to match, thus putting a stop to the waste associated with restricted output and artificially inflated prices. And soon enough seven "little TVAs" set up shop in other river basins with the authority to unify power, water, and land use policies.[19]

No agency was so singularly identified with the planning ethos as was the National Resources Planning Board (NRPB). Originally created as a subdivision of the Public Works Administration in 1933, when it was called the National Planning Board (it was later reincarnated as the National Resources Board, and once again as the National Resources Committee, and finally as the NRPB), the board was led by FDR's uncle, Frederic A. Delano, economist Wesley Mitchell, and University of Chicago political scientist and urban planner Charles Merriam. The NRPB was to plan the development of national resources in particular and the national economy more generally, including production, consumer expenditures, employment levels, and so on. Land use, land reclamation, and conservation of natural resources threatened by thriftless overexploitation, especially in agriculture and lumbering, were the board's special preoccupations. Much of its staff did important research and analysis into matters of soil erosion, flood control, and forestry and land reclamation. It called for the public purchase of submarginal land and actually managed to acquire some—in part thanks to the encouragement of Secretary Wallace, who was particularly interested in reclaiming forests, and in part through the work of the TVA. In 1940 the board issued a report entitled "The Structure of the American Economy," which outlined an ambitious scheme to make full use of workers and machines to ensure the country's economic security. The plan covered such diverse areas as land use, resettlement, rehabilitating and expanding the nation's systems of transportation, and the development of electrical power and other sources of energy.[20]

But by this time the voice in favor of economic planning had already grown faint within the councils of the New Deal. The NRPB had one last hurrah: it issued another report in 1943. Called "Security, Work, and Relief Policies," it became the bible for what remained of the New Deal's social democratic aspirations. The report sketched a vision of a postwar economy devoted to security—a kind of American version of the British Beveridge Plan, which had been recently announced in an official government report by William Beveridge of the London School of Economics, the basis of what became the welfare state in the United Kingdom after the war. While the NRPB report still flirted with the idea of national planning, it emphasized social insurance. How could the postwar economy guarantee that Americans would never again be so exposed to the risks and privations of a free-enterprise economy, which no degree of individual thriftiness could protect against? This "American Beveridge Plan" explicitly attacked the old nostrum that social insurance subverted the work ethic. It argued for an elastic program of federal public works that would expand to assure full employment when the private sector faltered. And, most of all, it advocated a vast expansion of social insurance against unemployment, disability, old age, and illness.

The NRPB report was an itemized rendering of what just a few months later the president, in his State of the Union address, would announce as his administration's commitment to a new "economic bill of rights"—one that would include the right to "a useful and remunerative job" and the right to earn enough "to provide adequate food and clothing and recreation." Without "economic security and independence," the president argued, political rights would be fatally weakened.[21] Soon enough FDR's rhetoric took on legislative form, inspiring the Full Employment Bill of 1945, introduced by Senator James E. Murray of Montana. The bill called for the president to prepare a yearly National Production and Employment Budget that would establish the number of jobs necessary to reach full employment and to what extent the gross national product would need to grow to achieve that goal. It assumed that the government would use its powers to spend, borrow, and invest to make up any deficit in full employment originating in the private sector.[22]

Ten weeks after the NRPB issued its version of the Beveridge Plan, the agency was abolished by Congress, thanks largely to the growing conservative opposition to any hint of "statism." Senator Murray's Full Employment Bill, renamed the Employment Act, was passed in 1946. The word *full* had been deleted, a deliberate omission signaling the end of any serious foray into the brave new world of economic planning. The act established no obligation on the part of the government—neither the Congress nor the president—to ensure full employment, and it was free to ignore recommendations for that purpose offered by the president's Council of Economic Advisers, a new body created by the act. As the New Deal wrapped up its affairs with the onset of war, it had given birth not to a planned economy but to a "broker state," one where the most muscular interest groups got their way. As one critic dourly noted, "From the viewpoint of national planning, the New Deal has been like Don Quixote who mounted his horse and rode off in all directions at once."[23]

After this denouement, collective thrift in the form of national economic planning lived out a ghostly existence. Its echoes could be heard in the recesses of mainstream Keynesian fiscal and monetary policy insofar as that toolbox of financial manipulations could, from afar, influence the flow of investment capital and the distribution of income and wealth. But no one any longer seriously proposed structural transformations in the economy or enlarging the capacities of the state either as a vehicle of investment or as a command post of directed economic development. Passage of the Environmental Protection Act in 1969, designed to grapple with the pollution of the country's air and water, represented a last practical attempt at using the powers of the state to confront the wastefulness of unregulated capitalism. Soon enough, however, the Environmental Protection Agency found itself hobbled by the contradiction between the economics of growth and the economics of thrift.

In the realm of ideas only John Kenneth Galbraith came close to offering up substantial arguments on behalf of planning. He had always steered clear of proposals that smacked too much of state management. However, his most celebrated works of the 1950s and 1960s, in particular *The Affluent Society* and *The New Industrial State*, criticized the neglect of the public sector. And when the country entered the economic slough of the 1970s, Galbraith's *Economics and the Public Purpose* boldly proclaimed the need for a kind of "public service socialism" that would empower the government to develop the nation's housing stock, its transportation network, and its health care facilities. He went even further, suggesting the overthrow of the military-industrial complex by "defense socialism," making defense contractors publicly owned; a "technostructure socialism" that would buy out shareholders in large corporations and take companies in key industries, like steel and auto, public; and finally a "socialism of ends" that would encompass the public planning of overall economic output, including public goods—all of which would amount to "socialism in support of the market."[24]

Economics and the Public Purpose was published in 1973. By then Galbraith and his notions of economic planning and a "socialism of ends" were irrelevant to the main drift of American politics and economic policy, which were decidedly headed in the opposite direction. That branch of collective thrift, stunted at birth, withered as the private economy recovered after the war and was undone by a renewed faith in the free market, which found in every intrusion of the state into economic affairs a mortal threat to freedom.

Social insurance, on the other hand, that kindred form of "collective thrift," lived on. It did so, first of all, because the memory of the Depression and its awful toll on people was as close to imperishable as the memory of any past event is likely to be in a country as inherently amnesiac as America. Social insurance also survived because it had the support of the most dynamic social movement of the first half of the twentieth century: without the labor movement, it is harder to imagine not only the Social Security Act but also the president's commitment to an economic bill of rights and the whole subsequent development of the welfare state. Married as they were, the labor movement and the social insurance state ended up nonetheless pursuing a strange career together, full of irony and paradox.

Social Insurance American Style

Once upon a time, the American labor movement was wary of all forms of state intervention in the labor market. The American Federation of Labor under the leadership of Samuel Gompers had good reason to suspect the intentions of the government, since its judicial and executive arms had been used again and again to enjoin and forcibly break up strikes and other forms of labor activism. With regard to matters of social security, trade unions had long pioneered in the arena of collective thrift. Beginning in the early nineteenth century, and together with various fraternal and mutual benefit societies to which they were often affiliated, trade unions had provided modest pensions and especially life and disability insurance for their members. The unpredictable and violent oscillations of the business cycle taught a tough lesson about the inherent riskiness of working-class life that no amount of Horatio Alger–like diligence could protect against. Workers would band together instead through their own organizations to provide for the future.

Up until the Great Depression, the trade union movement did not seek to off-load this burden onto the state. To the contrary, it jealously guarded the independence of these mutual benefit funds. Labor unions did so in part to steer clear of any dependency on the shifting whims of politicians and government officials, but they did so also because providing such insurance was an important way of winning and maintaining the loyalty of their own membership. Where they were powerful enough some trade unions succeeded in making pensions and even other forms of social insurance part of the collective-bargaining process, compelling employers to contribute to such funds.

Still, this occurred within the realm of what might be characterized as privatized collective thrift.[25]

The Great Depression changed all that. Both union and corporate pension plans collapsed. A new labor movement, the Congress of Industrial Organizations (CIO), situated at the core of American heavy industry, embraced the idea of the activist state. Indeed, without the CIO's vigorous political support for the New Deal, it is highly unlikely that what we think of as the modern administrative-welfare state could ever have achieved what it did. Elements within this new unionism—not only socialists and other secular leftists but also believers in Catholic social justice inspired by the two landmark papal encyclicals on this subject in 1890 and 1931—were well-disposed toward economic planning in general. Phillip Murray, who led the CIO after the resignation of John L. Lewis in 1940, proposed the creation of industrial councils to plan war production—councils on which the labor movement, along with other key economic players, would sit and make basic decisions about how and where capital was invested. The CIO even proposed a "national planning board" to oversee the conversion to peacetime production. The Murray Plan was widely debated but, like the NRPB's "American Beveridge Plan," it went nowhere. This was not the case, however, with regard to social insurance.[26]

Many segments of American society mobilized amid the Depression to win passage of the Social Security Act of 1935. They included middle-class reformers, social workers, and others who had been waging this fight, particularly in states like Ohio and Wisconsin, for many years, long before the crash of 1929. The Townsend movement (named after reformer and physician Francis Townsend) demanded a monthly stipend for the elderly—which would both help them survive and inject a revivifying dose of mass purchasing power into a moribund economy—and mobilized millions, inspiring lawmakers to create the Social Security Act of 1935. Elements of the business community joined in as well. All around them could be seen the wreckage of the corporate welfare schemes so popular in the 1920s, a picture grim enough that at least some businessmen welcomed state assistance in providing for the long-term well-being of their workforce. Still, major business organizations were at first adamantly opposed, labeling the Social Security Act an "immoral departure from the American way." Above all, the labor movement (eventually even the old-guard American Federation of Labor would get on board) saw the Social Security Act as the opening wedge of a broader campaign to have the government assume the burden of collective thrift, which the private economy had abandoned. Most saluted in 1934 when the president called for new ways to provide "security against the hazards and vicissitudes of life," promising in his message to Congress to "undertake the great task of furthering the security of the citizen and his family through social insurance."[27]

All by itself, the act was niggardly. Its actual monetary provisions in the form of unemployment insurance, disability payments, and pensions were meager and would remain so for years. Its coverage was far from universal, in either who or what it covered. Millions of agricultural workers were left out to keep southern politicians happy. Although many of its proponents wanted medical care included, it was not. Moreover, the whole system was defined by its beneficiaries' relationship to the workplace, for that is where the insurance funds were collected and where one earned the right to participate. Accepting the premise of "the family wage" meant women and others less regularly connected to or excluded from the labor market, African Americans particularly, were disadvantaged. Perhaps this outcome was virtually inevitable given the national reverence for the work ethic and self-reliance and the equally potent aversion to anything that smacked of a handout. Certainly keeping Social Security on short rations expressed a more basic instinct to keep the public household poor, the state weak. Be that as it may, designing the system in this way had two long-term consequences. First, it made Social Security nearly untouchable. During his campaign for the presidency in 1952, Dwight Eisenhower noted with finality that "should any political party attempt to abolish social security, you would not hear of that party again in our political history"; it had become the third rail of American politics.[28] But, second, the system's inherent biases and limitations severely hampered all future efforts to make social insurance truly universal. And this in turn would give new life to forms of privatized collective thrift that would entangle and bedevil the labor movement and corporate America for decades to come.[29]

At first, the labor movement, and the progressive wing of the New Deal more broadly, thought of the Social Security Act as just an initial victory. Before, during, and in the years immediately after the war, these circles campaigned tirelessly to extend the borders of the social insurance state. They lobbied to increase payments and widen the coverage of the original act and to some degree managed to accomplish that: by 1970 even the self-employed were included, and coverage had become nearly universal. The CIO's political action committee echoed Roosevelt's call for an economic bill of rights. It campaigned for increased federal aid for low-cost housing and even proposed a legislatively guaranteed annual wage. Most boldly—at least it seems audacious in hindsight—the labor movement and its various allies mobilized to establish a form of national health insurance. Theirs was a capacious vision of what that meant. It included not only insurance against illness but also providing good nutrition, healthful working conditions, and adequate housing. Looking after the future entailed providing for the health of the economy as well as for the well-being of the individual. A health care bill cosponsored by Congressmen Robert Wagner, James Murray, and John Dingell made its appearance in the late 1930s and was still setting off heated debate after the war. But its treading water for so long signaled that the main currents of American politics had shifted and were running against it.[30]

By 1946, the Republicans had recaptured the Congress, a process already well under way by the late 1930s. Together with their allies in the conservative wing, and especially the southern wing, of the Democratic Party, they had halted and even reversed the forward momentum of the New Deal, hence the abolition of the NRPB for its impertinence in suggesting the expansion of Social Security and the economic bill of rights. National health insurance ignited a firestorm of denunciation from these conservatives, along with their allies in the business community—in particular the American Medical Association, the drug company lobby, and the insurance industry. The assault was more than rancorous. It transformed a controversy over a specific piece of legislation into a life-and-death struggle to preserve the "American way of life."

This was the Cold War come home, and nothing could stand in its way. For many people—Republicans, southern Democrats, and others—the real thrust of their anticommunism was directed against the New Deal. They loathed its affinity for big government and for racial and ethnic cosmopolitanism as well as its inherent collectivism, embodied in its attachment to the labor movement. Liberal foundations—Ford, Rockefeller, and Carnegie especially—were denounced as "philanthropoids" for plotting to enlarge the scope of planning and social insurance. What began with the startling wartime popularity of Frederick Hayek's *Road to Serfdom* (serialized in *Reader's Digest* in 1944) eventually became an irresistible persuasion aimed at dismantling not only the welfare state but all forms of government interference with the private economy (except when powerful interests in that sector needed the state's financial assistance to bail them out of difficulties) as well. Coddling by the government would only undermine that indigenous frontier capacity for confronting risk, the arena in which Americans traditionally tested their moral and masculine wherewithal.[31]

All this and more was at play fueling the animus against national health insurance and any other attempt to make the social insurance state more generous. Critics called the plan for health insurance an "Un-American System blue-printed in the Kremlin Headquarters of the Communist Internationale." The American Medical Association described proponents of the Wagner-Murray-Dingell Bill as those "who seriously believe in a Socialistic State." Republican congressmen echoed these claims. Others struck even closer to the bone, attacking the act as "a threat against American manhood. . . . It is high time for Americans to get some of the brawn of their pioneer forebears and quit being dainty, steam-heated, rubber-tired, beauty-rested, effeminized pampered sissies."[32]

In the teeth of this onslaught the Truman administration vacillated and then gave up. And as the Democratic Party foreshortened its social ambitions, so too did the labor movement. The whole notion that economic well-being, now and in the future, should be treated as a right of citizenship was shelved indefinitely.

Health insurance was, after all, a thriving commercial business, and insurance companies and others were determined to keep it so. Meanwhile, congressional Republicans worked to rein in the political power of organized labor and soon enough managed to do so with the passage of the Taft-Hartley Act. On the defensive, unions turned instead to collective bargaining, an arena they knew better and where their leverage was greater.[33]

Even during the war, the government had encouraged unions and employers to make pensions, health insurance, and other "fringe benefits" part of the collective-bargaining process. This was suggested in lieu of wage increases, which the agencies in charge of wartime economic mobilization were determined to keep under strict control to ward off the danger of hyperinflation. Once it became clear after the war that the New Deal was in retreat, the labor movement sought to meet its members' needs for collective thrift through private negotiations with their corporate counterparts, forsaking the political arena. The great postwar strike wave—beginning in 1945, continuing through much of the following year, erupting periodically thereafter for the rest of the decade, and affecting virtually every major industrial sector—helped persuade corporate America to give in. So too did the government: the Truman administration and the courts ruled that such matters fell properly within the province of the nation's collective-bargaining statutes.[34]

Moreover, business itself turned out to be a willing convert. To begin with, most of the commercial world had come to terms with Social Security. Indeed, so long as it remained limited in scope, the government's program provided a useful minimum standard that shifted some of the burden of sustaining its workforce from private enterprise. Corporations could add on to that minimum, and there was good reason to do so, for it cemented loyalties to the company; at least it could help divide the allegiances of workers between the company and their union. Compelling reasons of state were also deemed important. *Business Week* noted that "management . . . is faced with a broad social demand—the demand for security. But if management does not use it wisely, the worker is likely to transfer his demand from the bargaining table to the ballot box." The National Association of Manufacturers recognized the same dynamic: either business would recapture the leadership in providing for the workers' welfare or the task of collective thrift would fall increasingly on the shoulders of the government, an outcome far more dreaded by the private sector.[35]

So it was that many key corporations like General Motors and United States Steel entered into pension and health insurance agreements with trade unions that gave the unions some say over the parameters, if not actual control over the execution, of those plans. From the standpoint of management that meant relinquishing what historically had been their unilateral and paternalist right to bestow or rescind the benefits of collective thrift. This was painful as it transformed a corporate gratuity into a contractual right. Still, business could count on the fact that no government regulations governed the funding, investments, eligibility rules, or security of these benefit plans until the passage of the Employment Retirement and Security Act in 1974. Non-union employers in the postwar era also instituted or reinstituted their own versions of privatized but collective thrift (many corporate welfare plans had collapsed earlier during the Depression), often in order to fend off the allure of unionization. In some cases, workers contributed a portion of these insurance funds out of their paychecks; in other cases, companies bore the whole load. At the end of the day, it was a way to keep the government at arm's length and the unions at bay.[36]

By midcentury, then, a system of sorts was in place—a quasi-public, quasi-private form of collective thrift that protected millions of Americans and left millions of others out in the cold. By 1976, Social Security provided two-thirds of all retirement benefits, while 21 percent came from industrial plans and 13 percent from individual insurance arrangements. In the late 1970s, 49 percent of the private sector workforce, or about 40 million people, were covered by private, mainly noncontributory pension arrangements. About two-thirds of the workforce under the age of sixty-five enjoyed some form of private health insurance; for about 60 percent of these workers, insurance was provided by their employers. On the other hand, the United States, alone among the countries of the industrialized West, offered no universal health insurance. In 1977, public expenditures by the U.S. government on health insurance as a percentage of national health costs were the lowest of all the Organisation for Economic Co-operation and Development countries.[37]

The term *system* is a bit too grandiose to be used to describe what existed. The arrangement was fragmented and incoherent and, most of all, alive with contradictions. In turning to the arena of private collective bargaining, the labor movement thought it would grow stronger, partly by reinforcing the commitments of existing members to the institution and partly by providing an incentive for unorganized workers to join. To some degree that happened. But precisely that same dynamic weakened the will to carry on the struggle for state-subsidized social insurance. Indeed, the organized sector of the working class disliked being taxed twice (once to fund their corporate pensions, once to fund Social Security), and this situation helped incite a more general resentment directed at the welfare state. So the new labor movement, which had once championed the needs of all working-class Americans, increasingly represented only the narrower interests of its members. This was a fatal shift because the labor movement had always been the main engine powering the movement for social insurance. There are many reasons for the drastic decline in trade union strength over the last half century, but this partial abandonment of the public sector must count heavily.

The only important exception to that general tendency was the establishment of Medicare in 1965 to meet some of the medical needs of the elderly, a landmark reform that the labor movement helped achieve. Medicare was the main contribution of President Lyndon B. Johnson's Great Society to broadening social insurance for the working and middle classes. The federal government assumed the role of subsidizing and socializing the costs of hospital care for those over sixty-five years old. The program significantly reduced the number of older persons living in poverty, but it inscribed the fundamental lessons of the Society Security system of which it was a formal amendment. It functioned as a supplement to private insurance and helped undergird the profits of insurance companies, doctors, and hospitals. Medicare notwithstanding, trade unions looked mainly to their partners in business to deal with the inherent long-term riskiness of the market economy.[38]

This growing dependency on the private sector created just that—a dangerous dependency. Labor had deluded itself that once corporate America was forced to contribute to its own retirement and health insurance plans, it would find the costs intolerable and opt for national insurance. That proved sadly mistaken, but the danger only became fully apparent at the turn of the twenty-first century. One major corporation after another announced that its pension and health care plans were bankrupt or near bankrupt, that they could no longer shoulder their financial obligations to their unionized (or in other cases their nonunionized) employees, or that their ability to compete on the world market was severely crippled by their commitments to their aging workforce. And this was ironic not only from the standpoint of a labor movement that had invested so heavily in this form of privatized collective thrift; it was ironic as well for a business establishment that for years and years resisted most efforts at improving and expanding the coverage of public social insurance. They had won that battle, only to discover that in the age of global capitalism they were losing the war. And whatever sentiments might have once bound a worker to his or her company—thanks to its generous provisions for the future—withered away in a storm of outrage when the company reneged on its promises.

Back to the Future

Compared with most other countries, America has been spared much national misfortune. However, to fully explain the counterreformation against the social insurance state that marked the last quarter of the twentieth century, one must reckon with the enveloping and deeply disturbing sense of a United States in decline. Feelings of this sort were particularly ripe during the 1970s and for good reason.

Military defeat in Vietnam was one shock. Devaluation of the dollar was another. Moreover, their convergence signaled an even more fatal fall from grace. The United States entered a period of secular economic stagnation and decline that lasted twenty years, at least.

Signposts of decline appeared everywhere: in the ransoming of the West by the Organization of Petroleum Exporting Countries (OPEC) to the price of oil in 1973; in the jettisoning of fixed exchange rates that same year; in the desperate rooftop evacuation of the American embassy in Saigon; in the resignation of a president to save himself from impeachment; in the depressing economics of runaway inflation and high unemployment soon dubbed "stagflation"; in the woeful drop of the rate of savings; in President Jimmy Carter's hapless jeremiad about the country's descent into a quagmire of cultural narcissism; in President Gerald Ford's callous indifference to New York City's fiscal emergency (captured in the immortal headline in the *Daily News*: "Ford to City—'Drop Dead'"); in an uncharacteristic liberal pessimism about the "limits of growth"; in the damping down of the heartland's smokestack industries, soon labeled "the deindustrialization of America"; in the wounding realization that the Japanese had traded places with the United States, assuming the lead in technological development and economic growth; in the demoralizing erosion of middle-class income, which one writer aptly named "the hidden crash"; in the depressing statistic that American steel, once accounting for more than 65 percent of the world's output, now chipped in 15 percent, less than that of Spain or South Korea; and in the feelings of national impotence aroused by the sight of American hostages in Iran and by the pathetic failure of the effort to rescue them.[39]

The period of worldwide growth that followed World War II had come to an end and with it the willingness and wherewithal of corporate America and the state to sustain even the level of public-collective thrift that the postwar economic boom made possible. Japan and Germany, for example, might prosper—but now only at the expense of other industrial countries. In America this meant first and foremost that its industrial core, the pride and joy of American supremacy for three-quarters of a century, was burdened with antiquated technologies, huge administrative and bureaucratic overhead, higher labor costs, and a looming crisis of overcapacity. Innovation, productivity, wages, and savings—every vital sign of economic growth—slowed, stopped, or regressed.

Years before it became a presidential invocation, many yearned for the return of "morning in America" to break through the gloom and demoralization of the 1970s. So it was that beginning in 1980, that is, in the age of President Ronald Reagan, the country headed back to the future. If only the nation could return to the old verities abandoned long ago in the headlong enthusiasm for the New Deal, America might be America again. This view was promoted with a vengeance, especially regarding collective thrift. But what began as a systematic attempt to limit the reach of the social insurance state by providing alternative forms of privatized collective thrift turned into an extraordinary exercise in thriftless financial speculation.

In the nostalgic glow of hindsight, the Reagan years come down to us as a period of near-legendary rebirth. And as a matter of fact, after an initial recessionary dip (the steepest of the postwar era), the economy grew robustly for most of the 1980s. But the rise in the country's GNP concealed a more sober reality. Upper-class and upper-middle-class Americans were the disproportionate beneficiaries of that economic good news. Neither the public domain nor the standard living among middle-income and poorer citizens fared nearly as well, especially compared with the immediately preceding postwar era. And this increasing inequality of income and wealth had serious repercussions on the fate of collective thrift.

So, for example, while 3 percent of the country's GDP had been spent on development and renewal of infrastructure between 1950 and 1970, that figure dropped by two-thirds in the early 1980s. Median family income did not improve between 1973 and 1987, as most of the gains in GNP accrued to the top 20 percent of the population as measured by income. Real wages were no higher in 1990 than they had been in 1967. Net business investment in the mid-1980s was below the average prevailing rate of the 1950s, 1960s, and even the dolorous 1970s. Thus the rate of both business investment and personal savings declined together. At the same time, the national deficit tripled, mainly due to a vast expansion in the military budget and the Reagan administration's tax cuts, a deficit that further impeded the rate of new capital formation. The increase in military spending helped account for the rise of the GNP, but it would be extremely myopic to count that a thrifty use of American economic resources. The growth in productivity—a vital measure of a society's potential to provide for the future—averaged 2.8 percent annually during the 1950s and 1960s but fell to 1.2 percent during the 1970s and 1980s. The federal minimum wage provided a poverty-level income in 1980 but provided 30 percent less than that by 1990. Between 1977 and 1987 the average after-tax income of the lowest 10 percent of the population fell by 10.5 percent. While 14 percent of American children lived in poverty in the late 1960s, that figure had grown to 20 percent when Reagan left office. At the end of the decade, *Business Week* summed up where things stood: "That the Great Divide between rich and poor in America has widened is perhaps the most troubling legacy of the 1980s."[40]

Morning in America, at least from the standpoint of general economic well-being, thus turned out not so sunny if you lived on the wrong side of the street. And this was true from the outset of the Reagan administration.[41] Soon after Reagan took office, his administration launched an assault on Social Security. This was one piece of a broader legislative agenda that included deregulation, tax cuts, and shrink-wrapping the federal budget, except for a massive increase in defense expenditures. Milton and Rose Friedman published *Free to Choose*, a best-selling polemic against the Social Security system. The economic rationale for slicing away at Social Security was positively Machiavellian. Actuarial projections for the fund were premised on current earning levels and the rate of growth in earnings. This meant that in an economy like the one then prevalent, in which wages essentially stagnated and where most income was flowing instead to wealthy holders of such assets as stocks and bonds, wage-earning forecasts looked particularly grim. In turn, those dreary estimates fueled support for junking Social Security, neatly justifying a policy favored precisely by those business and financial interests most responsible for whatever shortfall might actually emerge.

It being "morning in America" once again, much of the Reagan program went down easily enough. But cutting Social Security proved politically indigestible, as Eisenhower had long ago predicted it would. What happened instead, however, was even more promising, at least from the standpoint of the business and financial communities.[42]

The Reagan era heralded what some have characterized as the "financialization of the economy." Capital flowed at reduced amounts into new plant and equipment and even less into technological innovations and other forms of long-term productive investment, once the best evidence of capitalist thrift. As a matter of fact, the 1980s underperformed even the notoriously sluggish 1970s in this regard, falling far below the levels achieved during the years of the postwar boom. Instead, an inviting and bewildering array of short-term financial speculations absorbed the lion's share of liquid capital. Mergers and acquisitions financed by junk bonds and other high-risk securities, initial public offerings in the stock of companies more virtual than real, speculation in commercial real estate reminiscent of the 1920s, trading in the arcane "derivatives" of homelier forms of debt like mortgages and government bonds, hedging short-term investments in commodities and energy markets, and global speculations in the currencies and economies of far-flung nations (rechristened "emerging markets") all proved irresistible to financial institutions. From the standpoint of the economy as a whole it amounted to a kind of negative thrift. No matter, these core financial institutions were no longer content with the modest rates of return available in the country's industrial heartland; indeed, more, much more could be made speculating in the dismantling of American heavy industry. And thanks to deregulation and the triumph of free-market ideology, no one needed to worry overmuch about government supervision of even the most questionable dealings.[43]

Where was all the money to set in motion this adventure in wholesale financial speculation coming from? In an irony of historic proportions, a great deal of it was increasingly funded by those gigantic pools of capital collecting in the major centers of collective thrift. Corporate pension funds, public-employee pension funds, and, most infamously, savings and loan institutions found themselves neck deep in these highly risky undertakings. The Employee Retirement Income Security Act, which was designed to safeguard pension funds, also thereby helped channel savings—in an era noted for low growth, perilously low rates of individual savings, and low levels of capital formation—into the financial services industry.

The savings and loan debacle of the late 1980s best captured the black humor of this historic reversal. It was, after all, New Deal legislation that helped save savings banks, insuring them so that they could perform their true function as "thrifts" and make home building and ownership safe and widespread. The term itself, *thrifts*, was coined back then as a cautionary reminder that unchecked capitalism was not reliably thrifty. But the new, finance-driven economy of the Reagan era undermined that purpose. Regulations governing the rates that savings and loan associations could pay their depositors and, even more important, regulations governing these institutions' nonmortgage investments were lifted. President Reagan pronounced this "the Emancipation Proclamation for American savings institutions." Free of those constraints and anxious to compete for funds with other, higher-performing investment outlets, the whole savings and loan industry became a source of speculative money and was itself an object of speculation until it sank beneath a wave of bankruptcies, saved only by a $175 billion government bailout—that is, a bailout by the American taxpayers, in an involuntary act of socialized risk.

The "thrifts" were not alone. Beginning with the rise of Michael Milken (the "king of junk bonds" in the mid-1980s) and continuing through IPO frenzy of the 1990s, pension funds, those presumably providently cautious and far-sighted institutions charged with watching out for the future well-being of ordinary working people, were implicated in a global high-wire world of rogue traders, insider conspiracies, and market bubbles. In 1999, employee pension funds accounted for $13 trillion. Three-fifths of that was owned by U.S. policyholders.[44]

Watching the explosive growth of pension funds after the war, celebrated management guru Peter Drucker had prophesied something he called, perhaps partly in jest, "pension fund socialism." Others more to the left took that prospect seriously—in particular, Jeremy Rifkin and Randy Barber did so in their book *The North Will Rise Again*. Drucker viewed privatized collective thrift as an alternative both to the free market and to big government. Pension funds as collective but nongovernmental institutions operated within the framework of private enterprise yet were set up to provide social goods. But this turned out to be more fable than fact: such thinking grossly underestimated the purely capitalist and speculative motivations—"shareholder value"—driving these funds. Policyholders proved powerless to deploy savings as an economic lever to advance the interests of working families or their communities. Rifkin and Barber pointed out that unless unions assumed some of the prerogatives of management, the pension funds they invested in often as not undermined union strength, as they propped up antiunion corporations and financed corporate reengineerings that closed plants and helped companies relocate abroad. Moreover, the use of pension monies to fuel the reorientation of the economy was complemented by the deliberate fostering of a vast contingent workforce; "temps" were free agents to whom corporations owed no long-term obligations regarding their health, retirement, or welfare.[45]

Free-market theory and practice shifted the center of gravity of privatized collective thrift. Defined benefit plans, where the employer shouldered the risk and always contributed at least a portion of the retirement funds, were gradually supplanted by defined contribution plans, in which the employee assumed the burden of future financial calamities and the employer was less likely to pony up a share of the funds. In 1981, 37 percent of U.S. workers were covered by defined benefit pensions; by 1995 that percentage had dropped to 23 percent. Employer contributions to defined benefit plans fell from $61 billion in 1978 to $18.9 billion in 1990. At the same time, a new form of pension arrangement, soon known by its Internal Revenue Service designation as a 401(k) plan, further encouraged an individualist approach to thrift. It proved enormously popular. By 2002, 88 percent of workers with pensions were enrolled in 401(k) plans or in profit-sharing or stock option plans—that is, arrangements in which employees assumed the lion's share of the contribution and most of the risk. These arrangements seemed on the surface to resemble traditional forms of savings and self-reliance. Actually, the situation was quite different because 401(k)s simultaneously functioned as leverage for present consumption (the accounts could be drawn on for certain purposes before retirement) and as a tax-avoidance device and, therefore, were inherently more risky. An economy that had become so oriented to immediate gratification and speculative gambling found it difficult to really return to a world of delayed gratification and an economics of productive thrift.[46]

So long as the good times continued to roll on through the 1990s and even after the bursting of the dot-com stock market bubble, practical and ideological justifications for this state of affairs were easy to find. Secretary of the Treasury Paul O'Neill, gearing up for the frontal assault on Social Security that would usher in the second administration of George W. Bush, advised that "able-bodied adults should save enough on a regular basis so that they can provide for their own retirement and for that matter for their health and medical needs."[47] As conservative pundit George Will remembered, "Time was when Americans savored freedom's uncertainties and considered 'security' an unworthy goal for a free people."[48] As the new millennium began, however, more and more "able-bodied" people were tasting just this kind of uncertainty and finding it less savory than Will or O'Neill anticipated. By the mid-1990s, well over 40 million workers and their dependents were without health insurance. Corporations continued to shed their welfare plans so that a majority of businesses no longer offered health insurance of any kind. Termination of corporate pension plans began as a trickle in the 1980s but reached a flood tide in the opening years of the twenty-first century. Household names of American business—Bethlehem Steel, Lucent Technologies, Polaroid—found they could no longer afford what decades earlier they had promised their employees to keep them loyal and immune to the lure of "statism." Only 30 percent of the private sector workforce enjoyed pension coverage by the mid-1990s, and that percentage continued to drop as companies like General Motors and the country's major airlines tried to survive by abandoning the sinking ship of collective thrift.[49]

President Bush began his second term determined to privatize Social Security. He failed. Eisenhower proved prophetic again as the most popular legacy of the New Deal continued to function as the third rail of American politics. Nonetheless, collective thrift in both its public and private forms remained an endangered species. Consumer culture continued to eat away at the instinct to save for the future. The rate of individual household savings—already the lowest in the West by the 1970s—actually went negative in 2005. The "financialization" of the economy rewarded short-term speculation instead of long-term investment. A national infatuation with the stock market encouraged a broader inclination to seek individual or private solutions to all economic dilemmas. Worldwide industrialization inexorably undermined the resource and environmental base of future economic well-being, assuming that existing technologies, forms of industrial organization, and free-market deregulation remained in place.

In the United States at least, this global improvidence at the top, among the wealthy and the corporate elite, was blamed instead on the thriftless working poor who, it was argued, needed to do better at saving and planning for the future. The welfare reform of the Clinton administration gave this legislative force. This paring away at the welfare state was advertised as a way of improving the thriftiness of public finance. Such scrupulousness, however, was applied selectively with special emphasis on the poor. Welfare reform was more pointedly a reversion to the weak state, the natural default position of an economy headed back to the virginal condition of the unencumbered free market.

Meanwhile, the pension and health insurance funds of American corporations were in deep crisis; or, conversely, American corporations found themselves in crisis thanks in part to their pension and health insurance obligations. The population of the medically uninsured continued to grow. Stories of corporate malfeasance that frittered away the security of loyal employees still commanded headlines. The specter of global warming became steadily more frightening. Might these multiple dilemmas revive interest in new forms of social insurance and collective thrift? Proposals for socialized capital investments and planning run against the American grain. Once, under duress, they received a hearing. What made all the difference then was the mobilization of popular movements for social justice and their incorporation into a potent political coalition. If indeed modern capitalism is subject to an inherent thriftlessness, new collective remedies may be headed our way again.[50]

Notes

1. Alan Derickson, "Health Security for All? Social Unionism and Universal Health Insurance, 1935–1958," *Journal of American History* 80 (March 1994): 1333–56.

2. William Graham Sumner, *What Social Classes Owe Each Other* (1883; New York: Harper, 1961), 53.

3. Andrew Mellon, quoted in Otis L. Graham Jr., *Toward a Planned Society: From Roosevelt to Nixon* (New York: Oxford University Press, 1976), 4.

4. Rudolph Goldscheid, "A Sociological Approach to Problems of Public Finance," in *Classics in the Theory of Public Finance*, ed. Richard A. Musgrave and Alan T. Peacock (New York: St. Martin's Press, 1958).

5. Robin Blackburn, *Banking on Death, or Investing in Life: The History and Future of Pensions* (New York: Verso, 2002), 35.

6. Daniel Bell, *The Cultural Contradictions of Capitalism* (New York: Basic Books, 1976), 20.

7. Irving Fisher, quoted in Steve Fraser, *Every Man a Speculator: A History of Wall Street in American Life* (New York: HarperCollins, 2005), 399.

8. *Report of the President's Conference on Unemployment* (Washington, DC: Government Printing Office, 1921), 21–23, 159, 163–65.

9. Marc Allan Eisner, *The State in the American Political Economy* (Englewood Cliffs, NJ: Prentice Hall, 1995), 151–52, 153.

10. Arthur A. Ekich Jr., *Ideologies and Utopias: The Impact of the New Deal on American Thought* (New York: Quadrangle Books, 1969), 51–56.

11. Alan Brinkley, *The End of Reform: New Deal Liberalism in Recession and War* (New York: Knopf, 1995), 35.

12. Brinkley, *End of Reform*, 35; Eisner, *The State*, 163; Graham, *Toward a Planned Society*, 13.

13. Franklin Roosevelt, quoted in Eisner, *The State*, 165.

14. Graham, *Toward a Planned Society*, 18–19.

15. Richard Parker, *John Kenneth Galbraith: His Life, His Politics, His Economics* (New York: Farrar, Straus and Giroux, 2005); Eisner, *The State*, 170; Graham, *Toward a Planned Society*, 44–45; Ekich, *Ideologies and Utopias*, 118.

16. Rexford Tugwell, quoted in Brinkley, *End of Reform*, 34.

17. Brinkley, *End of Reform*, 39–40.

18. Franklin Roosevelt, quoted in Graham, *Toward a Planned Society*, 20–21, 39.

19. Fraser, *Every Man*, 450–52.

20. Brinkley, *End of Reform*, 247–49; David E. Wilson, *The National Planning Idea in United States Public Policy: Five Alternative Approaches* (Boulder, CO: Westview Press, 1980), 30, 32; Graham, *Toward a Planned Society*, 37–40.

21. Franklin Roosevelt, State of the Union address, January 11, 1944.

22. Brinkley, *End of Reform*, 251–55, 260–61.

23. Ibid., 255, 263; Wilson, *National Planning Idea*, 41; Graham, *Toward a Planned Society*, 67.

24. Parker, *John Kenneth Galbraith*; John Kenneth Galbraith, *Economics and the Public Purpose* (Boston: Houghton Mifflin, 1973), 221–22, 278–79; Wilson, *National Planning Idea*, 61, 66. From the Marxist Left, James O'Connor mounted an argument in *The Fiscal Crisis of the State* (New York: St. Martin's Press, 1973) that certain forms of planning had become a necessity in the age of monopoly capitalism.

25. Daniel Wadhwami, "Banking from the Bottom Up: The Case of Migrant Savers and the Philadelphia Savings Fund Society," *Financial History Review* 9 (April 2002): 41–63; Beth Stevens, "Labor Unions, Employee Benefits, and the Privatization of the American Welfare State," *Journal of Policy History* 2 (1990): 233–60; Jennifer Klein, *For All These Rights: Business, Labor, and the Shaping of America's Public-Private Welfare State* (Princeton, NJ: Princeton University Press, 2003), 16–17; Teresa Ghilarducci, *Labor's Capital: The Economics and Politics of Private Pensions* (Cambridge, MA: MIT Press, 1992), 17; Sanford M. Jacoby, *Modern Manors: Welfare Capitalism since the New Deal* (Princeton, NJ: Princeton University Press, 1997), 4.

26. Nelson Lichtenstein, "Labor in the Truman Era: Origins of the 'Private Welfare State,'" in *The Truman Presidency*, ed. Michael J. Lacey (New York: Woodrow Wilson International Center for Scholars and Cambridge University, 1989); Brinkley, *End of Reform*, 204.

27. Klein, *For All These Rights*, 79–81; Blackburn, *Banking on Death*, 53; Jacoby, *Modern Manors*, 206, 214.

28. Dwight Eisenhower, quoted in Blackburn, *Banking on Death*, 56.

29. Colin Gordon, "Why No Health Insurance in the United States? The Limits of Social Provision in War and Peace, 1941–1948," *Journal of Policy History* 9 (1997): 277–310; Klein, *For All These Rights*, 11–13, 81, 109.

30. Yair Aharoni, *No-Risk Society* (New York: Chatham House, 1981), 79–80; Stevens, "Labor Unions"; Jennifer Klein, "The Politics of Economic Security: Employee Benefits and the Privatization of New Deal Liberalism," *Journal of Policy History* 16 (2004): 34–65; Klein, *For All These Rights*, 138, 140, 151, 160, 172.

31. Aharoni, *No-Risk Society*; Alice O'Connor, "The Politics of Rich and Rich: Postwar Investigations of Foundations and the Rise of the Philanthropic Right," in *American Capitalism: Social Thought and Political Economy in the Twentieth Century*, ed. Nelson Lichtenstein (Philadelphia: University of Pennsylvania Press, 2006), 228–48.

32. Gordon, "Why No Health Insurance"; Derickson, "Health Security for All?"

33. Stevens, "Labor Unions"; Derickson, "Health Security for All?"

34. Gordon, "Why No Health Insurance."

35. Klein, "Politics of Economic Security"; Klein, *For All These Rights*, 5.

36. Klein, *For All These Rights*, 3–5; Ghilarducci, *Labor's Capital*, 20.

37. Aharoni, *No-Risk Society*, 79–80; Klein, *For All These Rights*, 258–59.

38. Klein, *For All These Rights*, 258–64; Wilson, *National Planning Idea*, 61.

39. Kevin Phillips, *Wealth and Democracy: A Political History of the American Rich* (New York: Random House, 2002), 83–88; Haynes Johnson, *Sleepwalking through History: America in the Reagan Years* (New York: Anchor Books, 1992), 118.

40. Karen Pennar, "The Free Market Has Triumphed, but What about the Losers?" *Business Week*, September 25, 1989, 178, quoted in Kevin Philips, *Wealth and Democracy: A Political History of the American Rich* (New York: Broadway Books, 2002), 47.

41. Robert M. Collins, *Transforming America: Politics and Culture in the Reagan Years* (New York: Columbia University Press, 2007), 76, 88, 90, 131; David Harvey, *A Brief History of Neoliberalism* (New York: Oxford University Press, 2005), 15–16, 25; Kevin Phillips, *The Politics of Rich and Poor* (New York: Random House, 1990), 8, 11, 14, 15, 18, 24, 70, 87, 110–11, 126–28, 200, 207; Paul Krugman, *The Age of Diminished Expectations* (Cambridge, MA: MIT Press, 1990), 1, 12, 21; Stephen Pimpare, *The New Victorians: Poverty, Politics, and Propaganda in Two Gilded Ages* (New York: New Press, 2004).

42. Blackburn, *Banking on Death*, 359.

43. Fraser, *Every Man*, chap. 18; Blackburn, *Banking on Death*, 163–64, 175; Kevin Phillips, *Wealth and Democracy: A Political History of the American Rich* (New York: Random House, 2002).

44. Blackburn, *Banking on Death*, 5–6, 131–32, 175; Ghilarducci, *Labor's Capital*, ix.

45. Blackburn, *Banking on Death*, 10, 11, 78; Ghilarducci, *Labor's Capital*, 78, 112, 129–30; Jacoby, *Modern Manors*.

46. Klein, *For All These Rights*, 265–67; Blackburn, *Banking on Death*, 79.

47. Paul O'Neill, quoted in Klein, *For All These Rights*, 273.

48. George Will, quoted in ibid., 25.

49. Derickson, "Health Security for All?"

50. Aharoni, *No-Risk Society*, 106; *Nation*, March 27, 2006.

19 }

Middle-Class Respectability in Twenty-First-Century America

WORK AND LIFESTYLE IN THE PROFESSIONAL-MANAGERIAL STRATUM

Steven Brint and Kristopher Proctor

Before the Great Recession of 2008, it appeared that we in the United States were living in a "postthrift" society. On many contemporary measures—from low individual savings rates to soaring levels of consumer debt to a ballooning national deficit—there were good empirical reasons to think so. It was tempting to conclude that the virtue of thrift in its classical sense as frugality had been largely forgotten. At least we heard little of it, especially from the educated professionals and managers who were once its chief proponents. Indeed, a popular notion existed that highly educated professionals were more liberal in their spending habits, as well as more free-thinking in their moral outlooks, than other Americans. They were cast by some as a "new class" or "new elite" opposed to traditional bourgeois virtues.[1]

The Great Recession changed the circumstances of professionals and managers. Some lost their jobs or their clients, and their savings rates, like those of other Americans, began to rise. Yet as the country crept out of its recessionary woes, professionals and managers—who were in any event among the least affected—began to return, however chastened and cautiously, to the styles of life they had practiced in the pre-crash years.

As other essays in this volume attest, the meanings of thrift have shifted with transformations in the structure and expression of capitalism throughout American history; accordingly, we find members of the professional-managerial stratum enacting thrift in different ways today than did their nineteenth-century predecessors. To see the importance of the professional-managerial stratum for the unfolding story of thrift in the present era, it is essential to understand how historical forms of thrift (and, in particular, frugality) are but one historical expression of society's sense of what it means to practice thrift in its original sense—as the attitudes and behaviors conducive to *thriving* in society.

Two Eras of Professionalism

Professionalism was transformed during the course of the nineteenth and early twentieth centuries. The professional stratum grew dramatically, as more and more people in new specialized occupations requiring advanced training—from agronomists and city planners to investment counselors and management consultants—claimed professional status based on their educational qualifications, the intellectual skills and formal knowledge those qualifications conveyed, and standards of ethical conduct promulgated by their professional associations.[2] In Magali Sarfatti Larson's apt phrase, many occupations engaged in "collective mobility projects" by finding a place in university curricula, adopting licensing requirements, and walling off jurisdictions of practice based on a monopoly of qualified practitioners.[3]

For the historian Burton Bledstein, the "culture of professionalism" during this period emphasized the material comforts, respectability, and career ambitions of middle-class life. Middle-class respectability and striving were combined with ideals of rationalism, mental concentration, self-control, and the dedicated commitment to work that was the mark of a distinctively intellectualized form of asceticism. "A person's work was more than an unrelated series of jobs and projects. . . Work was the person: a statement to the world of his internal resources, confidence, and discipline; his active control over the intrinsic relationships of a life, his steadfast character."[4] The model professional was "self-reliant, independent, ambitious, and mentally organized." He was also highly protective of the autonomy he was granted in the name of a "specialized grasp of a meaningful universe."[5] As compared with businessmen of similar economic standing, professionals shared little among themselves but a claim to autonomy on the job based on their advanced educational training and a penchant for rationalizing social relations around a body of formal knowledge.

At first, the ideology of fiduciary responsibilities to society continued as part of professionals' claim for respect and deference.[6] The classic expression of this ideology is found in a passage by R. H. Tawney written in the 1920s:

> [Professionals] may, as in the case of the successful doctor, grow rich, but the meaning of their profession, both for themselves and for the public, is not that they make money, but that they make health, or safety, or knowledge, or good government, or good law. . . . [Professions uphold] as the criterion of success the end for which the profession, whatever it may be, is carried on, and [subordinate] the inclination, appetites, and ambition of individuals to the rules of an organization which has as its object to promote the performance of function.[7]

For Tawney and many other advocates for the professions, these "functions" were activities that embodied and expressed the idea of larger social purposes. Of course, the expression of high-minded ideals in public settings might very well go hand in hand with conspicuous displays of extravagance at the private banquets that immediately followed. For all their expressions of devotion to ideals of service, it is an open question whether professionals were in fact any more self-denying than businessmen of similar social rank.

A second important ideal developed in the course of the late nineteenth and early twentieth centuries as an alternative to "social trustee professionalism." This ideal of "expert professionalism" emphasized the instrumental effectiveness of specialized, theoretically grounded knowledge, and it included comparatively little concern with collegial organization, ethical standards, or service in the public interest. Experts applied skills and judgment to problems defined by others. Experts justified themselves on the basis of productivity and progress, not on their contributions to values underlying social order. Gradually, and with an increasing pace from the 1960s on, expressions of the high-minded ideals of "social trustee professionalism" gave way and were replaced by this less socially conscious stance of "expert professionalism." Expert professionalism eschewed a broader social legitimacy and, therefore, provided no moral glue to bind a class.

As professional ideals and political outlooks splintered,[8] perhaps the only element that remained constant was the striving for middle-class respectability. But the contours of what it meant to embody "middle-class respectability" changed in the later twentieth century. Middle-class respectability required self-discipline in activities related to professional training, work, community life, and family social reproduction, but it allowed self-expression and pleasure seeking in activities related to consumption. There was, in this sense, a tension between self-restraint and self-expression, albeit a tension most professionals and managers found easy enough to reconcile.

Defining the Professional-Managerial Stratum

Some brief words of definition are in order. Professional occupations include all those involving nonroutine mental work, usually based on training in an academic discipline, leading to a high degree of autonomy in the workplace and requiring judgment based on both work experience and academic training for the analysis and solution of work-related problems.[9] Professional occupations range from certified public accountants and tax lawyers to fiction writers, ministers, and professors. They also include scientists and engineers, architects and urban planners, therapists, schoolteachers, nurses, and social workers. Educated managers share some of these occupational characteristics (autonomy, work on complex problems, formal training) but are, in addition, expected to keep the broad organizational vision in mind, to advocate organizational teamwork, and to show loyalty to the organizational chain of command. The consequences of holding organizational authority do in some respects distinguish managers from nonmanaging professionals. In terms of their political attitudes and party identifications, for example, the two are clearly distinct; managers are much more likely to say they are conservatives and to identify with the Republican Party.[10] Nevertheless, highly educated professionals and managers can be defined as a distinct stratum , even as a "social class" in the Weberian sense: They have common educational experiences and work in occupations of similar prestige. They interact on familiar and more or less equal terms. They live in the same neighborhoods. And their children intermarry.

The stratum is defined by the conjunction of occupational and educational characteristics. It includes all those in professional and managerial occupations who hold baccalaureate or higher level degrees. This grouping includes 80 percent of census professionals and 50 percent of census managers[11] —altogether just over 15 percent of the U.S. labor force.[12] Overlapping with the professional-managerial stratum in income and wealth are independent small business people who have made their way without the benefit of higher education. Below it lie the vast majority of Americans who work in technician, sales, clerical, blue-collar or service occupations. Above it stand the 1 percent or so of the wealthy whose fortunes derive from executive positions, celebrity, or inheritance.

Professional-Managerial Culture: Is Self-Expression All?

Many conservatives subscribe to the idea that highly educated professionals have become opponents of bourgeois virtues, because they follow the lead of intellectuals rather than businesspeople. But the empirical evidence does not support this claim. Far from following a liberal-spending and hedonistic ethos, highly educated professionals show a profile of moderation consistent with their interests in middle-class respectability. The same can be said for highly educated managers. We can show this by comparing their behavior on measures of economic and behavioral restraint to those of other Americans.

ECONOMIC RESTRAINT

Indebtedness is largely a function of (low) income. Consumer goods and services cost more than they have in the past. Controlling for inflation, the median earner in the United States has essentially the same income now and as he or she had twenty-five years earlier, and the incomes of the bottom fifth have declined.[13] Not surprisingly, a disproportionate increase in credit card debt has occurred among lower-income Americans—those with annual incomes less than $25,000.[14] Many low-income families are carrying credit card debt nearly half the size of the family's annual income. Bankruptcy follows a similar course. The average earnings of chapter 7 bankruptcy filers in 1996 were $19,800, and they held a slightly higher-than-average amount of credit card debt—$17,500.[15] People who declare bankruptcy are spread across the spectrum of American society, but they are distinct in one way: their incomes are much lower than those of the average family. The causes of low income are numerous but most often involve loss of work, high credit card balances, divorce, losses on housing, and unexpected or uninsured health expenses.[16]

Savings rates are also income-sensitive. The year 2005 was the first year since the Great Depression that Americans spent more than they earned.[17] The average personal savings rate was at −0.4 percent, down from +2 percent in 2004.[18] Following the stock market collapse of 2008, personal savings rates moved back into positive territory.[19] More than one-quarter of families live from paycheck to paycheck.[20] The only economic variable significantly related to savings is income; education is not positively related to savings once income is controlled.[21] If professionals and managers save more than others, it is because they have more income than others.

Although professionals and managers are not in the vanguard of economic waste, neither are they at the head of the class in wealth accumulation. Studies suggest that the classic wealth accumulator is a self-employed entrepreneur, who spends many hours on financial planning, knows as much as any expert about investing, and does not care for lavish material displays.[22] These wealth accumulators tend to live on 7 percent or less of their net worth each year, and surprisingly few drive expensive cars or own expensive suits, watches, or shoes. Many professionals earn high salaries, but they do not necessarily spend long hours on financial planning, and they do not necessarily live frugally. One study of high-income earners (those earning at least $100,000 in the mid-1990s) found a *negative* relationship between education and wealth accumulation. The authors suggest that social expectations make a difference:

> Doctors, lawyers, accountants and (other professionals) are expected to live in expensive homes. They also are expected to dress and drive in a style congruent with their ability to perform their professional duties. . . .Many people judge professionals by display factors. Extra points are given to those who wear expensive clothes, drive luxury automobiles, and live in exclusive neighborhoods. They assume a professional is likely to be mediocre, even incompetent, if he lives in a modest home and drives an old car.[23]

The same could be as aptly said of corporate managers. Net of other significant covariates, total real consumption is significantly higher for people with high incomes and college educations, for those who are married and have children, and for people who live in cities.[24]

BEHAVIORAL RESTRAINT

Professionals and managers are not, on balance, more hedonistic than other Americans, and on most measures they are less so. Social drinking, for example, is widespread in American society. According to the General Social Survey (GSS) 1991–99 (the last time these issues were addressed in the GSS), white-collar workers (including professionals and managers) were somewhat more likely than blue-collar workers to say they have ever had a drink (roughly 75 percent compared with 60 percent) but less likely to say they ever drank to excess. Perhaps because of travel, managers and business professionals (such as marketing specialists) were more likely than others to say they spent time in a bar at least once a month. Human services professionals (such as teachers and social workers) were less likely to say they had had a drink or spent time at a bar.[25]

The use of non-prescription drugs is much less common among Americans than social drinking. No groups are very likely to say they use non-prescription drugs, though, judging from police statistics, the use of hard drugs is more common among the poor. Many college students experiment with marijuana, but few use it later in life.[26] The use of sleeping pills and neuroenhancers, however, may be higher among professionals and managers than among people from other strata in American society[27].

Professionals have been slightly less likely than others to be gamblers or to participate in lotteries, though all strata in American society include a sizable portion of recreational gamblers. In the 1990s and early 2000s, more than 80 percent of Americans said they had gambled during the last year, but only about one-quarter said they gambled weekly.[28] Higher SES groups were less likely to gamble often, and they were more likely to wager small amounts.[29] Lottery participation rates were also high (near or above 50 percent) in all occupational groups.[30] but again higher SES groups were less likely to participate and those who did participate spent smaller amounts.[31]

By contrast, the attitudes of professionals and managers toward sex are comparatively liberal-minded; they have, for example, been less likely than members of other strata to frown on premarital sex, to think of homosexuality as intolerable, or to think that using pornography leads to moral breakdown.[32] These more liberal attitudes are associated, not only with higher levels of education, but with lower levels of religiosity, urban residence, and youth. Those who work in the arts and culture industries have distinctly more liberal attitudes about sex than other professionals or managers.[33] Conventional mores, however, tend to rule when it comes to sexual behavior. According to GSS data from the 1990s and early 2000s, married people regardless of job category rarely admit to sexual behaviors that break the vows of marriage. Minorities of unmarried professionals and managers reported behaviors that could be interpreted as treating sex in a casual manner. Such behaviors include having had a one-night sexual encounter in the last year (35 percent), having had sex with an acquaintance in the last year (31 percent), or ever having paid for or been paid for sex (9 percent). Less than one-quarter of professionals or managers said they had had twelve or more sexual partners in their lifetimes. The figures for unmarried professionals and managers were similar to those for unmarried people from other social strata.[34]

In sum, because educated professionals and managers have more to lose than most people, they are more likely to be prudent about finances and less likely than others to engage in behaviors that could become costly. Traditional norms of middle-class respectability, dating from the nineteenth century, remain strong in some areas, such as personal finance. They have changed in other areas due to the widespread acceptance of social drinking, recreational gambling, and sexual pleasure. These practices, evident in the 1920s among young, highly educated urbanites, became accepted in the broader U.S. adult population by the mid-1970s.[35]

Social Theory and Professional-Managerial Culture

What, then, are the truly distinctive patterns of work and lifestyle in the professional-managerial stratum? And how do these patterns reflect contemporary conditions for thriving?

Sociological theory provides a few useful heuristics for answering these questions. The work of Daniel Bell is particularly notable because Bell was the first sociologist to illuminate the duality in contemporary American culture between self-discipline at work and self-expression in consumption, a keynote also of our interpretation. Bell argued that self-discipline and deferred gratification were necessary to produce and reproduce economic success in a competitive capitalist society. At the same time, self-expression and pleasure seeking were avidly promoted by consumer marketing and encouraged also by affluence. Bell worried that consumer culture, following the trail blazed by nineteenth-century bohemian intellectuals' rejections of bourgeois virtues, could subvert the self-discipline required to maintain a highly productive capitalist economy. For Bell, the tensions between self-denial and pleasure seeking represented the "cultural contradictions of capitalism."[36]

Our interpretation is influenced by Bell's sense of tension between the spheres of work and leisure.[37] Unlike Bell, however, we see no contradiction between the norms of the workplace and those of the consumer marketplace. Indeed, self-discipline at work and pleasure seeking in consumption may reflect the natural disposition of people living in a society simultaneously defined by "bureaucratic-corporate" and mass-consumption values, and this combination should be particularly prevalent among those who are among the most responsible for, and have among the most to gain from, this society.[38] Moreover, an element of play exists in the work, and an element of work in the play, of professionals and managers. Nor is it always possible to separate discipline and pleasure; many people report strong feelings of pleasure in performing acts that might seem to require self-denial, such as helping others through community volunteering.[39] Thus, against Bell we argue that self-restraint and self-expression are neither decisively separated in the spheres of work and leisure nor necessarily opposed in orientation. Work governs the material conditions of life and provides discipline-based opportunities for self-realization; consumption and community relationships govern ideal representations of self (and family) and provide expression-based opportunities for self-realization. They are in harmony more than they are in tension, because self-realization is attainable mainly by those who are both highly self-disciplined and capable of non-conformity in thought and action.

Our interpretation also draws selectively on the work of Pierre Bourdieu. As an analyst of taste cultures, Bourdieu focused on the distribution of two forms of "capital." Economic capital (measured by income and wealth) disposed its holders toward conspicuous status display through purchase of expensive consumer goods, such as luxury homes and cars. By contrast, cultural capital (measured by high levels of education and particularly education in the arts and humanities) disposed its holders toward conspicuous displays of learning and refined taste.[40] Bourdieu's mapping of the distribution of "capitals" led him to identify a division of between managers and business-oriented professionals on one side, and professionals in the culture industries (academe, media, the arts) and the public and non-profit sectors on the other. We find some evidence of this division in American society, not only in consumption patterns but in political views. But we also find that some views Bourdieu associated with economic capital—such as orientation to economic status signals—influence many more people in the stratum than he suggests. Similarly, some views he associated with cultural capital—particularly the cosmopolitan interest in other cultures—have taken on a more defining role within the stratum than he seems to suggest.[41]

Time-Use Indicators

Time use studies show, in broad strokes, the distinctive interplay of self-discipline and self-expression in the professional-managerial stratum. The data presented in table 19.1 show that highly educated people worked longer hours on average than

TABLE 19.1 } American's Use of Time, 1985

BACKGROUND FA CTOR	Biological			Status			Role				Temporal		Ecological	
									Parenthood					
	Sex	*Age*	*Race*	*Educ.*	*Income*	*Occupa-tion*	*Work Hours*	*Marital Status*	*P18*	*P5*	*Season*	*Day of Week*	*Urban or Rural*	*Region*
	Female	Older	Black	College	High	Prof	High	Married	Yes	Yes	Summer	Weekend	Urban	South
Contracted Time														
Work	---	-,+	0	+	+	+	++++	0	0	-	0	----	0	+
Work Related Travel	-	-,+	0	+	+	0	+++	+	0	-	0	---	-	+
Committed Time														
House Work	++++	+++	-	-	0	0	---	+++	++	+	0	+	+	0
Child Care	+++	--	0	0+	0	0	--	+++	+++	+++	0	-	0	0
Shopping	++	0	-	+	0	0	--	+	0	0	0	0	0	-
Personal Time														
Sleep	0	0	0	-	0	-	--	0	0	0	0	+++	0	0
Meals	-	++	-	0	0	0	0	0	-	-	0	+	0	+
Groom	+	0	+	-	0	0	0	-	0	-	+	+	0	0

Free Time														
Education	0	---	0	+	0	0	--	---	-	--	-	-	0	-
Religion	+	++	++	0	-	0	-	0	0	0	-	+++	+	+
Organization	0	++	0	+	0	0	0	+	0	0	0	+	+	0
Cultural activities	0	--	-	++	+	0	0	0	0	0	+	++	0	0
Visiting	0	-	0	0	0	0	0	--	-	-	0	+++	0	0
Sports	--	-	0	0	0	0	0	-	0	0	+	++	+	0
Hobbies	0	0	0	0	0	0	-	-	0	-	0	+	0	-
Communication	+	0	0	0	-	0	-	-	-	0	0	+	0	-
TV	-	0+	++	---	--	-	-	0	-	0	--	++	0	+
Read	0	++	-	++	0	0	-	0	-	-	-	++	-	-
Stereo	0	0	+	-	-	0	0	-	0	0	-	0	0	0
Total free	0	+-	0	0	-	-	---	--	-	--	0	+++	0	-
Travel	-	-	0	++	++	+	+	0	+	-	0	0	0	-

Source: Robinson and Godbey (1997), p. 190.

Note: Symbols in this table should be interpreted as follows: Zero (0) means no significant relationship. One symbol (+ or –) represents correlation coefficients ranging from .05–.09; two symbols represent correlation coefficients ranging from .10–.19; three symbols represent correlation coefficients ranging from .20–.29; four symbols represent correlation coefficients above .30. Signs (+ or –) represent the direction of the correlation.

TABLE 19.2 } American's Use of Time, 2004

BACKGROUND FACTOR	Biological			Status			Role				Temporal		Ecological	
									Parenthood					
	Sex	*Age*	*Race*	*Educ.*	*Income*	*Occupation*	*Work Hours*	*Marital Status*	*P18*	*P5*	*Season*	*Day of Week*	*Urban or Rural*	*Region*
	Female	Older	Black	College	High	Prof	High	Married	Yes	Yes	Summer	Weekend	Urban	South
Contracted Time														
Work	--	--	0	++	++	++	+++	+	0	0	0	----	0	0
Work Related Travel	--	-	0	+	+	+	+++	+	0	0	0	---	+	0
Committed Time														
House Work	++	++	-	0	0	0	--	++	-	0	0	+	0	0
Child Care	++	--	0	+	+	0	0	++	++	++++	0	0	0	0
Shopping	++	0	0	0	0	0	0	0	0	0	0	+	0	0
Personal Time														
Sleep	0	0	+	--	-	-	--	--	0	-	0	++	0	0
Meals	-	++	--	++	0	0	0	++	--	0	0	+	0	0
Groom	++	0	+	0	0	0	0	0	0	0	0	0	0	0

Free Time														
Education	0	---	0	-	0	0	--	--	+	-	-	-	0	0
Religion	0	+	+	0	-	0	-	0	0	0	0	++	0	0
Organization	0	0	0	0	0	0	0	0	0	0	0	0	0	+
Cultural activities	0	-	0	0	0	0	0	0	0	0	+	++	0	0
Visiting	0	0	0	0	0	0	0	0	0	0	0	0	0	0
Sports	-	-	-	0	+	0	0	0	0	0	+	0	0	0
Hobbies	-	0	0	0	0	0	--	-	0	-	0	0	0	0
Communication	0	-	0	0	0	0	-	-	0	0	0	++	0	+
TV	-	++	++	--	--	--	---	-	-	--	0	+	0	0
Read	0	+++	0	+	0	0	--	0	--	--	0	+	0	0
Stereo	-	0	0	0	0	0	-	-	0	0	0	0	0	0
Total free	0	++	+	-	-	0	-	0	0	-	+	0	-	0
Travel	0	-	0	0	0	0	0	0	+	+	0	0	0	0

Source: American Time Use Survey (2004)

Note: Symbols in this table should be interpreted as follows: Zero (0) means no significant relationship. One symbol (+ or –) represents correlation coefficients ranging from .05–.09; two symbols represent correlation coefficients ranging from .10–.19; three symbols represent correlation coefficients ranging from .20–.29; four symbols represent correlation coefficients above .30. Signs (+ or –) represent the direction of the correlation.

others in both 1985 and 2005, but they also spent more time on child care and in volunteering. They engaged in more physical exercise. They spent more time reading than others, and they attended more (though not many more) arts events. They were able to expend time on these projects of self-improvement and social improvement because on average they slept less, relaxed less, and watched less television. Education was a better predictor of time use in each of these spheres than was either income or occupation. Professionals' investments in culture and community organizations were less evident in the middle of the first decade of the twenty-first century than in the mid-1980s, while their differential investments in work remained highly significant. Professionals continued to sacrifice sleep and television for longer work hours.

We can improve on the broad class comparisons time use data provide by filling in with more detailed studies. No single source of data exists to provide the range of information necessary for this purpose. Our portrait, like a mosaic, has been constructed from small bits of information built up, piece by piece, into a coherent whole. The single best source of data is the cumulative General Social Survey. Data on topics not covered by the GSS are drawn from a variety of sources, including the U.S. census of 2000, the American Time-Use Survey, the Consumer Expenditure Survey, specialized reports on arts and reading participation, and market reports from the financial services and travel and tourism industries. We also draw on many other specialized studies. As we report the findings of these studies, we interpret all percentage estimates of differences among groups using confidence intervals.[42] When we use the terms *more likely* and *less likely*, we mean to denote statistically significant differences, net of other covariates in the analyses.

Spheres of Self-Discipline and "Self-Denial"

We find high levels of self-discipline and "self-denial" in the realms of life that are most closely connected to career, community life, and the intergenerational reproduction of social status. These are areas in which restraint and visible effort are most highly prized.

KEEPING PACE: WORK AND WORK INTENSITY

In *Time for Life*, sociologists John Robinson and Geoffrey Godbey conclude, "While college-educated people may live in better homes, drive fancier cars, or wear designer clothes, they do not have more free time; indeed having abundant free time is not a badge of honor. Today's privileged class of college graduates does not have the privilege of free time."[43] Professionals and managers spend more time at work during the average day than other workers and are significantly more likely to say that they work more than 40 hour weeks.[44]

(This is far more true of men; women said they spent many fewer hours working.[45]) College education, high income, and professional and managerial occupations are all related to longer work hours.[46] Nevertheless these are mainly nine-to-five workers, perhaps adding a few hours in the evenings and on the weekends when deadlines are pending. Only those with the strongest ambitions and greatest responsibilities try to keep up with the pace of top executives with breakfast meetings at seven and business-related socializing after work.

Some observers believe that the work of professionals is more intense and stress-filled than that of other workers because of deadlines, multitasking requirements, and lack of supervision. On average, however, the work of industrial workers and technicians is at least equally demanding, and it lacks many of the attributes of professional work that attenuate stress. Social scientists find that work stress is a function of time pressures, accountability pressures, and consumer-demand pressures. Professionals and managers do not face the automatic time pressures of the assembly line, but they do often have targets that they must meet by deadlines.[47] Moreover, the proportion of professional and managerial workers regularly facing tight deadlines has been growing over time.[48] Those in human services (for example, teaching, social work, and health care) may spend three-fourths or more of their time in the company of clients, another characteristic of work environments associated with stress.[49] At the same time, professionals typically enjoy the advantages of greater autonomy (or control of work flow and time), which attenuate pressures that come from tight deadlines and work with clients.[50]

Self-discipline is closely linked to opportunities for self-fulfillment. When the GSS last asked the question in the mid-1990s, 80 percent of professionals and managers said that having a "fulfilling" job was very important to them; the reported importance of having these kinds of jobs rose with educational level.[51] Professionals can realize the goal of fulfilling work more often than other workers because they are more frequently employed in jobs designed with high levels of flexibility. These jobs combine high levels of multitasking, discretion, capacity to use intellectual abilities, and unregulated coordination with others.[52] They are most likely to be found in industries, such as finance and research, that produce complex products or involve complex work processes.[53]More generally, professionals and managers are connected to multiple sources of information in their work lives, and it is now common to see the busiest among them working on several screens at once on their computers or checking for information on their smart phones as they wait for meetings to start. The job designs of professionals and managers are more engaging and therefore more fulfilling, because they create more interesting and varied work, even if they periodically demand high levels of work intensity.

Popular resentments of professionals derive, at least in part, from the perception that professional work involves a play element that leads to self-actualization, while people like themselves are forced to engage in a meaningless grind of repetitive actions and encounters. These images can be easily exaggerated. Outside of the creative elite, the play element in professional work would be more accurately defined as choice among limited options. Professionals sort through a constrained set of alternatives, using their training and whatever seasoning they have gained from experience, to inform choices on a limited range of recurrent problems.

THE ABLE BODY: FITNESS AND HEALTH

The capacity to work hard and live fully requires good health. Regular, vigorous exercise also demands self-discipline. The elite of the industrial age expressed their status through physical solidity and even corpulence, but the elites of our health-conscious age express their status through physical vigor and youthful appearance. Indeed, fitness has been a major theme among professionals since the 1980s, when the popularity of jogging, health clubs, and health foods boomed.[54] The pursuit of youthful vitality through physical exercise is now a widely held norm throughout the upper classes.

Less than one-quarter of American adults engage in vigorous enough physical activity every week to achieve health-related benefits; some estimates run as low as 15 percent.[55] Net of covariates, higher levels of both education and income are significantly associated with regular physical exercise. Reports of physically unhealthy days or time lost from work due to poor health are less common too among high-income people and people with more education.[56] Some have speculated that education is primarily a source of information about the benefits of regular exercise, whereas income is primarily a source of the economic opportunities to participate in physical activities through memberships in tennis, golf, and health clubs.[57] Social status is not the only influence on physical fitness. Older people, women, and minorities exercise less than younger people, men, and whites.[58] They are also more likely to be among the 30 percent of Americans who are completely sedentary.[59] Similarly, age, gender, and minority status also influence self-reports of physically unhealthy days and time lost from work due to poor health.[60]

SERVICE TO OTHERS (AND SELF): COMMUNITY VOLUNTEERING

In the professional-managerial stratum, the old adage "to serve is to rule" does not quite apply. Here to serve is to express moral virtue. This is another arena requiring self-discipline, because every hour of service is an hour taken away from work or leisure. Among professionals and managers who volunteer, efficiency and competence continue to be prized, but they are joined by requirements to show that one is concerned with more than one's own life or narrow social circle. Almost 30 percent of Americans say they volunteer in community organizations, and those who volunteer say they average about an hour of service a week[61] Few such small investments in time are as important to social acceptability.

Volunteering is strongly related to education. More than twice as many college graduates (46 percent) as high school graduates (21 percent) say they volunteer.[62] Professionals working in the public and nonprofit sectors are more likely than others to volunteer in community organizations.[63] Highly educated people are also much more likely to hold leadership positions in voluntary organizations.[64] They are more likely to tutor and teach, to coach or supervise sports, and to provide counseling and medical care. They are particularly active in youth service and educational organizations as compared to less educated and older adults who favor involvement in church activities.[65] Church attendance and participation is a less important way to express moral virtue for highly educated professionals and managers than it is for less educated and lower-income workers.[66]

Most who engage in volunteering say they do it for idealistic reasons.[67] It would be a mistake, however, to think of volunteering as entirely a matter of self-denying service to others. Volunteering also satisfies social interests in making friends and developing organizational skills. It can be a precondition for acceptance in higher social circles because it provides both the symbolic capital—the assurance of moral concern and contribution to the collective good—that cements friendships with other community leaders and the admiration of those who are less involved.[68]

ORGANIZATION AND EDUCATION KIDS: STATUS TRANSMISSION

The journalist David Brooks coined the term *organization kid* to describe children of the professional-managerial stratum distinguished by the flurry of activities that mark their days: school and study, sports and music after school, tutoring others for effective community service, and religious activities for spiritual development.[69] Like their adult counterparts, these children are "fully scheduled." In Brooks's words, "Elite kids are likely to spend their afternoons and weekends shifting from one skill-enhancing activity to the next."[70] Behind the rise of the organization kid, Brooks suggests, lies the increasing competitive demands for being accepted to the "right" universities and the values parents attach to socialization for leadership in the organizational world that children will inhabit as adults.

An ethnographic study by the sociologist Annette Lareau showed that middle-class parents tend to conform to a logic of child rearing she characterizes as "concerted cultivation":

> They enroll their children in numerous age-specific organized activities that dominate family life and create enormous labor, particularly for mothers. The parents view these activities as transmitting important life skills to children. . . . This "cultivation" approach results in a wider range of experiences for children but also creates a frenetic pace for parents, a cult of individualism within the family, and an emphasis on children's performance.[71]

Middle-class parents often "were preoccupied with the pleasures and challenges of their work lives." They viewed childhood as a "dual opportunity": a chance both to play and to develop talents and skills of value later in life. One parent noted that playing soccer taught his son to be "hard nosed" and "competitive," skills that would be valuable in the workplace. Another noted the value of activities for learning to work with others.[72]

Quantitative studies using data from the Panel Study of Income Dynamics show that a mother's education exhibits a very strong positive effect on the hours per week her children spend in organized leisure activities and on the mean number of activities in which her children participate.[73] Another study using data from the Early Childhood Longitudinal Survey (kindergarten cohort) showed strong effects of both parents' education and family income on children's likelihood of participating in arts and crafts groups, performing arts groups, and sports clubs and of taking educational trips with their parents.[74]

This evidence on organizational involvements should not lead us to overlook the central importance of education itself as an element connecting professionals' life experiences with their strategies for intergenerational transmission of status. Professionals have relied on their educational qualifications, and, without businesses to hand down to their children, they naturally see education as an essential means for the reproduction of family social status. Professionals also tend to have the skills and information to help their children succeed in school. Drawing on a sample of couples from the National Survey of Families and Households, William Marsiglio found that both the father's and the mother's educational attainment were important net influences on the amount of time parents were engaged with preschool children. (The father's education was an important net influence on the amount of time he spent talking with and reading to his older children.)[75] Similarly, for a sample of California children aged three to ten, Suzanne M. Bianchi and John P. Robinson found that children of parents with bachelor's or advanced degrees read more and watched less television than the children of less educated parents. They also spent more time studying than the children of less educated parents.[76] Children growing up in the home of highly educated adults hear at least three times as many words in the average day as children growing up in the home of high school dropouts.[77]

Spheres of Self-Expression and Pleasure Seeking

Professionals and managers seek self-expression and pleasure in the realm of consumption. Owing largely to their higher levels of education, they express outlooks that are relatively cosmopolitan and tolerant of cultural and political differences. They are also comparatively likely (although not very likely) to cultivate pleasures of the mind.

THE PRESTIGE-ACQUISITION STYLE AND ITS ALTERNATIVES

Decades ago, the sociologist Michael Sobel identified four lifestyle patterns in the population at large. He called the dominant consumption pattern among affluent Americans the "prestige acquisition" lifestyle.[78] He found high to very high ratios of factor loadings to standard errors for the following consumer goods: housing expenditures, vacations, club memberships, reading material, dress clothing, household decorations, and furniture. While all three SES variables (income, occupation, and education) were strongly connected to this prestige-acquisition lifestyle, Sobel observed that the lifestyle was most strongly related to high income.

More recent consumer-expenditure data from the mid-2000s confirm that income is the strongest influence on the purchase of the consumer goods and services that go into a prestige-acquisition lifestyle. The highly educated consume about 1.5 times their share of discretionary goods and services. Professionals and managers also consume about 1.5 times their share of discretionary goods and services. But people in households earning $100,000 or more annually consume much more than that—about 2.5 times more than their share of the population. Those in households earning $150,000 or more annually consume nearly three times their population share—and in some expenditure areas (such as second homes, fees and admissions, and specialized apparel) much more than three times their share. Education is connected to the acquisition of information, but income is, not surprisingly, more closely connected to the acquisition of expensive objects. We can assume that high-earning medical specialists, corporate lawyers, successful architects, and investment consultants participate just as actively in the prestige-acquisition lifestyle as do business executives (see table 19.2).

Professionals and managers rate the importance of financial security highly: When the GSS last asked about the importance of financial security, 80 percent of professionals and managers said that it was "very important." As the sociologist Michele Lamont found, "signals of high socio-economic status are the only status signals that are really significant" for many upper-middle class men.[79] These interests in financial security continue a long tradition. As Burton Bledstein observed, "Historically, the middle class in America has defined itself in terms of three characteristics: acquired ability, social prestige, and a

TABLE 19.3 } Shares of Aggregate Expenditures on "Luxury Items" by Education, Occupation, and Income of Heads of Households, 2003

Expenditure	Masters or Higher Degree	Professional or Managerial Occupation	Income > $100k	Income > 150k
Percentage of Population	*10.1*	*24.9*	*12.8*	*4.4*
Annual Expenditure Share	*15.7*	*34.9*	*27.9*	*11.9*
Share Disproportion	*1.6x*	*1.4x*	*2.2x*	*2.7x*
Food Away from Home	15.5	35.3	29.0	11.6
Alcohol	16.0	35.9	28.7	12.8
Housing	16.0	34.5	26.3	11.3
Second Homes/ Other Lodging	24.6	43.2	44.2	24.3
Property Tax	20.0	37.6	31.9	14.7
Furniture	19.3	40.5	38.0	17.3
Floor Coverings	32.5	40.5	40.0	25.4
Misc. Household Equipment	17.8	38.2	34.7	15.1
Household Services	24.0	40.4	36.2	18.6
Other Personal Services	16.9	42.8	33.7	15.7
Vehicles	10.7	32.8	26.9	10.8
Men's Apparel	16.3	35.8	34.9	15.3
Women's Apparel	14.1	34.9	31.1	12.1
Other Apparel Products/ Services	20.0	42.0	36.3	19.3
Fees and Admissions	24.5	44.5	38.7	18.8
Other Entertainment (e.g. equipment, supplies)	15.5	39.2	29.1	14.1
Reading Materials	22.7	38.6	28.6	11.8
Education	26.0	46.5	39.9	21.1
Pension/Insurance	19.5	44.0	39.1	17.1
Cash Contributions (e.g. charity, gifts)	24.6	37.4	37.1	21.8

Source: Bureau of Labor and Statistics ("Consumer Expenditure Survey") 2005.

[comfortable] life style."[80] Yet professionals and managers, like other Americans, do not wish to be seen as materialistic. Only 20 percent of professionals and managers told the GSS in the mid-1990s that "having nice things" was "very important" to them.

Nor do all who desire the prestige-acquisition lifestyle have the resources to attain it. Instead, the opportunities are a byproduct of economic success, higher-than-average saving during early and middle adulthood, or inheritance. Consumer tastes consequently vary with age and income. The young are more interested in squeezing meager resources to make stylish statements. Those with lower incomes may continue the hipster or casual style of their college years. Others look to the purchase of solid and durable goods that Bourdieu associated with the need to "make a virtue of necessity" among the lower-middle and working classes. In an age of reduced prospects and reduced salaries, making a virtue of necessity has become more important to lower-income professionals, and the prestige acquisition lifestyle, however desirable, seems out of reach to many.

THE (COMPARATIVELY) OPEN MIND: TOLERANCE AND COSMOPOLITANISM

The value of freedom of expression can be seen in the extent to which the prerogative is accorded to others. The association between higher education and tolerance for unpopular views is one of the most consistent findings in social science. The first systematic study of support for civil liberties, by the sociologist Samuel Stouffer, found that college graduates were more much likely than others to tolerate unpopular opinions in the name of free speech and to be interested in protecting the civil rights and civil liberties of minorities.[81] These findings have been replicated in many studies over the last half century.[82] Within the professional-managerial stratum, somewhat higher levels of tolerance and support for civil liberties have been associated with employment in the public and nonprofit sectors.[83] Demographic variables, such as youth, urbanism, and low levels of religiosity, are also strongly related to tolerance and support for civil liberties.[84]

Cosmopolitanism, or interest in cultures outside one's own, is the active complement to passive support for the civil liberties of others. The highly educated are far more knowledgeable than the less educated about societies beyond the borders of the United States.[85] They also show greater willingness to explore other cultures. Foreign travel is a measure of cosmopolitan consumption patterns. About one out of nine adult Americans travel abroad during the year. Professionals and managers constitute two-thirds of foreign travelers. No doubt this disproportionate share of foreign travel partly reflects the higher incomes of professionals and managers. (The median household income of foreign travelers was nearly $100,000.) But the propensity to visit foreign lands likely also reflects the cosmopolitan interests of the highly educated. A recent study showed that professionals constitute the largest proportion of pleasure travelers to foreign countries, nearly four times their share of the adult population.[86] Other measures of cosmopolitanism reveal similar patterns. The World Values Survey asked respondents to identify to which of geographic group they belonged "first of all." Some 15 percent of respondents cited a supranational entity (the world or a continent); those most likely to do so were people living in large urban places (21 percent), having the highest education (18 percent), and born in the most recent cohort (21 percent).[87] Conversely, local and subnational regional identities were most common among people living in villages and among the least educated and the oldest cohorts.

THE CREATIVE CLASS?

Participation in the arts and cultural activities is not widespread in American society, nor does it take up much time for most people—much less than an hour every month on average.[88] Within the context of this meager diet, education is a strong predictor of participation.[89] For example, in the early 1990s, 77 percent of adults with postgraduate degrees attended at least one arts event during the year, compared with similar attendance by less than 10 percent of those without a high school diploma. Income also predicted arts participation, but it was not as important as education.[90] Other studies have shown a significant net association between professionals and highbrow artistic tastes;[91] and some have found that teachers, professors, and arts and communications professionals are particularly likely to say they enjoy classical music and to attend theatrical productions and art exhibitions.[92]

Reading is more common than arts participation, taking up more than half an hour a day among those with higher degrees.[93] Educated people are much more likely to be readers and to read "serious" literature. Male college graduates read about twice as much as male high school graduates each day. (Among women educational differences in reading are lower.) People in professional and managerial occupations are more likely to read literature than those in blue-collar and service occupations, even after education, income, and demographic characteristics are taken into account.[94] Reading largely takes the place of television watching. College graduates watch about one-third less television each day than less educated people—the difference between two and three hours a day on average. Yet even college graduates spend, on average, three times as many minutes per day watching television as they do reading.[95]

These data suggest that professionals and managers in the United States do not generally focus on esoteric cultural knowledge as important expressions of their status in society. According to GSS data from the mid-1990s (the last time the question was asked), one-third of professionals in culture industries and nearly the same proportion of professionals in human services cited "being cultivated" as a "very important" characteristic in friends. By contrast, fewer than 10 percent of science and engineering professionals and fewer than 20 percent of managers rated "being cultivated" as a very important characteristic in friends.[96] These findings were consistent with the higher than average, but nevertheless limited, appeal of creativity as a quality in friends.[97] In the same data series, professionals involved in human services and cultural industries were the only professional groups to report even one-third of the time that creativity was a "very important" characteristic in friends. Scientists, engineers, and managers were very unlikely to think of creativity as a very important quality.[98]

Professional-Managerial Culture and the Ethos of Global Capitalism

We have shown that some foundations of middle-class respectability have remained impressively constant since the birth of the modern professional stratum in the late nineteenth century: notably, comparatively long hours at work, the high value placed on financial security, and the expression of status through prestige acquisitions. But middle-class respectability has also evolved in ways that parallel the evolution of broader American cultural expectations and anxieties. Thriving in the professional-managerial stratum today requires new forms of self-discipline—including higher average levels of physical fitness, which has become a status symbol, and close attention to the organizational activities of children. Where community volunteering was once the special province of women, in an age of dual careers it has become expected of upper-middle class men as well. The horizon of members of the stratum has gradually expanded. Cosmopolitan tastes, once characteristic of city life, have become far more common in the suburbs.

Given their superior access to status-related information, it would be surprising if highly educated professionals and managers were less connected to the emerging trends in global capitalist culture than people in less connected social strata. In fact, the developing ethos of educated elites in the United States shows a close correspondence to what we might call the "competitive cosmopolitanism" of global capitalist society.

Economic competition is accepted and embraced by highly educated professionals and managers, no less than by business elites. Political scientist Pippa Norris's study of the World Values Survey indicated that highly educated, urbanized people living in economically developed democracies were the strongest supporters of free trade and free movement of labor, the cornerstones of neoliberal policies. Educated elites in other countries were also interested in competitiveness and efficiency, if only because they hoped to see their national industries succeed in a world economy strongly influenced by market priorities.[99] As Andrew Hacker has written:

> The abilities and outlooks associated with the analytical style (of the highly educated) can no longer be adequately thought of as "white" or "Western" or "European," but are in fact part of a dominant global culture, which stresses not only literacy and numerical skills, but also administrative efficiency and economic competitiveness.[100]

At the same time, the freer movement of capital, labor, and tourists across national boundaries encourages tolerance and cosmopolitanism, characteristics not often associated with earlier eras of European and American capitalism. Professionals' interest in the arts and literature and other cultures points the way toward the more cosmopolitan and interconnected world culture of the future and is shaped, in turn, by the gradual emergence of that culture. The indicators of cultural expansion and hybridization are already pervasive in the largest and most cosmopolitan cities and in institutions with ambitions for global leadership. The range of national influences on Western pop and rock music has grown to include reggae from the Caribbean, South American samba and bossa nova, bhangra from India, and rai from Algeria. Fusion food has become the standard fare in upscale restaurants in urban centers. At the leading universities in the world, such as the Swiss Federal Institute of Technology Zurich, the École Polytechnique, Columbia University, and the Massachusetts Institute of Technology, as many as 20 to 25 percent or more of students come from foreign countries.[101] No doubt cultural pluralism of this type appeals more to young, urban, and secular professionals than to others in the professional-managerial stratum. They are the leading edge of change.

The new "great powers" rivalry between the United States and China could lead to policies of economic and social retrenchment—and the regionalization of trade and cultural ties. If global integration continues, however, competition and cosmopolitanism will go hand in hand.[102] Indeed, it will be difficult for American industries to capture new global markets without a complementary broadening of cultural appreciation and sensitivity. To the extent that globalization advances, we are therefore likely to be impressed with the degree to which the culture of professionals and managers in twenty-first-century America is consistent with, and influenced by, the culture of global capitalism—efficient and expansive; profit-oriented, yet tinged with environmental and social consciousness; and diffusing Western organizational techniques while incorporating the diversity of the human population out of which new markets are formed.

Notes

1. On the "new class," see Irving Kristol, "Business and the 'New Class'" and "About Equality," in *Two Cheers for Capitalism* (New York: Basic Books, 1978); Alvin W. Gouldner, *The Rise of the New Class and the Future of Intellectuals* (New York: St. Martin's Press, 1979); and Norman Podhoretz, "The Adversary Culture and the New Class," in *The New Class?* ed. B. Bruce-Briggs (New Brunswick, NJ: Transaction, 1979). On "cultural elites, see David Brooks, "One Nation, Slightly Divisible," *Atlantic Monthly*, December 2001, 53–65; Gertrude Himmelfarb, *One Nation, Two Cultures* (New York: Knopf, 1999); Blake Hurst, "The Plains vs. the Atlantic," *American Enterprise*, March 1, 2002, 38; and John Podhoretz, "The Two Americas: Ironic Us, Simple Them," *New York Post*, March 13, 2001, 43.

2. Robert Wiebe, *The Search for Order, 1877–1920* (New York: Hill and Wang, 1967), chap. 5.

3. Larson, *Rise of Professionalism*, 66–79.

4. Burton Bledstein, *The Culture of Professionalism: The Middle Class and the Development of Higher Education in America* (New York: Norton, 1976), 146.

5. Ibid., 92.

6. Steven Brint, *In an Age of Experts: The Changing Role of Professionals in Politics and Public Life* (Princeton, NJ: Princeton University Press, 1994), chaps. 1–2.

7. R. H. Tawney, *The Acquisitive Society* (1920; New York: Harcourt Brace Jovanovich, 1948), 94–95.

8. Brint, *In an Age of Experts*, chaps. 3–5.

9. Eliot Freidson, *Professional Powers: A Study in the Institutionalization of Formal Knowledge* (Chicago: University of Chicago Press, 1986).

10 See Brint, *In an Age of Experts*, chaps. 2–5; Clem Brooks and Jeff Manza, "Class Politics and Political Change in the United States, 1952–1992," *Social Forces* 76 (December 1997): 379–409

11. National Center for Education Statistics, *Digest of Education Statistics 2003* (Washington, DC: NCES, 2003), table 379.

12. Bureau of Labor Statistics, *Current Population Reports: Educational Attainment in the United States: 2004* (Washington, DC: Bureau of Labor Statistics, 2005).

13. Robert H. Frank, *Luxury Fever: Why Money Fails to Satisfy in an Age of Excess* (New York: Free Press, 1999), 45.

14. Ibid.

15. G. J. Barker-Benfield, cited in Ibid., 48.

16. Theresa A. Sullivan, Elizabeth Warren, and Jay Lawrence Westbrook, *The Fragile Middle Class: Americans in Debt* (New Haven, CT: Yale University Press, 2000).

17. U.S. Department of Commerce, Bureau of Economic Analysis, *Personal Savings Rate* (Washington, DC: Bureau of Economic Analysis, 2006).

18. Ibid.

19. Jack Healy, "Consumers Are Saving More and Spending Less," *New York Times*, February 2, 2009, www.nytimes.com/2009/02/03/businesseconomy/03econ.html.

20. Frank, *Luxury Fever*.

21. Michael T. Walden, "Absolute and Relative Consumption of Married U.S. Households in 1960 and 1996," *Journal of Consumer Affairs* 36 (2002): 77–98.

22. Thomas J. Stanley and William D. Danko, *The Millionaire Next Door: The Surprising Secrets of America's Wealthy* (New York: Pocket Books, 1998).

23. Ibid., 75–76.

24. Walden, "Absolute and Relative Consumption."

25. Analyses of GSS data conducted by the authors. Analyses available on request.

26. Denise Kandel, Pamela C. Griesler, Gang Lee, Mark Davies, and Christine Schafran, *Parental Influences on Adolescent Marijuana Use and the Baby Boom Generation: Findings from the 1979–1996 National Household Surveys on Drug Abuse* (Washington, DC: U.S. Department of Health and Human Services, Substance Abuse and Mental Health Services Administration, 2001).

27. On neuroenhancers, see Margaret Talbot, "Brain Gain." *The New Yorker* (April 27, 2009). Retrieved from www.newyorker.com/reporting/2009/04/27/090427fa_fact_talbot.

28. John W. Welte. Grace M. Barnes, William F. Wieczorek, Cecile Tidwell, and John Parker, "Gambling Participation in the U.S.—Results from a National Survey," *Journal of Gambling Studies* 18 (2002): 324–27.

29. Dean Gerstein. Cindy Larison, Laszlo Engelman, Sally Murphy, Amanda Bilmer, Luciano Chuchro, Marianna Toce, Robert Johnson, Tracy Buie, and Mary Ann Hill, *Gambling Impact and Behavior Study: Report to the National Impact Study Commission* (Chicago: National Opinion Research Corporation, 1999).

30. Alvin C. Burns, Peter L. Gillet, Marc Rubinstein, and James W. Gentry, "An Exploratory Study of Lottery Playing, Gambling Addiction, and Links to Compulsive Consumption," *Advances in Consumer Research* 17 (1990): 298–305; J. R. B. King, "Participation in the National Lottery—Evidence from the Family Expenditure Survey," *Journal of Royal Statistics* 160 (1997): 207–12.

31. Gerstein et al., *Gambling Impact and Behavior Study.*

32. Analyses of GSS data conducted by the authors. Analyses available on request.

33. Brint, *In an Age of Experts*, 100–101.

34. Ibid.

35. Robert T. Michael, Edward O. Laumann, and Gina Bari Kolata, *Sex in America: A Definitive Survey* (Boston: Little, Brown, 1994), 236–7.

36. Daniel Bell, *The Cultural Contradictions of Capitalism* (New York: Basic Books, 1976).

37. Those who have attempted to describe a general "professional" or "professional-managerial" culture without examining the relationship between work and leisure have usually proved to provide a one-sided or inaccurate portrait. Ronald Inglehart posited a general shift from "materialist" to "postmaterialist" values, with professionals in the lead, because of their higher levels of education and relative youth. See Ronald Inglehart, *The Silent Revolution: Changing Values and Political Style among Western Publics* (Princeton, NJ: Princeton University Press, 1977), and *Culture Shift in Advanced Industrial Societies* (Princeton, NJ: Princeton University Press, 1990). Randall Collins proposed a theory of "class cultures" emphasizing two dimensions: authority at work and diversity of contacts. See Randall Collins, *Conflict Sociology: Toward an Explanatory Science* (New York: Academic Press, 1975), and *Theoretical Sociology* (New York: HarperCollins, 1988). For Collins, professionals shared with managers a high level of authority in society, leading to close identification with dominant institutions and dominant norms. However, many differed from managers in their diversity of contacts. Where managers were monitored for conformity by a small number of subordinates and superiors, professionals often worked on their own or in contact with diverse others. Focusing still more exclusively on work relationships, Erik Olin Wright built an analysis of professionals from the mix of "organizational" and "expert" skill sets they employed at work. See Erik Olin Wright, *Classes* (London: Verso, 1985). For Wright, professionals combining organizational and expert skills sets are identified as "professional-managers," while professionals employing only "expert" skill sets are "semi-autonomous" workers.

38. Steven Brint, *Schools and Societies, 2nd ed.* (Stanford: Stanford Univeristy Press, 2006), 142-3.

39. Robert N. Bellah, Richard Madsen, William M. Sullivan, Ann Swidler, and Steven M. Tipton. *Habits of the Heart: Individualism and Commitment in American Life* (Berkeley and Los Angeles: University of California Press, 1985), chap. 7.

40. Pierre Bourdieu, *Distinction: A Social Critique of the Judgment of Taste.* (Cambridge, MA: Harvard University Press, 1984), part 1. See also Pierre Bourdieu, "The Forms of Capital." Pp 241-58 in John G. Richardson (Ed.). *Handbook of Theory and Research for the Sociology of Education.* (New York: Greenwood Press, 1986).

41. For a critique of Bourdieu's work as it applies to the U.S. upper middle class, see Michele Lamont, *Money, Morals, and Manners: The Culture of the French and American Upper-Middle Class* (Chicago: University of Chicago Press, 1992).

42. For population estimates, confidence intervals of plus or minus 3 percent should be inferred in surveys of 1500 or more people; for subgroup estimates, confidence intervals of no less than plus or minus 5 percent should be applied. Confidence intervals for smaller subpopulations can be as wide as 8 to 10 percent.

43. John P. Robinson and Geoffrey Godbey, *Time for Life: The Surprising Ways Americans Use Their Time* (University Park: Pennsylvania State University Press, 1997), 217.

44. Bureau of Labor Statistics, *American Time Use Survey—2004 Results Announced by BLS* (Washington, DC: U.S. Department of Labor, Bureau of Labor Statistics, September 20, 2005).

45. Philip L. Rones, Randy E. Ilg, and Jennifer M. Gardner, "Trends in Hours of Work since the Mid-1970s," *Monthly Labor Review* 120 (April 1997): 3–14.

46. College-educated people overestimate their work hours on surveys by as much as two to three hours per week on average. William A. Sundstrom, "The Overworked American, or the Overestimated Work Week? Trend and Bias in Recent Estimates of Weekly Work Hours in the United States" (unpublished paper, Department of Economics, Santa Clara University, 1999); Harley Frazis and Jay Stewart, "What Can Time Use Data Tell Us about Hours of Work?" *Monthly Labor Review 127* (December 2004): 3–9. This overestimation of work hours may be partly due to the lack of clear boundaries between work and nonwork for many professionals, especially those who work part of the time at home. Overreporting increases with the number of hours reported. Workers who reported working sixty hours or more on surveys are found to work about fifty-three hours per week when diaries are used instead. John P. Robinson and Ann Bostrom, "The Overestimated Workweek? What Time Diary Measures Suggest," *Monthly Labor Review* 117 (August 1994): 11–23; see also Sundstrom, "Overworked American."

47. Pierre Boisard, Michel Gollac, Antoine Valeyre, and Damien Cartron, *Time and Work: Work Intensity* (Dublin: European Foundation for the Improvement of Living and Working Conditions, 2003).

48. Ibid.

49. Richard Karasek and Torres Theorell, *Healthy Work: Stress, Productivity, and the Reconstruction of Working Life* (New York: Basic Books, 1990).

50. Boisard et al., *Time and Work;* see also Eliot Freidson, *Professional Powers* (Chicago: University of Chicago Press, 1986).

51. Analysis of GSS data conducted by the authors. Analysis available on request.

52. Eileen Applebaum and Rosemary Batt, *The New American Workplace: Transforming Work Systems in the United States* (Ithaca, NY: Institute for Labor Relations Press, 1994); Cindy Zoghi, Alec Levenson, and Michael Gibbs, *Why Are Jobs Designed the Way They Are?* (Washington, DC: U.S. Department of Labor, Bureau of Labor Statistics, 2005).

53. Zoghi, Levenson, and Gibbs, *Why Are Jobs Designed.*

54. Robinson and Godbey, *Time for Life.*

55. Center for Disease Control 1997; U.S. Department of Health and Human Services, *Physical Activity and Health: A Report of the Surgeon General* (Atlanta, GA: Department of Health and Human Services, Centers for Disease Control and Prevention, 1996).

56. Centers for Disease Control and Prevention, "Health-Related Quality of Life Surveillance—United States, 1993–2002," Surveillance Summaries, *Morbidity and Mortality Weekly Report* 54, no. SS-4 (October 28, 2005): 15-6.

57. Joseph G. Grzywacz and Nadine F. Marks, "Social Inequalities and Exercise during Adulthood: Toward an Ecological Perspective," *Journal of Health and Social Behavior* 42 (June 2001): 202–20.

58. Ibid.

59. U.S. Department of Health and Human Services, *Physical Activity and Health.*

60. Centers for Disease Control and Prevention, "Health-Related Quality of Life Surveillance." See also Ronald C. Kessler, "A Disaggregation of the Relationship between Socioeconomic Status and Psychological Distress," *American Sociological Review* 47 (December 1982): 752–64.

61. Bureau of Labor Statistics, *American Time Use Survey—2004*; Bureau of Labor Statistics, *Volunteering in America 2005* (Washington, DC: U.S. Department of Labor, Bureau of Labor Statistics, 2005).

62. Bureau of Labor Statistics, *Volunteering in America 2005.*

63. Thomas Rotolo and John Wilson, "Employment Sector and Volunteering: The Contribution of Non-profit Sector and Public Sector Workers to the Volunteer Work Force," *Sociological Quarterly* 47 (February 2006): 21–40.

64. Sidney Verba, Kay Lehman Schlozman, and Henry E. Brady, *Voice and Equality: Civic Voluntarism in America* (Cambridge, MA: Harvard University Press, 1995); Bureau of Labor Statistics 2005.

65. Bureau of Labor Statistics, ibid.

66. Claude S. Fischer and Michael Hout, *Century of Difference: How America Changed in the Last One Hundred* Years (New York: Russell Sage Foundation Press, 2006), chap. 7.

67. Francie Ostrower, *Why the Wealthy Give: The Culture of Elite Philanthropy* (Princeton, NJ: Princeton University Press, 1997).

68. Helmut K. Anheier and Lester M. Salamon, "Volunteering in Cross-National Perspective: Initial Comparisons," *Law and Contemporary Problems* 43 (Autumn 1999): 43–63.

69. David Brooks,"The Organization Kid." *The Atlantic Monthly* 287 (April 2001): 40-54.

70. Ibid., 42.

71. Annette Lareau, "Invisible Inequality: Social Class and Childrearing in Black Families and White Families," *American Sociological Review* 67 (October 2002): 748.

72. Ibid., 771. Lareau argued that these child-rearing strategies are influenced by more than parents' education. "It is the interweaving of life experiences and resources, including parents' economic resources, occupational conditions, and educational backgrounds, that appears to be most important in leading middle-class parents to engage in concerted cultivation and working-class and poor parents to [emphasize] natural growth." Ibid., 771–72.

73. Annette Lareau and Elliot B. Weininger, "Work-Family Conflicts, Gender and Children's Organizational Leisure Activities" (unpublished paper, Department of Sociology, University of Maryland, 2005).

74. George Farkas and Jacob Hibel, "Being Unready for School: Factors Affecting Risk and Resilience," in *Early Disparities in School Readiness: How Do Families Contribute to Successful and Unsuccessful Transitions into School?* ed. Alan Booth and Ann Crouter (Mahwah, NJ: Erlbaum, 2007).

75. William Marsiglio, "Paternal Engagement Activities with Minor Children," *Journal of Marriage and the Family* 53 (November 1991): 973–86.

76. Suzanne M. Bianchi and John P. Robinson, "What Did You Do Today? Children's Use of Time, Family Composition, and the Acquisition of Social Capital," *Journal of Marriage and the Family* 59 (May 1997): 332–44.

77. Betty Hart and Todd Risley, *Meaningful Differences in the Everyday Experience of Young American Children* (Baltimore: Paul Brooks, 1995).

78. Michael Sobel, "Lifestyle Differentiation and Stratification in Contemporary U.S. Society," *Research in Social Stratification and Mobility* 2 (1983): 115–44.

79. Lamont, *Money, Morals, and Manners*, 64.

80. Bledstein, *Culture of Professionalism*, 41.

81. Samuel A. Stouffer, *Communism, Conformity, and Civil Liberties* (New York: Doubleday, 1955).

82. Ernest T. Pascarella and Patrick T. Terenzini, *How College Affects Students: Findings and Insights from 25 Years of Research* (San Francisco: Jossey-Bass, 1991), 274–84.

83. Brint, *In an Age of Experts*, chap. 5; Michael W. Macy, "'New-Class' Dissent among Social and Cultural Specialists," *Sociological Forum* 3 (Summer 1988): 324–56.

84. Brint, ibid., .

85. Paul W. Kingston. Ryan Hubbard, Brent Lapp, Paul Schroeder, and Julia Wilson, "Why Education Matters," *Sociology of Education* 76 (January 2003): 53–70.

86. Norris, "Global Governance and Cosmopolitan Citizens."

87. International Trade Administration, Office of Travel and Tourism Industries, *2004 Profile of U.S. Resident Traveler Visiting Overseas Destinations* (Washington, DC: ITA, 2005).

88. Bureau of Labor Statistics, *American Time Use Survey—2004*.

89. Paul DiMaggio and Francie Ostrower, *Race, Ethnicity, and Participation in the Arts.* (Washington, DC: Seven Locks Press, 1992); Herbert Gans, *Popular Culture and High Culture: An Analysis and Evaluation of Taste* (New York: Basic Books, 1974); Robinson and Godbey, *Time for Life*; Michael Hughes and Richard A. Peterson, "Isolating Cultural Choice Patterns in the U.S. Population," *American Behavioral Scientist* 26 (1983): 459–78.

90. Robinson and Godbey, *Time for Life*, 179–80.

91. Tally Katz-Gerro, "Cultural Consumption and Social Stratification: Leisure Activities, Musical Tastes, and Social Location," *Sociological Perspectives* 42 (1999): 627–46; Richard A. Peterson and Albert Simkus, "How Musical Tastes Mark Occupational Status Groups," in *Cultivating Differences: Symbolic Boundaries and the Making of Inequality*, ed. Michele Lamont and Marcel Fournier (Chicago: University of Chicago Press, 1992), 152–86.

92. Paul DiMaggio and Michael Useem, "Social Class and Arts Consumption: The Origins and Consequences of Class Differences in Exposure to the Arts in America," *Theory and Society* 5 (March 1978): 141–61; Peterson and Simkus, "How Musical Tastes."

93. Bureau of Labor Statistics, *American Time Use Survey 2005 Microdata File.* (Washington, DC: Bureau of Labor Statistics, 2005).

94. Nicholas Zill and Marianne Winglee, *Who Reads Literature? The Future of the United States as a Nation of Readers* (Cabin John, MD: Seven Locks Press, 1990), 64–6.

95. Bureau of Labor Statistics, *Volunteering in America 2005*.

96. Analysis of GSS data conducted by the authors. Analysis available on request.

97. Recently, economists and social observers have developed the idea of the "creative economy" and the "creative class" as the dynamic element in American capitalism. See, e.g.,

Richard Florida, *The Rise of the Creative Class* (New York: Basic Books, 2002). This idea has emerged as an alternative to the related conception of knowledge as the dynamic element in American capitalism and of "knowledge workers" as the key stratum. Daniel Bell, *The Coming of Post-industrial Society: An Essay in Social Forecasting* (New York: Basic Books, 1973). However, the American economy is dominated neither by "knowledge industries" nor "creative industries." On the former, see Steven Brint, "Professionals and the Knowledge Economy: Rethinking the Theory of Post-industrial Society," *Current Sociology* 49 (2001): 101–32; on the latter, see Toby Miller, "A View from a Fossil: The New Economy, Creativity, and Consumption—Two or Three Things I Don't Believe In," *International Journal of Cultural Studies* 7 (2004): 55–65. The dynamic industries in the U.S. economy are far too diverse to be characterized in such simplistic ways. Moreover, the cities that fit the "creative-economy" model best are not always the most prolific producers of jobs. Steven Malanga, "The Curse of the Creative Class," *City Journal*, 14 (Winter 2004): 1–10. Retrieved from www.city-journal.org/html/14-1-the-curse.html.

98. Analyses of GSS data conducted by the authors. Analyses available on request.

99. Pippa Norris, "Global Governance and Cosmopolitan Citizens," in *Governance in a Globalizing World*, ed. Joseph S. Nye and John Donahue (Washington, DC: Brookings Institution Press, 2001).

100. Andrew Hacker, "Transnational America," *New York Review of Books*, November 22, 1990, 24.

101. *Times Higher Education Supplement: World University Rankings*, November 28, 2006, http://www.thes.co.uk/worldrankings. The foreign-student enrollment figures cited here appeared in the 2005 rankings.

102. The term *multicultural* has developed positive connotations for college-educated Americans. Brooks and Manza, "Class Politics and Political Change"; Michael W. Link and Robert W. Oldendick, "Social Construction and White Attitudes toward Equal Opportunity and Multiculturalism," *Journal of Politics* 58 (February 1996): 149–68.

20 }

Thrift in the Other America

Wilson Brissett

The idea that there exist "two Americas"—divided by a vast gap in economic opportunity—has a long history in American politics, stretching back to the populism of William Jennings Bryan and reviving as recently as John Edwards's two failed bids for the Democratic presidential nomination in 2004 and 2008. The concept was crystallized for the late twentieth century, however, by Michael Harrington in his 1962 book *The Other America*. His argument is directly aimed at the persistence of poverty in the midst of widespread affluence in the United States of the postwar period. In a chapter near the end, titled "The Two Nations," Harrington offers a forceful account of the income inequality divide in America:

> The United States in the sixties contains an affluent society within its borders. Millions and tens of millions enjoy the highest standard of life the world has ever known. This blessing is mixed. It is built upon a peculiarly distorted economy, one that often proliferates pseudo-needs rather than satisfying human needs. For some, it has resulted in a sense of spiritual emptiness, of alienation. Yet a man would be a fool to prefer hunger to satiety, and the material gains at least open up the possibility of a rich and full existence.
>
> At the same time, the United States contains an underdeveloped nation, a culture of poverty. Its inhabitants do not suffer the extreme privation of the peasants of Asia or the tribesmen of Africa, yet the mechanism of their misery is similar. They are beyond history, sunk in a paralyzing, maiming routine.[1]

Harrington argues that American poverty is an entrenched, cultural phenomenon and that it silences the political voices of those who are trapped within it. This claim locates the problem of poverty on the grandest of moral scales—the abuse of the poor by the wealthy, according to Harrington, is corroding the very foundations of the Republic, which are rooted in the sovereignty of the people.

Since Harrington's book, some things have changed in the national discourse of the "two Americas." One is the expansion of the concept of "the Other America" beyond the boundaries of poverty as traditionally defined. Increasingly, the middle classes that used to fall within Harrington's "affluent" America are being classified with the poor. This category drift is also echoed in the growing preference among academics in the field of public policy for the term *low-income* (LI), or even *low- or moderate-income* (LMI) to identify the population in need of economic policy assistance. In addition to avoiding the social stigma of the traditional term, the use of LI and LMI also allows for the expansion of the population under discussion—it feeds the sense that everyone beneath the CEO level is under the grip of an American economic oligarchy. While this vocabulary shift may be partly driven by a renewed wave of populist rhetoric, it agrees with the account of "downward mobility" noted by commentators like Barbara Ehrenreich. Why this inequality persists, and is by all accounts increasing, is a pressing concern that goes to the heart of the moral landscape that dominates our economic thinking at the beginning of the twenty-first century.[2] Especially in light of the global financial crisis of 2008, which still seemed to be in its opening act as this chapter was being written, the question of "the Other America" (What is its composition? What will be its fate?) moves front and center. In an investment economy dominated by complex, risk-laden financial instruments and an employment market driven by flexible, relatively unstable jobs, where do the vast majority of Americans—who are not managing the assets or bringing home the executive pay—find themselves?

The idea of thrift is a significant point of entry into this larger problem. This is certainly true on a macro level, where analysis centers around the failure of credit markets as a result of the overextension of debt to consumers, corporations, and even nations. As the global system falters in response to inadequate liquidity, commentators everywhere bemoan the lack of proper savings across the vast economic infrastructure. But thrift pertains on the individual level as well. It often comes up in debates over why the gap between the superrich and everyone else persists. A closer look at the role of thrift (or its absence) among the LMI populations can help clarify the intimate relationship between moral and economic issues surrounding the income gap in America. Thrift understood as the personal practice of economic frugality has not fared well among LMI groups. In the midst of a larger national conversation about a widespread decline of saving across all income groups, it yet makes sense to speak of a "saving gap" between the top and bottom income earners in the United States.[3] This gap indicates, on the one hand, the degree to which income level is an accurate predictor of the saving practices of a family or individual; on the other hand, the gap points up the difference in the availability of financial systems and instruments that encourage saving and multiply the advantages of economic thrift. A great body of research shows that low-income earners save less, as a percentage of income, than their more wealthy counterparts, but it is important that we avoid simplistic conclusions about why this is so.[4] The problem of personal motivation is beyond the scope of this chapter (perhaps it is, in the end, beyond the scope of any academic study), but what we can do is review the institutional arrangements that discourage and encourage economic thrift in the United States among LMI populations as a way of outlining a significant aspect of the moral culture of economics in contemporary America. This way of proceeding will enable us to ask what becomes of "the Other America" in this age of individualist, free-agent economic structures by paying attention to the changes in notions and practices of thrift across the contemporary scene.

The Rise of Anti-Thrift Institutions

Institutional means of assisting low-income populations practice thrift and build assets have a long history in the United States. From the first decades after the Revolution, mutual aid societies and benevolent groups energetically strove to encourage saving among the working poor, especially in the big cities. Over the course of the nineteenth century, these voluntary, associational vehicles for thrift developed stronger organizational structures, and in the first decades of the twentieth century, the credit union movement institutionalized many of their best practices. Today credit unions remain perhaps the strongest institutional supporter of low-income thrift in the United States.[5] At the same time that these instruments for individual thrift were developing, new vehicles for collective thrift were also coming into existence in forms as varied as union activities, pension funds, and war bonds. This is, in a sense, an old story that developed from the stage of informal community activism and voluntary associations to that of formalized regional and national institutions.

What is new since World War II, amid the decline of the most important forms of collective thrift, is the rise in the number of economic institutions that counteract the practice of thrift among low-income groups. Certainly there have always been myriad temptations toward profligacy, from gambling to overconsuming—but cornerstone institutions (not least the government) traditionally opposed these forces with a message of prudent economizing. Over the last fifty years, this reality has begun to shift, and the result has been the rise to prominence of a host of anti-thrift institutions that compete for influence (and dollars) with those institutions that promote frugality. It is not that institutionalized forms of anti-thrift are entirely new, but their legitimation within changing legal and political parameters has given them a new place of power in the middle of the public sphere. And while this is not without consequences on a practical level, it also speaks to a deeper shift in normative economic thinking, because the arguments in favor of lotteries, easy credit cards, and ubiquitous payday loan centers outline very specific notions of the individual and the market. They presuppose a view of the individual as a radically independent choice maker whose best interest (politically or economically or otherwise) is always served by increased freedom of access to a wide range of options.

STATE LOTTERIES

Until very recent years, the most conspicuous new form of institutionalized prodigality was the state-run lottery system. While lotteries had been legal in some states in the nineteenth century, they were outlawed across the nation for the first half of the twentieth century. Beginning in 1964, though, lotteries began to make a comeback. New Hampshire was the first state to run its own lottery. Through the 1970s twelve more states began lotteries, and another eighteen adopted the practice in the 1980s.[6] Today, there are lotteries in forty-two states plus the District of Columbia. These lotteries represent big business for the states that operate them: as long ago as 1997, Americans spent $36 billion on lotteries, making them "one of the largest operations run by state governments."[7]

They have not become so popular and so large on simple demand alone. In the same year that Americans bought $36 billion worth of lottery products, U.S. states spent $400 million advertising their lotteries to potential customers. This despite the fact that in every state in which the lottery is legal, the state is the only authorized operator of the lottery, giving it monopoly status. Part of the dramatic shift in the states' relationship to thrift, as far as lotteries are concerned, is the states' unprecedented willingness to advocate (and not merely allow) gambling in this form, and further to authorize themselves as the sole beneficiaries of the proceeds of an activity formerly regarded as morally and financially questionable. Not only has the lottery been allowed, then, it has been welcomed and maximized by the authorities who previously sought to prevent its existence.

Now that the lottery is fully normalized, and the individual states are its most enthusiastic proponents, the question of consumer behavior in relation to the lottery remains. A 1999 survey seeking to trace the impact of lotteries found that "about half the adult population play the lottery in any one year."[8] The distribution of players, however, is striking. A strong majority of lottery players are casual, buying very few tickets and spending relatively little money. But the 20 percent of players who played the lottery most often accounted for 82 percent of lottery sales.[9] The researchers estimated that if all players of the lottery spent as much as the median player spent, "sales would fall by 76 percent."[10] Thus lottery sales are weighted heavily toward the most frequent players, but it also seems the most frequent players are those who are least able to afford it. A University of Chicago survey in 1999 demonstrated that lottery players with an income under $10,000 spent more than twice as much as players with an income over $100,000 and nearly three times as much as those with incomes between $50,000 and $100,000.[11] So it seems that not only does a certain group of players spend an inordinate amount of money on the lottery, but that this is the same group of players that has the lowest income among all players.

The lottery is clearly a new form of government involvement in public life. And while state profits from lottery sales increase the revenues available to a state for education, infrastructure, and other essential public services, studies have shown that the lottery amounts to a voluntary tax on the lowest income groups. At the very least, we have state governments vying to push low-income constituents to spend millions of dollars on gambling. Most states justify this operation to the public as a legitimate form of recreation and by highlighting that proceeds provide crucial state revenues. This line of argument, however, seems to ignore the impact of institutional arrangements on human behavior. At its worst, the lottery influences thinking on fate and the possibilities of the future—especially in economically hard times. In the wake of the 2008 mortgage crisis and accompanying economic downturn, for instance, more than half of states with lotteries reported an increase in sales.[12] Not only does this statistic indicate a level of dangerously wishful thinking—it also speaks volumes about the sense many people have that their lives and future happiness are placed at the mercy of a prevailing economic system that they are powerless to change. The placing of legitimate hopes in the lottery suggests that the ticket buyers register a certain hopelessness about the possibilities for advancement within the economic system as such. But we need to paint a fuller picture of the economic reality for low-income individuals before we can understand the full impact of any one element.

THE DEMOCRATIZATION OF CREDIT

At the same time that lotteries were becoming popular across America in the 1980s and 1990s, the banking industry was undergoing massive transformations at a very high level that would nonetheless have wide-reaching impact across the economic spectrum. In the early 1980s, the Reagan administration paved the way for new federal regulations making it easier for financial institutions to merge and consolidate a very broad range of services under one organization.[13] The result was heightened competition among banks in the new merger-friendly environment, and one of the major stages where this drama played out was the attempt to create new markets for existing services. As such, banks were willing to take on more risky customers than they previously would have. One of the most important ways banks sought to keep up in this more competitive environment was through the expansion of credit card services into LMI markets. This business proved very lucrative for the banks. Citicorp (owner of Visa and MasterCard) became "the most powerful financial institution in the world . . . largely due to the profitability of its credit cards and other consumer services."[14] Other banks followed the example, buying up smaller competitors and extending financial services, especially consumer debt, to a broader clientele. This development, sometimes labeled the "democratization of credit," has opened up many LMI Americans to a new form of financial uncertainty. And while the culture of credit can sometimes generate new forms of financial discipline, through the structural necessities of making regular payments, the credit crunch of recent decades seems to be driving families to make more and more difficult decisions about where to spend their money, or shift their credit.

The precariousness of credit card debt is evident most directly in its financial consequences: in 2005 Americans carried $800 billion in credit card debt.[15] Almost 50 percent of credit card holders missed a payment in 2007.[16] According to a 2005 survey by the Center for Responsible Lending, the average household credit card debt in LMI households was $8,650.[17] The situation among young people is just as startling: more than half of college students carry a balance on their credit cards, with an average balance of more than $2,000.[18] Beyond these statistics, which are rehearsed so often that they can numb the mind, is the wide reach of credit card debt's social impact. It has compounded the mortgage crisis, added to the financial woes brought on by rising health care expenses, and inhibited many from pursuing advanced education.[19] Most certainly, it creates patterns of financial behavior that limit the ability and inclination to practice even the most basic forms of thrift.

This is the great irony of the democratization of credit. The extension of easy consumer debt to more socioeconomic groups, instead of opening a new realm of economic freedom as it was supposed to do, seems to have severely limited not only the financial health but also the potential for social mobility of large swaths of Americans. It seems that the clearest benefits from this shift have fallen to the megabanks that hold the credit cards. The deregulation of financial practices brought about in the era of bank mergers—which led to the creation of increasingly "vertical" institutions that offer every type of financial product from individual accounts to a range of debt services—served first and foremost to enrich the banks that have pushed for the new rules and the executive leadership and stockholders that have implemented them.[20]

Again, the idea that offering easy consumer credit to all levels of the American economy can be described positively, as a process of "democratization," takes the flattening of the idea of the individual to new heights. Entirely divorced from the relational, social, and organizational forces that shape so much of social life, the *homo economicus* of easy credit is presented as the ultimate free decision maximizer, loosed within the brave new world of consumer debt to fulfill the true duty of the citizen by playing the role of purchaser. The democratization of credit promises to enable Americans of all socioeconomic levels to enjoy the free-ranging consumerist lifestyle modeled by the elite professional class, but the result more often than not has been a widening of the income inequality gap, as credit card profits have flowed up the scale to bank executives and their shareholders, and LMI individuals and families have seen their assets and net worth decline. The idea has been sold that everyone can live the lifestyle of the cosmopolitan professional elite and that credit can help reach this goal. Devoid of any recognition, however, of the different situation of the LMI population, the democratization of credit seems to have limited the choices and economic freedoms of a significant number of Americans.

PAYDAY LOAN CENTERS

It is little wonder, given the increasingly uncertain situation of many LMI Americans, that new forms of debt have arisen to offer possible solutions to the cash-flow needs of the nation. One of the most controversial new forms of debt is the payday loan—a cash advance given to a worker against the promise of the next paycheck, often secured with a postdated check from the borrower to be cashed by the lender on payday. The initial loan period is between one week and one month, and the lender usually charges a fee of $15 to $20 per $100 borrowed. The extraordinarily high interest rates, which typically run close to 400 percent, have drawn the attention and criticism that have shed unwanted light on the industry. Another aspect of payday loans that has drawn fire from the press and advocacy groups is the rate of revolving debt among its users. Borrowers have the option, if they are unable to pay their balance on payday, to roll the loan over to the next pay period, and they can do this multiples times, increasing the financial danger of this type of indebtedness. Despite the risks involved, however, payday loans have become very widely used—in 1990, there were almost no payday loans centers in the Unites States; in 2006, there were 15,000 such centers servicing $25 billion in debt.[21] Advocates and industry insiders argue that payday loans are providing a necessary financial service for which there is no substitute in the post–bank merger era, when the number of local bank branches has shriveled. Still, there has been widespread concern over the impact of payday lending.

The Federal Reserve in 2000 issued a regulation that all payday lenders must disclose the interest rates of the loans they issue; since then, eleven states have banned or limited the industry.[2] Following its own study in 2006, the Pentagon called for (and President Bush signed into law) a cap of 36 percent for interest rates charged on payday loans to military personnel.[23] Often leading the charge against the expansion of payday loan services have been Community Development Financial Institutions (CDFIs), which are federally designated (usually nonprofit) organizations that offer financial services and education to high-risk clients through a developmental model that offers an alternative to the practices of mainstream financial markets. CDFIs were in the front wave of criticism, for instance, when payday loan companies sought in 2005 to push a bill through the Maine state legislature that would have raised the fees payday loan centers could charge borrowers and exempted the lenders from following the state credit code.[24] A group of consumer advocates, including representatives from Coastal Enterprises Inc. (a Wiscasset, Maine–based CDFI), joined together to defeat the bill, and Maine remains one of the tougher markets for payday loan centers.

The significance of CDFI opposition to payday loan centers lies partly in the simultaneous presentation of alternative financial services, often provided by the CDFIs themselves. While payday loan centers operate openly on "market" principles, engaging risky clients in short-range loans on hard terms, CDFIs provide financial service for the same (low-income) demographic while intentionally developing extramarket instruments and procedures that seek to deliver a benefit in terms of community development through economic education and betterment. More will be said about the role of CDFIs in promoting thrift among low-income groups, but the difference between a community development approach and that of the mainstream payday loan centers is instructive. While the payday loan transaction seeks, in an economically minimalist fashion, to address an immediate financial need with a quick monetary solution, the CDFI experience seeks to confront a range of behavioral and cultural factors in the process of meeting the particular financial needs of its clients. The payday loan proposes to be a merely economic solution, but the normative consequences of its activities become clear in the critical responses of lawmakers, community activists, and even the military administration. CDFIs, on the other hand, make no secret of their normative motivation to bring social goods out of their financial services.

The common thread of these anti-thrift institutions—state lotteries, the democratization of credit cards, and payday loan centers—is the picture they provide of the economic status of the individual. The composite portrayal is that of the free-ranging subject, liberated to make her own financial decisions without having to worry about restriction or regulation. If the system is not working out for you, escape from the hard realities of it with the hope of a winning lottery ticket; if you can't manage to move up to the next socioeconomic level, perhaps the supplementation of a credit card will help you do it; if you run into temporary financial trouble, a short-term, high-interest loan can tide you over as a "onetime" fix. All these arrangements seem to be makeshift responses to deeper and more complex problems with the version of economic normativity that obtains in the early twenty-first-century United States. But are there countercurrents that offer alternatives to this narrow, individualistic account of how to manage in the midst of a system that seems to exclude large swaths of the population?

Community Development Finance Institutions: The Shape of Thrift Now

Telling the story of CDFIs will take us back before the debt developments of the 1980s and 1990s discussed in the previous section, and this is not incidental. One way of thinking about the growth of the current debt culture among LMI populations is that mainstream financial institutions have successfully moved into (and taken advantage of) markets that were pioneered in the 1970s and 1980s by community development organizations. There is a deep irony here, in the sense that CDFIs have long sought to establish "demonstrative impact" in their field, whereby the innovative financial products and services they provide could play a role in shaping the practices of mainstream financial institutions. Things have gone rather differently, though, and in some cases the reverse has happened. Mainstream financial institutions—in the wake of the bank merger wave and the consolidation of many smaller, local banks—have invaded the LMI markets initially opened by CDFIs, but they have not adopted CDFI practices. They have instead imported traditional financial instruments into CDFI territory and caused CDFIs to compete with them for customers.[25] As a result, CDFIs have often shifted their practices to look more like mainstream financial institutions in order to keep up with the banks and investment companies now competing with them.

HISTORY AND STRUCTURE OF THE INDUSTRY

The CDFI industry in its current form is a relatively recent development. While the credit union movement began growing in the first decade of the twentieth century, the scope of activities that CDFIs now offer was a much later development.[26] The oldest CDFIs trace their history back to President Lyndon Johnson's War on Poverty in the 1960s and the creation of the Office of Economic Opportunity, which established Community Development Corporations (CDCs). Their mission was to offer financial services to low-income communities that banks saw as too risky and so to spur economic development in the most impoverished regions of the nation.

CDCs were targeted at both rural and urban poverty, and two of the earliest and most successful were the Kentucky Highlands Investment Corporation (KHIC) in Appalachian Kentucky and the Bedford-Stuyvesant Restoration

Corporation in Brooklyn. These two organizations indicate the broad scope of activities in which CDCs engaged—KHIC mostly invested in small businesses poised for high growth (pioneering a community development venture capital model), while Bedford-Stuyvesant's primary project was administering a $100 million home mortgage fund raised from New York banks.[27] There were also numerous and successful community development credit unions and loan funds that filled out the financial services CDFIs provided their customers. The industry as a whole received a great boon with the federal Community Reinvestment Act (CRA) of 1977, which stipulated that banks must invest a percentage of their capital within the local community where they are based—this provided a strong new stream of capital for CDFIs. The golden era for CDFIs, though, was without a doubt the Clinton administration years, which saw the renewal and expansion of the CRA in 1995 and the creation of a federal CDFI Fund in 1994. Toward the end of the 1990s, programs like the New Markets Tax Credit and New Markets Venture Capital fund provided additional dollars for CDFI initiatives that sought to expand their operations, increase their capitalization, and keep up with mainstream financial institutions in a market that had become much more complicated over the last decade of the century.

The results of this growth were impressive. As of 2001, there were more than 550 CDFIs across the nation, which were managing more than $6.5 billion in assets.[28] A large portion of the CDFI industry is still involved in supporting various forms of "small thrift"—individual savings accounts, home and auto loans, and even small-business start-up loans. This kind of work has been the bread and butter of many CDFIs from the beginning, and many have simply expanded the kind of work they do in these sectors as the industry as a whole has grown and received more public attention and more government and foundation funding.

This growth, however, has also raised questions within the industry about where the future lies for CDFIs. Many advocates state the challenge of the future in stark terms: "The CDFI industry will need to re-engineer, reposition, and re-tool itself in order to be viable in the twenty-first century."[29] One of the largest trade organizations for CDFIs, the Opportunity Finance Network, rolled out a new public awareness campaign for CDFI leaders in 2006 and called it "Grow, Change, or Die." The biggest issue at hand in these discussions is the realization that "CDFIs are without a doubt constrained by their resistance to capital market compliance."[30] This had always been a direct and intentional aspect of the CDFI mission because CDFIs "often see themselves as a parallel system to conventional financial institutions."[31] But at the turn of the century, in the wake of the vast transformation of the banking industry and the increasing play of mainstream institutions for CDFI clientele, the restraints of this philosophy became more evident to industry leaders. And while some stressed the role of CDFIs as "intermediaries" who serve to adapt mainstream practices to unconventional clients, rather than as true innovators in the finance field,[32] others pushed forward in another way, insisting that the key to survival for CDFIs was the development of more sophisticated equity instruments that would increase capitalization and grow the ability of CDFIs to make long-term investments that could yield greater economic and social returns.[33]

COMMUNITY DEVELOPMENT VENTURE CAPITAL

One of the more concrete outcomes of these discussions was the growth of a new subfield—a sort of "big thrift" with a macrofocus—within the CDFI industry that was committed to making equity investments in high-growth industries within low-income census tracts as a means of creating quality jobs and spurring broad-based economic growth in areas of entrenched poverty. This type of CDFI investment had been pioneered by KHIC in the early 1970s. The Community Development Venture Capital (CDVC) model grew across the 1980s and especially the 1990s, but it has exploded onto the CDFI scene only within the last ten years, as key federal legislation has helped solidify industry practices and brought wider attention to the work of CDVCs.

The most important legislative accomplishment was the New Markets Venture Capital (NMVC) program approved by Congress in late 2000, just before President Clinton left office. This initiative, under the authority of the Small Business Administration (SBA), offered $150 million in public investment dollars (called *debentures*) and $30 million in operational assistance grants to six CDVCs that were able to raise matching funds from private sources.[34] The operational assistance grants were one of the more innovative aspects of the NMVC program—this money provided opportunities for the six New Markets Venture Capital Companies (NMVCCs) to engage in a full range of professional development activities with their portfolio companies, including leadership training, business model preparation, and marketing and technological assistance. The funding given to the six initial NMVCCs in 2002 and 2003 represented only half of the original appropriation, but the program was cut early on in the Bush administration, and the remaining seven NMVCCs were never selected or funded. Still, the six NMVCCs that participated in the program had, by 2006, invested nearly $50 million in seventy-five companies and leveraged additional investments of $136 million. They had also created more than 350 new jobs in economically distressed regions of the country.[35]

The question remains, though: Why support Community Development Venture Capital as a strategy to address poverty? Credit unions had for many years been providing low-income customers with account-level banking services, and Community Development Loan Funds (CDLFs) had been offering consumer, car, and home loans to the same groups. The rapid growth of the CDVC movement (more than doubling its capital investments between 2000 and 2004)[36] can be explained in part through the motivation to correct the "venture capital gap" that consolidates private equity investing within a few high-growth regions of the nation. In the first quarter of 2008, for example, forty-two of the top forty-eight deal-making venture capital firms were located in the states of California, Massachusetts, or New York.[37] This means that Silicon Valley and the Boston metroplex receive the lion's share of equity investing necessary to grow new business. The CDVC seeks to bridge this "venture capital gap" by establishing private equity funds in underserved regions that also qualify as federal low-income census tracts.

Thus CDVC pitches itself within the CDFI field as a better way of doing economic development, from a higher vantage point, and effecting larger-scale changes that promise to transform an area with broad economic growth. It is a kind of trickle-down model of community development work. Another common claim of CDVCs is that their funds produce market-rate returns. Indeed, while the initial NMVCCs have yet to finish their first round of investments, some funds are expecting returns as high as 30 percent—a performance that would be respectable even for the traditional field of venture capital investing. There can be no doubt, then, that the rise of CDVCs has pushed the CDFI industry significantly in the direction of conventional market products and services. Most CDVCs are even structured as private, for-profit limited partnerships that are sometimes subsidiaries of larger nonprofit organizations. The biggest players in the CDVC field argue vigorously that bringing home a profit is not at odds with the social mission of community development, and the field is really too young to take any substantial measure of its impact. Still, the drift of the CDFI industry toward this new form of equity investment delivers a certain message even before the outcomes can be assessed.

The shift toward CDVC investing can be seen as a move way from the hands-on, ground-level type of financial services traditionally provided by CDFIs. Instead of offering the "small thrift" services of checking and savings accounts, retirement plans, and home, auto, and small business loans to low-income groups, CDVCs put money into the hands of entrepreneurs and wait for their businesses to grow, hire new workers, and increase tax revenues in low-income regions—the "big thrift" of a more global economic vision. This is an innovative approach for sure, but one that also places the fate of the working poor solidly within the movement of market forces. The problem that has lately affected the American economy more broadly (income inequality, as the benefits of increasing productivity have been disproportionately channeled to economic elites) also becomes a potential danger within the community development world. Resisting this sort of inequality becomes much more difficult when the developmental model is more reliant on market instruments like private equity. The regulations are fewer, and the for-profit nature of the endeavor holds all the potential to crowd out the social goals that drove the innovation in the first place. Perhaps the CDVC industry will cool down in the coming years and take its place within the full range of CDFIs; perhaps new agreements and innovations will even allow CDVCs to more directly support the more hands-on work of the credit unions and CDLFs. It seems undeniable, though, that the advent and relative success of CDVCs has shifted the whole CDFI field, for better or worse, decidedly in the direction of the market practices of mainstream financial institutions.

The Contours of Thrift in the Other America

So where does thrift stand among nonelite groups in the United States today? A complex network of institutional actors and forces impinges on the simple question of frugality among the LMI populations, but understanding its bent also indicates the warp and woof of economic normativity in the first decades of the twenty-first century. We seem to be at the tail end of a long period of dominance by essentially conservative economic philosophy, a movement that has been crystallized in the drive to privatize and deregulate industries and submit ever more sectors of the society to the control of market forces. But liberal politics has gotten the bug as well, and the hybrid programs that have emerged to mix the goals of community development and conventional profitability were birthed in Democratic administrations. The question of the human, on both sides of the political divide, is increasingly posed in narrowly economic terms. Under this rational choice model of philosophical anthropology, the primary mission of the economic life of the nation becomes to free as many as possible to participate in as many markets as possible and let the drivers of self-interest and self-preservation work their magic. This has left large swaths of the population to fall in between the gaps of our broad national prosperity.

Of course even the elite professionals who do succeed are not *all* by themselves; they have a whole range of institutional aids—from the products and advice of investment firms to company-sponsored retirement plans—that enable them to thrive in the do-it-yourself economy. One way to see the more precarious position of many LMI workers is to understand that institutional actors—from financial service companies to advertising agencies—have tried to sell the LMI population on the elite professional lifestyle. And if they don't have the finances to maintain it, banks are more than willing to extend new and more "democratic" forms of credit to fill in the gaps. In effect, debt has been offered as a new enabler of economic citizenship and a bridge that can help LMI groups traverse the territory between the "two Americas." The crossing, however, has proved to be more difficult than many thought (and to have deeper consequences), and those "other Americans" who bought into it have often found themselves without the safety nets of those who are already living in the prosperous America on the other side.

In the context of the credit crisis of 2008, however, the market's mojo seems less reliable than it did ten or fifteen years ago, even for the professional class; each piece of the system (from overstretched borrowers to overeager brokers and investors) was acting in concert with the expectations of rational self-interest—and yet the accumulation of these myriad market impulses resulted in the near collapse of the global banking system. This seems to represent a serious blow for economic thinking as usual. Former chairman of the Federal Reserve Alan Greenspan, who for eighteen years led U.S. monetary policy from the perspective of laissez-faire economics, even admitted that he had been wrong on key aspects of economic orthodoxy: "Those of us who have looked to the self-interest of lending institutions to protect shareholders' equity, myself included, are in a state of shocked disbelief."[38] If Greenspan and his ilk were caught unawares by the utter failure of the market to regulate itself, the surprise has been a good bit more than academic among the vast population of homeowners (many LMI individuals among them) who now face foreclosure and worse on the downside of the mortgage selling frenzy. And yet for many LMI homeowners, the credit crisis is simply the most recent and the most extreme example of a contemporary American economy that seems to be structured mainly for the benefit of higher-income groups. In this sense, the subprime mortgage crisis plays like a cruel joke—the path to upward mobility (in the form of the American dream of home ownership) is extended to a broad population, who are told they can live like the middle class now, but after the Wall Street gang has made its money on the deal, reality sets back in and the easy road to economic security closes up just as quickly as it had opened. Following on the heels of the promise of the democratization of credit, the subprime crisis marks one more way that financial institutions have profited from making LMI groups believe that they can participate, at low cost to themselves, in a financial system that is really calibrated to the resources and needs of individuals with much higher incomes.

But even this group of financial elites is shrinking. The decline of the middle class, perhaps more than any other indicator, has challenged the received wisdom that the new globalized economy is fundamentally working for the elite professionals at the vanguard. While the system favors (perhaps is even designed for) their flexible, mobile, conspicuously consuming lifestyle, it is becoming more and more clear that for this group of movers and shakers also, the collective safety nets have been removed. This new set of circumstances has pointed up the reality that economic thought, talk, and practice are everywhere coded with moral significance. But beyond the ubiquitous accusations of "corporate greed" and the partisan bickering over whose politics created the crisis, we have an opportunity to examine at a deeper level the normative substratum that is widely shared across political lines in contemporary America. The idea of a do-it-yourself economy takes a serious hit when the banks and financial institutions leading the charge begin to need public assistance to stay afloat.

In this new context, the question of thrift can once again offer a language for understanding the shape of our economic situation in terms of a broader notion of the common good. The current era has not been shaped up to now by such thinking. New institutional support for a range of corporate and government activities has exacerbated a "debt culture," the consequences of which are felt most acutely among those with the least income. At the same time, efforts to support and grow healthy financial practices among LMI workers have drifted, in significant ways, toward the macromarket logic that fostered the current income inequality in the first place. Both of these movements have taken thinking about thrift in "the Other America" very far from the mutual aid societies, voluntary associations, and credit unions that sought to address this problem 100 or 200 years ago. Simply recycling these past forms will not begin to address the confusion we are experiencing now. But understanding how the concept of thrift has been narrowed by intensely individualistic, rationalist notions of human motivation can be a starting point for seeing more clearly the problems of the present. And if the language of thrift has often been at the forefront of innovative problem solving in economic struggles of the American past, perhaps a serious reconsideration of the capacious possibilities of thrift (understood as the conditions necessary for human thriving) can initiate the kind of thinking that will lead to an effective set of responses to the global financial crisis that looms in the first decade of this new millennium.

Notes

1. Michael Harrington, *The Other America: Poverty in the United States* (New York: Macmillan, 1962), 158.

2. Ronald T. Wilcox, *Whatever Happened to Thrift? Why Americans Don't Save and What to Do about It* (New Haven, CT: Yale University Press, 2008), 29.

3. Daniel Schneider and Peter Tufano, "New Savings from Old Innovations: Asset Building for the Less Affluent," in *Financing Low-Income Communities: Models, Obstacles, and Future Directions*, ed. Julia Sass Rubin (New York: Russell Sage Foundation, 2007), 17.

4. Ibid, 16.

5. Institute for American Values, *For a New Thrift: Confronting the Debt Culture* (New York: Institute for American Values, 2008).

6. Charles T. Clotfelter, Philip J. Cook, Julie A. Edell, and Marian Moore, "State Lotteries at the Turn of the Century: Report to the National Gambling Impact Study Committee," Duke University (April 23, 1999), 2, http://govinfo.library.unt.edu/ngisc/reports/lotfinal.pdf (accessed December 16, 2008).

7. Ibid., 7.

8. Ibid., 12.

9. Ibid.

10. Ibid.

11. Ibid., 32.

12. Katie Zezima, "Sweet Dreams in Hard Times Add to Lottery Sales," *New York Times*, September 13, 2008, A1.

13. Gary A. Dymski, *The Bank Merger Wave: The Economic Causes and Social Consequences of Financial Consolidation* (New York: M. E. Sharpe, 1999), 41.

14. Robert D. Manning, *Credit Card Nation: The Consequences of America's Addiction to Credit* (New York: Basic Books, 2000), 71.

15. The Center for Responsible Lending, "The Plastic Safety Net: The Reality behind Debt in America" (2005), 5, http://www.responsiblelending.org/pdfs/DEMOS-101205.pdf (accessed August 29, 2008).

16. Institute for American Values, "Debt Facts" (2008), http://www.newthrift.org/pressroom/debtfacts.pdf (accessed December 14, 2008).

17. Center for Responsible Lending,'The Plastic Safety Net," 7.

18. Institute for American Values, "Debt Facts."

19. Ibid.

20. Dymski, *The Bank Merger Wave*, 50.

21. Edward C. Lawrence and Gregory Elliehausen, "A Comparative Analysis of Payday Loan Customers," *Contemporary Economic Policy* 26 (2008): 299–316.

22. "Report Says Payday Loan Fees Cost Consumers $4.6 Billion," *Associated Press Newswires*, November 30, 2006.

23. "Maine's Loan Protection Should Expand," *Bangor Daily News*, December 4, 2006.

24. "'Payday Loan' Chains Look to Expand Maine Presence; State House: Proposed Changes Would Make the Industry More Lucrative," *Portland Press Herald*, March 31, 2005, A1.

25. Alan Okagaki and Kirsten Moy, "Changing Capital Markets and Their Implications for Community Development Finance," Capital Xchange (Washington, DC: Brookings Institution, 2001), 5, http://www.brookings.edu/articles/2001/07metropolitanpolicy_moy.aspx (accessed December 16, 2008).

26. Institute for American Values, *For a New Thrift*, 42–44; Charles D. Tansey, "Community Development Credit Unions: An Emerging Player in Low Income Communities," Capital Xchange (Washington, DC: Brookings Institution, 2001), 3, www.brookings.edu/articles/2001/09metropolitanpolicy_tansey.aspx (accessed December 16, 2008).

27. Okagaki and Moy, "Changing Capital Markets," 2.

28. Mark Pinsky, "Taking Stock: CDFIs Look Ahead after 25 Years of Community Development Finance," Capital Xchange (Washington, DC: Brookings Institution, 2001), 1, http://www.brookings.edu/es/urban/capitalxchange/pinsky.pdf (accessed December 16, 2008).

29. Okagaki and Moy, "Changing Capital Markets," 1.

30. Pinsky, "Taking Stock," 7.

31. Okagaki and Moy, "Changing Capital Markets," 3.

32. Pinsky, "Taking Stock," 10.

33. Nancy Andrews, "Equity with a Twist: The Changing Capital Needs of the Community Development Finance Field," Capital Xchange (Brookings Institution, 2001), 1–2, www.brookings.edu/articles/2001/04metropolitanpolicy_andrews.aspx (accessed December 16, 2008).

34. The program is outlined on the SBA Web site http://www.sba.gov/aboutsba/sbaprograms/inv/nmvc/INV_NMVC_INDEX.html (accessed August 30, 2008).

35. "The NMVC Program: Providing Equity Capital and Expertise to Entrepreneurs in Low-Income Urban and Rural Communities," Community Development Venture Capital Alliance, (2006), http://www.cdvca.org/policy/docs/July_2006_The_New_Markets_Venture_Capital_Program_prepared_by_CDVCA.pdf (accessed December 14, 2008).

36. "Industry Stats," Community Development Venture Capital Alliance, http://www.cdvca.org/(accessed December 14, 2008).

37. "The MoneyTree Report," PricewaterhouseCoopers and the National Venture Capital Association (2008), https://www.pwcmoneytree.com/MTPublic/ns/index.jsp (accessed July 29, 2008).

38. "Greenspan Concedes Error," *New York Times*, October 24, 2008, B1.

21 }

Thrift and Waste in American History

AN ECOLOGICAL VIEW

J. R. McNeill and George Vrtis

In the hearts and minds of most Americans there is, and has long been, a struggle between the rival impulses of restraint and indulgence, of thrift and consumption. Americans are not unique in this respect, but the unusual material abundance of modern American society relaxed constraints on consumption to a degree almost unknown elsewhere. Twentieth-century Americans found themselves in unchallenged possession of a large land, rich in resources, generally equable in climate, and well suited to the existent (and emerging) technologies of transport. Moreover, their society was guided by a state unfettered by dynastic ambitions, only moderately interested in foreign wars, and increasingly committed to economic growth as the salve for all tears in the social fabric. All this, combined with steady demographic growth and plenty of oil and coal, spelled unusual wealth and consumption. Americans eventually created a cultural format in which endless consumption rivaled spiritual grace as the path to worthiness and fulfillment.

The scale and intensity of the American economic experience provided startling ecological transformations, easily visible to observers who traveled the country or, in many cases, to those who remained in the same locale for as long as twenty years. This often provoked dismay and regret, and eventually anxieties about potential scarcities of certain raw materials or natural resources arose. Over time, these concerns found expression in the American conservation and environmental movements and thereby influenced natural resource policies at the national level. Despite these developments, however, the overwhelming direction of American society almost always led toward the consumption of ever greater levels of material goods and the generation of ever greater levels of waste. In terms of Americans' relationship with the natural world in the twentieth century, the struggle between thrift and consumption tilted hard toward the latter.

The Cornucopian Vision

To European explorers, colonists, and generations of settlers, the sheer abundance of the North American landscape seemed to almost defy their abilities to describe it. When Captain Arthur Barlowe visited one of the many barrier islands hugging the North Carolina coast in 1584, he described the island in ways that would be repeated again and again as Europeans and their descendants spread across the continent. "This Island," wrote Barlowe, "had many goodly woodes and full of Deere, Conies, Hares, and Fowle, even in the middest of Summer in incredible abundance."[1] Farther north in the coastal waters off New England, the Reverend Francis Higginson made a similar observation regarding the numbers of fish he observed. Writing in 1630, Higginson described the "aboundance of Sea-Fish" as "almost beyond beleeving." In fact, Higginson continued, "I should scarce have beleeved it except I had seene it with mine owne eyes."[2] Even more astonishing were the seasonal flights of passenger pigeons, which left more than one observer grasping for words to describe the immense flocks. Near the northern limits of Massachusetts, the surveyor Richard Hazen wrote of passing through three miles of countryside in 1741 where the "pigeons' nests were so thick that five hundred might have been told on the beech trees at one time."[3] Others described flocks containing so many millions upon millions of birds that they required hours to pass overhead and could even, as the naturalist John James Audubon described in 1840, cause branches and whole trees to give way where they landed.[4]

Much the same was written about many of North America's other native creatures, as well as its forests, grasslands, soils, and stocks of minerals. From the Atlantic seaboard to the shores of the Pacific Ocean, fur traders found beavers, raccoons, otters, martens, foxes, deer, and other animals in almost incredible numbers.[5] Nothing, though, stirred travelers' and settlers' imaginations like the huge herds of buffalo they encountered as they traversed the Great Plains. While ascending the Platte River in 1820, the botanist-explorer Edwin James described one such congregation: "Immediately upon surmounting this undulation we saw before us, . . . immense herds of bisons, grazing in undisturbed possession; and obscuring, with the density of their numbers, the verdant plain; to the right and left, as far as the eye was permitted to rove, the crowd seemed hardly to diminish, and it would be no exaggeration to say, that at least ten thousand burst on our sight in the instant."[6] Lumbermen drew on comparable superlatives to describe the magnificent forests of the Middle West, Rocky Mountains, and Pacific Northwest, just as ranchers, farmers, and miners often seemed to stumble in search of words to depict the rich grasslands, soils, and gold and silver deposits they found scattered across the country.[7]

Experiences and perceptions such as these did little to moderate resource use; in fact, combined with forces of European demographic and economic expansion, they surely encouraged it. Across the continent, individual species and whole ecosystems disappeared. Beaver were extirpated from much of New England by the late seventeenth century, and their numbers declined across the continent as fur traders pushed beyond the Great Lakes and into the trans-Mississippi West in the early nineteenth century.[8] By the late 1870s, the passenger pigeon had vanished from most of the eastern United States, and in 1914 the last known member of the species died in captivity at the Cincinnati Zoo.[9] By 1889, only a few hundred bison remained of a species that only three decades earlier had numbered in the tens of millions.[10] Forests, prairies, and mineral-rich mountainsides were all overrun as well. In places like the great northern woodlands of Michigan and Wisconsin, as well as the towering old-growth forests of California's Sierra Nevada and coastal ranges, whole forests were cut down and used to provide for industries such as farming and mining or to build cities like Chicago, San Francisco, and the countless other urban places that sprang into existence in the nineteenth century. Prairies gave way to farms and ranches; mountains were turned inside out in the search for precious metals; rivers were replumbed—and each of these developments generated a myriad of complex environmental problems, including soil erosion, flooding, and many new forms of pollution.[11] In all, much of the ecological abundance that had so impressed earlier European colonists and settlers was quickly disappearing or being degraded by the later decades of the nineteenth century. These rapid and large-scale ecological transformations—the life's work of millions—underpinned American prosperity and economic growth and seemed to most Americans a satisfactory course for their country.

Environmental Concern

As wildlife, timber, and other natural resources diminished—and pollution and environmental degradation mounted—Americans began to reconsider their relationship with the natural world. Although notions of thrift, stewardship, and conservation in relation to land use were not entirely new, they gained national attention beginning in the late 1800s. By then, local concerns over declining forests, dwindling wildlife populations, and increasingly polluted urban areas had begun to coalesce and slowly raise awareness about environmental issues at the national level. Between about 1890 and 1920, as both environmental threats and public awareness increased, efforts to conserve natural resources and improve Americans' waste-disposal practices gathered momentum and emerged as a powerful national political movement alongside other Progressive Era reforms.[12]

From the beginning, the American conservation movement represented many different interests. For many, the rapid and often profligate consumption of natural resources raised fears about future scarcities and possible limits to the nation's exuberant growth. This was particularly evident in terms of the nation's forests, where unregulated cutting had leveled vast stretches of woodlands and led to widespread soil erosion, flooding, and sometimes massive fires in the cutover lands. In response to such developments and to a growing body of knowledge on the state of the nation's forests and the importance in regulating water flow, Congress passed a bill in 1891 containing an obscure rider (section 24) subsequently known as the Forest Reserve Act. This act, as the historian Stephen Fox has pointed out, set a "bench mark in conservation history," empowering the president to set aside federal lands as "forest reserves."[13] The management of those lands was eventually defined by the 1897 Forest Management Act and deeply influenced by the first chief forester of the U.S. Forest Service, Gifford Pinchot. Under Pinchot's leadership and backed by the conservation-minded president, Theodore Roosevelt, forestry officials focused on the efficient, scientific, and sustainable management of the nation's forest reserves in order, as Pinchot put it, to provide "the greatest good to the greatest number for the longest time."[14] This focus on using scientific expertise to increase efficiency and provide for current and future generations, as the historian Samuel Hays has argued, is at the heart of the conservation movement.[15] It also infused notions of thrift into the nation's land-use policies for generations to come.

While many concentrated on the conservation of natural resources like timber and water, others turned their attention to the nation's wild animals. The dramatic decline of the passenger pigeon, the American bison, and, perhaps even more important, common game species such as white-tailed deer and waterfowl sparked efforts to protect wildlife. Sportsmen and wildlife enthusiasts formed organizations such as the American Ornithologists' Union (1883), the Audubon Society (1886), and the Boone and Crockett Club (1887), all of which were dedicated to conserving various wildlife species. At the federal level, Congress passed the Lacey Act in 1900, which outlawed the interstate transport of birds killed in violation of state laws. And in 1913, passage of the Weeks-McLean Migratory Bird Act empowered the Bureau of Biological Survey in the Department of Agriculture to regulate bird hunting and protect threatened species at the national level.[16]

The conservation movement also included, in addition to those concerned with the efficient use of resources and the protection of favored game species, several other interests whose relationship to the idea of thrift is less clear. Some, like the influential founder of the Sierra Club, John Muir, sought to preserve wilderness for aesthetic, spiritual, and biocentric reasons, arguing that certain landscapes ought to be set aside from all types of resource use. This sentiment found expression in the creation of national parks and wilderness areas, beginning with the establishment of Yellowstone National Park in 1872.[17]

Still others focused on more immediate concerns. The rapid growth of industrial cities like Pittsburgh, Cleveland, and Chicago created all sorts of new environmental problems that threatened peoples' health. Noise, dirty streets, smoke-filled air, polluted water, crowd diseases, poorly organized waste collection systems, unregulated dumping, lack of sanitation facilities and potable water—all these problems and more plagued industrial cities well into the early twentieth century. By then, however, efforts were under way to address these issues as cities turned to scientifically trained professionals to deal with sanitation, pollution control, public health, and water and air quality.[18]

The American conservation movement, then, was an important period of reconsideration in the nation's environmental history. Never before had environmental issues related to notions of conservation and thrift gained national prominence. And never before had such ideas influenced natural resources policy at the national level. In the decades following the Progressive Era, the various interests that made up the conservation movement would continue to grow and broaden and ultimately come together in the even more diverse environmental movement beginning in the 1950s.

While the environmental movement would ultimately become composed of a vast array of complex (and sometimes conflicting) impulses—everything from reforming the urban and industrial order to curbing the use of nuclear power and promoting environmental justice—one thread would continue to link the movement to its Progressive Era roots and attitudes about thrift. The idea of using natural resources more efficiently, of being wise, prudent, and farsighted stewards of the land, was carried forward into the age of environmentalism. Its legacy can be seen most clearly in the organizations, commissions, and national policies that emerged to promote more efficient natural resource management strategies and address possible material shortages. For example, the establishment of the U.S. Soil Conservation Service (1935), the Conservation Foundation (1948), and Resources for the Future (1952), as well as the assembly of the President's Materials Policy Commission in 1952 and the enactment of federal automobile fuel economy standards (known as CAFE standards) in 1975, all shared in the older conservationists' concerns over efficiency, thrift, and wise use.[19]

Thus, from the beginning, ideas about thrift were evident in both the conservation and environmental movements. They animated one current of these diverse movements and thereby influenced Americans' relationship with the natural world.

Material Realities I: Consumption and Production since 1900

Like all peoples at all times, modern Americans could not make something from nothing. Fortunately for them, the continental expanse of the United States contained bountiful natural resources appropriate for both an agricultural and an industrial economy: fertile soils, fresh water, timber, coal, oil, and minerals were there in generous quantities, just waiting, it seemed, to be used. In the twentieth century they would be used as never before, despite the anxieties developing in conservation and environmentalist circles. In an apparent paradox, Americans used natural resources more efficiently but, at the same time, they used more of them than ever before.

One important reason behind this apparent paradox was that the number of Americans producing and consuming things grew steadily. In 1900 the national population numbered some 76 million. By 1950 it had doubled to 152 million, and by 2000 it had nearly doubled again, reaching 282 million—making the United States the third most populous country in the world. This century-long quadrupling proceeded with remarkable steadiness, despite the effects of world wars, economic downturns, and changing immigration policies (figure 21.1). The global population also showed a fourfold increase over the twentieth century; the American experience in this respect was routine.

The American economic experience was more exceptional. The size of the U.S. economy grew about elevenfold between 1929, when the first careful estimates were made, and 2000 (figure 21.2). Over the course of the century as a whole, the growth likely came to about twenty-five-fold.[20] This enormous expansion resulted partly from mere population growth, but in greater

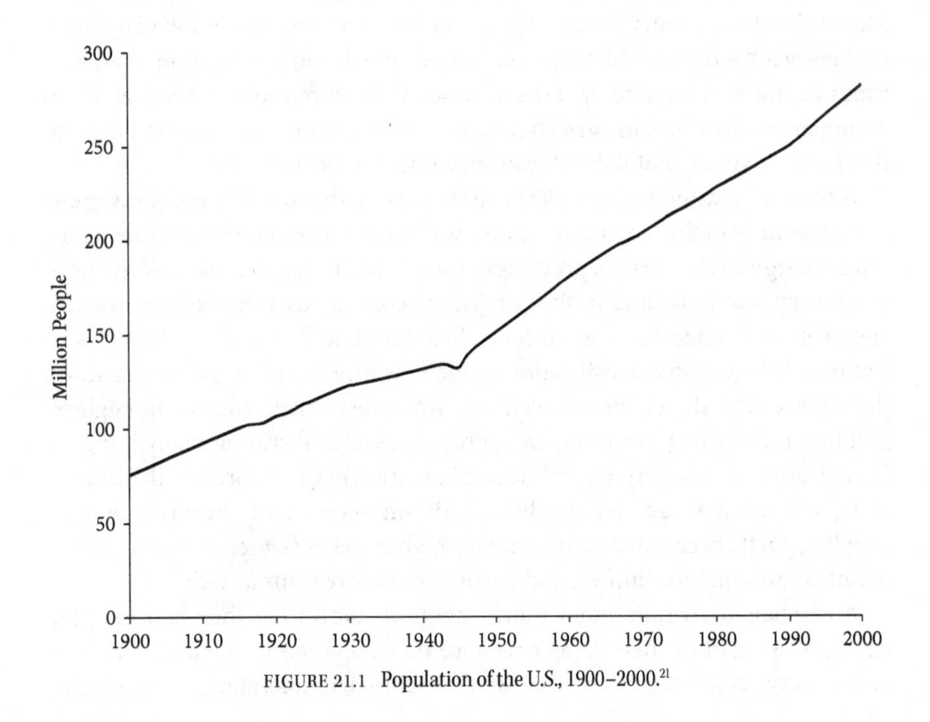

FIGURE 21.1 Population of the U.S., 1900–2000.[21]

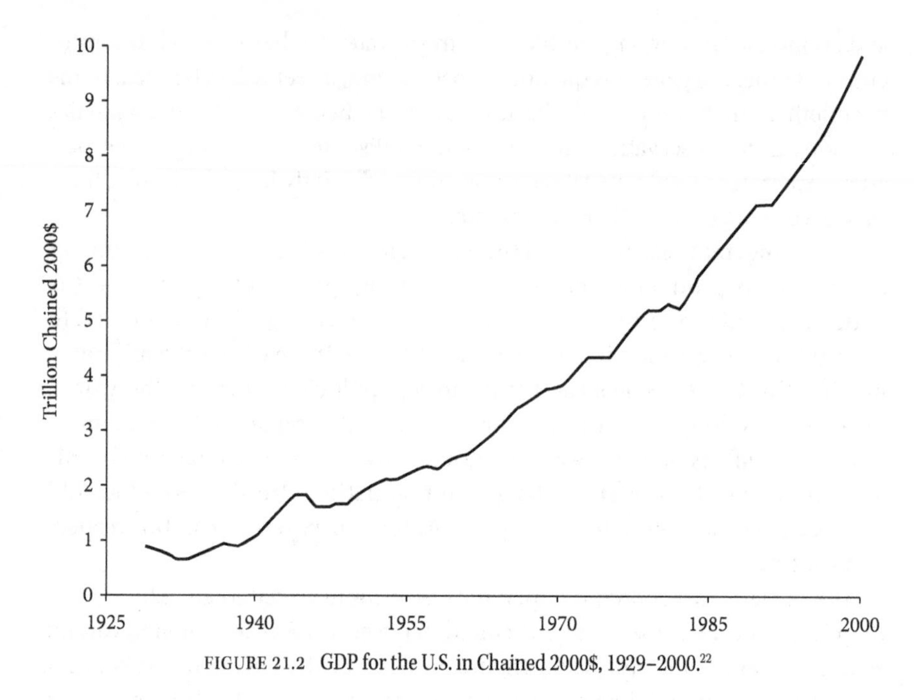

FIGURE 21.2 GDP for the U.S. in Chained 2000$, 1929–2000.[22]

measure from large gains in productivity per worker, which was a result of new technologies such as the electrified assembly line, introduced in Ford Motor Company plants in 1912. The resultant prosperity was unlike anything in American economic history—or, indeed, the world's. Americans had five times as much money to spend on personal consumption in 2000 as their grandparents had had in 1929 (figure 21.3). Production and consumption on this scale inevitably put natural resources under acute pressure.

A primary reason, perhaps *the* primary reason, that the U.S. economy grew so exuberantly in the twentieth century was the application of ever more inanimate energy to the various processes of work and transport. Most of the new machinery that took hold in the American economy used fossil fuels or used electricity generated from fossil fuels, hydroelectric dams, or nuclear power stations. This was an intensification of the new direction in economic history that emerged in the eighteenth century, when fossil fuels and steam engines first began to deliver power on an appreciable scale, liberating many humans from drudging muscular toil. While this liberation began in Britain, the United States carried it to greater heights, partly on account of abundant energy supplies, partly because of comparatively higher wages (which encouraged the use of laborsaving machines), and partly for other reasons as well.

Americans used four times more energy in 1900 than they had in 1850, largely as a result of their greater reliance on coal. Then in the next hundred years, energy consumption rose by another tenfold, thanks above all else to the

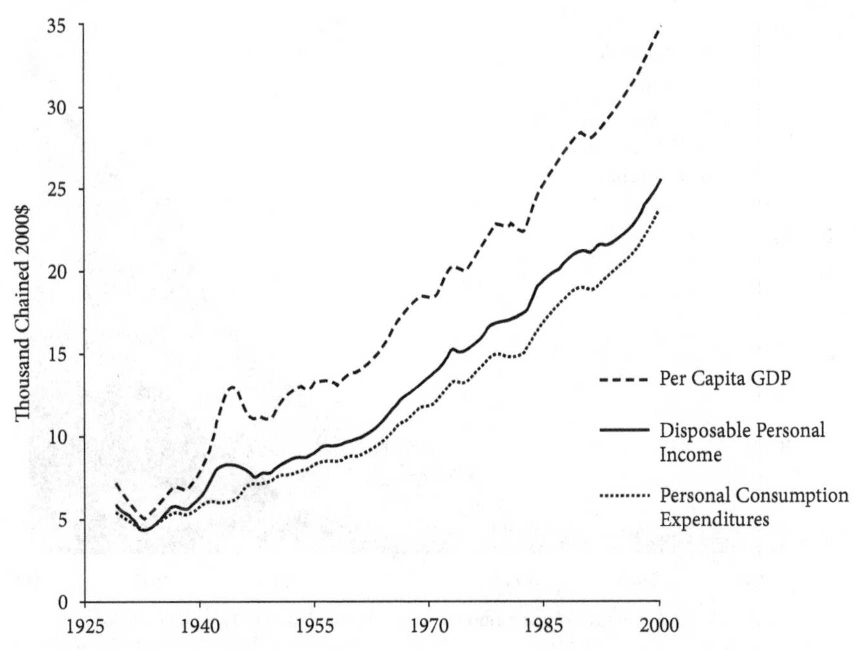

FIGURE 21.3 Per Capita GDP, Disposable Personal Income, and Personal Consumption Expenditures in the U.S., in Chained 2000$, 1929–2000.[23]

emergence of oil as the dominant fuel in transport and a major fuel elsewhere in the economy. By the late 1940s, oil had outstripped coal as the primary fuel in the U.S. economy (figure 21.4). Americans built a high-energy economy before anyone else, and on a larger scale than anyone else, thanks to abundant supplies of fossil fuels, flexible business and government structures that allowed new technologies to take root, and the entrepreneurial and political skills of coal and oil businessmen.

Although the American economy has consistently used ever more energy, with only momentary dips during the Great Depression of the 1930s and the oil crises of the 1970s, the economic efficiency of energy use has improved since the 1920s. That is, the amount of gross national product generated per unit of energy consumed has grown since about 1920. Or, put another way, the energy intensity of the American economy has declined since 1920. This is mainly a result of sectoral shifts away from agriculture and heavy industry and toward services, but it is also a result of technical advances in, for example, steel manufacture, pulp and paper mills, and electricity generation.[24]

The voracious consumption of energy revolutionized the lives of ordinary Americans after 1900. Per capita energy use remained very steady in the latter half of the nineteenth century, but it climbed with electrification in the early twentieth century. After falling during the Great Depression, per capita energy use rocketed upward during World War II (1941–45) and climbed yet faster during the 1960s.

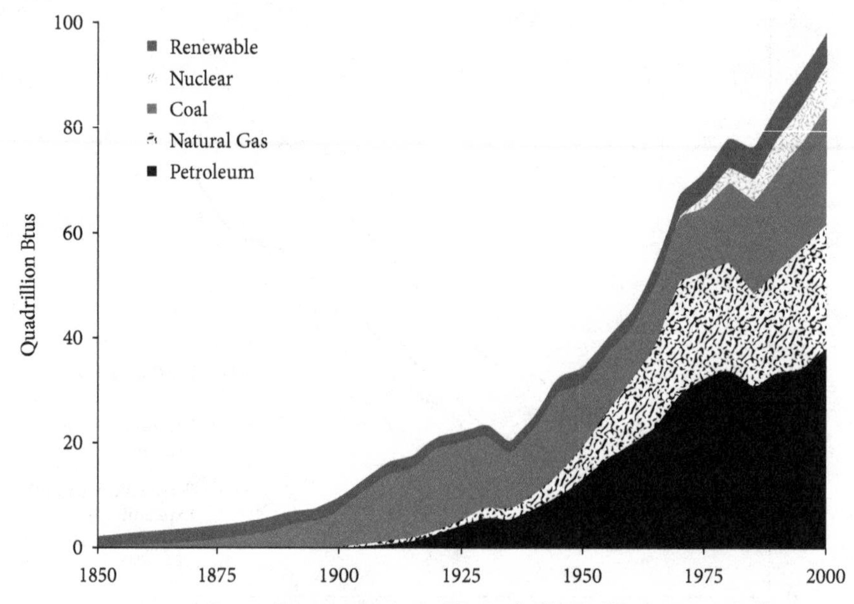

FIGURE 21.4 Energy Consumption in the U.S., Stacked by Fuel Type, 1850–2000.[25]

Since the early 1970s it has again stayed fairly steady; indeed, the absolute peak came in 1978–79 (figure 21.5). This trajectory reflects the saturation of American society with the personal automobile, the arrival of household appliances run on electricity (which assisted materially in a social revolution in the home), and, in general, a vast substitution of electricity and gasoline for muscular exertion.

Concern for thrift and anxieties about waste when it came to energy cropped up most frequently with respect to oil. As early as the 1920s, some in the oil business predicted exhaustion of supplies and urged conservation. But in the 1930s vast new oil fields were discovered, quelling anxieties, for the most part, until the politically induced price hikes of the 1970s. Americans responded mainly through efforts to expand supply rather than curtail consumption, although it should be noted that Americans cut back on energy consumption during the Great Depression (out of financial necessity rather than concern for supply), and they also briefly cut back on oil consumption after the oil shocks of the 1970s because prices rose steeply. But in the past, whether the 1930s or the 1970s, conditions soon returned to normal: that is, cheap energy, and consumption in absolute, if not per capita, terms grew once more. By and large efforts to expand supply, whether through more vigorous exploration within the United States (1930s) or through foreign policy measures that assured the flow of oil from the Persian Gulf and elsewhere, succeeded.[26] The first strategy is now surely exhausted (there are no new oil fields, even in Alaska, that contain more than a few months' supply for the United States); the second is currently in crisis, but it is imprudent to conclude it has run its course.

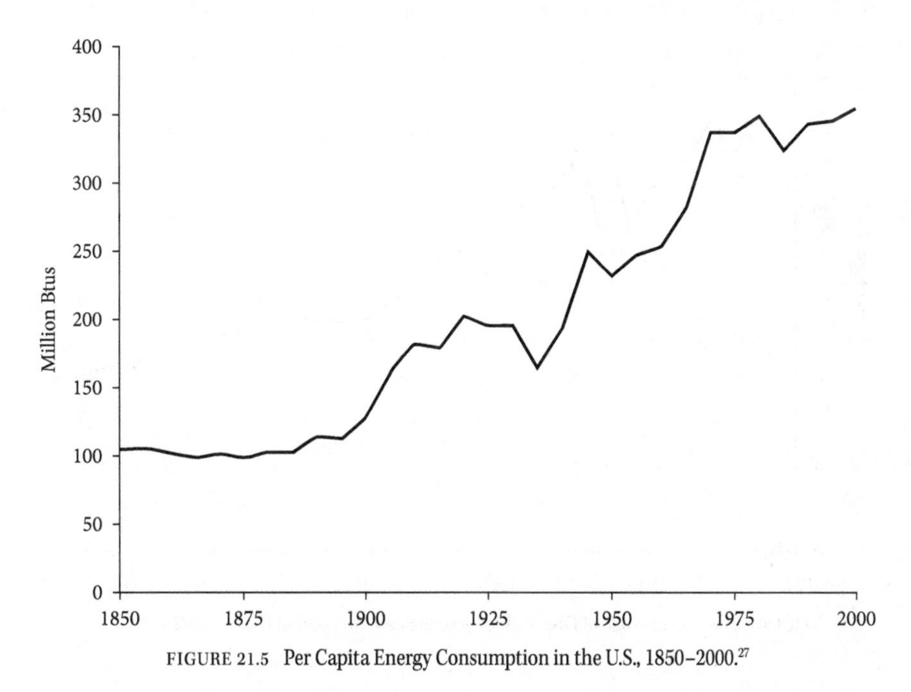

FIGURE 21.5 Per Capita Energy Consumption in the U.S., 1850–2000.[27]

Among the sectors of the American economy revolutionized by cheap energy was agriculture. In the nineteenth century American agriculture was, like agriculture everywhere, dependent on human or animal muscles, and most of the food raised went into nourishing those very muscles. As a result, urbanization and industrialization were constrained by food supply. As late as 1920, half of Americans lived on farms. But oil-powered machinery—tractors, harvesters, and combines—and oil-derived fertilizers began to raise yields, slowly at first and more rapidly from the 1940s onward. Thus the same acre came to produce two to four times as much wheat, corn, soybeans, or cotton, and farm laborers could produce ten times as much as their grandparents had. In economic terms, oil brought great efficiency gains to agriculture. In energy terms the reverse was true: mechanized, high-input agriculture used several calories of energy to produce a single calorie of food.

The substitution of energy for labor in agriculture helped make food cheap. After the 1930s, the United States had almost banished persistent hunger in its population. On average, families in the 1930s spent a quarter of their income on food; by 1999 they spent only 10 percent (figure 21.6). And they ate much more, although not necessarily better, food. The caloric intake of Americans rose by nearly a quarter from 1961 to 2000 (figure 21.7). The efficiency of the agricultural economy, combined with overall economic growth, made food a minor part of the household economy—a situation unprecedented in the history of the world. As a result, it seemed rational for Americans to throw away vast tonnages of food every day.

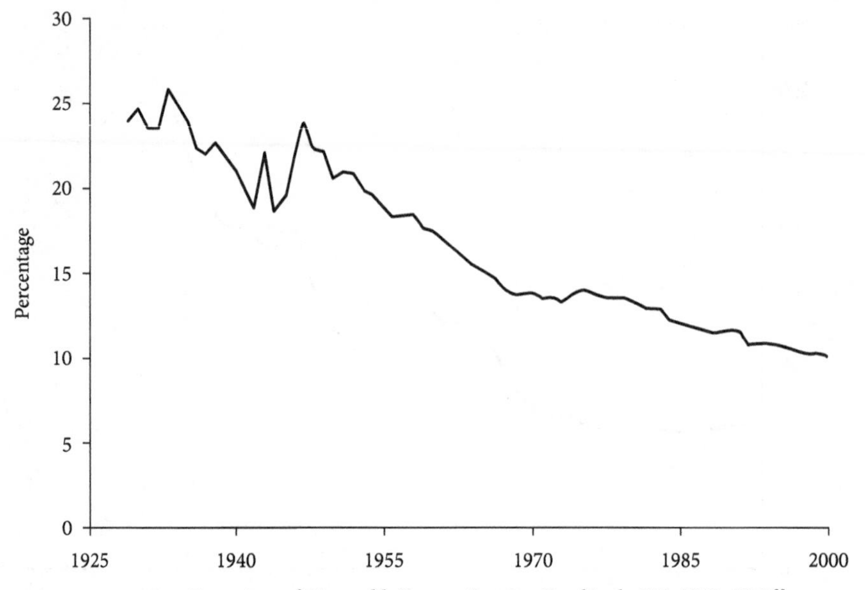

FIGURE 21.6 Percentage of Disposable Income Spent on Food in the U.S., 1929–2000.[28]

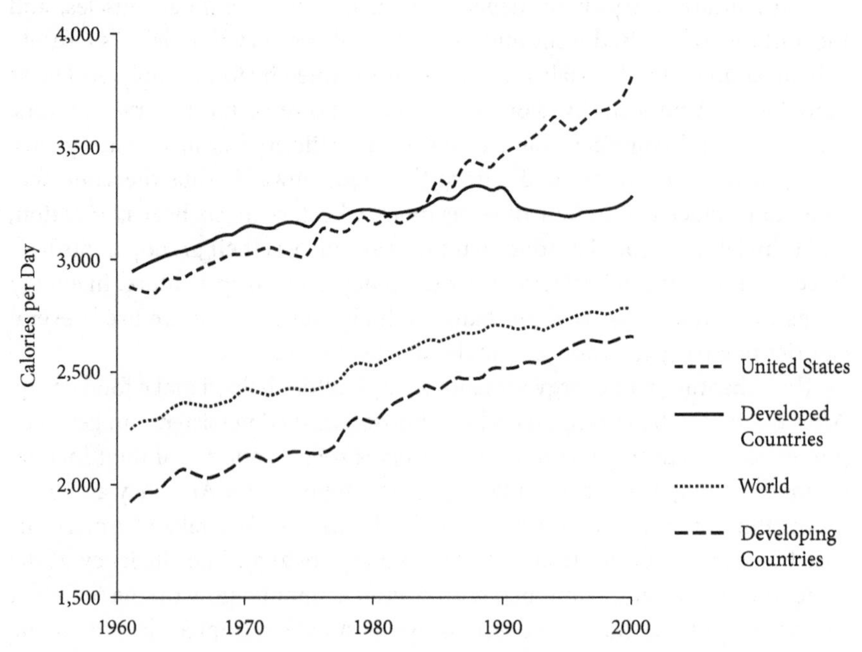

FIGURE 21.7 Daily Per Capita Consumption of Calories in the U.S. and Selected Other Regions, 1961–2000.[29]

In American agriculture, at least to the west of the Mississippi River, oil and water mixed. To make the most of fertilizers, pesticides, and specially bred crops, farmers needed water at the right times, in the right quantities, and in the right places. High-input agriculture also meant high inputs of irrigation water. Until the 1980s, American farmers, like their counterparts elsewhere around the world, used more than half of the total amount of freshwater withdrawals, while industry and domestic users divided the rest. (Lately, industry has overtaken agriculture as a water consumer.)[30] Americans used about eight times as much water at the end of the twentieth century as at the beginning. Their thirst grew fastest between 1950 and 1980, as farmers extended the domain of irrigation, particularly in California and on the Great Plains. Since 1980, however, Americans have managed to use less water—not merely in per capita terms but overall—despite population growth (figure 21.8). This is a remarkable departure from the overall trend of ever-more-intense resource use. It is explained partly by the introduction or extension of water pricing for irrigation and partly by gains in technical efficiency. There remains considerable scope for further increases in efficiency in the nation's water system—as in almost every other country.

The changes in agriculture freed (or obliged) tens of millions of people to leave farms for cities. There they took part in the growing industrialization of the country. From its agrarian origins, the United States had become the world's leading industrial producer by about 1890, and then the country embarked on a spurt of industrial growth checked only briefly by the Great Depression. Two world wars fought far from American soil (and factories)

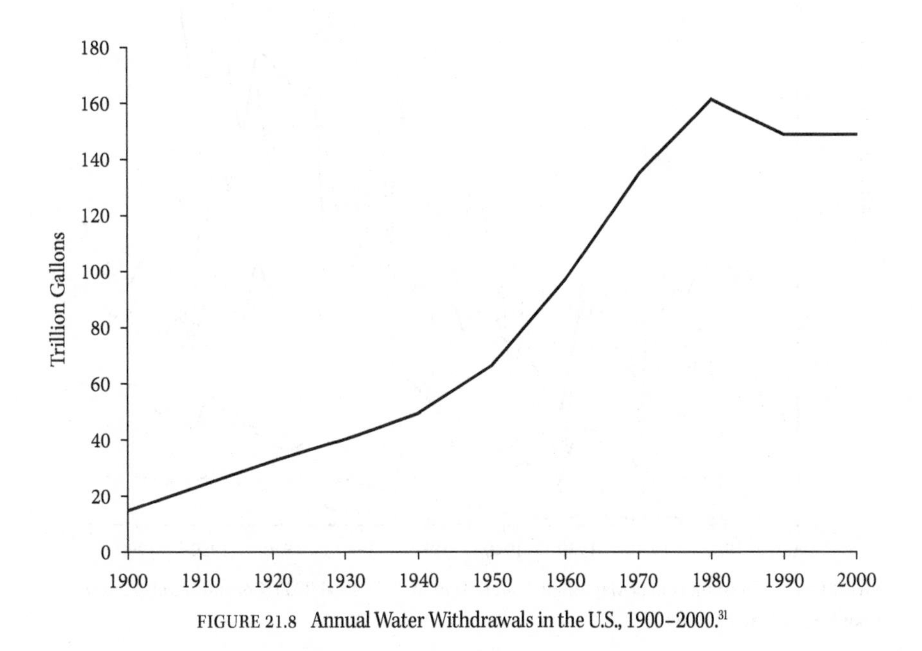

FIGURE 21.8 Annual Water Withdrawals in the U.S., 1900–2000.[31]

helped spur the process, as did military demand throughout the Cold War. But the principal driving force behind industrial growth was consumer demand from American households.

Aside from energy and water, American industry needed a congeries of raw materials, nearly everything from asbestos to zinc. Tens of millions of tons, eventually more than a hundred million tons, of iron went into manufacturing, as did lesser quantities of copper, aluminum, and other metals. The decline of the American steel industry in the 1970s checked the demand for iron, which thereafter, like freshwater use, bucked the general trend. But use of other metals continued to climb. So did consumption of wood and cement, used mainly in the construction industry (figures 21.9 and 21.10).

As with its use of water and energy, American industry became more efficient in its use of metals, wood, cement, and many other raw materials. Technical improvements meant, for example, that automobiles contained much less steel in 1995 than they did in 1955 and that a given ton of steel

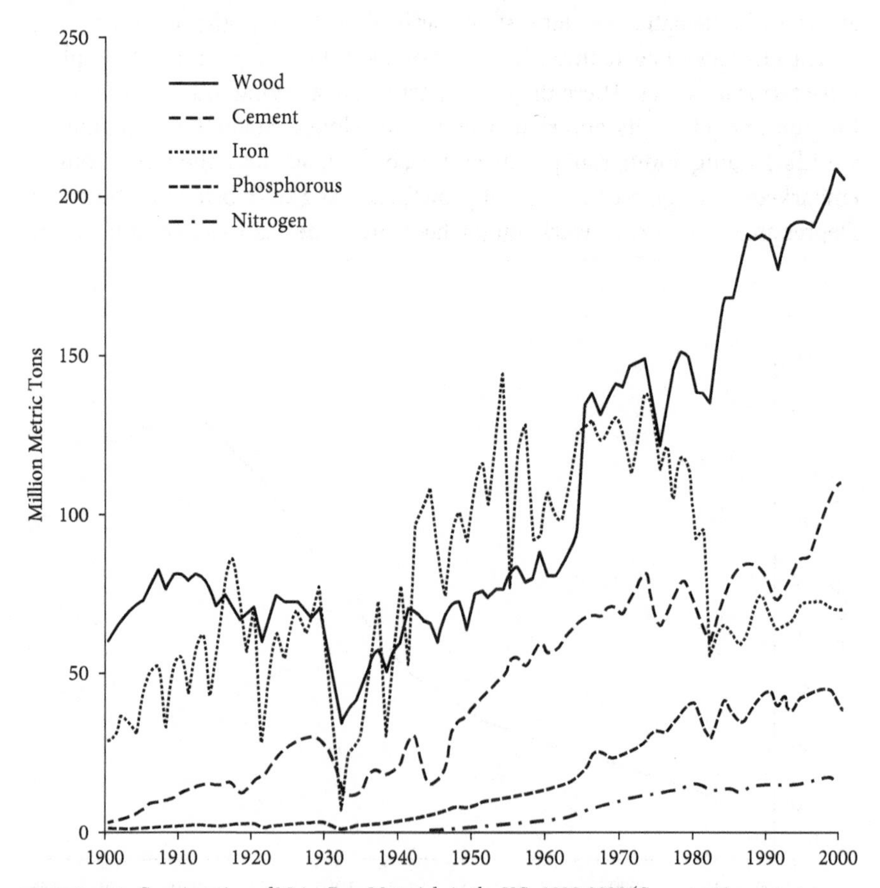

FIGURE 21.9 Consumption of Major Raw Materials in the U.S., 1900-2000 (Consumption *greater* than 8 million metric tons).[32]

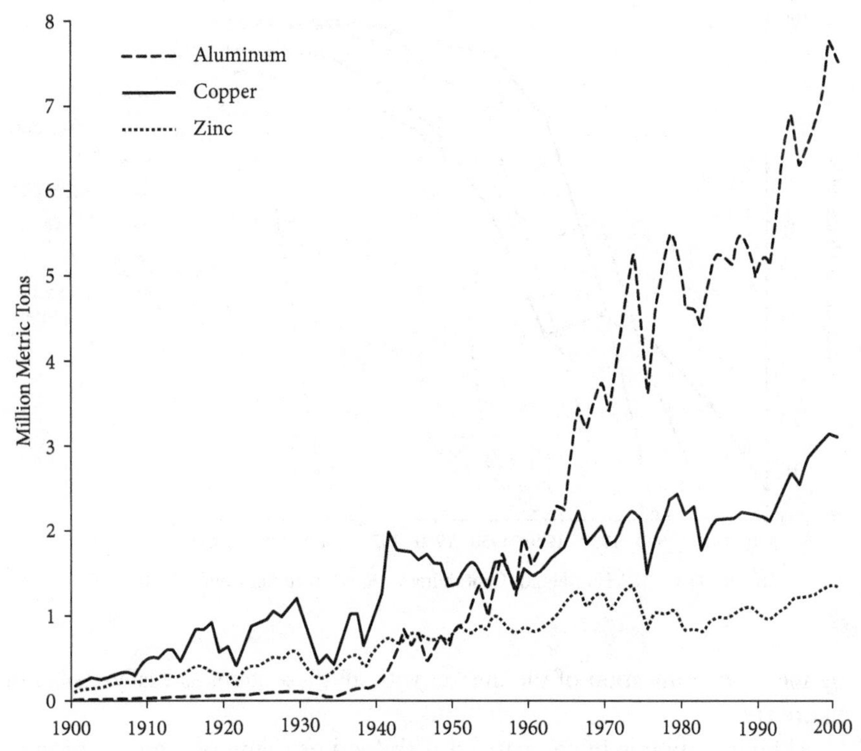

FIGURE 21.10 Consumption of Major Raw Materials in the U.S., 1900–2000 (Consumption *less* than 8 million metric tons).[33]

required far less iron ore. But these efficiency gains were largely masked (except for iron) by the overall expansion of production.

Although the military gobbled up a sizable share of raw materials (generally ranging from a tenth to a quarter between 1942 and 2000) and exports of manufactures accounted for some more (especially before 1975), most of the demand came from American households. The United States contained about 15 million households in 1900 and more than 100 million in 2000. This sixfold increase reflects both a fourfold population growth and the growing tendency among young adults to establish their own households. The number of households, as opposed to mere population, is important because of its effect on consumption. From the 1920s onward, households rapidly began to acquire so-called consumer durables, such as radios, TVs, telephones, refrigerators, washing machines, and dryers; beginning in the early 1980s, they added personal computers and VCRs (figure 21.11). As noted earlier, these appliances made household work a lot easier. They also raised the energy and materials demand of American households substantially, as did automobiles, owned by a quarter of American households in 1920, and three-quarters of households

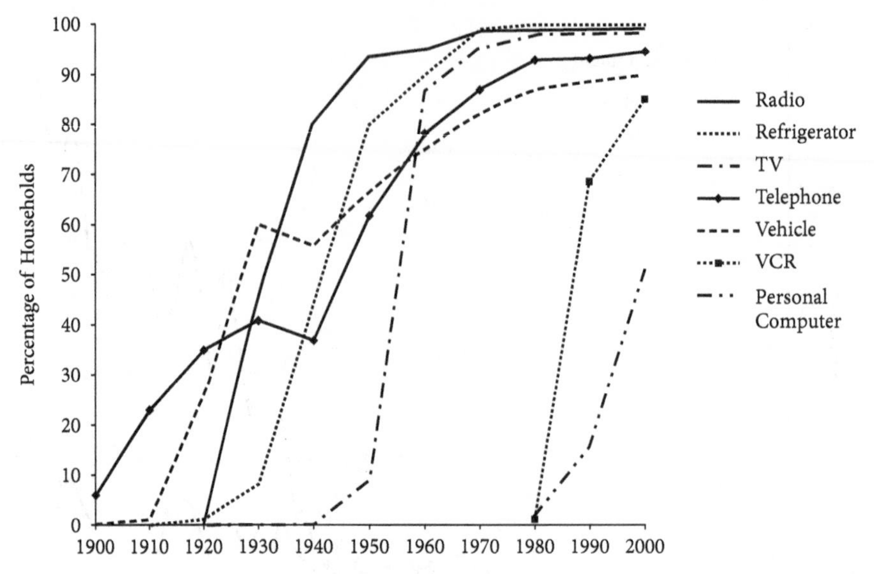

FIGURE 21.11 U.S. Households Containing Various Consumer Goods, 1900–2000.[34]

by 1960. The saturation of the market with all these items is easily visible in figure 21.11.

Although durable in comparison with food or shampoo, most consumer durables were not built to last. They were built to be replaced in a few years, either because they broke down or because they were made to seem inadequate when compared with newer models. At Ford Motor Company, for instance, the head of styling in the 1950s, George Walker, explained his company's strategy of planned obsolescence this way: "We design a car to make a man unhappy with his 1957 Ford 'long about the end of 1959."[35] This, of course, was true of countless items, from razor blades to tennis balls. Moreover, Americans used their household machines more and more because their operating costs (usually electricity or gasoline) were low and their services were agreeable and convenient: Americans came to wash their clothes more often, drive their cars more miles (figure 21.12), and, in many cases, own multiple radios, TVs, and personal computers. In many corners of American society, owning an elderly car or computer came to carry a stigma. Hence, in part, consumer behavior held enormous implications for Americans' use of raw materials.[36]

As the twentieth century wore on, the American continent could supply less and less of the economy's demand for raw materials. Happily for Americans, it was a large planet with plenty of timber, oil, rubber, and so forth available on world markets. While the United States remained self-sufficient in many raw materials, far more so than some other large countries—such as Japan, Germany, and Great Britain—it still drew

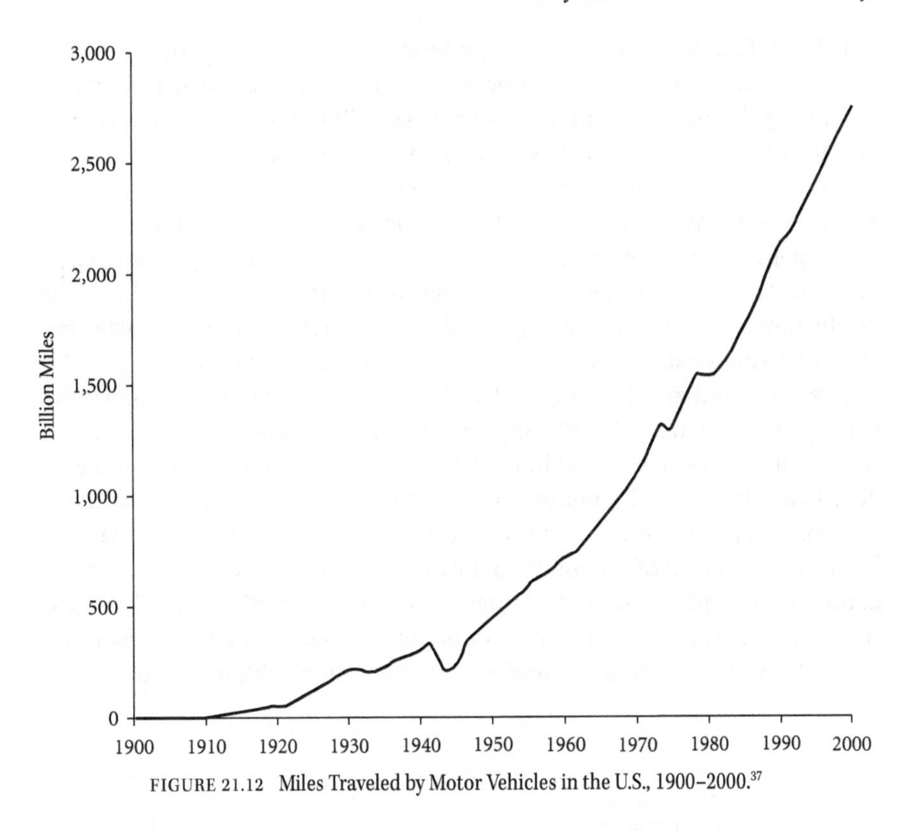

FIGURE 21.12 Miles Traveled by Motor Vehicles in the U.S., 1900–2000.[37]

increasingly on the rest of the globe and accordingly spread its "ecological footprint" far and wide.[38]

Material Realities II: Wastes and Recycling since 1900

All production and consumption is imperfectly efficient: it produces useless wastes. In general, where market signals are the dominant forces shaping consumption patterns, cheap raw materials, cheap energy, and cheap food mean a lot of wastes. Americans' wasteful behavior had long irritated foreign observers such as the Finnish-Swedish botanist Peter Kalm, who traveled through eastern North America in the 1740s. "In a word," wrote Kalm, "the grain fields, the meadows, the forests, the cattle, etc., are treated with equal carelessness; and the characteristics of the English nation, so well skilled in these branches of husbandry, is scarcely recognizable here. We can hardly be more hostile toward our woods in Sweden and Finland than they are here: their eyes are fixed upon the present gain, and they are blind to the future."[39] The patterns of the twentieth century demonstrate continuity in American attitudes and behavior in a radically different material environment.

Official figures on wastes and pollution date back only thirty-five to forty-five years. Since 1960, Americans have nearly tripled their production of municipal solid waste, increasing from 88 million tons in 1960 to 234 million tons in 2000. Overall, however, the total amount of refuse consigned to landfills has actually decreased in recent years. Landfill wastes peaked at 172 million tons around 1990 and then dropped to 165 million tons in 2000. While population increases account for a large share of the rise in aggregate discards, an increase in per capita figures during this period also drove the production of wastes. Between 1960 and 2000, the total amount of waste generated by Americans on a daily basis rose from 2.7 to 4.6 pounds per day (figures 21.13 and 21.14). Compared with that of other countries, Americans' per capita production of waste appears high. For example, according to one study of urban waste disposal in the late 1980s, residents of Los Angeles produced an astounding 6.4 pounds of garbage per day, whereas those of Paris and Toronto produced 2.4, and Rome just 1.5, pounds of garbage per day.[40]

The composition of the municipal waste stream reflects the "throwaway" nature of American society. Paper and plastics—which are the most common materials used in consumer packaging—accounted for nearly half of all the waste generated. Food scraps also remain high, amounting to

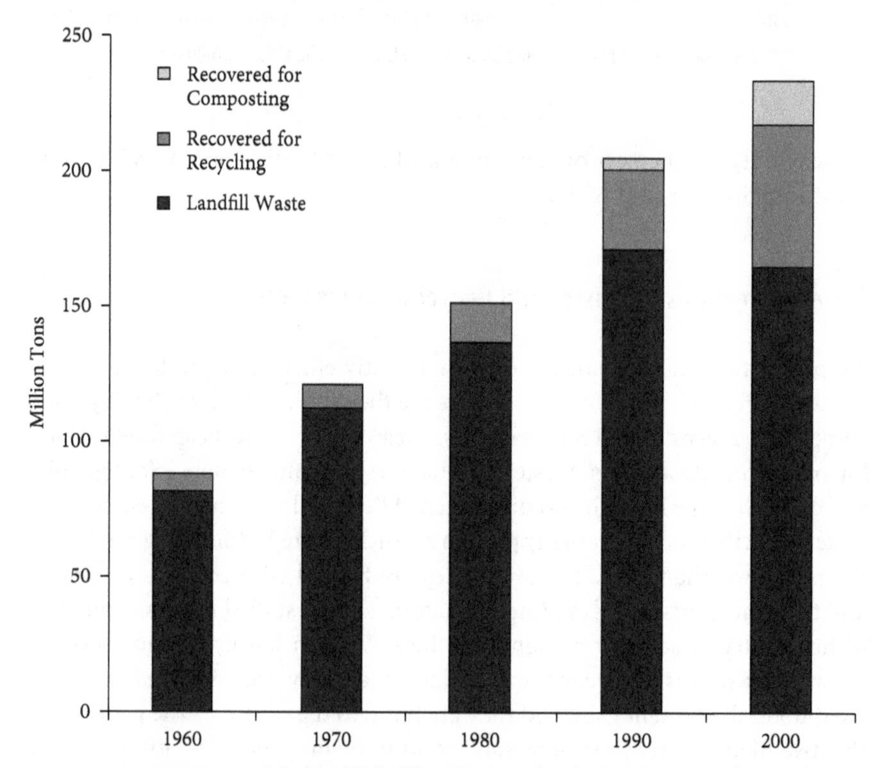

FIGURE 21.13 Municipal Solid Waste Generated in the U.S., 1960–2000.[41]

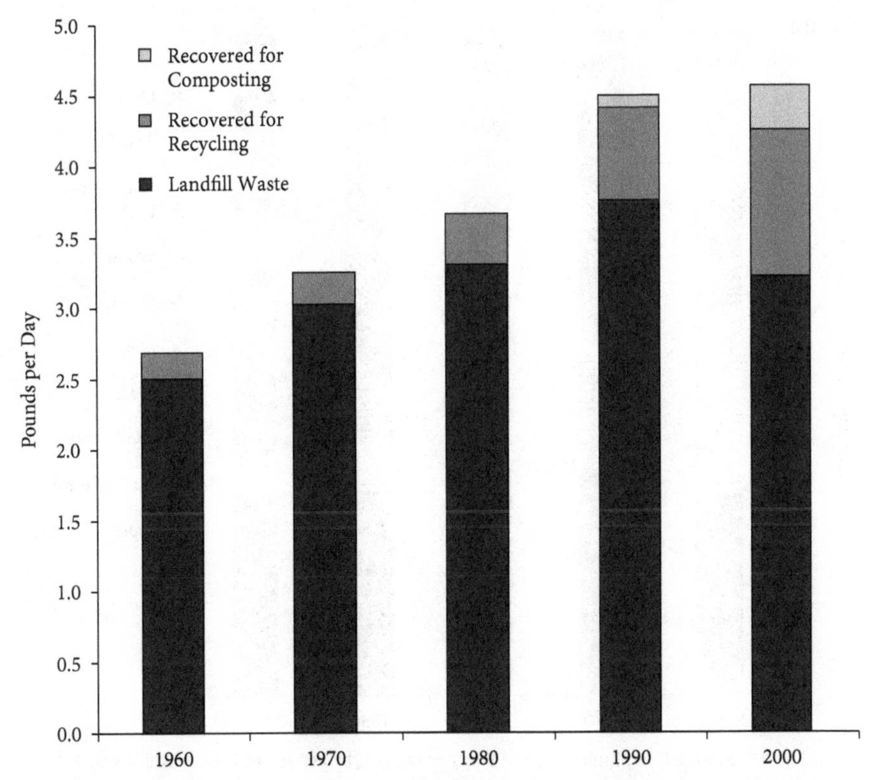

FIGURE 21.14 Per Capita Municipal Solid Waste Generated in the U.S., 1960–2000.[42]

nearly 16 percent of the total waste generated in 2000. On the other hand, the percentage of metals and yard trimmings discarded has declined substantially over the last forty years, reflecting the expansion of recycling programs, a shift toward plastic containers, and an increase in yard-waste composting. Though small in percentage terms, the increase in inorganic wastes (designated as "other" in figure 21.15) between 1960 and 2000 poses a complex array of waste disposal problems. The disposal of household wastes such as cleansers, solvents, paint, and many of the other items that bring comfort and ease to modern American life carry potentially harmful environmental consequences (see figure 21.15).

For communities in, say, western Nebraska, where land was cheap and waste production modest, incentives to limit garbage were low and the cost and inconvenience of living in a throwaway society almost negligible. In New York City, on the other hand, home to the largest landfill in the world—a garbage mountain on Staten Island—matters were otherwise: land was scarce, trash abundant, and garbage was a genuine problem. This situation was symbolized by the 1987 odyssey of a barge laden with New York trash. The "garbage barge," as it became known, sought a welcoming landfill but was turned

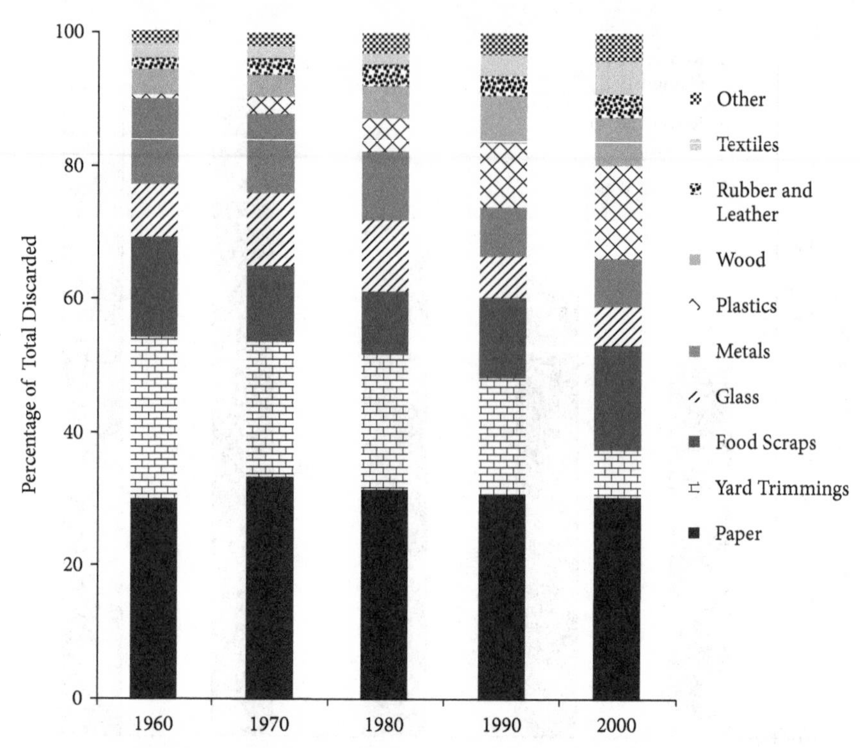

FIGURE 21.15 Materials in Municipal Solid Waste in the U.S., by Percent of Total Waste Discarded (Landfill Waste), 1960–2000.[43]

away in five states and three foreign countries as it sailed up and down the western Atlantic seaboard.[44]

One way to limit garbage problems was to recycle wastes. Recycling, in an informal sense, has always been part of the American economy. Bricks, nails, bottles, and rags were used and used again in the eighteenth century as in the twentieth, sometimes because new ones were too expensive and sometimes because discarding perfectly useful items offended sensibilities of thrift. Before the 1880s, Americans generally found old metal, glass, wood, and cloth valuable enough to keep and reuse. In urban areas, this informal recycling grew into a business, especially with respect to scrap iron and other metals. Families and firms sold their broken tools and machines to scrap dealers, who in turn sold scrap metal to foundries or steel mills for reuse. Immigrants often specialized as scrap dealers, since barriers to entering this profession were low and native-born Americans often scorned the trade as unhealthy or demeaning.[45]

From the 1880s, with the onset of a new cycle of industrialization built around iron and steel, Americans increasingly found it cheaper and easier to throw things away rather than save scrap for possible reuse. But as household recycling declined, business recycling arose. Scientific management in American business found waste deplorable, an opportunity lost. Consequently in many industries such as metallurgy, chemicals, and petroleum, business organizations sought and found profitable ways to reuse apparent wastes. Perhaps the greatest change came in the 1890s, with the adoption of the open-hearth process in steelmaking, which allowed steelmakers to reuse scrap without concern for impurities.

Both the recycling of household scrap and the reuse of industrial wastes worked best in thickly populated, heavily industrialized parts of the country, most notably what is now the rust belt of the Northeast. In the South and the West, where rag and scrap dealers had to travel longer distances to collect useful quantities that could be marketed, more was thrown away.

Despite the efforts of scrap dealers and the efficiencies achieved by scientific business management, by and large Americans probably recycled less and discarded more than most other peoples on the face of the earth. In 1860, for example, the visiting Japanese schoolmaster and writer Yukichi Fukuzawa was astonished to see bent nails tossed away, because in Japan iron was too scarce and costly to be discarded. In Tokyo, after a fire, people sifted through the ashes looking for old nails.[46] The main reason for Americans' more casual attitudes toward scrap and waste was their prosperity. As their affluence grew, more things were defined as trash and fewer things seemed worth husbanding. These definitions were fluid, subject to change as economic fortunes fluctuated. Informal recycling within American households surely expanded during the Great Depression, for example, even as the scrap businesses collapsed. Formal recycling efforts took shape especially during wartime, when metal, rubber, and other militarily useful goods had to be husbanded carefully so that relevant raw materials could be used in military production. Within weeks after the attack on Pearl Harbor, for example, the Boy Scouts, the Campfire Girls, and a host of other organizations were collecting scrap for use in war industries. In 1942 the Brooklyn Dodgers patriotically offered free admission to one of their baseball games to fans who brought ten pounds of scrap metal with them.[47] President Franklin Delano Roosevelt made repeated requests of Americans to donate useful scrap to military industries and to conserve fuel and materials, some of which (gasoline, rubber, and nylon) were made subject to rationing. Such efforts at recycling and conservation scarcely outlasted the war.

Modern recycling in the United States, as elsewhere, involved citizens' pressure on local governments rather than the government's encouragement of citizenry. Motivated by environmental concerns, Americans pressed for recycling programs focused on household consumer wastes, especially paper, metal cans, and bottles. Although these programs were slow to mature—especially in jurisdictions where distances were great, population was sparse, and landfill space was almost free—Americans recycled tens of millions of tons of waste by the 1980s; by 2000, the sum had reached 50 million tons annually, nearly a quarter of all wastes.

This post-1970 development owed little to any American ethic of thrift. Citizens who recycled their paper, plastic, glass, and metal wastes did so generally out of a sense of environmental responsibility. Businesses, on the other hand, continued to recycle because they found it good business to do so, as they had done for decades.

Businesses also found ways to reduce air and water pollution. One of the least welcome aspects of industrialization in the United States, as elsewhere, was pervasive pollution. Remarkably, people—at least in urban settings—grew accustomed to it, and children who grew up amid coal smoke and filthy rivers thought nothing of it. By 1900 most urban Americans accepted air and water pollution that routinely made millions of them sick and killed thousands every year. A few crusaders raised their voices against pollution, but for most it was an acceptable cost of industrial life, the life that brought them what prosperity and comfort they enjoyed. Although systematic data are scarce, it is likely that pollution levels in the United States rose across the board until the 1960s. Then, with the rise of the environmental movement, a remarkable reversal took place. Spurred by citizen agitation, the federal government enacted a spate of antipollution legislation that changed the incentives for many polluting industries. They found it good business to limit their pollution, avoid lawsuits and fines, and improve their "community relations."

As a result, emissions of many important pollutants declined sharply after 1970. Carbon monoxide emissions fell by half between 1970 and 2000, as did sulfur dioxide and volatile organic compound (VOC) emissions. Lead emissions, especially dangerous to human health, fell much more precipitously, as did the tiny particulates (soot) that cause or exacerbate lung diseases (figures 21.16 and 21.17).

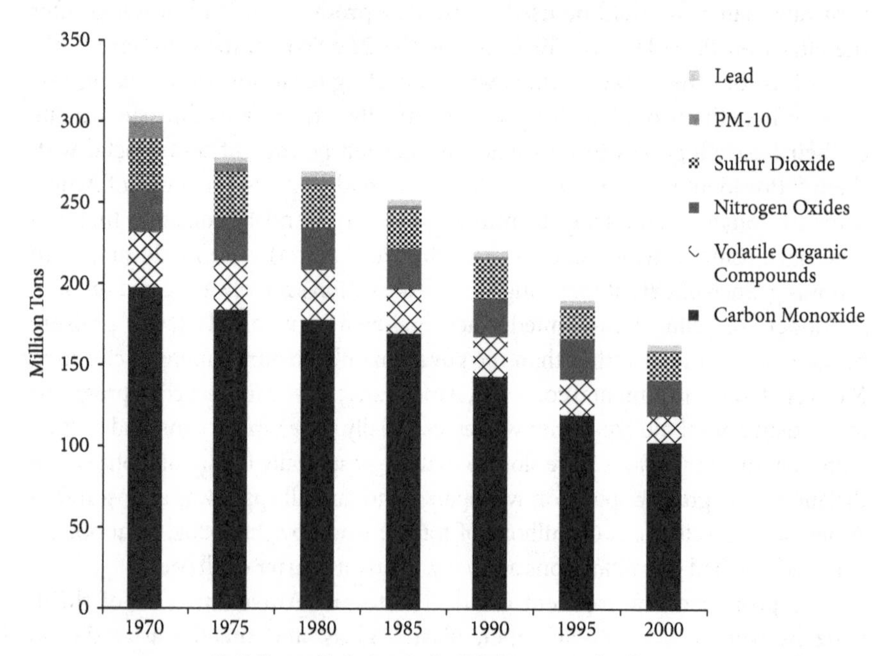

FIGURE 21.16 Air Pollutant Emissions in the U.S., Six Principal Pollutants, 1970–2000.[48]

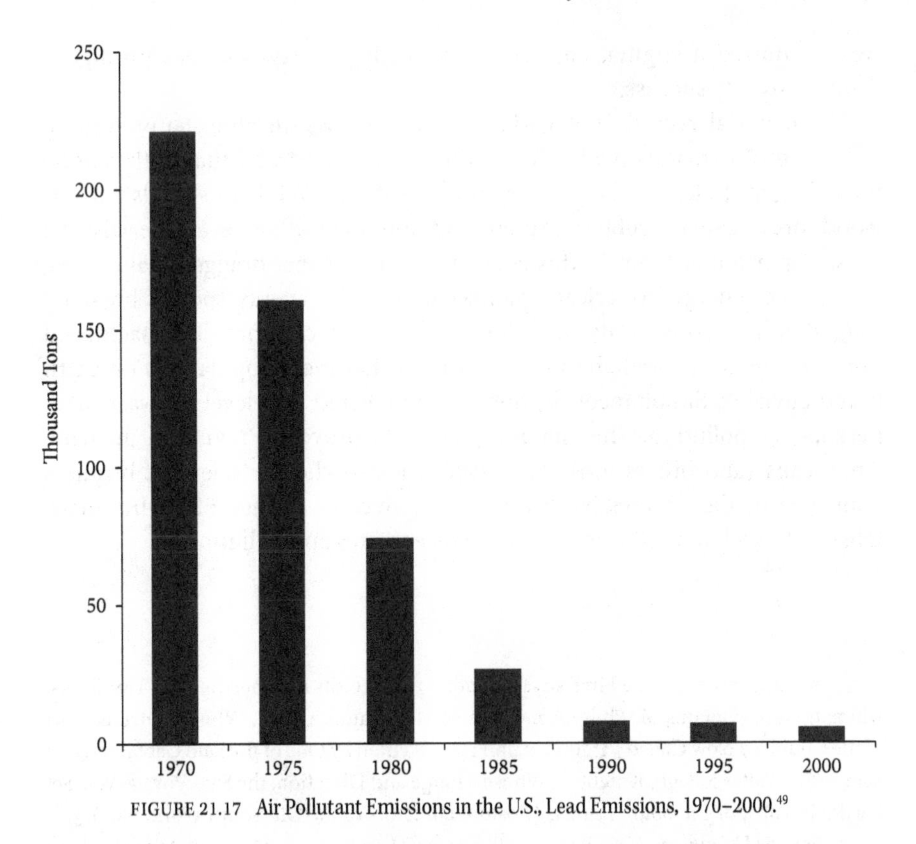

FIGURE 21.17 Air Pollutant Emissions in the U.S., Lead Emissions, 1970–2000.[49]

It turned out that under pressure, manufacturers could easily limit air pollution, just as they could easily, under the instruction of scientific management, recycle many of their own wastes profitably. The United States was not alone in this achievement: Japan, Germany, Britain, and many other countries formerly bedeviled by industrial pollution did much the same thing, as it was technically simple and politically popular.[50]

Conclusion

While American culture contained and still contains competing impulses toward thrift and profligacy, American nature inclined the population toward ebullient use and prodigal waste. Natural resources almost always seemed to exist in sufficient quantity to justify reckless use without conservation for tomorrow. Plentiful wide-open spaces available for use as "sinks" for wastes justified casual habits toward disposal and dispersal of garbage and pollution. When and where careful husbandry and thrift triumphed, it was more often than not a reflection of poverty and good business practices than of any sense of restraint. Indeed, in some segments of the population, thrift acquired a stigma, an association with poverty, whereas profligacy came to signify success.

The material record of American history shows an almost unremitting escalation of demands made on natural resources, a trend that both reflects prevailing attitudes and helps shape those attitudes. While this holds true for wood, ores, cement, rubber, leather, and countless other raw materials, the most important element in this escalation, the one that dragged many along with it, was energy. Americans pioneered the high-energy society, breaking long-standing constraints on consumption and comfort. They achieved unprecedented material abundance, in ways that most populations on earth found enviable. Simultaneously, they also pioneered new levels of waste and, perhaps, of pollution. This, naturally enough, provoked revulsion in many Americans (and others too), motivating them—whether scientific business managers in the Progressive Era or housewives in the age of environmentalism—to seek new efficiencies and reduce wastes and pollution.

Notes

1. Arthur Barlowe, "The First Voyage Made to the Coasts of America, with Two Barks, wherein Were Captains M. Philip Amadas, and M. Arthur Barlowe, Who Discovered Part of the Countrey Now Called Virginia, Anno 1584. Written by One of the Said Captaines, and Sent to Sir Walter Ralegh, Knight, at Whose Charge and Direction, the Said Voyage Was Set Forth," in vol. 4 of *Old South Leaflets* (Boston: Directors of the Old South Work, 1898), 3.

2. Francis Higginson, *New-England's Plantation* (London: n.p., 1630), quoted in William Cronon, *Changes in the Land: Indians, Colonists, and the Ecology of New England* (New York: Hill and Wang, 1983), 22.

3. Richard Hazen, quoted in David R. Foster, *Thoreau's Country: Journey through a Transformed Landscape* (Cambridge, MA: Harvard University Press, 1999), 167.

4. See Timothy Silver, *A New Face on the Countryside: Indians, Colonists, and Slaves in North Atlantic Forests, 1500–1800* (New York: Cambridge University Press, 1990), 30–31; Gordon G. Whitney, *From Coastal Wilderness to Fruited Plain: A History of Environmental Change in Temperate North America, 1500 to the Present* (New York: Cambridge University Press, 1994), 329; and Cronon, *Changes in the Land*, 23. For John James Audubon's observation, see Foster, *Thoreau's Country*, 169.

5. An idea of the vast numbers of fur-bearing animals that inhabited much of North America in the seventeenth, eighteenth, and nineteenth centuries can be derived from fur trade harvest statistics: see, e.g., John F. Richards, *The Unending Frontier: An Environmental History of the Early Modern World* (Berkeley and Los Angeles: University of California Press, 2003), 463–516, esp. 511; Milan Novak et al., *Furbearer Harvests in North America, 1600–1984* (Toronto: Ontario Trappers Association, 1987); Paul Chrissler Phillips, *The Fur Trade*, 2 vols. (Norman: University of Oklahoma Press, 1961); and Hiram Martin Chittenden, *The American Fur Trade of the Far West: A History of the Pioneer Trading Posts and Early Fur Companies of the Missouri Valley and the Rocky Mountains and of the Overland Commerce with Santa Fe*, 2 vols. (1902; Stanford, CA: Academic Reprints, 1954).

6. Edwin James, *Account of an Expedition from Pittsburgh to the Rocky Mountains, Performed in the Years 1819, 1820. By Order of the Hon. J. C. Calhoun, Secretary of War, Under the Command of Maj. S. H. Long, of the U. S. Top. Engineers*, in *Early Western Travels, 1748–1846: A Series of Annotated Reprints of Some of the Best and Rarest Contemporary Volumes of Travel, Descriptive of the Aborigines and Social and Economic Conditions in the Middle and Far West, During the Period of Early American Settlement*, ed. Reuben Gold Thwaites (Cleveland, OH: Arthur H. Clark, 1905), 15:239.

7. See, e.g., Michael Williams, *American and Their Forests: A Historical Geography* (New York: Cambridge University Press, 1989); Steven Stoll, *Larding the Lean Earth: Soil and Society in Nineteenth-Century America* (New York: Hill and Wang, 2002); and Andrew C. Isenberg, *Mining California: An Ecological History* (New York: Hill and Wang, 2005).

8. See, e.g., Cronon, *Changes in the Land*, 99; Richards, *Unending Frontier*, 463–516, esp. 509–15; Novak et al., *Furbearer Harvests*; and Phillips, *Fur Trade*. The types of large-scale environmental transformations depicted in this paragraph are nicely summarized in Alan Taylor, "Wasty Ways: Stories of American Settlement," *Environmental History* 3 (July 1998): 302–5.

9. Foster, *Thoreau's Country*, 172.

10. Andrew C. Isenberg, *The Destruction of the Bison: An Environmental History, 1750–1920* (New York: Cambridge University Press, 2000), 123–63, esp. 143.

11. See, e.g., William Cronon, *Nature's Metropolis: Chicago and the Great West* (New York: Norton, 1991); Gray Brechin, *Imperial San Francisco: Urban Power, Earthly Ruin* (Berkeley and Los Angeles: University of California Press, 1999); Geoff Cunfer, *On the Great Plains: Agriculture and Environment* (College Station: Texas A&M University Press, 2005); David Igler, *Miller and Lux and the Transformation of the Far West, 1850–1920* (Berkeley and Los Angeles: University of California Press, 2001); and Isenberg, *Mining California*.

12. Early concerns over resource use are evident in regional policy developments such as hunting and fishing regulations, dumping restrictions, and the protection of forested areas like the Adirondack Forest Preserve in New York State, which was established in 1885. See, e.g., Cronon, *Changes in the Land*, 101; and Whitney, *From Coastal Wilderness to Fruited Plain*, 329. For an excellent primer on the early conservation movement, including analyses and selections from original texts, see David Stradling, ed., *Conservation in the Progressive Era: Classic Texts* (Seattle: University of Washington Press, 2004). For a brief survey of the movement's intellectual antecedents, see Mark Dowie, *Losing Ground: American Environmentalism at the Close of the Twentieth Century* (Cambridge, MA: MIT Press, 1995), 9–18; and, more substantively, Roderick Frazier Nash, *Wilderness and the American Mind*, 4th ed. (New Haven: Yale University Press, 2001).

13. Stephen Fox, *The American Conservation Movement: John Muir and His Legacy* (Madison: University of Wisconsin Press, 1981), 110.

14. Gifford Pinchot, *The Fight for Conservation* (1910; Seattle: University of Washington Press, 1967), 48. For further reading on Pinchot and his ties to conservationist thought, see the recent work by Char Miller, *Gifford Pinchot and the Making of Modern Environmentalism* (Washington, DC: Island Press/Shearwater Books, 2001).

15. Samuel P. Hays, *Conservation and the Gospel of Efficiency: The Progressive Conservation Movement, 1890–1920* (1959; Pittsburgh: University of Pittsburgh Press, 1999).

16. Fox, *American Conservation Movement*, 151–59.

17. Robert Gottlieb, *Forcing the Spring: The Transformation of the American Environmental Movement* (Washington, DC: Island Press, 1993), 26–29; and Fox, *American Conservation Movement*, 115–47.

18. See Martin V. Melosi, *Garbage in the Cities: Refuse, Reform, and the Environment, 1880–1980*, rev. ed. (College Station: Texas A&M University Press, 2005); Martin V. Melosi, *The Sanitary City: Urban Infrastructure in America from Colonial Times to the Present* (Baltimore: Johns Hopkins University Press, 2000); Martin V. Melosi, ed., *Pollution and Reform in American Cities, 1870–1930* (Austin: University of Texas Press, 1980); Joel A. Tarr, *The Search for the Ultimate Sink: Urban Pollution in Historical Perspective* (Akron, OH: University of Akron Press, 1996); and Gottlieb, *Forcing the Spring*, 47–75.

19. On the development and evolution of the American environmental movement, see Samuel P. Hays, *A History of Environmental Politics since 1945* (Pittsburgh: University of Pittsburgh Press, 2000); Samuel P. Hays, *Beauty, Health, and Permanence: Environmental Politics in the United States, 1955–1985* (New York: Cambridge University Press, 1987); Gottlieb, *Forcing the Spring*; and Dowie, *Losing Ground*. For three useful and relatively short introductory works on the environmental movement, see Benjamin Kline, *First Along the River: A Brief History of the U.S. Environmental Movement*, 2nd ed. (San Francisco: Acada Books, 2000); Hal K. Rothman, *The Greening of a Nation? Environmentalism in the United States since 1945* (Fort Worth, TX: Harcourt Brace, 1998); and Kirkpatrick Sale, *The Green Revolution: The American Environmental Movement, 1962–1992* (New York: Hill and Wang, 1993). On the 1952 President's Materials Policy Commission, commonly known as the Paley Commission (after its chairman, William S. Paley), see U.S. President's Materials Policy Commission, *Resources for Freedom: A Report to the President*, 5 vols. (Washington, DC: U.S. Government Printing Office, 1952).

20. Derived from figures in Angus Maddison, *The World Economy: Historical Statistics* (Paris: Organisation for Economic Co-operation and Development, 2003), 85–86.

21. (Source: U.S. Census Bureau, U.S. Department of Commerce, *Statistical Abstract of the United States, 2003*, Mini-Historical Statistics, Table No. HS-1 Population: 1900 to 2002, 1–2, available at http://www.census.gov/statab/hist/HS-01.pdf, (accessed 2006)).

22. Note: Chained dollars is a statistical measure used by economists to represent the real purchasing power of a dollar with reference to a particular year, in this case the year 2000. (Source: Bureau of Economic Analysis, U.S. Department of Commerce, *National Income and Product Accounts Tables*, Current-Dollar and "Real" GDP, available at http://www.bea.gov/bea/dn/gdplev.xls, (accessed 2006)).

23. (Source: Bureau of Economic Analysis, U.S. Department of Commerce, *National Income and Product Accounts Tables*, Table 7.1 Selected Per Capita Product and Income Series in Current and Chained Dollars, available at http://www.bea.gov/bea/dn/nipaweb/TableView.asp#Mid, (accessed 2006)).

24. Jesse H. Ausubel and H. Dale Langford, eds., *Technological Trajectories and the Human Environment* (Washington DC: National Academy Press, 1997).

25. Note: A Btu (British thermal unit) is a standard unit of energy measurement; one Btu is the amount of heat required to raise the temperature of one pound of liquid water by one degree F. (Sources: (1850–1945): Energy Information Administration, U.S. Department of Energy, *Annual Energy Review 2004*, Table E.1 Estimated Energy Consumption in the United States, Selected Years, 1635–1945, available at http://www.eia.doe.gov/emeu/aer/pdf/pages/sec13_e.pdf, (accessed 2006). (1950–2000): Energy Information Administration, U.S. Department of Energy, *Annual Energy Review 2004*, Table 1.3 Energy Consumption by Source, 1949-2004, available at http://www.eia.doe.gov/emeu/aer/pdf/pages/sec1_9.pdf, (accessed 2006)).

26. The 1930s was the most rewarding decade for oil exploration in the continental United States. American oil production reached its peak in 1970. See K. S. Deffeyes, *Hubbert's Peak* (Princeton, NJ: Princeton University Press 2001), 137.

27. (Sources: (1850–1945): Based on data from the U.S. Census Bureau, U.S. Department of Commerce, *Historical Statistics of the United States: Colonial Times to 1970* (Washington, DC: U.S. Government Printing Office, 1975),vol. 1, 8; and Energy Information Administration, U.S. Department of Energy, *Annual Energy Review 2004*, Table E.1 Estimated Energy Consumption in the United States, Selected Years, 1635–1945, available at http://www.eia.doe.gov/emeu/aer/pdf/pages/sec13_e.pdf, (accessed 2006). (1950–2000): Energy Information Administration, U.S. Department of Energy, *Annual Energy Review 2004*, Table 1.5 Energy Consumption, Expenditures, and Emissions Indicators, 1949–2004, available at http://www.eia.doe.gov/emeu/aer/pdf/pages/sec1_13.pdf, (accessed 2006)).

28. (Source: U.S. Census Bureau, U.S. Department of Commerce, *Statistical Abstract of the United States, 2003*, Mini-Historical Statistics, Table No. HS-19 Food Consumption Per Capita and Food Expenditures: 1929 to 2001, 31-2, available at http://www.census.gov/statab/hist/HS-19.pdf, (accessed 2006)).

29. (Source: Food and Agriculture Organization, United Nations, FAOSTAT Database, Agriculture, Food Supply, available at http://faostat.fao.org/faostat/form?collection=FS.CropsAndProducts&Domain=FS&servlet=1&hasbulk=0&version=ext&language=EN, (accessed 2006)).

30. Peter H. Gleick, *World's Water, 2002–2003: The Biennial Report of Freshwater Resources* (Washington, DC: Island Press, 2002), 247.

31. (Sources: (1900–1990): Peter H. Gleick, *The World's Water, 2002–2003: The Biennial Report of Freshwater Resources* (Washington, DC: Island Press, 2002), 308. (2000): U.S. Geological Survey, *Estimated Use of Water Supply in the United States in 2000*, Table 14 Trends in Estimated Water Use in the United States, 1950–2000, available at http://pubs.usgs.gov/circ/2004/circ1268/htdocs/table14.html, (accessed 2006)).

32. (Source: U.S. Geological Survey, *Historical Statistics for Mineral and Material Commodities in the United States*, available at http://minerals.usgs.gov/ds/2005/140/, (accessed 2006)).

33. (Source: U.S. Geological Survey, *Historical Statistics for Mineral and Material Commodities in the United States*, available at http://minerals.usgs.gov/ds/2005/140/, (accessed 2006)).

34. Figure modeled after Bjorn Lomborg, *The Skeptical Environmentalist: Measuring the Real State of the World* (New York: Cambridge University Press, 2001), 78, Figure 37. (Sources: (Number of Households): U.S. Census Bureau, U.S. Department of Commerce, *Historical Statistics of the United States*, vol. 1, 41; and U.S. Census Bureau, U.S. Department of Commerce, *Statistical Abstract of the United States, 2003*, Table No. 66 Households, Families, Subfamilies, and Married Couples: 1980 to 2002, 49, available at http://www.census.gov/prod/2004pubs/03statab/pop.pdf, (accessed 2006). (Radio, Telephone, TV and VCR): U.S. Census Bureau, U.S. Department of Commerce, *Historical Statistics of the United States*, vol. 2, 783, 796; and U.S. Census Bureau, U.S. Department of Commerce, *Statistical Abstract of the United States, 2003*, Table No. 1126 Utilization of Selected Media: 1970 to 2001, 721, available at http://www.census.gov/prod/2004pubs/03statab/inforcomm.pdf, (accessed 2006). (Refrigerator): Stanley Lebergott, *Pursuing Happiness: American Consumers in the Twentieth Century* (Princeton: Princeton University Press, 1993), 113; and Energy Informa-

tion Administration, U.S. Department of Energy, *Appliance Reports*, U.S. Data Table 2001, Table 1 Appliances in U.S. Households, Selected Years, 1980–2001, available at http://www.eia.doe.gov/emeu/reps/appli/us_table.html, (accessed 2006). (Vehicle): Lebergott, *Pursuing Happiness*, 130; and U.S. Census Bureau, U.S. Department of Commerce, *Statistical Abstract of the United States, 2003*, Mini-Historical Statistics, Table No. HS-27 Housing Units—Historical Trends for Selected Characteristics: 1940 to 2000, 46, available at http://www.census.gov/statab/hist/HS-27.pdf, (accessed 2006). (Personal Computer): Energy Information Administration, U.S. Department of Energy, *Residential Energy Consumption Survey*, Trends Analysis, Household PCs by Year, available at http://www.eia.doe.gov/emeu/recs/recs97/appusage.html#pcusage, (accessed 2006); and U.S. Census Bureau, U.S. Department of Commerce, *Statistical Abstract of the United States, 2001*, Table No. 1158 Households with Computers and Internet Access by Selected Characteristics: 2000, 720, available at http://www.census.gov/prod/2002pubs/01statab/inforcomm.pdf., (accessed 2006)).

35. George Walker, quoted in Lizabeth Cohen, *A Consumer's Republic: The Politics of Mass Consumption in Postwar America* (New York: Knopf, 2003), 294.

36. For further reading on the history of modern American consumer society, see the following recent works in this growing field of study: Avner Offer, *The Challenge of Affluence: Self-Control and Well-Being in the United States and Britain since 1950* (New York: Oxford University Press, 2006); Gary Cross, *An All-Consuming Century: Why Consumerism Won in Modern America* (New York: Columbia University Press, 2000); and Lawrence B. Glickman, ed., *Consumer Society in American History: A Reader* (Ithaca, NY: Cornell University Press, 1999). For a provocative earlier analysis of American consumer society, see the now-classic work by Vance Packard, *The Waste Makers* (New York: David McKay, 1960).

37. (Source: U.S. Census Bureau, U.S. Department of Commerce, *Statistical Abstract of the United States, 2003*, Mini-Historical Statistics, Table No. HS-41 Transportation Indicators for Motor Vehicles and Airlines: 1900 to 2001, 77-8, available at http://www.census.gov/statab/hist/HS-41.pdf, (accessed 2006))

38. For a detailed study regarding tropical latitudes, see Richard P. Tucker, *Insatiable Appetite: The United States and the Ecological Degradation of the Tropical World* (Berkeley and Los Angeles: University of California Press, 2000).

39. Peter Kalm, *The America of 1750: Peter Kalm's Travels in North America*, ed. Adolph Benson, 2 vols. (1753–61; New York: Dover, 1966), 1:308.

40. Melosi, *Garbage in the Cities*, 205–6.

41. (Source: U.S. Environmental Protection Agency, *Municipal Solid Waste Generation, Recycling, and Disposal in the United States: Facts and Figures for 2003*, 2, available at http://www.epa.gov/epaoswer/non-hw/muncpl/pubs/msw05rpt.pdf, (accessed 2006)).

42. (Source: U.S. Environmental Protection Agency, *Municipal Solid Waste Generation, Recycling, and Disposal in the United States: Facts and Figures for 2003*, 4, available at http://www.epa.gov/epaoswer/non-hw/muncpl/pubs/msw05rpt.pdf, (accessed 2006)).

43. (Source: U.S. Environmental Protection Agency, *Municipal Solid Waste Generation, Recycling, and Disposal in the United States: 2003 Data Tables*, Table 3 Materials Discarded in the Municipal Waste Stream, 1960 to 2003, available at http://www.epa.gov/msw/pubs/03data.pdf, (accessed 2006)).

44. Martin Melosi, *Effluent America: Cities, Industry, Energy, and the Environment* (Pittsburgh: University of Pittsburgh Press, 2001), 68. See also Melosi, *Garbage in the Cities*; and Tarr, *Search for the Ultimate Sink*.

45. Carl Zimring, *Cash for Your Trash: Scrap Recycling in America* (New Brunswick, NJ: Rutgers University Press, 2005).

46. Yukichi Fukuzawa, *The Autobiography of Yukichi Fukuzawa* (1899; New York: Columbia University Press, 1960), 115–16.

47. Zimring, *Cash for Your Trash*, 81.

48. (Source: U.S. Environmental Protection Agency, *Air Emissions Trends: Continued Progress through 2004*, Table on National Air Pollutant Emissions Estimates for Major Pollutants, available at http://www.epa.gov/air/airtrends/2005/econ-emissions.html, (accessed 2006)).

49. (Source: U.S. Environmental Protection Agency, *Air Emissions Trends: Continued Progress through 2004*, Table on National Air Pollutant Emissions Estimates for Major Pollutants, available at http://www.epa.gov/air/airtrends/2005/econ-emissions.html, (accessed 2006)).

50. J. R. McNeill, *Something New Under the Sun: An Environmental History of the Twentieth-Century World* (New York: Norton, 2000), 50–83.

22 }

Disputing Abundance

THE ANTIGLOBALIZATION PROTEST MOVEMENT AND OUR CHANGING NATURAL IMAGINARY

Joshua J. Yates

"Ya Basta! (enough) is our first and fundamental point of unity, our 'one no' that precedes our 'many yeses.'"

—AMORY STARR

At first glance, globally familiar zones of protest pageantry conjure an array of unrelated media images: streets filled with costumed activists, some dressed as giant endangered sea turtles and mad cows, others as Zapatista rebels and Uncle Sams–turned–Grim Reapers, still others as a veritable cornucopia of genetically modified vegetables; members of the Ruckus Society rappel down the sides of skyscrapers and bridges, hanging large banners denouncing the World Trade Organization, the International Monetary Fund, and the World Bank as "the Unholy Trinity," while back on the ground, demonstrators dance to the syncopated rhythms of beating drums and trilling whistles. Except for the intermittent staging of rallies and teach-ins, the overall atmosphere is a cross between Mardi Gras and Woodstock. Most of the faces are young, but some are clearly veterans of mass demonstration. Many of the faces cannot be seen, however. Covered, eyes peer out from behind water-soaked bandanas and makeshift gas masks; some peaceful and nonviolent in their obstruction, duct taped arm to arm, forming human chains hundreds strong, while others, like the Wombles (White Overalls Movement Building Libertarian Effective Struggles) and the anarchists' Black Block, raise havoc with the storefront windows of familiar corporate icons: Starbucks, Niketown, and McDonald's. A phalanx of police in full riot gear advances, converging on the scene. The picketers, having anticipated the confrontation, prepare themselves for the clash. With power fists, peace signs, and placards raised high, they shout out in unison, "Ya basta!" "People before profits!" "The world is not for sale!" In the final moment, to the gratification of scores of personal video recorders, water cannons and pepper spray fill the air.

Such dramatic scenes are now commonplace and display the most effervescent side of what is often labeled the antiglobalization protest movement.

Some observers view these activists ambivalently. As symptomatic of growing pains in the "new" economy, they are understood to be expressing the fears, anxieties, and inevitable displacements that occur during moments of massive social-structural change. Far more characteristically, however, these protesters are simply dismissed out of hand. The *New York Times* columnist Thomas Friedman has been among the most vociferous of critics, referring variously to the movement as "The Coalition to Keep Poor People Poor"; as a group of the "largely well-intentioned, but ill-informed being led around by the ill-intentioned and well-informed"; and most caustically, when he described them as "a Noah's ark of flat-earth advocates, protectionist trade unions and yuppies looking for their 1960's fix."[1] Most within the movement understandably bristle at these popular caricatures, and many disavow the antiglobalization label altogether. Among the activists themselves, this movement is known as the global justice movement, the anticorporate movement, or simply the "Movement" (a name I will use interchangeably with the antiglobalization protest movement in what follows).

The lack of serious analysis is not altogether surprising. For starters, the substance of the Movement's critiques are—whatever their intentions—quite often simplistic, ill-informed, and naive, while the tenor of its rhetoric commonly veers from understandable social and environmental concern to sanctimonious alarmism and apocalyptic brooding. The animating spirit of the Movement is a curious mixture of Arcadian optimism and Malthusian pessimism. Indeed, this "Movement of movements" presents a baffling assortment of causes and constituencies, perplexing for its apparent unification of hitherto separate and often opposed interests. In American politics it is hard to imagine stranger bedfellows than family farmers and environmentalists, or labor unions and Third World trade activists, and yet these are the constituencies the Movement claims to represent. Given such proclivities, it is no wonder that objective scholarly treatments have been few, and that where they have existed, they have been limited primarily to scholar-activists concerned with more effectively advancing the cause.

This chapter examines the discourse of leading Movement activists and organizations, arguing that they represent a significant phenomenon worthy of serious scholarly attention, if for reasons other than those suggested by the activists themselves. However accurate its critique of the dominant model of economic globalization may be, and however credible its alternative, the cultural significance of the Movement lies elsewhere. It can be found in the employment of what herein are called the "rhetorics of thrift"—both as a form of moral protest and as the basis of an alternative way of life, or orthopraxy. Perhaps counterintuitively, the antiglobalization protest movement serves as an illuminating backdrop against which to trace the surprising cultural career of thrift in American society: where once thrift was thought necessary to free, prosperous, market-based societies, today it is commonly dismissed as either outmoded or inimical to free markets, to societies premised on a virtual, corporate-dominated, technologically produced abundance. In the Movement's rendering, thrift is enlisted in the resistance to the very society it was once counted on to create. The rhetorics of thrift, whether as protest or praxis, challenge the reigning ideology of abundance, what activists believe to be the deeply flawed (even catastrophic) presumption at the heart of our present social and economic order. Disputing abundance as a realistic depiction of the current state of affairs under the conditions of late capitalism, the antiglobalization protest movement gives expression to long-standing intellectual and moral debates about the character of material well-being and its relationship to both the natural world and the ordering of economic life. A study of the movement's rhetoric of thrift thus illuminates the changing and ever-contentious conceptions of human and planetary flourishing in the West.

The Antiglobalization Protest Movement: A Portrait

The antiglobalization protest movement did not begin on the streets of Seattle. According to some activists its history predates even the Bretton Woods institutions (i.e., the World Bank and the International Monetary Fund), whose fifty-plus years of existence have attracted so much of the Movement's vehemence. According to this perspective, the present mobilization is but the most recent (and ostensibly shortest) round in a "fight" that has been going on since the 1500s. In the words of Vandana Shiva, one of the Movement's leading spokespersons, "The first globalization was colonialism, and it lasted 500 years. The second globalization was so-called 'development,' and it lasted 50 years. The third globalization was 'free-trade' and it only lasted 5 years."[2] Today's struggle against the World Bank and the World Trade Organization (WTO), the neoliberal ideology of the so-called Washington Consensus, and corporate domination is, on this view, but the latest episode in the epoch-long battle against the exploitative forces of capitalism. And yet, its activists are clearly hopeful that this new, unfolding global chapter holds possibilities for real progress in their ongoing fight. "So while the movement is very, very old," writes the scholar-activist Amory Starr, "it has entered a new phase in which some genuinely global movements, recognizing themselves in others and others in themselves, are forging not only some notions of solidarity, but a unified voice saying 'ya basta' (enough!), and articulating detailed visions of 'another world.'"[3]

While its origins are manifold, the Movement's most direct antecedents can be traced to a handful of key movements and events.[4] In the Global North, its ideological heritage comes most clearly from the new social movements of the 1960s and 1970s—burgeoning feminism, environmentalism, anticorporate animus, the peace movement, and Third Worldism. Movement activists often point to the Club of Rome's ominous report, "The Limits to Growth," and the successful international boycott of Nestlé as defining moments of early inspiration, mobilization, and formation. Perhaps less well understood, but still significant given the anarchist impulse so evident in the Movement, were the "Autonomen" that surfaced across Europe throughout the 1980s.[5] Although often more militant, the Autonomen employed many of the direct-action tactics used by those in the Movement today: teach-ins, mass street blockades, "squats," culture jamming, and property crime. In the Third World societies of the Global South, what were initially discrete, local movements of resistance—against, for instance, the International Monetary Fund's structural adjustment policies, or certain World Bank–sponsored development projects such as the Sardar Sarovar dam in India's Narmada Valley—gradually became symbolic instances of burgeoning global resistance movements. In 1985, the Brazilian landless workers movement (Movimento dos Trabalhadores Rurias Sem Terra) was formalized, establishing linkages to similar movements around the world. The First Continental Encounter of Indigenous Peoples was held in 1990 and is now networked with other indigenous groups worldwide. In both the Global North and the Global South, family farming, fair trade, and food sovereignty movements have also been critical precursors, with José Bové's ransacking of a McDonald's in the small French town of Millau perhaps the most famous and thoroughly eulogized act of cultural resistance within the Movement.

By most accounts, 1992 was the pivotal year. Events that year are generally perceived to have initiated the chain reaction from which the antiglobalization movement would eventually emerge so colorfully in Seattle. Besides seeing the creation of the WTO, it was also the year of both the Earth Summit held in Rio de Janeiro and the Zapatista uprising in Chiapas, Mexico.[6] However, it was not until the mid-1990s that the Movement came fully into the public eye, most notably in the United States around the Kathie Lee Gifford sweatshop scandal, effectively launching the antisweatshop movement. In 1996, the Institute for Policy Studies issued the widely cited report, "The Top 200: The Rise of Corporate Global Power," further galvanizing the Movement. The report found that 51 of the biggest 100 economies in the world were not nations but corporations. Measured in terms of gross domestic product or annual sales, General Motors was bigger than Denmark, General Electric bigger than Portugal, IBM bigger than Singapore, and so on.[7] In 1997, the worldwide financial crisis, which came to be known as the "Asian Flu," seemed to confirm on a massive scale the expressed concerns of the emerging movement. In 1998, the Jubilee Movement to forgive Third-World debt began to gain real currency among American and European policy makers, and the

People's Global Action "nonorganization" was launched, at the instigation of Zapatistas, with its Global Day of Action (an event that witnessed a day of simultaneous protests against the WTO in thirty countries on five continents). In 1998 the budding protest network also experienced one of its first major successes when its direct action blockade not only shut down the Multilateral Agreement on Investments (MAI) negotiations in Montreal, Canada, but also contributed to the eventual scrapping of the MAI altogether. Finally, 1998 was the year that the antibiotech movement took off in earnest with the widespread consumer rejection of genetically modified foods in Europe, South America, and Asia.

When viewed against even this brief chronological sketch of the Movement's rise and formation, the massive protests on the streets of Seattle—what is known within the Movement as "N30" (November 30, 1999)—takes on a slightly different, more qualified aspect. "The significance of the 'N30' Seattle Protests," writes Starr, "was not the beginning of a new global movement, but the entrance of U.S. citizens into the movement."[8] Since Seattle, the Movement has continued to stage similar global street protests at nearly every major meeting of the WTO, the World Bank and the International Monetary Fund, the World Economic Forum, the Organisation for Economic Co-operation and Development, and the G8.[9]

To be sure, the multiplicity of issues and constituencies represented in such global street protests can appear more like a protest bazaar than a unified social movement. There is, however, a common denominator among what looks to be multiple marriages of convenience. To borrow an image from astronomy, the Movement can be likened to a stellar constellation. Up close, various points within the constellation can be seen to be made up of clusters of stars (even entire galaxies), each one autonomous, with its own history and development—a whole cosmos of its own. But when viewed from a greater distance each cluster contributes to a larger image—in this case the nodal points of resistance in the fight against economic globalization.

The main points in the constellation include (1) resisting the corporate-dominated institutions promoting international free trade and the ideology of neoliberalism that underwrites them; (2) fighting poverty and economic inequality and promoting more equitable and sustainable development, the chief expression of which has come from groups dedicated to debt relief; (3) battling the privatization and commoditization of everyday life, nature, and the "commons" (understood here to include everything from water and air to the airwaves and other public spaces, to traditional seed varieties and genetic codes—even outer space); and (4) protesting environmental degradation and the diminution of biodiversity due to overconsumption and lack of public regulation. If we move to a yet greater distance, these four points merge into two general clusters: social and economic justice and environmental sustainability. The Movement's dynamism and grassroots appeal have clearly come from the powerful confluence of these two main factions. But as will be shown, this conflux of social justice and environmental movements is unified by more than a penchant for highly stylized displays of resistance. Beyond the aesthetic politics, these movements are also, and more significantly, unified in the substance of their resistance, that is, in their *rhetorics of thrift*.[10]

The Rhetorics of Thrift

THRIFT AS PROTEST

It has been said that term *globalization* is a shibboleth.[11] This is certainly the case for antiglobalization protesters, for whom the bywords of economic globalization—for example, free trade, integrated markets, flexible capital, comparative advantage—express a single coded meaning: the imperative of unlimited growth. Against these bywords, the activists have marshaled an army of their own catchphrases and slogans—"The world is not for sale!" "People before profits!" "The world is full!" and "No logo." But the most visceral of these is "Ya basta!" (Enough!)—*enough* of injustice and inequality, of environmental destruction and overconsumption, of the overweening hubris of technological civilization.

But what is immediately striking for our purposes is how the cultural idiom of "Ya basta!" embodies a reformulation of the language of thrift, albeit broadly conceived. This is striking in light of the fact that the language of thrift is employed by the Movement to resist and subvert capitalism, whereas historically thrift was perceived to be an economic virtue vital to its very development and maintenance. As we shall see, among these activists, even thrift narrowly understood as frugality comes to connote the spirit of "Ya basta!" As the ethicist James Nash writes, thrift as frugality is "a subversive virtue, a revolt against an economic system that depends upon intensive production and consumption to keep the system going and growing."[12] Whether understood broadly or narrowly, the value of thrift in the context of the Movement is that it counsels limits. In their general repugnance over the contravention of both biological and normative limits, the antiglobalizers lament what is being lost and identify what therefore must be saved, preserved, conserved, or otherwise safeguarded. But the semantic distance between saying "No more!" in the interests of protecting something and of saying "Not ever!" in the name of some inviolable principle is negligible. With the momentum of prudential logic, the rhetoric of thrift-as-protest terminates in its most emphatic and disciplining voice, asserting what finally must be *off* limits, even forbidden. Thrift becomes a form of moral interdiction.

At the micro level the object of thrift-as-protest is personal consumption. Again, we see thrift in the defiant praxis of countless consumer prohibition campaigns, from the Rainforest Action Network's "Don't buy old growth!" to the Adbusters Media Foundation's "Buy Nothing Day," the motto of which is "The more you consume, the less you live." At a macro level, there is no doubt that *the* animating concern of the Movement, as well as *the* precipitating factor of its existence, is the creation and progressive implementation of a series of regional and international free-trade regimes, most notably with the creation of the WTO. It is here more than anywhere else that scores of groups have emerged, guided by their thrift-inflected protest. U.S. groups like Public Citizen and Global Exchange, the French group ATTAC (Association pour la Taxation des Transactions pour l'Aide aux Citoyens, or Association for the Taxation of Financial Transactions for the Aid of Citizens), and the Canadian-based Polaris Institute, to name but a handful of the more prominent, are hard at work to make international capital flows serve the broader public interest, proposing four interrelated regulatory reforms: regulating capital movements, reforming international institutions, managing exchange rates, and coordinating macroeconomic policy.

However, even more important than publicizing the details of these broad public policy agendas is saving that which antiglobalists believe is most imperiled by the new international trade regimes: namely, democracy. The Polaris Institute puts the matter forcefully: "The pivotal lesson that emerged from this social movement experience was that transnational corporations had effectively secured control over the reins of public policy making in this country (and elsewhere) to the point where citizens were becoming politically disenfranchised. In effect, a form of corporate governance had been established."[13] The International Forum on Globalization (IFG) developed a series of full-page campaign ads that paints the matter in even bolder strokes: "The World Trade Organization (WTO) is emerging as the world's first global government. But it was elected by no-one, it operates in secrecy, and its mandate is this: To undermine the constitutional rights of sovereign nations."[14]

But the specter of market totalitarianism darkens even more than the horizon of popular government and national self-determination. In its shadow, which IFG's members believe is increasingly hard to avoid, national polities and local cultures alike increasingly face the very real prospect of having their distinctive cultural traditions and practices turned into dusty relics on museum shelves or, worse, into relics on the shelves of tourist gift shops—that is, commodities on the world market. One of the main aspirations of corporate-led globalization is to create a single, worldwide regulatory and development environment, a situation that affords the greatest efficiencies and lowest costs and therefore the highest profitability for investors. For Movement activists, this homogenizing process has resulted in the death sentence of local cultures. Leaders of IFG maintain that in the "new-economy" countries as varied as India, Kenya, Thailand, and Sweden,

> are all meant to adopt similar tastes, values, and life-styles. They are to be served by the same few global corporations, the same fast-food restaurants, hotel chains, and clothing chains; wear the same jeans and shoes; drive similar cars; receive the same films, music, television shows; live in the same kind of urban landscapes; and engage in the same kind of agricultural and industrial development schemes, while carrying the same personal, cultural, and spiritual values—a global monoculture. This trend is already visible to any traveler. Every place is becoming more and more like every other place. Cultural diversity is going the way of biodiversity.[15]

This last remark underscores how the Movement's many diverse grievances overlap. For in the assessment of the protesters, the loss of local cultures, especially in terms of the loss of local knowledge and capacities, is directly correlated with the degradation and loss of local environments. They are inexorably intertwined in the minds of activists. Local ways of life are bound up with local ecosystems. "For thousands of years," explains a the Web site for Food First,

> small farmers have grown food for their communities, planting diverse crops in healthy soil, recycling organic matter, following nature's rainfall patterns, and maintaining the earth's rich bio-diversity. Their accumulated knowledge of their local environments—a treasure beyond price—has been passed on from one generation to the next. Today, our family farm systems and the men and women who work tirelessly to sustain them face unprecedented economic, political, and social abuse. Industrial agriculture is replacing family farms with corporate farms, farmers with machines, and mixed crops with monocultures, and has traded local food security for global commerce.[16]

Food First argues that "ecologically sound food production is based on diversity: of cultures, farming systems, crops, and animals, as well as genetic diversity, natural biodiversity, and healthy ecosystems." Others agree and point out that according to the Food and Agriculture Organization (FAO), the world has already lost 75 percent of its crop diversity because of the globalization of industrial agriculture.[17]

But the loss of self-government and the homogenization of local cultures into a single mold stems, according to the protesters, from more than mere corporate greed. The problem comes from a kind of reductionism of human reality to the economic sphere. It is a dominant worldview that conceives of society not as merely *possessing* an economy but *as* essentially (and entirely) *an* economy. Its anthropology similarly reduces persons to economic maximizers. Activists believe that this market totalism has been an especially pernicious imposition under the humanitarian guise of development. Wolfgang Sachs, a leading intellectual in IFG circles, writes:

> Turning the South's societies into economic competitors not only required the injection of capital and the transfer of technology but a cultural transformation, for many "old ways" of living turned out to be "obstacles to development." The ideals and mental habits, patterns of work, and modes of knowing, webs of loyalties and rules of governance in which the South's peoples were steeped were usually at odds with the ethos of an economic society.[18]

His concern is that in a world being reshaped by global capitalism, few can opt out of this one-size-fits-all structure, for the horizon of viable alternatives for securing the means to life and well-being has been fatefully narrowed.

Yet Movement activists are quick to report that lines are being successfully drawn in the sand. One such protest front where the Movement claims important victories concerns what they refer to as the "commons." Activists within IFG break the commons into three categories:

> The first category includes the water, land, air, forests, and fisheries on which everyone's life depends. The second includes the culture and knowledge that are collective creations of our species. Finally, more modern common resources are those public services that governments perform on behalf of all people to address such basic needs as public health, education, public safety, and social security, among others. All these common heritage resources are under tremendous strain as corporations seek to privatize and commodify them. Together, these three categories of resources form the foundations of all wealth.[19]

The commons rank among those areas that activists believe should simply be off limits to the market. "Efforts by persons or corporations to monopolize ownership of an essential common heritage resource, such as water, a seed variety, or a forest, . . . should be deemed unacceptable."[20] Emblematic of the Movement's successes in resisting such encroachments on the commons is what has become known as the Cochabamba Water War, which pitted the forces of economic globalization (or "globalization from above" in Movement parlance) against the local citizens of Cochabamba, Bolivia (or "globalization from below"). The citizens successfully fought against the Bolivian government's decision to privatize the water utilities. Within a short time of taking over, Bechtel, the American-based multinational that sought the water rights, was forced to withdraw its operations. In the midst of the conflict, the Cochabamba Declaration on the Right to Water was drafted.[21] Its first three principles are as follows:

1. Water belongs to the earth and all species and is sacred to life, therefore, the world's water must by conserved, reclaimed, and protected for all future generations and its natural patterns respected;

2. Water is a fundamental human right and a public trust. . . . Therefore, it should not be commodified, privatized, or traded for commercial purposes . . .;
3. Water is best protected by local communities and citizens. . . . Peoples of the earth are the only vehicle to promote earth democracy and save water.

Activists believe that in the context of such struggles, statements like the following one made by the IFG activists are hardly excessive: "We could end up with Mitsubishi running social security, Bechtel controlling the world's water, Deutschebank running the jails (and maybe the parks), Disney running the British Broadcasting Corporation, Merck running the Canadian healthcare system."[22] They believe that without more acts of resistance like that which occurred in Cochabamba, there is reason to fear that the grip of privatization will continue to grow tighter, further restricting the options of local people and national polities alike. "The unfettered hegemony of Western productivism," writes Sachs, "has made it more and more impossible to take exit roads from the global racetrack; thus, the maneuvering space for countries in times of uncertainty is dangerously limited."[23] The protesters press for massive resistance to such fatalism. As we shall see shortly, to Margaret Thatcher's famous neoliberal acronym TINA ("there is no alternative"), they counter, "a better world *is* possible" (emphasis added).

Alongside the concerns over the putative loss of the commons, local culture, or democratic voice is the most pressing concern of all: the destruction of the environment. The moral to commonly traded stories of impending environmental doom and disaster has been clear: if we don't change our way of life, we will face a serious crisis *in the future*. But what is perhaps novel in the protesters' telling is their insistence that the moment of crisis is now *imminent*. In other words, we have already reached the moment of decision beyond which there is no return. (We may perhaps have already surpassed it.) "We begin with the premise that life on earth entered its most precarious phase in history," states the Foundation for Deep Ecology. "We speak of threats not only to human life, but to the lives of all species of plants and animals, as well as the health and continued viability of the biosphere. It is the awareness of the present condition that primarily motivates our foundation's activities."[24]

According to this more urgent and foreboding tale, humanity has crossed an epochal threshold of danger and entered into an era of what sociologists call "manufactured risk."[25] In this situation, the consequences of human knowledge and actions on both social relations and the natural world are as great as, if not greater than, the consequences of social relations and the natural world on humanity. Sachs states it more simply: "For time immemorial humanity defended itself against nature. Now nature must defend itself against humanity."[26] David Korten, a leading economist of the antiglobalization movement, agrees:

> We have crossed a monumental historical threshold. Because of the fivefold economic expansion since 1950 the environmental demands of our economic system have filled up the available environmental space of the planet. In other words we live in a "full world." We could argue whether a particular limit was hit at noon yesterday or will be passed at midnight tomorrow, but the details are far less important than the basic truth that we have no real option other than to adapt our economic institutions to the reality of a "full world."[27]

Korten's phrase "full world" echoes what the Center for a New American Dream and many other groups are at pains to make clear: "The earth does not hold endless stores of natural resources, nor is it capable of absorbing limitless levels of pollution."[28] The utter dependence of our present way of life on a "gigantic throughput of fossil energy," writes Sachs, which requires first the ruthless extraction of natural resources and then the harmful elimination of largely nonbiodegradable waste, has outstripped the "earth's capacity to serve as mine and dumping ground." Indeed, if all countries were to follow the advanced industrial example, "five or six planets would be needed to serve as 'sources' for the inputs and 'sinks' for the waste of economic growth."[29] And yet, to the great dismay and alarm of the activists, most of the countries in the world are moving down this exact track at very high speeds, with China and India in the lead.

The idea of risk is (and has always been) most closely concerned with the relationship between human planning and the forces of nature. But what makes a situation of manufactured risk different and acutely worrisome for activists is, to put it elliptically, that nature itself is no longer itself. They assert that few aspects of our surrounding material environment have not been in some way altered irrevocably. Nothing has caused the antiglobalizers more angst in this regard than the havoc-wreaking potential of biotechnology. Consider another full-page advertisement from IFG's Turning Point series: "Over the next few years, the biotechnology industry will dump hundreds of thousands of genetically engineered plants and animals into the environment. This brings grave risk of destructive—and irreversible—genetic pollution. It's time for an immediate moratorium on this practice."[30] In the face of such incalculable risk, the protesters speak emphatically with the voice of interdiction.

A similar Turning Point ad declares: "HIV and the Ebola virus crossed from primates to humans. The 1918 influenza virus started in pigs. Now, biotechnologists who shuffle live organs and genes between human and animals could end up unleashing deadly new diseases without hope of a cure."[31] In our folly, the IFG hopes to persuade us, humanity is gaily crossing the ecological

Rubicon. The power of their interdiction is, on this view, grounded in the nihilism of the alternative. The world is full, and, as popular Movement graffiti exclaims, "Growth is madness."

The image of the contemporary world portrayed by the antiglobalization protesters is a cross between that found in Aldous Huxley's *Brave New World*, George Orwell's *1984*, and Albert Camus's *The Plague*—a world on the edge of self-inflicted catastrophe. Its leading public officials and experts have failed (whether from naïveté, greed, or pure hubris) to acknowledge certain natural and normative limits, indeed, have encouraged their ever-greater transgression. Against this folly, the antiglobalization protesters have mobilized in resistance, employing the rhetoric of thrift in their protest. For the very things that make life livable—our food, air, water, health, not to mention basic political and economic rights—they believe have been put at tremendous risk. To this the protesters say again: "Ya basta! Enough!"

THRIFT AS ORTHOPRAXY

But the antiglobalization activists are not simply satisfied with protest. Recalling the epigram at the start of the chapter, they are not only saying no, but yes. While it may not aspire to a cohesive political philosophy, the Movement offers a positive vision (or visions) of what the French group ATTAC calls *altermondalization*. The most systematic statement of the alternative globalization on offer is given in IFG's *Alternatives to Economic Globalization*. Its authors, again many from among the Who's Who in the Movement, write, "Unified by a deep commitment to universal values of democracy, justice, and respect for life, this alliance functions with growing effectiveness without a central organization, leadership, or defining ideology. It also takes different forms in different settings."[32] But the initial point of unity around which all in the Movement rally is in the common belief that "a better world is possible."[33] What will it take to bring about this new and improved world, and what might it look like? To bring it about, they must debunk myths propagated by the forces of economic globalization and expose the real costs of our putative progress; they must also create alternative measures of genuine progress; but above all, bringing this new world into being will take thrift. That is, the antiglobalization protesters must offer a viable alternative way of life for a better world based on frugality, sustainability, subsidiarity, conservation, and precaution. The burden of the rhetorics of thrift shifts its weight from protest to orthopraxy.

Debunking Myths

As the apocalyptic warnings about risk demonstrate, the first step toward convincing humanity that a better world is possible is to shake our confidence in the present world, making a new one seem necessary but also plausible. To accomplish this, activists go to great lengths to fight what they see as the ideological grip of a number of principal myths that now order our world. A number of these myths should already be apparent:

> MYTH: Sustained economic growth as measured by GDP is the foundation of human progress and is essential to alleviate poverty and protect the environment.
>
> MYTH: Free markets and free-trade result in the most efficient and socially optimal allocation of resources.
>
> MYTH: Economic globalization—moving toward a single, integrated world market in which goods and capital flow freely across national borders—spurs competition, increases economic efficiency and growth, and is generally beneficial for everyone—helping poor people/raising all boats, etc.
>
> MYTH: This globalizing world is "brand new."
>
> MYTH: "There is no alternative"—Margaret Thatcher's famous acronym TINA—is the biggest of them all.

Jerry Mander, founder and director of IFG, summarizes the central implication of these globalization myths: "We are now being asked to believe that the development processes that have further impoverished people and devastated the planet will lead to diametrically different and highly beneficial outcomes, if only they can be accelerated and applied everywhere, freely, without restriction; that is, when they are globalized. That's the bad news. The good news is that it is not too late to stop this from happening."[34]

To this end, many in the Movement target Disney, McDonald's, Nike, the Gap, and other powerful mythmaking corporations. Others take aim at myths propagated within the academic field of economics and by professional economists who they perceive to be the priestly class of neoliberalism. The True Cost Economics Manifesto declares:

> We, the undersigned, make this accusation: that you, the teachers of neoclassical economics and the students that you graduate, have perpetuated a gigantic fraud upon the world. You claim to work in a pure science formula and law, but yours is a social science, with all the fragility and uncertainty that this entails. We accuse you of pretending to be what you are not. You hide in your offices, protected by your jargon, while in the real world forests vanish, species perish, human lives are ruined and lost. We accuse you of gross negligence in the management of our planetary household. We will have our clash of paradigms, we will have our moment of truth, and out of each will come a new economics—open, holistic, human scale. On campus after campus, we will chase you old goats out of power. Then, in the months and years that follow, we will begin the work of reprogramming the doomsday machine.

According to the Adbusters Media Foundation, the group behind the manifesto, the myths of neoliberalism are ready for unmasking. Conventional economics is "a bucket full of water that's ready to tip. All it needs is a jolt. So let's kick it over."[35]

Counting the Costs, Redefining Progress

One of the chief myths the protesters hope to undermine is encapsulated by the key economic indicator of our time, the gross domestic product, or GDP. According to Ted Halstead and Clifford Cobb, two prominent activist-intellectuals:

> The GDP is the statistical distillation of the worldview of conventional economics. It is basically a measure of total output, and it assumes that everything produced is good by definition. It is a balance sheet with no cost side of the ledger; it does not differentiate between costs and benefits, between productive and destructive activities, or between sustainable and unsustainable ones. It is a calculating machine that adds but does not subtract.[36]

Wendell Berry, agrarian writer and sometimes friend of the Movement, has dubbed this the lost art of subtraction.[37] The activists are trying to renew this art by reclaiming the cost side of the ledger. Recall Adbusters's True Cost Economics project cited earlier. In its "true cost" pricing indexes, the project adds up the costs of everything from industrial farming to obesity to aviation to global warming. According to Adbusters, the true costs of these aspects of our modern, technologically based civilization are much higher than we have been led to believe or even imagine. "According to a 2002 US Surgeon-General report," they inform us, "61 percent of Americans are significantly overweight. This obesity generates $117 billion in annual medical bills and triggers 300,000 premature deaths each year."[38] Likewise, according to a 2001 Iowa State University study on the conventional food-delivery system cited by the project, "The average piece of produce in that state travels 1,494 miles to get to the consumer. Compared to Iowa-based regional and local systems, the conventional system used far more fuel, and released five to 17 times more carbon dioxide into the atmosphere."[39] The true costs of present-day aviation are also higher than we might expect because our economic measures, like the GDP, are blind to certain real costs: "Aviation gives rise to a number of adverse environmental impacts. These include aircraft noise, contributions to local air quality problems and climate change, and other negative effects on townscape, landscape, biodiversity, heritage and water."[40] Quoting a physicist at Boeing about the pollution generated from the takeoff of a single 747, the IFG alliance drives the point home: the departure of one 747 is "like setting the local gas station on fire and flying it over your neighborhood."[41]

The GDP measures economic growth. But as activists counter, "growth" in this case is best understood as the shifting of functions from the nonmarket economy of household and community, where economists cannot see them, to the market, where they can. As Halstead and Cobb describe it, "The garden plot becomes the supermarket; home sewing of clothes becomes the sweatshop; parenting becomes childcare; visits on the side porch become the entertainment industry and psychiatry. Up and down the line, the things people used to do freely for and with one another turn into products and services. The market grows by cannibalizing the family and community realms that nurture and sustain it."[42] Furthermore, Halstead and Cobb go on to argue, not only is the use of GDP as the primary indicator of well-being misleading, it can be downright perverse. Because such things as car crashes, divorces, and new prison construction appear as economic gain, the GDP "denies what people intuitively know—that just because more money is changing hands does not mean that life is getting better."[43]

Against the GDP and other conventional measures of material and social progress, a number of groups have offered alternative indicators such as the Genuine Progress Indicator, the Human Development Index, the Living Planet Index, the Well-being Index, and the ecological footprint. In contrast to the GDP, the Genuine Progress Indicator (GPI), for instance, also counts the value of housework, caring for children and the elderly, volunteerism, and the hours spent on free time or family and community activities—all of which can be viewed as good for the economy although no money changes hands. According to the 2001 GPI, for instance, the value of American economic activity grew by 1.6 percent, as opposed to the GDP's 3.9 percent.[44] The ecological footprint, on the other hand, measures the amount of productive land area required to sustain one human being. According to those who use it, there are about 1.9 hectares of productive land per person in the world, but the average ecological footprint is already 2.3 hectares. The largest footprint, 9.57 hectares, belongs to U.S. citizens, proponents claim, whereas people in Bangladesh need just 0.5 hectares. China's inhabitants are now somewhere in the middle at 1.36 hectares. What are we to conclude? We need more planet Earths if we are to sustain our current levels of consumption. This fact is totally missed, according to activists, by conventional indicators.

For the antiglobalizers, the novelty of alternative progress measures like the GPI and the ecological footprint is found in how they show, in the words of World Watch, how people are "handcuffed by the sets of choices available to them."[45] In other words, reform requires resistance, but it also depends on empowerment. People need to be shaken out of their enthrallment to the seductively hegemonic structures of the market and given plausible alternatives. This, activists avow, is among the highest priorities of the Movement. The objective of the Polaris Institute, for instance, is "to enable citizen movements to re-skill and re-tool themselves to fight for democratic social change in an age of corporate driven globalization."[46] Its very name is self-consciously evocative of the North Star, once the compass point of orientation for sailors trying to get their bearings at sea. The Ruckus Society, one of the main groups responsible for coordinating many of the high-visibility tactics of the street protests in Seattle, sees itself "as a toolbox of experience, training, and skills. We provide instruction on the application of tactical and strategic tools to a growing number of organizations and individuals from around the world in skill shares and trainings that are designed to move a campaign forward."[47] Public Citizen's Global Trade Watch website sums it up nicely: "Animating many facets of our work is the concept of the 'public citizen'—a person who, once empowered with information and tools to affect change, makes being an activist part of her or his daily life."[48]

A Way of Life for a Better World

The third and final step in articulating and implementing an alternative globalization is to provide actual examples of viable alternatives. Again turning to IFG's *Alternatives to Economic Globalization*, activists have condensed the wide spectrum of Movement affirmations into a handful of key precepts for which they collectively stand, including economic democracy, subsidiarity, ecological sustainability, protection of the commons, and the precautionary principle, to name five of ten.[49] At their core, these precepts promote the following: *restraint* via genuine public regulation of markets; *temperance* by privileging local self-sufficiency over global excess; *conservation* through proper stewardship of nature; *preservation* by safeguarding humanity's common stock of resources; *prudence* as the taking of proper precaution and care for the future; and, finally, *frugality* through economical, industrious, and simple living. Taken together or individually, these precepts find their principle formulation in the moral-linguistic register of thrift.

Environmental sustainability is a kind of "eco-" or "green" thrift. It presumes that if we are not careful, we will exhaust the ecological resources on which we depend. Sustainability in this way involves future-oriented conservation planning, which in turn requires both public regulation and a certain degree of self-imposed limits on consumption and wastefulness. Almost all the protesters are working toward this balance. But there is another, perhaps less familiar dimension to the promotion of conservation. It comes as an endorsement of the so-called precautionary principle: "In order to protect the environment," explain the IFG activists, "the precautionary approach shall be widely applied. . . . Where there are threats of serious or irreversible damage, lack of full scientific certainty shall not be used as a reason for postponing cost-effective measures to prevent environmental damage."[50] Greenpeace highlights the importance of the precautionary principle by enumerating the harm done when it has not been implemented:

> The release of ozone-depleting chlorofluorocarbons (CFCs) long after the first alarm bells started ringing in the 1970s, the buildup of persistent and bioaccumulative chlorinated pesticides in the environment and in our food, or the continuously increasing emissions of climate change–inducing CO_2 are cases in point. Some of these consequences have been asthma, cancer, birth defects and species extinction as well as global climate change, stratosphere ozone depletion and worldwide contamination from toxic substances and nuclear materials.[51]

In an age of manufactured risk, activists propose the precautionary principle as the only rational and responsible—and prudent—response to our uncertainty.

Subsidiarity, or the primacy of the local, is also a form of thrift. For many in the Movement, the idea of subsidiarity is partially summed up by the popular slogan "Think globally, act locally." In essence, subsidiarity privileges local decision-making power. It is a kind of self-sufficient temperance. However, this principle is believed endangered. The majority of people on the planet still live in and through local, community-based activities like fishing and farming or by means of other types of traditional subsistence. But the forces of economic globalization, say those in the Movement, are "rapidly dismantling" these local sufficiencies, "favoring instead economies based on export with global corporations in control."[52] Following the principle of subsidiarity does not mean that global-level interaction would be completely prohibited, merely restricted. Mander and Goldsmith, editors of *The Case against the Global Economy: And for a Turn toward the Local*, maintain that subsidiarity "doesn't mean that all trade is undesirable; only that its role must be limited to providing those things that cannot be provided for locally."[53] Moreover, "going global" by the terms set by economic globalization has led to destructive and exploitative intemperance, which needs to be fought at a global level. But Helena Norberg-Bodge, another leading activist, makes this key qualification:

> We need to distinguish between efforts merely to counter further globalization and efforts that can bring real solutions. The best way to halt the runaway global economy would undoubtedly be through multilateral treaties that would enable governments to protect people and the environment from the excesses of trade. But such international steps would not in themselves restore the health to economies and communities. Long-term solutions to today's social and environmental problems require a range of small, local initiatives that are as diverse as the cultures and environments in which they take place.[54]

The Foundation for Deep Ecology concurs: "Respect for diversity leads us to recognize the ecological wisdom that grows specific to place and context.

Thus, supporters of the deep ecology movement emphasize place-specific, ecological wisdom and vernacular technology practices."[55]

The principle of subsidiarity is closely connected to the significance of indigenous peoples. The significance of indigenous peoples within the antiglobalization movement cannot be overstated for three reasons: First, no group of people has been more oppressed by globalization, whether in its colonial phase or in the present free-market phase. Second, the most desired caches of natural resources (especially fossil fuels) are often found on their aboriginal lands. Third, "a better world is possible" precisely because these peoples' alternative ways of life actually exist. It is worth quoting Amory Starr at length:

> While incomplete and imperfect, experiments in Fair Trade, food policy councils, self-housing associations, worker-owned cooperatives, neighborhood assemblies and decentralized energy production and water harvesting show the viability in generating the social and scientific technologies that will ensure dignified lives for all. While these experiments have been fruitful, the movement's confidence that another world is possible is rooted in the recuperation from centuries of ridicule of the social and economic methods of indigenous peoples. Hundreds and thousands of distinct peoples lived for millennia providing for their own material, spiritual, social, and political needs. Those who survived colonialism are now continuing a complex process of agentic creolization despite conditions of seductive cultural invasion, genocidal state-corporate land grabs, and biopiracy. Diverse communities spent thousands of years using the scientific method in agriculture, medicine and ecosystem management. They also refined economic, political, social, and educational systems. These advanced traditions, developed in societies in which the market (to the extent that it existed) was subordinate to social criteria, are now posed as "alternatives" by movements which dare to redefine progress as something other than surrendering history, culture, and life to business. Survivors of postmodern capitalism are embracing these traditions as methods of achieving their most sophisticated aspirations for sustainable, accountable, diverse, and engaged social life.[56]

In this way, indigenous peoples epitomize the promise of subsidiarity. They are, in the Movement's eyes, laboratories of orthopraxy.

Alongside the appeal of indigenous peoples is the push for a more simple, modest, frugal life in the wealthy countries of the Global North, where "Enough!" is said not only in resistance but in affirmation of a set of modest habits and mores. "Creating a sustainable future requires a new way of thinking," states the Declaration of Independence from Overconsumption. "We must re-examine our desires, transform our perceptions, and develop a new ethic." What might these new habits and mores be? The declaration emphasizes frugality, industry, economy, and simplicity. Poor Richard would be proud.

The New Road Map Foundation, which produced this declaration, acknowledges that humans are inescapably consumers and, as a result, take their "sustenance from and return waste to the environment." However, the foundation fears that we postindustrial societies have become *over*consumers, "taking more than we can productively use—or more than the environment can sustainably provide." Overconsumption, they say, has become our way of life. "We put our faith in 'more,' " writes Vicki Robin, the declaration's principle author, "but it's never enough; we report being no happier now than we were in 1957, when cars were fewer, houses were smaller and microwaves and VCRs and personal computers did not even exist. Worse yet, our lifestyle, which threatens our social fabric and the very web of life on which we depend, has become the envy of much of the world."[57] What is the solution? Robin goes on to quote Robert Muller, retired assistant secretary-general of the United Nations: "The single most important contribution any of us can make to the planet is a return to frugality."[58] The New Road Map Foundation continues its boostership of classic thrift in another section of the declaration, entitled "Reframe the Game: Saving Money," in which it promotes " 'creating a nest egg,' 'saving for a rainy day,' [and] 'recession-proofing your life.' " Ensuring a secure financial cushion in retirement, "independent of shaky pensions or social security," the declaration adds, "benefits you, the economy and the planet."[59] By getting out of debt, saving money, and building financial security, we will consume less and be more satisfied in life. The Center for the New American Dream exclaims, "Our Motto: 'More fun, less stuff.' "[60] Or, again, there is the "Buy Nothing Day" slogan: "The more you consume, the less you live."

In the end, the Movement employs the rhetorics of thrift, whether as protest or as orthopraxy, in the effort to conceive of individual and collective prosperity on radically new terms.

The Curious Career of Thrift: From Scarcity to Abundance and Back?

By most accounts, the place of thrift in American culture is not what it once was. To be sure, it remains for a minority of Americans a virtuous practice central to a responsible work ethic. For others, however, thrift is no more than an austere survival tactic—a necessary virtue in hard times—as it inevitably was for the generation coming of age during the Great Depression. For many more, however, the word *thrift* evokes images of stinginess and greed perhaps best epitomized in Charles Dickens's famous lines about Ebenezer Scrooge: "Oh! But he was a tight-fisted hand at the grind-stone, Scrooge! a squeezing, wrenching, grasping, scraping, clutching, covetous, old sinner!"[61] Yet, as the onetime popularity of Benjamin Franklin's Poor Richard suggests, this was not always the case (or, more precisely, not so one-sidedly the case). Thrift was once an economic virtue at the heart of mainstream American culture, commonly held to be essential to early capitalist prosperity. Yet not only has thrift largely been displaced from the mainstream, appearing mainly at the cultural margins of late capitalism, it is now being employed to protest and counter the very projects to which it was once thought to be in service.

So we face a puzzle. How do we explain thrift's curious cultural career as evidenced by the Movement's rhetorics of thrift? Much remains to be worked out in the telling of this story, but its provisional line of analysis can be put summarily as follows: thrift, a practice once widely believed essential to early capitalism's vision of individual and collective thriving, made sense in an age characterized by the material conditions of *scarcity*. But today, so the story goes, we live in an age of material *abundance* where thrift can appear unnecessarily constraining and inhibiting, if not downright miserly. Of course, many people, not to mention a cottage industry of cultural critics, are quite aware of the enormous variety of social problems that haunt our plentitude. Curiously enough, however, it is not the modern-day scions of the Puritans or Benjamin Franklin who have spoken loudest in the language of thrift, but rather those more directly descended from the beatniks and the 1960s radicals.

This third, and final, section of the chapter offers a speculative historical explanation of thrift's rather unexpected employment by the antiglobalization protesters; it does so by placing the substantive concerns of Movement activists not only within long-standing debates about modern political economy but also, and more significantly, in relation to changing assumptions about the character of the natural world (and our relationship to it). Thus situated, we can see how the protest of the antiglobalization activists goes deeper than a mere aesthetic distaste of mass consumer society, youthful rebellion, or even reactionary politics. It touches upon the deep structures of culture itself.

HUMAN THRIVING AND THE CHANGING "NATURAL" IMAGINARY

We begin where some very superior scholarship has left off. The economist Albert O. Hirschman and the moral philosopher Charles Taylor have each explored the particular political and intellectual rationales for capitalism that occasioned the transvaluation of acquisitiveness and material ambition into modern virtues.[62] Hirschman showed how this new disposition toward economic life, although heralded in different ways by the likes of Montesquieu, Bernard Mandeville, and Adam Smith, was nevertheless premised on a single idea: modern realism's radical preoccupation with life as it *actually is* rather than how religion or tradition insisted it *ought to be*. The significance of this shift was, as we know, revolutionary, and Taylor has captured its consequences for contemporary social life in what he calls the "modern social imaginary"—that is, "the ways people imagine their social existence, how they fit together with others, how things go on between them and their fellows, the expectations that are normally met, and the deeper normative notions and images that underlie these expectations."[63] But what has been left largely implicit in these important accounts—and what must be apprehended directly if we are to understand the full intellectual and cultural significance of the antiglobalization protest movement (at least its American variants)—is what we might, adapting Taylor, call the modern "natural" imaginary.[64]

The full story of thrift can only be told against the changing social *and* natural imaginaries of Western modernity. Here we only have space to consider, and in the most perfunctorily fashion, the initial change in natural imaginaries that occurred with the shift from the classical and medieval worlds to the "disenchanted" world of early modernity. As we shall see, thrift only becomes an essential economic virtue against the backdrop of material scarcity, and then, only when a certain understanding of human agency becomes operative.

FEAST AND FAMINE: ABUNDANCE AND SCARCITY

From time out of mind it has been taken as axiomatic that the primary state of human existence is one of want, that the primary posture of daily life is a struggle for subsistence, and that history is the repetition of various cycles of feast and famine, birth and death, rise and decline. The historian Polybius provides the classical statement of this law of recurrence. "From time to time," he writes, "as a result of floods, plagues, failures of crops or other similar causes, there occurs a catastrophic destruction of the human race, in which all knowledge of the arts and social institutions is lost. Such disasters, tradition tells us, have often befallen mankind, and must reasonably be expected to recur."[65] Humanity is thus doomed to repeat the same basic pattern of development and decay. Nature is in this sense both stable and predictable—hunger both precedes and follows the harvest.

However, this never-ending pattern of scarcity and abundance and the fatalism that often accompanied it were enveloped by, and to some degree in tension with, a divinely infused cosmos. In its Christian formulation, the divine economy of the world was ordered by what Arthur Lovejoy has referred to as "the principle of plentitude." This principle describes a reality in which "the extent and abundance of creation must be as great as the possibility of existence and commensurate with the productive capacity of a 'perfect' and inexhaustible Source, and that the world is the better, the more things it contains."[66] The plentitude of which Lovejoy speaks is the "plenum," or fullness of God, and is necessarily unlimited in its potentiality. Its superabundance is expressed in the biblical mandate to be fruitful and multiply. Yet, in another important sense, it is a fullness that cannot be improved upon by human agency. The vision of nature that emerges from this principle is a dynamic yet harmonious set of natural correspondences, sufficient to the needs of all creatures properly situated within a vertical order of hierarchical complementarity (à la the Great Chain of Being).

This vision of sublime amplitude, however, was always tempered by the experience of ongoing, and often severe, depravation. In the dominant classical picture, this was a result of the fact that the world was only a pale and imperfect reflection of the cosmic harmony of the eternal Forms. According to Jewish and Christian theology, the world, although originally plentiful, was fallen, misdirected, and suffering under divine curse. The full access to God's plenum was thus temporarily foreclosed. Under such conditions, the Earth's continents had become an archipelago of hard labor, and the span of a human life was determined by the limits of physical exhaustion. "In the sweat of your face," declares the biblical Creator, "you shall eat bread till you return to the ground."

Accordingly, these premodern cosmologies conditioned ancient and medieval attitudes regarding economic life in the West for millennia. On the whole, economic life was a functional necessity—a matter of mundane prudence perhaps—but hardly a realm of spiritual or even worldly virtue. On the contrary, the desire to accumulate wealth was viewed with strong suspicion. Where the Greeks ruminated about the problem of *pleonexia*, the Christians preached against the sin of avarice. This suspicion was at least partly founded on the presumption that the content of the world (whether imperfect or fallen) did not change. From Augustine to the medieval Scholastics, the reigning Christian theory of economics presumed a zero-sum world. In a way that sounds remarkably similar to the classical economists, Augustine claims, "If one does not lose, the other does not gain."[67]

In the premodern natural imaginary of the West, although varied in its particulars depending on place and time, the world was thus full of tensions: On the one hand, it was ultimately conceived as a divinely unified, self-sufficient, and ordered cosmos; on the other, the actual experience of the world was of constant change, uncertainty, and mystery. Nevertheless, such tensions were made meaningful by belief in the will of divine agency. In this way, the lot of human existence was simultaneously (though not equally) that of abundance and scarcity. There were to be sure many moments of plenty, feasting, and rest, but such moments were always truncated by much longer periods of dearth, hunger, and toil—at least until, in the Christian story, humans reached the end of history when the gates to paradise would be reopened and access to God's plenum would be fully restored.

DEBATING SCARCITY: HUMAN MASTERY AND THE TURN TOWARD ABUNDANCE IN EARLY MODERNITY

With that complex concatenation of historical transformations we have come to refer to as modernity, the social and natural imaginaries of the West underwent a seismic shift. Of the initial articulators (and propagators) of the changing moral registers and intellectual tempers, few were as significant as Machiavelli. His reformulation of classical realism in a modern idiom highlighted the growing quest for human control over the world. In politics, his preoccupation with society as it actually is (again, not as it ought to be) issued a challenge that would be taken up across Europe as the basis of modern political order, most famously by Thomas Hobbes. But Machiavelli also heralded the beginning of an alteration in the natural imaginary. "Fortune is a woman," he quipped, who can be controlled by force, liberating men from its grip.[68] Here we catch a glimpse of the natural world stripped of its enchantments and transcendence—perceived "as it actually is." Taking up the Machiavellian outlook in the natural sciences, Francis Bacon argued against the theoretical, speculative character of premodern science, claiming that we have the intelligence necessary if not for overcoming Adam's curse, then certainly for making its demands less onerous. The goal of modern science was, according to Bacon, to seek the "relief of man's estate." Humans were no longer subject to the dictates of fate or fortune. They had come of age. "For man by the Fall," says Bacon, "fell both from his state of innocence and his dominion over creation." He continues:

> Both of these, however, can even in this life be to some extent made good; the former by religion and faith, the later by arts and sciences. For the curse did not make the creation entirely and forever rebellious; but in virtue of that ordinance "in the sweat of thy face shalt thou eat thy bread," by every kind of effort. . . it will at length and in some measure be subdued so as to provide man with his bread, with the necessities of human life.[69]

In a similar vein, Bacon's slightly younger contemporary René Descartes wrote:

> It is possible to arrive at knowledge that is very useful in life and that in place of the speculative philosophy taught in the Schools, one can find a practical one, by which, knowing the force and actions of fire, water, air, stars, the heavens, and all the other bodies that surround us. . . we could. . . use these objects for all the purposes for which they are appropriate, and thus make ourselves, as it were, masters and possessors of nature.[70]

In the optimistic sentiments of both men, we can see the great transvaluation in values in full progress, and the evolution of our natural imaginaries along with it.

By the time of Adam Smith, the West had developed a natural imaginary that stood fully in between, but well on its way from, the premodern to the modern world. On the one hand, the Enlightenment (especially in its Scottish version) retained a form of the principle of plentitude, though redacted in deist terms as the beneficence of natural harmony. Radically enough, it is one in which competitive self-interest ("rightly understood") was the basis of that harmony. "The administration of the great system of the universe, the care of the universal happiness of all rational and sensible beings," explains Smith in *The Theory of Moral Sentiments*, "is the business of God, and not of man. To man is allotted a much humbler department, but one much more suitable to the weakness of his powers, and to the narrowness of his comprehension—the care of his own happiness, of that of his family, his friends, his country."[71] Smith believed that the divine has so ordered human nature that when freed to "truck and barter," society prospers and misery is reduced to a minimum. This is, of course, the import of Smith's most enduring metaphor: the "invisible hand," which Alexander Pope summarized in his well-cited verse "Thus God and Nature link'd the gen'ral frame / And bade Self-love and Social be the same."[72]

On the other hand, however, this early modern natural imaginary depicts a world that could be improved by human agency. If the iron law of scarcity still ruled over the everyday lives of most people in the world, the new and fully modern conceit was the idea that humans could actually change this state of affairs. To wit, they could master fate itself. For Smith, it is the progress of this mastery that he effectively credits with separating the prosperous societies from the poor and miserable ones. In the opening pages of *The Wealth of Nations*, Smith contends:

> Among civilized and thriving nations [as opposed to miserably poor ones] though a great number of people do not labor at all, many of whom consume the produce of ten times, frequently of a hundred times more labor than the greater part of those who work; yet the produce of the whole labor of society is so great, that all are often abundantly supplied. And the workman, even of the lowest and poorest order, if he is frugal and industrious may enjoy a greater share of the necessaries and conveniences of life than it is possible for any savage to acquire.[73]

The moral is clear. What distinguishes the prosperous nation from the impoverished (and hence the civilized from the uncivilized) is principally the way wealthy societies actively manage and organize their labor at a collective level, and how (most) individuals in such societies actively manage their personal affairs through thrift. The full import of Smith's claim needs underscoring: it is only against a backdrop of material scarcity that thrift makes sense, and only then, when persons understand themselves as having a kind of autonomy from, and agency toward, the world around them.

From Smith to the more adamant Enlightenment proponents of human progress, like Voltaire and Condorcet, it is still a world of scarcity, but only for the time being. With the proper economic practices and structures, like a modern division of labor and thrift, humanity could—and would—overcome it. The golden age was not in the misted past, on this view, nor was it in an otherworldly future, but in the *near* future, in an extended modern present. This belief was compelling enough to inspire Voltaire's poetic redescription of Eden in "The Worldling." The state of nature was not the garden paradise it was purported to be. On the contrary, the condition of Adam and Eve was best described as primitive, ignorant, and deplorable. He limns:

> Both weary of the marriage yoke
> You supped each night beneath an oak
> On millet, water, and on mast,
> And having finished your repast,
> On the ground we were forced to lie,
> Exposed to the inclement sky:
> Such in the state of simple nature
> Is man, a helpless, wretched creature.[74]

If anything substantiates a genuine earthly paradise for Voltaire, it is the myth not of prelapsarian Eden but of 1736 Paris. Of his life there, Voltaire says, "I have, I own, a worldly mind / That's pleased abundance here to find."[75]

However, the optimism of this changing natural imaginary can be overstated. While figures like William Godwin (and later socialists) believed that the problem of scarcity inhered not to nature as such but to the inequity of human institutions—not least that of private property—and could thus be overcome with the right political organization, the classical economists abjured. John Stuart Mill supplied perhaps the most famous objection. "The necessity of restraining population is not," he argued, "as many persons believe, peculiar to a condition of great inequality of property. A greater number of people cannot, in any given state of civilization, be collectively so well provided for as a smaller. The niggardliness of nature, not the injustice of society, is the cause of the penalty attached to over-population."[76] The figure most commonly associated with this view, though, is Thomas Malthus. "A finite earth cannot support the unchecked increase of any form of life," he maintained, "animal or plant and must necessarily prescribe such limits to the production of the means of subsistence as to prevent the full potential growth of human population." Nature had historically taken care of population problems, according to Malthus, through vice, poverty, and moral restraint. The industrialization of society, however, had presumably undercut the power of the first two, leaving only moral restraint on which to fall back. At the heart of his pessimism was a "law of diminishing returns," which states that as populations increase typically due to higher crop yields, land fertility inevitably declines; as land fertility declines, rent for good land goes up; as rent increases, wages for labor go down. The net effect is a catch-22 that sounds remarkably similar to the classical and Christian cycle of recurrence, where scarcity always follows abundance in this world. Yet the Malthusian principle of population is clearly the obverse of Lovejoy's principle of plentitude.

PERPETUAL FEAST: FROM SCARCITY TO ABUNDANCE

Whether humanity had in fact embarked upon the path to mastery over nature and therefore to lasting abundance or, rather, whether the surplus of the industrializing world would prove just as intermittent and fleeting as it had been in the pre-industrial—these would be open questions for more than a century. By the early twentieth century, however, the question appeared firmly settled in favor of the Enlightenment optimists and against the pessimism of the classical economists. By most accounts, Malthus was simply dead wrong. The unprecedented generation of wealth produced by industrial society demonstrated that the old problems of scarcity had been, or at least would very shortly be, solved once and for all.

One of the first to articulate full confidence in an abundance-based natural imaginary was the historian Simon Patten. In his 1907 book, *The New Basis of Civilization*, Patten traces what Smith referred to as "the progress of opulence" to its culmination in the industrial societies of the West. In a fit of Promethean exuberance Patten explains that the pessimistic views of the classical economists were not mistaken, merely obsolete. For they "were writing the epilogue of one drama while the curtain was rising upon the prologue of another presenting a new cast of characters. Many of the obstacles that were insuperable a century ago are falling before the young genius of the Mechanical Age. Militarism, bad sanitation, inadequate protection from heat and cold, a high birth-rate off-setting a high death rate—all these obstructions . . . have been reduced."[77] As a consequence, what were seen to be virtues and vices in a world of scarcity need to be reevaluated. "All civilizations before the Nineteenth Century, like the primitive societies of the Western world today and the backward despotisms of the East," he writes,

> were realms of pain and deficit in which the traditions and experiences of men were molded out of the general menaces of life and happiness. . . . But are these sad endings the fit sequel of man's ill-doing in a one-time perfect world, as certain moralists have affirmed, or are suffering and defeat the outcome of the purely physical conditions of existence? If the latter, improvements in the environment will construct a new basis of civilization by lessening deficit and destroying the old status between men and nature.[78]

This last line is crucial for it illustrates a profound intensification of expectations moderns had of their own powers toward the natural world.

That the mid-twentieth century was undoubtedly the high tide of the paradigm of abundance is evident in the founding of its most defining economic institutions. In his opening speech at the 1944 Bretton Woods Conference, which established what we know of today as the International Monetary Fund and the World Bank, U.S. secretary of Treasury Henry Morgenthau called for "the creation of a dynamic world economy in which the peoples of every nation will be able to realize their potential in peace and enjoy, increasingly, fruits of material progress on an earth infinitely blessed with natural riches." He stressed the "elementary economic axiom that prosperity has no fixed limits. It is not a finite substance to be diminished by division."[79] Such were the founding sentiments of the global economic order.

The paradigm of abundance found its most influential champion in John Maynard Keynes. Nowhere does he summarize the perspective more boldly than in his Great Depression–era essay, "Economic Prospects for Our Grand Children." There Keynes contends: "From the earliest times of which we have record—back to two thousand years before Christ—down to the beginning of the 18th Century, there was no very great change in the standard of living of the average man living in the civilized centers of the earth. Ups and downs certainly. Visitations of plague, famine, and war. Golden intervals. But no progressive violent change."[80] But in the world of modern, industrial society, even shocks as great as those experienced in the Great Depression were merely growing pains. "We are suffering," he claimed, "not from the rheumatics of old age, but from the growing pains of over-rapid changes, from the painfulness of readjustment between one economic period and another."[81] Although some of his contemporaries were tempted to return to the pessimism of the classical economists, Keynes insisted that this was a mistake, for "in the long run . . . mankind is solving its economic problem."[82] Still, his is not a call for unalloyed optimism. In solving his economic problem—the problem of subsistence—mankind would now have to confront a different set of what Keynes believed were his more permanent challenges. "For the first time since his creation," proclaims Keynes, "man will be faced with his permanent problem—how to use his freedom from pressing economic cares, how to occupy the leisure, which science and compound interest will have won for him, to live wisely and well."[83] It is as if humans had found the key to reopen the gates of Paradise on their own, without divine assistance, and now, finally, they could enjoy the plentitude that had been so long barred from them.

It is at this point that we are able to bring thrift squarely back into the discussion. For while we might expect Keynes to encourage thrift as a way of living "wisely and well" amid abundance, as Smith did more than a century before, he does not. In fact, he does the opposite. Echoing Patten, Keynes writes: "We shall be able to rid ourselves of many of the pseudo-moral principles which have hag-ridden us for two hundred years, by which we have exalted some of the most distasteful of human qualities into the position of the highest virtues."[84] For Keynes, thrift is akin to hoarding and an overly obsessive preoccupation with the future. It may have been a rational response to existence in an age of scarcity, but it is irrational in an age of abundance.[85] "The 'purposive' man," he writes, "is always trying to secure a spurious and delusive immortality for his acts by pushing his interest in them forward in time. He does not love his cat, but his cat's kittens. . . . For him jam is not jam unless it is a case of jam tomorrow and never jam today. Thus, by pushing his jam always forward into the future, he strives to secure for his act of boiling it an immortality."[86] According to the Keynesian "paradox of thrift," moreover, thrift is an even greater hindrance for society as a whole, at least during recessions. As Paul Samuelson writes in an early edition of his authoritative textbook, *Economics*: "It is a paradox because in kindergarten we are all taught that thrift is *always* a good thing. Benjamin Franklin's *Poor Richard's Almanac* never tired of preaching the doctrine of saving. And now comes a new generation of alleged financial experts who seem to be telling us that black is white and white is black, and that the old virtues may be modern sins." For Keynes and other midcentury theorists of abundance, our modern technologically produced bounty had finally freed humanity to pursue their most authentic virtue—"to once more value ends above means and prefer the good to the useful."[87] The conclusion could not have been clearer: human mastery of the natural world had mastered scarcity and, in doing so, rendered what virtue the old Victorian notion of thrift once had obsolete.

By the 1970s and 1980s, thanks in large measure to the influence of Keynesianism in the United States and Europe, and the fifty-year influence of the Bretton Woods institutions in the area of international development, the paradigm of abundance had been thoroughly globalized. Ironically, it was during these same decades that Keynesianism (not to mention its more thoroughly socialist counterparts) came under severe attack by detractors who accused it of being a hindrance to the worldwide realization of abundance. Its promotion of the welfare state, government protectionism, and the nationalization of major industries were charged with being inefficient and unproductive, leaving billions still trapped in poverty. According to its detractors, the Keynesian world was still, paradoxically enough, enthralled to practices and ideas in which poverty remained man's normal lot. What was needed was the realization of the promise of Bretton Woods: a "new world economic order" in which all the barriers to free trade would come down; then, and only then, so its advocates contended, could Smith's "progress of opulence" be universally achieved.[88] It is no coincidence that it was also at this precise moment when many of the social movements that would eventually coalesce into the antiglobalization protest movement were first being formulated.

With the fall of the Soviet Union and the end of the Cold War, the prospect of realizing the promise of a new, and unfettered, world capitalist order appeared to be within the world's grasp for the first time in human history. Nothing seemed to stand in the way. Yet, as we know, the euphoria of the moment did not last long. A host of long-standing problems—from racial inequality to extreme poverty to ethnic violence and failing states—reasserted themselves with new force, while entirely new problems like global climate change darkened the horizon of the new millennium. Initially, however, staunch champions of the new world economic order like Thomas Friedman remained confident about the future despite some early setbacks. In his first book on the topic of globalization, *The Lexus and the Olive Tree*, Friedman quotes a Merrill Lynch ad to suggest (just as Keynes had during the Great Depression) that the setbacks were merely growing pains and not the rheumatics of old age:

> It was born when the Wall fell in 1989. It's no surprise that the world's youngest economy—the global economy—is still finding its bearings. The intricate checks and balances that stabilize economies are only incorporated with time. Many world markets are only recently freed, governed for the first time by the emotions of the people rather than the fists of the state. From where we sit, none of this diminishes the promise offered a decade ago by the demise of the walled-off world.... The spread of free markets and democracy around the world is permitting more people everywhere to turn their aspirations into achievements. And technology, properly harnessed and liberally distributed, has the power to ease not just geographical borders but also human ones. It seems to us that, for a 10-year-old, the world continues to hold great promise. In the meantime, no one said it was going to be easy.[89]

Indeed, standing a decade yet further on, things look even more difficult and uncertain for this "world" (now twenty years old)—so much so that even Freidman has had to temper his optimism. His latest book, *Hot, Flat, and Crowed: Why We Need a Green Revolution—And How It Can Renew America*, expresses the changing mood and mind-set. As his title suggests, environmental concerns have moved onto the agendas of our political leaders and public intellectuals and into the cultural mainstream. As a result, one is more likely to hear the language of "sustainability" being preached today than the gospel of "abundance." This is as true for multinational corporations as it is for environmental activists. When people start believing that the world really is "full" and that Earth is a scarce, unrenewable resource, it is no wonder that thrift is once again regaining its virtue.

All this raises the question about whether we are witnessing another shift in our natural imaginary? It is too early to tell. Whether the emergence of the discourse of sustainability represents a transformation comparable to that which occurred with the shift in natural imaginaries from one dominated by a paradigm of scarcity to one dominated by a paradigm of abundance, or whether it merely augurs a further intensification of that shift, the fact remains that we are bearing witness to transformations in our understanding of what it means to thrive and the forms of restraint upon which any substantive vision of thriving must necessarily depend.

Conclusion: Disputing Abundance

Against this all-too-brief sketch of the intellectual reformulations of the Western natural imaginary, we may now be in a better position to appreciate the cultural significance of the antiglobalization movement, and thus its rather surprising reliance on the language of thrift.

Simply put, the Movement's rhetorics of thrift dispute the ideology of abundance that has come to define the modern natural imaginary of the West and, by doing so, to challenge economic globalization's vision of human thriving that has emanated from it. In the world being fashioned by global capitalism, human thriving is understood to depend on unlimited economic growth, which in turn is contingent on a never-faltering rise in consumption—indicators of which are everywhere measured in terms of GDP. In such a world, thrift is no longer plausible as a means to human thriving—it can even seem problematic for rational people and rationalized societies. Against this prevailing ideology, Movement activists contend that the corporate-dominated, technologically produced abundance is, at best, an artificial abundance that has come at an unrecoverable cost—increasing global inequality, environmental destruction, and a loss of the commons; at worst, it is bringing humanity down a path of manufactured risk, a path that will certainly lead to the wholesale degradation of life on the planet, and quite possibly to its own demise. Unsurprisingly, the protesters contend that they are the true realists because they alone are willing to acknowledge the "true costs" of our present way of life—alas, the world as it actually is.

Whether they will be proved correct, of course, remains to be seen. In the meantime, there are good reasons to be skeptical about certain aspects of their critique, as well as of the alternatives they claim to offer.[90] But what is hopefully apparent is why we might take them seriously, at least culturally speaking. The antiglobalization protesters call our attention to long-standing intellectual and moral disputes that grow out of our evolving social and natural imaginaries, and which bear on the abiding question of economic life: the question of what it means and takes to thrive. In this way, the protesters have shown how this question and the disputes that surround it remain saliently and profoundly our own.

Notes

1. Thomas Friedman, "The Coalition to Keep Poor People Poor," *New York Times*, April 24, 2001, A19.

2. Vandana Shiva, quoted in Amory Starr, *Global Revolt: A Guide to the Movements against Globalization* (London: Zed Books, 2005), 19.

3. Ibid., 19–20.

4. Amory Starr's *Global Revolt* informed much of this brief summary of Movement antecedents.

5. For a helpful discussion of these movements, see George Katsiaficas, *The Subversion of Politics: European Autonomous Social Movements and the Decolonialization of Everyday Life* (Atlantic Highlands, NJ: Humanities Press, 1997).

6. These events energized both environmental justice and indigenous peoples movements while at the same time bringing them in closer contact with other global causes.

7. The full impact of this and other reports is difficult to estimate, but in exposing the disparities of wealth between nation-states and multinational corporations in such stunning terms, the report certainly contributed to the internal justification of the Movement.

8. Starr, *Global Revolt*, 19.

9. One of the most important developments in the further solidification of the Movement in recent years has been the creation of the World Social Forum (countering the World Economic Forum). In 2002, at the second meeting of the Forum, some 51,000 people attended from 123 countries; see www.forumsocialmundial.or.br.

10. What I am calling the *rhetorics* of thrift are central to the antiglobalization protest movement in two forms: thrift as protest and thrift as orthopraxy. The distinction is, of course, merely analytical. In terms of thrift itself, it is perhaps also important to emphasize that the term is used here broadly, in ways that include but also transcend thrift as it has classically been understood—that is, as a purely economic practice synonymous with fiscal frugality. In short, I am interested in what we might call the spirit of thrift.

11. See Zygmunt Bauman, *Globalization: The Human Consequences* (New York: Columbia University Press, 1998), 1.

12. James Nash, "On the Subversive Virtue: Frugality," in *Ethics of Consumption: The Good Life, Justice, and Global Stewardship*, ed. D. A. Crocker and T. Linden (Lanham, MD: Rowman and Littlefield, 1998), 418.

13. http://www.polarisinstitute.org/aboutus (accessed June 13, 2010).

14. The Turning Point Project, "Invisible Government," advertisement no. 3 in a series on Economic Globalization (personal collection), but see http://bss.sfsu.edu/fischer/IR%20 305/Readings/invisibl.htm (accessed June 14, 2010).

15. John Cavanagh and Jerry Mander, eds., *Alternatives to Economic Globalization: A Better World Is Possible* (San Francisco: Berrett-Koehler, 2004), 38. Together with Jerry Mander and Edward Goldsmith, eds., *The Case against the Global Economy: And For a Return to the Local* (San Francisco: Sierra Club Books, 1996), these two books represent what many activists consider the most definitive statements of the Movement.

16. http://www.foodfirst.org/node/241 (accessed June 13, 2010).

17. This statistic is stated in Cavanagh and Mander, *Alternatives to Economic Globalization*, 41, but a source for it is not cited.

18. Wolfgang Sachs, "Neo-Development: 'Global Ecological Management,'" in *The Case against the Global Economy*, ed. Jerry Mander and Edward Goldsmith (San Francisco: Sierra Club Books, 1996), 240.

19. Cavanagh and Mander, *Alternatives to Economic Globalization*, 88.

20. Ibid. Another of the Turning Point ads (this one entitled "Who Plays God in the 21st Century?") expresses the basic concern with respect to our genetic makeup: "The genetic structures of living beings are the last of Nature's creations to be invaded and altered for commerce. Now they're being seized for corporate ownership."

21. This can be found in Starr, *Global Revolt*, 33.

22. Cavanaugh and Mander, *Alternatives to Economic Globalization*, 37.

23. Sachs, "Neo-Development," 240.

24. http://www.deepecology.org/mission.htm (accessed June 13, 2010).

25. See Anthony Giddens, *Runaway World: How Globalization Is Reshaping Our Lives* (New York: Routledge, 2000).

26. Sachs, "Neo-Development," 245.

27. David Korten, "The Failures of Bretton Woods," in *The Case against the Global Economy: And for a Turn toward the Local*, ed. Jerry Mander and Edward Goldsmith (San Francisco: Sierra Club Books, 1996), 22–23.

28. http://whitedwarf.org/affluenza/cnad/justice.html (accessed June 13, 2010).

29. Activists base this claim in what is called the "ecological footprint": "the amount of renewable and non-renewable ecologically productive land area required to support the resource demands and absorb the wastes of a given population or specific activities." Redefining Progress, "Ecological Footprint Analysis," www.rprogress.org/newprojects/ecolfoot.

30. Turning Point Project, "Genetic Roulette," advertisement no. 3 in a series on Genetic Engineering (personal copy); see also http://www.biocentury.com/biotech-pharma-news/coverstory/1999-11-01/spectacular-claims—fight-or-flight-a2 (accessed June 13, 2010).

31 .Turning Point Project, "Where Will the Next Plague Come From?" advertisement no. 4 in a series on Genetic Engineering (personal copy).

32. Cavanagh and Mander, *Alternatives to Economic Globalization*.

33. "A Better World Is Possible" is both the subtitle of *Alternatives to Economic Globalization* and the motto of the World Social Forum.

34. Jerry Mander, "Facing the Rising Tide," in *The Case against the Global Economy: And for a Turn toward the Local*, ed. Jerry Mander and Edward Goldsmith (San Francisco: Sierra Club Books, 1996), 4.

35. See "Economists Lead the Change: Robert Costanza," www.adbusters.org/metas/eco/truecosteconomics/economists/costanza.html (accessed December 15, 2006).

36. Ted Halstead and Clifford Cobb, "The Need for New Measurements of Progress," in *The Case against the Global Economy: And for a Turn toward the Local*, ed. Jerry Mander and Edward Goldsmith (San Francisco: Sierra Club Books, 1996), 199.

37. Wendell Berry, *Life Is a Miracle: An Essay against Modern Superstition* (Washington, DC: Counterpoint, 2000).

38. Andrew Gumbel, "Fast Food Nation: An Appetite for Litigation." *Independent*, June 4, 2002, news.independent.co.uk/world/americas/article179042.ece (accessed December 15, 2006); cited in Adbusters Media Foundation, "True Cost Pricing, Cost of Obesity in the US," http://adbusters.org/metas/eco/truecosteconomics/true_cost.html (accessed December 15, 2006).

39. Rich Pirog et al., "Food, Fuel, and Freeways: An Iowa Perspective on How Far Food Travels, Fuel Usage, and Greenhouse Gas Emissions," presented to the Leopold Center for Sustainable Agriculture at Iowa State University, Ames, Iowa, June 2001, www.leopold.iastate.edu/pubs/staff/ppp (accessed December 15, 2006); cited in Adbusters, "True Cost Pricing."

40. "Valuing the External Costs of Aviation," a report commissioned by the Department for Transport, London, www.dft.gov.uk/stellent/groups/dft_aviation/documents/page/dft_aviation_503315.hcsp (accessed December 15, 2006); cited in Adbusters "True Cost Pricing."

41. Cavanagh and Mander, *Alternatives to Economic Globalization*, 43.

42. Halstead and Cobb, "The Need for New Measurements of Progress," 200.

43. Ibid., 199.

44. See Redefining Progress Web site, www.rprogress.org.

45. http://www.worldwatch.org/node/815 (accessed June 13, 2010).

46. http://www.polarisinstitute.org/aboutus (accessed June 13, 2010).

47. http://ruckus.org/section.php?id=71 (accessed June 13, 2010).

48. http://www.citizen.org/trade/about/ (accessed June 13, 2010).

49. For a complete list, see chap. 4 of Cavanagh and Mander, *Alternatives to Economic Globalization*. These precepts were gleaned by the IFG staff from a survey of scores of groups in the Movement.

50. Cavanagh and Mander, *Alternatives to Economic Globalization*, 101.

51. http://www.greenpeace.org/international/en/campaigns/trade-and-the-environment/the-precautionary-principle/ (accessed June 13, 2010).

52. Ibid., 82.

53. Mander and Goldsmith, The *Case against the Global Economy*, 391.

54. Helena Norberg-Hodge, "Shifting Direction: From Global Dependence to Local Interdependence, *The Case against the Global Economy*, 393–94.

55. http://www.deepecology.org/movement.htm (accessed June 13, 2010).

56. Starr, *Global Revolt*, 50–51.

57. http://www.sacredlands.org/independence.htm (accessed June 13, 2010).

58. Robert Muller, *Safe Passage into the Twenty-First Century: The United Nations Quest for Peace, Equality, Justice, and Development* (New York: Continuum, 1995); this address was given at the United Nations on April 6, 1994.

59. http://www.sacredlands.org/independence.htm (accessed June 13, 2010).

60. http://www.newdream.org/about/mediaclips/pittpostgazoct192004.php (accessed June 13, 2010).

61. Charles Dickens, *A Christmas Carol* (London: Chapman and Hall, 1897), 10.

62. The idea of "paradistole" is offered by Jerry Z. Muller in *The Mind and the Market: Capitalism in Western Thought* (New York: Anchor, 2003), a superb intellectual history in the line of Albert O. Hirschman's book *The Passions and the Interests: Political Arguments for Capitalism before Its Triumph* (Princeton, NJ: Princeton University Press, 1997).

63. Charles Taylor, *Modern Social Imaginaries* (Durham, NC: Duke University Press, 2004), 25.

64. As with the rhetorics of thrift, so with social and natural imaginaries; they are integrally related and only separated here analytically. It perhaps also needs to be stressed that by "natural" imaginary, I mean to include not only the mental conceptualizations of the physical environment but also our orientation to it—again, it has much to do with our expectations of nature.

65. Polybius, *The Rise of the Roman Empire* (New York: Penguin, 1974), 304. For Polybius, what is true for nature is true for human endeavors, especially political projects: "For just as rust eats away iron, and woodworms or shipworms eat away timber, and these substances even if they escape any external damage are destroyed by the processes which are generated within themselves, so each constitution possesses its own inherent and inseparable vice." Ibid., 310.

66. Arthur O. Lovejoy, *The Great Chain of Being* (Cambridge, MA: Harvard University Press, 1936), 52.

67. Augustine, *Expositions on the Book of Psalms*, vol. 8 of *A Select Library* (New York: 1888), 320–21, quoted in Muller, *The Mind and the Market*, 6.

68. Niccolò Machiavelli, *The Prince* (New York: Bantam Classics, 1986), 86.

69. Francis Bacon, "Aphorisms Concerning the Interpretation of Nature and the Kingdom of Man," in *Novum Organum* (LaSalle, IL: Open Court, 1994), 2:52.

70. René Descartes, *Discourse on Method*, trans. Laurence J. LaFleur (New York: Macmillan, 1960), 33.

71. Adam Smith, *The Theory of Moral Sentiments* (New York: Cambridge University Press, 2002), 348.

72. Alexander Pope, "Epistle 3: Of the Nature and State of Man with Respect to Society," in *The Works* (London, 1751), ll. 313–14, quoted in Peter J. Bowler, "Malthus, Darwin, and the Concept of Struggle," *Journal of the History of Ideas* 37 (October–December 1976): 644.

73. Adam Smith, *The Wealth of Nations* (New York: Random House, 2000), xxiv.

74. Voltaire, "The Worldling," From The Works of Voltaire, A Contemporary Version, (New York: E.R. DuMont, 1901), A Critique and Biography by John Morley, notes by Tobias Smollett, trans. William F. Fleming. Vol. X The Dramatic Works Part 1 (Zaire, Caesar, The Prodigal, Prefaces) and Part II (The Lisbon Earthquake and Other Poems). Chapter: THE WORLDLING. Accessed from http://oll.libertyfund.org/title/2240/211136 on 2011-01-21.

75 .Voltaire, "The Worldling."

76. John Stuart Mill, *Principles of Political Economy with Some of Their Applications to Social Philosophy*, 7th ed., ed. William J. Ashley (London: Longmans, Green, 1909), 1.13.5.

77. Simon N. Patten, *The New Basis of Civilization* (Cambridge, MA: Belknap Press, 1968), 14.

78. Ibid., 10.

79. Henry Morgenthau, opening speech at Bretton Woods, Vermont, July 1, 1944, quoted in Korten, "Failures of Bretton Woods," 1.

80. John Maynard Keynes, "Economic Possibilities of Our Grandchildren," in *Essays in Persuasion* (London: Macmillan, 1930), 360.

81. Ibid., 358.

82. Ibid., 364.

83. Ibid., 367.

84. Ibid., 370.

85. Paul Anthony Samuelson, *Economics* (Boston: McGraw-Hill, 1958), 237.

86. Keynes, "Economic Possibilities," 370.

87. Ibid., 372.

88. Of course there were countercurrents running the whole way from Malthus to the Club of Rome's "Limits to Growth" report.

89. Merrill Lynch ad, quoted in Thomas Friedman, *The Lexus and the Olive Tree: Understanding Globalization* (New York: Farrar, Straus and Giroux, 1999), xiii–xiv.

90. Peter Lindert and Jeffrey G. Williamson, "Does Globalization Make the World More Unequal?" in *Globalization in Historical Perspective*, ed. Michael D. Bordo, Alan M. Taylor, and Jeffrey G. Williamson (Chicago: University of Chicago Press, 2003); see also Benjamin Friedman, *The Moral Consequences of Economic Growth* (New York: Vintage Books, 2005), 361–68.

23 }

Conclusion: Thrift and Thriving

TOWARD A MORAL FRAMEWORK FOR ECONOMIC LIFE

Joshua J. Yates and James Davison Hunter

The Witch of Wall Street

Hetty Robinson Green was the first female tycoon in American history. Almost unknown today, Hetty's robber baron–era success would have rivaled the wealth and notoriety (if not quite the celebrity) of Oprah and Madonna. Yet during her lifetime, Hetty Green's notoriety did not stem from her fabulous wealth, though in that respect she stood peer to Vanderbilt, Astor, Rockefeller, Morgan, and Carnegie. She was instead infamous for her pathological obsession with thrift. There is an old joke about the tightwad who "pinches the dollar so hard it makes the eagle scream"; Hetty Green made this an art form. She was quite possibly the greatest miser in American history.

Hetty's frugality was legendary: she wore only drab, durable clothing, which she washed herself and then only sparingly; she lived on oatmeal, which she heated on the radiators of the cheap boardinghouses in which she lived; she traveled by public transportation and was well known for clipping coupons, for incessant haggling, and for violent rages when she felt she was being overcharged—which was nearly always. After reading the morning newspaper she would roll it up and send her son out to resell it. She became so preoccupied with people taking advantage of her wealth that she often feigned poverty. On one tragic occasion, her son badly injured his leg in a sledding accident. Fearing she would be exploited when the doctors realized who she was, she took her son, dressed as a pauper, to a doctor as a charity patient. As the story goes, however, Hetty was recognized before her son could be treated, and the doctor refused the free care. The leg eventually had to be amputated.

Yet, in matters of business and investing, Hetty was as shrewd and ruthless as she was sparing, earning her the nickname "the Witch of Wall Street." When asked about the secrets to her success, she replied famously: "I don't believe much in stocks. I never buy industrials. Railroads and real estate are the things I like. Before deciding on an investment, I seek out every kind of information about it. There is no secret in fortune making. All you have to do is buy cheap and sell dear, act with thrift and shrewdness and be persistent."[1] Thrifty, shrewd, and persistent she was—in spades. Inheriting around $10 million in her thirties, by the time she died some fifty years later at the age of eighty-one, Hetty had increased her fortune to $100 million (equal to about $1.5 billion in today's dollars).

Despite her investing acumen and monetary achievements, however, Hetty spent her last days moving through a succession of low-rent rooming houses and cheap hotels—all to avoid paying New York State taxes—and it is rumored that she died of a stroke caused by an argument over the merits of buying skimmed milk. However much her philosophy of fanatical parsimony paid off in financial terms, Hetty Green appeared as eccentric and cranky to her contemporaries as she does to us. Yet, it was not Hetty's thriftiness per se that made her seem so peculiar, even tragic. There is something about her life that seems to undermine the very ends of thrift. She had few friends, constantly suspicious as she was of people's motives in friendship; her penny-pinching had contributed to the loss of her son's leg; and as far as we know, she did not contribute much to philanthropy. And what, after all, is the virtue of thrift if it does not contribute to individual and collective flourishing?

To be sure, Hetty Green is an extreme case. It is only fair to ask whether it was thrift she was practicing after all. It is doubtful any of thrift's greatest champions, from Benjamin Franklin to today's financial self-help writers, would have recognized it as such. Still, Green's example is instructive in how it calls attention to the confusion that attends contemporary attempts to think about thrift. For one thing, the discourse of thrift as personal frugality has come to seem passé. Although this could change in the wake of the 2008 subprime mortgage turned credit crisis, the term itself has nearly faded from popular use, except perhaps as a synonym for secondhand clothing shops. Hetty Green's life thus invites a basic question: What is the contemporary significance of a study of thrift from the Puritans to the present? Having reached the end of our study, we are now in a position to offer an answer.

The Story of Thrift

In this volume, the story of thrift in America has been shown to be a *story within a story*. The first story examines thrift conventionally understood as fiscal frugality, what we have called "classic thrift." Though scrimping and saving has been a virtue of necessity for humans since time out of mind, classic thrift became a guiding ethical ideal of middle-class respectability in the middle to late 1800s. With the exception of its momentary rejuvenation during the Great Depression (again by necessity), by the middle of the twentieth century it had lost its appeal and normative authority, becoming marginalized in American economic life thereafter.

The second, more expansive story reveals, in one historical case after another, how remarkably rich, dynamic, and versatile thrift has been in practice. Extending well beyond commonsense notions, thrift in this broader sense has been more concerned with ends than with means. This is thrift viewed in light of its unexpected but compelling etymology: *thrift originally referred to the condition of "thriving."* This meaning has always been the subtext of thrift, however conceived, and at times has been used to critique the more narrowly conceived applications of thrift as individual frugality. Here thrift can be seen to move beyond the instrumentalities of "more or less" and begs the question: What does it mean to thrive? In short, thrift for what? More or less for what end?

As we said at the outset, such questions reveal thrift's distinctive moral gravity and the original contribution of this volume: thrift is a lens through which we see how economic decisions and activity, far from being morally neutral, have been shot through by evolving and contrasting visions of the good life and society from the beginning of American history. This was the point of the historical typology of thrift and moral order we set forth in the introduction: from Puritan thrift and the "Holy Common Wealth" to classic thrift and the Victorian-Individualist Synthesis, from consumer and collective thrift and the Managerial-Civic Compromise to free agent and green thrift and the Free Agent-Expressivist Experiment, the meaning of thrift varies according to the changing pictures of human thriving. Economic life is thus fundamentally and irreducibly moral.

This historical reappraisal of thrift since the Puritans raises some pressing questions for us in the present. In particular, it focuses our attention on the state of those normative dimensions of economic life today and encourages us to consider what resources it offers us in the face of mounting political, social, and financial challenges. What we see is not reassuring. Americans have grown confused and inarticulate about the specifically ethical requirements of economic life in recent years, much to our individual and collective detriment. However, we have also seen how thrift (its grammar if not its idiom) offers us a common language by which to talk together about the nature of a good, sustainable, and humane economy. If there is a moral to the story of thrift, it is that our ability to sustain and extend the conditions for genuine human thriving depend first and foremost on our ability to sustain and extend a conversation about the inescapably normative dimensions of economic life. This is the promise of thrift well-understood.

Of course, discerning this moral and putting it into practice are two different things. Anyone attempting to heed the moral of "thrift well-understood" must contend with the acute normative perplexity of late modern capitalism.

The Normative Perplexity of Late Capitalism

Consider how, despite the fact that economic questions define so much of modern existence, we find it difficult to engage these questions satisfactorily. For starters, the subject of economy is both theoretically and practically complex, and most Americans simply do not possess the technical knowledge necessary to grasp the manifold intricacies of our economic system. Moreover, the average American encounters a dizzying assortment of sound bites and statistics about the financial state of his society every day, each disconnected from all the others and absent of any kind of coherent whole. These snippets make the issues only more confusing. Rarely are we offered any framework for thinking about the greater interdependencies that tie the multitude of economic and policy concerns together. For their part, economic specialists—from economists to policy analysts to financial planners—serve to mystify matters through their highly technical, abstract, and specialized analysis. As with the television, the microwave, and the personal computer, the typical person is left taking the logic of this thing we call "the market" on a leap of faith. As long as it works, we consider ourselves relieved from the burden of caring how it works, despite a nagging, largely latent anxiety that our fabled abundance may be more precarious than we would like to believe.

Even the growing refinement of our statistical measuring devices, as they are used by our most able economic experts, has not produced any significant consensus on the state of our national economic affairs—in fact, quite the opposite. Polarization over these issues is suggested by the titles of two recently popular books: *It's Getting Better All the Time* and *The Coming Economic Collapse*. We cannot agree on the problems, let alone how they ought be solved.[2]

Wherever ethical considerations take a place of importance in economic discussion, however, dialogue is quickly dominated by the special interests of activist organizations trading in the politicization of key issues. No doubt, much of this discourse is animated by authentic and principled positions, but the structures of the public sphere cater to the shrill partisanship of a zero-sum politics.

As a result, we find ourselves unable to develop viable solutions to many of our most pressing social issues, not to mention generally incapable of articulating the exact nature of those issues. We are all too familiar with many of the vexing economic matters of the day: dismally low personal savings rates, spiraling federal deficits, double-digit unemployment, the growing gap between rich and poor, the stagnating middle class, skyrocketing medical costs—the list is long.

The example of personal savings is suggestive of the difficulties that attend them all. Most Americans are aware they are not saving enough to provide for their future, yet they do not lower their spending to put more aside. To be sure, many people have simply failed to manage their money well. Yet, the reasons for indebtedness are not always capricious. As Robert Frank suggests in this volume, many families spend too much on housing not because of the lust for luxurious space but because they want to live in a good school district. Parents find themselves forced to choose between competing goods, and children typically win out over retirement. This is more than a problem of individual willpower; an effective solution must address the inherent collective action problems too big for any individual or family to overcome.

The case of personal savings reveals just some of the difficulties involved in addressing the present quandaries of economic life. Common to them all, and arguably the most significant, is the fact that Americans lack a shared language and associated ethos—not to mention the supporting institutional framework—that might create the conditions and incentives capable of fostering individual self-restraint while generating the collective will to overcome significant structural dilemmas. Instead, Americans exhibit an abstracted, fragmented, polarized idiom on matters that are essential to the quality of their individual and collective well-being.

Plainly put, the central ethical quandary of contemporary economic life is that there is no publicly available consensus on, no shared vision regarding, the relationship between moral and material progress. While this is not an unprecedented situation (it has recurrently been the situation during transitions between past moral orders), it is in one crucial way distinct. Its radical departure from times past is in its institutionalization of normative incoherence that undercuts consideration of the more immediate questions about the ends to which we direct our economy, that is, to questions about human thriving. In short, it is enormously challenging to foster a sustained, meaningful, and compelling engagement with the inescapably ethical dimensions of economic life.

This is not to suggest that people do not talk in deeply moral, even moralizing terms about economic matters. On the contrary, the quandaries of economic life have done little to hamper our propensities for social critique. Whatever our politics, whether liberal or conservative, progressive or libertarian, complaints about inequity, profligacy, wastefulness, greed, and debt abound. Indeed, this polyphony of complaint is but a further extension of the central quandary itself.

It is true, as T. J. Jackson Lears warns us, that excoriations of the market or condemnations of wasteful extravagance often obscure matters more than they illuminate them.[3] But as this volume has repeatedly shown, the penchant for moralism with respect to economic matters is no mere distraction from the story of thrift in American history. Ideologically charged evaluations of the profligacy of Americans have been a central and perennial aspect of the relationship between moral order and economic life. Censure, admonition, and exhortation are an essential, though insufficiently appreciated, part of the story of thrift. The flip side of the question What does it mean to thrive? is What does it mean to *fail* to thrive? A significant part of thrift's history has involved arguments surrounding our historic attempts to answer both questions.

As we have seen repeatedly throughout the volume, criticism of the dominant forms of economic life has taken some distinctive (if by now familiar) forms. Though moral approbation of material gain has a long and varied history in the West, the archetypal form of social critique in American history has been the tradition of the Puritan jeremiad. The late historian Steven Innes wrote of this in part I, on what he called the "Puritan dilemma." The Puritan was caught between two competing imperatives: "diligence in worldly business and yet deadness to the world." "The central irony of the Puritan dilemma," wrote Innes, "was that it was inescapable; industry, thrift, and self-discipline might well lead to the temptations of wealth and worldliness, but a Puritan who foreswore the virtues of productivity in fear of these temptations was no longer a Puritan."[4] Generations of Puritan preachers and civic leaders underscored the paradox and, in the process, developed the rhetorical tradition of the jeremiad, one of the most powerful forms of social critique in American history. Innes concluded that the marvelously industrious culture that grounded its strenuous efforts in a robust theology of vocation was also a culture that "managed to create a self-critical ideology that effectively interpreted material success as spiritual failure."

With the shift in moral orders from the Puritan vision of the "Holy Common-Wealth" to what we are calling the Victorian-Individualist Synthesis, there came a shift in the dominant social ethic and, as we have seen, with thrift itself. Mirroring this shift, the jeremiad tradition constantly exhorting the faithful to remember (their covenant with God), repent from sinful (profligate) ways, and return to godly faithfulness (thrift) in all of life gradually became secularized and narrowed to an overriding concern with individual responsibility as regards private material security and philanthropy. Popular advice literature, sermons, tracts, editorials, and most famously Ben Franklin's Poor Richard were paradigmatic in this regard. Again and again in the course of American history, changes in the structure of capitalism meant changes to (and doubtless confusions about) the moral bases for answering more fundamental questions about human thriving. Over time, the rhetorical tradition of the jeremiad, as well as other forms of moral complaint and reform, came to give voice to tensions both within and between legitimating moral orders.

To return to the central quandary of contemporary economic life, the defining issue at this point in American history is not our inability to muster powerful forms of social critique or calls to reform. Again, they are common enough. The trouble is, rather, with our systematic inability to make any particular call to reform credible and publicly compelling. Ultimately, this ineptitude weakens the moral authority of our governing institutions. In the best of times, Americans routinely experience the inability of their institutions to mobilize common action across differences. In part, this is a willing price they pay for democracy. In times of acute crisis, however, they often confront stunning failures on the part of their experts and institutions to project any sense of moral authority in ways that inspire common action across the divisions of class, race, religion, age, and gender. Whatever its strengths, individual self-interest is clearly not enough to engender trust and confidence in our institutions by itself, nor to inspire the collective practices and habits of self-limitation and sacrifice that are always essential to their continued vitality.

It is clear that our need for some compelling evaluative orientation has not subsided in this sometimes prosperous, sometimes precarious new economy. While market forces in free societies have done exceedingly well in producing the material conditions of abundance, they have rarely (if ever) helped us discern the best ways of managing that abundance for our greatest individual or collective good. Again, the 2008 financial crisis and the following recession made this startlingly apparent. Even if one agrees with a thesis recently put forward by economist Benjamin Friedman that, in most instances, "Countries where living standards improve over sustained periods of time are more likely to seek and preserve an open, tolerant society, and to broaden and strengthen democratic institutions," sustaining that achievement is no easy task. Indeed, it is especially difficult when we lack a shared basis to discuss the larger implications of both our economic achievements and failures for the commonweal (to invoke an older parlance).[5]

Yet none of the reasons for the normative perplexity of our time—not the technical complexity, polarization, and moralism of our political culture, or the accompanying ethical inarticulacy with respect to economic matters—can be fully comprehended without attending to a single overriding matter: the shift from scarcity to abundance. Our evolving conception of the material conditions of abundance has been the persistent, if largely latent, backdrop to the evolution of thrift in American history. More than anything else, the experience of this shift has profoundly altered our conceptions of what it means to thrive, just as it has generated a succession of dilemmas within which the normative perplexities of economic life take shape and against which the varieties of moral evaluation and social critique have been mobilized.

The Dilemmas of Abundance

In the midst of the Great Depression, John Maynard Keynes famously wrote an essay that astonished many of his contemporary readers. In an essay provocatively entitled, "The Economic Possibilities of Our Grandchildren," Keynes wrote to counter the widespread and increasingly pessimistic view that interpreted the enormous social dislocations of the period—its breadlines, foreclosures, and indigence—as the end of a century-long era of unprecedented economic growth. To the contrary, he argued, "We are suffering not the rheumatics of old age, but from the growing pains of over-rapid changes, from the painfulness of readjustment between one economic period and another."[6] The hard times were not the end of a brief interlude of prosperity but the birth pains of a new yet more prosperous future epoch, though the advanced nations of the world were admittedly stumbling across its threshold. According to Keynes, humankind had in fact solved its age-old economic problem: the problem of subsistence. The challenge for future generations would thus no longer be the perennial threat of hunger and material deprivation. From now on, the problem would be one altogether unprecedented, and also somehow more humanly central and enduring. "Thus for the first time since his creation," proclaimed Keynes, "man will be faced with his real, his permanent problem—how to use his freedom from pressing economic cares, how to occupy the leisure, which science and compound interest will have won for him, to live wisely and agreeably and well."[7] Put simply, the real challenge for the future, for his grandchildren and great-grandchildren, would be how to thrive amid their abundance.

Keynes may have been wrong in key respects, but the extraordinary economic growth that would come by midcentury would prove him profoundly insightful in this key respect. Of course, he was not alone in his appraisal of either the opportunities or the challenges that would come with abundance. There were both boosters and knockers of abundance well before (and long after) Keynes made his predictions. Still, it was his ideas more than any others that came to represent a paradigm shift in how we have come to think about our material condition, and it is clear from our contemporary vantage point that his challenge remains pointedly our own. We are, after all, his grandchildren and great-grandchildren.

How Americans have encountered the challenge to thrive amid abundance has depended on the particular view of moral progress and the associated ethic they have brought to the question. Different dilemmas have occupied different eras. From the point of view of Puritan or classic thrift, the problem was how to achieve prosperity through diligent work, and then how to keep and steward affluence without allowing it to corrupt the very faith, virtues, and disciplines that made such a material achievement possible in the first place. Again, this is Innes's Puritan dilemma. From the point of view of consumer and collective thrift, the dilemma was how to ensure that abundance continued to increase through scientific management, corporate centralization, and individual consumption, and yet ensure that more and more of the nation's citizens were able to secure a basic share in the collective prosperity and security. From the point of view of today's advocates of a free-agent ethic, the overriding concern is how to maximize economic growth in a globally competitive and uncertain environment, whereas, how to minimize the detrimental aspects of economic growth on people and the planet has been the overriding concern of what we have called "reactionary thrift."

Though the dilemmas of abundance have manifested themselves in distinctive ways in various eras, they have recurrently coalesced around three overlapping issues: indebtedness and the rise of a debt culture, the negative externalities of economic growth, and the psychological anxieties of abundance. Such dilemmas form the main axes of controversy and social critique and, in this way, clarify as well as heighten the normative perplexity of contemporary economic life.

THE RISE OF A DEBT CULTURE

The fear of falling behind, of owing more than one can afford to pay, or of simply lacking the means to make ends meet has been a perennial feature of human existence. Likewise, credit and debt collection systems have been ubiquitous features of human society past and present. Yet, most traditional cultures have either severely proscribed lending and collecting practices or, in the case of cultures influenced by the biblical religions, often prohibited practices like usury altogether. Regardless of the particular form these systems took, nearly all had in common their general condemnation of indebtedness—at least in principle.

If our time is unrivaled in the particular way it has come to democratize and even esteem the use of credit, it is wholly unique in how it has normalized indebtedness. Debt no longer carries the stigma of the prodigal. Far from it. Whether making our monthly mortgage payments, financing our educations, purchasing our groceries, or making donations to our favorite charities, debt has become an acceptable and appropriate way of underwriting daily living. It has become so normalized over the past century that, like death and taxes, it is one of the few utterly unremarkable constants of modern life.

Yet old fears linger. We can still feel the admonitory force of Ben Franklin's advice, "He who goes aborrowing, goes asorrowing."[8] Under fear of defaulting on the burden of what Lendol Calder has termed the "hard payments" of buying on credit, many worry about how routine indebtedness saps individual virtue and forfeits the most precious of democratic achievements, our liberty, independence, and in Daniel Walker Howe's phrase, "the self-government of the American commonwealth." John Adams famously summarized this civic republican ideal in a letter to Thomas Jefferson: "Without Virtue there can be no political Liberty."[9] For many of the founders, personal thrift was among the chief virtues of the democratic citizen. For those like Thomas Jefferson (who suffered the consequences of personal indebtedness firsthand), the virtue of thrift carried over into public and political life: "I place economy among the first and most important virtues, and public debt as the greatest of dangers.

To preserve our independence, we must not let our rulers load us with perpetual debt."[10] Ralph Waldo Emerson echoed this sentiment in the early years of the Republic. "By diligence and self-command," wrote Emerson, "let him put the bread he eats at his own disposal, that he may not stand in bitter and false relations to other men; for the best good of wealth is freedom."[11]

There are more than a few contemporary observers who echo these classic concerns about debt's adverse impact on individual virtue and material well-being, and, in turn, on civic life more generally. Long before the subprime mortgage crisis and the "Great Recession" made such worries headline news, there were, of course, ample reasons to fear that the liberalization and mass promotion of credit was leading to a highly ambiguous achievement: the normalization of a debt culture, not in a time of economic stagnation or crisis but in a time of plenty.

In the years leading up to the economic crisis, the national savings rate, though never high relative to that of other wealthy nations, had actually become negative for the first time since the Great Depression. Careful observers will of course note that personal savings rates have recently surged to their highest levels in more than fifteen years while household debt fell also for the first time since we started keeping track of such data according to the Federal Reserve. Nevertheless, the average total household debt (including credit cards, mortgage, home equity, student loans, and more) still equaled $54,000 in 2009. Of this, rotating credit card debt alone accounted for more than $15,000.[12] And this is to say nothing of the number of home foreclosures, which rose to more than 1 million in 2007, or bankruptcies, which were expected to reach 1.1 million in 2008 (twice the 2006 number).[13]

The litany of indebtedness, however, does not end here. On top of mounting levels of individual and household debt have been growing yearly federal budget deficits and a spiraling national debt. Prior to the 1980s, the U.S. government typically kept spending and revenues in balance, except during wartime or periods of high unemployment. Since then, budget deficits have been more the rule than the exception, this despite a brief period of reported surplus in the late 1990s. By 2008, the annual budget deficit reached $438 billion, an all-time high in dollar terms, according to estimates from the Congressional Budget Office (CBO).[14] But a year later, the CBO estimated the deficits to be $1.6 trillion, which translates to 11.2 percent of GDP.[15] Given a $14 trillion gross domestic product, however, it can be quite difficult for the typical American to comprehend what is at stake in such deficits.[16] It can also be hard for the economically astute observer. The Harvard economist Benjamin Friedman explains the downside: "When the government spends more than it takes in from taxes, the Treasury has to borrow in the financial markets to cover the overage." This means that the government ends up borrowing from the money that Americans have invested in bonds, securities, savings accounts, and mutual funds. This has the negative side effect of siphoning off private saving that would otherwise have been available for investment in physical and human capital, both of which are highly correlated with economic growth. Friedman supplies the basic math: "It is a simple matter of accounting arithmetic that what a country saves, less whatever part of that saving its government absorbs to finance any budget deficit, must equal what the country invests."[17] In light of present financial straits we are left wondering what will happen if that stock of private savings itself is decimated or if credit markets should contract so severely that the federal government is actually unable to borrow to cover its costs.

What America had been unable to make up for at home it has increasingly sought abroad. While our federal debt has now surpassed the $13 trillion mark (and is expected to reach $19.6 trillion by 2025), our total societal debt (including both public and private sectors, as well as the average American household) is estimated at $53 trillion, making what was once the world's largest creditor nation the world's largest debtor nation.[18] This is a fact with potentially serious political ramifications. David Walker, then U.S. comptroller general, declared in 2007:

> Foreign interests have more control over the U.S. economy than Americans, leaving the country in a state that is financially imprudent. More and more of our debt is held by foreign countries—some of which are our allies and some are not. The huge holdings of American government debt by countries such as China and Saudi Arabia could leave a powerful financial weapon in the hands of countries that may be hostile to U.S. corporate and diplomatic interests.[19]

For other observers, foreign ownership of our debt is a sign of confidence in the U.S. economy. Purchasing U.S. Treasury securities, accordingly, is simply a smart investment. Nonetheless, both the magnitude of our debt and the proportion owned by foreign countries raises the question of how economically and politically vulnerable the United States is to forces that may not have its best interests in mind. Not to put too fine a point on it, the globalization of American indebtedness is emerging as a critical geopolitical issue.

But to the growing national indebtedness and the worries over the influence of foreign creditors, one must also add the accumulating burden of interest payments and numerous unfunded liabilities (like Social Security), not to mention the price of the wars in Afghanistan and Iraq, exorbitant health care costs, and so on. "'Crisis' may be an overused word," concludes one "pro-thrift" activist, "but it may be fair to say that much of America, using borrowed money to cover the costs of today's needs and wants, and without adequate savings, is now experiencing a crisis of over-indebtedness."[20]

Finally, Americans have also confronted with increasing distress the unwelcome fact that their crisis of overindebtedness somehow contributed to a global economic meltdown. Few people anticipated either the speed by which the speculative mortgage bubble would burst or the enormity of the bust, leaving hundreds of banks, brokerages, and investment firms—and millions of overindebted Americans—in default while the federal government became the sole proprietor of America's financial sector. Although it is still too early to know what will come of this worldwide economic conflagration, we can be sure that it will be some time before Americans dig themselves out from its repercussions.[21]

Not everyone thinks that debt is such a bad thing or that Americans are worse off for their lack of saving. Some, like *Atlantic* contributing editor Virginia Postrel, suggest that we might even be better off because of it. In her article "The Case for Debt," Postrel claims: "The expansion of consumer credit is one of the great economic achievements of the past century. One institution after another has made borrowing easier and cheaper for rich and poor alike." She points out that while there has always been a fear that our ever-growing indebtedness would inevitably lead to disaster, that dreaded day has never come.[22] Perhaps. But even if one believes that debt is on the whole a positive thing for society, there nevertheless seems to be ample reason to conclude that certain kinds of debt are not. Would anyone now defend the merits of the so-called NINA loans, those "no interest, no assets" lending vehicles that did indeed make borrowing easier and cheaper for rich and poor alike? In short, there is such a thing as *bad* debt. The issue of bad debt is of enormous individual and public concern at present, and it raises pressing questions for Americans. At what point does otherwise good debt go bad? When is there too much debt? What can be done privately and publicly to protect ourselves from the downside of debt? What about all the bad debt generated by the subprime crisis? Should the American citizenry foot the bill for bailing out all those imprudent home buyers, lenders, and brokerages that created it? Does it really have a choice? It seems fair to say that regardless of where one comes down on the issue of debt generally, the normalization of indebtedness comes with the risk of occasional, and sometimes profoundly painful, structural adjustment.

THE NEGATIVE EXTERNALITIES OF ECONOMIC GROWTH

A second area of abiding concern has been less preoccupied with individual well-being, focusing instead on the general welfare of society as a whole. Two issues have recurrently stood out as the main negative externalities of abundance: a concern with social and economic inequality and a concern with environmental degradation. Debates about these issues inevitably ignite controversies over the dominant premise of advanced capitalism: that the solution to most social problems comes through continued economic growth.

With material abundance come inevitable questions about its equitable distribution or at least about what would constitute a just and nondiscriminatory distribution of opportunities for social and economic mobility. Does the configuration of our economic system foster greater equality or generate new inequalities? Such questions shaped liberal politics well before Marx first warned that a specter of inequality haunted (and would soon revolutionize) modern societies.

Concern over the theme of inequality has ebbed and flowed over the course of the twentieth century in America. In the decades after the Second World War, all socioeconomic classes saw an extraordinary period of economic growth. However, the issue of inequality has returned with growing urgency in the present. While incomes grew about 3 percent yearly for all income categories between 1947 and 1973, according to Robert Frank, "the top 1 percent of earners has captured more than 70 percent of all earnings growth during the last two decades."[23] Frank is not alone among economists who believe there is reason for worry. Benjamin Friedman, in his recent book extolling the moral consequences of economic growth, nevertheless contends that "America is at an economic cross-roads. As we have seen, living standards for the majority of citizens grew little from the early 1970s to the early 1990s, and along the way inequality widened significantly."[24] Few things seem to illustrate the disparities more than the widely publicized fact that CEOs now make more than 400 times as much as their average worker. Such excessive discrepancies in compensation have led the journalist-activist Bill McKibben (no friend to the political or economic status quo) to extreme conclusions. Discussing how economists calculate a "Gini coefficient" to measure income inequality across a society, he writes, "The U.S. coefficient has risen steadily since the late 1960s, to the point where many economists believe wealth is more stratified today than any time since the Gilded Age."[25]

Alongside concerns of growing domestic inequality has been even more urgent alarm over the growing global divide between rich and poor. Arguably, before 1820 there were not the vast divides in wealth and poverty that we see around the world today. According to Jeffrey Sachs, "China, India, Europe, and Japan all had similar income levels at the time of the European discoveries of the sea routes to Asia, Africa, and the Americas. Marco Polo marveled at the sumptuous wonders of China, not at its poverty. Cortés and his conquistadores expressed astonishment at the riches of Tenochititlán, the capital of the Aztecs. The early Portuguese explorers were impressed with the well-ordered towns of West Africa."[26] Since then, however, during a period of economic growth unimaginable previously, where the total gross world product grew, according to Sachs, nearly fiftyfold, the beneficiaries of that growth both within countries and across regions are extremely uneven. Today, for instance, the gap between the wealthiest society, the United States, and the poorest region, sub-Saharan Africa, is twenty to one in terms of per capita income, with the average American living off $30,000 a year compared with $1,300 a year for the average African.[27]

Concern with global inequality has been sharpest with respect to the "poorest of the poor," the so-called bottom billion of humanity who face extreme poverty, and extending to those who live just above mere subsistence (which includes another 1.5 billion people). Altogether, 40 percent of humanity live lives ruled by the iron hand of scarcity.[28] The good news is that as a *proportion* of the world's population, the number of the very poor is shrinking. The bad news is that because of population growth, *absolute* numbers are higher than ever before and seem to be falling further and further behind the top billion. The recurring scandal of inequality, both foreign and domestic, is that it grows more acute as the world becomes more prosperous.

Alongside worries about domestic and international inequality, we see heightened anxieties over a cluster of environmental matters. Among the most vexing issues on the consumption side is depletion of natural resources, especially fossil fuels. It is hard to imagine what the world would look like today without cheap coal and petroleum, yet in light of the dawning significance of "peak oil" and the growing expense of extraction in both financial and human capital (not to mention the heightened geopolitical entanglements of extraction), such a question begins to feel like more than a counterfactual curiosity. On both the production and disposal sides, the massive destruction of our planet's biodiversity and carrying capacity through deforestation, strip mining, overfishing, and rampant urbanization—not to mention through catastrophic accidents like the Gulf of Mexico oil spill of 2010—have become among the most poignant concerns of the early twenty-first century.

Once again, these worries are long-standing. In the tradition of Emerson and Thoreau, the forester Aldo Leopold wrote in the 1940s: "We face the question of whether a higher 'standard of living' is worth its cost in things natural, wild, and free."[29] From early conservationists like Leopold and John Muir (founder of the Sierra Club) to Rachel Carson, Edward Abbey, E. F. Schumacher, Wendell Berry, and other champions of the contemporary American environmental movement, concerns about ecological degradation have been a critical subtext to what environmental historians J.R. McNeill and George Vrtis have called in this volume, the "cornucopian vision" of boundless material amplitude.

This is not to imply there is nothing important and new in these concerns. For one thing, environmental concern has become more mainstream during the past few decades. Americans routinely recycle (at least children routinely remind their parents they ought to); we have implemented important pieces of public policy such as the Clean Air Act and the Clean Water Act; and we have established numerous large-scale environmental reclamation projects, such as the federally sponsored Superfund initiatives. Clearly, the most significant development is growing alarm and controversy surrounding global climate change. At issue here is the link between economic growth, emissions from hydrocarbon-based energy sources, and global warming.

These environmental matters are compounded as other societies emulate the standard of living in America and Western Europe. Recognizing this as one of the greatest challenges confronting the world in coming decades, Benjamin Friedman writes, "Bringing the rest of the world up to the standard of living that prevails today in Portugal, the last country on the list of the richest thirty, would more than double the total world output."[30] To glimpse the double-edged significance of such profound economic growth, one only has to ponder what it will mean for the already overloaded carrying capacity of the planet should both China and India begin to rival U.S. rates of car ownership. Short of massive innovations in efficiency and in alternative forms of energy, increases in carbon dioxide emissions, not to mention conflicts over extracting the remaining world petroleum reserves, would be astronomic in both environmental and financial terms. And, here again, debates over inequality come to the fore. Should disproportionate rates of consumption of natural resources by wealthy societies, as well as their disproportionate rates of carbon dioxide emissions, be reduced so developing countries can grow without ruining the planet?

Needless to say, debates about the negative externalities of the market have been fodder for countless op-eds, scholarly articles and books, and twenty-four-hour cable news stories. In the tradition of the muckrakers, best-selling exposés of corporate sweatshops and environmental destruction flourish. In the name of the public interest, would-be social movements seek to mobilize the masses for resistance and reform. Yet we are left with a number of distressing questions: Which problems are the most pressing? How can we be sure which activists are correct? Have we finally reached the limits to economic growth? Are we to believe the worst predictions of a coming environmental catastrophe? Or, do we write them off as merely the newest half-baked doomsday theories that will in time prove to be as groundless as previous predictions of our coming demise? Can we remain confident in our ability to grow our way out of trouble through some combination of technological innovation, policy adjustment, and the coordination of demand through price mechanisms of the market? Moreover, even if we trust continued economic growth and greater abundance, can we anticipate future side effects of our technological, governmental, and economic solutions to today's problems?

THE ANXIETIES OF ABUNDANCE

On top of the abiding worries over excessive indebtedness and the negative social and environmental consequences of economic growth is the fact of discontent itself. A spate of academic studies have come out in recent years, revealing what many Americans know from personal experience: although the American standard of living is among the highest in human history, the number of citizens who describe themselves as happy has not increased for more than fifty years. There are a number of possible reasons for this. Specifically, Americans report increasing difficulty balancing the demands of making a living with the needs of family and private life. They are in constant fear of falling behind as most are but a single paycheck away from serious financial difficulty. There is evidence that they are also overwhelmed by the seemingly endless escalation of choices they confront daily. The psychic burden of decision making weighs heavily upon them. On top of these personal anxieties, Americans confront growing uncertainty about the health of the national economy. Not surprisingly, as Americans cope with the significance of these issues, the percentage of those who experience apprehension, stress, and depression is rapidly growing.

Again, such concerns are not new. Thinkers as early as the 1700s anticipated the mixed psychological blessings of abundance, what historian Simon Schama once fittingly described as the "ordeal of prosperity."[31] They worried about three issues in particular: the fundamental meaninglessness of ever-expanding choices, the insatiability of ever-rising expectations, and the restiveness that comes with a polity increasingly characterized by invidious social comparisons based on consumption.

The most consistent worry of intellectuals throughout the modern period has been, according to historian Jerry Mueller, "that the market (sometimes in tandem with other forces in modern society, such as science and technology) would lead to a life filled with choices but devoid of meaning."[32] Many shared the Aristotelian concern with *pleonexia*, in Mueller's words, "the danger that arises from the open-ended desire for acquisition without limit." Rousseau was among the earliest to worry about the way the economic development of modern societies diminished human happiness by artificially inflating needs.[33] In Hegel's terminology this was the problem of "negative infinity"—the fear that "individuals might become mere playthings of the want-creating machine that was the market."[34] Without adequate grounding in cultural frameworks that could counter this tendency by offering an independent notion of appropriate wants, the general concern was that the individual might "be attracted to one commodity after another, in an endless round of joyless consumption."[35]

A related and similarly persistent concern has been what many thinkers have referred to as "the revolution of expectations" that came with modern capitalist development. This refers to the striking way one generation's luxuries become the next generation's necessities. In her chapter, Joyce Appleby discusses this process in the years of the early Republic. Tobacco, tea, coffee, sugar, and the like were all considered luxuries on the eve of our founding, yet "within a generation," she writes, "comforts were calibrated as necessities, and luxuries had been redesignated as comforts."[36] With few exceptions, the logic of this cycle has repeated itself for every succeeding generation. What before the Second World War were objects of conspicuous consumption for Veblen's affluent leisure class—that is, all manner of laborsaving appliances—became the standard of middle-class respectability in the postwar era. The same could be said today for the democratization of information technologies, only the time horizon has shrunk dramatically. Where the phone, television, radio, and even early models of the personal computer were once the province of entire family units and controlled by supervising adults, today they are a routine part of the almost entirely private lives of adolescents. Although critics have widely disagreed whether new wants in themselves are a problem, most agree that the endless creation of ever-new consumer wants and goods is ultimately unsatisfying if it does not fit into some larger set of purposes than mere accumulation. The pursuit and achievement of happiness depend on something more than material security and comfort, at least after some basic threshold of subsistence has been reached. Without this, the escalation of expectations will be insatiable and thus at some level intolerable.

Among the first and most insightful observers to reflect upon the social-psychological dimensions of the emerging capitalist economy of desire was Alexis de Tocqueville. He famously observed how the taste for material well-being that came with increasing social equality and prosperity accounted for "the singular melancholy that the inhabitants of democratic lands often display amid their abundance, and the disgust with life that sometimes seizes them in the midst of an easy and tranquil existence." He was amazed by the striking display of restlessness he witnessed among Americans. Considering the future prospect of democratic societies elsewhere, he identified a powerful aspect of the social psychology of democratic and commercial societies: the inevitable tensions that would arise between absolute and relative standards of living. In such societies, people tend to achieve a basic equality in the law and a certain *absolute* baseline of social and economic equality, yet they cannot attain the equality they desire *relative* to their fellow citizens. As a result, Tocqueville writes: "Hopes and desires are more often disappointed, souls more aroused and more restive, and cares more burning" among prosperous democratic peoples.[37]

Today, the emerging field of "happiness studies" draws from all three sets of concerns—that is, the meaninglessness of expanding consumer choices, the revolution of expectations that accompanies such expansion, and the tension between absolute and relative needs. Though relatively new and largely impressionistic on many points, this research repeatedly shows a counterintuitive relationship between levels of happiness, fulfillment, and personal satisfaction, and the objective conditions of material abundance. It turns out that wealth does indeed make a difference to people's happiness, but only to a point—the point of subsistence.[38] Beyond this, the logic of diminishing returns seems to take over. Increases in absolute living standards simply may not matter once we escape the physical deprivations of poverty, at least for most consumer decisions. There are a number of possible reasons for this. The remarkable human capacity to adapt to changing circumstances is often cited as a prominent explanation by behavioral scientists, again harkening back to theories about the revolution of expectations. Another has to do with the difference between absolute and relative living standards invoked by Tocqueville, and recently discussed by Juliet Schor and Robert Frank.

In the end, what may account for widespread ambivalence and discontent is the simple fact that with material plenty comes an overwhelming abundance of choice. Behavioral psychologist Benjamin Schwartz has recently argued precisely this.[39] Instead of more time and greater opportunity to pursue one's vision of the good life, the typical individual feels beleaguered by the burdens of an expanding universe of choice on matters mundane and trivial (which of the twenty-five varieties of toothpaste to buy) but also on matters of consequence (whether to prioritize one's retirement or the education of one's children). This burden is made heavier by the seductive, but intentionally unsettling, messages of mass advertising and popular entertainment and are aggravated by growing income disparities both within and across social reference groups and, increasingly, by unprecedented indebtedness. Under it all, the psychic burdens of abundance are borne by the individual alone. It is no wonder that Americans have witnessed a tenfold increase in "unipolar depression" in the past two generations,[40] and that the use of psychoactive drugs has skyrocketed; it helps explain how it could possibly be that in one observer's words: "We live in a favored age yet do not feel favored."[41]

A Provisional Achievement

We are fortunate to live in an age of plenty, yet its ongoing dilemmas continue to make our experience a mixed and incomplete blessing. This double-sided fact has provoked the emergence of two overarching and opposing perspectives on how we ought to conceive of the material reality modern capitalism has created. The dominant position—that held by what we will call the Party of Abundance—is generally optimistic that the combination of human scientific and technological ingenuity, political freedom, and the momentum of accumulated abundance will in due time resolve the dilemmas that plague us. Dilemmas we face today, its advocates reassure, will not be the dilemmas our children will face tomorrow. They posit an image of material reality that is dynamic, prolific, and boundless. The opposing position—that held by what we call the Party of Scarcity—is skeptical we will ever fully escape these dilemmas, believing they are chronic features of the way in which humans have come to produce and organize our abundance in the modern world. Moreover, they are certain these dilemmas will prove unsustainable over time, thereby revealing the very idea of abundance to be a grand illusion. On this view, our material reality is certainly precious, exhaustible, and finite.

Ever ambivalent, most Americans view the situation as somewhere between the poles of abundance and scarcity. We feel the pull of both perspectives. With the Party of Abundance, we recognize that those fortunate to live in America and the world's other wealthy societies enjoy a standard of living that would have once been the envy of emperors. The journalist Greg Easterbrook, squarely in the abundance camp, has captured our privileged condition in bold strokes:

> Today we live a long time, in fairly comfortable circumstances; enjoy goods and services in almost unlimited supply; travel where we wish quickly and relatively cheaply; talk to anyone in the world; know everything there is to know; think and say what we please; marry for love, and have sex with whomeverwill agree; and wail in sorrow when anyone dies young, for this once routine event has become a wrenching rarity. All told, except for the clamor and speed of society, and for trends in popular music, your great-great-grandparents might say the contemporary United States is the realization of utopia.[42]

While we rarely have occasion to think in such historically comparative terms, it is hard not to be moved by the force of these basic facts.

Confident that we can today extend the share of abundance even further, Jeffrey Sachs explicitly draws upon Keynes's famous essay with which we began. He writes: "Today we can invoke the same logic to declare that extreme poverty can be ended not in the time of our grandchildren, but in our time. The wealth of the rich world, the power of today's vast storehouses of knowledge, and the declining fraction of the world that needs help to escape from poverty all make the end of poverty a realistic possibility."[43] As with Keynes before him, Sachs is making a claim that from the vantage point of any previous generation in world history would have been simply unimaginable. But Sachs assures us: "Our generation can choose to end extreme poverty by the year 2025."[44]

Yet the benefits of abundance are ostensibly greater (or go deeper) than even Sach's optimism suggests. According to Benjamin Friedman, the most important contribution of our plentitude may be its most overlooked: the connection between moral improvement and economic growth. In *The Moral Consequences of Economic Growth*, he contends that "even when people plainly acknowledge that more is more, less is less, and more is better, economic growth rarely means simply more. The dynamic process that allows living standards to rise brings other changes as well." He maintains that growth is valuable for how it affects society's moral character. In particular, societies that achieve a certain level of *sustained* economic growth are on the whole more open, tolerant, democratic, and free. Societies that suffer periods of economic stagnation or decline very often become more closed, intolerant, and oppressive.[45]

As representative voices in the Party of Abundance, Easterbrook, Sachs, and Friedman offer us morally compelling reasons for the fixation with economic growth. The reigning maxim of political economy since Adam Smith, its achievements and ambitions are surely worthy of acclamation if not even measured exuberance.

Yet, one can readily concede the historical achievement of abundance and still share reservations with the Party of Scarcity about the dilemmas this achievement has created for us. At issue are worries about what appear to be the clear limits, failures, and future risks of abundance. In *Deep Economy*, journalist Bill McKibben challenges the reigning economic wisdom, submitting that the achievement of abundance through economic growth has in fact led us to a critical impasse. He summarizes his argument with a parable. "For most of human history," he writes, "the two birds More and Better roosted on the same branch. You could toss one stone and hope to hit them both. . . . But the distinguishing feature of our moment is this: Better has flown a few trees over to make her nest." In this way, McKibben affirms the achievement of abundance but questions the ideology of economic growth that dogmatically insists more always continues to be better. According to the view expounded by McKibben, we have reached a point of diminishing returns; from now on, we will have to face the stark choice between them: "It's More or Better."[46] For McKibben and other members of the Party of Scarcity, continuing up the road of economic growth is unsustainable and ultimately disastrous. Instead, they exhort us to change our mind-sets and daily habits, and perhaps most important of all, to change "our sense of what constitutes progress."[47] They counsel individual restraint and collective limits.

Yet, even the partisans of abundance admit concern about the dilemmas discussed here, though they resist the ethically charged dichotomizing of more and better. "Until the day when everyone is released from basic want," concedes the otherwise Whiggish Easterbrook, "a sword will hang over Western abundance."[48] Friedman, a more academically qualified but no less ardent supporter of economic growth, worries that Americans are actually no longer doing what is necessary to maintain their abundance: "A rising standard of living for the great majority of our citizens has in fact been the American norm, and it is we, today, who are failing to achieve it."[49]

Regardless of where one comes down on these dilemmas, whether one is closer to the Party of Abundance or the Party of Scarcity, we can discern a glimmer of consensus on at least one basic point: *our abundance is a provisional achievement*. The unrivaled material abundance enjoyed by advanced industrial societies in the twentieth century, and an ever-greater portion of humanity in the twenty-first, is a hard-won accomplishment. Only because of generations of concerted investment of human ingenuity, capital, and effort have we managed to wrest our collective fate significantly away from the caprice of nature and the stern demands of physical survival. Appreciation of the historical circumstances that made our prosperity possible in the first place thus makes clear that this achievement was neither inevitable, nor has it been accomplished once and for all. *Abundance is itself a scarce resource in the longue durée of human history.* This is a fact that seldom receives the recognition it deserves. Its achievement has come, moreover, with a host of unintended consequences, some of which call into question our ability to extend its benefits to greater classes of people now and into the future. The fundamental, underlying, and abiding dilemma we face is how to secure and sustain the hard-won but provisional abundance for ourselves, for the rest of humanity, and for succeeding generations.

Toward a Moral Framework of Economic Life

It is now possible to return to the basic assertion of the volume. What perhaps began as a curious topic of inquiry ends up being a perspicuous lens into a deeper cultural reality. To reiterate the central point: economic life is fundamentally and unavoidably moral. Through this historical appraisal we gain insight not only into the meaning of material well-being but also into the changing understandings of the good life and the good society more generally. This multifaceted investigation of thrift has offered a vivid and richly illustrative portrait of the changing relationship between capitalism and moral order in American history.

A crucial but largely latent part of this narrative picture involves the world-historic shift from social and economic conditions of scarcity to those of abundance. Reflecting on how this shift in material conditions became the primary experiential prism through which Americans think about what it means to thrive, in terms of both their individual quality of life and the collective standard of living, helps us better account for the perplexity that unsettles our otherwise unrivaled material prosperity in the best of times. This much should be clear. What remains to be shown is whether such a reconsideration of thrift might offer any constructive response to this situation. Can thrift help us overcome the chronic ambivalence and inarticulacy of the average American in the face of abundance's abiding dilemmas?

THE CONVENTIONAL WISDOM AND THE LESSONS OF THRIFT

The great Puritan divine Cotton Mather memorably lamented the consequences of prosperity for the Plymouth colony when he wrote: "Religion begot prosperity, and the daughter devoured the mother."[50] Max Weber famously reworked the Puritan jeremiad into the sober, clinical analysis of social theory when he argued that the birth of capitalism sealed the fate of its midwife, if not its parent. The paradoxical truth about the fabled Protestant ethic, apparently, is that it has been sowing the seeds of its own destruction for more than three centuries. In the material shift to abundance, so one can extend the logic, those seeds found conditions enormously conducive to their bountiful, if contradictory, fruition. Of course, the deterioration of previous economic ethics was never simply a matter of unintended consequences. As capitalism took root and matured, powerful institutional forces gave rise to vested interests that actively sought to displace older notions of restraint. Still, to the extent that thrift played a role in aiding and abetting capitalist development in its take-off phase, it had a hand in undermining itself. Irrespective of particular details, the history of thrift since the Puritans brings into sharp relief the question—some insist impasse—of whether we can at last call the process of demoralization complete. Have we finally reached the exhaustion of the Protestant ethic? If so, can "victorious capitalism," again to invoke Weber, be sustained and enlarged without the support of the character type and the authority of the accompanying moral order that once legitimated it?[51] Traditionalists clearly think not and urge a return to a more responsible, diligent, and abstemious ethic. For their part, radicals typically have no wish to revitalize the Protestant ethic, but they do share the criticism that the status quo will have disastrous consequences. Yet, both the traditionalist and the radical represent minority positions.

For nearly fifty years, the conventional wisdom has embraced the neoliberal wager at the heart of what we have called the Free-Agent-Expressivist Experiment, the dominant moral order of late, global capitalism. Its boosters have been adamant that an unfettered, "self-regulating" market is the best and only way to produce the economic growth necessary for addressing the dilemmas before us. Claiming the mantle of Adam Smith, they insist that the combination of rational decisions of utility-maximizing individuals in a market free from governmental intrusion undercuts the need for any corresponding character type or robust ethic of restraint, at least any ethic that we all need to share. Some boosters might concede that the market needs moral individuals to work optimally, but they contend that the market is itself amoral. Such has been the reigning assumption for the past quarter century in the world's leading financial institutions, and, until recently at least, it seemingly had the force of epic economic growth behind it.

The lessons of thrift expounded throughout this volume seriously challenge this recently dominant view, although not only in ways traditionalists and radicals might expect. To begin with, neoliberal claims to normative neutrality are belied by the default promotion of a very definite character type and corresponding ethic: that of the "free-agent" subject, who perforce enacts the cultural imperatives of autonomy, self-interest, and self-cultivation through highly disciplined efforts in both work and leisure. Moreover, such a subjectivity depends upon specific ideological and institutional backing, which has only recently begun to be questioned. In what some believe, perhaps prematurely, to be the death knell of the neoliberal project, former chairman of the Federal Reserve Alan Greenspan confessed before a congressional hearing on the subprime mortgage crisis: "Those of us have who looked to the self-interest of lending institutions to protect shareholders' equity, myself included, are in a state of shocked disbelief."[52] At the very least, its seems safe to say that Greenspan signaled a crisis for the Free-Agent-Expressivist Experiment. For the moment, even some of its most ardent champions can no longer deny how economic life is never free from moral limits, evaluation, or sanction.

Nonetheless, the real constructive potential of thrift will not be found, as the traditionalists would have it, in a return to long-standing admonitions about frugality and individual responsibility. Culturally speaking, there is no going back to the fabled Protestant ethic or any of its derivative ethics of restraint. Yet neither will the constructive potential of thrift be found in a wholesale repudiation of economic growth as the radicals would have it.

The lessons of thrift encourage a different view of our situation and thus a different response to it. A more apt view is that while some forms of growth are critically necessary for human thriving, they are not in themselves sufficient to secure it. Why? Because the imperative of growth cannot direct us as to the *ends* of growth—to what it means to thrive amid the ambiguities of plenty. On its own, more (or less) growth, or for that matter, more (or less) regulation, will merely intensify the general state of normative perplexity and thus deepen the dilemmas of abundance. For economic growth to lead to sustained and expanding opportunities for human thriving, it is necessary for it to be informed by some basic and commonly held ethical framework. This is what the formerly reigning economic perspective denied in its naive claim to be value-free. In reality, the pervasive and dogmatic faith in economic growth via free markets has replaced our older and equally dogmatic moral traditions, but without offering any explicit, let alone adequate, alternative conception of the good life or the good society. Its radical individualism has instead denuded our sense of crucial interdependences, mutual obligation, and the commonweal.

To employ a maritime metaphor, without an adequate normative framework for thinking about the ends of growth we are adrift in a vast ocean, lacking the capacity to orient ourselves sufficiently. As long as conditions are good, we have little to fear and are free to float along. But conditions are never so unstintingly kind. Sooner or later we discover that we are not as free as we think, but pushed along by powerful currents and unpredictable winds. Neither are we as secure. The fear of capsizing (we do not all sail in equally seaworthy vessels) and of being cast away at sea is ever-present. Something like this is very close to our predicament today, in which we suffer the acute diminishment of our capacities for constructive engagement with the economic realities that shape our entire way of life and occasionally threaten to sink it.

If Americans desire less perplexity, less passive acquiescence to economic forces, they will need to acknowledge and not duck the inescapable normativity of economic life. In short, they will need to generate a language and an institutional framework that would provide some measure of ethical consensus.

It has been the burden of this volume to suggest that Americans need not invent such a language; that thrift—that is, thrift "well-understood"—can help us become articulate about what it means to thrive in light of the provisionality and dilemmas of our abundance.

THE PROMISE OF THRIFT WELL-UNDERSTOOD

As we have seen throughout this collection, when Americans have considered the normative dimensions of economic life, they have historically done so through the varied idioms of thrift. Whereas thrift has most commonly been understood pragmatically, as a synonym for saving and scrimping, we have seen how it has also functioned respectively as an analogue of wise stewardship, careful husbandry, collective welfare, countercultural protest, even calculated efficiency. Yet, the original contribution of the volume has been to show what ties all of these disparate thrift ethics together—which we see in light of thrift's etymology. The fact that thrift originally referred to the condition of "thriving" has allowed us to connect the evolving practices of thrift with the changing pictures of what it has meant to thrive throughout American history.

Far from a sterile academic exercise, we believe that careful attention to the ends of thrift holds forth the possibility of bringing all parties—left, right, and center—onto preciously scarce common ground. Questions about what it means to thrive necessarily precede the technical aspects of economy and policy prescription just as they transcend the narrow partisanship that bedevils public discourse today. Instead, they focus our attention on the cultural foundations of capitalism that too often go unarticulated and neglected—issues like trust and virtue, but also of meaning and authority, moral judgment and evaluation. If anything else, highlighting the connection between thrift and thriving holds out the possibility of meaningful debate and disagreement because it can clarify genuine differences on the most important matters. Yet, it could potentially illuminate points of common concern and agreement that would otherwise go unrecognized and therefore unrealized.

Under the rubric of human thriving, moreover, thrift does not lose its association with prudential calculation; rather, frugality finds its proper place within the richer context of the *humane* ends of economic activity. Like thrift, the concept of the humane is an inescapably normative matter. Also a moral quality of the middle range, it aspires to something more robust than mere polite regard, yet not to perfect goodness. Its particular moral register calls forth qualities such as civility, propriety, and mutual obligation—that is, for a common fund of generalized goodwill and a commitment to the common good as befitting human dignity. The humane is not something that can be taken for granted; it is an achievement ever in need of maintenance and renewal. The answer to the question to which thrift points—*What does it mean to thrive?*—can only be found in the common effort to make our material abundance not only more sustainable but, by definition, more humane.

In making these claims, it is necessary to offer important qualifications. First, the argument here is not that if we simply start invoking the language of thrift we will automatically find agreement on solutions to the many problems we face. No particular thrift ethic, past or present, is sufficient to address a ten-figure federal deficit, overcome our dependence on fossil fuel, reform Social Security and health care, or restore investor confidence. They are simply not all solvable by thrift, whatever its formulation. Second, as the story of Hetty Green was intended to illustrate at the outset, the term *thrift* is loaded with so much preconception and ideological baggage that it may not be congenial to any constructive project. Finally, we are also not promoting any one historical type of thrift over others, though we think there are things to learn from them all. We are promoting, rather, the *grammar* common to all the historical idioms of thrift. This grammar, as we have suggested, is essentially about the basic conditions of thriving, and as such offers us a fruitful starting point to renew and revive a common language of economic life.

When we view it in light of this grammar, we inevitably draw upon the best of the historical forms of thrift depicted in this volume and the highest aspirations of each: Puritan thrift's concern with the common good and with ends that transcend private, material (even worldly) well-being; classic thrift's emphasis on individual responsibility, delayed gratification, and benevolence; consumer thrift's trade-offs with time, as well as its concern with self-refinement; collective thrift's championing mutual obligation, social justice, and civic virtue; green thrift's stewardship of the environment and natural resources; and even the free-agent ethic's celebration of self-expression, autonomy, and mobility. At their best, what each of these features illuminate are the noninstrumental ends of economic life—responsibility, reciprocity, propriety, stewardship, authenticity, and citizenship. In this broad sense, historic appraisal of thrift's surprising grammar gives us fresh insight not only into the evolving meaning of material well-being but into the changing understandings of the good life and the good society more generally. We also see how each era possesses its own conventional wisdom and characteristic mistakes. Historical consideration of preceding epics and ethics in this way expands the horizons of our moral imaginations regarding the possible answers to what it means to thrive.

Americans stand at a crossroads when it comes to economic life, this much is certain. On the one hand, it is becoming apparent that the prevailing ideological paradigm of neoliberalism can no longer be taken for granted. On the other hand, there is no obvious alternative paradigm ready to take its place. The overwhelming response to this situation has been vacillation between the search for technocratic solutions to neoliberalism's failures (whether in the form of government bailouts or a new enthusiasm for regulation) and op-ed moralizing about rapacious CEOs, swindling Wall Street traders, incompetent or colluding government regulators, and materialistic and irresponsible consumers. This mood swing is understandable, but it is futile without attention to the deeper deficit of our moral culture. The underlying and abiding problem is that we have no public consensus on the relationship between moral and material progress. We have highly developed theories and procedures regarding private interest, but radically fragmented ideas and practices when it comes to the public interest. Rarely are we offered any conceptually and morally salient framework for thinking about the greater interdependencies, and thus rights *and* responsibilities, that tie private economic and public goods together. Americans thus confront a historic opportunity to reformulate such a framework by reconsidering what it means (and takes) to thrive. Of course, reexamining the "grammar" of thrift is only a beginning. Unless it is accompanied by a supporting institutional framework that supports new ways of conceiving and practicing economy, talk of thrift will likely lapse into a platitude, or worse, another brand of moralism. Still, the promise of thrift is real and offers conceptual and ethical resources for renewing a common language by which we can talk together in the face of our many dilemmas about the nature of a prosperous, just, sustainable, and humane economy.

Notes

1. Quoted in Richard Falon, ed., *Forbes Greatest Investment Stories* (New York: Wiley, 2001), 157. See also Charles Slack, *Hetty: The Genius and Madness of America's First Female Tycoon* (New York: HarperCollins, 2004).

2. Stephen Moor and Julian L. Simon, *It's Getting Better All the Time* (Washington, DC: Cato Institute, 2001); Stephen Leeb and Glen Strathy, *The Coming Economic Collapse* (New York: Warner Business, 2006).

3. T. J. Jackson Lears, "The American Way of Debt," *New York Times*, June 11, 2006.

4. Cotton Mather, *Magnalia Christi Americana*, 2 vols. (Boston, 1853), 1:63.

5. Benjamin Friedman, *The Moral Consequences of Economic Growth* (New York: Knopf, 2005), 399.

6. John Maynard Keynes, "The Economic Possibilities for Our Grandchildren," in *The Collected Writings of John Maynard Keynes*, vol. 9, *Essays in Persuasion* (London: Macmillan, 1972), 321.

7. Ibid., 328.

8. Benjamin Franklin, *Poor Richard Improved* (Philadelphia, 1758).

9. *The Adams-Jefferson Letters*, ed. Lester J. Capon (Chapel Hill: University of North Carolina Press for the Omohundro Institute, 1987), 550.

10. *The Writings of Thomas Jefferson*, vol. 7, ed. H. A. Washington (Washington, DC: Taylor and Maury, 1853), 19.

11. Ralph Waldo Emerson, "Prudence" (1841), in *Essays and Lectures* (New York: Library of America, 1983), 364.

12. http://money.cnn.com/2008/12/11/news/economy/flow_of_funds/index.htm (accessed February 1, 2010); http://2.bp.blogspot.com/_pCDyiFUv9XU/SoTnRhbNIVI/AAAAAAAAH_s/taQ3BCxwZok/s1600-h/Savings+Rate.jpg (accessed February 1, 2010); http://www.creditcards.com/credit-card-news/credit-card-industry-facts-personal-debt-statistics-1276.php (accessed June 11, 2010).

13. Personal bankruptcies are rising, up 28 percent from 2007. More than 22,000 Americans file for bankruptcy every week, according to the American Bankruptcy Institute, which predicts this number will continue to climb as the nation plunges deeper and deeper into a recession. Available online at http://consumer.abiworld.org/ (accessed December 17, 2008).

14. Congressional Budget Office, "Monthly Budget Review" (October 7, 2008), www.cbo.gov/ftpdocs/98xx/doc9818/10-2008-MBR.htm (accessed October 31, 2008).

15. http://www.cbo.gov/ftpdocs/105xx/doc10521/2009BudgetUpdate_Summary.pdf (accessed June 4, 2010).

16. *The World Fact Book 2006*, s.v. "United States," http://www.cia.gov/library/publications/the-world-factbook/print/us.html (accessed October 31, 2008).

17. Friedman, *Moral Consequences of Economic Growth*, 408.

18. http://www.reuters.com/article/idUSN08846252010060 8 (accessed June 13, 2010). See also http://www.brillig.com/debt_clock/ (accessed June 4, 2010). In September 2008, Time Square's National Debt Clock actually ran out of spaces. To make room for our current debt level, the digital dollar sign had to be removed. According to the Associated Press, a new clock is being built that will make room for a quadrillion dollars of debt. See *Time* magazine report online, October 14, 2008, www.time.com/time/business/article/0,8599,1850269,00.html (accessed October 31, 2008).

19. http://business.timesonline.co.uk/tol/business/markets/united_states/article2120735.ece (accessed December 17, 2008).

20. David Blakenhorn, *Thrift: A Cyclopedia* (New York: Institute for American Values, 2008), 299–300.

21. "When the American economy enters a downturn," writes Joseph Stiglitz, "you often hear experts debating whether it is likely to be V-shaped (short and sharp) or U-shaped (longer but milder). Today, the American economy may be entering a downturn that is best described as L-shaped. It is in a very low place indeed, and likely to remain there for some time to come." See "Reversal of Fortune."

22. Virginia Postrel, "The Case for Debt," *The Atlantic*, (November 2008), 46.

23. In Juliet Schor, ed., *Do American Shop Too Much?* (Boston: Beacon Press, 2000), 38–39.

24. Friedman, Moral Consequences of Economic Growth, 401.

25. Bill McKibben, *Deep Economy: The Wealth of Communities and the Durable Future* (New York: Time Books, 2007), 12.

26. Jeffrey Sachs, *The End of Poverty: Economic Possibilities for Our Time* (New York: Penguin, 2005), 26.

27. Ibid., 28, 30.

28. See Paul Collier, *The Bottom Billion: Why the Poorest Countries Are Failing and What Can Be Done About It* (New York: Oxford University Press, 2007).

29. David Shi, *The Simple Life: Plain Living and High Thinking in American Culture* (New York: Oxford University Press, 1985), 264.

30. Friedman, Moral Consequences of Economic Growth, 394.

31. Quoted in Daniel Bell, *The Cultural Contradictions of Capitalism* (New York: Basic Books, 1996), 290.

32. Jerry Mueller, *The Mind and the Market: Capitalism in European Thought* (New York: Knopf, 2002), 395.

33. Ibid., 142.

34. Ibid., 395.

35. Ibid., 396.

36. Joyce Appleby, chapter 6.

37. Alexis de Tocqueville, *Democracy in America* (Chicago: University of Chicago Press, 2000), 514.

38. See Friedman, Moral Consequences of Economic Growth, chap. 4.

39. See Benjamin Schwartz, *The Paradox of Choice: Why More Is Less* (New York: Harper Perennial, 2005).

40. Greg Easterbrook, *The Progress Paradox: How Life Gets Better While People Feel Worse* (New York: Random House, 2003), 165.

41. Ibid., xx.

42. Ibid., xv.

43. Sachs, The End of Poverty, 3.

44. Ibid., 1.

45. Friedman, Moral Consequences of Economic Growth, 399.

46. McKibben, *Deep Economy*, 1.

47. Ibid., 2.

48. Easterbrook, *The Progress Paradox*, 68.

49. Friedman, Moral Consequences of Economic Growth, 436.

50. Quoted in Jerry Mueller, *The Mind and the Market* (New York: Anchor Books, 2002), 8.

51. Max Weber, *The Protestant Ethic and The Spirit of Capitalism* (New York: Dover Publications, 2003), 181.

52. "Greenspan Concedes Error," *New York Times*, October 24, 2008, B1.

INDEX